1|6|14
71.99

Euro-Jews and Afro-Arabs

The Great Semitic Divergence in World History

Ali A. Mazrui

Edited by
Seifudein Adem

UNIVERSITY PRESS OF AMERICA, ® INC.
Lanham • Boulder • New York • Toronto • Plymouth, UK

Copyright © 2008 by
University Press of America,® Inc.
4501 Forbes Boulevard
Suite 200
Lanham, Maryland 20706
UPA Acquisitions Department (301) 459-3366

Estover Road
Plymouth PL6 7PY
United Kingdom

Library of Congress Control Number: 2007935042
ISBN-13: 978-0-7618-3857-9 (paperback : alk. paper)
ISBN-10: 0-7618-3857-0 (paperback : alk. paper)

Contents

Preface and Acknowledgments   v

SECTION I   THE GREAT SEMITIC DIVERGENCE

1   Towards the Europeanization of the Jews and the Africanization
of the Arabs: An Introduction   3

2   Semitic Divergence and African Convergence   23

SECTION II   EURO-JEWS IN WORLD HISTORY

3   The Talmudic Tradition in Comparative Perspective   45

4   Muslims between the Jewish Example and the Black Experience:
American Policy Implications   67

5   Blacks, Jews and Comparative Diasporas   96

6   Is Israel a Threat to American Democracy?   115

SECTION III   AFRO-ARABS IN WORLD HISTORY

7   Afrabia: From Arabo-Hebraic Divergence to
Afro-Arab Convergence   129

8   The Black Arabs in Comparative Perspective   142

9   The Multiple Marginality of the Sudan   175

10   Africa and Egypt's Four Circles: Nasser's Legacy   192

11 Afro-Arab Crossfire: Between the Flames of Terrorism and
the Force of Pax Americana   206

12 Eurafrica, Eurabia, and African-Arab Relations: The Tensions
of Tripolarity   218

SECTION IV   THE SEMITES BETWEEN SIN AND VIRTUE

13 Comparative Slavery: Western, Muslim and African Legacies   249

14 Comparative Racism: Zionism and Apartheid   270

15 Comparative Terrorism: Arab, Jewish and African (Usama,
Sharon and Shaka)   296

16 Black Intifadah: The Mau Mau War and the Palestinian Uprising   314

17 Between Intifadah and Al Qaeda: East African Perspective   323

SECTION V   ISLAM IN WORLD AFFAIRS

18 Muslims in a Century of Four Ethical Revolutions   335

19 Africa and Islam in Search of Seven Pillars of Wisdom   352

20 Islam and the United States: Streams of Convergence, Strands
of Divergence   380

SECTION VI   CONCLUSIONS

21 The Semitic Impact on Africa: Arab and Jewish Influences   417

22 Euro-Jews and Afro-Arabs in World History: A Conclusion   439

Appendix   I. Prosperous Minorities as Targets of Prejudice   447

Appendix   II. Is "Jewish Uniqueness" a Dangerous Doctrine?   451

Appendix III. The Nuclear Club: Is There a
Judeo-Christian Monopoly?   455

Index   461

Preface and Acknowledgements

I have known about the Arabs from my earliest years. This is because I grew up in a family, which was not only Muslim but identified with Arab ancestry across several centuries. In reality the family had become much more African than Arab—Swahili speakers rather than Arabic speakers. But the racial nature of British colonial rule in East Africa tended to encourage African Muslims to identify themselves as "Arab" if they could get away with it.

British rule divided Kenya into four racial categories—European, Asian, Arab, and African. It was not always easy to determine where Africanity ended and Arabness began, or where Arabness ended and Muslim identity began. I had my earliest education in Arab primary and secondary schools. In reality it was a school for Muslim students in Mombasa almost regardless of race—Arab, African and those descended from Baluchistan in Pakistan.

My first contact with Jews was probably at the Arab School—but it was unconscious contact. The Arab School in Mombasa had a number of European teachers who taught me on subjects which ranged from geography to English literature, and from mathematics to my own native language, Kiswahili. Yes, I was taught literary Kiswahili partly by an Englishman.

But to the present day I do not know which of my teachers in the Arab School were British Jews and which were British Gentiles. I am, of course, indebted to them all.

After the Arab School my first regular job was at a technical institute called the Mombasa Institute of Muslims Education (MIOME) in my hometown. The Institute was intended to teach Muslims in Kenya skills, which were more relevant to the twentieth century. Although all the students at the Institute were Muslims (and intended to be so), almost all instructors were Europeans recruited from Britain in subjects like mathematics, electrical engineering, mechanical engineering and the pure sciences. To the present day, I do not know how many of those British instructors as a Muslim technical institute in colonial Kenya were Jewish and how many were Gentiles. Colonial Africans like myself tended to regard all Europeans in Kenya as "white folks," and were not sensitized to the nuance between Jew and Gentile among local Europeans in a colonial situation.

On the other hand, the editor of this volume, Seifudein Adem, grew up in Ethiopia where Jewishness was not just a European phenomenon, but was also fundamentally a local Ethiopian presence. Seifudein learned about the Jews from three sources—biblically (through the Old Testament), imperially (through the impact of Europeans on Ethiopia) and ancestrally (through the presence of the Falasha Jews in the body politic of Ethiopia). As an Ethiopian, Seifudein Adem was as exposed to the Arabs in his youth as was author, Ali Mazrui. Bust editor Seifudein Adem, was more consciously exposed to the Jewish presence in Ethiopia than Mazrui was in Kenya.

Ali Mazrui was subsequently educated in Great Britain (Huddersfield, Manchester and Oxford) and in the United States (Columbia University in New York). Mazrui's exposure to Euro-Jews began to have a more direct impact on his intellectual and political consciousness. At British educational institutions Mazrui was still not sophisticated enough to identify which of his instructors was Jewish and which Gentile. It was not until Mazrui arrived in New York City, and studied at Columbia University, that he became more aware of the Jewish factor in the total Western experience.

Since then Mazrui has studied how Jews who originated from the Middle East eventually become European Jews. He has also studied (partly autobiographically) how Arabs and Africans merged into a shared identity—AFRABIA. In this book we now record the dual saga about Afro-Arabs, on one side, and Euro-Jews on the other.

My concept of AFRABIA goes back at least until 1973 when almost all of Africa broke off relations with Israel in solidarity with Egypt at war. This Afro-Arab alliance against Israel made me wonder whether Africa and the Arab world were two regions gradually merging into one, at least in the diplomatic arena. I articulated the beginnings of the thesis in a lecture I gave at Haile Selassie I University in Addis Ababa. I did not realize it at the time, but this was my last visit to Ethiopia before their revolution of 1974. Emperor Haile Selassie I was overthrown in 1974.

Since then I have lectured on "AFRABIA" in both Africa and the Middle East. I am particularly grateful to Abdalla Bujra based in Addis Ababa, Ethiopia, and to Ahmed Fituri in Libya and Ismael Serageldin in Egypt for their insightful stimulation and encouragement on this subject.

The idea of comparing the Africanization of the Arabs with the Europeanization of the Jews occurred to me in the course of a seminar I was giving at Cornell University. It was part of a class I was teaching at Africana Studies and Research Center on the subject of "Islam in Africa and its Diaspora." I am grateful to my Cornell students for their comments and criticisms on the two concepts of "Afro-Arabs" and "Euro-Jews."

To my editor, Seifudein Adem, I am particularly indebted for meticulous editing of my papers and for his negotiations with the publishers. Without Seifudein this book might not have materialized at all.

This book is partly indebted to the historical and ancestral experiences of author Ali Mazrui and editor Seifudein Adem. The research has been funded primarily by Binghamton University, State University of New York, in association with the Africana Studies and Research Center at Cornell University.

Editorially this book has benefited not only from Seifudein Adem but also from Thomas Uthup, Patrick Dikirr, and Ruzima C. Sebuharara who have enhanced the bibliographical references from chapter to chapter. Amadu Jacky Kaba has also enhanced our statistics and Abdul S. Bemath has prepared the index.

The manuscript secretarially benefited from the labor and skills of Anna-Marie Palombaro, the late Nancy Levis, Nancy Hall, and Barbara Tierno.

Graduate assistants who have contributed in this endeavor include Ramzi Badran, Senthilkumar Mehalingam and Dellvin Williams.

We are greatly indebted for a whole range of insights to these and other experts of the African condition.

Ali A. Mazrui
April 2007

Section I

THE GREAT SEMITIC DIVERGENCE

Chapter One

Toward the Europeanization of the Jews and the Africanization of the Arabs: *An Introduction*

The Semitic peoples are defined in three ways—by language, by genealogy and by religion. Linguistically, the Semites are those whose mother tongues are the Semitic languages. These languages are divided primarily into three categories. The Northwestern (or Northern Central) category includes ancient and modern Hebrew and the ancient languages of Aramaic and Phoenician.

Southern Central Semitic languages include Arabic and Maltese, while the Southern Peripheral includes South Arabic, Amharic and one or two other languages of Ethiopia.

The Semitic language of Akkadian does not fit into these three categories. It is often regarded as a separate category (Northern Peripheral or Northeastern).[1]

When Semitic peoples are defined genealogically, they often respond to their lineage cultures. In Israel, if the mother is Jewish the child is Jewish. In Saudi Arabia or Egypt, if the father is Arab the child is Arab.

The third definition of a Semite is religious. This is easiest when defining the Jews. Jews are people whose original language was Hebrew or Aramaic and whose ancestral religion is Judaism. Over the centuries, the Jews have become less and less of a linguistic group and more of a purely religio-cultural identity.

There is also a religious definition of "Semites" which links up with at least mythological genealogy. By their respective myths of ancestry, Jews and Arabs are descended from the patriarch Abraham. The Jews are descended from Isaac (Ishak) and the Arabs from Ishmael (Ismail). Jews and Arabs might, therefore, be regarded as Abrahamic peoples.

More recently the term "Abrahamic" has been theologized and not merely limited to genealogy. It is not just Arabs and Jews who are "Abrahamic," but also the three monotheistic religions which were first "revealed" to them. Thus, Judaism, Christianity and Islam have more recently been designated as Abrahamic religions.[2]

When the Prophet Muhammad began to preach the message of Islam in the year 610 of the Christian era, the number of Jews had declined from previous highs of probably as much as four to five million to between one to one and a half million.[3] The Arabs at that time were confined mainly to the Arabian Peninsula, while the Jews were already partly scattered in the Diaspora.

The reduction of the Jewish population was partly due to massacres by the Roman Empire in the first and second centuries, but more Jews were lost through conversion, mostly to Christianity.[4] The number of Arabs, on the other hand, has increased as a result of the spread of the Arabic language and Islam. As a result, today there are about seventeen Arabs for every single Jew in the world. There may also be close to eighty-four Muslims for every Jew.[5]

In addition to numbers, there is another crucial divergence which occurred between Jews and Arabs. As they dispersed across their own Diaspora, the Jews became more and more part of European history. A process of Europeanization began to affect this branch of the Semitic peoples.

On the other hand, the emergence of Islam initiated the process of the partial Africanization of the Arab branch of the Semites. Across the centuries, Arabs and Africans began to converge into one people. When Islam first arrived in Africa more than fourteen centuries ago, there were very few Arabs even in the Hamito-Semitic areas of North Africa and the Horn.

Today there are *close to a* quarter of a billion Arabs in the African continent.[6] That is to say, there are more Arabs in Africa than in the rest of the Arab world outside Africa. This is quite apart from the spread of Islam in Africa. We have called this Afro-Arab convergence as a transition toward AFRABIA.

What are the different stages of this Afro-Arab interpenetration? And what were the different historical processes which have resulted in the Europeanization of the Jews? Let us begin with the Jewish story.

EURO-JEWS IN THE MAKING

The initial stage towards the Europeanization of the Jews was the first major Jewish experience of exile. This was the Jews' first Diaspora, which occurred after the Babylonian conquest of the Kingdom of Judah in 586 BCE. Jews were forced into exile, often deported as slaves. Cyrus the Great of Persia subsequently conquered Babylon in turn. In 539 BCE Cyrus allowed the Jews to return to Judah.[7] However, many Jews preferred to remain abroad. The first Diaspora was born.

After the Babylonian exile, the only Israelites who retained Jewish identity were the survivors of Judah. The ten tribes of Israel proper had been dispersed earlier after the Assyrian conquest of 722 BCE. These exiles did not crystallize into a Diaspora because they were gradually assimilated by other people and lost their Jewish identity. It was the Babylonian exiles who initiated the process of Diasporization.[8]

The second major stage in the process of the Europeanization of the Jews began with the conquest of Palestine by Alexander the Great in 332 BCE. This initiated a cultural phenomenon which came to be known as Hellenistic Judaism, which responded to the cultural stimuli of classical Greece and which flourished from the fourth century BCE to the second century of the Christian era. There were major centers of Hellenistic Judaism in Asia Minor, Syria, Babylonia and, most impressively, in Alexandria in Egypt.[9] This port city of Egypt flourished into the largest, most productive and culturally most creative Jewish Diaspora in this early history of Judaism. It is estimated that 40 percent of the population of Alexandria in that period were Jews.[10] This was the second major stage in the story of the gradual Jewish integration into European civilization.

By the middle of this Hellenistic period, five million Jews lived outside Palestine; four-fifths of them were in the Roman Empire.[11] In other words, Diaspora Jews by this Hellenistic period were already outnumbering Jews in Palestine even before the destruction of Jerusalem in the year 70 of the Christian era.

The cultural period of Hellenistic Judaism overlapped with Roman rule over the Jews. The Roman years of 63 BCE to 135 CE included one of the earliest attempts to establish a Jewish state. These proto-"Zionists" of yesteryears included Herodians, Zealots and some quasi-mostic groups. These early aspirants for a Jewish state included an expectation of a Messiah to lead them to it.

Then came the era of Rabbinic Judaism (2nd to 18th century CE). This changed the nature of Diasporization, but did not reverse it. Jews as a Mediterranean people declined, while Jews as a European people gained new impetus during this period.[12]

The last Patriarch, Gamaliel IV, died in 425 CE, leading to the political fragmentation of the Mediterranean Jewry. But the continuing ritual role of the Jewish calendar, and the supportive roles of the rabbi, did indeed help to ensure the survival and expansion of European Jewry.

In the course of the middle Ages there developed a fourth major stage in the Europeanization of the Jews. Just as the Christian Church had split between Greek Orthodox and Roman Catholic, the Jews came to be distinguished between the *Sephardi* and *Ashkenazim*. The Sephardi were products of the Andalusian-Spanish community, culturally linked to Babylonia, and conditioned to some extent by the Arabic-Muslim wider environment.

The Ashkenazim were more distinctly European. They were basically Franco-German Jewry, who had evolved out of Latin-Christian culture and who could trace their ancestry to both Palestine and Rome.[13]

Jewish incorporation into European society was in fits and starts, two steps forward and one step back. In 1306 France expelled most Jews; in 1442 Spain did the same, along with the expulsion of the Moors (Spanish Muslims).[14] By the 18th century there was widespread persecution of the Jews in Europe. Conditions were so bad that many Jews converted to Christianity (apostasy) or pretended to be converted to Christianity (Marranism).[15] There also arose pseudo-messianic movements and Jewish extremism.

But the persecution of the Jews also helped to stimulate the Jewish Enlightenment (Haskala) in Eastern and Central Europe.[16] Messianic beliefs declined while the quests for individual achievement and collective Jewish fulfillment on this earth gathered momentum. This was the period when Moses Mendelssohn produced *Jerusalem* (1783), a work which defended Judaism not just as the spiritual heritage of the Jews, but above all as a universal religion of reason.[17]

The Jewish Enlightenment led to Jewish religious reform in Western Europe, accelerating during the Napoleonic period (1800–1815). The Jews who were back in France concentrated on doctrinal reform. In Germany the reform paid special attention to the aesthetic aspects of ritual and worship. German Reform Judaism crystallized into a denomination. German reform did not spread much in Europe beyond Germany, but it found receptive constituencies in the New World, especially in the United States.[18]

Somewhere between Orthodox Judaism and Reform Judaism emerged Conservative Judaism, which also began in Germany in 1845.[19] These cumulative trends were helping Jews to accommodate themselves to Western culture without permitting themselves to be assimilated. Even Orthodox Jews in Europe were culturally Europeanized while remaining adherents of Judaism in their spiritual life.

It was during these tumultuous and innovative years of the nineteenth century that a Jewish boy was born who was to have a greater impact on European and world history than any other single Jew, with the exception of Jesus Christ. This nineteenth century young Jew was called Karl Marx.[20] By a strange destiny, he was to propagate influential ideas which were at once products of his brilliant European mind and his profound Jewish legacy.

EURO-JEWISH GENIUS: MARX AND OTHERS

We have decided to focus on Karl Marx as a particularly fascinating example of the Europeanization of the Jews. Although baptized as Jewish by his mother and descended from a long line of Rabbis, Karl Marx was not just secular, not merely atheist, but anti-religion generally.

He unleashed one of the most influential ideological movements in modern times—a set of ideas which transformed the twentieth century fundamentally. At one time, more than a third of the human race lived under systems of government influenced by the ideas of Karl Marx. And within Europe this was a case of one single ethnic Jew transforming the power-politics of the whole continent. Yet the ideas of Karl Marx still bore the stamp of his own Jewish history and of the worldview of Judaism.[21]

> "Religion is the sigh of the oppressed creature and the soul of soul-less conditions. . . . It is the opium of the people."[22]

So said Karl Marx, the last of the great Jewish prophets. It is intellectually legitimate to raise the question whether Marxism itself is a secular religion. It is also intellectually legitimate to ask whether that particular secular religion shows rabbinic and Judaic impact in the great tradition of the Jewish prophets.

The name Marx is a shortened form of Mordechai, later changed to Markus. Karl's father—Heinrich Marx—was born in 1782, the third son of Meier Halevi Marx who became Rabbi of Trier. Karl Marx's paternal grandmother was also descended from Rabbis. As David McLellan put it in his biography of Karl Marx:

> In fact almost all the rabbis of Trier from the sixteenth century onwards were ancestors of Marx.[23]

Marx's father converted to Protestantism for purely economic and professional reasons the year before Karl was born. When Karl was baptized in 1824, his mother Henrietta described herself as Jewish. Later on Karl Marx's youngest daughter, Eleanor, though only half Jewish, said with defiant pride at a workers' meeting in the East End of London "I am a Jewess."[24]

Marx himself showed signs of anti-Semitism—as in his pamphlet *On the Jewish Question*.[25] But does Marx's whole system of ideas originate in his rabbinic ancestry? Does his lifestyle lie in the prophetic tradition? Does his appearance affirm that prophetic credential?

Marx owed a lot to the German philosopher, Hegel. When Jewish history is Hegelianized the link with historical materialism is at its most pronounced. Nachman Krochmal (1785–1840)—whose life overlapped with that of Marx—carried this Hegelianization of Jewish history to a new level.[26] As a neo-Hegelian, Krochmal viewed the Jewish people as the bearer of the historical process. Krochmal added a cyclical dynamic to history. The Jews were the only nation to rise again and again, re-invigorated after every decline. The Jews alone had a direct link with the Absolute Spirit.[27]

It followed therefore that the Jews were a source of special creativity, for each ascent was to a higher level of self-realization.

For Karl Marx the cyclic movement of history was not given to a nation like the Jews. It was given to an economic class in a constant movement between thesis, antithesis and synthesis. For Karl Marx the chosen people are not the Jews but the proletariat.

The idea that the Jews are the Elect of God has been recurrent in Jewish liturgy. "For you are a people holy to the Lord your God, and the Lord has chosen you to be a people of his own possession, out of all the nations that are on the face of the earth."[28]

For Karl Marx the proletariat was not the Elect of Gold but the Elect of History. And salvation is not for the individual (as in Christian liberalism or Reform Judaism), but for the whole people. For Marx salvation is through revolution on this earth.

There is the alternative interpretation that Marx's concept of the proletariat is messianic. For Jews "the Messiah as envisioned by the prophets, transmitted by the tradition, and embraced by the consciousness of the Jewish people, is the capstone of Judaism."[29]

For Marx, the messianic role is not to be played by an individual but by the supreme class of historical destiny—the proletariat.

In the Old Testament God is often cruel in order to be kind. Noah had to have an ark to save only a fraction of God's creation. Most could not be saved from God's angry floods. For Karl Marx, history (like God) has to be cruel in order to be kind. But for Marx the curse is not on the sexual sinners, but on the economic exploiters. History's damnation is not upon the first born. History's curse is upon the privileged of each epoch of class struggle.

But other aspects of Marx's prophetic tendencies are closer to Christianity than Judaism. In Karl Marx the Original Sin is of greed. It was greed which was responsible for:

• causing class formation
• causing class struggle
• causing revolution
• causing death

Marx then allowed a cycle of redemption before greed once again disrupted society. There is an underlying fatalism in Marx's theory of historical materialism. This is the inexorable march of class-struggle.

The Hegelian aspects of Marxism are also partly Biblical. The negation of the negation is a Hegelian principle. And the Bible says that out of death life often arises. Adam would have had eternal life, but for his sin. Was it the sin of greed or disobedience? Jesus's death on the cross much later was the negation of Adam's death:

> As by one sole man
> sin entered the world,
> And death by sin,
> And thus death passed to all men,
> Because all have sinned. . . .[30]
> As from one sole transgression
> there followed condemnation for all,
> So from one sole deed of justice,
> there followed justification for life.[31]

In the Divine Dialectic Jesus and Adam become two Adams—two men who determined the whole course of human history. The fifteenth chapter of the First Corinthians is more explicitly about this doctrine of two Adams. Thus is it written:

> There was made the first man, Adam, living soul
> The last Adam, life giving spirit[32]

If therefore Marxism shows the impact of aspects of the Old Testament, and even of the New, to what extent did the Soviet Union turn its back on religion by going Marxist? And yet for a while Western and Soviet political cultures confronted each other—and militarized their rivalry to new levels of potential destructiveness.

Was it Judeo-Christian Western alliance arming itself against a Judeo-Marxist Soviet Bloc? Were two sister civilizations unnecessarily on a collision course?

The Soviet Union has been and gone. Is Judeo-Marxism likely to be as enduring as the Judeo-Christian legacy? It seems unlikely—but who thought Christianity would last at the time of crucifixion? The future can be trusted to keep its own secrets until the fullness of time.

In the context of a longer span of history, Judeo-Marxism might be regarded as a particularly striking example of the Europeanization of Jewishness. As we mentioned earlier, Karl Marx was next only to Jesus Christ as an ethnic Jew who changed the world.

What we might now note is that the greatest of the ethnic Jews who changed the world were, in any case, "renegade Jews" who combined their

Jewishness with some dissident otherness. We know that Jesus Christ, while not disowning his Jewish heritage, started something which became an entirely new religion. We know Karl Marx rejected all religion. And yet Karl Marx's ideas, style and personal appearance have led to his being described as "the last of the Great Jewish Prophets."[33]

Sigmund Freud was another ethnic Jew whose ideas have profoundly affected the modern world. He helped to give us the tools for understanding the human mind. Once again, this Freud, a European Jew, delved into issues of origins and the secrets of the soul. He even attempted to psychoanalyze Moses in retrospect![34]

Benedict de Spinoza (1632–1677) was another European Jew who had a profound impact on Western thought, though not necessarily in the wider world. Once again, this was an ethnic Jew whose greatness was partly based on his being a dissenter. He is celebrated as a Dutch-Jewish rationalist of Portuguese ancestry. Indeed, one description of him is that he "was, and to some degree remains, the prototype of the emancipated secular Jew."[35] His belief in the supremacy of reason often led to his being accused of atheism.[36]

Albert Einstein (1879–1955) was another European Jew who was a genius and whose ideas have helped to change physics. His letter to President Franklin D. Roosevelt of the United States resulted in the Manhattan Project and the American pursuit of the atomic bomb. Einstein was widely regarded as a spiritual man, but not necessarily a religious man. Was he a "renegade Jew"? At one time, Einstein had renounced his membership in the Jewish community at the age of fifteen.[37] However, he " discovered for the first time I was a Jew" in his midthirties and was even offered the presidency of Israel.[38]

As we shall indicate in a later chapter, Jewish achievements in Western history go well beyond this handful of individuals who belong to the absolute top of human intelligence. The number of Jews who have won the Nobel Prize since it was established a century ago is staggering for a community so small (well below 15 million worldwide).[39]

What is clear is that in modern times Jews have been at their best when they have been Europeanized or Westernized. It has been the combination of a Jewish heritage with Western assimilation which has produced the most outstanding intellectual results.

Moreover, the greatest of all Jews in the last two thousand years have been those who were leaning towards dissident otherness—from Jesus Christ to Karl Marx, from Spinoza to Freud.

We must conclude that the Europeanization of the Jews, while diluting the Judaism in them, has also resulted in the intellectual flowering of the Jews in modern history. But how does this study of Euro-Jews compare and contrast with the other story about the evolution of Afro-Arabs? It is to this Afro-Arab story that we must now turn.

THE GENESIS OF AFRABIA

We have already sought to demonstrate that Jews and Westerners have historically been two peoples in the slow process of becoming one. Is it similarly true that Arabs and Africans are two peoples who have historically been converging towards becoming one people? Let us explore this second scenario of the trend towards Afrabia.

Let us begin with the pre-Islamic links between the Arabs and the Africans. These early connections are part of the origins of the Semitic peoples generally. As we mentioned earlier, native speakers of the Arabic language belong to the Southern Central Semitic family. The distinctly separate language of South Arabic of ancient Yemen is closely related to the Ethiopian languages of Amharic and Tigrinya.

We might, therefore, say that long before Arabs and Africans were connected by the shared experience of Islam, the two peoples were connected by the shared experience of Semitic languages. Yemen and Ethiopia are even bonded by their rival claims for the Queen of Sheba. Most Biblical scholars place the Queen of Sheba in Yemen. Most Ethiopians and African historians, on the other hand, regard Sheba as Ethiopia's own Queen who gave birth to Emperor Menelik I.[40]

The Qur'an itself refers to pre-Islamic relationships between the Arabs and Eastern Africans. The Qur'an refers to an invasion of Arabia by *as'haab el feel* (meaning "the people of the elephant"). It is almost certain that these invaders of Arabia were Ethiopians who were led by commanders riding elephants. Although this invasion was before the advent of Islam, God seemed to have been against the invaders. The Almighty sent birds to afflict the elephants. Was it pestilence breaking out among the invaders?

Further evidence of pre-Islamic Afro-Arab relationships was the presence of an African Diaspora in the Arabian peninsular before Muhammad was born. After all, it was Muhammad's own close companion who bought the freedom of the enslaved Ethiopian, Bilal. This emancipated Black man lived to become one of the closest companions of the Prophet Muhammad. He subsequently had the historic role of being the first Muezzin to call believers to prayer at the Grand Mosque in Mecca after Muhammad conquered Mecca from pre-Islamic idol-worshippers in the year 630 C.E. It is believed that Bilal eventually died in Syria and is buried in Damascus or Aleppo.[41]

Mecca was already an important trading city in the sixth century of the Christian era. There is little doubt that the trade which Mecca conducted included commerce with neighboring African countries across the Red Sea and possibly trading further into the African hinterland.

A much older historic connection between the Arabian peninsula and Africa was the fact that what became the peninsula of the Arabs was once part and parcel of the African land mass. As this book will later clarify, there was no Red Sea in very distant prehistoric times. It took a massive earthquake in antiquity to tear off the Arabian peninsular and create the great Rift Valley. To the present day, the geology of the Arabian peninsula shows striking affinity with the geology of eastern Africa and the Horn.

However, there is no doubt that the rise of Islam created much more complex relationships between Africa and the Arabs. In the seventh century of the Christian era, Islam arrived in Africa in two vastly different ways. Islam initially arrived in Ethiopia as a supplicant for religious and political asylum. In Mecca followers of the young religion of Islam were being persecuted by fellow Arabs, who were resisting the new religion as a threat to their polytheistic and idolatrous traditions. Uthman bin Affan (who later become the third Caliph of Islam after Muhammad's death) led a group of Muslim refugees to seek asylum in Christian Abyssinia.[42] A historic religious contact was made.

Barely two decades later, Islam was triumphant in Mecca and in much of the rest of the Arabian peninsular. And long before the end of the seventh century, Islam arrived in another African country, but this time Islam came as conqueror. The Arabs annexed Egypt and initiated two processes of monumental historical significance. One process was *Islamization*, meaning the spread of the Islamic religion initially in Egypt and North Africa. The second process was *Arabization*, meaning the spread of the Arabic language. Over the centuries, Egypt—which was Christian at the time of the Arab conquest— eventually, became overwhelmingly Muslim. Over more centuries, Egyptians became native speakers of the Arabic language. In time, so did much of the rest of North Africa and the Nile Delta. Africa had become an Afro-Arab continent.

Here a major distinction arises between the destinies of the Jews and of the Arabs. When Uthman bin Affan and his band of refugees arrived in Ethiopia, their predicament was similar to that of early Jews on the run into exile, seeking religious asylum. But when the Arabs arrived in Egypt as conquerors, they started a process of assimilating their subjects into the conquering culture, rather than being assimilated by their host countries.

This constituted a major difference between the expansion of the Arabs and the dispersal of the Jews. It was a major reason why the Jews are now less than one-seventeenth of the global population of the Arabs.

Why did the Jews in Europe remain limited in numbers while the Arabs in Africa dramatically grew in population? One primary reason was that the Arabs in Africa were exporting their culture and spreading their religion, whereas the Jews in Europe were engaged in the politics of cultural and religious survival. Far from trying to proselytize, the Jews attempted to be religiously inconspicuous.

A second reason for the growth of the Arabs in Africa, as contrasted with the Jews in Europe, was that Arabness was defined by language, whereas Jewishness was defined by religion. An Arab is he or she whose mother tongue is Arabic and who identified himself or herself with the Arabs. A Jew, on the other hand, is an individual who is personally a follower of Judaism or culturally identifies with the Jewish heritage. Until the creation of the state of Israel in 1948, the Jews had mostly lost their ancestral languages (Hebrew and Aramaic), while still struggling to save their religion in Europe.

A third reason as to why Arabs grew dramatically in population in Africa while the population of European Jews stagnated was that the Arabs were exogamous, responsive to racial intermarriage, while the Jews were endogamous, leaning towards marrying within their own community. Interracial marriage in Arab lands tended to produce more children than intracommunal matrimony among European Jews.

A fourth reason for Arab expansion was that Arab men were often polygamous in Africa, whereas Jews in Europe were almost always monogamous. Polygamous men produced more children than monogamous ones. Historically, in Palestine Jews had been polygamous, but Jews in Christian lands had to limit number of wives. Indeed, until the establishment of Israel as a state and consequent migration, Yemenite Jews preserved several of the ancient marriage and divorce customs, including polygamy.[43]

A fifth reason for why Arabs multiplied much more greatly in Africa than Jews did in Europe was the difference between patrilineal Arabs and matrilineal Jews. In Arab culture, if the father is Arab the child is Arab, regardless of who the mother is. In Jewish culture, if the mother is Jewish, the child is Jewish, regardless of whom the father is. But in a single lifetime a man can make more babies than a woman. Arab men have been known to be still making babies in their sixties, if not seventies. All their babies become fellow Arabs. But Jewish women normally stopped bearing babies in their forties at their oldest. Jewish matrilinealism, therefore, produced fewer Jews by descent in Europe than did Arab patrilinealism in Africa.

A sixth reason for Arab expansion of population is that Arabs owned slaves for centuries and children of a slave-owning father with his women slaves were themselves free offspring (according to Islamic law) and of Arab identity (according to Arab culture).

Jews, on the other hand, ceased to be slave owners after they left Palestine, although some of them did become slave traders in the Atlantic slave traffic centuries later. Indeed, there were some Jewish owners of Black slaves in the Caribbean as late as the nineteenth century prior to general emancipation.[44]

With regard to slave-owning Arabs in Africa, their slaves were not always Black. The slaves could be from Asia or Eastern Europe or from Black Africa.

The Arab slave system was fundamentally multiracial. Egypt was ruled by former slaves for centuries (the Mamluk Dynasty), but the composition of the Dynasty was multiracial from the start.

A seventh reason as to why Arabs multiplied faster in Africa than Jews did in Europe was because Arabs were far less race conscious and ethnic conscious than Jews. Black children of a white Arab father were still fully recognized as Arabs, regardless of evidence of race mixture. Egypt from the 1952 revolution until the end of the twentieth century had four Presidents— Muhammad Naguib, Gamal Abdel Nasser, Anwar Sadat and Husni Mubarak. The first and third presidents had black mothers and their appearance confirmed it. That was not an issue in Egyptian politics.

Kuwait has had a black Prime Minister who was a prince with a black mother. The Prime Minister was indeed obviously a black man.

In Washington, D.C., Saudi Arabia was represented for decades by Prince Bandar bin Sultan—who, in turn, was a Black man in appearance and by maternal descent.

Jews have tended to be more ethnically exclusive and racially conscious. A Black Prime Minister of Israel is very unlikely in the foreseeable future.

Although Judaism as a religion had deeply influenced Christianity and Islam, Jews as a people did not elicit many cultural imitators. The Jewish religion was a spiritual model to millions of non-Jews, but the Jewish people were not much of a role model to gentiles. While conditions in Muslim Africa were such that there were many non-Arabs who claimed to be Arabs, conditions in Europe had the reverse effect on Jews—many Jews pretended to be non-Jews (including Karl Marx's father and Spinoza's family before they left Portugal for the Netherlands).

However, there was one area of life where Jews excelled from almost the earliest days of their Diaspora. They certainly became influential intellectuals in the Muslim world—often serving as advisers to Sultans and Emirs, and translators of the riches of ancient Greek civilization.[45]

These were the years when Muslims believed in creative synthesis and were ready to learn from other people and other cultures. The Muslim world was ready to be stimulated in mathematics by India, in architecture by Persia, in philosophy by ancient Greece, in law by the Old Testament and Roman law. Islamic civilization as a collectivity became a role model for the Western world. To the present day the West calls its numerals "Arabic numerals"— having abandoned the Roman numerals for most purposes of life and scholarship. Individual Jews made a contribution over the years to both Islamic and European civilizations.

What about Arab and Muslim scholars on the African continent across the ages? Were there any to compare in genius with such ethnic Jews as Spinoza,

Sigmund Freud and Albert Einstein? Perhaps the most brilliant of Arab scholars was Ibn Khaldun, who was born in Tunis in 1332 C.E. and died in Cairo in 1406.

Ibn Khaldun is widely regarded as the father of secular philosophy of history and the founder of the study of sociology. The twentieth century English historian, Arnold Toynbee, described Ibn Khaldun's masterpiece, Al-Muqaddimah, as a "philosophy of history which is undoubtedly the greatest work that has ever been created by any mind in any time or place."[46]

Noted Arab historian Philip Hitti has said of Toynbee:

> No Arab writer, indeed no European, had ever taken a view of history at once so comprehensive and philosophic.[47]

Also a genius of a different kind from Arab Africa was Ibn Battutah — who was born in Tangier, Morocco, in 1304 and died in 1368/9 C.E., also in Morocco. He was probably the greatest of medieval travelers from any culture. He covered some 75,000 miles, detailing his observations from society to society with meticulous care. He covered almost all the Muslim countries and explored as far afield as China and Sumatra. His book, *Rihla*, (Travels), is widely regarded as the most ambitious travel book of all time.[48]

In more modern times Jews in Europe have far outstripped Arabs and Muslims in intellectual, scholarly and scientific performance. While less than 15 million Jews worldwide have won dozens of Nobel Prizes in almost all Nobel fields, 1.2 billion Muslims across the world have won only a handful. In modern times, Arabs and Muslims have lagged far behind Jews in manifest brilliance. But Arab Africa continues to be the location of two of the oldest universities anywhere in the world — Al-Azhar University in Cairo, Egypt,[49] and the University in Fez, Morocco. Each of them is over a thousand years old. Both institutions are steeped in ancestral learning and tradition, from across the ages. The most influential centers of learning in the Muslim world are not in Mecca and Medina, where Islam was born, but on the African continent — where Islam first arrived as a refugee and later arrived as a conqueror in the seventh century of the Christian era. The relentless convergence of *Afrabia* has encompassed the norms of scholarship, as well as the principles and traditions of culture.

CONCLUSION

We have sought to demonstrate in this chapter two processes — how one branch of the Semitic people (the Jews) became increasingly indistinguishable from Europeans and Westerners; and, secondly, how another branch of the Semites (the Arabs) became intermingled with Africa and the Africans.

When Islam first arrived in Africa in the seventh century there were almost no Arabs in Africa apart from a few traders and settlers scattered here and there. Today there are many millions of Arabs on the African continent. There are indeed more native speakers of the Arabic language in Africa than in the rest of the Arab world.

Similarly, there is more territory under Arab control within the African continent than outside. The largest Arab city in population is in Africa; Cairo also happens to be Africa's own largest city.

When Africa's Arab population is added to Africa's Black Muslim population, the total would make Africa the first continent in the world to have an absolute Muslim majority. Paradoxically, Nigeria alone may have more Muslims than any Arab country, including Egypt.[50]

Afrabia, as a convergence between Africa and the Arab world, has now produced identifiable people who may be designated as Afrabians (rather than just "Africans" or "Arabs"). Genealogical Afrabians are those who combine in their veins both African and Arab genes and blood. Such Afrabians would include many Northern Sudanese and at least two presidents of Egypt since the 1952 Egyptian revolution—Muhammad Naguib and Anwar Sadat.

Cultural Afrabians would be those Africans who have no Arab blood in them but have been substantially assimilated into Arab or Islamic culture. Most sub-Saharan Muslims in Africa belong to this category.

Ideological Afrabians are those Africans who have neither Arab genes nor been assimilated into Arab or Islamic culture, but are ideologically committed to trans-Saharan Pan-Africanism. They believe in the solidarity between Black Africa and Arab Africa—a concept of "one Africa indivisible." Such ideological Afrabians in history included Kwame Nkrumah, the founder President of post-colonial Ghana.

The fourth category is that of locational Afrabians. These would include Black Africans who do not culturally or ideologically identify with the Arabs but are citizens of a member of the Arab League (e.g., Southern Sudanese). Such locational Afrabians would also include non-Black Arabs who are citizens of non-Muslim African countries. A Coptic Egyptian who has become a citizen of South Africa would be an Afrabian in this locational sense.

Of these four categories, perhaps the fastest growing is that of cultural Afrabians—indigenous Black Africans who have substantially assimilated Islamic and Arab culture. The Muslim population of Black Africa is growing, both by expanding conversion and by biological increase within African Muslim families. On balance, sub-Saharan Muslims have larger families than sub-Saharan Christians and larger than Muslims north of the Sahara.

The number of genealogical Afrabians may also be expanding with the growing number of interracial marriages between Arabs and Africans. The convergence between Arabism and Africanity is still relentlessly moving towards the consolidation of Afrabia.

In this chapter we have already traced the different milestones in history towards the Europeanization of the Jews. There was the Babylonian exile following the conquest of the Kingdom of Judah by Babylonia. Some of the Jews remained in exile, even after Persia under Cyrus made it possible for the Jews to go back home.

The second milestone in the Euro-Diasporization of the Jews began after Alexander the Great conquered Palestine in 332 C.E. This conquest triggered the flowering of Hellenistic Judaism, inspired by ancient Greece.

The Roman period of 634 B.C.E. to 135 C.E. reactivated nostalgic Jewish dreams for establishing a Jewish state. These dreams failed. There followed Rabbinic Judaism from the second century of the Christian era to the eighteenth. The Mediterranean Jewry fragmented, while the Euro-Jewish Diaspora expanded.

The fourth stage in the Europeanization of Jews was the historic split between Sephardic Jews (linked to Andalusia and the legacy of Muslim Spain) and Ashkenazi Jews (more distinctly European—basically Franco-German and influenced by Latin-Christian culture).

The incorporation of the Jews into European civilization was in fits and starts—with a number of anti-Semitic pogroms and periodic mass expulsions of Jews from time to time. But even the persecution contributed to the flowering of the Jewish Enlightenment (Haskala) in Eastern and Central Europe.

The Jewish Reform led to the emergence of Reform Judaism and to the Conservative School alongside the older Orthodox versions of Judaism. Reform and Conservative Judaism were particularly successful in the United States.

And then European Jews invented modern *Zionism*—a new campaign for the establishment of a Jewish homeland. The movement was led by Theodor Herzl. Its initial headquarters were in Switzerland and then moved to Cologne and Berlin. It was ironic that a movement which dreamt about guiding Jews out of Europe to a distant homeland had its headquarters in Germany—the land which, under the Nazis, later tired to rid Europe of all its Jewish population.

In its original conception, Zionism sought to reverse the historic Europeanization of the Jews. Instead of Jews and Europeans converging to create one people, Zionism originally aspired to divorce Jews from Europeans all over again. A Jewish homeland in Palestine was supposed to attract the millions of Jews from the Diaspora back to the ancestral homeland in Palestine.

For a long time, Jews in the nineteenth and twentieth centuries were divided on whether Zionism was a sensible policy for world Jewry.[51] Many Orthodox Jews opposed the "modern nation of Israel as a Godless and secular state, defying God's will to send His Messiah at the time he preordained."[52]

In 1885 American Rabbis issued the Pittsburgh Platform—a declaration that Jews were no longer to look forward to a return to Israel. But in 1937 the Rabbis of the United States reversed themselves. The Central Conference of American Rabbis abrogated the anti-Zionist Pittsburgh Platform and encouraged instead the quest for a Jewish homeland.[53]

And yet many American and European Jews were still profoundly worried about Jews disengaging themselves from Europe and the West. Many Jews regarded Zionism as a declaration of divided loyalties—and dangerously close to disloyalty to the United States and to the European countries of which Jews were citizens or residents.

In 1943 the American Council for Judaism was founded with a platform which insisted that being a Jew was a religious affiliation and not a political identity. The Council was against the Zionist movement.

Few people knew before the end of World War II that while the Zionists were struggling hard to facilitate a Jewish exodus from Europe by voluntary emigration, the Nazis in Germany were facilitating a Jewish exit from Europe by extermination. When the full scale of the Nazi Holocaust against the Jews was exposed, support for the Zionist movement escalated. The anti-Zionist American Council for Judaism went moribund.

Many right-wing Christian Westerners supported the Zionist movement in the 1930s and 1940s in the hope of getting rid of their own Jews from Western countries. But the creation of the State of Israel did not result in a wholesale exodus of Jews from the Western world to Palestine. On the contrary, it resulted in giving to European Jews a chunk of Arab land. Zionism did not result in the de-Semiticization of Europe. It initiated instead the Europeanization of Palestine—for better or for worse.

The great historic saga of Euro-Jews is still unfolding—against the background of the even larger saga of a continental Afrabia. The final goal of AFRABIA is a little behind the destination of JEWOPE. But the historic movement towards those two destinies is surely irreversible. The struggle continues.

NOTES

1. For a guide to Semitic languages, see Robert Hetzron, *The Semitic Languages* (New York: Routledge, 1997), and on the linguistic origin and dispersal of Semitic languages, see Angel Sáenz-Badillos (transl. by John Elwolde), *A History of the He-*

brew Language (Cambridge and New York, NY: Cambridge University Press, 1993), pp. 3–8, and Thompson, *Early History of the Israelite People: From the Written and Archaeological Sources* (Leiden and New York: Brill, 1992), pp. 72–176.

2. The Abrahamic approach is exemplified, for instance, in F. E. Peters, *The Children of Abraham: Judaism, Christianity, Islam* (Princeton, NJ: Princeton University Press, 2004), Rev. Edition, with a foreword by John Esposito; Robin Wright, "At Cathedral, Iran's Khatami Urges Dialogue," *The Washington Post* (September 8, 2006) and an opinion piece by John Kearney, entitled "My God is Your God," *The New York Times* (January 28, 2004).

3. The Jewish population had declined from about 4.5–5 million in the first century to 1.2–1.5 million in the 6th century, and further declined to 1–1.2 million in the eighth century; see Maristella Botticini and Zvi Eckstein, "From Farmers to Merchants, Voluntary Conversions and Diaspora: A Human Capital Interpretation of Jewish History," Working Paper (August 2005), Tables 3 and 5, p. 11 and 18, manuscript available at www.colorado.edu/Economics/seminars/eckstein.pdf, accessed October 12, 2006.

4. Botticini and Eckstein, "From Farmers to Merchants, Voluntary Conversions and Diaspora," pp. 1 and 10.

5. The number of Jews worldwide is estimated at 14. 4 million; see John W. Storey and Glenn H. Utter, *Religion and Politics: A Reference Handbook*, (Santa Barbara, CA: ABC-CLIO, 2002), p. 119. The number of Arabs is estimated at 250–300 million, according to http://en.wikipedia.org/wiki/Arabs (accessed October 24, 2006).

6. The population of current African members of the Arab League, according to the CIA World Factbook is: Egypt (79 million), Libya (5.9 million), Sudan (41 million), Morocco (33 million), Tunisia (10.1 million), Algeria (33 million), Mauritania (3.2 million), Somalia (8 million estimate), Djibouti (487 thousand), Comoros (690 thousand), leading to a total of 213–214 million. It must be remembered that population figures in many of these countries is not accurate.

7. Elias J. Bickerman, "The Historical Foundations of Postbiblical Judaism," in Louis Finkelstein, Ed., *The Jews: Their History* (New York: Schocken Books, 1970, 1972), Fourth Edition, p. 73.

8. Jews had been exiled to Babylon after the destruction of the first temple in 586 BCE, and many chose not to return even when they had the opportunity to do so; see Jonathan Magonet, *The Explorer's Guide to Judaism* (London: Hodder and Stoughton, 1998), p. 53.

9. For some discussions on Jews in some of these Hellenistic and Roman urban centers, see John R. Bartlett, Editor, *Jews in the Hellenistic and Roman Cities* (London and New York: Routledge, 2002).

10. Jews occupied two of the five quarters in the city of Alexandria; see Cecil Roth, *A History of the Jews* (New York: Schocken Books, 1961), Revised Edition, p. 90.

11. A critical look at Jewish population estimates is provided in Brian McGing, "Population and Proselytism: How many Jews were there in the ancient world?" Bartlett, Editor, *Jews in the Hellenistic and Roman Cities*, pp. 88–106.

12. On the development of Rabbinic Judaism, see, for example, Jacob Neusner, *The Four Stages of Rabbinic Judaism* (London and New York: Routledge, 1999) and

Lawrence H. Schiffman, *From Text to Tradition: A History of Second Temple And Rabbinic Judaism* (Hoboken, N.J.: Ktav Pub. House, 1991).

13. The Sephardhi spoke the Judaeo-Spanish language of Ladino while the Ashkenazim spoke a Judaeo-German vernacular called Yiddish; see Magonet, *The Explorer's Guide to Judaism,* p. 54.

14. There were eighteen major expulsions from European countries between 1290 and 1496 alone, see Magonet, *The Explorer's Guide to Judaism,* p. 55.

15. The Marranos were concentrated in the Iberian countries; for some accounts, see B. Netanyahu, The Marranos of Spain: From the Late 14th to the Early 16th century, According to Contemporary Hebrew sources (Ithaca, NY: Cornell University Press, 1999) and Cecil Roth, *A History of the Marranos* (New York: Schocken Books, 1974, 1975).

16. Relatedly, consult Shmuel Feiner, *Haskalah and History: The Emergence of a Modern Jewish Historical Consciousness*, Translated by Chaya Naor and Sondra Silverston (Portland, OR and Oxford: Littman Library of Jewish Civilization, 2002).

17. See Moses Mendelssohn, *Jerusalem, Or, On Religious Power And Judaism*, translated by Allan Arkush (Hanover: Published for Brandeis University Press by University Press of New England, 1983).

18. Relatedly, consult Steven M. Lowenstein, "The 1840s and the Creation of the German-Jewish Religious Reform Movement," in Werner E. Mosse, Arnold Paucker, Reinhard Rürup, Editors, *Revolution and Evolution, 1848 in German-Jewish History* (Tübingen: Mohr, 1981.)

19. For an account of the beginnings of Conservative Judaism, see Moshe Davis, *The Emergence of Conservative Judaism* (Philadelphia: Jewish Publication Society of America, 1963).

20. For a biography, see David McLellan, *Karl Marx: His Life and Thought* (New York: Harper & Row, 1973).

21. The influence of Judaism on Marx's life and thought is analyzed in Murray Wolfson, *Marx, Economist, Philosopher, Jew: Steps in the Development of a Doctrine* (New York: St. Martin's Press, 1982).

22. This quotation is from Karl Marx, *Critique of Hegel's 'Philosophy of Right,'* in Robert C. Tucker, Editor, *The Marx-Engels Reader*, p. 12.

23. McLellan, *Karl Marx*, p. 3.

24. McLellan, p. 5.

25. Marx, "On the Jewish Question," in Tucker, Editor, *The Marx-Engels Reader*, pp. 24–51.

26. Krochmal's conception of history is detailed in Jay M. Harris, *Nachman Krochmal: Guiding the Perplexed of the Modern Age* (New York: New York University Press, 1991), pp. 103–155.

27. Harris, *Nachman Krochmal,* pp. 75–81.

28. Deuteronomy 14:2.

29. Heinrich Graetz, *The Structure of Jewish History*, translated by Ismar Schorsch (New York: Jewish Theological Seminary of America and Ktav Publishing House, 1975), p. 73. Consult also Shlomo Avineri, *The Making of Modern Zionism The Intellectual Origins of the Jewish State* (New York: Basic Books, 1981), pp. 30–31.

30. Romans 5: 12

31. Romans 5: 16

32. Corinthians 15: 45; consult Alfred Firmin Loisy, *The Birth of the Christian Religion and the Origins of the New Testament,* translated from the French by L.P. Jacks, (New York: University Books, 1962), p. 84.

33. Ali A. Mazrui, Program 3, *The Africans: A Triple Heritage* (BBC/PBS television series, 1986).

34. Relatedly, see Sigmund Freud, *Moses and Monotheism* (New York: Vintage Press, 1955, 1939) and Richard J. Bernstein, *Freud and the Legacy of Moses* (Cambridge and New York: Cambridge University Press, 1998).

35. Steven B. Smith, *Spinoza, Liberalism, and the Question of Jewish Identity* (New Haven: Yale University Press, 1997), p. 201.

36. Smith, *Spinoza, Liberalism, and the Question of Jewish Identity,* p. 49. Also see Leo Strauss, *Spinoza's Critique of Religion* (New York: Schocken Books, 1965).

37. Frederic V. Grunfeld, *Prophets Without Honor: A Background to Freud, Kafka, Einstein and Their World* (New York: Holt, Rinehart and Winston, 1979), p. 153.

38. Einstein did decline the honor; see Grunfeld, *Prophets Without Honor*, p. 184.

39. Columnist Charles Krauthammer has pointed out that 20 percent of Nobel winners have been Jewish; see his "Everyone's Jewish," *Washington Post* (September 25, 2006).

40. The importance of the Queen of Sheba in various traditions is described in Lou Silberman, "The Queen of Sheba in Judaic Tradition;" W. Montgomery Watt, "The Queen of Sheba in Islamic Tradition;" Edward Ullendorf, "The Queen of Sheba in Ethiopian Tradition;" and Paul F. Watson, "The Queen of Sheba in Christian Tradition," in James B. Pritchard, ed., *Solomon and Sheba* (London: Phaidon, 1974), pp. 65–145.

41. An unusual account of this black Muslim's life may be found in H. A. L. Craig, *Bilal* (London and New York: Quartet Books, 1977).

42. For a discussion of this journey, see W. Montgomery Watt, *Muhammad at Mecca* (Oxford: Clarendon Press, 1953), pp. 101–117.

43. See Aharon Gaimani, "Marriage and Divorce Customs in Yemen and Eretz Israel," *Nashim: A Journal of Jewish Women's Studies & Gender Issues*, (March 2006), Issue 11, pp. 43–83, and for the section on polygamy, pp. 61–65.

44. The limited role of Jews in British and Dutch slave trade is described in, for example, Eli Faber, *Jews, Slaves, And The Slave Trade: Setting The Record Straight* (New York: New York University Press, 1998) and Saul S. Friedman, *Jews and the American Slave Trade* (New Brunswick, NJ: Transaction Publishers, 1998).

45. For surveys of several Jewish personalities in Islamic lands, consult Moshe Gil,*Jews in Islamic countries in the Middle Ages*, translated by David Strassler (Leiden and Boston: Brill, 2004), pp. 273–489. Jews prominent in court life are described in Walter J. Fischel, *Jews in the Economic and Political Life of Mediaeval Islam* (New York, Ktav Pub. House, 1969).

46. Arnold Toynbee, *A Study of History, Volume* III (Oxford, UK: Oxford University Press, 1934), p. 322.

47. Philip Hitti, *History of the Arabs: From the Earliest Times to the Present* (London: Macmillan, 1953), p. 568.

48. For samples, see Said Hamdun & Noël King, Editors and Translators, *Ibn Battuta in Black Africa* (Princeton, NJ: Markus Wiener, 2005).

49. Relatedly, see Bayadrd Dodge, *Al-Azhar: A Millenium of Muslim Learning* (Washington, DC: Middle East Institute, 1961).

50. The estimation of the numbers of Muslims in Nigeria is somewhat controversial because of political issues over the census. According to an Associated Press report, "Muslim Mobs, Seeking Vengeance, Attack Christians in Nigeria," *New York Times* (May 13, 2004). "Many of Nigeria's 126 million people, [are] split almost evenly between Muslims and Christians. . ." However, another report estimates the percentage of Muslims in Nigeria at 75 percent; see http://www.islamicweb.com/begin/population.htm, accessed May 28, 2004. The CIA World Factbook July 2006 estimate of Nigeria's population is 131 million (50 percent Muslim) and that of Egypt at 78.8 million (90 percent Muslim).

51. A brief description of this opposition may be found in Yakov M. Rabkin, *A Threat from Within: A Century of Jewish Opposition to Zionism* (Black Point, NS: Fernwood, 2006), pp. 15–21, and specifically in one American case, Thomas A. Kolsky, *Jews against Zionism: The American Council for Judaism, 1942–1948* (Philadelphia: Temple University Press, 1990).

52. Encylopedia Brittanica, "Diaspora" available at http://www.search.eb.com/ (accessed October 14, 2006).

53. See Norton Mezvinsky, "Reform Judaism and Zionism: Early History and Change," in Roselle Tekiner, Samir Abed-Rabbo, and Norton Mezvinsky, Editors, *Anti-Zionism: Analytical Reflections*, p. 315, and pp. 327–328.

Chapter Two

Semitic Divergence and African Convergence

One of the big questions of the contemporary world is whether the era of *economic globalization* is simultaneously the era of *cultural re-tribalization.*

As we witness the enlargement of economic scale in the world, we are also witnessing cultural revivalism which range from the collapse of the Soviet Union, the disintegration of Yugoslavia, the rise of Hindu nationalism, the ferocity of the Palestinian intifadah, and major ethnic conflicts in Africa.

But is there a causal connection between the *globalization* and the *re-tribalization*? Is the enlargement of economic scale, for example, one of the forces, which are propelling people to reconsolidate their cultural identities?

We define "re-tribalization" in this chapter as a return to primordial values and identities. A return to ethnicity is rediscovery of ancestral loyalties; a return to religion is a rediscovery of sacred anchors. A return to Yoruba nationalism in Nigeria is rediscovering ancestry; the rise of the Sharia is rediscovering sacred anchors.

Let us look more closely at what is globalization in its widest meaning, and how it has affected Africa.[1] We shall then put *globalization* alongside *structural adjustment* as forces for cultural re-tribalization. Thirdly, we shall explore the new forces of *counter-terrorism* and the risks it carries for new forms of factionalism in Africa.

Economic globalization stems from all the forces which are transforming the global market and creating new economic interdependencies across vast distances. *Informational globalization* stems from all the forces which are exploding into the information superhighway—expanding access to data and mobilizing the computer and the Internet into global communication. *Comprehensive globalization* results from all the forces which are turning the world into a global village—compressing distance, homogenizing culture, accelerating mobility, and reducing the relevance of political borders. Under this comprehensive definition, globalization is the gradual villagization of the world.[2]

Under this third definition of globalization as the slow villagization of the world, the process has been going on for centuries—although the word is new. Before the West became the major engine of globalization in modern history, other people played a powerful role towards the villagization of the world—the Semitic peoples. Arabs and Jews were probably the pioneers of turning the world into a global village.

The Arabs became a vanguard of globalization firstly through the spread of Islam as a world religion; and secondly through the temporary rise of Islamic science and civilization.[3]

The Jews became a vanguard of globalization not through the spread of their religion (JUDAISM) but through their own dispersal. They were dispersed with many skills—Jewish jurists in Muslim Spain, Jewish poets in Byzantium, Jewish royal advisors in Persia, Jewish moneylenders in Europe.[4]

And then Europe and the Western world became the vanguard of modern globalization; the Jewish gene-pool produced disproportionate ethnic Jewish geniuses—including Spinoza, Karl Marx, Sigmund Freud, and Albert Einstein.

By this time Jewish identity had flowered best in the European Diaspora. World Jewry had disproportionately been Europeanized. This wing of the Semitic peoples continued at the pinnacle of scientific skills, while their Arab cousins declined in scientific performance.

The Israelis have won almost every war in the Middle East not because 80 per cent of Israelis are Jews, but because over 40% are European Jews—the new vanguard of globalization.

The Arab side of the Semitic people intermeshed less with Europe than with Africa. If the Jews historically became the Semites of European partnership, Arabs became the Semites of African partnership. Today there are more Arabs in Africa than outside Africa. There are therefore more speakers of the Arabic language in the African continent than in the Middle East. There are more Muslims in Black Africa than in the Arab world.[5] And in Nigeria there are more Muslims than in any Arab country.[6]

The Jewish Semites became part of the forces of power in the new globalization. The Arab Semites became part of the world of marginalization. The Jews retained their skills of the Middle Ages and modernized them impressively. The Arabs lost their skills of the Middle Ages, and could not even defend themselves against the Jews. This is the wide historic divergence of the Semitic peoples.

Are Africans caught in the crossfire? And how has Islam in Africa fared in the face of these forces of globalization and rivalry?

NORTH-SOUTH DIVIDE AND DIGITAL DIVIDE

In this twenty first century almost all economies of the world are bound of course to be significantly affected by the computer revolution and the commercialization of the Internet. But cultures differ in their responsiveness to the computer and the Internet. Indeed, while some cultures are calculus-friendly (at ease with mathematics) other cultures are calculus-challenged (ill-at-ease with mathematics).

In the United States there is increasing evidence that immigrants from South Asia (especially India and perhaps Pakistan) have responded faster to the computer culture than most other Americans. Indeed, India is already emerging as one of the great digital powers of the twenty-first century.

On American campuses there is indeed evidence that Korean-American students seem to be more calculus-friendly than Italian-American students. And Jewish-American students seem to be more at ease with the digital revolution than African-American students.

The question arises whether such differences also occur between the various cultures of Africa. Are some Southern cultures in Nigeria more calculus-friendly than some Northern cultures? Will this difference affect their comparative performance in the computer revolution? Is a digital divide in Nigeria likely to aggravate the North-South divide? It is tempting to conclude that Islam is anti-digital. In Sudan, on the other hand, are Muslim Northerners more at home with the computer culture than non-Muslim Southerners?

Mathematical prowess differs by individuals as well as by cultures. Calculus-friendly cultures produce a larger proportion of people who are comfortable with mathematics. This does not mean that calculus-challenged cultures produce no brilliant mathematicians at all. It only means that they produce far fewer. But is Islam—mother of algebra and co-parent of the Arabic numerals—lagging behind in the digital age?

Nor should we forget economic factors. Sometimes what may appear like cultural reasons for the digital divide may in fact be due to economic differences and financial access. If Southern Ghana (mainly Christian) is economically richer per capita than Northern Ghana (mainly Muslim), then the digital divide between North and South is likely to have economic as well as cultural reasons. Indeed, at this stage of this kind of research, we cannot be sure which reasons are weightier than which—economic or cultural.

Nor should these issues imply that Muslim Northerners in neighboring Nigeria are out skilled by Christian-led Southerners on all fronts. While there is indeed evidence that Southerners are more economically skilled than Northerners, most of the post-colonial period reveals that Northerners are better at the political game.[7] Even the electoral successes of Moshood Abiola in 1993 and of Olusegun Obasanjo in 1999 were due largely to the Northern support they received. Indeed, Obasanjo was rejected electorally by his fellow Yoruba in 1999, and supported substantially by Northerners.[8] The only question which arises is whether Northerners were "too clever by half" when they supported Obasanjo. Was Obasanjo a good political investment for the North? Or was he a miscalculation? Democracy has its risks.

The secret of ultimate stability in Nigeria does not simply lie in increasing the political power of the South—as the Obasanjo election might have done. It also lies in increasing the economic leverage and benefits of the North. There are wide-ranging proposals about how to increase the political power of the South—from rotation of the presidency to a confederal constitution.[9] But few minds have addressed the problem of how to increase the economic wealth per capita of the North and enhancing the North's economic leverage. Structural adjustment distrusts interference with market forces. A new sacred adjustment may be needed. We shall return to that theme later.

When privatization is more widely implemented, Northerners (especially Muslims) would have to be protected in Nigeria with a quota system and other safeguards. Methods of training young Northerners to become better entrepreneurs may have to be explored—ranging from special training to special loans to make their businesses more competitive. It is important to make those Northerners who are Muslim not just passive shareholders in the economy but energetic participants in wealth-creation.

Closing the digital divide between North and South may be part of closing the more general skill divide in the economy between the two regions. And closing the skill divide may be a precondition for closing the gap in *wealth per capita* between North and South. It is not enough to have a few highly visible Northern billionaires (the so-called "Kaduna Al-Hajis," as their critics call them). The people of the North generally need a fairer share of the wealth of their country. Does the legacy of *Lord Lugard* have to be vanquished—or simply be redefined for a new era? Islam—which once led the West in mathematics—may need to rediscover the culture of numbers in Muslim Africa.

BETWEEN DIVISION OF LABOUR
AND DIVISION OF CONTROL

The concept of a division of labour is familiar enough on a farm of mixed husbandry in Africa. There is sometimes a gender division of labour when women cultivate the crops while men are in charge of the cattle. Or men go to the mines or cities to work for wages, while their wives look after the family farm and the children.

While division of labour as a concept is so familiar, *division of control* in society may be less clearly articulated. In Malaysia political power is overwhelmingly in the hands of the ethnic Malays, while economic leverage is disproportionately in the hands of the ethnic Chinese.

What was the de facto deal struck between Blacks and whites in South Africa after Nelson Mandela's release? In order to avert a racial war, the whites said to the Blacks: "You take the crown, we shall keep the jewels."

The whites transferred political power to the Blacks but retained the bulk of economic control. The whites retained the best businesses, the best mines, the best jobs, the best shops in the major cities. The Blacks acquired the power to govern within those constraints. The Blacks had received the political crown; the whites retained the economic jewels. Here again is a situation not of a division of labour but of a division of control—similar to the deal between ethnic Malays who are Muslims and ethnic Chinese in Malaysia.

The question arises whether in a *de facto* kind of way a similar division of control had developed between the North and the South in countries like Uganda and Nigeria. Here we are confronting problems of *sub-regional marginalization* within a country. Was the North in postcolonial Nigeria and Uganda to be the hub of political power, while the South was the hub of economic activity and wealth? Were Northerners the equivalent of ethnic Malays—numerically strong, militarily protected, culturally Muslim but entrepreneurally less developed? Were Southerners in Nigeria or Uganda the equivalent of ethnic Chinese in Malaysia—more westernized, more entrepreneurial and better endowed in material resources? Was this the *de facto* division of control between North and South? Was the North supposed to have the political crown while the South kept the bulk of the economic jewels?

If this was Nigeria's national compact of division of control in much of the second half of the twentieth century, is it breaking down in the twenty-first century? In Uganda the division of control collapsed after Yoweri Museveni captured power in 1986.

Whenever this *de facto* division of control is seriously challenged, Nigeria's stability is at risk. The Igbo-led military coup of January 1966 challenged the division of control. Suddenly Northerners saw that they were not only economically marginal. They would now become politically marginal as well.

The root cause of the Nigerian civil war was not the anti-Igbo riots in the North late in 1966. It was the destabilization of the North-South division of control by the Ironsi-led military coup of January 1966. Also causal was the uneven distribution of economic skills between the Igbo and the Northern indigenous.[10] Even more dramatic has been the gap in economic performance between Northern Ugandans and Southern. The North is far behind.

With the democratic election of former military ruler Olusegun Obasanjo (a Southern Christian) to the presidency in Nigeria in 1999, another challenge to the North-South division of control has been posed. Will Northerners feel that their historic economic marginalization would once again be compounded by political marginalization? Democracy is always a gamble.

Brilliant Nigerian minds have spent a lot of time exploring how to share political power in Nigeria more justly. Nigerian federalism has been studied with great sophistication. Some reformers have called for *confederation* in Nigeria.[11]

But not enough time has been spent by Nigerian intellects exploring how to share economic power and economic skills more justly across ethnic and regional lines. The most dangerous economic inequalities in Nigeria are not class inequalities. They are economic inequalities *between ethnic groups and between regions.*[12] Particularly difficult to handle is the problem of the maldistribution of economic skills. Have the Bretton Woods institutions been insensitive to such realities in the past?

Privatization of state industries could result in an *ethnic take-over*. For example, if Southern ethnic groups in Nigeria are stronger entrepreneurs than Northern ethnic groups, the privatization of the oil industry could result in a Southern private take-over of the oil industry. In Uganda Yoweri Museveni's enthusiastic embrace of the free market has made it doubly hard for him to stabilize the North.

The Northern sense of economic marginalization has been aggravated. The breakup of commodity Marketing Boards in Uganda and Nigeria also resulted in opening up entrepreneurial opportunities. When the market forces are allowed free-play, these opportunities are often swallowed up dramatically by southern entrepreneurs.

Against the background that one of the causes of the Biafra war was Igbo entrepreneurship in Northern Nigeria, it is most important that any new ventures in privatization should include a minimum quota for Northern entrepreneurs—the sort of prescription often repugnant to champions of the free market.

A form of affirmative action is needed in Nigeria if we still believe in saving the Union and preserving national integrity.

In Cote d'Ivoire there is a similar North-South divide which coincides with religious differences. Under the Presidency of Felix Houphouet-Boigny the North-South divide was softened by wise power sharing. Cote d'Ivoire has more Muslims than Christians—but Christians dominated both the economy and the political system. From 1990 to 1993 Felix Houghouet-Boigny made Alassane Dramane OUATTARA, a Northern Muslim, Prime Minister.

Outtara had a break in his political career working for the International Monetary Fund as Deputy Managing Director from 1994 to 1999. He returned to the Ivory Coast to bid for the Presidency. Liberalization, however, did not translate into real democratization.

BETWEEN THE SHARIA AND GLOBALIZATION

The coming of the Nobel Prize to West Africa in 1986 was a symptom of yet another major force—the force of cultural globalization, which has recently coincided with the digital revolution. As we indicated, globalization consists of the forces which are leading the human race towards a global village. But since the 1990s globalization has also carried the seeds of cultural revivalism—ranging from ethnic resurgence to religious revival. In Northern Nigeria globalization has converged with the legacy of Lord Lugard.

Nigeria has the largest concentration of Muslims on the African continent. It has more Muslims than any *Arab* country, including Egypt. Since Olusegun Obasanjo became President in May 1999, some predominantly Muslim states in the Nigerian federation have taken steps towards implementing the Sharia in their own states, although the country as a whole is supposed to be a secular republic.[13] This has caused consternation among non-Muslim Nigerians. Indeed, in Lord Lugard's own Kaduna state, this Christian consternation exploded into inter-communal riots which cost hundreds of lives early in the year 2000.[14] But the momentum for SHARIACRACY still continues. Is Shariacracy an inevitable part of the legacy of Lord Lugard?

Many different reasons have been advanced for the rise of Sharia advocacy and Sharia implementation in Northern Nigeria. One explanation is that the Nigerian federation is getting more decentralized, and part of the decentralization is taking the form of cultural self-determination and revivalism. In Yorubaland this cultural self-determination is taking the form of Yoruba nationalism and retribalization. In Igboland it is taking the form of new demands for confederation. In the Muslim North cultural self-determination is taking the form of SHARIACRACY. Did Lord Lugard's Indirect Rule during the British colonial era lay the foundations of Shariacracy in the year 2000?

Another explanation for the rise of Sharia militancy is to regard it as a political bargaining chip. As the North is losing political influence in the Nigerian federation, it is asserting new forms of autonomy in preparation for a new national compact among the contending forces which Indirect Rule helped to demarcate.[15]

What has not been discussed is whether the rise of Sharia militancy itself is a consequence of globalization. One of the repercussions of globalization worldwide has been to arouse cultural insecurity and uncertainty about identities. Indeed, the paradox of globalization is, as we indicated, that it both promotes enlargement of economic scale and stimulates fragmentation of ethnic and cultural scale.[16] The enlargement of economic scale is illustrated by the rise of the European Union, and by the North American Free Trade Agreement (NAFTA).

The fragmentation of cultural and ethnic scale is illustrated by the disintegration of the Soviet Union, the collapse of Czechoslovakia into two countries, the rise of Hindu fundamentalism in India and the rise and fall of the Taliban and Islamic fundamentalism in Afghanistan, the collapse of Somalia after penetration by the Soviet Union and the United States, and the reactivation of genocidal behavior among the Hutu and Tutsi in Rwanda and Burundi.

Because globalization is a special scale of Westernization, it has triggered off identity crises from Uzbekistan to Somalia, Afghanistan to Northern Nigeria. Fragile ethnic identities and endangered cultures arc forced into new forms of resistance. Resisting Westernization becomes indistinguishable from resisting globalization. In Nigeria the South is part of the vanguard of Westernization and therefore the first to respond to globalization. When, in addition, the South appears to be politically triumphant within Nigeria under Obasanjo's presidency, alarm bells are sounded in parts of the North. This may not necessarily be Northern distrust of Yoruba or Igbo cultures. It may be Northern distrust of Westernization. Is Southern Nigeria a Trojan horse for globalization? And is globalization in turn a Trojan horse for Westernization? Paradoxically, a Westerner called Lord Lugard had helped to nurse Northern distrust of cultural Westernization.[17]

The Sharia under this paradigm becomes a form of Northern resistance not to Southern Nigeria, but to the forces of globalization and to their Westernizing consequences.[18] Even the policy of *privatization* of public enterprises and liberalization of the economy is probably an aspect of the new globalizing ideology. Privatization in Nigeria may either lead to new transnational corporations establishing their roots or to private Southern entrepreneurs outsmarting Northerners and deepening the economic divide between North and South. Again the Sharia may be a Northern gut response to these looming clouds of globalization and the de facto structural adjustment.

In Nigeria, the Sharia is caught between the forces of domestic democratization and the forces of wider globalization. On the one hand, Lord Lugard had helped to protect Islam in Northern Nigeria—and Islam had been an earlier form of cultural globalization within a worldwide community of believers.[19] On the other hand, the legacy of Lord Lugard had helped to heighten Hausa-Fulani identity, and was therefore a parochializing force. Both Globalization and Lugardization in Northern Nigeria had therefore contributed to the rise of Shariacracy.

In Uganda the North-South divide does not coincide with the religious divide, in spite of the fact that one arm of Northern resistance calls itself "the Lord's Resistance Army."

In Sudan the North-South divide does coincide with a religious divide. But unlike in Nigeria, the South in Sudan does not lead in economic skills. Southern Sudan is beginning to lead in economic *resources*. The discovery of oil in Southern Sudan has compounded the civil war between the North and South. In Sudan the North had previously tried to monopolize both political power and economic control. But a new "gold rush" has been precipitated by the discovery of oil. Piety and politics have now been compounded by petroleum.[20]

But where does terrorism fit into this global equation? How has the historic and fateful divergence of the Semitic peoples translated itself into terrorist confrontations? How is Africa affected by this additional mode of conflict?

AFRICA AND THE MIDDLE EAST: DIVERGENT RESPONSES

Why has terrorism continued to escalate in the Middle East while it has declined in Africa? Why is Africa talking about "Truth and Reconciliation" with the White man and Reparations from the Western World—while the Arabs and much of the rest of the Muslim world are angrier than ever against the West?

Why do Arab militants regard "Pay Back Time" in terms of retribution against the West—while so many African nationalists regard "Pay Back Time" in terms of reparation from the West?

Let us now look much more closely at the dynamics of politics in Africa and the Middle East from the point of view of reparation versus retribution.

The 2001 conference in Durban against racism and xenophobia took the issues of reparations forward.[21] But the terrorist events in New York on September 11 might have caused a setback to the cause of Reparations. Both Durban and September 11 have demonstrated once again a link between Africa and the Middle East, and the link has been affected by the forces of globalization.

I would like to explore the issue of reparations, on one side, and terrorist retribution, on the other, as alternative methods of "PAY BACK." I would like to place Africa alongside the Middle East in comparative perspective. Africa and the Middle East are in any case overlapping regions. Comparing them in this way is particularly appropriate in the context of globalization. Imperialism in the Middle East created conditions in which "PAY BACK" time threatened to be revenge. Imperialism in Africa, on the other hand, created conditions in which reparations appeared to be a more appropriate form of "PAY BACK."

Imperialism in the Middle East provoked the worst levels of anti-Western terrorism after formal liberation from European colonial rule. The British had been in power in Egypt, Iraq, Jordan, Sudan and elsewhere. The French had been in power in Syria, Lebanon, Algeria, Morocco, Tunisia and elsewhere. Palestine had been a United Nations trusteeship under British administration.

Imperialism in Africa provoked the worst levels of anti-Western terrorism before formal liberation from European colonial rule: that is to say, before Independence Day. Let us also relate the comparison to comparative rage. Imperialism in Africa triggered the most explosive anti-Western anger *before* European colonialism left Africa. Imperialism in the Middle East triggered off the most explosive anti-Western anger *after* European colonialism had left the Arab world.

What the colonial powers and white minority governments had condemned as "terrorism" in Africa included the Mau Mau war in Kenya, and the liberation wars in Algeria, Angola, Zimbabwe, Mozambique, and South Africa. What the Western world has condemned as "terrorism" in the Middle East has included hostage taking in Lebanon, high jacking of planes in the 1970s, as well as suicide bombs in the streets of Israel. The most spectacular was the destruction of the World Trade Center and the attack on the Pentagon on September 11, 2001.

In what sense are we to conclude that while the impact of imperialism in the Middle East created conditions for *violent* "PAY BACK" against the West, the impact of imperialism on Africa has been to create conditions which are ideal for "PAY BACK" in terms of reparations from the West?

PAY BACK AND SITUATIONAL DIFFERENCES

Some of the differences between Africa and the Middle East are situational, while other differences are primarily *cultural*. The postcolonial situation in the Middle East included a *permanent loss* of territory imposed by outsiders. The postcolonial situation in Africa involved *recovery* of territory—including recovery of land previously parceled out by apartheid in South Africa. This was won back to Africa.

Africa had also been spared the forceful creation of a Jewish state in Uganda and Kenya earlier in the twentieth century. Joseph Chamberlain, the Colonial Secretary at the time, had offered Theodor Herzl, the leader of the Zionist movement, a piece of Uganda and a piece of Kenya at the beginning of the twentieth century for the creation of a new Jewish state. (The boundaries of Uganda early in the twentieth century included parts of present-day Kenya.)

Had the Zionist movement accepted the offer, and a permanent Jewish state been established in East Africa, it is conceivable that African anger against the West today would be comparable to anti-Western rage in the Middle East.

But the Zionist movement in 1903 could not reach consensus about creating "Israel" in East Africa—and therefore the postcolonial situation in Africa today involves no permanent loss of territory.[22]

A related situational difference is that while the postcolonial conditions in Africa meant a clear end of foreign occupation, the postcolonial situation in the Middle East carried new forms of foreign occupation. It involved NOT just the creation of the state of Israel but also the occupation by Israel of the West Bank of Jordan, the occupation of Gaza, the annexation of the Golan Heights of Syria, the annexation of the whole of Jerusalem and the occupation for a while of a piece of Southern Lebanon. While the postcolonial period in Africa is truly post-occupation, the postcolonial period in the Middle East has entailed new forms of territorial annexations. This has immensely politicized the historic divergence of the Semitic peoples.

Where does the United States fit into this equation? When European powers occupied Africa and parts of Asia, *the image of America was that of an anti-colonial force* in world affairs. The United States put a lot of pressure on its European allies to speed up the process of giving independence to the colonies.

Even as late as 1956—when Britain, France and Israel invaded Egypt in response to Egypt's nationalization of the Suez Canal—the Eisenhower Administration turned against its allies.

The United States forced Israel to withdraw from the Sinai, and forced Britain and France to give up Port Said in Egypt. The British Prime Minister had a nervous breakdown—Anthony Eden gave way to Harold McMillan.

Egypt's Nasser emerged as a world figure—partly because the United States would not support the Anglo-Franco-Israeli invasion of Egypt. Nasser had been militarily defeated, but emerged politically triumphant. The Eisenhower administration—wittingly or unwittingly—had helped the Egyptian president rise to global stature.[23]

John F. Kennedy as President dismissed the concerns of the white settlers elsewhere in Africa when they objected to the phrase "AFRICA FOR THE AFRICANS." When Kennedy was asked by reporters at a news conference if he agreed with the phrase, first uttered by his Assistant Secretary of State, "Soapy" Williams at a press conference in Nairobi, Kennedy retorted, "I don't know who else Africa would be for."[24] The United States was on the side of the aspirations of African nationalists.

But two things were happening which future historians would later have to dis-entangle. The United States was expanding towards greater globalization and towards a greater role of interventionism in other parts of the world.

In the second half of the 20th century the United States began to be seen more and more as an imperial power, and a supporter of Israeli policies of occupation and repression.

Why is the U.S. being blamed for Israeli policies? Where is Osama bin Laden's anti-Americanism coming from?

a. Massive economic aid from the United States to Israel in billions.[25]
b. Provision of sophisticated American weapons to Israel
c. The United States shielding Israel from U.N. censure
d. The United States making U.N. Security Council impotent in punishing Israel
e. The United States weakening anti-Israeli Arab forces by buying off the government of Egypt with a billion U.S. dollars every year. Egypt is the largest Arab country and used to be the biggest single threat to Israel militarily. The U.S. largess has bought off Egypt effectively.[26]
f. Preventing Iraq from rising as an alternative to Egypt in challenging Israel. Taking advantage of Iraq's invasion of Kuwait to weaken Iraq permanently—whereas Pearl Harbor was not used to weaken Japan permanently, nor was Hitler's aggression used to weaken Germany permanently.

THE UNITED STATES is the main source of military support for the enemy of the Arab World, Israel, and the USA is also the main destroyer of Arab capacity to rise militarily. This latter policy includes weakening Egypt and enfeebling Iraq.

The American base in SAUDI ARABIA since 1991 is perceived as turning sacred Islamic soil into an extension of the PENTAGON. The American base in Saudi Arabia is seen not as a shield against such external enemies as Saddam Hussein, but a shield against an internal Iran-style Islamic revolution in Saudi Arabia. A situation of gross military frustration has been created, especially in Palestine and Iraq, but also on the sacred sands of Saudi Arabia.[27]

PAY BACK AND CULTURAL DIFFERENCES

But the differences between Africa and the Middle East in relation to political rage are not only due to divergent post-colonial situations.

There are also basic differences in *culture* between the Arabo-Hebrew Semitic peoples (both Arabs and Jews) on one side, and the majority of Black people in sub-Saharan Africa.

One major difference is the martyrdom complex which is much more developed among Middle Eastern peoples than among the Bantu and other peoples of sub-Saharan Africa.

The Jews have developed memories of the Holocaust into a major doctrine of Jewish martyrdom in history.[28] As for readiness to commit collective suicide, the Israeli nuclear program is partly based on the premise of the Samson option—a readiness to defend Israel even if it means destroying itself and much of the rest of the region.

Among Muslims of the Middle East (both Arab and Iranian) there is also the martyrdom complex in varying degrees.[29] Historically it has been more developed among Shia Muslims than among Sunni.[30] Suicide bombers against Israel and American troops in Lebanon started among Shiite Lebanese.

But anger against Israel and the United States has now resulted in the extension of the martyrdom complex to the Sunni population of the Middle East.

It is probable (though not yet proven) that the daredevils who destroyed the World Trade Center and the Pentagon were indeed Middle Easterners.

Because culturally the Middle East has a martyrdom complex, which is much more highly developed than among any groups in sub-Saharan Africa, it is the Middle East, which has been readier than Africa to commit suicidal political violence against the West. In the postcolonial period it is the Middle East, more than Africa, which has been ready to engage in acts of suicidal terrorism against the West.

Another major cultural difference between the Middle East and Africa concerns *comparative hate retention*. Cultures differ in hate-retention. Some cultures preserve a grudge across centuries. The Irish of Northern Ireland quarrel every year about a Protestant victory of the Orange Order against Catholics four centuries ago. The Irish have a high hate-retentive capacity.

The Armenian massacres of 1915 by the Ottoman Empire are still remembered bitterly by Armenians—and from time to time this memory results in the assassination of a Turkish diplomat somewhere in the world.[31] The Jews also have high hate-retentiveness, but they have sublimated it through the martyrdom complex. The Holocaust is given a sacred meaning rather than merely remembered as hate.

Because the Arabs have a vastly different history from Jews in the last fourteen centuries, the Arabs' experience as a persecuted people is relatively recent. Their hate-retention and their martyrdom complex is not as well developed or as sophisticated as that of the Jews. But Arabs and Jews do both share a fascination with the martyrdom complex. Now contrast this culturally with Black Africa. A major reason why Black Africa has not produced much postcolonial political violence against the West is Africa's short memory of hate.

Mahatma Gandhi used to prophesy that it would probably be through Black people that the unadulterated message of soul force [*satyagraha*] and passive resistance might be realized.[32] If Gandhi was indeed right, this could be one more illustration of comparative hate-retention.

The Nobel Committee for Peace in Oslo seems to have shared some of Gandhi's optimism about the soul force of the Black people. Africans and people of African descent who have won the Nobel prize for Peace since the middle of the twentieth century have been Ralph Bunche (1950), Albert Luthuli (1960), Martin Luther King Jr. (1964), Anwar Sadat (1978) Desmond Tutu (1984) and Nelson Mandela (1993). And now Kofi Annan and his UN leadership have joined the galaxy (2001). Neither Mahatma Gandhi himself nor any of his compatriots in India ever won the Nobel Prize for Peace, though Indians have won other categories of the Nobel Prize. Was Mahatma Gandhi vindicated that the so-called "Negro" was going to be the best exemplar of soul force? Was this a case of African culture being empirically more Gandhian than Indian culture?

In reality Black people have been at least as violent as anything ever perpetrated by Indians. The Horn of Africa has had its fair share of violence. So have other parts of black Africa. What is distinctive about Africans is their short memory of hate.

Jomo Kenyatta was unjustly imprisoned by the British colonial authorities over charges of founding the Mau Mau movement. A British Governor also denounced him as "a leader unto darkness and unto death." And yet when Jomo Kenyatta was released he not only forgave the white settlers, but turned the whole country towards a basic pro-Western orientation to which it has remained committed ever since. Kenyatta even published a book entitled *Suffering Without Bitterness.*[33]

Ian Smith, the white settler leader of Rhodesia, unilaterally declared independence in 1965 and unleashed a civil war on Rhodesia. Thousands of people, mainly Black, died in the country as a result of policies pursued by Ian Smith. Yet when the war ended in 1980 Ian Smith and his cohorts were not subjected to a Nuremberg-style trial. On the contrary, Ian Smith was himself a member of parliament in a Black-ruled Zimbabwe, busy criticizing the post-Smith Black leaders of Zimbabwe as incompetent and dishonest.[34] Where else but in Africa could such tolerance occur?

The Nigerian civil war (1967–1970) was the most highly publicized civil conflict in postcolonial African history. When the war was coming to an end, many people feared that there would be a bloodbath in the defeated eastern region. The Vatican was worried that cities like Enugu and Onitcha, strongholds of Catholicism, would be monuments of devastation and bloodletting.[35]

None of these expectations occurred. Nigerians—seldom among the most disciplined of Africans—discovered in 1970 some remarkable resources of self-restraint. There were no triumphant or triumphalist reprisals against the vanquished Biafrans; there were no vengeful trials of "traitors."

We have also witnessed the phenomenon of Nelson Mandela.[36] He lost twenty-seven of the best years of his life in prison under the laws of the apartheid regime. Yet when he was released he not only emphasized the policy of reconciliation—he often went beyond the call of duty. On one occasion before he became President a few white men were fasting unto death after being convicted of terrorist offences by their own white government. Nelson Mandela went out of his way to beg them to eat and thus spare their own lives.

When Mandela became President in 1994 it was surely enough that his government would leave the architects of apartheid unmolested. Yet Nelson Mandela went out of his way to pay a social call and have tea with the unrepentant widow of Hendrik F. Verwoed, the supreme architect of the worst forms of apartheid, who shaped the whole racist order from 1958 to 1966. Mandela was having tea with the family of Verwoed.[37]

Was Mahatma Gandhi correct, after all, that his torch of soul force (satyagraha) might find its brightest manifestations among Black people? Empirical relativism was at work again.

In the history of civilizations there are occasions when the image in the mirror is more real than the object it reflects. Black Gandhians like Martin Luther King Jr., Desmond Tutu and, in a unique sense, Nelson Mandela have sometimes reflected Gandhaian soul force more brightly than Gandhians in India. Part of the explanation lies in the soul of African culture itself—with all its capacity for rapid forgiveness.[38]

Yet "PAY BACK" as an African demand is a claim for Reparations—contrasting sharply with "PAY BACK" as political retribution against the West by other damaged regions of the world.

CONCLUSION

In an article for University of California students' journal *UFAHAMU* I once coined the term AFRABIA. In recent years this article has been circulating widely among third World oriented Arabs in the Middle East. More recently I have distinguished between the following AFRABIANS:

Afrabians of the Soil (but not of the Blood): Gamal Abdel Nasser of Egypt was a good example

Geneological Afrabians: Those Africans in whose veins there might flow the blood of both Arabs and Black Africans e.g. Anwar Sadat, Muhammad Neguib and most of Swahili people of Kenya and Tanzania.

Ideological Afrabians: Those Africans who idiologically believe in the oneness of Africa (both Arab and Black Africa) like Kwame Nkrumah of

Ghana—those who believe that Arabs and Africans are two people slowly becoming one; just as Jews and Europeans are two people who may already have become one.

We have sought to intimate in this chapter that long before the West became the major engine of globalization, the Semitic peoples (especially Arabs and Jews), were the vanguards of the of the villagization of the world. The Arabs helped to universalize Islam, which today commands the adherence of 1.2 billion people. Muslim civilization also carried the torch of mathematics for a while, banquething algebra and the Arabic numerals to the West, and introduced Europe to the intellectual gems of ancient Greece.

The Jews brilliantly dazzled Royal courts from Spain to Persia with their talents and wisdom, and later helped to orientate the modern mind through Spinoza, Freud, Marx, Einstein and others.

The Jews retained their position at the pinnacle of worldly skills; the Arabs and Muslims declined in those talents. The Jewish identity went into partnership with Europe; Arab identity went into partnership with Africa.

Jews became part of the power of globalization; Arabs and Africans became casualties of marginalization. The fateful Semitic divergence cast its shadow on the human race.

Islam in Africa was caught up with the forces of ethnic politics; and Islam in the world was caught up with the debate about terrorism and counter-terrorism.

It was once hoped by *Semitic optimists* that the creation of Israel in 1948, and the return of the Jews to the Middle East, would begin to heal the fateful Semitic divergence. Indeed, with Jews and Arabs living side by side, could a Semitic *re-convergence* begin?

Such Semitic optimists have yet to be vindicated. On the contrary, the Semitic pessimists have so far been vindicated in their conviction that creating a separate state for the Jews was not a reunification of the Semitic peoples but a permanent institutionalization of the Semitic divergence.

Exporting Ethiopian, Algerian, Egyptian and other Jews to Israel has also institutionalized the divergence of Jewish identity from Africa, just when Arab identity is more deeply interlocked with Africanity through the new African Union.

On the other hand, individual Jews (in or outside Israel) can make a lot of difference. As of now, it is inconceivable for the United Nations to have an Israeli as Secretary-General. The state of Israel is almost antithetical to the world body. But it is not inconceivable to have a Jew for Secretary-General. Boutros Boutros-Ghali was an Egyptian Christian who became Secretary-General. His First Lady was a Jew. James D. Wolfensen, the former President of the World Bank, is Jewish and was widely regarded by Arabs and Africans as probably the most progressive World Bank President ever.

There may not be much hope for real peace from the State of Israel, but James D. Wolfenson proves that there is hope in world Jewry. Jewish influence on globalization could be progressively used to start reversing the forces of marginalization in the world at last.

Amen!

NOTES

1. For some recent discussions on globalization, see Mohammed A. Bamyeh, *The Ends of Globalization* (Minneapolis: University of Minnesota Press, 2000); Mark Rupert, *Ideologies of Globalization: Contending Visions of A New World Order* (London and New York: Routledge, 2000); and Colin Hays and David Marsh, eds., *Demystifying Globalization* (New York: St. Martin's Press in association with Polsis, University of Birmingham, 2000).

2. Relatedly, see Marshall McLuhan and Bruce R. Powers, *The Global Village: Transformations in World Life and Media in the 21st Century* (New York: Oxford University Press, 1989).

3. For a comprehensive reference guide to the spread of Islam, see Everett Jenkins, Jr., *The Muslim Diaspora: A Comprehensive Reference To The Spread Of Islam In Asia, Africa, Europe, And The Americas* (Jefferson, N.C.: McFarland, 1999–2000).

4. Consult Evyatar Friesel, *Atlas of Modern Jewish History* (New York: Oxford University Press, 1990).

5. Figures on distributions of Muslim populations by nation state may be found in Azim A. Nanji, ed., *The Muslim Almanac* (New York, London et al: Gale Research, 1996), xxix–xxxv.

6. Nearly 50 percent of the estimated 128 million Nigerians are estimated to be Muslims; see Arthur S. Banks and Thomas C. Muller, eds., *Political Handbook of the World, 1999* (Binghamton, NY: CSA Publications, 1999) p. 723, and *The World Guide 1999/2000* (Oxford, UK: New Internationalist Publications, 1999), p. 429.

7. Since the country became independent in 1960, Nigeria has been ruled by Northerners for more than thirty years.

8. See Minabere Ibelema, "Nigeria: The Politics of Marginalization," *Current History* (May 2000), pp. 99, 637, 213.

9. For some analyses of political problems and solutions, consult, for example, Toyin Falola, *Violence in Nigeria: The Crisis of Religious Politics and Secular Ideologies* (Rochester, NY: University of Rochester Press, 1998); Paul A. Beckett and Crawford Young, *Dilemmas of Democracy in Nigeria* (Rochester, NY: University of Rochester Press, 1997); and S. Egite Oyovbaire, *Federalism in Nigeria: A Study in the Development of the Nigerian State* (New York: St. Martin's Press, 1985, 1984).

10. For an account of this coup, see Henry E. Nwigwe, *Nigeria—The Fall of the First Republic* (London: Motorchild Press, 1972).

11. See Note 18, above.

12. These are exacerbated when there are inconsistent and *ad hoc* revenue and expenditure policies; see Akpan H. Ekpo, "Fiscal Federalism: Nigeria's Post-Independence Experience, 1960–90," *World Development* (August 1994), pp. 22, 8, 1129–46.

13. According to Richard Dowden, "Death by Stoning," *New York Times Magazine* (January 27, 2002), p. 28, ten of the twelve northern states have introduced Sharia law.

14. See the reports in *The Guardian* (February 22, 2000), p. 1 and *Christian Science Monitor* (May 26, 2000), p. 1.

15. An overview of the North-South and other cleavages bedeviling Nigeria may be found in *The Economist* (January 15, 2000), pp. 14–15; also see *The Economist* (July 8, 2000), p. 47. For longer analyses on earlier conflicts caused by the Sharia issue, see Toyin Falola, *Violence in Nigeria: The Crisis of Religious Politics and Secular Ideologies* (Rochester, NY: University of Rochester Press, 1998), especially pp. 77–113; Simeon O. Ilesanmi, *Religious Pluralism and the Nigerian State* (Athens, OH: Ohio University Center for International Studies, 1997), pp. 174–207; M. H. Kukah and Toyin Falola, *Religious Militancy and Self-Assertion: Islam and Politics in Nigeria* (Aldershot, UK, and Brookfield, VT: Avebury Press, 1996), pp. 117–39; and Pat A. T. Williams, "Religion, Violence, and Displacement in Nigeria," *Journal of Asian and African Studies*, p. 32, 1–2 (June 1997), pp. 33–49.

16. Consult, relatedly Benjamin Barber, *Jihad Vs. McWorld.*(New York: Times Books, 1995).

17. For an overview of this important figure in Nigerian history, consult Dame Margery F. Perham, *Lugard* (2 volumes), (London: Collins, 1956–60).

18. For an earlier example, consult Abdullah Mu'aza Saulawa, "Islam and its Anti-Colonial and Educational Contribution in West Africa and Northern Nigeria, 1800–1960," *Hamdard Islamicus* (1996), pp. 19, 1, 69–79 and Falola, *Violence in Nigeria,* pp. 74–77.

19. See Michael Crowder, "Lugard and Colonial Nigeria: Towards an Identity," *History Today* 36 (February 1986), pp. 23–29.

20. The United States has become involved in mediation efforts; see a report in *The Washington Post* (Wednesday, May 15, 2002), p. 24.

21. For an optimistic view of this conference, see Pierre Sane, "In Defence of Durban; Racism is Back on the Agenda," *UNESCO Courier*, Volume 54, Number 10 (October 2001), pp. 10–12, and for a critical view, see Charles Krauthammer, "Disgrace in Durban," *The Weekly Standard*, Volume 7, Number 1 (September 2001), pp. 15–16.

22. This issue is discussed in David J. Goldberg, *To the Promised Land: A History of Zionist Thought from its Origins to the Modern State of Israel* (London and New York: Penguin Books, 1996), pp. 83–89.

23. A full treatment of the Suez crisis can be found in a collection of essays edited by William Roger Louis and Roger Owen, *Suez 1956: The Crisis and Its Consequences* (Oxford: Clarendon, 1989).

24. This episode is recounted in Robert K. Massie, *Loosing The Bonds; The US and South Africa in the Apartheid Years* (New York: Nan A. Talese, Doubleday, 1997), p. 115.

25. For a discussion on aid to Israel, see Mohammed Rabie, *The Politics of Foreign Aid: U.S. Foreign Assistance and Aid to Israel* (New York, Westport, CT, and London: Praeger, 1988).

26. See Duncan L. Clarke, "US Security Assistance to Egypt and Israel: Politically Untouchable?" *Middle East Journal* Volume 51, Number 2 (Spring 1997), pp. 200–14. Data on US aid to all countries between 1945–1997 may be found in United States Agency for International Development, *US Overseas Loans and Grants and Assistance from International Organizations July 1, 1945–September 30, 1997* (Washington, DC: Office of Budget, Bureau of Management, US AID, 2000).

27. A report in *The Washington Post* (January 18, 2002), 1, indicated that the Saudis were beginning to get antsy about the US presence and may ask the US to withdraw, although Secretary of State Colin Powell denied in *The Washington Post* (January 19, 2002), p. 15, that such a request had not been made.

28. The Jewish attitude and history toward martyrdom is discussed in Avner Falk, *A Psychoanalytic History of the Jews* (Cranbury, NJ: Farleigh Dickinson and Associated Universities Press, 1996), pp. 328–29, and pp. 467–68.

29. On martyrdom in Islam, see chapter 2 in Rudolph Peters, *Jihad In Classical and Modern Islam: A Reader* (Princeton, NJ: Markus Wiener, 1996).

30. The Iranian Revolution in 1979 drew special attention to this aspect; consult, for instance, Donald A. Braue, "Shi'i Martyr Consciousness And The Iranian Revolution," *Encounter* Volume 43 (Autumn 1982), pp. 377–393.

31. Readers interested in these massacres may consult Hamo B. Vasilian, ed., *The Armenian Genocide: A Comprehensive Bibliography And Library Resource Guide* (Glendale, VA: Armenian Reference Books Co., 1992).

32. See Sudarshan Kapur, *Raising Up A Prophet: The African-American Encounter With Gandhi* (Boston: Beacon Press, 1992), pp. 89–90.

33. Jomo Kenyatta, *Suffering Without Bitterness* (Nairobi and Chicago: East African Publishing House and Northwestern University Press, 1968).

34. For an overview of the transition from white rule to black rule in Zimbabwe, consult Anthony Parsons, "From Southern Rhodesia to Zimbabwe, 1965–1985," *International Affairs* Volume 9, Number 4, (November 1988), pp. 353–61; also see Victor De Waal, *The Politics of Reconciliation: Zimbabwe's First Decade* (London and Cape Town: Hurst and David Philip, 1981).

35. Readers interested in a guide to the Biafra war may consult Zdenek Cervenka, *The Nigerian War, 1967–70: History of The War, Selected Bibliography and Documents* (Frankfurt Am Main: Bernard & Graef, 1971).

36. See the report on Nelson Mandela in the *New York Times* (March 23, 1999), p. 1.

37. *New York Times* (March 23, 1999), p. 6.

38. For an article recommending the African experience for the Middle East, see the op-ed piece by Mark Mathabene, "The Cycle of Revenge Can be Broken," *New York Times* (July 5, 2002), p. 21.

Section II

EURO-JEWS IN WORLD HISTORY

Chapter Three

The Talmudic Tradition
in Comparative Perspective

'Emotion is black—reason is Greek!' This quotation from Leopold Senghor has become one of the central epigrams of negritude. Senghor has argued that the genius of Africa is not in the realm of intellectual abstraction; it is in the domain of emotive sensibility.

As we shall indicate later, some of the assumptions of negritude underline the whole Black Studies movement in the United States. We shall pay special attention to Black Studies as an effort to intellectualize negritude. But precisely because Black Studies has a major intellectual component in its *raison d'être*, it diverges from Senghor's dictum.

When under attack Senghor reformulates his views on this dictum. His interpretation of original Africa has sometimes exposed him to the charge of having deprived the traditional African of the gift of rationality. Senghor defends himself with his usual ingenuity. But ultimately he still insists on regarding the African as basically intuitive, rather than analytical. He has said:

> Young people have criticized me for reducing Negro-African knowledge to pure emotion, for denying that there is an African 'reason'. . . . I should like to explain myself once again. . . . European reasoning is analytical, discursive by utilization; Negro-American reasoning is intuitive by participation.[1]

Elsewhere Senghor emphasizes that this 'analytic and discursive reason' was part of the Greco-Roman heritage of Europe at large. 'One could even trace the descent of Marxism from Aristotle!' Senghor asserts.

Descartes had asserted that the ultimate proof that I exist is that I *think*. In his own famous words, "I think, therefore I am." According to Senghor, however, African epistemology starts from a different basic postulate. For the black African the world exists by the fact of its reflection upon his emotive self. 'He does not realize that he thinks; he feels that he feels, he feels his existence, he feels himself.'[2] In short, black-African epistemology starts from the premise, 'I feel, therefore I am.'

What about the genius of the Jews? If emotion is black and reason is Greek, the secret of the Jewish miracle in history is the fusion of emotion with reason. The Talmudic tradition is at the heart of this miracle.

To a certain extent the Talmudic tradition is a fusion of religion, ethnicity, and intellectual pursuits. Through the Talmudic tradition the national consciousness of the Jewish people was both intellectualized and sacralized.

The Black Studies movement in the United States, weak and uncertain as it is, was also born out of the national consciousness of a people. Like the Talmudic tradition, the Black Studies movement also seeks to intellectualize the national consciousness of its people. But among the questions which remain is whether Black Studies is also an effort to sacralize black identity. Is 'blackness' in the United States evolving into a religious as well as a racial experience? In that regard is blackness ever likely to become a neat equivalent of Jewishness, combining sacred and ethnic symbols of identification?

For the time being only members of the Nation of Islam, the Black Muslims of America, have attempted to combine religious with ethnic modes of identification in a manner reminiscent of the Jews. But while Judaism over the centuries has emphasized the nearness of Jews to God, the Nation of Islam tended for a while to emphasize the distance of whites from God.

Judaism was autocentric, emphasizing the self in the face of a hostile environment. The Nation of Islam was for a while eco-centric, emphasizing the hostility of the (white) environment even more than the self. The Nation of Islam was more preoccupied with denouncing the racial 'gentiles', the white people, than with praising the black people. To the Nation of Islam it was more fundamental that whites be exposed as devils than that blacks be accepted as the chosen people. For a while the dominant emotion among black Muslims was anger against the enemy rather than pride in one's self.

But the Nation of Islam has been changing. The challenge which came from Malcolm X before he broke off from the movement was a major stage in this evolution of the black religion. After going on a pilgrimage to Mecca and discovering how multiracial Islam abroad was, Malcolm was no longer convinced that white people were irredeemably devils. He was shifting the emphasis away from hostility against whites to pride in one's self. Shortly afterwards Malcolm was assassinated.

In 1975 Elijah Muhammed, the leader of the Nation of Islam, himself died of natural causes. The shift from eco-centrism (in rebellion against the environment) to autocentrism (inspired by self-confidence) has continued in the movement. To that extent the similarity with at least early Judaism has become somewhat greater, including a number of rituals affecting diet and sexual behaviour. What has been lacking in the Nation of Islam is a vigorous intellectual tradition, in spite of the relative success of some of their religious publications.

On the one hand, America has witnessed the Black Studies movement as an effort to intellectualize blackness. On the other hand, the Nation of Islam has emerged as an effort to sacralize blackness. What is missing is a viable movement which combines both intellectual and religious strengths. If the Talmudic tradition is a fusion of religion, ethnicity, and analytical power, there is as yet no black equivalent. There is as yet no pooling of resources between the Black Studies movement as an intellectual effort and the Nation of Islam as a religious endeavour in black America. Only a combination of the strengths of the two movements could produce a black equivalent to a tradition which takes pride in the history of the Jews, seeks to understand and analyze the heritage of codified morality, studies the implications of covenant with sacred origins, finds solace *and* strength in the collective martyrdom of its members over the centuries, and constantly reexamines the historic role of its peopole in human affairs generally.

How relevant has the Talmudic tradition been for Jewish specialization in intellectual pursuits? How do Jews compare with blacks in such pursuits?

BLACK BRAIN, JEWISH INTELLECT

Comparisons of intellectual performance between races and ethnocultural groups have been part of the history of racism itself. Yet there is little doubt that in the modern period of history the black man has been scientifically marginal, in the sense of being on the outer periphery of scientific and technological achievement.

By contrast the Jewish impact on the intellectual heritage of mankind has been immense. The great Jewish figures who have influenced the evolution of ideas and morals ranged from Jesus Christ to Karl Marx. The ethical component of modern civilization includes a disproportionate contribution form the ideas of Jewish thinkers and prophets. Even if we restricted ourselves to recent times, it is possible to argue that of the five people who have done the most to determine the shape of the modern mind, three are Jews. The five names are those of Isaac Newton, Charles Darwin, Karl Marx, Sigmund Freud and Albert Einstein. Of these five only Newton and Darwin were non-Jewish by descent, although Newton may have been converted secretly to Maimonide Judaism. This is in fact one of the most remarkable things about Jewish history — the Jewish propensity for producing intellectual geniuses. To the present day a disproportionate number of the towering figures in the academic world in the United States are Jews.

What explanation can be advanced for this remarkable intellectual phenomenon? Do the Jews bring into question the old debate about genetic differences in intelligence between one race and another? If we claim that all races are endowed with an equal distribution of intelligence, how then can we explain the Jewish miracle? If we used the number of towering minds as a measure of distribution of intelligence in a given race, and we concluded that the Jews were extra-endowed with intellectual gifts, would not the same reasoning force us to conclude that the blacks were deficient in such gifts? Is Jewish mental superiority the ultimate proof of black inferiority?

The debate is not as antiquated as it might at first sound. Arguments about genetic differences in relation to intelligence have re-entered academic discussions in the Western world.

One memorable day when I was still at Makerere University in Uganda my secretary buzzed my telephone to announce a long distance call from Durban in South Africa. 'Durban?' I asked in surprise, as I had no special connections there. When the call was put through it turned out to be an editor of a South African magazine. The editor wanted me to review a particular book. Considering the trouble he took to make a rather expensive long distance call, I became curious about the whole assignment. The book he referred to was one by a man called Barnett Potter. The title of the book was *The Fault, Black Man*, a phrase adapted from Shakespeare's *Julius Caesar*. 'The fault, dear Brutus, is not in our stars, but in ourselves, that we are underlings.' The South African editor said that the book had created a stir in southern Africa, and he wanted me to write a rebuttal. The central assertion of the book was 'The fault, black man, is not in your stars but in yourself that you are an underling.' The argument was that the black man had been ruled and dominated by others not because of bad luck but because of something inherently within himself. I agreed to write the rebutting review of the *book,* and arrangements were made for me to receive it from London.

The book itself did not pretend to be scholarly or even sophisticated, but the white man who had written it used the evidence of greater scholars than he could pretend to be. He used in part Arthur Jensen's article in the *Harvard Educational Review* asserting that research among American schoolchildren had indicated that blacks performed less well than whites intellectually for reasons which were partly genetic. Jensen's article had reactivated a long-standing debate concerning the question of whether races differed genetically in intellectual competence.[3]

Barnett Potter linked the findings of Jensen's research to the tribute paid to the Jewish community by C. P. Snow, the British physicist and novelist. C. P. Snow had drawn attention to the remarkable achievements of the Jews in the sciences and the arts. A crude measure like examining the names of Nobel Prize winners would indicate that up to a quarter of those winners bore Jewish names. Why should a population of little more than 15 million Jewish people in the world produce one quarter of the best scientific and scholarly performance in a world of approximately 3,000 million people?

Or is there is there something in the Jewish gene-pool which produces talent on quite a different scale from, say, the Anglo-Saxon gene-pool? I am prepared to believe that may be so. . . . One would like to know more about the Jewish gene-pools. In various places—certainly in Eastern Europe—it must have stayed pretty undiluted, or unaltered for hundreds of years.[4]

Lord Snow did not seem aware of the partial contradiction of his statement. The Jews who performed particularly impressively in recent times, and won Nobel Prizes, were not in fact primarily from Eastern Europe where Snow regarded the Jewish gene-pool to be particularly pure and 'unaltered for hundreds of years'. On the contrary, the best Jewish intellectual achievements in recent times have been overwhelmingly from Western Jews, in many ways the least pure in 'gene-pool' among all the Jews of the world.

Whatever the partial contradiction in C. P. Snow's analysis, there is indeed a phenomenon to be explained in the Jewish intellectual edge in Western history. Barnett Potter, as a white gentile, used the Jewish intellectual edge as proof that blacks were genetically inferior. But he too fell short of the logic of his own position. If Jewish intellects in the Western world itself have performed disproportionately in relation to white gentiles, are we also to conclude that white gentiles are genetically inferior intellectually to their Jewish neighbours? Certainly Barnett Potter would regard that conclusion as too high a price to pay for the comfort of proving that the fate of the black man was not in his stars but in his genes.

FROM THE TALMUD TO NEGRITUDE

What could be the explanation both for the Jewish intellectual edge and for the black scientific marginality?

This is perhaps where the Talmudic tradition claims some degree of relevance. Over a period of time a people that was governed by codified laws and a covenant began to put a special premium on analytical, judicial, and speculative skills. A structure of motivation evolved among Jews which conferred social rewards on intellectual performance. This was inevitably accompanied by processes and structures of socialization which exposed a significant proportion of children to analytical and abstract aspects of Jewish culture.

Among the Jews in the Diaspora a reinforcing factor may have been some prior intellectual selection at the time of Jewish dispersal two millennia ago. Was the composition of the Jews who went into exile abroad disproportionately intellectual? C. D. Darlington has argued as follows in connection with one important part of the dispersal:

> The Jews who moved into the Western parts of the Persian Empire were . . . . a highly selected remnant. . . . They were a group of skilled and partly intellectual classes differing from all other such classes in two vital respects. First, they were largely cut off from intermarriage with the other classes of the societies in which they lived. And, secondly, they were entirely liberated from the control of their own former military governing class. The Jewish intellectuals were thus free.[5]

Darlington suggests that a disproportionate number of intellectuals among those who fled from Palestine, combined with relatively strict endogamy, helped to maintain and accumulate a gene-pool of intellectual excellence.

This issue is also connected with the whole question of the relationship between professional specialization and intellectual alternative avenues of professional life were closed to Jews in Europe, the community began to specialize in commerce and later the liberal professions. The cumulative effect of specialization provided not a Darwinian natural selection, but a specialized cultural selection. Succeeding generations of Jewish intellectuals produced in turn children who were intellectually oriented. Specialization could provide the opportunity for the discovery of brilliance.

Also related as a factor is the whole tradition of Jewish prophets and of rules which are not only observed but continually enunciated and often intellectualized.

It might also be fortunate that Judaism does not demand celibacy of its rabbis. Had Jewish priests been expected to be celibate as Catholic priests, the Jewish intellectual contribution to world civilization might well have been significantly reduced. It has been estimated that many of the most impressive Jewish scholars have been sons or grandsons of rabbis. The tradition of the prophets has again helped to consolidate prior intellectual specialization.

With regard to black scientific marginality, there have been a number of different responses to the phenomenon. Among some black people, one response has been to deny that they have been scientifically marginal. Those who react in this way among black people then proceed to mention a number of famous black names in the intellectual history of the world. These would range from Aleksandr Pushkin, 'the father of Russian literature', to Alexandre Dumas, the French literary romantic. Both had the blood of black people in their ancestry, and many black men have taken pride in that.

The tendency to deny that there has been a black scientific marginality has been specially manifest among black Americans. It might well be that the precise nature of their humiliation from the slave days has created a resolve among their cultural nationalists to affirm black greatness in history.[6]

This kind of response is not unknown among black Africans either. In Ghana, while it was still under the presidency of Kwame Nkrumah, a number of postcards were issued with paintings depicting major achievements that had taken place in Africa These included a painting with figures in the attire of ancient Egypt, showing the first paper to have been manufactured. The caption was 'Ancient African History: Paper was Originated in Africa'. Then there is a painting of 'Tyro, African Secretary to Cicero, [who] Originated Shorthand Writing in 63 BC. Then there are cards asserting that the science of chemistry originated in Africa, that Africans taught the Greeks mathematics and the alphabet. According to these postcards reproduced from The Archive of Accra, Ghana, many other scientific inventions also originated in Africa. The Ghanaian postcards under Nkrumah were in a way in the tradition of black American cultural assertiveness, but transposed to the African continent.[7]

An alternative response to black scientific marginality is not only to affirm it but also to take pride in it. Black countries ruled by France produced a whole movement called negritude, which reveled in the virtues of a non-technical civilization. In the words of the poet Aime Cesaire:

> Hooray for those who never invented anything
> Who never explored anything
> Who never discovered anything!,
> Hooray for joy, hooray for love
> Hooray for the pain of incarnate tears.
> My negritude is no tower and no cathedral. . . .[8]

Clearly this response to scientific marginality is fundamentally different from the tendency to trace a black ancestry in the genealogy of Robert Browning, or of Pushkin or Alexandre Dumas.

The Black Studies movement in the United States has been influenced by both forms of response to black marginality. On the one hand, the movement asserts that too much distortion has taken place in the study of black history as a result of the white man's scholarship. Black contributions to world civilization have therefore been grossly underestimated. Only a Black Studies movement, controlled by blacks, can help to restore this balance.

On the other hand, the Black Studies movement has also been influenced by negritude with its emphasis on black cultural distinctiveness rather than black intellectual competitiveness. Let us now turn more fully to this linkage between the logic of negritude and the assumptions of the Black Studies movement.

NEGRITUDE AND NEGROLOGY

It is with French-speaking Africa and with Martinique that the word 'negritude' is normally associated. And it is among French-speaking blacks at large that negritude as a movement has found its literary proponents. The term itself was to all intents and purposes virtually coined by Aime Cesaire, the poet of Martinique, as he affirmed:

> My negritude is no tower and no cathedral
> It dives into the red flesh of the soil.[9]

Cesaire's poem was first published in a Parisian review in 1939. In Africa itself the movement's most distinguished literary proponent came to be Leopold Senghor, the poet-president of Senegal. It has been Senghor who has helped to give shape and definition to negritude as a general philosophical outlook. In his own words,

Negritude is the whole complex of civilized values—cultural, economic, myth-making, the gift of rhythm, such are the essential elements of negritude, which you will find indelibly stamped on all the works and activities of the black man.[10]

Senghor's definition as given here, though illuminating, is not in fact complete. Negritude is not merely a description of the norms of traditional black Africa; it is also a capacity to be proud of those values even in the very process of abandoning them. Sometimes it is a determination to prevent too rapid an erosion of the traditional structure.

Whether we take Senghor's own definition, or give it greater precision, it is clear that a believer in negritude need not be a French-speaking literary figure. 'Negritude is the awareness, defence and development of African cultural values,' Senghor has said elsewhere.[11] Such awareness, defence, and development need not, of course, take the form of a poem in French. To limit the notion of negritude to a literary movement is to miss what the literary outburst has in common with other forms of black cultural revivalism. The word 'negritude' might indeed owe its origin to a literary figure, but the phenomenon which it purports to describe has more diverse manifestations. In any case the term negritude is too useful to be allowed to die with a literary movement.

Not that a romantic literary preoccupation with an idealized Africa is likely to come to an end all that soon. There will be black poems of such a romantic bias for at least another generation. What need to be defined now with a wider vision are the boundaries of the phenomenon as a whole.

If negritude is indeed 'the awareness, defence and development of African values', we could usefully divide it into two broad categories. We might designate one category as literary and the other as anthropological negritude. Literary negritude would include not only creative literature but also certain approaches in African social and political—which characterize the black peoples or, more precisely, the Negro-African world. All these values are essentially informed by intuitive reason. . . . The sense of communion, the gift of historiography. An African historian who succumbs to methodological romanticism in his study of ancient African empires like Songhai and Mali is, in this sense, within the stream of literary negritude.

Anthropological negritude is on the whole more directly related to concrete cultural behaviour than literary negritude normally is. In its most literal form anthropological negritude is a romanticized study of an African 'tribal community' by an African ethnologist. The book *Facing Mount Kenya* by Jomo Kenyatta even on its own would have been enough to make young Kenyatta a proponent of anthropological negritude.

But there is more to this side of negritude than a formal study of a 'tribe'. There is a link between, say, Elijah Masinde, the prophet of *Dini ya Msambwa* in East Africa, and Aime Cesaire, the sophisticated poet of Martinique. At any rate, literary negritude and certain African messianic movements are different responses to one interrelated cultural phenomenon. Both the Greco-Roman aspect of European civilization and the Judeo-Christian side of it have sometimes forced the African into a position of cultural defensiveness. These two mystiques have come into Africa wrapped, to some extent, in Europe's cultural arrogance. The Greco-Roman mystique contributed to the birth of literary negritude as a reaction; the Judeo-Christian sense of sacred superiority contributed to the birth of Ethiopianism and African syncretic churches at large. The latter phenomena have intimate links with, or are themselves manifestations of, anthropological negritude.[12]

Sterling Stuckey has asserted persuasively that W.E.B. DuBois, the black American intellectual giant, was 'easily the most sophisticated proponent of negritude until the advent of Cesaire and Senghor'. Stuckey has also recommended a study of DuBois's cultural views which should, *inter alia,* seek to determine how the DuBois variant of negritude differed from that projected by the Harlem Renaissance writers.[13]

It is right that the new wave of Black Studies in the United States should explore its links with the negritude movement, for those two waves of intellectualized black assertiveness have a good deal in common. Leopold Senghor, the chief of negritude in Africa, has argued that there is a fundamental difference between the white man's tools of intellectual analysis on the one hand and the black man's approach to intellectual perception on the other.

Senghor has said: 'European reasoning is analytical, discursive by utilization; Negro-African reasoning is intuitive by participation.'[14]

Senghor, partly because of the complexity of his ideological position on culture, is not always consistent in his views on comparative epistemology as between European and Black-African modes of thought. But it is arguable that the logical conclusion of Senghor's position is that no European or white scholar can hope to understand fully the inner meaning of a black man's behaviour. This is the meeting point between negritude as the cultural essence of black civilization and negrology as the principles by which the black man was to be studied. For both Leopold Senghor and the militant wing of the Black Studies movement in the United States there are indeed certain socio-scientific principles of interpretation without which the black man cannot be adequately understood. The question is whether these principles can be mastered by a scholar who is not himself black. In his address to the Second International Congress of Africanists in Dakar in December 1967, President Senghor intimated that such principles of scholarly interpretation could be mastered by others if those scholars are sufficiently sensitive to the peculiar characteristics of the culture they are studying. Some of the advocates of Black Studies in the United States are more skeptical. For them only black scholars can fully command the principles of negrology.[15]

But if negrology is the science of studying the black man, should it not be sufficiently neutral to be accessible to diverse minds? Senghor would say that such a definition of 'science' is itself ethnocentric. He first quotes Jacques Monod, a Nobel Prize winner, who in his inaugural lecture at the College de France in 1967 asserted:

> The only aim, the supreme value, the 'sovereign good' in the ethics of Knowledge is not, let us confess, the happiness of mankind, less so its temporal power, or its comfort, nor even the 'know thyself of Socrates; it is the objective Knowledge of itself.

Senghor, after quoting this passage, says he disagrees with it fundamentally. With all due respect to those who hold this 'ultra-rationalist' position, knowledge for its own sake is 'alienated work'. For Senghor, as a child of African civilization, both art and science had a purpose—to serve man in his need for both creativity and love.[16]

Black Studies in the United States are of course also conceptualized in terms of purpose and social function. What about African studies in the United States? Should Americans study Africa for its own sake? Or should they study it in order to deepen the foundation of relations between Africa and the United States? Or should they study Africa in order to improve relations between whites and blacks within the United States? The second and third motives need not be mutually exclusive, but it may be necessary to decide on priorities and emphases.

There is a danger that if Africa is studied primarily in order to improve relations between whites and blacks within the United States, Africa itself might not be even remotely understood by either the blacks or whites in America. There may be a temptation to concentrate on only those aspects of African studies which are relevant to the domestic scene in America. African history might overshadow all other aspects of African studies. And with all due respect to Dr Stuckey, and to the importance of history, contemporary African cannot be understood simply by reference to its history. A preponderance of historian in African studies in the United States today would tend to distort American understanding of Africa as effectively as a preponderance of social anthropologists in African studies in Britain once distorted British understanding of the forces at work in Africa.

Studying Africa for the sake of black-white relations in American may also exaggerate the importance of white-black relations within Africa. Southern Africa might engage a disproportionate share of the attention of Americans studying Africa. White-black relations within Africa do indeed remain vitally important. But problems of black ethnicity north of the Limpopo, of the growth of new institutions in new African states, of economic development and changing cultural norms, are at least as deserving of scholarly attention. To study Africa primarily as a branch of American negrology may distort American understanding of Africa for generations to come.

If, as Senghor asserts, all science must be purposeful, American academics should be sure which purposes would be served by which branches of science. Black Studies should indeed be undertaken primarily to add rationality to relations between blacks and whites in the United States, and should therefore be accessible to both white and black students. But African studies in the United States should be undertaken primarily to add rationality to American understanding of Africa. The relevance of African studies for the domestic American scene should be indirect. By helping all Americans to understand Africa better, African studies should by extension also understand each other better.

The assumption of negritude and the principles of negrology might be correct in assuming that complete understanding be history is impossible. The world of scholarship cannot afford to accept Alexander Pope's poetic assertion:

> A little learning is a dang'rous thing;
> Drink deep, or taste not the Pierian spring:
> There shallow draughts intoxicate the brain;
> And drinking largely sobers us again.[17]

Even a partial understanding of the black man in both Africa and the New World must be, from the point of view of white education, preferable to the ignorant intolerance of yesteryear. A little learning may be a dangerous thing, but a lot of prejudice might be worse.

More profound than any diplomatic disagreement about the place of African studies in relations between Africans and Americans is the continuing problem of comparative intellectual performance between whites and blacks. Among the whites the Jewish component at once sharpens the contrast with blacks and deepens the poignancy in their relations.

BLACK POWER AND BRAIN POWER

Among sections of black Americans there is a view that 'the Jews are the brains of the white race'. They have been recognized as among the leading thinkers and writers, and they are suspected in such circles of being 'shrewd enough to manipulate the rest of the whites—to say nothing of the so-called Negroes'.[18]

It would also seem that the Jews are suspected among black militants of having a stranglehold on public opinion in the United States through their control of mass media. Either through outright ownership of radio and television stations, or through their massive advertising capability and power to withdraw advertisements, the Jews helped to 'dictate' the editorial policies of certain radio and television stations as well as magazines and newspapers:

> They hire Gentiles to 'front' for them so as not to antagonize the public; but on crucial issues, such as the Suez Canal, they control the thinking of the people.[19]

Then in 1968 and early 1969 the issue of the control of schools in New York City exploded into another area of Afro-Jewish antagonism. The black communities of New York City were agitating for the adoption of a system of education which would permit greater local controls of schools. The black community wanted a greater say in who taught in black schools and what was taught in them. In a sense it was a clash between Black Studies and the Talmudic tradition. Ultimately, however, local control of hiring and firing became the issue. This resulted in a head-on collision between black educational reformers and the teachers' union in New York City. Unionism of teachers in black schools were indeed Jewish. The idea of entrusting hiring and firing to local black communities was therefore a direct challenge to the security of tenure of Jewish teachers. The teachers' union won the first round of the tension, denying the local communities the demands they were making to control hiring and firing as well as curriculum. The issue brought to the fore once again the profound distrust by certain sections of black opinion of Jewish control of the educational system in some parts of the country. Open anti-Jewish speeches began to be heard more often from black militants. The so-called Jewish stranglehold on neighbourhood schools was sometimes linked to the disproportionate Jewish presence in the top sector of the American university system. The two levels of Jewish participation created an impression of a disproportionate intellectual influence upon the minds of others. The Talmudic tradition and its achievements in producing high-level intellectual quality was up against the Black Studies movement as a struggle to achieve educational and intellectual autonomy for black people.

John F. Hatchett, a black member of staff at New York University, was dismissed from his job for 'anti-Semitic' public statements. James Turner, the director-designate of the Black Studies Center at Cornell University, reportedly expressed a desire to have Hatchett on his staff. This in turn was taken on both sides of the Atlantic as further evidence of growing black anti-Semitism. Matthew Hodgart, professor of English at the University of Sussex, visited Cornell and wrote a report for *The Times* of London drawing attention to, among other things, these anti-Semitic tendencies. When challenged later in the correspondence columns of *The Times,* Hodgart emphasized afresh the signs of what he called 'black racism' in the United States.

> The Black Liberation Front, which does not represent the majority of black students at Cornell, is racist: it practices a rigid segregation by refusing to allow its members to associate with white students. The black militant movement, with which the B.L.F. is in sympathy is openly anti-Semitic. James Turner, the Director-designate of the Cornell Afro Center, has reportedly expressed a desire to have on his staff John F. Hatchett, a black teacher who was dismissed from New York University for anti-Semitic public statements.[20]

Jewish synagogues were also included among the institutions from which black militants were demanding 'reparations' because of their part in the historical 'exploitation of blacks'. The idea of reparation emerged in Detroit in April 1969 at the black economic development conference. Mr. James Forman, director of international affairs for the Student Non-violent Coordinating Committee, was addressing the all black audience when he suddenly read an unscheduled 'black manifesto' demanding 500 million dollars in reparations from white churches and synagogues. The manifesto called for a southern land bank, four major publishing and printing industries located in Detroit, Atlanta, Los Angeles, and New York, an audio-visual network based in Detroit, Chicago, Cleveland, and Washington, .D.C, a research-skills centre on the problems of black people, a labour strike and defence fund, a black university, and an international black fund-raising effort.[21]

In the reparations issue the Christian churches have been at least as involved as the Jewish synagogues. The picture is part of increasing black pressure on certain aspects of Jewish life in the United States. By early 1969 it was already being suggested that while in Eastern Europe Jewish migrations to Israel, when permitted, were due to official pressure from the authorities there, in the United States Jewish migration to Israel was in part a response to black militancy and black pressures on the Jews. Speaking in March 1969 at a special conference on emigration to Israel attended by 700 people at the Park Sheraton Hotel, Jacques Torczyner, president of the Zionist Organization of America, said he knew of 'several instances in which Jewish merchants relinquished their businesses because of black extremists' pressure'.

Uzi Narkis, director-general of the Department of Immigration and Absorption of the Jewish Agency, reported at the meeting of 4,300 Jews from North America, including 500 Canadians, settled in Israel the previous year, the highest since the establishment of Israel as a nation in 1948. He added that 25,000 American Jews had settled in Israel since 1948 and predicted that 7,000 more would settle there by the end of 1969. There was clear feeling that one factor behind the renewed attraction of Israel for Israel for American Jews was the racial situation in the United States.[22]

Jews in New York were sensing this more immediately perhaps than Jews in many other centres, but then there were more Jews in New York than in the entire state of Israel. 20 April is Hitler's birthday, and so in April 1969 a whole page of the *New York Times* was taken over by a massive photograph of Hitler. The advertisement was from 'The Committee to Stop Hate', an inter-denominational organization. The caption under the massive picture of Hitler says 'April 20th is his birthday. Don't make it a happy one. Adoph Hitler would love New York City's latest crisis. Black against Jew. Jew against black. Neighbor against neighbor.'[23]

Whether the crisis over New York schools was an aspect of Jewish intellectual dominance or something simpler, the fact remains that it became an important contributory factor to the rise of Afro-Jewish tensions in the United States, as has affirmative action in most major universities in the United States, especially since Jews are often thought to be over represented and blacks to have less than their fair share.

THE FOETUS OF THE FUTURE

From the 1840s onwards a man of Jewish extraction wrote or co-authored a number of historic publications. These included *The Manifesto of the Communist Party*. The man's name was Karl Marx. His Jewish father had converted to Christianity. A century later Marx was to capture the imagination of many black intellectuals struggling against the consequences of centuries of oppression.

There was one vital difference between the heritage of Marx and the heritage of black people. The majority of black people were heirs to an oral tradition, a transmission of song and oral wisdom ranging from Yoruba proverbs to black American blues. But Marx was at once a European and an heir to the Talmudic tradition, in spite of his father's opportunistic conversion to Christianity. Both the European and the Talmudic aspects of Marx put him within a vigorous stream of literary culture. The difference between Africa's oral tradition and the Euro-Talmudic literary tradition had immense relevance for the comparative performance of blacks and Diaspora Jews in recent history.

In the absence of the written word in most African cultures, many tentative innovations or experiments of a previous era were not transmitted to the next generation. The trouble with an oral tradition is that it transmits mainly what is accepted and respected. It does not normally transmit heresies of the previous age. A single African individual in the nineteenth century who might have put across important new ideas among the Nuer of the Sudan, but whose ideas were rejected by the consensus of his own age, is unlikely to be remembered today. Oral tradition is a tradition of conformity, rather than heresy, a transmission of consensus rather than dissidence.

Imagine what would have happened to the ideas of Karl Marx if in the nineteenth century Europe had been without the alphabet. If Karl Marx were simply propounding his ideas orally, from one platform to another, European oral tradition would have well-known figure in polite society in his own age. John Stuart Mill makes no reference to Marx in his own writings, betraying a total ignorance of Marx's contribution to the political economy of the nineteenth century.

Marx had many revolutionary followers, especially in continental Europe. He wrote interesting newspaper features for an American readership. Even that kind of effectiveness, however, presupposes the availability of an alphabet to get his ideas more widely publicized. In spite of that his fame for much of his own life was relatively modest. His fame by the second half of the twentieth century was greater than that of any other single figure in the nineteenth century. The fame that Karl Marx now enjoys, and the influence he has exerted on political, sociological, and economic thought in the twentieth century, would have been impossible had his ideas not been conserved by the written word and translated to a more receptive generation than his own.

The absence of the written word in large numbers of African societies was therefore bound to create a sense of isolation to some extent in a temporal sense, keeping one African century from another in terms of stimulation and

interaction, suppressing innovative heresies, burying genius under the oblivion of the dominant consensus of a particular age.

In addition to the absence of literacy was the absence of numeracy. It was
not simply the lack of the written word that delayed scientific flowering in
Africa; it was also the lack of the written numeral. Jack Goody has drawn attention to the relationship between writing and mathematics, and the implications of the absence of both in some African societies. Goody draws attention to the fact that the development of Babylonian mathematics depended
upon the prior development of a graphic system, though not necessarily an al-
phabetic one. And Goody then refers to the short time he spent in 1970 re-
visiting the Lo-Dagaa of Northern Ghana, 'whose main contact with literacy
began with the opening of a primary school in Birifu in 1949'. Goody proceeded to investigate their mathematical operations. He discovered that while
boys who had no special school background were efficient in counting a large
number of cowries (shell money), and often did this faster and more accu-
rately than Goody could, they were ineffective at multiplication.

> The concept of multiplication was not entirely lacking; they did think of four
> piles of five cowries as equaling twenty. But they had no ready-made table in
> their minds (the 'table' being essentially a written aid to 'oral' arithmetic) by
> which they could calculate more complex sums. The contrast was even more
> true of subtraction and division; the former can be worked by oral means
> (though the literate would certainly take to pencil and paper for the more com-
> plex sums), the latter is basically a literate technique. The difference is not so
> much one of thought or mind as of the mechanics of communicative acts.[24]

The absence of mathematics at the more elaborate level was bound to hamper considerably the black world's scientific development.

As for the more specific differences between blacks and Jews in intellectual history, part of the explanation may lie in the distinction between selective and comprehensive discrimination. When a people permitted to excel in
others—as the Jews were in the last 600 years of Western history—they may
attain striking achievements in those pursuits that are open to them. Certainly
in the fields of 'money-lending' and commerce, fields which were deemed
vulgar in polite European society at one time, the Jews in Europe acquired
skills quite early. Shakespeare's Shylock was only a bizarre exaggeration of
Jewish business acumen, caution and economic activism.

Selective discrimination against Jews had its ups and down in Europe. Jews
were allowed some professional avenues in some periods and lost them in
other epochs. But on balance, selective discrimination against Jews in, say,
politics contributed to Jewish excellence in the permitted professions of commerce, scholarship, and the arts. The Napoleonic legal code in the nineteenth

century was among the milestones of fitful Jewish emancipation in modern Europe; it released once again Jewish energies as discrimination was relaxed. In the words of Isaiah Berlin:

> The Jews had every reason to feel grateful to Napoleon . . . [for] his newly prom-ulgated legal code, which claimed as the source of its authority the principles of reason and human equality. This act, by opening to the Jews the doors of trades and professions which had hitherto remained rigidly barred to them, had the ef-fect of releasing a mass of imprisoned energy and ambition, and led to the' en-thusiastic—in some cases over-enthusiastic—acceptance of general European culture by a hitherto segregated community.[25]

But while fitful and selective discrimination against Jews released Jewish energies, comprehensive discrimination against blacks crippled the victims and stultified their innovative functions. It goes back to the slave trade.

A distinct factor worth bearing in mind when examining black intellectual marginality is indeed this impact of the slave trade, and later of imperialism, on the black world's capacity to innovate. The slave trade drained Africa of large numbers of its population. Those that reached the Americas, and sur-vived to be effective slaves, were a fraction of those who were captured in the first instance for enslavement. The drastic depopulation of important parts of Africa was bound to have significant consequences on the continent's capac-ity to achieve major successes in the different branches of knowledge. Later, when Africa fell more directly under alien domination, imperialism once again delayed in at least some respects the capacity of Africa to attain new levels of scientific and technological initiatives.

Here the picture gets a little more complicated. It is possible to argue that while slavery did harm Africa's potential for scientific innovation, imperial-ism later on helped to create a new infrastructure for potential inventiveness. After all, imperialism, while it was indeed a form of humiliating political bondage, nevertheless proceeded to reduce the spatial, cultural, and tempo-ral isolation which had previously been part of Africa's scientific marginal-ity. European imperialism, almost by definition, ended for some societies that isolation in space and culture which had previously been an element of their very being. New values, as well as new modes of travel and mobility, created new intellectual possibilities. The arrival of the written word and of the numeral again began to establish a foundation for a new African entry into the mainstream of scientific civilization. Imperialism could be inter-preted to be in part a mitigation of the consequences of the slave trade. Im-perialism, by introducing new intellectual horizons, was inadvertently, and in spite of itself, laying the groundwork for a future intellectual liberation of the black man.

The final factor to be borne in mind in evaluating black scientific marginality is an exercise in humility—that is to say, that we might not know enough of the causes of intellectual flowering and maturation among human beings generally. It was Levi-Strauss who reminded us how recent in absolute terms was the history of manifest human genius. The history of mankind is much older than the history of the revelation of major human intellects. Levi-Strauss argued;

> I see no reason why mankind should have waited until recent times to produce minds of the caliber of a Plato or an Einstein. Already over two or three hundred thousand years ago, there were probably men of a similar capacity, who were of course not applying their intelligence to the solution of the same problems as these more recent thinkers; instead they were probably more interested in kinship![26]

Even if we reduce the life of mankind from Levi-Strauss's 300,000 to 50,000 years, the question he raises is still significant. Why, out of the 50,000 years of the existence of the human race, do we have to look to the last 4,000 years for major indications of intellectual and scientific genius? The answer to that very question may have to await a future genius to unravel.

It was within those 4,000 years that the Talmudic tradition was born. Out of that tradition emerged a small segment of mankind, the Jews, destined to exert an unparalleled influence on the thinking processes of other men. From Jesus Christ to Karl Marx, from the Talmudic tradition to Einstein's theory of relativity, a Semitic heritage has manifested itself periodically in human genius.

The question which confronts us is whether within the next 4,000 years—and perhaps much sooner than that—another segment of the human race with a heritage of suffering, the blacks, will attain similar levels of intellectual performance and influence. For such a role the black people of both Africa and the black diaspora may have to shift from an oral tradition to a tradition of codified law, from a culture of consensus to a culture of prophecy, from a romanticization of a tribal past to an anticipation of a messianic future, from the chains of intellectual bondage to the ropes of intellectual mountaineering.

A black Talmudic tradition is needed, at once different in content from its Jewish counterpart and comparable in functions. The Black Studies movement may be the genesis of that black Talmudic tradition. In time the Black Studies movement may change beyond all recognition. It may become not merely a tolerated appendage in prestigious universities, not merely a cynical concession to black sensibilities in quality schools, not merely a forum of black rhetoric, but the beginnings of black intellectual independence which could spread from the ghetto. It could help to broaden still further the socialization processes to which the next generation of blacks would be exposed.

The black Muslim movement as a sacralization of black consciousness and the Black Studies movement as its intellectualization may indeed find that elusive point of fusion. On such a day a black prophecy would indeed be fulfilled, and a still Newer Testament would yet reveal even further the genius of Johovah working itself out in may.

CONCLUSION

Historically, no cultural group in the world, per head of population, has exerted more influence than the Jews. The total number of Jews worldwide is less than 15 million. Yet, Jewish contributions to higher education, high culture, journalism, diplomacy, statecraft, politics and science have been staggering. There are more than twice as many African-Americans as there are Jews globally. Yet, the influence of African-Americans on United States politics and policies is only a fraction of the influence of their Jewish compatriots.

And Jews outperform not just African-Americans but also White American gentiles per head of population. This is the phenomenon of Jewish exceptionalism and Jewish intellectual edge that has produced a stunning number of Jewish winners of the Nobel Prize for Literature, chemistry, physics, medicine and peace. Is this explanation due to genes or culture? It is culture, but with a strange combination. It is overwhelmingly Western Jews who have performed so superbly. Western Jews perform better than Westerners who are not Jews, and better than Jews who are not Westerners. The answer then is in the synthesis of Jewish tradition and Western civilization, a kind of creative impurity.

Over 80 per cent of the Jews of the world are Westerners. The largest Jewish country in population is not Israel but the United States. The US has about six million Jews. Israel has less than five million. One Latin American country (Argentina) has more than a quarter of a Million Jews. Brazil has about half of those. In Africa the largest concentration of Jewish presence is in South Africa, which ranks 10th in the world in the number of Jews.

Historically, Jews can be compared with the Japanese. There is indeed such a thing as Japanese exceptionalism. Japan became the leader of the industrial revolution in Asia, and is now the second industrial power in the world. The Japanese culture synthesises discipline, orderly hierarchy, thrift and savings, work ethic and social cohesion. In technology, the genius of Japanese exceptionalism is the genius of efficient improvement rather than the genius of original invention.

The exceptionalism of the Jews, on the other hand, is often the genius of original invention. Arguably, five of the greatest shapers of modern thought were Isaac Newton, Karl Marx, Charles Darwin, Sigmund Freud and Albert Einstein. Three of the five were Jewish. Interestingly, Israelis are more like Japanese than Western Jews in history. Jewish Nobel Laureates have continued to be disproportionately from the Jewish Diaspora rather than from Israel.

Israelis, like the Japanese, have been brilliant in improving the inventions of others, rather than in original inventiveness of their own. This raises the tantalising question whether Jews under siege (the Israelis) are inherently less inventive than Jews in dispersal like the Diaspora of the West? Israelis may be way ahead of the Arabs in technological sophistication but are the Israelis way behind Jews in the Western world in scientific inventiveness? Regarding the five thinkers who molded modern thought Charles Darwin was indisputably a gentile.

In spite of the name, Isaac Newton was probably also a Christian gentile. Although descended from a line of Rabbis, Karl Marx was only ethnically Jewish; he was not an adherent of Judaism. Sigmund Freud was also ethnically Jewish without being a believer. Was Jesus Christ also ethnically Jewish without being doctrinally Jewish? Is it conceivable that the most influential Jews in the history of Ideas have been disproportionately renegade Jews?

At least partially, such Jews have been in rebellion against their ancestral religious heritage. Whether Albert Einstein was also a Jewish dissenter in private is a matter of dispute. Potentially, even more controversial is the thesis that Jewish genius in modern history has flourished best when it has been synthesised with Germanic culture, the term 'Germanic' being culturally wider than the term 'German culture'.

The synthesis of the Judaic and the Germanic cultures certainly applies to Albert Einstein, Karl Marx and Sigmund Freud in their impact on modern history. Although born a German, Albert Einstein subsequently became a United States citizen, and did his greatest work as an American. Einstein came to symbolise the enormous Jewish contribution, not only to science but also to modern America.

Two hundred years ago, gentile Americans of mainly British stock created the United States' constitutional order. In the 20th century onwards some Jewish-Americans of diverse national origins became the architects of America's new intellectual order. The founding fathers of the new American intellectual heritage have been disproportionately Jewish and white. Is the American heritage becoming increasingly Judeo-Jeffersonian? A 1995 book, *Jews and the New American Scene*, noted that during the last three decades Jews in the United States have made up 50 per cent of the top 200 intellectuals, 40 per cent of partners in the leading law firms, 59 per cent of the directors, writers, and producers of the 50 top-grossing motion pictures from 1965 to 1982, and 58 per cent of directors, writers, and producers in two or more primetime television series.

The Israeli daily, Jerusalem Post, has also noted that the Jewish influence in the US is "far disproportionate to the size of the community." It is also public knowledge that, "Jews alone contributed 50 per cent of the funds for (President Bill) Clinton's 1996 re-election campaign." The moral of this story is simple: Jewish power in the United States is due to the successful Jewish counter-penetration into the citadels of American power.

African-Americans are twice the population of world Jewry, but they have not penetrated the American citadels of power sufficiently. Americans from South Asia and the Orient are counter-penetrating the Silicone Valley of Technology. Muslim-Americans are outstripping Jews in numbers, but cannot hold a candle to Jewish power. The United States as a global empire can only be checked by the United States as a domestic democracy. Darker Americans have much to learn from Jews about how to tame imperial America by becoming empowered Americans.

NOTES

1. L.S. Senghor, *Negritude et Huamnisme* (Paris: Seuil, 1964), p. 24 and *On African Socialism* (London: Pall Mall, 1964) p. 74.

2. *Ibid.*

3. Arthur R. Jensen, "How Much Can We Boost I.Q. and Scholastic Achievement?," *Harvard Educational Review*, Vol. 39, No. 1, Winter 1969. See also the subsequent debate with J.S. Kagan, M. Hunt, J.F. Crow, Carl Beseiter, D. Elkind, Lee J. Cronback, W.R. Brazziel, Arthur Stinchcombe, and Martin Deutsch, *Harvard Educational Review*, Vol. 39, No. 2, Spring 1969, and Vol. 39, No. 3, Summer 1969. Similar debates have since occurred in the United States in response to the racist views of Nobel Prize winner W. Schockley of Stanford University in California.

4. *New York Times*, April 1, 1969.

5. C.D. Darlington, *The Evolution of Man and Society* (London: George Allen and Unwin, 1969), p. 188.

6. Consult, for example, J.A. Rogers, *World's Great Men of Color*, Vols. 1 and 2, originally published in 1946. Reprinted in 1972 (New York: Collier Books, 1972).

7. These issues are discussed in a related context in Mazrui, *World Culture and the Black Experience* (Seattle, Washington: University of Washington Press, 1974). For information and illustration of the cards produced in Nkruman's Ghana which emphasized African contributions to world civilization I am indebted to Mrs. Simon Ottenberg, who later entrusted to my care her only set of those cards.

8. This rendering is from Gerald Moore (ed.), *Seven African Writers* (1962), p. viii.

9. *Ibid.*

10. Senghor, *"Negritude and African Socialism."* In *St. Anthony's Papers on African Affairs*, No. 2, edited by Kenneth Kirkwood (London: Chatto and Windus), p. 11.

11. *Chants pour Naett* (Senghor, 1950). This English rendering is from John Reed and Clive Wake (eds), *Senghor: Prose and Poetry* (London: Oxford University Press, 1965), p. 97.

12. The connection between literary negritude and separatist religious movements is discussed in a related context in my professorial inaugural lecture, 'Ancient Greece in African Political Thought', delivered at Makerere University College, Kampala, on 25 August 1966.

13. Stuckey, 'The Neglected Realm of African and Afro-American Relationships: Research Responsibilities for Historians', *Africa Today,* Vol. 16, No. 4, 1969, p. 4.

14. Senghor, *On African Socialism* (London: Pall Mall, 1964), p. 74.

15. See Senghor, 'The Study of African Man', *Mawazo* (Kampala), Vol. 1, No. 47, 1968, pp. 3–7.

16. Ibid., p. 7.

17. Alexander Pope, *Essay on Criticism.*

18. Cited by Eric Lincoln, *The Black Muslims in America* (Boston: Beacon Press, 1961), pp. 165–166.

19. Ibid., p. 166.

20. *The Times* (London), 23 and 26 May; and Miss J. Hodgart, 29 May 1969.

21. See *The Christian Science Monitor,* 10 May 1969.

22. 'Black Militants Seen as Factor in Migration to Israel', *New York Times,* 31 March 1962.

23. *New York Times, 7* April 1969.

24. Jack Goody, 'Evolution and Communication: The Domestication of the Savage Mind', *The British Journal of Sociology,* Vol. 24, No. 1, March 1973, p. 7.

25. Berlin, *Karl Marx: His Life and Environment* (London and New York: Oxford University Press, 1972 edition), 25.

26. C. Levi-Strauss, 'The Concept of Primitiveness', in R. B. Lee and 1. DeVore (eds), *Man the Hunter* (Chicago: Aldine, 1968), p. 351.

Chapter Four

Muslims between the Jewish Example and the Black Experience: American Policy Implications

This chapter is indebted to the author's previous work on American Muslims and policy formation in the United States. Muslims in the United States face three cultural crises relevant to their roles as citizens—the crisis of identity, the crisis of participation and the crisis of values and code of conduct.

The crisis of identity involves their determining who they are and how to reconcile their multiple allegiances. The crisis of participation involves decisions about how far to be active in community life and public affairs. The third crisis of values concerns a general code of ethical conduct and of policy preferences—ranging from Muslim attitudes to abortion to Muslim concerns about homosexuality. We plan to take each of these three crises in turn, but bearing in mind that in real life they are inter-related and intertwined.

In relation to these three concerns of identity, participation and code of conduct, American Muslims are best studied comparatively. As identities, Jews and Muslims are mutually exclusive categories. One cannot be both a Muslim and a Jew. On the other hand, Blacks and Muslims are overlapping identities. Indeed, up to a third of the population of Muslims in the United States are either African American or African.[1]

As U.S. Muslims struggle to define themselves in America, they may have lessons to learn from both the Black experience and Jewish self-definitions.

On the issue of political participation, Jews and Blacks in the United States are contrasting paradigms. American Jews may well be the most active participants of all major groups in the American political process. Jews participate not merely in the final voting, but also in the choice of candidates for the primaries, in the debates of the issues, and in making political financial contributions to the candidates or parties of their choice. Between elections Jews are also exceptionally participatory in trying to influence policy-options in Congress, the White House and in State legislatures.

On the other hand, African Americans are among the least participatory of all American voters. The majority of them do not have faith in the electoral process or in the political system as a whole. A large proportion of African Americans are also too poor to read newspapers, follow political trends, or have the time to be politically active citizens.[2] American Muslims are caught between these two paradigms of massive Jewish engagement and substantial Black disengagement from the political process.

The most emotional issues for Jews and Muslims have in the past been related to foreign policy. Jews vote in American elections partly on the basis of which candidate is more committed to the state of Israel. American Muslims are emotionally involved in such foreign policy issues as Palestine, Kashmir, Iran, Afghanistan and Iraq.[3]

African Americans, on the other hand, are much more concerned with such domestic issues as affirmative action, vouchers for schools, the politics of urban renewal, from welfare to workfare, and racial discrimination in such fields as law enforcement and the judicial process.[4]

Jews and Muslims in the United States are therefore divided mainly on foreign policy issues. They are certainly on opposing sides in the Israeli-Palestinian conflict. African Americans and Muslims are united mainly on race and civil liberties. Since September 11, 2001, the prejudices of "driving while black" have been compounded by the bigotry of "flying while Muslim."

Because of their well-earned success, U.S. Jews are a powerful minority in the American political process. Because of their history as a disadvantaged racial group, African Americans are a relatively marginalized minority in the American political order. U.S. Muslims would like to be like the Jews in level of success (vertical admiration) but are not keen to be integrated with them (horizontal empathy).

In the American system African Americans are not a collective role-model (because of vertical marginalization). But U.S. Muslims and African Americans have been exploring ways of solidarity (horizontal inter-linkage). Let us explore more fully the relationships between Islam and the Black experience, on the one hand, and Islam and the Jewish experience, on the other hand.

COMPARATIVE IDENTITY AND THE JEWISH QUESTION

Muslims in the United States have begun to outnumber Jews in the twenty-first century.[5] The two groups were already numerically neck-and-neck (about 6 million each) in the year 2000. However, contemporary Muslim influence on U.S. foreign and domestic programs continues to be only a fraction of the influence exercised by Jewish Americans. This is partly because

Jewish identity is consolidated enough to be focussed and probably because Jewish Americans are more strategically placed in the economy, in the media, in institutions of higher learning, and in the political process.[6]

From the point of view of response to public affairs, Muslims in the United States respond to four principal identities in themselves. Muslims respond to the emotional pulls and sentiments of their own national origins (e.g. as Pakistanis, Indonesians, Iranians, Somali, or Egyptians.)[7]

Second, Muslims also act in response to their racial identities, given the race-conscious nature of American society. Among U.S. Muslims the racial factor has historically been particularly immediate among African Americans, who currently constitute more than thirty percent of the Muslim population of the United States. Third, U.S. Muslims try to influence policy as Muslims per se—such as the activities of the American Muslim Council, which is based in Washington D.C. The Council has served as a lobby on both the Congress and the Federal Government on issues which have ranged from Bosnia to the Anti-Terrorism Act or the Patriot Act and their implications for civil liberties. Since September 11, 2001, U.S. Muslims have also felt exposed to new kinds of Islamophobia.[8]

Fourth, American Muslims may also act, quite simply, as Americans. As concerned or patriotic U.S. citizens, they may take positions on the size of the federal budget, or on how to deal with the trade imbalance with China, or on the future role of the North Atlantic Treaty Organization, or how to deal with large-scale corporate corruption.

In all these four identities (national origins, race, religion, and U.S. citizenship) American Muslims have become more organized and less inhibited since the last quarter of the twentieth century than they ever were before—with the possible exception of the followers of the Nation of Islam who have never been politically inhibited since they first came into being in the 1930s. Even the impact of September 11, 2001, has not forced U.S. Muslims back into a low-profile national role.

In some respects U.S. Muslims view U.S. Jews as a role model—a successful minority. Are Muslims in the United States comparable to Jewish Americans? What do they have in common and where do they differ? Both Muslims and Jews are anxious to avert being completely overwhelmed by the dominant Christian culture. Both Muslims and Jews are nervous about intermarriage across the religious divide. Both Muslims and Jews wish to retain a degree of cultural autonomy and distinctiveness within the wider educational system.

These generalizations about Muslims apply to Muslim immigrants from Pakistan, Egypt, Nigeria, Saudi Arabia, Bangladesh, Indonesia, Malaysia, Brunei, and elsewhere. On such issues they are concerned as Muslims. These groups have formed such Pan-Islamic organizations as the American Muslim Council, the Council on American-Islamic Relations (CAIR), the American Muslim Alliance, the Association of Muslim Social Scientists, the Association of Muslim Engineers, the International Institute of Islamic Thought in Washington, D.C., and the Islamic Society of North America (ISNA). This author is a member of the Governing Board of the American Muslim Council, Washington, D.C. and has been Chair of the Center for the Study of Islam and Democracy, Washington, D.C.

The annual conference of ISNA attracts up to twenty-thousand participants. This is clearly a Pan-Islamic event and not confined to national origins.

The American Journal of Islamic Social Sciences (published from Washington D.C.) does sometimes carry articles of relevance to policy and politics. Volume 12 No. 3 of Fall 1995, for example, included short pieces on "Islam and the West" and "Business Ethics: The Perspective of Islam." The journal is a joint publication of the Association of Muslim Social Scientists and the International Institute of Islamic Thought.

But in what sense are Muslims in the United States different from Jews? Although both American Jews and American Muslims have diverse national origins, Jews in the United States have become Jews first and national origins second, whereas Muslims are still national origins first and Muslim identity second.

It is partly a function of time. After all, Iranian Jews may be as Iranian as they are Jews. They will one day become more Jewish than Iranian in the United States. Will Pakistani Muslims in America one day become more Muslim than Pakistani? Is it a case of socio-religious evolution?

Muslim identity in the United States is more recent than Jewish identity. It remains to be seen whether Islam will overshadow national origins. Today Polish Jews, British Jews, and Jewish Moroccans are identified as Jews in America. But while Muslims and Jews share a cultural predicament in the United States, they do not share the same status in the political economy. The Jews are well-represented in the Congress. They are also well represented in the print media and television, and they have a substantial presence in the commanding heights of university education. This is quite apart from the Jewish economic muscle in banking, trade, and production.

With regard to the numbers game, The New York Times put it in the following terms as far back as August 1995:

Muslims now outnumber Episcopalians
   [Anglicans] 2–to-1. With six million
   adherents, Islam is expected to overtake
   Judaism as the largest non-Christian religion
   in the United States by the end of the decade.[9]

The Muslim community in the United States is also facing a crisis of participation. Blacks are an example of under-participation. Jews are a model of effective participation.[10] But is it religiously legitimate for the believer to be politically active in a system of government which is not only non-Islamic but is potentially anti-Islamic from time to time? Should a Muslim agree to vote under the United States constitution and against the background of the role of the United States' controlling if not intimidating many Muslim countries? In the 1990s alone American bombs and missiles fell on Iraq, Afghanistan, Sudan, and even Pakistan.

We could use some of the categories of medieval Islamic jurists who divided the world between Dar el Islam (the Abode of Islam) and Dar el Harb (the Abode of War). Are Muslims in America an enclave of Dar el Islam lodged in the body politic of Dar el Harb? Where does the political participation of Dar el Islam fit into the political process of Dar el Harb? Or should we abandon altogether these medieval Islamic divisions of the world as being outdated? What is clear is that deliberate Muslim self-marginalization in the United States would give additional power to the pro-Israeli lobby, reduce the protection of Palestinians in the American political process, and dilute the foundations of religious tolerance in the United States.

Once again Muslims are caught between the lessons of the Black experience and the attraction of the Jewish example. African Americans outnumber not just Jewish Americans but Jews of the whole world added together. Indeed the population of African Americans is on its way towards being double the population of world Jewry.[11]

And yet partly because African Americans grossly underutilize the American political process, and have allowed themselves to be taken for granted by both the Democrats and the Republicans, the influence of African Americans is only a fraction of its own potential—and certainly far less than the influence of their Jewish compatriots.[12]

COMPARATIVE IDENTITY AND THE AFRICANA QUESTION

But meanwhile Islam continues to expand in numbers in the United States, both within the world of the Nation of Islam and among mainstream denominations. What is the lure of Islam to the Black experience?

Among Diaspora Africans of the Western hemisphere there have been two routes toward re-Africanization. One route is through Pan-Islam—the transition chosen by Elijah Muhammad and Malcolm X. The other is the route directly through Pan-Africanism—the transition chosen by Marcus Garvey and the Rastafari Movement. Ras (Prince) Tafari were the title and name of Haile

Selassie before his coronation as Emperor of Ethiopia. The land of Bilal (the first African convert to Islam) is in competition with the legacy of Muhammad.

One question which arises is why Islam and the legacy of Bilal have made much more progress among North American Blacks than among Blacks in the West Indies. The second question is why African traditional religion, or beliefs rooted in sacred Africanity, sometimes appear to be more visible in the Caribbean than among Africans of North America.

One major variable was the tendency of African-Americans to equate Brown with Black. No sharp distinction was made in the Black American paradigm between Brown Arabs and Black Africans. Indeed, until the second half of the twentieth century, almost all "coloured people" in North America—whether they came from Africa or Asia or elsewhere-where treated with comparable contempt. When someone like W.E.B. DuBois argued that it was not Blacks who were a "minority" but whites, he had added up the teeming millions of Asia with the millions of Africa to give the coloured races a massive majority in the global population.

If the transition from Brown Asian to Black African was so smooth within the Black American paradigm, the transition from Africanity to Arabness continues to be even easier. Indeed, of all the religions associated with Asia, the one which is the most Afro-Asian is indeed Islam. The oldest surviving Islamic academies are actually located on the African continent—including Al-Azhar University in Cairo, over a thousand years old. The Muslim Academy of Timbuktoo in what is today Mali is remembered by Pan-Africanists with pride.

In Nigeria there are more Muslims than there are Muslims in any Arab country—including the largest Arab country in population, Egypt. On the other hand, there are more Arabs in Africa as a whole than in Asia. Indeed, two thirds of the Arab world lies in the African continent.[13]

Given then the tendency of the Black American paradigm to draw no sharp distinction between being Black and being "coloured," Islam's Africanness was not too diluted by its Arab origins. Elijah Muhammad, Malcolm X and Louis Farrakhan have sometimes equated Islamization with Africanization. North American Black Muslims have seen Mecca as a port of call on the way back to the African heritage, as well as a stage on the way back towards God.

Islam in the Caribbean, on the other hand, is partly in competition with Ethiopia as a Black Mecca. Moreover, race consciousness in the Caribbean does not as readily equate Black with Brown as it has historically done in the United States. The Caribbean historical experience was based on a racial hierarchy (different shades of stratification) rather than racial dichotomy (a polarized divide between white and "coloured").[14] Arabs in the Caribbean racial paradigm therefore belonged to a different pecking order from Africans. Indeed, Lebanese and Syrians were more likely to be counted as white rather than Black. Because of that, the Arab origins of Islam were bound to be seen as being in conflict with Islam's African credentials.

Moreover, the Caribbean has a highly visible East Indian population, a large proportion of whom are Muslims.[15] When I gave a lecture in Georgetown, Guyana, some years ago, on the subject of "Islam in Africa," the overwhelming majority of my audience were not Afro-Guyanese (eager to learn more about Africa) but Indo-Guyanese (eager to learn more about Islam). In the Black population in Guyana and Trinidad, there is a tendency to see Islam neither as African nor as Arab—but as Indian. The result is a much slower pace of Islamic conversions among Caribbean Africans than among African-Americans. Caribbean Blacks are less likely to see the Muslim holy city of Mecca as a spiritual port of call on the way back to the cultural womb of Africa. On the contrary, Mecca is more likely to be perceived as a stage of cultural refuelling on the way to the Indian sub-continent. Ironically Ethiopia, the land of Bilal, is the defacto "Mecca" of the Rastafari followers.

Indigenous African religiosity has often prospered better in the Caribbean than in Black America. Why? One reason is that cultural nationalism in Black America is rooted in romantic gloriana rather than romantic primitivism. Gloriana takes pride in the complex civilizations of ancient Africa; primitivism takes pride in the simplicity of rural African village life. In the words of Aime Cesaire, the Caribbean romantic primitivist of Martinique who coined the word negritude:

> Hooray for those who have invented neither powder nor the compass,
> Those who have tamed neither gas nor electricity,
> Those who have explored neither the seas nor the skies. . .
> My negritude [my Blackness] is neither a tower nor a cathedral;
> It plunges into the red flesh of the soil.

While this idealization of simplicity can capture the Caribbean mind, it seldom inspires the imagination of the African American. The dominant North American culture is based on the premise of "bigger, better and more beautified." Black rebellion against Anglo-racism therefore seeks to prove that Africa has produced civilizations in the past which were as "big and beautified" as anything constructed by the white man. Muslim civilization is seen as an African legacy.

In this cultural atmosphere of gloriana, African indigenous religion appears capable of being mistaken for "primitivism." Indigenous African rituals appear rural and village-derived. While Yoruba religion does have an impressive following in parts of the United States, and its rituals are often rigorously observed, the general predisposition of the Afro-American paradigm of nationalism is afraid of appearing to be "primitive."

The Islamic option is regarded by many African-Americans as a worthier rival to the Christianity of the white man. Parts of the Qur'an seem to be an improvement upon the white man's Old Testament. The Islamic civilization once exercised dominion and power over European populations. Historically Islamic culture refined what we now call "Arabic numerals," invented Algebra, developed the zero, pushed forward the frontiers of science, and built legendary constructions from Al-Hambra in Spain to the Taj Mahal in India. Black America's paradigm of romantic gloriana is more comfortable with such a record of achievement than with the more subtle dignity of Yoruba, Igbo or Kikuyu traditional religion.

There is a related difference to bear in mind. Cultural nationalism in Black America often looks to ancient Egypt for inspiration—perceiving pharaonic Egypt as a Black civilization. Caribbean Black nationalism has shown a tendency to look to Ethiopia. The Egyptian route to Black cultural validation again emphasizes complexity and gloriana. On the other hand, the Ethiopian route to Black cultural validation can be Biblical and austere.

The most influential Ethiopic movement in the African Diaspora has indeed become the Rastafari movement, with its Jamaican roots. This reveres Bilal's land of Ethiopia without Bilal's legacy. Named after Haile Selassie's older titled designation, the Jamaican Rastafari movement evolved a distinctive way of life, often austere, but sometimes drugged. Curiously enough, the movement's original deification of the Emperor of Ethiopia was more Egyptian than Abyssinian. The fusion of Emperor with God-head was almost pharaonic. The ancient Kings of Egypt built the pyramids as alternative abodes. The divine monarchs did not really die when they ceased to breathe; they had merely moved to a new address. To die was, in fact, to change one's address and modify one's life-style. In this sense the original theology of the Rastafari movement was a fusion of Egyptianism and pre-Biblical Ethiopianism. The resulting life-style of the Rastas, on the other hand, has been closer to romantic simplicity than to romantic gloriana. In North America the Rasta style is still more likely to appeal to people of Caribbean origin than to long-standing African Americans with their grander paradigm of cultural pride. Bilal's land sometimes casts a stronger spell than Bilal's Islamic legacy.

Pan-Africanism and Pan-Islamism are still two alternative routes towards the African heritage. The Ethiopanism of the Rastas converges with Bilalism as Black Islam. After all, Islam first arrived in the Americas in chains—for it was brought to the Western hemisphere by West African slaves. If Alex Haley is correct about his African ancestor, Kunta Kinte was a Muslim. So Haley assures us in Roots. In reality the Haley family under slavery was better able to preserve its African pride than to protect its Islamic identity. Slavery damaged both the legacy of African culture and the legacy of Islam among the imported Black captives. But for quite a while Islam in the Diaspora was destroyed more completely than was Africanity.

Yet I still remember my halal breakfast with Boxer Muhammad Ali in the Bilal Restaurant in Philadelphia in December 1992. The legacy of Bilal is Black Islam. The legacy of Bilal's country is Ethiopianism. Islamization and Africanization in North America are still perceived as alternative routes to the cultural bosom of the ancestral continent.

Within the political process of the United States, on the other hand, African American Muslims are, or can be, a bridge between other Muslims and the African American community at large. The comparison with the Jewish experience remains part of the national background. While Jews are the America of achievement, African Americans are the America of potential.

In population size, American Muslims generally are more like Jewish Americans—7 million or less. In power and national influence American Muslims are more like African Americans—very limited representation in the citadels of power. Neither Muslims nor Blacks have a single Senator on Capitol Hill.

In the economy and the liberal professions, non-Black American Muslims are becoming more and more like Jewish Americans—driven by the pursuit of the American dream and the achievement motive.[16] In access to the news-media and influence on mainstream opinion, American Muslims are more like African Americans—relatively marginalized.

In universities and research institutions nationwide the Jewish presence is remarkable in size and impact. The Black presence in higher learning is well below its potential and its impact is still modest. The Muslim presence is just beginning.

The Jewish presence in the higher echelons of the civil service of the United States, and among career diplomats, is impressive and constitutes a major in-put into policy-formation. The Black presence in diplomacy and the civil service has increased considerably in response to affirmative action policies, but it is still a fraction of the Jewish leverage. The Muslim presence in the American foreign and diplomatic service has at best just begun.

American Muslims generally and African Americans historically have continued to be adversely affected by a crisis of under-participation. Many Blacks have lost faith in the American political process for racial reasons. Many Muslims have disengaged from the political process for religious reasons. As cultural minorities in a liberal democracy should Blacks and Muslims re-examine their policies on participation?

TOWARDS RE-ENGAGING MUSLIMS AND BLACKS

The largest Muslim minority in the world is in South Asia. This is the minority of some 100 million Muslims in the Republic of India.[17] In spite of the periodic massacres of Muslims by Hindus in India, political participation by Muslims in the wider political process is one of the shields protecting Muslim interests.[18]

One of the factors which have influenced most political parties in India to be tolerant towards Muslims has been the voting leverage and participation of this 12% of the population. Had Indian Muslims opted out of politics completely Indian Muslims would have been more marginalized and perhaps even more victimized than ever.

The following distinctions need to be made concerning Muslims and U.S. laws:

I. a. Can Muslims live in the United States without obeying U.S. Laws?— Can they refuse to pay U.S. taxes, even if the taxes are not remotely Islamic?
    b. Can Muslims become U.S. citizens without allegiance to the U.S. Constitution which is not Islamic?
    c   Can Muslims insist that their money should not be used in wars against Muslim countries abroad?
II. Since Muslims in America cannot long endure without obeying U.S. laws, should they not try to influence the process of making those laws? Voting for Members of Congress and for the President constitutes part of the process of influencing the making of those laws—and not merely obeying the laws. Even those militant opponents of Muslim voting in U.S. elections do have to obey U.S. laws.
III. The Third domain is not merely Muslims voting but also Muslims running for office. This would be a process of Muslim empowerment. If elected, Muslims would not only be more directly affecting the making of the laws. The Muslims would also be influencing the implementation of the laws and their enforcement. Overtime the judicial and legal system of the United States would become more sensitized to the Muslim experience and related issues.

The central underlying question is that once American Muslims have recognized that they have to obey the laws of the United States, almost all of which have nothing to do with the Shari'a, the next question is whether Muslims should strategize to help influence the making of those laws and their implementation in the hope of making those laws more sensitive to the multicultural and multireligious nature of the population of the United States.

Fifthly, there is the nagging question: If Muslims cannot be voters in the United States, can they even be lawyers or legal consultants? Do opponents of Muslims voting in U.S. elections have sons or daughters training to become U.S. lawyers?

If it is haram to be a voter in a U.S. election, is it ten times haram to be trained as an expert in U.S. law and practising it? Is a Muslim-American lawyer who is devoting his or her time defending Muslim clients committing at least a double haram?

On the other hand, if we concede that Muslims may become attorneys and lawyers in the United States, why should not Muslims become voters also? Voting is connected with law at many different stages and in many different respects.

What we have here is the complex inter-relationship between law-making (legislature), law interpretation (the judiciary), law implementation (the executive). Voting is part of the process of choosing who makes these laws, who interprets them, and who implements them. The logic of the legal process is intertwined with the logic of the electoral process.

The logic of saying that it is haram to seek to influence law- making in the United States would make it haram to have Muslim lawyers practising under U.S. law. It would also make it close to haram to obey the laws of the land. Such advice would be dangerous indeed for a Muslim minority living almost anywhere in a primarily non-Muslim country.

The conclusion to be drawn is that it is to the unmistakable advantage (maslaha) of a Muslim minority to seek ways of influencing governance in the direction of greater enlightenment.

Like Jews, Muslims located in the United States have world-wide obligations since they are geographically located in the most powerful country in the world—with an immense capacity to either harm or benefit the rest of the co-religionists world-wide.

The United States could either do such positive things as helping Afghanistan get rid of Soviet occupation or do such negative things as bombing Khartoum and Tripoli when there is suspicion of so-called Sudanese and Libyan "terrorism."

The United States can either look the other way and let Iran arm Bosnian Muslims against Serbian genocide or the United States can pass illegal legislation penalizing Third countries for trading with Iran and Libya. American Jews have succeeded in making the United States and its courts be a defender of Jewish interests worldwide.

American Muslims need to be active enough to monitor and influence American policy in a similar way not only in domestic affairs but also in foreign affairs. The self-denial of voting power by some U.S. Muslims is an exercise in political castration.

Had the United States in the 20th century had very few Jewish citizens, the history of Israel and the Middle East would have been vastly different. Without a large and powerful Jewish lobby within the United States, U.S. generosity towards Israel would probably have substantially evaporated. At the very minimum the United States would have spent less money on arming Israel, used fewer vetoes to defend Israel at the United Nations, been more attentive to Palestinian and Arab concerns, and been more publicly critical of Israeli atrocities. Jewish activism in U.S. politics produced pro-Jewish results.

American Muslims may never equal the power of the Jews in the U.S. system, but the Muslims may one day help provide some counterbalance in policy-formation. Muslim participation and empowerment within the U.S. political system is therefore vital not only for the sake of Muslims themselves but also for the sake of the wider ummah world wide, and for the sake of enriching the pluralism and global representativeness of American civilization.

But how should Muslims vote? For one thing Muslims should avoid the mistake which African Americans have made for much of the twentieth century—that of being predictably for one political party and having nowhere else to go. In recent decades African-American votes have been too predictably identified with the Democratic Party—with the result that neither party has tried very hard to court their vote. They have simply tried not to alienate them completely.

Muslim voters should behave differently. They should use the vote as a leverage to reward those who take Muslim concerns seriously and to punish those who ignore those concerns. In some years more Democrats may deserve Muslim support than Republicans; in other years the Republicans may turn out to be the more Muslim-friendly.

In the Congressional elections of the years until 2020 Muslims should vote candidate by candidate—and not by political party. The American Muslim Alliance has the ambition of having one Muslim senator elected by the year 2008.

Muslims in each Congressional constituency, in each Senatorial constituency, should examine the candidates according to (a) their record (b) their policies and pledges (c) their degree of sensitivity to Muslim concerns at home and abroad.

At the Congressional and Senate levels in the years until 2020 Muslims should vote by candidates and not by party affiliation.

IN SEARCH OF ELECTORAL CARROTS AND STICKS

What about the presidential election when it ever comes? Since this is a crisis of political participation, we must confront the issue head on. There will always be two specific candidates close to the elections. Will one of them be more Muslim-friendly than the other?

In the elections of 2000 should Muslims have rewarded Bill Clinton by voting for Al Gore—rather than invest in the unknown quantity of George W. Bush? Bill Clinton had gone further than any other president in U.S. history to give Islam some standing as an integral part of American society. But this was Clinton not as a Democrat but as a pro-Muslim initiator. He had started the process of going beyond the political convention of treating the United States as a Judeo-Christian community only. In personal behaviour Clinton fell below Islamic standards of family values, but in official behaviour he was a particularly ecumenical President of the United States.

Under his watch, President Clinton recognized a major Islamic institution within the U.S.—the fast of Ramadhan. He sent an open letter to believers wishing them a blessed fast. Under the Clinton watch, the White House for the first time ever celebrated Idd el Fitr to mark the end of Ramadhan at which the first lady recognized the increasing expansion of the Muslim community within the United States and wished Muslims well.

Under Clinton's watch, the United States decided to look the other way when the Islamic Republic of Iran was arming the Government of Bosnia in the face of an illegally-imposed arms embargo by the United Nations in spite of Serbian aggression.

Under Clinton's watch the first Muslim chaplains of the U.S. military were appointed—with the major participation of the American Muslim Council. Under Clinton's watch Arab and Muslim Americans met with the President of the United States and discussed issues of Arab and Muslim concern. Under Clinton's watch Muslim representatives were received by Anthony Lake of the National Security Council and explored with him the implications of U.S. policy towards Bosnia.

Indeed, under Clinton's watch enemies of Islam began to accuse the White House of extending hospitality to Hamas and socializing with mujahiddeen. Bill Clinton stuck his political neck out for Muslims of America. While in foreign policy Clinton was no less friendly to Israel than any other U.S. president, in domestic policy he was more Muslim-friendly than any other president in the history of the United States. Did Muslims repudiate Clinton by voting for the Republican George W. Bush?[19]

To be or not to be politically active in a non-Muslim society. The burden of our analysis has been that U.S. Muslims cannot afford to be politically neutral. But they should reward the party which has helped them, and punish a party which betrays their interests. In the year 2000 Muslims did not reward the Democrats for a Muslim-friendly Clinton administration. The Muslims gambled on George W. Bush instead.

In terms of national origins, Arab Americans have been politically active since before Israel was born. Americans of Arab origin have included Christians (such as the consumer advocate Ralph Nader) as well as the more politicized Muslim Arabs. In the struggle to prevent the partition of Palestine before 1947–8 both Christian and Muslim Arabs lobbied hard in favour of "undivided Palestine." To the present day the Arab American population in the United States is more Christian than Muslim, on balance.[20]

But after Israel was created the "Palestinian cause" in the United States became increasingly identified with Muslims on their own. This coincided with a period of unprecedented Jewish rise in influence in the American political process—to the second half of the twentieth century.

Although the number of Arabs within the U.S. population rose from 1948 (the year of Israel's creation) to 1967 (the year of the Six-Day war), Arab impact on U.S. foreign policy probably declined during that period. This was almost certainly in direct proportion to the impressive expansion of the influence of the pro-Israeli lobby on Capitol Hill and on sections of the Federal Government during those years. Many Arab Americans also chose to keep a low profile out of fear of Zionist extremists and of other zealots of Middle Eastern politics.

What has changed in the last quarter of the twentieth century is that Arab Americans are less inhibited, feel less politically intimidated, and are more sophisticated in skills of utilizing the American political process. However, they are still subject to some of the tensions and divisions of the wider Arab world. They have also become more vulnerable to prejudice and ethnic profiling since September 11, 2001.

The foreign policy issue on which South Asian Muslims in the United States feel most strongly about is perhaps Kashmir. There is constant lobbying on Capitol Hill for either resolutions to censure India for human rights violations in Kashmir or for legislative action in search of a solution. There is also a constant flow of brochures, pamphlets, news-updating on Kashmir not only targeted at Congress, but also distributed widely to campuses, news media, and other contributors to policy-formation. Now that India and Pakistan have become nuclear powers, there is anxiety that Kashmir might become a nuclear trigger in the years ahead.

While the majority of South Asian Muslims in the United States favour self-determination for Kashmir or union with Pakistan, there is a minority of Muslim citizens of India who would rather see Kashmir remain part of India. It is worth remembering that India today has more than a 100 million Muslims (the fourth largest concentration of Muslims after Indonesia, Pakistan, and Bangladesh). Many Muslims of India are ambivalent about Kashmir. Do they want Kashmiris to have self-determination and risk depriving India of its

only state with a Muslim majority? Or would they rather have Kashmir remain part of India and strengthen the plight of other Muslims in India? Muslims from India who have become U.S. citizens betray the same ambivalence
about Kashmir.

However, those American Muslims who favour the status quo for Kashmir
have decided to keep a low profile—especially since most of them are ap-
palled by the human rights violations often perpetrated by the Indian troops
in Kashmir and by Hindu militants in Gujerat. The most vocal American
Muslims on Kashmir are those who favour self-determination for the embat-
tled people of that province.

From the point of view of racial identity, the great majority of Muslims in
the United States are of course people of colour. Their position on apartheid
in South Africa before the 1990s was almost unanimous. There was Muslim
consensus that the United States should impose and maintain sanctions
against the racist regime in Pretoria (as it then was). The American Muslim
Council went into a kind of strategic alliance with TransAfrica, led by the
African American activist Randall Robinson. TransAfrica was by far the
more active U.S. organization against apartheid. But many Muslims supported Robinson. And the American Muslim Council held a major conference
in the 1980s on the theme "Islam against Apartheid" with major international
speakers, including Muslim activists from South Africa itself.

The United States was persuaded (especially by TransAfrica and its allies)
to impose wide-ranging sanctions on the racist regime in South Africa. The
sanctions lasted until after Nelson Mandella was released and the African National Congress was legalized in the 1990's. Imam Warith Dean Mohammed,
the African American Sunni crusader, played an important role in consolidat-
ing the Muslim crusade against apartheid and racism.

The most race-conscious of all those who call themselves Muslims in the
United States are, however, the followers of the Nation of Islam, currently led
by Minister Louis Farrakhan. Foreign policy was part and parcel of the birth
of the movement, for the founder was an immigrant reportedly born in
Mecca, who arrived in the United States in 1931. Was Farrad Muhammad an
Arab? In pigmentation he was very fair, but he identified himself with the
Black people of the city of Detroit.

Farrad Muhammad disappeared without a trace in 1934. His successor as
leader of the Nation of Islam was Elijah Muhammad.[21] The foreign policy
tests came with the outbreak of World War II. Elijah Muhammad enjoined his
followers that as Muslims they had no obligation to fight for the flag of the
United States. He was imprisoned from 1942 to 1946 because of that position.

The dilemma between Islam and the flag in the United States continued afterwards. The boxing champion Muhammed Ali, a follower of the Nation of

Islam, refused in 1967 to fight for the United States in Vietnam. He was convicted and stripped of his championship in retaliation. He in turn reportedly threw away his Olympic gold medal in protest. It was not until 1971 that the Supreme Court of the United States revoked his conviction and helped to restore his championship title, by protecting his religious freedom and freedom of expression under the American Constitution. At the 1996 Olympic games in Atlanta Muhammed Ali was also ceremonially honoured with a replacement of his ostensibly "lost" Olympic medal.

I and other AMC colleagues spent five hours with Minister Louis Farrakhan at his home in Chicago, Illinois, in January 1996. This was of course after the Million Man March of October 1995. Did the Million Man March have foreign policy implications? Minister Farrakhan told us that soon after the march he had received congratulations from Muamar Qaddafy, the Head of State of Libya. Qaddafy was most impressed by the success of the march.

Farrakhan also told us about his plans to tour both the Muslim world and Africa. He started the tour the following month—stirring much debate in the United States when he was reported to have visited Iran, Iraq, Syria, and Libya, which were regarded with particular hostility by the U.S. government.

When Libyan sources reported that Muammar Qaddafy had offered Louis Farrakhan one billion dollars for his movement, and Farrakhan confirmed this on his return to the United States, there were demands in Congress that Farrakhan be compelled to register as a "foreign agent." Farrakhan retorted that he would be prepared to discuss such a possibility if several members of Congress would similarly register as agents of the state of Israel. In any case, Qaddafy's proposed one billion dollars to the Nation of Islam was for schools, clinics, and social services, and not for political lobbying or political activism, Farrakhan insisted.[22] The wrangling continued inconclusively.

When U.S. Muslims behave as Muslims (heirs of the Hijrah), and when they behave as concerned Americans (heirs of the Mayflower), they have operated under a number of paradoxes. Let us examine those paradoxes affecting codes of conduct.

BETWEEN POLITICAL VALUES AND A MORAL CODE

The first paradox is that while American secularism is good news for Muslims (separating church from state), American libertarianism is bad news for Islam (such as the latest American debate as to whether same-sex marriages should be legally recognized nationwide as they already are in Hawaii).

The Democratic Party in the United States is more insistent on separating church from state, including its opposition to prayer in schools. This draws some Muslim parents towards the Democrats, since the Muslim parents do not want their kids to be under peer pressure to attend Christian prayers.

On the other hand, the Republicans are stronger on traditional family values and are more opposed to sexual libertarianism. This draws many Muslims (especially immigrant Asians) to the Republican party. Most Muslims share Republican concerns about abortion and gay rights.[23]

The second paradox concerns the legacy of the Clinton Administration. We have mentioned that while Clinton's administration had been no more pro-Israel than any other U.S. administration since Lyndon Johnson, this same Clinton administration had domestically made more friendly gestures towards U.S. Muslims than any previous administration. We referred to the President's greetings to Muslims during the fast of Ramadhan in 1996. We referred to the First-Lady hosting a celebration of Idd el Fitr (the Festival of the End of Ramadhan) in the White House in April 1996 and 1998. Vice President Al Gore visited a mosque in the Fall 1995. And the first Muslim chaplain to serve the 10,000 Muslims in the US Armed Forces was sworn into the Air Force under Clinton's watch. Clinton also appointed the first Muslim Ambassador of the United States.

President Clinton received in the White House a delegation of Arab Americans to discuss wide ranging issues, domestic and international. We referred to the National Security Advisor, Anthony Lake, receiving a delegation of Muslims (including this author) in 1996 to discuss the ramifications of the Bosnian crisis.

The Clinton gestures towards Muslims were sufficiently high profile that a hostile article in the Wall Street Journal in March 1996 raised the spectre of "Friends of Hamas in the White House"—alleging that some of the President's Muslim guests were friends of Hamas, and supporters of the Palestinian movement. The critic in the Wall Street Journal (Steve Emerson) had a long record of hostility towards U.S. Muslims. His television programme on PBS entitled Jihad in America (1994) alleged that almost all terrorist activities by Muslims worldwide were partially funded by U.S. Muslims. President Clinton's friendly gestures to Muslims probably infuriated this self-appointed crusader of Islamophobia.[24] But did Clinton start a process of recognizing Islam as part of America which may survive even the impact of September 11, 2001?

The third paradox facing U.S. Muslims is that in foreign policy the Republicans in recent U.S. history before September 11, 2001, had been greater friends of Muslims than have Democrats—whereas in domestic policies the Democrats are probably more friendly to Muslims than the Republicans. We shall return to that thesis soon.

The fourth paradox concerns the two Islams in America—indigenous and immigrant. But let us first return to the first paradox. In the United States

Western secularism has protected minority religious groups by insisting on separation of church and state. That is a major reason why the Jews in the United States have been among the greatest defenders of the separation of church and state. Any breach of that principle could lead to the imposition of some practices of the religious majority—like forcing Jewish children to participate in Christian prayers at school.

In discussing the role of American Muslims qua Muslims (heirs of the Hijrah), we have to look more closely at their moral concerns in relation to American culture. Curiously enough, American secularism is indeed good news for Muslims in America. The bad news is the expanding arena of American libertarianism. Secularism in the political process does indeed help to protect minority religions from the potential intrusive power of the Christian Right. On the other hand, expanding American libertarianism in such fields as sexual mores alarms both the Christian Right and Muslim traditionalists in the United States.

These moral concerns in turn have consequences on how American Muslims relate to the wider political divide between Republicans and Democrats in both foreign and domestic policies.

Since the 1990s more and more American Muslims are registering to vote and seeking to influence candidates in elections. On such social issues as family values and sexual mores, Muslims often find themselves more in tune with Republican rhetoric and concerns. On the need for a more strict separation of church and state, which helps to protect religious minorities, it is the more liberal Democrats who offer a better protection to Muslims. Let us look at these contradictions more closely.

The First Amendment permits religious minorities to practise their religions in relative peace. Of course, like all doctrines, secularism has its fanatics who sometimes want to degrade the sacred rather than permitting it. But at its best a secular state is a refuge of safety for minority religions. It is in that sense that American secularism is a friend of Muslims living in the United States.

But while secularism is a divorce from formal religion, Muslims see libertarianism as a dilution of spirituality. One can be without a formal religion and still be deeply spiritual in a humanistic sense. John Stuart Mill and Bertrand Russell were without formal religion, yet each had deeply spiritual values. Albert Schweitzer, the Nobel Laureate for Peace, was at times an agnostic—but he was deeply committed to the principle of reverence for life—even protecting the lives of insects in Africa.

Religion has been declining in influence in the West since the days of the Renaissance and the Enlightenment. But it is mainly from the 20th century that spirituality in the West has taken a nose-dive. From an Islamic perspective, America has become not only less religious—but dangerously less spiritual. America has become not only more secular but dangerously more libertarian.

It is the libertarianism which is regarded as a danger to Muslims living in the Western hemisphere. There is the libertarian materialism of excessive acquisitiveness (greed), libertarian consumption (consumerism), the materialism of the flesh (excessive sexuality), the materialism of excessive self-indulgence (from alcoholism to drugs). These four forms of libertarianism could result in a hedonistic way of life, a pleasure-seeking career.

What is more, Muslim parents fear that American libertarianism is likely to influence the socialization and upbringing of the next generation of Muslim children—excessive levels of acquisitiveness, consumerism and diverse forms of sexuality. It is because of all these considerations that Islam within the United States feels threatened less by American secularism than by American libertarianism.

BETWEEN IDEOLOGY AND PRAGMATISM

But there are also the political and ideological shifts in power in the Western world as a whole—between liberals and conservatives, between Tories and Socialists, between Democrats and Republicans. American Muslims have been sensitive to those shifts internationally. What does the end of the Cold War mean for the Muslim countries? In much of the Western world in recent times it is not simply a case of more conservative parties winning elections; the whole political system in France and Britain has been moving to the right. Muslims worldwide have wondered about the implications of all these developments and changes for Islam today.

American Muslim leaders follow global trends with mixed feelings. What used to be major socialist or internationalist parties have not only shrunk in support—they have also diluted their left-wing orientation. Communism is crippled. A party of the right may lose an election -as the Tory Party has done in Britain in the last General Election—but it lost to a Labour Party which is a much more conservative force today than it was thirty or fifty years ago.

Indeed, the leader of the British Labour Party had already got the party to get rid of clause 4 in its constitution—a clause which had for so long committed the party to the socialist ambition of nationalizing the means of production, distribution and exchange. In France when the late socialist President Mitterand was ailing, so was his old style of socialism. The system had not only moved to the right—it had become a little more racist. There is also more Islamophobia in France today than there has been at any other time in the 20th century. The move to the right has coincided with greater anti-Muslim and anti-immigrant sentiments.[25]

What about the United States? Is it simply a case of the Republicans winning greater control of the Congress? Or are all three branches of government moving to the right with only minor variations between the two parties? Was the Clinton style of "New Democrat" a reflection of the force of conservative influence? Is the U.S. system as a whole going conservative—and how is it going to affect Muslims? Is the shift short term or long-term?

In France the move to the right has triggered off some degree of xenophobia or hostility towards foreigners. French cultural xenophobia has included Islamophobia. In Germany xenophobia has included Turkophobia, or hostility towards the Turks—which in turn has included elements of Islamophobia. Turkish houses have been fire-bombed and Turks have died at the hands of German neo-Nazis. U.S. Muslims are bracing themselves for similar chauvinism against immigrants. After the Oklahoma City bombing, there were at least 227 hate crimes against Muslims, according to the Council for American Islamic Relations. Muslims braced themselves for more hate crimes after the atrocities against the U.S. embassies in Kenya and Tanzania in 1998 and since September 11, 2001.

In the United States changes in regime between Republicans and Democrats has had historical paradoxes. In Middle Eastern politics Republican Administrations in the twentieth century sometimes showed greater ability to stand up to Israel than have Democratic administrations. American Muslims have noted that.

In 1956 it was Republican President Dwight Eisenhower who insisted on a halt to the occupation of parts of Egypt by Britain, France and Israel—and compelled the Israelis to withdraw from the Sinai which they had occupied in the Suez War of 1956.

It was the first President George Bush who put his foot down against the indirect use of American money on illegal Jewish settlements on Arab occupied lands. George Bush did lead Desert Storm against Iraq in the Gulf War of 1991—but perhaps no U.S. President (Republican or Democrat) would have permitted Iraq to annex Kuwait. What is more, a Democratic president might have authorized a march onto Baghdad.

On the other hand, it was a Democratic President Harry S. Truman who gave the U.S. green light in 1947 for the creation of the State of Israel—setting the stage for fifty years of Arab-Israeli wars, for Palestinian suffering and for mutual hatreds.

It was Democratic President Lyndon Johnson's administration which helped Israel (with logistical intelligence) win the June war of 1967 in six days which resulted in the occupation of Arab lands in Gaza, Sinai, Golan

Heights, and the West Bank. It has been Democratic President Bill Clinton who came closer than any U.S. President towards giving silent legitimization to Jewish settlements in occupied Arab territories. Bill Clinton did once even consider recognizing Jerusalem as the capital of Israel. A brief temptation. The Clinton Administration was for a while more militant in trying to isolate Iran internationally than previous U.S. administrations had been since the Islamic revolution in 1979. The election of Muhammad Khatami as President of Iran in 1997 began to tip the scale. Khatami was more liberal.

It was, on the other hand, Republican Richard Nixon who took a position sympathetic to Pakistan and against India in the Indo-Pakistani conflict in 1971 when Nixon was in power. Nixon was hated in India for it. What all this means is that in foreign policy, the Republicans before George W. Bush were often greater friends of the Muslim world than the Democrats. Did September 11, 2001, change this particular equation?

But domestically the Democrats are the party of minorities and the secular state. And so although Muslims have not emerged very explicitly as a political minority, the party most likely to be sensitive to domestic diversity is the Democratic Party. If Muslims are discriminated against or harassed at home within the United States, the Democrats are more likely to come to the rescue than the Republicans.

In foreign policy, on the other hand, the Republicans in the twentieth century were greater friends of the Muslim world, than were the Democrats. The anti-terrorist legislation proposed and signed by the Clinton Administration was probably both a matter of domestic policy and foreign policy. The divide between Republicans and Democrats was therefore even. Since September 11, 2001, Muslim and Arab profiling has been done by a Republican Administration.

AMERICAN ISLAM: IMMIGRANT AND HOME-GROWN

In places like Britain, France and Germany both Islam as a civilization and local Muslims as residents are widely regarded as foreign even when the Euro-Muslims are citizens of the European countries. In the United States, on the other hand, half the Muslim population will soon consist of descendants of families who have been Americans for hundreds of years. A third of Muslims in the United States are already African Americans. This creates a different situation from that of Europe.

In Europe both Islam and Muslims may be regarded as foreign; but in the United States such an equation is increasingly difficult. Islam may be new, but its followers will include millions who have been part of American history for two or three hundred years. African-American Muslim population is expanding significantly.

But even the immigrant half of the Muslim population of the United States is operating in a country of immigrants any how—unlike the immigrant Muslims of France, Britain and Germany.

In the United States it has been possible for an immigrant with a heavy foreign accent to become the most outstanding non-presidential American statesman of the second half of the 20th century—Henry Kissinger, the brilliant Jewish Secretary of State.

So even the immigrant Muslims in the USA are, in that special American sense, less foreign than the Muslim immigrants in Europe. But there is no doubt of the reality that the United States faces a TALE OF TWO ISLAMS.

We define "indigenous" in the United States in this article as people who have been American for at least two centuries. We might therefore conclude that indigenous American Muslims are mainly African Americans, with a small percentage of white Americans.

We regard immigrant Americans in this essay as those who have been part of American society for less than a century. Immigrant American Muslims are mainly from Asia, the Middle East and Africa in recent times. Some are from Muslim Europe.

While indigenous American Muslims are highly sensitive to issues of domestic policy in the United States, immigrant American Muslims are more sensitive to the foreign policy of the United States.

The problem of low income families among indigenous Muslims may be above the national average—this is to say, there are too many poor families. On the other hand, the proportion of families in the professional class among immigrant Muslims (teachers, lawyers, doctors, engineers and others) may be above the national average.

Indigenous Muslims (especially African Americans) tend to rebel against the mythology of the American dream as a pursuit of personal advancement in conditions of economic freedom. Immigrant Muslims, on the other hand, seem to be like Jewish Americans—disproportionately persuaded that there is more opportunity than oppression in capitalism.

Indigenous American Muslims are new to Islam but old to America (though Islam did once arrive in the Americas with enslaved Africans in chains). Today African American Muslims are fully Americanized but not always fully Islamized. Warath Dean Mohammed is among those who is both fully American and fully Muslim.

With immigrant Muslims the situation is the reverse. They are old to Islam but new to America. They are often substantially Islamized but not yet fully Americanized.

Indigenous American Muslims are overwhelmingly unilingual—speaking only English (standard or dialect or both) though they often learn some modest Arabic for purposes of Islamic ritual. Immigrant Muslims are often bilingual and even trilingual. At home they may even speak more than one European language. Lebanese Americans may speak French, Arabic as well as English.

Indigenous American Muslims are weak economically, but as African Americans they have considerable potential political leverage. After all, the population of African Americans generally is much larger than the population of the Jews of the whole world added together. And yet at the moment the influence of African Americans on US foreign policy is only a fraction of the influence of Jewish Americans. Will the difference in leverage narrow in the 21st century? Will African-American influence reflect the political importance of Islam among American Blacks?

If indigenous Americans are currently economically weak but potentially strong politically, the immigrant Muslims may be in the reverse predicament. They may be politically weak but with considerable potential for economic and professional leverage.

The population of indigenous Muslims may expand as a result of the new Republican attacks on welfare, medicaid, and on the safety nets which had once been provided for the Black poor. More poor Blacks may turn to Islam. On the other hand, the population of immigrant Muslims may decline as a result of more strict laws against immigration from all parts of the world. Muslim immigration may also suffer from how the new anti-terrorist legislation is actually implemented on the ground. Individual immigration officers might be encouraged to be particularly harsh to visa candidates from the Muslim world in the aftermath of September 11, 2001.[26]

But when all is said and done, the two sets of Muslims in the United States (indigenous and immigrant) are in the process of being forged into the largest Muslim nation in the special hemisphere of Christopher Columbus, the Americas. In 1492 the Islamic presence in Spain was ended. In 1492 Christopher Columbus opened up the Americas for the West. Five hundred years later an Islamic presence was trying to establish itself in the lands which Columbus helped to open up for Spain and the West. Was history indulging her ironic sense of humour all over again? The heirs of the Hijrah became simultaneously heirs to the Mayflower.

In foreign policy the four identities of U.S. Muslims play their part. The issue of national origins, the membership of a racial group, the power of religious affiliation, and the moral concerns of U.S. Muslims as ordinary Americans—such a confluence of identities is part of the politics of pluralism, part of policy-formation in a liberal democratic order.

But in the final analysis the cultural dimension of the American Muslim experience is not simply this crisis of identity. It is also the simultaneous and interrelated crises of participation and code of conduct. It still remains a drama in three Acts. First Act: Am I an American Muslim or a Muslim American? Which comes first—and under what circumstances? Second Act: Do I accept to be a participant in the American constitutional process? Third Act: Is my code of conduct as a Muslim compatible with my code of conduct as an American? The heritage of the Hijrah and the legacy of the Mayflower are in search of a moral synthesis.

We have sought to demonstrate in this essay that one approach towards understanding Muslims in the American public space is to view Muslims comparatively. The Muslim predicament in America is caught between the lessons of the Black experience and the power of the Jewish example.

Jews are the America of achievement. Blacks are the America of potential. Muslims are caught between the pursuit of their potential and the lure of ultimate achievement. The struggle for readjustment continues.

NOTES

1. Jonah Blank of the *U.S. News & World Report* points out that, "The two largest Muslim groups in the United States are native-born African–Americans (42 percent) . . ." (Source: Jonah Blank, "The Muslim Mainstream." U.S. Department of State. International Information Programs. July 20, 1998. http://usinfo.state.gov/usa/islam/a072098.htm).

2. According to the United States Census Bureau, African Americans voter participation in congressional elections in 1998 was 40 percent, a 3% increase from 1994. (U.S. Census Bureau. "African Americans Defy Trend of Plunging Voter Turnout, Census Bureau Reports." July 19, 2000). In the 2000 presidential elections, "The voting rate for African American citizens increased by 4 percentage points, to 57 percent, . . . The voting rate for all citizens was 60 percent. (U.S. Census Bureau. "Registered Voter Turnout Improved in 2000 Presidential Election, Census Bureau Reports." February 27, 2002). According to Human Rights Watch:

> Among Florida's African American residents, the impact of the state's disenfranchisement laws is particularly dramatic: 31.2% of black men in Florida—more than 200,000 potential black voters—were excluded from the polls. Assuming the voting pattern of black ex-felons would have been similar to the vote by black residents in Florida generally, the inability of these ex-offenders to vote had a significant impact on the number voting for Vice President Gore.

(Source: "US Election 2000. Losing the Vote: The Impact of Felony Disenfranchisement Laws." Human Rights Watch. November 8, 2000). The poverty rate of African Americans in 2000 was 22.1%, significantly higher than the national average of 11.3%

during that same year. (U.S. Census Bureau, "Nation's Household Income Stable in 2000, Poverty Rate Virtually Equals Record Low, Census Bureau Reports" September 21, 2001). In higher education, the total 1,640,700 blacks enrolled in degree granting institutions in the United States in 1999, comprised 11.5% of all students enrolled. (Source: U.S. Department of Education, National Center for Education Statistics, Higher Education General Information (HEGIS), "Fall Enrollment in Colleges and Universities" surveys; and Integrated Postsecondary Education Data System (IPEDS), April 2001).

3. Reporting on Jewish Americans' lobby for Israel, Lisa Richardson of the *Los Angeles Times* writes that:

> The success of Jewish groups in helping to defeat two longtime African American members of Congress has further frayed the damaged relationship between leaders of black and Jewish organizations. In the wake of Tuesday's ousting of Rep. Cynthia A. McKinney in a Georgia Democratic primary, some African American political activists and leaders are expressing outrage at Jewish organizations that targeted McKinney because she had expressed pro-Palestinian sentiments about the Middle East crisis. McKinney lost to Denise Majette, a former state judge who is also black but benefited from out-of-state contributions from Jewish groups and crossover voting by Republicans. Also this year, another black member of Congress, Rep. Earl F. Hilliard of Alabama, who had pro-Arab support, was defeated by Artur Davis, who was funded by backers of Israel.

(Source: Lisa Richardson, "Political Ties Between Blacks and Jews Strained." *Los Angeles Times.* August 23, 2002). Jeff Phillips reports that 88.7% of Muslim Americans want an independent Palestinian state. (Source: Jeff Phillips, Muslims 'Key' to US Elections." U. S. Department of State. International Programs. August 29, 2000. www.usinfo.state.gov/usa/islam/phillips.htm).

4. For more analysis of African Americans political participation in the United States, see Jeremy D. Mayer, *Running on Race: Racial Politics in Presidential Campaigns 1960–2000.* Random House. (August 20, 2002).

5. In August 1995, the *New York Times* estimated the US Muslim population to be 6 million. See front page article on Islam in American, *New York Times*. (August 28, 1995). A television program *Frontline* also points out that, "The estimated 5–7 million Muslims in the U.S. include both immigrants and those born in America. (three-quarters of whom are African Americans)." (Source: "Portraits of Ordinary Muslims: United States" *Frontline.* Aired on PBS Television on May 9, 2002).

6. In an article in the Saudi Arabian English language online newspaper, *arabnews.com,* Mark Weber, Director of the Institute for Historical Review, examines the achievements and political influence of Jewish Americans in the United States, and points out the following:

- "As Jewish author and political science professor Benjamin Ginsberg has pointed out: . . . Since the 1960s, Jews have come to wield considerable influence in American economic, cultural, intellectual and political life. Jews played a central role in American finance during the 1980s, and they were among the chief beneficiaries of that decade's corporate mergers and reorganizations.

- Today, though barely two percent of the nation's population is Jewish, close to half its billionaires are Jews. The chief executive officers of the three major television networks and the four largest film studios are Jews, as are the owners of the nation's largest newspaper chain and the most influential single newspaper, the New York Times. . . . The role and influence of Jews in American politics is equally marked. . .
- Jews are only three percent of the nation's population and comprise eleven percent of what this study defines as the nation's elite. However, Jews constitute more than 25 percent of the elite journalists and publishers, more than 17 percent of the leaders of important voluntary and public interest organizations, and more than 15 percent of the top ranking civil servants.
- Two well-known Jewish writers, Seymour Lipset and Earl Raab, pointed out in their 1995 book, *Jews and the New American Scene*: . . .

  During the last three decades Jews [in the United States] have made up 50 percent of the top two hundred intellectuals . . . 20 percent of professors at the leading universities . . . 40 percent of partners in the leading law firms in New York and Washington . . . 59 percent of the directors, writers, and producers of the 50 top-grossing motion pictures from 1965 to 1982, and 58 percent of directors, writers, and producers in two or more primetime television series.
- The influence of American Jewry in Washington, notes the Israeli daily *Jerusalem Post*, is "far disproportionate to the size of the community, Jewish leaders and U.S. official acknowledge. But so is the amount of money they contribute to [election] campaigns." One member of the influential Conference of Presidents of Major American Jewish Organizations "estimated Jews alone had contributed 50 percent of the funds for [President Bill] Clinton's 1996 re-election campaign. . . . ." Source: Mark Weber, "A Look at The Powerful Jewish Lobby." *www.arabnews.com.* *(*July 14, 2002).

Richard Cohen, columnist for the *Washington Post* also notes in an article that, "At the elite Ivy League schools, Jews make up 23 percent of the student body. They are a measly 2 percent of the U.S. population." (Source: Richard Cohen, "A Study in differences " *Washington Post* May 28, 2002).

7. For an overview of Muslims in America, see Yvonne Y. Haddad, *The Muslims of America* (New York: Oxford University Press, 1991).

8. Other groups and organizations established by Muslims in the United States to correct stereotypes and influence policy include the Committee for American Islamic Relations, based in Washington, D.C. and the Muslim Public Affairs Council; see "Muslims Learn to Pull Political Ropes in US," *Christian Science Monitor* (February 5, 1996) p. 10.

9. James, Brooke, "Amid Islam's Growth in the U.S., Muslims Face a Surge of Attacks," *The New York Times* (Front page) Monday, August 28, 1995.

10. According to an article by the *Religion Writers Association*, "In the 2000 election, Dr. Saeed [Dr. Agha Saeed is President of the American Muslim Alliance] counted nearly 700 Muslim candidates across the United States, of which 152 were elected. This year he estimates that about 70 American Muslims are running for of-

fice,. . . ." (Source: "9/11 fallout: Muslims fall back from seeking office" www.*religionwriters.com.* August 26, 2002). For more analysis on American Muslims political participation in recent years, see Alexander Rose, "How Did Muslims Vote in 2000?." *The Middle East Quarterly.* Summer 2001. Volume VIII).

According to the Joint Center for Political and Economic Studies, the total number of black elected (federal, state, sub-state regional, county, municipal, judicial and law enforcement and education) officials in the United States in 2000 was 9,040. (Source: "Black Elected Officials." Joint Center for Political and Economic Studies http://www.jointcenter.org/DB/detail/BEO.htm).

Of the Jewish Americans' political participation, Stephen Steinlight, of the American Jewish Committee, writing on immigration issues and a concern of diminished Jewish political power in the United States, points out that, "Not that it is the case that our disproportionate political power (pound for pound the greatest of any ethnic/cultural group in America) . . . Jewish voter participation also remains legendary; it is among the highest in the nation. Incredible as it sounds, in the recent presidential election more Jews voted in Los Angeles than Latinos." (Source: Stephen Steinlight, "The Jewish Stake in America's Changing Demography" Center for Immigration Studies. October 2001).

11. According to the *U. S. Census Bureau*, the number of residents in the United States who reported as African American alone or in combination with one of more other races in the 2000 Census was 36.4 million (Source: U. S. Census Bureau, "African American History Month: February 2002." January 17, 2002). According to the Prime Minister of Malaysia, Dr. Mahathir bin Mohamad, there are currently 13 million Jews in the whole world. (Source: Mahathir bin Mohamad, "The Muslim world is hopelessly weak." *International Herald Tribune.* July 30, 2002).

12. In the 2000 presidential election, 90% of African Americans voted for the Democratic candidate, Al Gore. (Source: Source: "National Coalition's Efforts Lead to Upsurge in Black Voter Turnout." National Coalition on Black Civic Participation. November 10, 2000).

13. According to the *World Factbook,* as of July 2001, the total estimated population of Algeria, Egypt, Libya, Morocco, Sudan and Tunisia was 182.9 million (Source: compiled from the *CIA World Factbook*, 2001). These six African countries alone, which are part of the Arab League make up the majority of that organizations' widely reported total population of 281 million.

14. For more analysis on racial stratification in the West Indies, see J. A. Rogers, *Nature Knows no Color-Line.* Third Edition Copyright 1952 (pp. 23–26). Renewed 1980 by Helga M. Rogers. Printed in the United States.

15. For example, as of July 2001, Trinidad and Tobago and Guyana have populations of 1.16 million (40.3% East Indian) and 697,181 (49% East Indian) respectively. Moreover, Trinidad and Tobago and Guyana have Muslim populations 5.8% and 9% respectively. (Source: compiled from the *CIA World Factbook*, 2001).

16. According to a study by the Center for Immigration Studies, in 2000 Muslims constituted 73% of Middle Eastern immigrants to the United States. (This study includes as Middle Easterners immigrants from Afghanistan, Bangladesh, Pakistan, North African countries and Mauritania). According to the Study, Middle Eastern immigrant

men in the United State have median earnings of $39,000, slightly more than the $38,000 average for native workers. Moreover, 19% of Middle Eastern immigrants own their own businesses, compared to 11% of natives. (Source: Steven A. Camarota, "Immigrants from the Middle East: A Profile of the Foreign-born Population from Pakistan to Morocco." Center for Immigration Studies. August 2002).

17. India's Muslim population is now estimated at 150 million. (Source: Thomas L. Friedman, "Where Freedom Reigns." *New York Times.* August 14, 2002).

18. For more analysis on Hindu-Muslim relations in India, see Peter Van Der Veer and Kevin Michael Doak, *Religious Nationalism: Hindus and Muslims in India.* University of California Press (February 1994).

19. According to an American Muslim Alliance (AMA) post-election survey: "more than 80% of the Muslim Americans cast their votes for George W. Bush [in the November 2000 Presidential Election]. About 10% voted for Ralph Nader." In Florida, where the Presidential Election was won officially by "537 votes out of 5.8 million cast" (J. Lantigua, "How the GOP Gamed the System in Florida." *The Nation,* April 30, 2001), the AMA reports that "Of the 100,000 Muslims in Florida, about 60,000 are eligible voters, . . . an exclusive exit poll of Florida Muslims, 91% of those polled indicated that they had voted for George W. Bush." (Source: AMA Election Report, "Muslim Vote" Freemont, California. Nov. 12, 2000 http://www.amaweb.org/election2000/ama_election_report.htm).

20. The Arab American Foundation reports that, of the nearly 3 million Arab Americans in the United States, Christians comprise 77% (Catholic 42%, Othodox 23% and Protestant 12%) and Muslims comprise 23 percent. (Source: Helena Samhan, "Arab Americans." *www.aaiusa.org/definition.htm.* Article originally printed in *Grolier's Multimedia Encyclopedia*, 2001).

21. For a biography, see Malu Halassa, *Elijah Muhammad* (New York: Chelsea House, 1900).

22. See the reports in the *Amsterdam News*, Feb. 3, 1996; *New York Times*, Feb. 22, 1996; *Afro-American*, Feb. 10, 1996; *Chicago Tribune*, Feb. 22, 1996; *Chicago Defender*, Feb. 1, 1996, among others.

23. According to a Zogby International survey of 1,781 Muslims entitled, "American Muslim Poll, Nov/Dec 2001," Muslim and Republican Party voters in the United States share similar social values. According to Zogby International: "American Muslims are conservative on many issues. They support the death penality (68%); oppose gay marriages (71%); support making abortions more difficult to obtain (57%); oppose physician assisted suicide (61%), and support banning the sale and display of pornography (65%). . . . American Muslims support prayer (53%) and the display of the Ten Commandments (59%) in schools, and they support vouchers to send children to private schools (68%). (Source: Zogby International. News Release, "American Muslim Poll. Nov/Dec 2001." Dec. 19, 2001. www.projectmaps.com/PMReport.htm).

24. Steve Emerson's article appeared in the *Wall Street Journal.* March 13, 1996. P.14.

25. Even liberal intellectuals in France opposed the freedom of Muslim girls to wear headscarves. For one analysis of this event, see Norma C. Moruzzi, 'A problem with headscarves: contemporary complexities of political and social identity'. *Politi-*

cal Theory. November 1994) pp. 653–72. In addition, the European Union is preparing to take harsh immigration measures against third world countries. According to the *Singapore Strait Times* newspaper:

> Efforts to forge Europe-wide policies to tackle illegal immigration suffered a setback when EU governments split publicly over linking aid to cooperation on tackling illegal migration. At a meeting on Monday the foreign ministers of France, Sweden and Finland opposed British, Italian, Dutch, Spanish and German-backed plans to make the European Union's 9.3 billion euro ([Singapore] S$15.7 billion) development aid budget conditional on repatriation agreements. "The EU does not go this far when it comes to violations of human rights and the war on terrorism, so it is sending the wrong signals going so much further on illegal immigration," said Swedish Foreign Minister Anna Lindh. . . . The dissenters however want the EU to focus on giving incentives in extra aid and technical support to Third World countries that help stem the flow of asylum seekers and economic migrants. Shocked by a surge in support for anti-immigration populist parties across Western Europe, EU leaders are rushing to find ways to get tough on the influx of an estimated 500,000 illegal migrants a year into the bloc.

(Source: *Singapore Strait Times*, "EU nations split over linking aid to migration curbs." June 19, 2002).

26. The number of temporary visas issued to Middle Easterners (except Israel) & South Asians by the U.S. State Department between Sept. 11, 2001 and March 31, 2002 and temporary visas issued the same time last year, declined by 41.2%, from 315,120 to 196,190. (Source: Joseph A. D'Agostino, "U.S. Has Given 50,000 Visas Since 9–11 To New Visitors From the Middle East." *Human Events*, Week of April Dec.8, 2001).

Chapter Five

Blacks, Jews and Comparative Diasporas

This chapter is indebted to the author's earlier writings in Islamic and Africana Studies. In the heat of the debate about multiculturalism and diversity in the wider American society, one thing may so easily be overlooked— the increasing diversity within the African-American community itself. Never has the Black population in the United States been as diverse as it is today. The richness lies in a wider range of sub-ethnicity, a wider range of religious affiliation, a wider spectrum of ideology, and a more complex class structure. Are we facing a convergence of different Diasporas?

If Global Africa means people of African ancestry all over the world, the Black population of the United States is a microcosm of Global Africa. Today this Black population includes people from literally every Black country in the world—from every member of the African Union, every member of the Organization of American States, and from other parts of the Black world as well. If there is indeed a microcosm of global Africa, it is to be found within the shores of the United Sates of America—from Hutus to Haitians, from Baganda to Barbadians, from natives of Afro-Muscat to decedents of Afro-Mississippi. Black America is Global Africa in microcosm. The Black experience has a new dialectic of diversity.

In some cases there is a transition from the concept of "Africans in America" to the succeeding generation of "African-Americans." Thus, while Ali Mazrui is still an "African in America," his children are already African-Americans or are in the process of becoming so.

The geographic origins of the Black population in the United States have been diversified as a result of a number of factors. First, the immigration policies of the United States have been liberalized in the second half of the twentieth century as compared with the first half, thus admitting more Black immigrants. Secondly, the racial situation within the United States has been desegregated enough to make the country more attractive to middle class Blacks from other lands. Thirdly, post-colonial problems in Africa and the Caribbean have created a brain drain to the Northern hemisphere, including the United States. Haiti has experienced the exodus not just of the intelligentsia, but also of members of the poorest sectors of society (the Haitian boat people). For a while the problem of apartheid in South Africa also created a brain drain of refugees to Europe and North America. While many of these South Africans are now returning home, or planning to do so, a large proportion have become Americans and will remain in the United States.

Partly because of the stimulus of new immigrants, and partly for other reasons, the religious landscape of Black America has also become more diverse. Haitians have not only strengthened Catholicism; some of them have also arrived with residual "voodoo" culture of their own. More ancestral traditional religions directly from Africa have become more legitimate in some African-American circles. Yoruba religious culture has been particularly influential. Religion, too, has its Diasporas.

Within the Protestant tradition there is also more diversity now in Black America than there was in the first half of the twentieth century. Immigrants from Africa and the Caribbean have enriched Protestant diversity in the country, ranging from Anglicans from Nigeria to followers of Simon Kimbangu form the Democratic Republic of the Congo (formerly Zaire). In addition, African versions of the Eastern Orthodox tradition are now better represented in the United States. The Ethiopian Orthodox Church and the Coptic Church now have stronger leadership in the United States.

The Rastafarian movement from the Caribbean has also been part of the American scene in the second half of the twentieth century. It is as much a cultural phenomenon as it is a religious one.

The term Diaspora originated with the Jews. Black Jews are not a new phenomenon in the United States. Sometimes these are basically Old Testament Christians who have become more and more Abrahamic. African-American Jews have sometimes had difficulty being recognized by Israel under the Law of Return. The Black Jews of Ethiopia (the so-called Falasha) were also slow in gaining full recognition in Israel, but most of the Ethiopian Jews were at last moved to Israel in the 1980s under Operation Moses and subsequent transfers. A few Ethiopian Jews have migrated to the United States and become Americans.

Islam has wider pan-African implications. There are now virtually as many Muslims as Jews in the United States, but the Muslims are of course much less visible and much less influential than are the mainstream U.S. Jews. Islam provides some direct African-American linkages with both Africa and the Middle East. But there are also areas of contrast between African-Americans and West Indians in relation to both Islam and indigenous African religion. Let us look at the sociology of religion in the African Diaspora more closely. It inevitably intertwines with other Diasporas.

BLACK RELIGIOUS ALTERNATIVES

Among Diaspora Africans of the Western hemisphere there are two routes toward re-Africanization. One route is through Pan-Islam—the transition chosen by Elijah Muhammad and Malcolm X. The other is the route directly through Pan-Africanism—the transition chosen by Marcus Garvey and the Rastafari Movement. Ras (Prince) Tafari were the title and name of Haile Selassie before his coronation as Emperor of Ethiopia.

One question which arises is why Islam has made much more progress among North American Blacks than among Blacks in the West Indian Diaspora. The second question is why African traditional religions, or beliefs rooted in sacred Africanity, sometimes appear to be more visible in the Caribbean than among Africans of North America.

One major variable was the tendency of African-Americans to equate Brown with Black. No sharp distinction was made in the Black American paradigm between Brown Arabs and Black Africans. Indeed, until the second half of the twentieth century, almost all "coloured people" in North America—whether they came from Africa or Asia or elsewhere—where treated with comparable contempt. When someone like W.E.B. DuBois argued that it was not Blacks who were a "minority" but whites, he had added up the teeming millions of Asia with the millions of Africans to give the coloured races a massive majority in the global population.

If the transition from Brown Asian to Black African was so smooth in the Black American paradigm, the transition from Africanity to Arabness continues to be even easier. Indeed, of all the religions associated with Asia, the one which is the most Afro-Asian is indeed Islam. The oldest surviving Islamic academics are actually located in the African continent—including Al-Azhar University in Cairo, which is over a thousand years old. The Muslim Academy of Timbuktu in what is today Mali is remembered by Pan-Africanists with pride. Timbuktu was at its height under the Songhai empire (1325 to 1591) and the Mali empire (1100 to 1700)—overlapping periods.

In Nigeria there are more Muslims than there are Muslims in any Arab country—including the largest Arab country in population, Egypt. On the other hand, there are more Arabs in Africa as a whole than in Asia. Indeed, up to two thirds of the Arab world lies in the African continent. In that sense, Africa is an Afro-Arab continent.

Given then the tendency of the Black American paradigm to draw no sharp distinction between being Black and being "coloured," Islam's Africanness was not too diluted by its Arab origins. Elijah Muhammed, Malcolm X and Louis Farakhan have sometimes equated Islamization with Africanization. North American Black Muslims have seen Mecca as a port of call on the way back to the African heritage, as well as a stage on the way back towards God.

Islam in the Caribbean, on the other hand, has been handicapped by two factors. Firstly, race consciousness in the Caribbean does not as readily equate Black with Brown as it has historically done in the United States. The Caribbean historical experience has been based on a racial hierarchy (different shades of stratification) rather than racial dichotomy (a polarized divide between white and "coloured"). Arabs in the Caribbean racial paradigm therefore tend to belong to a different pecking order from Africans. Indeed, Lebanese and Syrians in the West Indies are more likely to be counted as white rather than Black, especially if they are Christian. Because of that, the Arab origins of Islam are less likely to be equated with Africanity, although there are exceptions, like the more radical nationalism of Afro-Trinidadian Islam led by Yasseen Abubakar.

Moreover, the Caribbean has a highly visible East Indian Diaspora, a large proportion of whom are Muslims. When I gave a lecture in Georgetown, Guyana in the past, on the subject of "Islam in Africa," the overwhelming majority of my audience was not Afro-Guyanese (eager to learn more about Africa), but was Indo-Guyanese (eager to learn more about Islam). Among most Blacks in Guyana and Trinidad, there is a tendency to see Islam neither as African nor as Arab, but as Indian. The result is a much slower pace of Islamic conversions among Caribbean Africans than among African-Americans. Fewer Caribbean Blacks are likely to see the Muslim holy city of Mecca as a spiritual port of call on the way back to the cultural womb of Africa. On the contrary, Mecca is more likely to be perceived as a stage of cultural refueling on the way to the Indian sub-continent.

In contrast, indigenous African religion has often prospered better in the Caribbean than in Black America. Why? One reason is that cultural nationalism in Black America is rooted in romantic gloriana rather than romantic primitivism. Gloriana takes pride in the complex civilizations of ancient Africa; primitivism takes pride in the simplicity of rural African village life. In the words of Aime Cesaire, the Caribbean romantic primitivist who coined the word negritude:

> Hooray for those who have invented neither powder nor the compass,
> Those who have tamed neither gas nor electricity,
> Those who have explored neither the seas nor the skies. . .
> My negritude [my Blackness] is neither a tower nor a cathedral;
> It plunges into the red flesh of the soil.

While this idealization of simplicity can capture the Caribbean mind, it seldom inspires the imagination of the African American. The dominant North American culture is based on the premise of "bigger, better and more beautified." Black rebellion against Anglo-racism therefore seeks to prove that Africa has produced civilizations in the past which were as "big and beautified" as anything constructed by the white man.

In this cultural atmosphere of gloriana, African indigenous religion appears capable of being mistaken for "primitivism." Indigenous African rituals appear rural and village-driven. While Yoruba religion in the Diaspora does have an impressive following in parts of the United States, and its rituals are often rigorously observed, the general predisposition of the Afro-American paradigm of nationalism is afraid of appearing to be "primitive."

The Islamic option is regarded by African-Americans as a worthier rival to the Christianity of the white man. Parts of the Qur'an seem to be an improvement upon the white man's Old Testament. The Islamic civilization once exercised dominion and power over European populations in Spain and later over Eastern Europe under the Ottomans. Historically Islamic culture refined what we now call "Arabic numerals," invented Algebra, developed the zero, pushed forward the frontiers of science, and built legendary constructions from Al-Hambra in Spain to the Taj Mahal in India. Black America's paradigm of romantic gloriana is more comfortable with such a record of achievement than with the more subtle dignity of Yoruba, Igbo or Kikuyu traditional religion.

There is a related difference to bear in mind. Cultural nationalism in Black America often looks to ancient Egypt for inspiration—perceiving pharaonic Egypt as a Black civilization. Caribbean Black nationalism has shown a tendency to look to Ethiopia. The Egyptian route to Black cultural validation again emphasizes complexity and gloriana. On the other hand, the Ethiopian route to Black cultural validation can be Biblical and austere. These are comparative Diasporas in search of ancestral reaffirmation.

The most influential Ethiopic movement in the African Diaspora has become the Rastafari movement, with its Jamaican roots. Named after Haile Selassie's older titled designation, the Jamaican movement evolved a distinctive way of life, often austere. Curiously enough, the movement's original deification of the Emperor of Ethiopia was more Egyptian than Abyssinian. The fusion of Emperor with God-head was almost pharaonic. The ancient Kings of Egypt built the pyramids as alternative abodes. The divine monarchs did not really die when they ceased to breathe; they had merely moved to a new address. To die was, in fact, to change one's address and modify one's lifestyle. In this sense the original theology of the Rastafari movement was a fusion of Egyptianism and pre-Biblical Ethiopianism. The resulting life-style of the Rastas, on the other hand, has been closer to romantic simplicity than to romantic gloriana. In North America the Rasta style is still more likely to appeal to people of Caribbean origin than to long-standing African Americans with their grander paradigm of cultural pride.

Pan-Africanism and Pan-Islamism are still two alternative routes towards the African heritage. After all, Islam first arrived in the Americas in chains— for it was brought to the Western hemisphere by West African slaves. If Alex Haley is correct about his African ancestor, Kunta Kinte was a Muslim. So Haley assures us in Roots. In reality the Haley family under slavery was better able preserve its African pride than to protect its Islamic identity. Slavery damaged both the legacy of African culture and the legacy of Islam among the imported Black captives. But for quite a while Islam in the Diaspora was destroyed more completely than was Africanity.

But now Islamization and Africanization in North America are perceived as alternative routes to the cultural bosom of the ancestral continent. It remains to be seen whether the twenty-first century will see a similar equilibrium in the Caribbean, as the search continues for more authentic cultural paradigms to sustain the African Diaspora of tomorrow.

In the new America since September 11, 2001, African American Muslims have sometimes undergone a transition from being members of a disadvantaged Black race to being members of a disadvantaged religious group. As Muslims they are part of a group which includes U.S. citizens of such diverse national origins as the Middle East, South Asia, South-East Asia, post-colonial Africa and parts of Europe.

The literature about Islam in the United States sometimes distinguishes between "immigrant American Muslims" (meaning those who came to the United States since the nineteenth century), and "indigenous American Muslims" (meaning mainly African American Muslims whose folks have been Americans for much longer than two centuries).

AMERICAN ISLAM: IMMIGRANT AND HOME-GROWN

In places like Britain, France and Germany, both Islam as a civilization and local Muslims as residents are widely regarded as foreign even when the Euro-Muslims are citizens of the European countries. In the United States, on the other hand, half the Muslim population will soon consist of descendants of families who have been Americans for hundreds of years. A third of the six million Muslims in the United States are already African Americans. This creates a different situation from that of Europe.

In Europe both Islam and Muslims may be regarded as foreign; but in the United States such an equation is increasingly difficult. Islam may be new, but its followers will include millions who have been part of American history for two or three hundred years. African-American Muslim population is expanding significantly.

But even the immigrant half of the Muslim population of the United States is operating in a country of immigrants any how—unlike the immigrant Muslims of France, Britain and Germany.

In the United States, it has been possible for an immigrant with a heavy foreign accent to become the most outstanding non-presidential American statesman of the second half of the 20th century—Henry Kissinger, the brilliant Jewish Secretary of State.

So even the immigrant Muslims in the U.S.A. are, in that special American sense, less foreign than the Muslim immigrants in Europe. But there is no doubt of the reality that the United States faces a TALE OF TWO ISLAMS.

We have already defined "indigenous" in the United States in this paper as people who have been American for several centuries. We must therefore conclude that indigenous American Muslims are mainly African Americans, with a small percentage of white Americans.

We regard immigrant Americans in this essay as those who have been part of American society since the nineteenth century. Immigrant American Muslims are mainly from Asia, the Middle East and Africa, in recent times. Some are from Muslim Europe.

While indigenous American Muslims are highly sensitive to issues of domestic policy in the United States, immigrant American Muslims are more sensitive to the foreign policy of the United States.

The problem of low income families among indigenous Muslims may be above the national average—this is to say, there are too many poor families. On the other hand, the proportion of families in the professional class among immigrant Muslims (teachers, lawyers, corporate managers, doctors, engineers and others) may be above the national average.

Indigenous Muslims (especially African Americans) tend to rebel against the mythology of the American dream as a pursuit of personal advancement in conditions of economic rivalry. Immigrant Muslims, on the other hand, seem to be like Jewish Americans—disproportionately persuaded that there is more opportunity than oppression in capitalism.

Indigenous American Muslims are new to Islam, but old to America (though Islam did once arrive in the Americas with enslaved Africans in chains). Today African American Muslims are fully Americanized but not always fully Islamized. Warath Deen Mohammed is among those who are both fully American and fully Muslim.

With immigrant Muslims the situation is the reverse. They are old to Islam, but new to America. They are often substantially Islamized but not yet fully Americanized.

Indigenous American Muslims are overwhelmingly unilingual—speaking only English (standard or dialect or both) though they often learn some modest Arabic for purposes of Islamic ritual. Immigrant Muslims are often bilingual, and even trilingual. At home they may even speak more than one European language. Lebanese Americans may speak French, Arabic as well as English.

Indigenous American Muslims are weak economically, but as African Americans they have considerable potential political leverage. After all, the population of African Americans generally is much larger than the population of the Jews of the whole world added together. And yet at the moment the influence of African Americans on US foreign policy is only a fraction of the influence of Jewish Americans. Will the difference in leverage narrow in the 21st century? Will African-American influence reflect the political importance of Islam among American Blacks?

If indigenous Americans are currently economically weak, but potentially strong politically, the immigrant Muslims may be in the reverse predicament. They may be politically weak but with considerable potential for economic and professional leverage.

The population of indigenous Muslims may expand as a result of the new Republican attacks on welfare, Medicaid, and on the safety nets which had once been provided for the Black poor. More poor Blacks may turn to Islam. On the other hand, the population of immigrant Muslims may decline as a result of more strict laws against immigration from all parts of the world. Muslim immigration may also suffer from how the new anti-terrorist legislation is actually implemented on the ground. Individual immigration officers might be encouraged to be particularly harsh to visa candidates from the Muslim world in the aftermath of September 11, 2001. Recent evidence indicates, for example, that the number of temporary visas issued to Middle Easterners (except Israel) and South Asians by the U.S. State Department between Sept. 11, 2001 and March 31, 2002, and temporary visas issued during the same time last year, declined by 41.2 percent, from 315,120 to 196,190.[1]

But when all is said and done, the two sets of Muslims in the United States (indigenous and immigrant) are in the process of being forged into the largest Muslim nation in the Western hemisphere. In 1492, the Islamic presence in Spain was ended. Also in 1492, Christopher Columbus opened up the Americas for the West. Five hundred years later, an Islamic presence was trying to establish itself in the lands which Columbus helped to open up for Spain and the West. Was history indulging her ironic sense of humor all over again? The heirs of the Hijrah became simultaneously heirs to the Mayflower.

But Muslims in the United States are now part of the fabric of American society. Ideologically they are challenged by the values of American capitalism and liberal democracy. Politically they are often challenged by rivalry with American Jews (part of the Jewish Diaspora). Let us now explore these challenges of values and politics in the context of the American experience.

MUSLIMS BETWEEN BLACK AND JEWISH DIASPORAS

Muslims in the United States face three cultural crises relevant to their roles as citizens—the crisis of identity, the crisis of participation and the crisis of values and code of conduct.

The crisis of identity involves their determining who they are and how to reconcile their multiple allegiances. The crisis of participation involves decisions about how far to be active in community life and public affairs. The third crisis of values concerns a general code of ethical conduct and of policy preferences—ranging from Muslim attitudes to abortion to Muslim concerns about homosexuality. We plan to take each of these three crises in turn, but bearing in mind that in real life they are inter-related and intertwined.

In relation to these three concerns of identity, participation and code of conduct, American Muslims are best studied comparatively.[2] (See also [3], [4], [5], [6], [7], [8], and [9]) The Jewish Diaspora is strongest in America. As identities, Jews and Muslims are mutually exclusive categories. One cannot be both a Muslim and a Jew. On the other hand, Blacks and Muslims are overlapping identities. Indeed, up to a third of the six million populations of Muslims in the United States are either African American or African. According to one survey of U.S. Muslims, 30 percent are black, 33 percent South Asian, and 25 percent Arab. The survey did not include followers of the Nation of Islam.[10] Other estimates put the African American Muslim population at a higher percentage (as high as 42 percent).[11]

As U.S. Muslims struggle to define themselves in America, they may have lessons to learn from both the Black experience and Jewish self-definitions. The Jews invented the Diaspora experience. They have both suffered and triumphed.

On the issue of political participation, Jews and Blacks in the United States are contrasting Diasporic paradigms. American Jews may well be the most active participants of all major groups in the American political process. Jews participate not merely in the final voting, but also in the choice of candidates for the primaries, in the debates of the issues, and in making political financial contributions to the candidates or parties of their choice. Between elections, Jews are also exceptionally participatory in trying to influence policy-options in Congress, the White House and in State legislatures. [12],[13] According to one report by Nathan Diament, a Lobbyist for the Orthodox Jwish movement, Jewish voting turnout is as high as 80 percent.[14]

On the other hand, African Americans are among the least participatory of all American voters. The majority of them do not have faith in the electoral process or in the political system as a whole. A large proportion of African Americans are also too poor to read newspapers, follow political trends, or have the time to be politically active citizens. According to the United States Census Bureau, African Americans voter participation in congressional elections in 1998 was 40 percent, a 3 percent increase from 1994.[15] In the 2000 presidential elections, "The voting rate for African American citizens increased by 4 percentage points, to 57 percent; the voting rate for all citizens was 60 percent."[16] (See also [17]) This number could have been higher had African American voters not been prevented from casting their ballot. In this regard, Human Rights Watch observes "Among Florida's African American residents, the impact of the state's disenfranchisement laws is particularly dramatic: 31.2 percent of black men in Florida—more than 200,000 potential black voters—were excluded from the polls. Assuming the voting pattern of black ex-felons would have been similar to the vote by black residents in Florida generally, the inability of these ex-offenders to vote had a significant impact on the number voting for Vice President Gore."[18] American Muslims are caught between these two Diasporic paradigms of massive Jewish engagement and substantial Black disengagement from the political process.

The most emotional issues for Jews and Muslims have in the past been related to foreign policy. Jews vote in American elections partly on the basis of which candidate is more committed to the state of Israel. Reporting on Jewish Americans' political activity on the basis of Congressional representatives' view of the Israeli-Palestinian dispute, Lisa Richardson of the *Los Angeles Times* writes that:

> The success of Jewish groups in helping to defeat two longtime African American members of Congress has further frayed the damaged relationship between leaders of black and Jewish organizations. In the wake of Tuesday's ousting of Rep. Cynthia A. McKinney in a Georgia Democratic primary, some African American political activists and leaders are expressing outrage at Jewish organizations that targeted McKinney because she had expressed pro-Palestinian sentiments about the Middle East crisis. McKinney lost to Denise Majette, a former state judge who is also black but benefited from out-of-state contributions from Jewish groups and crossover voting by Republicans. Also this year, another black member of Congress, Rep. Earl F. Hilliard of Alabama, who had pro-Arab support, was defeated by Artur Davis, who was funded by backers of Israel.[19] (See also [20] and [21])

The importance of Israel for most Jews is encapsulated in the words of Eric Cantor, the House Chief Deputy Whip (and the only House Jewish Republican) "For the mainstream Jewish community, Israel is of paramount importance."[22]

American Muslims are emotionally involved in such foreign policy issues as Palestine, Kashmir, Iran, Afghanistan and Iraq.[23] Jeff Phillips, reporting for the BBC in Washington on a survey of U.S. Muslims, pointed out that 88 percent of Muslim Americans wanted an independent Palestinian State.[24] In particular, Arab Americans have been approached for their political support, since their numbers may be pivotal in some battleground states in the 2004 Presidential race.[25] Jews and Muslims feel strongly about ancestral origins.

African Americans, on the other hand, are much more concerned with such domestic issues as affirmative action, vouchers for schools, the politics of urban renewal, from welfare to workfare, and racial discrimination in such fields as law enforcement and the judicial process.[26] (See also [27] and [28]) Poverty among African Americans, which may be associated with these problems, is another major concern. The poverty rate of African Americans in 2000 was 22.1 percent, significantly higher than the national average of 11.3 percent during that same year.[29]

Jews and Muslims in the United States are therefore divided mainly on foreign policy issues. They are certainly on opposing sides in the Israeli-Palestinian conflict. African Americans and Muslims are united mainly on race and civil liberties. Since September 11, 2001, the prejudices of "driving while black" have been compounded by the bigotry of "flying while Muslim." The difficulties faced by Muslim travelers at airports—including this author—were reported in *Washinghton Post*.[30]

Because of their well-earned success, U.S. Jews are a powerful minority in the American political process. Because of their history as a disadvantaged racial group, African Americans are a relatively marginalized minority in the American political order. U.S. Muslims would like to be like the Jews in level of success (vertical admiration), but are not keen to be integrated with them (horizontal empathy).

In the American system, African Americans are not a collective role-model (because of vertical marginalization). But U.S. Muslims and African Americans have been exploring ways of solidarity (horizontal Afro-Islamic interlinkage). Let us explore more fully the relationships between Islam and the Black experience, on the one hand, and Islam and the Jewish experience, on the other hand.

Muslims in the United States have begun to outnumber Jews in the twenty-first century. However, their numbers vary. According to one study conducted by Professor Ihsan Bagby of Shaw University in Raleigh, North Carolina (as part of a larger study of American congregations called "Faith Communities Today," coordinated by Hartford Seminary's Hartford Institute for Religious Research, there are approximately 6 million Muslims in the U.S. with over 2 million of these being regularly participating adult attenders at the more than

1,209 mosques/masjids in the United States.[31] The television program *Front-line* also points out that "The estimated 5–7 million Muslims in the U.S. include both immigrants and those born in America (three-quarters of whom are African Americans)."[32] The two groups were already numerically neck-and-neck (about 6 million each) in the year 2000. However, contemporary Muslim influence on U.S. foreign and domestic programs continues to be only a fraction of the influence exercised by Jewish Americans. This is partly because Jewish identity is consolidated enough to be focused and probably because Jewish Americans are more strategically placed in the economy, in the media, in institutions of higher learning, and in the political process. A number of observers (including Jews themselves) have pointed to the disproportionate numbers and influence of Jews in various sectors of the U.S. government, commerce, education, and entertainment. For example:

- "It is one of the worst-kept secrets in American Jewish politics that the campaign contribution is a major key to Jewish power." (Goldberg, p. 266)[33]
- "Jews provided at least half the money donated to the DNC [Democratic National Committee] in the 1998 and 2000 election cycles. At the RNC, Lew Eisenberg, who is Jewish, was finance chairman until he became finance chairman of the host committee for the Republican National Convention recently. At Bush-Cheney fundraisers in Washington, California, New York and Florida, rabbis gave the invocations. Ira N. Forman, executive director of the National Jewish Democratic Council, said that Jews are the most politicized ethnic group in the country." "Karl Rove has a Jewish strategy," Forman said. "It's largely about money — but it goes way beyond that." (Blumenfeld, p. A1)[34]
- "Although less than two percent of the US population is Jewish, of the 100–member Senate body, ten are Jewish. These are Carl Levin, Arlen Specter, Frank Lautenberg, Herb Kohl, Joe Lieberman, Dianne Feinstein, Barbara Boxer, Russell Feingold, Ron Wyden and Charles Schumer." (See, for a list of past and current Jewish Senators, Maisel and Forman, *Jews in American Politics*, pp. 449; a complete roster for all major political positions is available in the same publication, pp. 449–470.)[35]
- ". . . the American Israel Public Affairs Committee. Long regarded as the most effective foreign-policy lobby in Washington, AIPAC has an annual budget of $19.5 million, a staff of 130, and 60,000 members. Those members constitute a powerful grass-roots network that can be activated almost instantly to press Congress to take this action or that." (Massing, p. 18)[36]
- "Jews played a central role in American finance during the 1980s, and they were among the chief beneficiaries of that decade's corporate mergers and reorganizations. Today, though barely two percent of the nation's population

is Jewish, close to half its billionaires are Jews. The chief executive officers of the three major television networks and the four largest film studios are Jews, as are the owners of the nation's largest newspaper chain and the most influential single newspaper, the New York Times." (Ginsberg, p. 1)[37]

- "Jews are only 3 percent of the nation's population and comprise 11 percent of what this study defines as the nation's elite. However, Jews constitute more than 25 percent of the elite journalists and publishers, more than 17 percent of the leaders of important voluntary and public interest organizations, and more than 15 percent of the top ranking civil servants." (Ginsberg, p. 103)[38]

- "During the last three decades Jews [in the United States] have made up 50 percent of the top two hundred intellectuals . . . 20 percent of professors at the leading universities, 27 percent of high civil servants, 40 percent of partners in the leading law firms in New York and Washington . . . 59 percent of the directors, writers, and producers of the 50 top-grossing motion pictures from 1965 to 1982, and 58 percent of directors, writers, and producers in two or more primetime television series." (Lipset and Raab, pp. 26–27)[39]

- "At the elite Ivy League schools, Jews make up 23 percent of the student body. They are a measly 2 percent of the U.S. population." (Cohen, p. A17)[40]

From the point of view of response to public affairs, Muslims in the United States respond to four principal identities in themselves. Muslims respond to the emotional pulls and sentiments of their own national origins (e.g. as Pakistanis, Indonesians, Iranians, Somali, or Egyptians.)[41]

Second, Muslims also act in response to their racial identities, given the race-conscious nature of American society. Among U.S. Muslims the racial factor has historically been particularly immediate among African Americans, who currently constitute more than thirty percent of the Muslim population of the United States. Third, U.S. Muslims try to influence policy as Muslims per se— such as the former activities of the American Muslim Council, which is based in Washington, DC. Other groups and organizations established by Muslims in the United States to correct stereotypes and influence policy include the Committee for American Islamic Relations, based in Washington, D.C., and the Muslim Public Affairs Council.[42] The Council once served as a lobby on both the Congress and the Federal Government on issues which have ranged from Bosnia to the Anti-Terrorism Act or the Patriot Act and their implications for civil liberties. Since September 11, 2001, U.S. Muslims have also felt exposed to new kinds of Islamophobia. Incidents of bias against Muslims have also increased due to, among other reasons, the war in Iraq, as noted by Mary Beth Sheridan in "Bias Against Muslims Up 70 percent." [43] (See also [44])

Fourth, American Muslims may also act, quite simply, as Americans. As concerned patriotic U.S. citizens, they may take positions on the size of the federal budget, or on how to deal with the trade imbalance with China, or on the future role of the North Atlantic Treaty Organization, or how to deal with large-scale corporate corruption.

In all these four identities (national origins, race, religion, and U.S. citizenship), American Muslims have become more organized and less inhibited since the last quarter of the twentieth century than they ever were before — with the possible exception of the followers of the Nation of Islam who have never been politically inhibited since they first came into being in the 1930s. Even the impact of September 11, 2001, has not forced U.S. Muslims back into a low-profile national role. As U.S. Muslims face a crisis of identity, partly based on their countries of origin, let us bear in mind estimates of such origins. According to some estimates, U.S. Muslims are about a third Black, a third South Asian (Pakistan, India and Bangladesh), a quarter Arab and the rest other groups. Other estimates put the African American Muslim component as high as 42 percent, but this is strongly contested.

As U.S. Muslims face a crisis of participation, they see Jews as exceptionally participatory and American Blacks as reluctant participants. According to some estimates, Jewish voters have a continuing record of 80 percent turnout. On the other hand, according to the U.S. Census Bureau, African American voting participation in Congressional elections in 1998 was 40 percent, half that of the Jews put a 3 percent increase from 1994. In the 2000 Presidential elections, African American participation was exceptionally high, but it was still below the overall national level of all groups, and certainly well below the level of Jewish participation.

The Muslim dilemma continues to be a dilemma between the Jewish model and the Black experience. Muslims would like to be similar to the Jews in performance, but would not seek Jewish partnership for now. A Muslim "yes" to Jewish performance; but a Muslim "no" to Jewish partnership for now. Muslim attitude toward African Americans is the reverse. They would like a partnership with Blacks, but not the performance of Blacks to date. A Muslim "no" to Black performance to date, but a Muslim "yes" to Black partnership as soon as possible.

What about the attitude of African American Muslims to the comparison between Jews and other African Americans? It would be unnatural if any African American (Muslim or non-Muslim) did not wish for the Black race a level of worldly achievement attained by the Jews, provided it was not at the cost of other people. But what is the scale of Jewish achievement in the United States?

It has been estimated that as the twentieth century was coming to a close, Diaspora Jews in the U.S.A. made up 50 percent of the top two hundred intellectuals, 20 percent of professors at the top universities, 40 percent of partners in leading law firms in New York and Washington, D.C., and nearly 60 percent

110   *Chapter Five*

of the directors, writers, and producers of the 50 top-grossing pictures from the 1960s to 1980s, and 58 percent of directors, writers and producers in some major primetime television series. This is a performance which U.S. Muslims could not but envy. It is also well above the performance of white gentiles.

On the other hand, according to the African American scholar, Manning Marable of Columbia University, African Americans only comprise 6.1 percent of all U.S. faculty in 2001, and even that figure could include adjuncts and part-timers. In the highest ranking research institutions, African Americans have comprised only 3.6 percent. As for the most prestigious American Academy of Arts and Science, African Americans comprise only 1.6 percent.[45] Barack Obama, the Kenyan-American who was elected to the United States Senate in 2004, is only the third Black to serve in the U.S. Senate since Reconstruction, and only the fifth ever.

In contrast, Jews in the U.S. Senate are not only always there, but are often a tenth of the total Senate membership (ten out of 100 Senators). Jews in America constitute a Diaspora triumphant. And yet Jews are a mere 2 percent of the population of the United States, while African Americans are some 12 percent. Indeed, the population of African Americans is more than twice the population of the Jews of the whole world, including Israel.

It is, therefore, not surprising that Muslims in the United States [including African American Muslims] should wish for a Jewish level of performance without necessarily seeking, for the time being, Jewish bonds of partnership. Most Muslims (including Black Muslims) would say "yes" to Jewish performance and "no" to Jewish partnership for the time being.

On the other hand, U.S. Muslims aspire to forge a partnership with African Americans as soon as possible, but are not yet inspired by Black success in using the American system to Black advantage. The dilemma persists for American Muslims (including African American Muslims). The overwhelming Muslim answer is "yes" to Black partnership, but "no" to Black performance in the U.S. system so far.

We know that as long as the Israeli-Palestinian problem persists, a sensible partnership between Muslims and Jews is bound to be elusive. What is less well known is that the Israeli-Palestinian bloody stalemate is also a threat to a partnership between Muslims and African Americans. Too close an alliance between African Americans and Muslim Americans is regarded as a threat by Jewish Americans. As Lisa Richardson observed in the Los Angeles Times:

The success of Jewish groups in helping to defeat two longtime African American members of Congress has further frayed the damaged relationship between leaders of Black and Jewish organizations. In the wake of [the 2002] ousting of Representative Cynthia A. McKinney in a Georgia Democratic Primary, some African American political activists and leaders are expressing outrage at Jewish organizations that targeted McKinney because she expressed pro-Palestinian sentiments about the Middle East crisis. McKinney lost to Denise Majette, a former state judge, who is also Black but benefited from out-of-state contributions from Jewish groups and crossover voting by republicans. Also [in 2002] another Black member of Congress, Representative Earl F. Hilliard of Alabama, who had pro-Arab support, was defeated by Arthur Davis, who was funded by backers of Israel.[46]

For as long as the Israeli-Palestinian problem is unresolved, African American leaders are expected to be pro-Israel or lose their offices. A partnership between African Americans and Muslim Americans arouses defensive reactions from Jewish Americans.

Muslims in the United States also face a crisis of values. Among immigrant Americans the social values they espouse resemble closely the social values of Republicans—often the less liberal Republicans. Muslim support for the death penalty is 68 percent, opposition to the sale of pornography 65 percent, opposition to physician assisted suicide 61 percent, support for making abortion less easily available 57 percent, support for vouchers to send children to private schools 68 percent, support for prayer in schools 53 percent, and support for displaying the Ten Commandments in schools 59 percent.

African American Muslim values are closer to the values of other African Americans—with greater emphasis on issues like job opportunities, affirmative action, and reform of the judicial system—all of them more liberal than the social values of immigrant Muslims.

A CONCLUSION

In foreign policy, the four identities of U.S. Muslims play their part. The issue of national origins, the membership of a racial group, the power of religious affiliation, and the moral concerns of U.S. Muslims as ordinary Americans—such a confluence of identities is part of the politics of pluralism, part of policy-formation in a liberal democratic order.

But, in the final analysis, the cultural dimension of the American Muslim experience is not simply this crisis of identity. It is also the simultaneous and interrelated crises of participation and code of conduct. It still remains a drama in three Acts. First Act: Am I an American first or a Muslim first? Which comes first—and under what circumstances? Second Act: Do I accept to be a participant in the American constitutional process? Third Act: Is my code of conduct as a Muslim compatible with my code of conduct as an American? The heritage of the Hijrah and the legacy of the Mayflower are in search of a moral synthesis. But the answers partly depend upon other Diasporic identities—racial, religious, geographic and cultural.

We have sought to demonstrate in this essay that one approach towards understanding Muslims in the American public space is to view Muslims comparatively. The Muslim predicament in America is caught between the lessons of the Black experience and the power of the Jewish example. The Diasporas of Africa and Judaism are challenging the Diaspora of Mecca and Medina.

I am indebted to Dr. Thomas Uthup and Dr. Amadu Jacky Kaba for bibliographical guidance.

NOTES

1. D'Agostino, Joseph A., "U.S. Has Given 50,000 Visas Since 9–11 To New Visitors From the Middle East." *Human Events* (Week of April Dec. 8, 2001).
2. Malik, Iftikhar H., *Islam and Modernity: Muslims in Europe and the United States* (London and Sterling, VA: Pluto Press, 2004), pp. 156–180.
3. Wormser, Richard, *American Islam: Growing Up Muslim in America* (New York: Walker & Co., 2002).
4. Hasan, Asma Gull, *American Muslims: The New Generation,* 2nd ed., (New York: Continuum, 2002).
5. Haddad, Yvonne Yazbeck, Ed., *Muslims in the West: From Sojourners to Citizens* (Oxford and New York: Oxford University Press, 2002).
6. Haddad, Yvonne Yazbeck and Jane I. Smith, *Muslim Minorities in the West: Visible and Invisible* (Walnut Creek, CA: AltaMira Press, 2002).
7. Haddad, Yvonne Yazbeck and John L. Esposito, Eds., *Muslims on the Americanization Path?* (Oxford and New York: Oxford University Press, 2000).
8. Afridi, Sam, *Muslims in America: Identity, Diversity and the Challenge of Understanding* (New York City, NY: Carnegie Corporation of New York, 2001).
9. Smith, Jane I., *Islam in America* (New York: Columbia University Press, 1999).
10. *The Baltimore Sun* (April 27, 2001), p. 4.
11. Leonard, Karen, "South Asian Leadership of American Muslims," in Haddad, Ed. *Muslims in the West: From Sojourners to Citizens*, p. 233.
12. Medoff, Rafael; foreword by Edward I. Koch, *Jewish Americans and Political Participation: A Reference Handbook* (Santa Barbara, CA: ABC-CLIO, 2002).
13. Maisel, Sandy and Ira N. Forman, Eds., *Jews in American Politics* (Lanham, MD: Rowman & Littlefield Publishers, 2001).
14. Nathan Diament. Quoted in Dana Milbank and Mike Allen, "Move Could Help Bush Among Jewish Voters," *The Washington* Post (April 15, 2004), p. 16.
15. U.S. Census Bureau. "African Americans Defy Trend of Plunging Voter Turnout, Census Bureau Reports" (July 19, 2000). Retrieved May 1, 2004 from http://www.census.gov/Press/www/2000/cb00–114.html.
16. U.S. Census Bureau. "Registered Voter Turnout Improved in 2000 Presidential Election, Census Bureau Reports." February 27, 2002. Retrieved on May 1, 2004 from http://www.census.gov/Press-Release/www/2002/cb02–31.html.

17. Lusane, Clarence "Hands across the Atlantic: Comparison of Black American and Black British Electoral Politics," in James Jennings, Ed., *Race and Politics: New Challenges and Responses for Black Activism* (London and New York: Verso, 1997), pp. 114–119.

18. Human Rights Watch "US Election 2000. Losing the Vote: The Impact of Felony Disenfranchisement Laws," November 8, 2000. Retrieved from (http://www .hrw.org/campaigns/elections/results.htm) on May 1, 2004.

19. Richardson, Lisa, "Political Ties Between Blacks and Jews Strained." *Los Angeles Times.* (August 23, 2002), retrieved on May 1, 2004 from (http://www.latimes .com/news/nationworld/nation/la-na-tension23aug23002048.story).

20. Glod, Maria, "Comments On Jews Shadow Moran," *The Washington* Post (April 19, 2004), p. B01.

21. Medoff, *Jewish Americans and Political Participation*, pp. 189–208.

22. Cantor, Eric, Quoted in Dana Milbank and Mike Allen, "Move Could Help Bush Among Jewish Voters," *The Washington* Post (April 15, 2004), p. A16.

23. See Malik, *Islam and Modernity*, pp. 176–177.

24. Phillips, Jeff, "Muslims 'Key' to US Elections." August 29, 2000. http://news .bbc.co.uk/1/hi/world/americas/901033.stm (accessed April 20, 2004).

25. Broder, David, Op-ed piece, "Mobilizing Arab Americans," *The Washington Post* (October 22, 2003), p. 29.

26. Tate, Katherine, *Black Faces in the Mirror: African Americans and Their Representatives in the U.S. Congress* (Princeton, NJ: Princeton University Press, 2003).

27. Mayer, Jeremy D., *Running on Race: Racial Politics in Presidential Campaigns 1960–2000.* (New York: Random House, 2002).

28. Jackson, James S., Ed., *New Directions: African Americans in a Diversifying Nation* (Washington, DC; Ann Arbor, MI: National Policy Association and Program for Research on Black Americans, University of Michigan, 2000).

29. U.S. Census Bureau, "Nation's Household Income Stable in 2000, Poverty Rate Virtually Equals Record Low, Census Bureau Reports" (September 21, 2001). Retrieved on May 1, 2004 from http://landview.census.gov/Press-Release/www/release/ archives/income_wealth/000393.html.

30. *The Washington Post* (September 14, 2003), p. 8.

31. http://www.cair-net.org/mosquereport/, accessed April 19, 2004.

32. *Frontline.* Aired on PBS Television on May 9, 2002, "Portraits of Ordinary Muslims: United States." Retrieved on May 1, 2004, from (http://www.pbs.org/wgbh/pages/ frontline/shows/muslims/portraits/us.html).

33. Goldberg, J. J., *Jewish Power: Inside the American Jewish Establishment* (Reading, MA: Addison-Wesley, 1996), p. 266.

34. Blumenfeld, Laura, "Terrorism Jars Jewish, Arab Party Loyalties," *The Washington Post* (December 7, 2003) p. A1.

35. Maisel and Forman, *Jews in American Politics*, pp. 449; a complete roster for all major political positions is available in the same publication, pp. 449–470.

36. Massing, Michael, "Deal Breakers," *The American Prospect* (March 11, 2002) Vol. 13, No. 5, p. 18.

37. Ginsberg, Benjamin, *The Fatal Embrace: Jews and the State* (Chicago: University of Chicago Press, 1993) p. 1.

38. Ginsberg, Benjamin, *The Fatal Embrace,* p. 103.

39. Lipset, Seymour Martin and Earl Raab, *Jews and the New American Scene* (Cambridge, MA: Harvard University Press, 1995), pp. 26–27.

40. Cohen, Richard, "A Study in Differences," *Washington Post*, (May 28, 2002), p. A17.

41. Afridi, *Muslims in America,* p. 4. Other works that may be consulted on American Muslims include Wormser, *American Islam* and Hasan, *American Muslims*.

42. Robert Marquand and Lamis Andoni, "Muslims Learn to Pull Political Ropes in US," *Christian Science Monitor* (February 5, 1996) p. 10.

43. *Washington Post* (May 3, 2004), p. A 12.

44. Fred Halliday, *September11: Two Hours That Shook the World: Causes and Consequences* (London: Saqi Books, 2002), pp. 121–131.

45. Marable, Manning, "Blacks in Higher Education: An Endangered Species," http://www.manningmarable.net/) (July 2002, accessed April 6, 2004).

46. Lisa richardson, "Political Ties Between Blacks and Jews Strained," *Los Angeles Times*, August 23, 2002.

Chapter Six

Is Israel a Threat to American Democracy?

There will be no "world without terrorism" for as long as the Palestinian-Israeli dispute is unresolved. It is by far the biggest trigger of rage against the United States among all issues.

Muslims are victims of violent injustice elsewhere in the world without the globalization of anger against the United States. Muslims in Kashmir, India, are victims of Indian security forces trying to prevent them from having self-determination.

Muslims in Chechnya are victims of Russian security forces trying to prevent them from having self-determination. Muslims in Macedonia are trying to cope with discrimination from Christian Macedonians. Muslims in Kosovo are denied a separate state by the international community and face the risk of reintegration with Yugoslavia against their will.

Muslims in Afghanistan faced the Soviet Union before and defeated it. The Afghans have now experienced military action by the United States.

If Muslims have been victimized elsewhere by other powers, why is the victimization of Muslims in the Middle East such a powder keg?

A ZIONIST SHADOW ON THE U.S. CONSTITUTION

Israeli militarism, occupation of Arab lands and repression of Palestinians are the main causes of not only anti-Israeli terrorism but also anti-American terrorism. No issue in the world since apartheid in South Africa has caused greater international rage than Israeli repression of Palestinians.

Even in dusty Khartoum—the New York Times reports—several hundred thousand people have marched in the streets denouncing Israel and the USA—

and some cheered Osama bin Laden. On April 17, 2002, President Husni Mubarak of Egypt declined to see Secretary of State Colin Powell and sent Egypt's Foreign Minister instead to meet him. Mubarak had a diplomatic cold.

If Israeli repression and militarism provokes suicide bombers and give rise to movements like Hamas and al- Qaeda, Israeli political culture becomes increasingly racist—and the Attorney General of the United States begins to curtail civil liberties in the United States.

1. There are now detainees without trial in the USA in their hundreds, sometimes physically tortured.
2. Prisoners' access to attorneys is restricted
3. There have been search and seizure in cultural institutions of Arab and Muslim Americans. What is probable cause? Being Muslim!
4. The attorney-client confidentiality is at risk for those suspected of terrorism. What happened to the principle of innocent until proven guilty?
5. Military tribunals may be set up for civilian suspects: even secret trials have been considered.
6. CNN and other networks have been summoned to the White House to be lectured about giving undue publicity to Osama bin Laden. What happened to editorial independence?

And now steps are being taken towards militarizing domestic life in the United States. New military reforms establish a military command for within the United States.

If Israeli atrocities and repression cause terrorism in the United States, and terrorism in turn threatens civil liberties in America, a chain of causation is established. The behaviour of the state of Israel threatens not merely democracy within the Jewish state. Israel threatens democracy in America as well.

We keep on hearing that Israel is the only democracy in the region. But it is in the interest of the United States that Israel should be the only democracy.

Because of Israeli intransigence, Arab public opinion is more anti-American than most Arab dictators. Had the Arab world been more democratic, their governments would have had to be more militantly anti-Israel and anti-American than they are.

The United States has a vested interest in an Arab world which is not democratic. For Arab dictators are a safety valve to keep their populations less explosively anti-American.

Almost all the 20 Arab governments of the Arab League apart from Syria, Libya, Iraq, and Sudan are obedient to the United States. But such pro-American obedience would have been voted out of office had the Arab world enjoyed free elections.

Similarly, only a military regime in Pakistan under General Musharaff could have cooperated so fully with the United States in its invasion of Afghanistan. No elected government in Pakistan would have been able to defy the pro-Islamic and pro-Taliban segments of Pakistani opinion with such impunity.

The United States gained from lack of democracy in Pakistan.

Into the Arab heartland Western powers decided to create a Jewish state in 1948—with President Harry S. Truman playing a critical role in making it happen.

It did not stop with the creation of the Jewish state.

1. Israel expanded after the 1948 war
2. Eisenhower prevented expansion in 1956
3. Further Israeli occupation of Palestinian territory after 1967 war
4. Annexation of Jerusalem by Israel in 1967
5. Creating Jewish settlements on Arab land continually
6. Blowing up and destroying Arab homes as a hidden strategy of ethnic cleansing.

WHY IS THE U.S. being blamed for Israeli policies? Where was Osama bin Laden's anti-Americanism coming from?

1. Massive economic aid from the United States to Israel in billions
2. Provision of sophisticated American weapons to Israel
3. The United States was shielding Israel from U.N. censure
4. The United States was making U.N. Security Council impotent in punishing Israel.
5. The United States was weakening anti-Israeli Arab forces by buying off the government of Egypt with a billion U.S. dollars every year.
   Egypt is the largest Arab country and used to be the biggest single threat to Israel militarily. The U.S. largess has bought off Egypt effectively.
6. The U.S. was preventing IRAQ from rising as an alternative to Egypt in challenging Israel. Taking advantage of Iraq's invasion of Kuwait to weaken Iraq permanently—whereas Pearl Harbor was not used to weaken Japan permanently, nor was Hitler's aggression used to weaken Germany permanently.

THE UNITED STATES is both the main source of military support for the enemy of the Arab World, Israel, and the USA is also the main destroyer of Arab capacity to rise militarily. This latter policy includes weakening Egypt and enfeebling Iraq.

We must solve the Palestine problem if terrorism is to end. To the moralist, terrorism against the United States is born out of evil. To the political analyst terrorism is born out of rage and frustration.

Solving the Israeli-Palestinian brutal stalemate is indispensable for the creation of a world without terrorism. It is also indispensable for making the United States a more benevolent super power, and Israel a less racist power.

Finally, the Jews to whom 1.2 billion Muslims owe a lot doctrinally and to whom a similar number of Christians are equally indebted, will one day rediscover their global role. The Jews—who invented globalization—may one day help to make globalization more humane. AMEN.

TOWARDS THE RACIALIZATION OF ZIONISM

But for the time being many friends of Israel are anxious that the repressive forces in the Jewish state are getting stronger—and a distinctly Israeli form of racism may be evolving. This is a minority. But within that racially anti-Arab minority there may be a smaller and more ominous sub-group.

There is a school of thought in Israel which is already becoming fascist. This issue is debated more frankly in Israel itself than in the United States. Lovers of democracy in Israel are alarmed by the fascist trend. There is even an Israeli word for this kind of Semitic fascism. Professor Yeshayahu Leibovitz of the Hebrew University has called it: Judeo-Nazism. As editor of the Encyclopedia Hebraica, Leibovitz has grappled with many trends in the Jewish experience. But he has now raised the issue of whether the concept of Judeo-Nazism is any longer a contradiction in terms.[1]

Israelis are warning each other that the unthinkable is not necessarily impossible. Specific sociological conditions in inter-war Germany fostered right wing extremism among the Germans. The history of German extremism started with a people who believed they had been humiliated and humbled.

The Treaty of Versailles which ended World War I created among the Germans a martyrdom complex which later favoured the rise of extreme nationalism. The martyrdom complex—strong among the Israelis today and powerful among the Germans in the inter-war years—can degenerate into paranoia. We now know that lovers of democracy in the German population underestimated the danger. The whole world paid a heavy price for German paranoia.

Jews—like the Germans—have been impressive contributors to world civilization. But both people are human, and therefore psychologically vulnerable. The danger of extremism is real.

The stages toward extremism through which the German psyche passed were as follows:

1. Martyrdom Complex
2. Paranoia
3. Extreme Nationalism
4. Racial Exclusivity
5. Militarization
6. Territorial Expansionism

It is very unlikely that Israelis will pass through similar stages. There are in any case major constraints to Zionist extremism. The question nevertheless remains whether the danger of fascism in Israel is real enough to alarm Israeli patriots themselves.

Israel was genuinely born out of the ashes and anguish of the Holocaust. It was a more genuine martyrdom than was the Nazi sense of humiliation in the inter-war years.

But when does the martyrdom complex evolve into paranoia? In two stages in the case of the Jews:

a. Monopolizing the Holocaust as an experience of the Past
b. Pre-empting imaginary Holocausts of the future

A 1980's American immigrant into Israel from a religious family in New York prayed for a new persecution of Jews in the Diaspora so that they are forced to go to the fortress Israel:

> "The hatred the Gentiles feel towards the Jews is eternal. There never was peace between us and them except when they totally beat us or when we shall totally beat them. Maybe if they will give someone like Sharon the chance to kill . . . until the Arabs will understand that we did them a favour letting them remain alive. . . . We are powerful now and power should talk now. The Gentiles only understand the language of power."[2]

Prime Minister Yitzhak Shamir declared in April 1988:

> "We say to them, from this hilltop and from the perspective of thousands of years of history, that in our eyes they are like grasshoppers."[3]

Menachin Begin's earlier denunciation of Palestinians as "two-legged animals" has formed part of the same drift towards racist perceptions and perspectives in powerful circles in Israel.

Is Zionist nationalism stifling Israeli liberalism? Opinion polls of Israeli attitudes to the Palestinian uprising in the occupied territories is one measure. The death of over 500 Palestinians since the Intifada began has not alarmed enough Israelis. Indeed, the majority of Israelis seem to want even stiffer measures against the Palestinians.

When is soft Israeli arrogance towards the Arabs paternalistic? As an Israeli originally from Aden put it:

> "We know that the Arab is an obedient good creature as long as he is not incited and no one puts ideas into his head. . . . He just has to be told exactly what his right place is. . . . They must understand who the master is. That's all."[4]

When united to fanaticism and nationalism, arrogance can take the form of militant racism. Take the case of the young rabbi who denounced the "filth" of mixed marriages and the "hybrid children" such marriages produce—"a thorn in the flesh of the Jewish society in Israel."[5]

This rabbi recommended school segregation and exclusion of Arabs from the universities. Echoes of apartheid are unmistakable.

As for the trend towards militarization, Israel has indeed become the most efficient war machine since Nazi Germany. In war after war the Jewish state has demonstrated staggering proficiency both in the air and on land. The six-day war in June 1967 was its most dazzling military success. Did this military success increase territorial appetite?

A state created in the teeth of the opposition of indigenous people became a state surrounded by hostile neighbours. It was only a matter of time before the moral cost had to be paid. A Director-General of Israel Broadcasting Authority (radio and television) during years of apartheid was a "long time admirer of South Africa and a frequent visitor there." He even wrote an "emotional article" expressing his preference for South Africa over Black Africa, complete "with citations of research proving genetic inferiority of blacks"—a view which "seems to reflect the feeling of many in the Israeli elite."[6]

The journal of Mapam (left wing of Labour Alignment) published an explanation of the superiority of Israeli pilots. Blacks and Arabs were inferior in "complex, cognitive intelligence." That was why "American Blacks succeed only in short distance running"[7]

Israeli neo-Nazism reversed the scale of genetic values favoured by German Nazis. Both forms of extremism exaggerated the impact of the Jewish factor. The Nazis thought the Jewish impact was negative. The Israeli extremists erred the other way.

Why has the United States outdistanced Europe in modern culture? The proportion of Jews in the American population has enhanced American creativity, according to this Israeli school of thought.[8]

By implication German inventiveness before the Holocaust was due to the Jewish creative infusion into the German population. An Israeli labour party journal refers to "genetic experiments" at Tel Aviv University—which have shown that "genetic differences among Jewish communities [Poland and Yemen are cited] are smaller than those between Gentiles and Jews."[9]

"In earlier years the Rabbinate had cited biblical authority to justify expulsion of the Arabs ("The foreign element") from the land, or simply their destruction, and religious law was invoked to justify killing of civilians in war or raid." [10]

American Rabbi Isaac Bernstein argued that religious law gives power and legitimacy to Israel to "dispossess the Arabs of the conquered territories." [11] Another Rabbi, Rabbi Lubovitcher of New York, deplored that Israel did not conquer Damascus during the 1973 October War.[12]

A doctrine emerged called "secure and defensible borders." After almost every war Israel attempted to get more territory. Whose secure and defensible borders? Because of Israel's military supremacy, only Israel had such secure borders. The Arabs were easily penetrable by Israeli air and rocket power.

The transition from chosen people to chosen race gathered momentum. Rabbi Elazar Valdman of Gush Emunim wrote in the journal Nekudah of the West Bank settlers:

> We will certainly establish order in the Middle East and in the world. And if we do not take this responsibility upon ourselves, we are sinners, not just towards ourselves but towards the entire world. For who can establish order in the world? All of those Western leaders of weak character?[13]

The question which inevitably has now arisen is whether Israel's taste for imperial expansion can long be sustained without hurting Israeli democracy. Can the sadism against Palestinians be long enjoyed without creating Israeli masochism? Is Zionism becoming a cancer not just on the body politic of Arab stability but also on the body politic of Jewish sense of justice?

CAN A STATE BE JEWISH AND DEMOCRATIC?

In the course of this twenty-first century Israel will have to choose between remaining a Jewish state and remaining a democracy. Such a dilemma already exists but it will get worse.

The proportion of Arabs in Israel is higher than the proportion of Blacks in the United States. Yet while Blacks in the United States have reached high echelons in the executive branch, Arabs in Israel are marginalized in government.

Arab Israelis have done well in the legislative branch, but have effectively been kept out of major executive and judicial positions. There is no Arab equivalent of Thurgood Marshall or Justice Clarence Thomas.

The Arab population in Israel—now eighteen percent—is on its way towards becoming a quarter of the population. There will indeed come a time when Israel has to choose between being a Jewish state and being a democratic state.

More recently there is increasing support in the state of Israel for a policy which is euphemistically called "transfer." It is basically a policy of ethnic cleansing. More and more Israelis are dreaming of a kind "final solution to the Palestinian problem"—the transfer of all Palestinians of the West Bank [and presumably Gaza] to new refugee camps in the rest of the Arab world. What to do with those Palestinians who are already Israeli citizens poses difficult problems for these ultra-Zionists.[14]

But American civil liberties and Israeli democracy are not the only victims of the cruel behavior of the State of Israel towards Palestinians. There is also the additional risk of reactivating international anti-Semitism. It is to this dimension that we should now turn.

ISRAEL AS A CAUSE OF ANTI-SEMITISM

The state of Israel was created partly as a permanent asylum for Jews who might otherwise suffer persecution in other parts of the world. The Zionist movement was originally conceived as a quest for a piece of land without people to accommodate people without land. As it turned out, Palestine was hardly "a piece of land without people." Millions of Arabs have remained displaced to accommodate Jews from elsewhere.

Political Zionism was originally intended as a defense against anti-Semitism. Fifty years after the creation of the State of Israel, has Zionism now become a cause of new forms of anti-Semitism? Is the state of Israel becoming a cause of hatred for other Jews around the world?

This appears to be the conclusion which has been reached by the Chief Rabbi of Great Britain. On the last day of February 2002 Dr. Jonathan Sacks urged strong action to prevent "violence and bloodshed" against Jews in England. He argued that the Israeli-Palestine conflict had sparked off levels of anti-Semitism not seen in Britain since the years of the Holocaust. He referred to an increasing number of attacks on synagogues and "virulent anti-Israel campaigns on some English university campuses which have left many Jewish students fearful for their safety." [The TIMES (London) March 1, 2002, page 2]

The Chief Rabbi complained that the leading liberal newspapers in Britain such as THE GUARDIAN, THE INDEPENDENT and THE STATESMAN had started publishing op-ed articles questioning Israeli's right to exit. According to the Chief Rabbi, the websites of THE INDEPENDENT and THE STATESMAN had become what he describes as a focus of anti-Semitic discussion.

At the University of Manchester, England, Jewish students claimed to have been spat upon and denounced as "Nazis" and "baby butchers" during a bitter dispute at the students' union about whether Israel should be declared an apartheid-state.

Rabbi Sacks claimed that until recently he had never experienced anti-Semitism in Britain. But he saw new evidence that anti-Semitism was returning not only to Britain but also to other parts of Europe.

"The fact that I have chosen to speak indicates the depth of my concern. We know from all of history that words turn into deeds, prejudice into violence, and eventually violence into bloodshed. . . . You cannot deny people the right to criticize any nation-state [such as Israel]. But what we are seeing goes beyond that, and has become an attack on Jews, not just the state of Israel . . . That Jewish students on campus should have to go in fear is unacceptable." [THE TIMES (London) March 1, 2002]

After the massacre in Jenin in April 2002, THE INDEPENDENT in London accused Israel of a "monstrous war crime" [April 16). In the correspondence columns of THE GUARDIAN (London) there have been many letters about whether negative reactions to Israeli policies are leading to a revival of European anti-Semitism. One pained statement came from David Grossman as early as October 22, 2001. He said:

"I am highly critical of Israel's behaviour, but in recent weeks I have felt that the [British] media's hostility to it has not been fed solely by the actions of the Sharon government. A person feels such things deeply, under the skin, I feel them with a kind of shiver that percolates down to the cells of my most primeval memories. . . ."[15]

In Black Africa, where Israel had many friends, there is new questioning. John Nagenda has said the following in a Uganda newspaper:

"The Israelis latterly scored over 300 Palestinian deaths to less than 20 against them, but still insisted that it was Arafat and his Palestinians who were the aggressors. Where is God?"

"It must be crystal clear that Sharon's blind rage policy daily leads Israel to more insecurity, not less. . . . By Bush giving carte blanche, the American President is a bad, not a good friend of Israel. Does Bush know many Israelis? Did he go to prep school with many of them? Are many of them members of his clubs?"[16]

By giving Israel carte blanche, the United States was also a bad friend to world Jewry. Is the U.S. feeding into global anti-Semitism?

In April 2002 World Jewish leaders held an emergency meeting in Brussels to discuss what was described as "the rash of anti-Semitic violence that has swept Western Europe." The Secretary-General of the World Jewish Congress said: "We are now facing an unprecedented increase in anti-Semitism on this continent." Israel's military action against Palestinians was identified as a factor. [*New York Times*, April 23, 2002]

In the final analysis, blind U.S. policy, which is uncritical of Israel, is dangerous to American lives—as well as to Jewish safety. It is also a potential threat to American democracy.

Israel was created as a refuge from anti-Semitic hate. It has become one of the main causes of anti-Semitic rage against innocent Jews in other parts of the world. It is also in danger of compromising its own democratic order, as well as the constitution of its closest friend, the United States of America.

CONCLUSION

The issue of Israel started causing damage to American democracy long before September 11, 2001. Few topics have caused more self-imposed censorship on the American media than any criticism of the State of Israel. Journalists, reporters and editors have to watch carefully what they say about Israel. What is at stake is the potential wrath of the pro-Israeli lobby, and also potential loss of revenue from angry advertisers who withdraw their commercials or angry Jewish subscribers to public television or National Public Radio. The Print media in the United States also routinely censors themselves against any criticism of the State of Israel.

The issue of Israel has also detracted from academic freedom on American campuses. There have been cases when scholars have been denied tenure because of their pro-Palestinian writings or lectures. The United States may be the only country in the world in which it is safer to criticize the host country itself (i.e. the United States) than to criticize a particular external power (i.e. Israel). While some scholars have lost their jobs for criticizing the government of Israel almost no scholar runs much of risk at an American University for criticizing the U.S. administration of the day.

Perhaps Israel ought never to have been created. Millions of Jews were opposed to its creation in the first place. Those Jews have now been vindicated. The creation of the Jewish state has cost thousands of lives and may cost many more. If the world had realized the potential human cost, even the unrepresentative United Nations of 1947–1948 might never have voted for the partition of Palestine.

But now that Israel has been created, there should be no attempt to destroy it physically. Most Israelis today are innocent of the original massive miscalculation, and do not deserve to suffer for that mistake.

However, the Jewishness of Israel will be destroyed by its own contradictions. In a few decades Israel will have to choose between remaining a Jewish state and remaining a democracy. The two will be incompatible.

Already the effort to maintain the Jewishness of Israel is racializing Jewish attitudes to Palestinians. Rightwing views in Israel even from Rabbis and religious figures are getting increasingly racist. And under Prime Ministers like Ariel Sharon, Israeli policies are narrowing the gap between the behavior of Nazis towards Jews and the behaviour of Israelis towards Palestinians. Terms like the following are entering the vocabulary of international censure of Israel—"Judeo-Nazism" and "Nazi-onism." Israeli Jews, who were once the unique martyrs of human history, are now becoming just one more oppressor of other people. Human kind is the poorer for this Israeli deterioration.

NOTES

1. Cited by Noam Chomsky, *The Fateful Triangle: The United States, Israel, and the Palestinians* (Boston: South End Press, 1983).

2. Report by Israel Writer Amos Oz based on interviews and published in Davar Noam Chomsky, *The Fateful Triangle*, pp. 446–7.

3. "Search for Partners: Should the US Deal with the PLO?" *Time Magazine* April 11, 1988. See what is a "Grasshopper," letter to NYT, April 20, 1988.

4. Report by Amos Oz in a series of articles in *Davar*, Ibid, Chomsky, *The Fateful Triangle*, p. 447.

5. Consult report by Eliahu Salpeter, Ha'aretz, No. 4, 1982.

6. Benjamin Beit-Hallahmi, "Israel and South Africa" *New Outlook*, March/April 1983; Hotam, April 18, 1975 and October 1, 1982.

7. Chomsky, p. 152.

8. Davar, September 8, 1981. Chomsky pp 151–152.

9. Charles Hoffman, "A Monkey Trial, Local Style," *Jerusalem Post*, March 22, 1983.

10. Chomsky, *The Fateful Triangle,* p. 153. See also Military rabbinate publications *Peace in the Middle East?* pp. 108–9; Shahak, *Begin and Co.*, Said, *Question of Palestine*, p. 91.

11. Chomsky, p. 153, Bernstein, *Dialogue* (New York) Winter 1980.

12. *Al Hamishmar*, January 4, 1978.

13. Cited by Danny Rubenstein, *Davar*, October 8, 1982.

14. The increasing popularity in Israel of the idea of "transfer" of the Palestinian population was covered in "60 Minutes II," ABC Television [U.S.A.] Wednesday April 10, 2002.

15. "Diary," *THE GUARDIAN*, October 22, 2001. Cited in a letter by Arnold Wesker, *THE GUARDIAN* (London) March 1, 2002.

16. "Sharon's Blind Rage is Leading Israel to Hell," *THE NEW VISION* (Kampala), February 23, 2002.

Section III

AFRO-ARABS IN WORLD HISTORY

Chapter Seven

Afrabia: From Arabo-Hebraic Divergence to Afro-Arab Convergence

This chapter is a work in progress. It addresses the great Semitic divergence. On one side it addresses how the Jews over the centuries gradually merged with Europe and the West, and, on the other side, how the Arabs over the centuries gradually merged with Africa.

The great Semitic divergence is the relentless Europeanization of the Jews simultaneously with the partial Africanization of the Arabs.

It is particularly appropriate that this lecture occurs so close to Eid el Kabir or Eid el Adha. For Muslims, the Kaaba symbolizes in part the legacy of Abraham (Ibrahim). And at least for some Muslims the sacrifices of the lamb and sheep during Eid-Hajj partly celebrates Ibrahim's readiness to sacrifice his son—and the permission he received from God at the last minute to sacrifice a ram or lamb instead.

This story is shared between the Qur'an and the Bible and in relation to the two sons of Abraham, Isaac [Ishaq] and Ishmael [Ismail]. Some regard Isaac as the ancestor of all modern Jews, and Ishmael as the grandfather of all modern Arabs. The Bible is more emphatic that Ismail's mother was Egyptian.

There is a new term which has gained currency in recent decades—and the term is "the Abrahamic Religions." This vocabulary recognizes Abraham as a founding father of the three great monotheistic religions—Judaism, Christianity and Islam.

However, is there a revival of an older term, but with a revised meaning? Are there Abrahamic peoples, as well as Abrahamic religions? While Abrahamic religions are inter-related faiths, Abrahamic peoples belong to inter-related languages. These are the Semitic peoples—with special reference to the Arabs and the Jews.

But while this particular lecture will pay more attention to the Afro-Arab convergence than to the Euro-Jewish convergence, we must at least indicate an outline of the Europeanization of the Jews.

The dispersal of the Hebrews among the Gentiles began with Babylonian exile in 586 B.C.

Cyrus the Great of Persia is credited with having liberated the Jews—when he conquered Babylon. In 538 B.C. Cyrus permitted the Jews to go back home to ancient Israel, but many dispersed Jews decided to remain in exile.

This is where the city of Alexandria comes into play. In the first century B.C. forty percent of the population of Alexandria was Jewish. The Jews of Alexandria were regarded as culturally and intellectually the most scintillating and innovative part of the Diaspora in early Jewish history.

In those days Alexandria was more part of Europe than it was part of either the Arab or Muslim worlds. Indeed, Islam as the religion of the Prophet Muhammad had yet to be born. It was also centuries before the Arab conquest of Egypt. It might, therefore, be said that the Europeanization of the Jews began in Alexandria before the Christian era.

By the first century of the Christian era, the Jews in the Diaspora already outnumbered those still resident in Israel. Up to five million Jews already lived outside Palestine—four quarters of which were in the Roman Empire, including Alexandria.

The major centers of Jewish presence from then on alternated and shifted between Babylonia, Persia, Byzantium and then more clearly European centers of Spain, France, Russia, Germany, Poland and eventually the United States of America.

The worst rebellion against the Jewish presence in Europe occurred in Germany in the twentieth century, as well as in other countries dominated by the Nazis during World War II.

Paradoxically, this Jewish Holocaust had two paradoxical long-term consequences. On one side the Nazi Holocaust gave greater support and sympathy to the Zionist movement—which was committed to the mission of reversing the Diaspora formation through the creation of a new Jewish state in Palestine.

On the other hand, the Jews who remained in the Diaspora became more powerful after the Holocaust than they ever were before the Nazis.

By the end of the twentieth century, out of 15 to 16 million Jews in the whole world, less than a quarter were in Israel, forty percent were in the Untied States and most of the rest were in Russia and other European countries. The Europeanization of world Jewry had become basically the Westernization of the Jews presence in the world.

The integration of the Jews into Western society resulted in massive Jewish penetration into the citadels of power, especially in the United States. Although Jews are less than three percent of the population of the United States, Jews sometimes constitute a tenth of the United States' Senate. They have disproportionate power in the economy, in the academy, and in such major institutions of opinion-formation as the New York Times and the electronic media. This particular branch of the legacy of Abraham (the descendants of Isaac) had substantially fulfilled the Biblical prophecy about Abraham, "And your offspring shall possess the gates of their enemies, and by your offspring shall all the nations of the earth gain blessing for themselves, because you have obeyed my voice."[1]

Arabs can be fully assimilated into Western society provided they are Christian and fair skinned. Arab-Americans who have been elected to the U.S. House of Representatives include Nick Joe Rahall II (West Virginia), Darrell Issa (California) and Ray LaHood (Illinois). John E. Sununu is serving as a member of the U.S. Senate, and John Baldacci as Governor of Maine. The most famous Arab-American is probably Ralph Nader, who has run as a serious third party presidential candidate in the U.S. elections of 2000 and 2004.

While Jews have risen to senior membership of the U.S. Cabinets as members of a minority religion in the country (Judaism), no Arab has risen to such American political prominence as a member of the minority religion of Islam.

Let us now turn to the other part of the great Semitic divergence—the Africanization of the Arabs. In reality there are reciprocal forces at work. Across the centuries the Arab world has become Africanized demographically and territorially. The majority of the population of the Arab world is now in Africa—that is, demographic Africanization.

And secondly the bulk of the territory under Arab control and settlement is now in Africa. There are more square miles or kilometers under Arab control in Africa than in the rest of the Arab world. This is the territorial Africanization of the Arab world.

But while the Arab world is getting Africanized demographically and territorially, the African world is getting Arabized culturally, as well as religiously. The Arab impact on Africa consists not only in the spread of Islam, but also in the emergence of new languages deeply influenced by the Arabic language, and the penetration of Arab ideas and concepts even in African languages of people who are not religiously Islamized.

While the Euro-Jewish convergence has been mainly about how the Jews politically penetrated the Western world while allowing themselves to be culturally Westernized, the Afro-Arab convergence may involve a whole redefinition of geographical areas of the world. In the future will it be possible to talk about the Arab world without talking more and more about Africa? Will we talk much about Africa without talking about the Arabs?

By far the most ambitious idea floating in the new era of African-Arab relations is whether the whole of Africa and the whole of the Arab world are two regions in the process of merging into one. Out of this speculative discourse has emerged the concept of AFRABIA.

Three tendencies have stimulated new thinking about African-Arab relations. One tendency is basically negative but potentially unifying—the war on terrorism. The new international terrorism may have its roots in injustices perpetrated against such Arab people as Palestinians and Iraqis, but the primary theater of contestation is blurring the distinction between the Middle East and the African continent.[2] In order to kill twelve Americans in Nairobi in August 1998, over two hundred Kenyans died in a terrorist act at the United States Embassy in Nairobi. In 2002, a suicide bomber in Mombasa, Kenya, attacked the Israeli-owned and Israeli-patronized Paradise Hotel. Three times as many Kenyans as Israelis died.

African countries like Uganda, South Africa, Tanzania and Kenya have been under American pressure to pass anti-terrorist legislation—partly intended to control their own Muslim populations and partly targeted at potential Al-Qaeda infiltrators. Uganda and Tanzania and others have already capitulated to American pressure.

Independently of the war on terror, Islam as a cultural and political force has also been deepening relationships between Africa and the Middle East. Intellectual revival is not only a Western idiom. It is also the idiom of African cultures and African Islam. The hot political debates about the Shariah (Islamic Law) in Nigeria constitute part of the trend of cultural integration between Africa and the Middle East.

The new legitimation of Muammar Qaddafy as an African Elder Statesman has contributed to the birth of no less a new institution than the African Union. In my own face-to-face conversations with the Libyan leader, I have sometimes been startled by how much more Pan-Africanist than Pan-Arabist he has recently become. At least for the time being Qaddafy is out-Africanizing the legacy of Gamal Abdel Nasser.

The third force which may be merging Africa with the Middle East is political economy. Africa's oil producers need a joint partnership with the bigger oil producers of the Middle East. In the area of aid and trade between Africa and the Middle East, the volumes may have gone down since the 1980s. But most indications seem to promise a future expansion of economic relations between Africa and the Middle East.[3] In the Gulf countries of the United Arab Emirates and the Sultanate of Oman the concept of "AFRABIA" has begun to be examined on higher and higher echelons. Let us look more closely at this concept in the light of the revival of both intellectual discourse and new approaches to Pan-Africanism.

WHO ARE THE AFRABIANS?

It was initially Trans-Saharan Pan-Africanism which gave birth to the idea of Afrabia. The first post-colonial waves of Pan-Africanists like Nkrumah believed that the Sahara Desert was a bridge rather than a divide.

The concept of AFRABIA not only now connotes an interaction between Africanity and Arab identity; it is seen as a process of fusion between the two. While the principle of Afrabia recognizes that Africa and the Arab world are overlapping categories, it goes on to prophesy that these two regions are in the historic process of becoming one.

But who are the AFRABIANS? There are in reality at least four categories. Cultural Afrabians are those whose culture and way of life have been deeply Arabized but falling short of their being linguistically Arabs. Most Somali, Hausa, and some Waswahili are cultural Afrabians in that sense. Their mother-tongue is not Arabic, but much of the rest of their culture bears the stamp of Arab and Islamic impact.

Ideological Afrabians are those who intellectually believe in solidarity between Arabs and Africans, or at least between Arab Africa and black Africa. Historically such ideological Afrabian leaders have included Kwame Nkrumah, the founder president of Ghana; Gamal Abdel Nasser, arguably the greatest Egyptian of the twentieth century; and Sékou Touré, the founding father of post-colonial Guinea (Conakry). Such leaders refused to recognize the Sahara Desert as a divide, and insisted on visualizing it as a historic bridge.

Demographic Afrabians are those Arabs and Berbers whose countries are members of both the African Union and the Arab League. Some of the countries are overwhelmingly Arab, such as Egypt and Tunisia, while others are only marginally Arab, such as Mauritania, Somalia and the Comoro Islands. What these countries have also in common is a predominantly Muslim population.

As for genealogical Afrabians, these are those who are biologically descended from both Arabs and Black Africans. In North Africa these include Anwar Sadat, the President of Egypt who concluded a peace treaty with Israel and was assassinated in 1982 as a consequence. Anwar Sadat's mother was Black. He was politically criticized for many things, but almost never for being racially mixed.

Genealogical Afrabians in sub-Saharan Africa include Salim Ahmed Salim, the longest serving Secretary-General of the Organization of African Unity.

Genealogical Afrabians also include the Mazrui clan scattered across Coastal Kenya and Coastal Tanzania. It should be noted that Northern Sudanese qualify as Afrabians by both geographical and genealogical criteria.

These four sub-categories of Afrabians provide some of the evidence that Africa and the Arab world are two geographical regions which are in the slow historic process of becoming one.

But the merger of the Arab world with Africa is a slow integration across generations. What is more urgent is cooperation based on reconciliation in the immediate future. Tensions in places like Darfur in Sudan make such short-term accord more difficult. Nevertheless, let us examine African-Arab relations with two models of historic reconciliation involving other societies. The Anglo-American model traces the transition from hostility to fraternity in the relations between the people of Britain and those of the United States from the late eighteenth century to the two World Wars. Are there lessons to be learnt which are relevant for relations between Arabs and Africans historically? The Anglo-American reconciliation was slow but eventually deep.

The second model of reconciliation traces the transition from enmity to friendship between the United States and Japan from 1941 to this new century. Are there other lessons to be learnt in this Americo-Japanese model which are also pertinent for African-Arab relations in historical perspective? Let us look at these two models of reconciliation more closely. The Americo-Japanese reconciliation has been quicker, but more shallow.

Forgiveness between Arabs and Africans may be somewhere between the U.S.—British model (slow but deep) and the U.S.—Japanese model (quick but shallow). African-Arab reconciliation may be less slow than the Anglo-American fraternity and significantly deeper than the Americo-Japanese reconciliation. Afro-Arab reconciliation involves not only memories of the Zanzibar revolution but, even more fundamentally, memories of Arab involvement in the slave trade in Africa. Can the pain of the past be forgotten?

Global trends in the New Global Order are dictating speed in African-Arab reconciliation and integration. Historical continuities and geographical contiguities may lend greater depth to the future relationship between Africa and the Arab world. But conscious steps need to be taken in pursuit of any new forms of solidarity. Forgiving the past is one thing; forging a new future is a bigger imperative.

AFRABIA BETWEEN GEOGRAPHY AND CULTURE

The French once examined their special relationship with Africa—and came up with the concept of EURAFRICA as a basis of special cooperation. We in turn should examine the even older special relationship between Africa and the Arab world—and call it AFRABIA.

After all, the majority of the Arab people are now in the African continent. The bulk of Arab lands are located in Africa. As we have observed, there are more Muslims in Nigeria than there are Muslims in any Arab country, including Egypt. In other words, the Muslim population of Nigeria is larger than the Muslim population of Egypt. The African continent as a whole is in the process of becoming the first continent in the world with an absolute Muslim majority.

But AFRABIA is not just a case of the spread of languages and the solidarity of religion. Whole new ethnic communities were created by this dynamic. The emergence of Cushitic groups like the Somali in the Horn of Africa are one case in point. Oman, Yemen and Saudi Arabia were also instrumental in helping to give birth to whole new ethnic groups on the eastern seaboard of Africa. Swahili culture and the Swahili city states captured a whole epoch in African history and legacy. Oman is central to the modern history of the Swahili heritage.

The brave peoples of Eritrea are also a reluctant bridge of AFRABIA. Even the Berbers of North Africa are a special case of Afrabia. The very name "Africa" probably originated in a Berber language, and was initially used to refer to what is now Tunisia. The continent got its name from what is now "Arab Africa." Is there a stronger argument for AFRABIA?

Then there have been the migrations and movements of populations between Africa and Arabia across the centuries. There is evidence of Arab settlements on the East African coast and in the Horn of Africa well before the birth of the Prophet Muhammad. And the fact that the first great muezzin of Islam was Seyyidna Bilal is evidence that there was an African presence in Mecca and Medina before Islam. Bilal was there before he was converted— a symbol of an older Arabian link with Africa. AFRABIA is a pre-Hijjriyya phenomenon.

Islam itself is almost as old in Africa as it is in Arabia. In Ethiopia Muslims came to seek religious asylum during the Prophet Muhammad's early days when he and his followers were persecuted in Mecca. Archeological excavations in Eastern Africa have discovered remains of mosques which go back to the earliest decades of Islam. Islam as a factor in AFRABIA does indeed go back some fourteen centuries!

There is the impact of language on AFRABIA. The language with the largest number of individual speakers in the African continent is still Arabic. The most influential indigenous African languages are Swahili (Kiswahili) in East Africa and Hausa in West Africa—both of them profoundly influenced by both Arabic and Islam, a manifestation of AFRABIA.

Linguistic links between Africa and Arabia are, in fact, much older than Islam. Everybody is aware that Arabic is a Semitic language, but not as many people realize that so is Amharic, the dominant indigenous language of Ethiopia. Indeed, historians are divided as to whether Semitic languages started in Africa before they crossed the Red Sea, or originated in the Arabian peninsula and later crossed over to Africa. The very uncertainties themselves are part of the reality of AFRABIA.

BLACK CONTINENT, RED SEA?

A central thesis of ours in this part of the lecture is that the Red Sea has no right to divide Africa from Arabia.

Where then is Africa? What is Africa? How sensible are its boundaries? Islands can be very far from Africa and still be regarded part of Africa—provided they are not too near another major land mass. But a peninsula can be arbitrarily dis-Africanized.

Madagascar is separated from the African continent by the 500–mile wide Mozambique channel. Greater Yemen, on the other hand, is separated from Djibouti by only a stone throw. Yet Madagascar is politically part of Africa, while Greater Yemen is not.

Much of the post-colonial African scholarship has addressed itself to the artificiality of the boundaries of contemporary African states. But little attention has been paid to the artificiality of the boundaries of the African continent itself. Why should North Africa end on the Read Sea when Eastern Africa does not end on the Mozambique channel? Why should Tananarive be an African capital when Aden is not?

There has been discussion in Africa as to whether the Sahara desert is a chasm or a link. Continental Pan-Africanism asserts that the Sahara is a sea of communication rather than a chasm of separation. Yet there are some who would argue that North Africa is not "really Africa." Why? Because it is more like Arabia?

But in that case, why not push the boundary of North Africa further east to include Arabia? Why not refuse to recognize the Read Sea as a chasm, just as the Pan-Africanist has refused to concede such a role to the Sahara Desert? Why not assert that the African continent ends neither on the southern extremity of the Sahara nor on the western shore of the Red Sea? Should not Africa move northwards to the Mediterranean and North-eastwards to the Persian Gulf? And, should this new concept be called AFRABIA?

The most redundant sea in African history may well be the Red Sea. This thin line of ocean has been deemed to be more relevant for defining where

Africa ends than all the evidence of geology, geography, history and culture. The north-eastern boundary of Africa has been defined by a strip of water in the teeth of massive ecological and cultural evidence to the contrary.[4]

The problem goes back three to five million years ago when three cracks emerged on the east side of Africa. As Colin McEvedy put it:

> One crack broke Arabia away, creating the Gulf of
> Aden and the Red Sea, and reducing the area of contact
> between Africa and Asia to the Isthmus of Suez.[5]

Before the parting of the Red Sea, there was the parting of Africa to create the Red Sea as a divide. Three cracks had occurred on the African crust—yet only the one which has resulted in a sea was permitted to "de-Africanize" what lay beyond the sea. The other two cracks resulted in "rift valleys," straight sided trenches averaging thirty miles across. The eastern and western rifts left the African continent intact—but the emergence of a strip of water called the Red Sea resulted in the geological secession of Arabia.

But what a geological crack had once put asunder, the forces of geography, history and culture have been trying to bind together again ever since. Who are the Amhara of Ethiopia if not a people probably descended from South Arabians? What is Amharic but a Semitic language? What is a Semitic language if not a branch of the Afro-Asian family of languages? Was the Semitic parental language born in Africa and then crossed the Red Sea? Or was it from the Arabian peninsula originally and then descended upon such people as the Amhara, Tigre and Hausa in Africa? How much of a bridge between Arabia and Africa are the Somali? All these are lingo-cultural questions which raise the issue of whether the geological secession of Arabia three to five million years ago has been in the process of being neutralized by AFRA-BIA, the intimate cultural integration between Arabia, the Horn and the rest of Africa.

In the linguistic field it is certainly no longer easy to determine where African indigenous languages end and "Semitic" trends begin. There was a time when both Hamites and Semites were regarded as basically alien to Africa. In due course Hamites were regarded as a fictitious category—and the people represented by the term (like the Tutsi) accepted as indisputably African. What about the Semites? They have undoubtedly existed in world history. But are they "Africans" who crossed the Red Sea—like Moses on the run from the Pharaoh? Or are the Semites originally "Arabians" who penetrated Africa? These agonizing problems of identity would be partially solved overnight if the Arabian peninsula was part and parcel of Africa, or if a new solidarity of Afrabia took roots.

ON CULTURE AND CONTINENT

The cultural effort to re-integrate Arabia with Africa after the geological divide five million years previously reached a new phase with the birth and expansion of Islam. The Arab conquest of North Africa was a process of overcoming the divisiveness of the Red Sea.

Twin processes were set in motion in North Africa—Islamization (a religious conversion to the creed of Muhammad) and Arabization (a linguistic assimilation into the language of the Arabs). In time the great majority of North Africans saw themselves as Arabs—no less than the inhabitants of the Arabian Peninsula. In short, the Islamization and Arabization of North Africa were once again cultural countervailing forces trying to outweigh the geological separatism perpetrated by the birth of the Red Sea millennia earlier. North Africans have been cast in a dilemma. Are they as African as the people to the south of them? The question which has yet to be raised is whether the Arabs east of the Red Sea are as African as the Arabs north of the Sahara.

But if the Red Sea could be ignored in determining the north-eastern limits of Africa, why cannot the Mediterranean also be ignored as an outer northern limit? There was indeed a time when North Africa was in fact regarded as an extension of Europe. This goes back to the days of Carthage, of Hellenistic colonization, and later of the Roman Empire. The concept of "Europe" was at best in the making at that time. In the words of historians R.R. Palmer and Joel Colton:

> There was really no Europe in ancient times. In the
> Roman Empire we may see a Mediterranean world, or even
> a West and an East in the Latin and Greek portions.
> But the West included parts of Africa as well as Europe. . .[6]

Even as late as the seventeenth century the idea that the land mass south of the Mediterranean was something distinct from the landmass north of it was a proposition still difficult to comprehend. The great American Africanist, Melville Herskovits, has pointed out how the Geographer Royal of France, writing in 1656, described Africa as a "a peninsula so large that it comprises the third part, and this the most southerly, of our continent."[7]

The old proposition that North Africa was the southern part of Europe had its last desperate fling in the modern world in France's attempt to keep Algeria as part of France. The desperate myth that Algeria was the southern portion of France tore the French nation apart in the 1950s, created the crisis which brought Charles de Gaulle to power in 1958 and maintained tensions between the Right and the Left in France until Algeria's independence in

1962, with an additional aftermath of bitterness in the trail of Charles de Gaulle's career.

This effort to maintain Algeria as a southern extension of a European power took place at a time when in other respects North Africa had become a western extension of Arabia. From the seventh century onwards Arabization and Islamization had been transforming North Africa's identity. Because Africa's border was deemed to be the Red Sea, the Arabs became a "bicontinental" people—impossible to label as either "African" or "Asian." Indeed, the majority of the Arab people by the twentieth century were located west of the Red Sea (i.e. in Africa "proper") although the majority of the Arab states were east of the Red Sea (deemed as Western Asia).

The Arabic language has, as we indicated, many more speakers in the present African continent than in the Arabian peninsula. And Arabic has indeed become the most important single language in the present African continent in terms of speakers.

The case for regarding Arabia as part of Africa is now much stronger than for regarding North Africa as part of Europe. Islamization and Arabization have redefined the identity of North Africans more fundamentally than either Gallicization or Anglicization have done.

In spite of the proximity of the Rock of Gibraltar to Africa, the Mediterranean is a more convincing line of demarcation between Africa and Europe than the Red Sea can claim to be a divide between Africa and Asia. All boundaries are artificial but some boundaries are more artificial than others. Afrabia has at least two millennia of linguistic and religious history to give it geocultural reality.

CONCLUSION

This chapter has been partly about the great Semitic divergence—how the Isaac wing of the Abrahamic legacy got Europeanized and how the Ishmaeli descendants of Abraham got Africanized.

We live in an age when a people's perception of themselves can be deeply influenced by which continent or region they associate themselves with. Until the 1950s the official policy of the government of Emperor Haile Selassie was to emphasize that Ethiopia was part of the Middle East rather than part of Africa. Yet it was the Emperor himself who initiated the policy of re-Africanizing Ethiopia as the rest of Africa approached independence. Ethiopian self-perceptions have been getting slowly Africanized ever since.

Yet cultural similarities between Ethiopia and the rest of Black Africa are not any greater than cultural similarities between North Africa and the Arabian peninsula. Nevertheless, a European decision to make Africa end at the Red Sea has decisively dis-Africanized the Arabian peninsula, and made the natives there see themselves as west Asians rather than North Africans.[8]

Before the parting of the Red sea, there was the parting of Africa to create the Red Sea. Several million years ago the crust of Africa cracked and the Red Sea was born. As we indicated, this thin strip of water helped to seal the identity of whole generations of people living on both sides of it.

Yet cultural change has been struggling to heal the geological rift between Africa and Arabia. Did the Semites originate to the east or the west of the Red Sea? Are upper Ethiopians originally South Arabians? Has Islam rendered the Red Sea a culturally irrelevant boundary? Has the Arabic language made the boundary anachronistic? Is it time that the tyranny of the sea as a definer of identity was at least moderated if not overthrown? We have sought to demonstrate that Africa and the Arab world have in any case been slowly merging into one vast region.

In any case, the tyranny of the sea is in part a tyranny of European geographical prejudices. Just as European map-makers could decree that on the map Europe was above Africa instead of below (an arbitrary decision in relation to the cosmos) those map-makers could also dictate that Africa ended at the Red Sea instead of the "Persian Gulf." Is it not time that this dual tyranny of the sea and Eurocentric geography was forced to sink to the bottom?

The most difficult people to convince may well turn out to be the inhabitants of the Arabian peninsula. They have grown to be proud of being 'the Arabs of Asia" rather than "the Arabs of Africa." They are not eager to be members of the new African Union even if it were led by Libya. Will they at least embrace the concept of AFRABIA?

And yet if Emperor Haile Selassie could initiate the re-Africanization of Ethiopia, and Gamal Abdel Nasser could inaugurate the re-Africanization of Egypt, prospects for a reconsideration of the identity of the Arabian peninsula may not be entirely bleak. In the New Global Order it is not only Europe which is experiencing the collapse of artificial walls of disunity. It is not just the United States, Mexico, and Canada which will create a mega-community. It is not just South East Asia which will learn to readmit Indo-China to the fold. Also momentous in its historical possibilities is the likely emergence of AFRABIA—linking languages, religions and identities across both the Sahara Desert and the Red Sea in a historical fusion of Arabism and Africanity in the New World Order.

But will AFRABIA be a case of rich Arabs in a union with poor Africans? Actually, there are rich countries in Africa, poor countries in the Arab world—

and vice versa. Africa's mineral resources are more varied than those of the Arab world—but African countries like Congo (Kinshasa) have been more economically mismanaged than almost any country in the Arab world.

AFRABIA of the future will include post-apartheid South Africa—richer and more industrialized than almost any other society in either Africa or the Arab world. The AFRABIA of the future may economically be led by the oil-rich and the mineral-rich economies—but in a new order where equity and fairness will count as much between societies as they have sometimes done within enlightened individual countries. Relentlessly Africa and the Arab world continue their historic march towards merger, their historic destiny of integration.

NOTES

1. Genesis, 22.4, Verse 15.
2. According to Joseph A. D'Agostino (2001), among the 25 nations (they include Afghanistan, Algeria, Bahrain, Djibouti, Egypt, Eritrea, Indonesia, Iran, Iraq, Jordan, Kuwait, Lebanon, Libya, Malaysia, Morocco, Oman, Pakistan, Qatar, Saudi Arabia, Somalia, Sudan, Syria, Tunisia, the United Arab Emirates, and Yemen) classified by the U.S. State Department as where Al Qaeda operates, are nine African countries (Algeria, Djibouti, Egypt, Eritrea, Libya, Morocco, Somalia, Sudan and Tunisia. Joseph A. D'Agostino, "7,000 Men Recently Entered from Al Qaeda 'Watch' Countries," *Human Events Online*, Week of December 17, 2001).
3. According to the United Nations Economic Commission for Africa, financial aid from Arab countries to Africa increased from $0.1 billion in 1970 to $0.3 billion in 1999. ("Economic Report on Africa 2002: Tracking Performance and progress," Overview Section. United Nations Economic Commission for Africa. http://www.uneca .org/era2002/index.htm)
4. The issue of whether the Red Sea is a legitimate boundary of Africa is also discussed in Mazrui, *The Africans: A Triple Heritage* (London: BBC Publications and Boston: Little, Brown Press, 1986) Chapter 1.
5. C. McEvedy, *The Penguin Atlas of African History* (Harmondsworth, Middlesex: Penguin Books, 1980).
6. See R.R. Palmer in collaboration with Joe Colton, *A History of the Modern World* (New York: Knopf, 1962), 2nd edition, p. 13.
7. See Melville Herskovits' contribution to Wellesley College, *Symposium on Africa* (Wellesley College, Massachusetts, 1960), p. 16.
8. This question also features in Ali A. Mazrui's television series, *The Africans: A Triple Heritage* (London: British Broadcasting Corporation and Washington, D.C.: WETA, Public Broadcasting System, 1986), Programme No. 1, "The Nature of a Continent."

Chapter Eight

The Black Arabs in Comparative Perspective

In discussing the spread of Islam in the Nuba Mountains of the Republic of the Sudan, Mr. R. C. Stevenson referred to two parallel processes of social change—"one linguistic and cultural, by which the people of the land acquired Arabic as their language and certain Islamic cultural conceptions and became connected with the Arab tribal system; and the other racial, by which the incoming Arab stock was absorbed in varying degrees, so that today a modicum of Arab blood flows in their veins."[1]

It is this combination of acculturation and inter-mating between races which might be called a process of bio-cultural assimilation. Some degree of integration between groups is achieved by the process of mixing blood and fusing cultural patterns.

SYMMETRY IN BIO-CULTURAL ASSIMILATION

There are two concepts here which need to be further refined. One is the concept of symmetrical acculturation and the other is the concept of symmetrical miscegenation. Symmetrical acculturation arises when a dominant group not only passes on its culture to the groups it dominates but is also significantly receptive to the cultural influence of its subjects or captives. Symmetrical acculturation is arrived at when cultural transmission is a two-way affair. Complete symmetry is impossible to achieve, and even if achieved, would be impossible to measure. What needs to be approximated is a significant reciprocal influence.

There have been occasions in history when acculturation has been asymmetrical, and yet the receiving group has been the politically dominant. The classic example is that of Greek influence on the Roman conquerors. After the decline of Greece and the rise of Rome, Greek subjects succeeded in partially Hellenizing the Roman conquerors.[2]

A more common example is the kind of asymmetry in which the politically dominant culture transmits itself to its subjects and captives but receives little in return. The British cultural influence in much of Africa has been of the second category. We might call this descending asymmetry, and call the Greek-Roman example a model of ascending asymmetry.

As for symmetrical miscegenation, this would arise in a situation where two racial communities inter-marry and produce a comparable number of both men and women who crossed the racial boundary to seek partners from another community. In very isolated circumstances, and even there with some qualifications, such symmetry is conceivable. It may be conceivable in a situation where one race or ethnic group is patrilineal and the other is matrilineal. The matrilineal group might not mind its women crossing the border and marrying men from the other country. The patrilineal group, in like manner, might permit the men to be exogamous. But in such situations claims as to whether the mother or the father has first priority to the children, and how descent is to be determined, might become an issue as soon as the married couple appear to be on the verge of separating. For as long as they are together, it is conceivable for a child to enjoy dual racial citizenship. Supposing the father is a patrilineal Arab and the mother is a matrilineal Jew. To the matrilineal race the child is regarded as sharing the race of its mother (a Jew); while the patrilineal wing recognizes the child's racial affinity to its father (an Arab). Tensions in such situations are conceivable, precisely in the duality of citizenship and the pulls of potentially conflicting loyalties. Symmetrical miscegenation in such an instance could indeed be approximated.

A much more prevalent phenomenon is that of asymmetrical miscegenation. Certainly, in the great majority of cases where black people have intermarried with non-black people, a lack of symmetry has been a continuing characteristic.

In this chapter, we shall pay special attention to racial mixture as between the Arabs and black Africans. We intend to do this in a broad comparative perspective, relating the Afro-Arab experience to the different histories of racial mixture in the United States, in Latin America and in South Africa. These three, when combined with the Afro-Arab model, provide four distinct patterns of the relationship between miscegenation and social structure.[3]

All four models of miscegenation are asymmetrical but in significantly different ways. In each case the dominant ethnic group has produced many more husbands in the racial mixture than wives. Over sixty percent of the so-called black population of the United States has white blood. But overwhelmingly the white blood has come through white males rather than white females. Until recently, mating between whites and blacks in North America usually meant white men and black women.

The Latin American model is less straightforward, but it is still basically asymmetrical. It is the fairer-skinned males that have easy access to darker-skinned females, rather than the other way round. A factor which has in some respects accentuated the asymmetry in Brazil is the sexual prestige of the mulatto girl among white Portuguese.

> Gilberto Freyre has written that prolonged contact with the Saracens led to the idealization among the Portuguese of the type of the 'enchanting Mooress', a seductive ideal with dark eyes, enveloped in sexual mysticism . . . Freyre suggests that dark-skinned women were preferred by the Portuguese for love, or at least for physical love.[4]

Within the African continent the asymmetry in miscegenation originated partly in the phenomenon of slavery itself. Both in South Africa and in Arabized black Africa, slavery was the breeding ground of asymmetrical miscegenation. The Boers in the Cape, and the Arabs in Zanzibar and the Sudan, helped themselves to female African slaves or concubines and produced children. The transmission of Afrikaner blood in South Africa and of Arab blood in Zanzibar and the Sudan was definitely through the dominant Afrikaner or Arab male.

But in spite of the fact that all the four models of race relations that we are going to discuss are based on asymmetrical miscegenation, the fate of the children varies in fundamental ways among those four models. Do the children of a mixed marriage between a dominant race and an under-privileged race follow the father into the amenities of dominance or do they follow the mother into the handicaps of under-privilege? Or do they in fact become a category apart?

It is the contention of this chapter that the answers to these questions are different in each case when we are looking at the North American, the Latin American, the South African, or the Afro-Arab models. The precise fate of children in mixed unions has a great deal of relevance for the whole issue of a biological approach to national integration. Does racial or ethnic mixture reduce cleavages between groups and in what way? The answers differ in the four models, and their pertinence to the integrative process has to be correspondingly differentiated.

Before we look at the four models, let us examine more closely the Arab presence in Africa, as a whole. Let us examine more specifically those Arabs who have intermingled directly with black Africans.

I have already argued elsewhere that Egypt is at once the least African of the Arab countries within the African continent, and the most pan-African among them. Egypt is the least African because of its longer exposure to

Western influences. Egypt is in many ways the most Westernized of all African countries apart from South Africa, and her capital city, Cairo, is among the most cosmopolitan.

Yet, in spite of being the least African of the Arab countries in the continent, Egypt can still be described as the most pan-African. The initiative for this status was derived from Nasser's foresight and leadership. Nasser's pan-Africanism consisted in granting scholarships to African students, allowing Cairo to become the first major centre of refuge for nationalists from colonial Africa, converting Cairo Radio into an instrument of anti-colonialism in Africa as well as the Arab world, involving himself in the conference diplomacy of African states, establishing cultural links with Muslims elsewhere in the continent, undertaking, the responsibility of looking after illustrious destitutes, like the children of Lumumba on Lumumba's death, and participating in the struggle to make Africa an effective component of the movement of the non-aligned.

In general, among all Arab states within the African continent, it is quite clear that Egypt has been more involved in many more African enterprises than any other Arab state. To that extent it has proved its credentials for pan-African involvement. It has even gone as far as to participate in the Nigerian civil war, on the side of those who wanted to maintain Nigerian unity.

In many ways, Egypt is less African than Algeria, or Morocco or even Tunisia. Egypt's pull towards the rest of the Arab world, and its status as the largest country in the Arab world, came to enforce upon its an outward-looking perspective, which reduces its roots within the African continent. It is pan-African by ideology and sympathy rather than by historical roots.

What all this confirms is that there are *degrees* of African-ness. In any case, the Arabs in the north might be natives of Africa even if they are not fully "Africans." Yet by what criterion are they to be regarded as natives of the continent? One answer I have heard given in Ghana is the following: The Arabs by now must be recognized as natives *of Africa* because they have been in Africa since the seventh century.[5] But sometimes even more important than duration of stay is rapidity and depth of assimilation and extent of intermingling with the local population. It is sometimes too readily assumed that the population of Egypt today consists mainly of descendants of Arab conquerors who arrived there thirteen hundred years ago. Of course, such an assumption about the actual racial composition of Egypt is, to say the least, naive. It is perhaps still true to say that the most dominant "racial" strain in the population of Egypt today is descended from the indigenous Egyptian inhabitants—the societies that produced the Pharaohs and perhaps Cleopatra. As we know, there have been other races immigrating into Egypt in the last thirteen hundred years. This is typical of the Mediterranean as a whole and its capacity for migrations. But the important fact to grasp is that the bulk of the population of Egypt is Arab by cultural assimilation and not by blood descent from Arab conquerors. The numbers of the conquerors at that time were a small fraction of the population of Egypt. It is true that the population of Egypt itself then was modest, but the few Arabs from the deserts of the Arabian peninsula who exercised authority over this former province of the Byzantine empire were little more than a fraction of the *subjects* over whom they exercised that power.

The Muslim conquests of the sixth century had taken on two mighty empires simultaneously. The Byzantine empire of which Egypt was a province, and the Persian empire. Egypt and Persia were conquered at roughly the same time in the first wave of Muslim expansionism from the peninsula. The Persians were converted to Islam, but the Persian language survived as a separate language. The strength of Persian civilization withstood the Arab impact, absorbing religious aspects and interacting with others, but still retaining a distinctive personality as Iranian rather than Arab.

The Arab conquest of Egypt, on the other hand, succeeded not only in Islamizing the people they found there, but also in gradually Arabizing them. In Egypt there was cultural asymmetry, as the conquering civilization exerted its dominance over the population, and finally made Egyptians feel that they were indeed Arabs.

In Persia, on the other hand, the interaction between Iranian civilization and the new Arabism and Islam was more symmetrical. Persia has made an impressive contribution to Islamic civilization. The range is from architecture to the *Arabian Nights,* from Persian carpets to poetry. At the same time Persia became deeply Islamized, and because of that, partially Arabized. In the Persian case the two mighty civilizations, ancient Iranian and Islamic, interacted substantially on a level of balance and reciprocity.

In Egypt, on the other hand, the new wave of Islam and its original language, Arabic, found an old civilization in decay—tired and petty in its sectarian squabbles. Over a period of time the Egyptians became Arabs.

Is what is going on in the Sudan today a repetition of what went on in Egypt earlier, a gradual conversion of a country to Arabism through bio-cultural assimilation? The answer once again has to be sought in a wider comparative framework.

MISCEGENATION: DESCENDING, AMBIVALENT AND DIVERGENT AND ASCENDING

We must again remind ourselves that acculturation and intermarriage do not necessarily result in social intermingling between the races or even in a system of desegregation. It very much depends upon the precise systems of descent observed by the race in question, and by the general racial attitudes of the dominant race in a particular society.

One might say that there are four active models of relationship between blood mixture and social structure at large. One is the North American model. Within this model, whenever there is mating between a white person and a black person, the offspring is invariably "black." We may call this the model of *descending miscegenation.* Over two-thirds of African Americans have Caucasian blood flowing in their veins, and yet they are categorized as blacks. Until recently, there were states in the United States which presumed to characterize a person's race according to calculation of how much "Negro blood" the person had. Certainly the law of white-dominated Florida used to define a "Negro" as recently as the 1960s as a person with "one-eighth or more of African or Negro blood." And the laws of Florida, like the laws of eighteen other states in the American union in the 1960s, specifically prohibited "miscegenation."[6]

The second model of racial mixture in relation to social structure is that of Latin America. In Brazil especially, the offspring of mating between a black person and a white person produces a mulatto or mestizo, but the mestizo could either enjoy the same rights as the white person or the same handicaps as the black person depending partly on social class or on the actual colour he or she inherits from the parents. We may call this the model of *ambivalent miscegenation.* In other words, much of the prejudice in Latin America is colour prejudice rather than race prejudice. Of course, very often the two coincide, but they need not. And even where they coincide a different emphasis can often be discerned. Class stratification in Brazil does correlate substantially with the shades of skin colour—the fairer your child is the better are its chances of social success in the future.

This does contrast with model number one of North America where the emphasis is on purity of blood, regardless of how fair the child is. Indeed, a person might have a skin which is indisputably white, but if the legal calculators of blood in the old Florida were to discover that one-eighth of this white man's blood was "African or Negro blood" the white-skinned person would become re-classified as a black man.[7]

During the colonial phase of Brazil's history, Francisco Manuel de Melo once noted that "Brazil is the Inferno of Negroes, the Purgatory of White Men, and the Paradise of Mulattoes of both sexes."[8]

It is unlikely that de Melo was ever right in this formulation. Brazil might indeed have been, and to some extent still remains, an inferno for Negroes. But it is clearly the white men that are in paradise, and the mulattoes that are in purgatory. The mulatto, a person of mixed parentage, could either end up in the hell of the black people or in the paradise of the white people, depending upon the precise shade of his or her colour.

Census figures in Brazil have tended to adopt the three categories of whites, Negroes and "mestizos," the mixed group that allows also for the inclusion of Indian blood. But Brazilian census figures in these terms have always been bedeviled precisely by this phenomenon of racial mobility—the capacity of a person to move upwards in race classification if his or her physical features and skin-colour permit it.

> Many light mulattoes, refined, educated, and of good appearance, must appear to be white. Mestizos appearing to be white are included as whites, contrary to the practice in the United States, where one eighth of Negro blood classifies one as Negro.[9]

This important distinction has struck other writers too. Donald Pierson has noted that while the American criterion was based on racial descent, the Brazilian was based on physical appearance. Pierson draws attention to the phenomenon of many "Negro" grandparents having grand-children who are "white."

It is this consideration which leads to the conclusion that while in the United States the progeny of mixed marriages is classified as belonging to the less privileged group, the progeny of mixed marriages in Brazil could be classified either with the privileged or with the under-privileged depending upon physical features, social class and shade of skin-colour.

> In the white group, then, one finds not only true whites but also white phenotypes, that is, Afro-white and Indian-white mestizoes reverting to white type. In the Negro group there are Negroes and Negro-phenotypes and cafuzos [Indian-Negro] reverting to Negro type. Finally, the mestizo classification shows the greatest lack of precision, for mulattoes, mixtures of Negro and white, are not distinguished from caboclos, mixtures of Indian and white.[10]

And then we come more specifically to the African continent in our quest for categories of relationship between racial mixture and social structure.

In South Africa we see a third category. Under the legacy of South Africa, the progeny of mixed marriages between whites and blacks are neither automatically black, as they are in the United States, nor are they necessarily entitled to upward mobility if physical features permit, as they are in Brazil. Even after apartheid, the South African model decrees that the progeny of a mixed marriage between white and black belongs to a group apart. The group is that of the Coloureds. We might call this the model of *divergent miscegenation.*

Over three-quarters of the Coloured population of South Africa live in the Cape. The concentration of this mixed population coincides roughly with the settled districts of the Western Cape during the slave period. The Coloureds have been defined as "the product of a dual process of Westernization and miscegenation between Whites, Hottentots and slaves."

The total subordination of the woman slave to the whims of her master, and the interest of the master in producing highly prized mulatto slaves, promoted a good deal of racial intermingling. In culture the bulk of the coloured population is a sub-group of the Afrikaner culture. Indeed, the great majority are native Afrikaans speakers.

Under the conditions of the United States the Coloureds would have belonged more firmly to the "Black" population. Any mixture of blood follows the line of less privilege. Under Latin-American conditions the Coloured population of South Africa would have been divided between the blacks and the whites, according to physical features inherited from the parental groups. Some coloureds would definitely have been accepted fully as part of the Afrikaner population, while others would have had to find solidarity with the black population. But since South Africa is neither the United States nor Latin America, the Coloureds have remained a group apart, distinct both from the pinnacle of racial privilege and from the base at the bottom of the pyramid.[11]

The fourth model of assimilation would bring us at last to the phenomenon of places like the Sudan and Zanzibar. The population of the Sudan as estimated on January 17th, 1956, was 10,262,536. At the time of the census 39% of the total population was deemed to be *"racially"* Arab. The "racial" definition of Arab was in terms of membership—or claimed membership, of an Arab tribe. This constituted biological intermingling between the "races," real or claimed.

But in a country like the Sudan there is also the linguistic definition of Arab to be taken into account. By this linguistic definition a person is an Arab if his or her mother tongue is Arabic. Muddathir 'Abd Al-Rahim has estimated that 51% of the Sudanese speak Arabic as their first language and must, according to the census figures, be deemed to be Arabs. The linguistic definition hinges not on biological integration but on cultural or linguistic assimilation.

But, although 'Abd Al-Rahim emphasizes the linguistic definition of an Arab, he does draw attention to the remarkable racial intermingling in many parts of the Sudan. The two southern provinces of Bahr al-Ghazal and the Upper Nile are almost exclusively populated by Nilotics. There are also relatively unmixed communities, in the biological sense, in parts of Northern Sudan. But the central parts of the country illustrate considerable genetic mixture.

Although Arab tribes predominate in the provinces of Khartoum, Blue Nile, Kordofan, and Northern Province, the Beia in Kasala, Westerners in Darfur, and the Nilo-Hamites in Equatoria, it is obvious that considerable racial mixing has taken place, particularly in the central parts of the country. A clear indication of this is the wide range of colours and features among the Sudanese Arabs (over half of the total population) who are, on the whole, much darker than other Arabic-speaking peoples north of the Sahara and across the sea in Arabia.[12]

If in the Sudan the utilization of the linguistic definition of Arab increases the number of Arabs from 39% of the population to 51 of the population, in Zanzibar after the revolution of 1964 a linguistic definition of Arab would have nearly *halved* the Arab population. In other words, while the Sudan has more native Arab speakers than it has people with Arab blood, pre-revolutionary Zanzibar had more people with Arab blood than it had native Arabic speakers. Many Arabs in pre-revolutionary Zanzibar were native speakers of Kiswahili, a Bantu language.

What all these differences indicate is that the distinction between Arabs and Black Africans is not dichotomous but has the complexity of a continuum. That was one reason why the Organization of African Unity was born in 1963 as a multi-pigmentational enterprise. The Arabs as a people defy straight pigmentational classification. They vary in colour from the white Arabs of Syria and Lebanon, the brown Arabs of the Hadhramout to the black Arabs of much of the Sudan and of some of the Eastern parts of the Arabian peninsular. Within Africa itself the range of colour among the Arabs is indeed from white to black also, though each colour cannot as smoothly be allocated to a specific geographical area. Even within Egypt on its own the range of colour is virtually as wide as it is in the Arab world as a whole.

This is what brings us to the relevance of this model of Afro-Arab intermingling, as contrasted with the model of Afro-Saxon intermingling in the United States, and with the Afro-Latin intermingling in Brazil and the Afro-Afrikaner intermingling in South Africa. With the Arabs the idea of "half-caste" is relatively alien. If the father is Arab, the child is Arab without reservations. If we visualize an Arab marrying a Black Nilotic woman in the fourteenth century and visualize the son being born, the son would be Arab. If we imagined in turn that the son again married a Nilotic woman who bore a son—this son, too, would be an Arab. If we then assumed that the process is repeated, generation after generation, until a son is born in the last years of the twentieth century with only a drop of his blood still ostensibly of Arab derivation and the rest of his blood indubitably Nilotic, the twentieth century child is still an Arab.[13]

It is this phenomenon which has saved the Arab-Black division in Africa from being a dichotomous gulf—and converted it instead into a racial continuum of merging relationships.

In Pan-African literature it has been more the African Americans than either the Arabs or the Black Africans that have grasped this fact of the racial continuum. Edward Blyden, the nineteenth century Liberian intellectual of West Indian birth, put it in the following terms:

> With every wish, no doubt, to the contrary, the European seldom or never gets over the feeling of distance, if not of repulsion, which he experiences on first seeing the Negro. . . . The Arab missionary, on the other hand, often of the same complexion as his hearer, does not, require any long habit to reconcile the eye to him.' He takes up his abode in Negroland, often for life, and, mingling his blood with that of the inhabitants, succeeds in the most natural manner, in engrafting Mohammedan religion and learning upon the ignorance and simplicity of the people.[14]

Blyden here captures the paternalism which characterized missionary work both by Arabs and by Europeans. But the essential contrast here is between the repulsion reluctantly felt by well-meaning Europeans, on the one hand, and the Arab capacity for "mingling his blood with that of the inhabitants," on the other.

What Blyden has also captured is the difference between the social distance purposefully created by European missionaries in the areas in which they worked, and the more integrative approach to proselytism adopted by Muslim missionaries. The Christian missionary even today may indeed walk among the people to comfort the sick, educate the ignorant, convert the heathen, and reform the sinner. But he does not mix his blood with them. If he is a Protestant, and has already been ordained, he has probably taken the precaution of getting himself a wife from home prior to coming to Africa in any case. According to the dominant interpretations of the religion, Christianity favours either the self-discipline of no wife at all (celibacy) or the "faithfulness" of one wife only (the more prevalent principle of monogamy). The Catholic missionary priest, a celibate, is a biological specimen apart in the village in which he is proselytizing. The ordained Western Protestant missionary has a wife, carefully obtained from home both as an assistant in the great enterprise of spreading the gospel and serving the unfortunate in distant lands, and as a safeguard against the temptations of Satan in the loneliness of life among the heathens.

By contrast, Muslim missionaries did not have to be monogamous, and were hardly ever celibate. Nor did they regard it as necessary to arm themselves with a wife from their own community before venturing into the "darkness of Africa." In the words of Blyden:

> The Muslim missionary often brought to the aid of his preaching the influence of social and domestic relationships—an influence which in all efforts to convert a people is not to be entirely ignored.[15]

What Blyden here is suggesting is the efficacy of biological integration as a method of cultural assimilation. He even quotes Dean Stanley's assertion

> The conversion of the Russian nation was effected, not by the preaching of the Byzantine clergy, but by the marriage of a Byzantine princess.[16]

It is arguable that the three most important ways of spreading a culture to other lands are, firstly, by purposeful cultural transmission and proselytization, secondly, by the flow of trade and its incidental consequences in the field of culture contact, and thirdly, by actual migration of people from one land to settle in another. It is arguable that imperialism is a means towards a means. Conquest and imperialism help to determine the magnitude of trade, cultural transmission, or migration.

TRADERS, FARMERS AND MARRIAGE

Special emphasis needs to be placed on the phenomenon of trade and the incidence of culture contact caused by trade. In the impact of Europe on Africa, the missionary and the trader were distinct specimens, though often in alliance. But in the case of the impact of Islam and Arab civilization on Africa, the missionary and the trader were often the same person.

Islam very often spread casually as a result of contact between individuals, and as a result of ordinary social intermingling between a Muslim and a non-Muslim. The Arab shopkeeper in a small town in Tanzania or the Sudan could converse about Islam to his "animistic"customers, and sometimes influence them towards conversion. The Arab shopkeeper may marry among the same alien people he serves commercially, and through the influence of kinship and marriage he may at the same time unofficially proselytize for Islam. Or the Arab trader may be a nomadic business man, moving from town to town selling his wares. Again migratory trade has often served the function of being a mobile mission in Islam at the same time.

But in the European penetration of Africa the missionary has tended to precede the trader, and both in turn have helped to prepare the way for the Flag.

William C. McLeod once discussed the trader and inter-marriage in a context related to the subject of this paper. McLeod put forward the hypothesis that a trading man was more ready than a settler to get married to groups other than his own. He referred to those analysts who insisted that there was a difference between the Nordic and Latin races in their attitudes to non-white peoples. The standard assertion has been that the Nordic Germanic peoples, by their very cultural background, tend to be racially endogamous and rather averse to "miscegenation." The Latin peoples, partly because of their cultural universalism, are less exclusive in their social and matrimonial habits. Certainly the difference between the North American model we discussed of descending miscegenation, and our Latin American model of ambivalent miscegenation, has sometimes been explained in terms of the differences in culture between universalistic Latins and more socially exclusive Germanic peoples.

But McLeod argues that the comparison has been based on a fallacy:

> In contrasting the French and the English, [popular writers] make the cardinal error of comparing French traders not with British traders but with British agriculturists; and the needs of a French colonial regime which never developed to the point where the trading interests lost control of the needs of dominantly agricultural settlements. French and British traders alike married Indian women and gave rise to numbers of half-breeds; and both groups were able to adapt themselves to Indian ways of life and the Indian manner of thinking.[17]

As for the Spaniards and the Portuguese, McLeod asserts that they are indeed capable of intense racial prejudice. But their attachment to religion has tended to make the religious differences a greater barrier to adequate social intercourse than racial differences.

> The Moor and the Jew in Spain and Portugal were hated only so long as they refused to become Christians; Christianized they were. racially absorbed by both the aristocratic and the commoner strata of the population.[18]

And yet in conceding the "relevance of Iberian Christianity to their racial attitudes," McLeod was beginning to concede the relevance of Latin culture at large for differential behaviour as between the Latin and the Germanic peoples.

But what McLeod's analysis wishes to emphasize is the relevance of those aspects of culture which are to do with cooking, keeping house, and general domestic arrangements. McLeod's theoretical thrust in this hypothesis is that these very mundane aspects of culture, often determined by whether the man has settled in one place for good or regards himself as a transient nomad, have been far more important in determining racial orientations in matrimonial matters than the wider concepts of culture concerned with God and values.

> Farmers needed wives who knew the ways of European housekeeping and husbandry, who knew how to milk cows, fry eggs, and so on. Indian women would not do. The farmer, even in Virginia, so late as 1632, often preferred to pay the expense of importing women of questionable repute from the European cities, at considerable cost, than to take Indian women who would be helpless on a farmer's homestead. Champlain offered one hundred and fifty franks as a dowry to each French Canadian farmer who would marry an Indian girl, but his offer was in vain.[19]

Herbert Moller, writing more than a decade later, re-affirmed McLeod's thesis. Moller took the position that the greater extent of inter-racial mingling in Spanish and Portuguese America could not be attributed to an inherently different attitude on the part of the Latin peoples in their relations with "the natives." The history of race relations in New France would, according to Moller, be an effective witness against such a position. During the second half of the seventeenth century, when the early French colonists had an exceedingly high sex ratio, there was no prejudice against alliances with Indian women. Only four marriages between French men and Indians were recorded at the time, but "left-handed marriages are known to have been frequent." But by the turn of the century, the sex ratio in the eastern parts of Canada was beginning to be fairly balanced, partly because the number of males was not radically increased by new immigration. With the balance came a decline in mixed marriages in Canada.

On the other hand, the western parts of Canada still remained strongly masculine, and so did Louisiana. "There concubinage with young Indian squaws was the rule through the eighteenth century."

Similarly, argues Moller, British colonists had relatively easy ideas about miscegenation for as long as there was a great shortage of white women, and moral attitudes had not been deeply influenced by white women.

There is an underlying suggestion sometimes in Moller's analysis that the predicament of the new colonists, still unsure of the future and even of survival in very strange new circumstances, is sociologically comparable to the position of the trader settling in a village and being guided by the likely impermanence of his abode.

But once the agricultural pattern of life began to gain roots and the people were at last settlers, the aversion to mixed marriages began to rise perceptibly among North American colonists. Moller asserts that the kind of racial prejudices which grew up in North America were not imported from Europe. Such antipathies were, according to the writer, virtually non-existent in the Europe of the seventeenth and eighteenth centuries. Racial aversions of the form which was found in subsequent decades of North American history, were, so to speak, native to the American experience.

> The most plausible explanation, so far, for the increasing avoidance of inter-racial marriage in the British colonies has been the need of agriculturalists and tradesmen for wives 'who knew the ways of European housekeeping and husbandry', whereas traders, both French and British could afford to marry Indian women.[20]

Moller's own important contribution to the debate was his thesis regarding the influence of the white woman on racial attitudes. There has been a lot of literature so far emphasizing sexual insecurity in the white male as a major reason for his aggressive response to any suggestion of interaction between a black man and a white woman. Moller, on the other hand, argues that it was to some extent the sexual insecurity of the white woman combined with fears of unknown worlds of inter-racial sexuality which sharpened the phenomenon of racial repugnance among certain sections of white colonists in North America.

Herbert Moller had added female hypogamy as another causal factor behind white repugnance and emotions of disgust over the phenomenon of inter-racial relations. The argument here is that women as a rule refrain from matrimonial and social relations with men of a lower social class or stratum than their own. The majority of women persist in this attitude even if the price is life as an old maid and complete celibacy. In the history of Europe, whenever there was a surplus of women in the upper or middle classes, fathers had to confront the issue of how best to provide for their unmarried daughters.

Significant here is the tendency of women to identify themselves completely with the class and status of their husbands or lovers, while men do not share this urge to any comparable degree. Hypogamy as marriage beneath one's station is considered with greater aversion by women than by men.

> Whereas in Europe this feminine attitude prevented women from marrying beneath their social status, it worked in America against their marrying into culturally or socially inferior races. Moreover, through their enhanced influence on family and community life, women became more or less unintentionally the foremost agents in the establishment of racial barriers. Thus the development of aversion to racial miscegenation in the thirteen colonies can be traced to the invasion of feminine sentiments into colonial society.[21]

Valuable as McLeod's and Moller's contributions to theories of race relations might be, they both overemphasize white attitudes to the relations between men and women and did not pay enough attention to white attitudes to the offspring of mixed mating. It is true that disapproval of mixed marriage is a profound conditioning factor on subsequent attitudes to the children produced by mixed marriages. But that very attitude to the children is itself a changing phenomenon and has to some extent to be treated as an important additional variable in its own right.

It may be true that traders are more tolerant of mixed marriages than settled agriculturalists. It may also be true that much of the initial success of mixed marriages between Arabs and black Africans was partly attributable to the fact that the Arabs were structurally nomadic in the sense of being engaged in trade in eastern Africa and the Sudan. Yet this is not the whole story. Many Arabs settled in Zanzibar permanently, and still intermingled biologically with the black societies among whom they had established residence.

Similarly, in the Sudan, migrations of Arab tribesmen often resulted in Arab settlements, and involvement in trades and agriculture, rather than commerce as such. There was a significant process of migration with whole populations settling in new areas. Fadl Hasan has even suggested that until the end of the fifteenth century the processes of Arabization and Islamization were "almost entirely accomplished by tribal migration." Inhabitants of the Sudan became Arabized and assimilated into the Arab tribal system.

> . . . the dominance of Arabic culture suggests, among other factors, that the Arab invaders arrived in large numbers and came to exercise a considerable influence over the life of the local population. Indeed, when Bruce traveled the country of the Ja'aliyyin towards the end of the eighteenth century, he saw no distinction between the indigenous population, who were already Arabized, and the Arabs (probably meaning nomads), except that the former continued to live in mud houses beside the river bank, while the latter lived in tents.[22]

Not all those who claimed Arab descent, or who included themselves more specifically in a particular tribal genealogy, did in fact have Arab blood flowing in their veins. The fluidity of genealogies and tribal affiliations exaggerated the degree of biological Arabization. What is clear is that the distinction which McLeod and Moller made between attitudes to miscegenation among agriculturalist settlers and such attitudes among traders was much less vindicated in the field of Afro-Arab relations than it might have been between blacks and whites in North America.

An important differentiating characteristic is the much stronger patrilineal principle in Islam and Arab culture as contrasted with the culture of the Germanic peoples. The idea that the father determined the tribal affiliation of the descendants was the critical difference between the Afro-Arab model of ascending miscegenation and that first model we discussed of the North American tendency to regard the offspring of mixed marriages as belonging to the race of the under-privileged—i.e. descending miscegenation.

BLACK SLAVES AND WHITE MASTERS

Critical in the comparative histories of the two models is the attitude to the offspring of slave girls mated by their masters. In the case of the American experience, the law in the slave states asserted that if one of the parents was a slave, the offspring would follow the status of the enslaved mother rather than the free father. The American historian Herbert Aptheker adds a footnote in the following vein:

Generally, of course, where the parents were slaves and free, the mother was a slave and the father was a white man, often a slave owner, who, thus in accordance with the law had both pleasure and profit.[23]

In his book, *Black Reconstruction in America, W. E. B.* DuBois refers, in parenthesis, to the consequences of that law in more vivid terms:

> The law declares that the children of slaves are to follow the fortunes of their mother. Hence the practice of planters selling and bequeathing their own children.[24]

Perhaps because they knew of this rigid prejudice against miscegenation in the Germanic section of the New World under our first model, black Americans who went to Africa were impressed by the Afro-Arab racial continuum. In the United States the divide was dichotomous—it was between white men and Blacks. And a person could not pass as "white" if he was mixed enough to be "brown." In Africa, however, the division was between Arabs and black Africans—and yet there were many Arabs who were as black as black Africans. And so W. E. B. DuBois could make the following observation:

> Anyone who has traveled in the Sudan knows that most of the 'Arabs' he has met are dark-skinned, sometimes practically black, often have Negroid features, and hair that may be almost Negro in quality. It is then obvious that in Africa the term 'Arab' . . . is often misleading. The Arabs were too nearly akin to Negroes to draw an absolute colour line.[25]

Slavery was a factor behind the mixed populations in the Sudan, Zanzibar, South Africa, Latin America as well as the United States. But again there was a fundamental difference between the mating of black slaves by white masters, and the mating of black slaves by Arab masters.

Within our first model of descending miscegenation based on experience in North America, we have already discussed the phenomenon of white masters making love to their slave girls, partly with a view to improving the quality of the offspring so that their own lighter skinned children may later be sold at a higher price. After all, lighter coloured slaves often fetched a better price than very black ones.

Experience in Latin America, with special reference to Brazil, was somewhat less straightforward. It varied to some extent historically, depending partly upon the decrees of the Government of the day. There were times and families which accepted the offspring derived from the mating of slave girls by white masters into the very body of the family, to be brought up as members thereof. But there was always an important section of opinion, sometimes triumphant in the legal process, which regarded the practice of accepting mixed children as members of white families as something which eroded the essential basis of the caste society. In the words of Florestan Fernandes:

> The incorporation of the element of colour in the legal nucleus of a great family would bring with it a form of recognition of social equality between the *white man* and the *Negro* or *mulatto.* In order to avoid this, petitions were drawn up opposing inter-marriage and subordinating marital relations to endogamic standards. . . . The prohibitions did not affect sexual relations but only marital relations. Not only were the slave sex partners not elevated to the social position of the masters, but children born of these unions remained in the same condition as their mothers.[26]

Through much of the colonial period of Brazil the Crown disapproved of concubinage, and the Brazilian Church declared itself against such practices. Yet concubinage in Brazil remained alive for a long time, and was practiced not only by masters but sometimes even by priests. Also widespread was a situation whereby children born of such unions assumed the status of their bonded mothers. For as long as slavery continued there was a strong tendency in Latin America, as in North America, towards *descending mis*cegenation.

In this respect, the experience of South Africa in the eighteenth century was similar. A slave woman who won the favours of her master in bed and produced fair-skinned children, could indeed quite often improve her own status and the status of her children. But this would be an improvement within the slave system, becoming relieved of some chores, enjoying extra privileges, and perhaps even supervisory power over other slaves. The children also perhaps became better fed than the children produced of unions of slave with slave. But the persistent pattern in South Africa in the 18th and 19th centuries, as elsewhere in the world of white slave ownership, was to regard children of slave girls as being themselves slaves, regardless of whether the father was free or not. Descending miscegenation continued to be the rule in conditions of slave ownership. As Van den Berghe put it in relation to South Africa's experience:

> The close symbiosis of masters and slaves, and the total subordination of the female slave to her male owners made for extensive intermixture. Other incentives accelerated the process. Through miscegenation the female slave could improve her condition and the status of her children. The White Master, on his side, had, apart from sexual gratification, an economic interest in increasing and 'improving' his human stock by producing highly priced mulatto slaves.[27]

Later on, when slavery was abolished, the idea of Coloured People in South Africa being a group apart both from Whites and Blacks began to consolidate itself. Divergent miscegenation became the new pattern. But in the background was the whole experience of regarding children born of a union between a master and a slave girl as being themselves slaves.

BLACK SLAVES AND ARAB MASTERS

The difference between this phenomenon of slavery in the white world and the phenomenon of slavery in the Arab world has had important consequences for the status of children of mixed mating. In Islam any child born to a slave girl by her master is legitimate; the legitimacy in this case confers upon the child descent from his father, including the status of a free-born and rights of inheritance; and this descent confers upon the child. links with the father's tribe. In slave conditions Islam insists on ascending miscegenation. If the father is Arab the child is Arab, regardless of whether the mother is a wife or concubine, and regardless of the nationality or race of the mother.

If a similar system of descent had been operable in the United States, the majority of those who are now called "Blacks" would, in fact, have belonged to the "White" community. They would have acquired this paternal descent simply because most of the children of mixed unions in the United States have involved white fathers and black mothers. If the Germanic and Anglo-Saxon cultures had had as sharp a principle of paternal descent as the Arabs, the population of under-privileged black people in the United States today would have been much smaller. The bulk would have been assimilated upwards into the dominant and privileged community.

In South Africa, the application of the Arab principle that the father's tribe determines the child's tribe would have tilted the balance of population as between English-speaking whites and Afrikaans-speaking whites, as well as affecting attitudes to gradation of colours within the. system as a whole.

The racial prejudice of the Whites is solely responsible for the social existence of a distinct Cape Coloured group, a fact recognized by many moderate' Afrikaners today, and indeed by some Hertzogites as early as the twenties. Except for the concern with colour of South African 'Whites' (many of whom have themselves 'Coloured blood'), Afrikanerdom would be nearly twice as large as it is today, and would outnumber the English-speaking Whites by well over two to one. For every six White Afrikaners there are approximately five Coloured Afrikaners and four English-speaking Whites. In the entire population there are four non-Whites to one White, if colour is the criterion; but, if mother tongue is taken as the criterion, there are only two nonEuropeans to one European.[28]

In the Latin American model of racial mixture the application of the Arab principle of paternity would have made another kind of difference — it would have obliterated to some extent the categories of mestizo and mulatto as significant ones. Given that the child follows the father in tribal or racial affiliation, the so-called white population would have become more varied in skin colour; and conceivably also the non-white would also have had a variety of colours. But the balance between the groups—white, black, Indian would have had a different basis. Variation in colours would still have been significant but the relative populations of the different groups would be substantially changed, reducing in the process the number of those who were relatively under-privileged.

But in Islam the colour of the offspring is certainly no reason for denying its paternity and descent, even in a situation where the mother is a fair skinned Arab and so is the father. Reuben Levy, a Cambridge professor, draws our attention to the following hadith:

> The extreme case is quoted, or invented, of a Bedouin Arab who came to the Prophet declaring that his wife had given birth to a Negro child, and hinting that he wished to repudiate it. Muhammad, however, refused him permission to do so. . .[29]

Levy also draws our attention both to the legitimacy of children born in concubinage and to the concern of the tribe as a whole in ascertaining the paternal link with the tribe.

> In Islam it is sufficient for the father to acknowledge cohabitation with his wife or slave to establish the legitimacy of the child. . . . Seeing that concubinage is lawful in Islam, it is not necessary for the mother of a child to be married to its father in order for it to be declared legitimate.
>
> The powers of the father over his children are very great, [but] he cannot sell them into slavery. . . . Normally, indeed, the legitimacy of a boy is a matter of some concern to the father's family or tribe.[30]

Arab patrilinealism in Zanzibar, reinforced by Islamic prescriptions, resulted on the one hand in the cultural assimilation of the Africans into Islam, and on the other into the biological Africanization of the Arab immigrants. The local indigenous populations imbibed imported culture to a considerable extent, while the future composition of the Arab population on the island absorbed important African strains biologically.

But when, in addition, the racial intermingling led to the emergence and consolidation of the Swahili language as the national language of Zanzibar, problems of differentiating Arab from non-Arab became compounded. The result was considerable ethnic fluidity. We know that social mobility is the capacity of a person to move from one class to another; but Zanzibar had in addition racial mobility in the sense of capacity of a person or even whole sub-groups to move from one racial category into another.

Before the revolution, the Arab minority in Zanzibar was described as "Sub-Saharan Africa's second largest alien oligarchic minority"—following in proportional size only the white community of South Africa. But if the South African method of descent had been applied to Zanzibar, and the Zanzibari method of descent had been applied to South Africa, South Africa's proportion of Whites would have been greater than it is today—and Zanzibar's proportion of Arabs would have been much smaller than it was at the time of the revolution.

The substantial issue to be borne in mind is precisely the ethnic fluidity which was characteristic of Zanzibar's racial situation. In the 1930s and 1940s. the Arab population in Zanzibar shot up significantly, not because new immigrants had arrived from the Persian Gulf, nor because the Arabs' natural rate of reproduction bad suddenly taken a sharp turn upwards. In 1924 the Arabs as a percentage of the total population of Zanzibar consisted of 8.7%. By 1948 the Arabs were up to 16.9%.

> A small fraction of this increase was doubtless Arab. But the vast bulk of the increase in the Arab population had to come from within Zanzibar society, from among segments of the population which had previously opted for categories of self description other than Aiab. Between 1924 and 1931 large numbers of former non-Arabs changed their minds, as it were, about the ethnic category most suited to their own descent and decided to 'join' the Arab community.[31]

On the coast of Kenya during the colonial period similar shifts in racial categorization took place. The Arab population of the coast of Kenya was barely twenty thousand by the 1948 census. The population rose by a few thousand in the early 1950s simply because groups of Arabized coastal tribes, previously designated as non-Arab, were at last given recognition by the British Colonial authorities as Arabs. They had themselves been pressing for such recognition from the British Colonial authorities, though their credentials were challenged by those who were already recognized as Arabs. The British Colonial authorities, perhaps partly influenced by the bewildering fluidity of intermingling between Arabs and Africans, decided to confer the more prestigious title of "Arab" upon the new claimants from the coast.

The advantages which Kenya coastal Arabs enjoyed as against Kenya coastal Africans were sometime more substantial than mere prestige. Terms of service for jobs were, during the colonial period, categorized into European terms of service, Asian terms of service, and African terms of service. The Arab sector, by its racial ambivalence, was sometimes eligible for the

Asian terms of service, and sometimes not. Certain banks in Mombasa classified all Arabs as Africans, and paid them accordingly. East African Railways and Harbours also classified many Arabs as Africans and paid them accordingly. And yet in much of the civil service within Kenya, Arab civil servants were often regarded as being eligible for Asian terms of service. The pigmentational and racial ambivalence of the Arabs converted them into marginal persons.

In the entertainment world there were also differentials in privileges among the groups. A symbolic differential concerned films (movies) which were given the grade of X by the censors in colonial Kenya. X-films in Kenya meant "Not to be shown to Africans and children under sixteen." The term "African" at the initial introduction of the censorship law encompassed Arabs, and so they too for a while were kept out of film shows bearing the title X. It took a demonstration organized by a prominent Mombasa Arab, Shariff Abdulla Salim, to force the "Majestic" cinema in Mombasa to admit a group of militantly defiant local Arabs. Once the breach was made at the "Majestic" cinema, gradually the term X as a category of censored film implied only Africans and children under sixteen, and no longer Africans, Arabs and children under sixteen. But where did Africanness end and Arabness begin?

The ambiguity resulted in conferring significant powers of racial categorization on the gatekeepers and ticket-sellers at the cinemas. An African could indeed acquire the privilege of seeing an exciting sex film, or a film involving violence, if he could convince the booking-office clerk or the gatekeeper at the "Regal" or "Majestic" cinema that he was an Arab and not an African. On the other hand, a black Arab might have to argue his way, or even bribe his way into the cinema, if the clerk insisted in regarding him as an African. There were special cinema shows exclusively for women. These shows which were "strictly for ladies" were less subject to racial discrimination in colonial Mombasa.

In the Sudan, ethnic fluidity has also been a persistent feature of the whole process of acculturation. It is true that the initial impetus of Arabization did include the coming of large numbers of Arabs. It is also true that Arab immigration continued in varying volumes over many years. But Sudanese Arabs themselves, to the present day, often grossly exaggerate the numbers of Arabs who came in. Much of the population of northern Sudan is a population of Arabized Africans, rather than Arabs as such. Whole groups began to identify with particular Arab tribal names, and genealogies grew up, of varying authenticity, establishing the Arabness of the different groups.

Unfortunately we know remarkable little of the way in which Arabization was accomplished. The whole of our knowledge is derived from two different types of sources: the first, a limited number of contemporary medieval Arabic writings and the second, a large body of Sudanese genealogical traditions which in their present form were compiled at a much later date.[32]

Fadl Hasan warns us that the genealogical traditions which are at the moment current in the northern Sudan indicate a high degree of Arabization. The adoption of Arab genealogies by the inhabitants of the Sudan is very widespread. The fact that there is a preference for adopting such genealogies indicates at the minimum a high degree of cultural Arabization.

> However, any conclusions that are drawn from these genealogies as to tribal origin, must be accepted with some reserve.[33]

The sheer fluidity of ethnic affiliations, and the cultural pull of the dominant identity, have resulted in a high degree of integration in northern Sudan. Denominational differences in religion assumed a greater political significance in the Sudan than the racial categories of the northern population. Disputes as to whether such and such a family is really Arab by descent or not, and evaluations of family prestige partly in terms of lighter shades of colour, have all remained an important part of the texture of Sudanese life in the north. Prejudices based on colour have by no means disappeared. There are black Arabs, deeply black, whose credentials are fully respected in relation to their Arab genealogies. There are others who may be a shade lighter, and yet have their Arab credentials disputed by at least some families. The political sociology of shades of colour remains a part of the Sudanese scene. But the phenomenon of intermarriage and miscegenation, on the basis of patrilineal descent, have resulted in a more integrated model of racial mixture than that afforded by either the North American experience, the Latin American experience or the experience of South Africa.

SOUTHERN SUDAN: TOWARDS A BIO-CULTURAL SOLUTION?

Is the policy of inter-marriage relevant for the problem of southern Sudan? Will the Arab model of descent, practiced in terms of racial mixture, provide one long-terra solution to the southern problem?

There have been signs in the Sudanese scene indicating a groping for the utilization of racial mixture as an integrative device. Official circles in Khartoum have sometimes been reported to have encouraged a more relaxed attitude in the north to the idea of Arab girls being married to black southerners.

Arab attitudes to inter-marriage have been asymmetrical. When the Arab man marries into a different community no special stigma is attached to the union, and the children, in any case, become Arab. But, when an Arab woman is married to a non-Arab man, a different set of suppositions arise. The logic of patrilineal descent necessarily entails that there should be disapproval of an Arab girl marrying a non-Arab (be the bridegroom an African or a European). After all, the children of such a union would not themselves be Arab. In Northern Sudan is there a relaxation of this resistance to give away Arab daughters to non-Arab husbands?

But here an additional complicating factor enters the scene. Islam recognizes no racial distinctions in regard to marriage; but it emphatically recognizes religious distinctions. Racially mixed marriages among Muslims are fully valid in Islam; but religiously mixed marriages are more complex. The Muslim man may marry either a Jewess or a Christian woman without necessarily converting her. Islam in India extended this tolerance to the idea of marrying a Hindu woman without necessarily converting her. But a marriage between a non-Muslim man and a Muslim woman is not valid in *orthodox* Islam. There are Muslim jurists who argue that the marriage of a Muslim woman to a non-Muslim man is irregular rather than void. There are supporters of this interpretation in some parts of the Muslim world, including Pakistan and the Sudan itself. But the dominant feeling among Muslim jurists is that the marriage of a Muslim woman to a non-Muslim man is, according to Sharia, null and void.

Ameer Ali, the Indo-Pakistani Islamic jurist, recommended a flexible interpretation of this prohibition. And D. F. Mulla more recently has reaffirmed the proposed distinction between an irregular marriage and a void marriage. Asaf Fyzee, yet a third Islamic jurist, accepts the distinction, but insists that in the case of a marriage between a Muslim woman and a non-Muslim man, the marriage is not merely irregular but it is void.

> The present position appears to be that the *Nikah of* a Muslim man with an idolater or fire-worshipper is irregular and not void. Mulla goes on to say, however, that the marriage of a Muslim woman with a non-Muslim is only irregular, not void. This is, it is submitted, an inaccurate statement *of* the law. The marriage of a Muslim woman with a non-Muslim is declared by the Koran to be *batil,* void and not merely irregular. Thus it would seem that reform, in consonance with the view of Ameer Ali, can only be introduced by legislation.[34]

Discussion in the Sudan has also been conducted on the distinction between an irregular marriage and a void marriage. The reformers and modernizers, particularly those sympathetic to the marriage of northern Muslim girls to Christian southerners (preferably highly educated), have encouraged a more liberal interpretation of the Sharia. But, on the whole, northern Sudanese parents have tended to be orthodox in such matters. Southern suitors for northern girls have been confronted with stipulations from some parents that they should be practicing Muslims for a period of at least two years before they could be regarded as eligible husbands for Muslim girls. Problems of circumcision have also sometimes intruded. The majority of non-Muslim southerners are not circumcised, and this influences questions of eligibility for marriage to northern girls.

Islam is clear in its prescription that the Muslim male ought to be circumcised. Circumcision in Islam does not command quite the degree of sacred covenant that it does in Judaism. This is partly because the Jews, in their isolation as a minority in other parts of the world, gradually converted the circumcision rite into an overpowering symbol of their separate identity. Nevertheless, male circumcision in Islam is important enough to be practiced among Muslims all over the world, regardless of other differences. It is certainly a powerful influence in Arab Islam and is often regarded as a prerequisite for masculine eligibility in matrimony.

The reported policy of the Khartoum Government to encourage flexibility on marriage customs between northerners and southerners aroused a good deal of suspicion among the more nationalistic southerners. That the policy was motivated by the ambition of bio-cultural assimilation was something which the more politically conscious southerners immediately grasped. The *official* encouragement of such flexibility was, to some extent, counter-productive. It created at least temporary resistance among the more politically conscious southerners, and exposed those who married northern girls to the risk of nationalist ridicule and political disapprobation.

Southern nationalists might have been more tempted to encourage the marriage of northern girls if there was a feeling that such an enterprise was *officially* disapproved of. In such circumstances, the marriage of a northern girl to a southern man would become a kind of defiant assertion of parity of esteem with the north. It would have been similar to situations in North America where black desires for white mistresses were sometimes motivated by political ambitions to assert parity of dignity with the white community — taking white girls to bed became a symbolic political protest.

But in the Sudan the actual official encouragement of intermarriage made the phenomenon more suspect, and might therefore have been counter-productive.

Nevertheless, from the main perspective of Arabs marrying others, the theses of this paper remain basically secure. The union of an Arab male with a non-Arab Sudanese woman, where it is legitimate, produces more Arabs rather than half-castes. The dominant group increases in size. It becomes possible to envisage a situation when more and more Sudanese become, linguistically and by claimed descent, Arab Sudanese.

The two Sudanese civil wars have themselves had consequences relevant to this whole process of inter-marriage. Arab soldiers in the south have taken mistresses, or married southern girls. Where the offspring is illegitimate, the child could either remain with the mother, as is often the case, or later be claimed by the father for Arabization and Islamization in the north. The Sudanese, both Arab and black African, are, on the whole, strongly patrilineal. This has tended to encourage fathers to claim their children, particularly if they are boys, for inclusion into their original family. The Dinka seem to be at least as patrilineal as the Arabs. In general, it would seem that if the father is Dinka the child is almost certainly also Dinka, especially if it is a boy.

A more distinct example is that of the Dinka of north-western Sudan, who have close contacts with Baggare Arabs who come down annually in search of water and good pastures. During the Miriam wars with the Dinka, the Dinka captured Arab girls and some young Arab men. Many of these were integrated to some extent with the society which had captured them. In the villages of Jorbioc and Akuang Akuet, there are Arab Dinkas with names such as Ngong. In appearance many betray their mixture, but they are Dinka by language and culture.[35]

But, in the final analysis, inter-marriage between Arab and southerner in the south is still in its initial stages, and cannot yet be regarded as a substantial contribution to the integration of the country as a whole. Nevertheless, the issue of biological intermingling when coupled with cultural assimilation has to be regarded as an important dimension in the slow process of nation-building.

One facilitating factor for the biological approach to national integration in the Sudan is the fact that regionalism and race are beginning to be cross-cutting. Arabized southerners are already part of the scene, and groups like the Dinka have relatives in the north. Some calculations of Dinka in the north put them at more than a million. Inter-marriage between Arabs and Dinka has taken place both in the north and in the south.

Estimates of the population of the Dinka in the Sudan as a whole are varied. The Nuer are sometimes included as a sub-section of the Dinka, partly because the languages are mutually intelligible. When the Nuer are included, the population of the Dinka may be up to nearly ten million. This makes the group the largest single tribe in the Sudan as a whole, both north and south. It also allows for the possibility of significant Dinka influence in the Sudanese nation should the present composition of the Sudan survive the civil wars and other pulls to which it is subjected. If one out of every five Sudanese is a Dinka, and if the tradition of inter-marriage between the Dinka and the Arabs is increasing, the possibilities of nationally significant racial integration are indeed real.[36]

CONCLUSION

Much of what is going on in the Sudan today is in part a repetition of what went on in Egypt earlier, the gradual conversion of a country to Arabism and its culture. The process includes both conflict and integration. The Sudanese process appears noticeable partly because the majority of Arabs in the world are fairer than black Africans. What is often overlooked is that when Egypt was conquered by the Arabs, the Arabs from the deserts of the peninsula were darker than the Egyptians they were subjecting. The Arabs from the peninsula were also darker than the Syrians whom they converted to Islam in that first wave of conquest. The Fertile Crescent and Egypt, partly because of their diplomatic prominence over the centuries, began to be identified with the leadership of the Arab world. Because they were fair, it was assumed that the very origins of Arabness implied light Mediterranean skin.

But the purest Arabs come from further south in the Arabian pensinsula, and these are darker. Moreover, the Arabs of the peninsula proper, have intermingled more with racially dark-skinned people than have the Arabs of the Fertile Crescent to the north.

If the Sudanese Arabs are dark, so are many of the inhabitants of Mecca and Medina. They may not be as dark as the Sudanese, though some of them are. The Arabs of Mecca and Medina are a blend of Asia and Africa, while the Lebanese and Syrians, for example, may be a blend of Europe and Asia.

In their expansionism the Arabs have insisted on asymmetry both in culture and in miscegenation. This is certainly true also with regard to the Arab impact on the Sudan. Arabic is a conquering language, sometimes absorbing a little of the local languages, but in its very pride tending towards ultimate triumph. Patrilinealism, as we shall indicate, operates in terms of permitting and even encouraging Arab men to marry women from other communities, but forbidding or discouraging Arab women from marrying others.

The example of Zanzibar, on the other hand, is distinct. The Arabs in Zanzibar stood for asymmetrical miscegenation, but they also stood for symmetrical acculturation. The Arabic language was not an irresistible conqueror, flattening out local linguistic opponents. On the contrary, many Arabs of Zanzibar actually ceased to be Arabic speakers—and became native speakers of the basically Bantu language of Kiswahili. The Arabs of Zanzibar had allowed themselves to become less "Arab" than the Egyptians and Sudanese had done—and yet at the time of the revolution the Zanzibar Arabs were regarded as less native to their part of Africa than northern Sudanese were deemed to be in theirs.

The passionate hatred of the Arabs at the time of the revolution within Zanzibar was, in some ways, one of the most remarkable anomalies in contemporary

African history. There seems to have been more passionate hatred of the Arabs in Zanzibar than there was hatred of the white man in Tanganyika. It is true that there were differences in situations. Some of the worst brutalities committed by white people against local Tanganyikans were committed by the Germans before the British assumed control following World War I. The British, the new rulers, turned out to be also exclusive in their social habits. But they were not as arrogant or as cruel as the Germans in the history of Tanganyika. Nevertheless, there is no escaping the fact that the British were a small minority of people, conferring privileges on local Indians and local Europeans, exercising considerable hegemony over Africans, and clearly demanding separate treatment.

The Arab oligarchy in Zanzibar, on the other hand, mixed socially with the Africans, called many Africans uncle or nephew or cousin, shared the same religion with them, prayed shoulder to shoulder in mosques, appreciated the same jokes, sometimes frequented the same brothels.

Yet, by 1958, it was already clear that a deep anti-Arab animosity in large sectors of the African population in Zanzibar, had consolidated itself. When racial riots erupted in 1961, there was no doubt that all the years of mixed marriages and reciprocal acculturation had not resulted in minimizing hostility. The question which arises is whether that hostility may have been partly due to the very inter penetration between the groups which had taken place. Had the British, by keeping themselves completely apart, averted in the short run those depths of feeling? It is true that in Kenya there was sufficient anti-British hostility to erupt into a Mau Mau insurrection, but again, was it significant that the Mau Mau movement took place among the Kikuyu, the most acculturated of Kenya's peoples at the time, partly because of their very nearness to the British authorities? Elsewhere in Kenya resentment of the white man was there, but with nothing of the depth illustrated on that tragic island of Zanzibar in January 1964 against the Arabs. The problem which this raises. is whether tension and hostility increases rather than diminishes when the dominant group narrows the cultural gap between itself and the under-privileged group.

According to this thesis, the Arabs of Zanzibar expedited their vulnerability to African challenge as they themselves became more culturally African. The adoption of the Swahili language as the dominant language of Zanzibar, and the decline of Arabic except in a section of the Arab population, was, in some ways, an establishment of cultural parity between Arabian culture and the Bantu linguistic cultures. But did this bring the revolution nearer? Are there occasions when economic imbalance is indeed stabilized precisely by cultural compartmentalization? Where a dominant group looks and speaks differently, and displays a very different way of life, it may perhaps have to face less of a challenge than if it mixes more fully with the population and reduces the social and cultural distance.

In the latter situation where the cultural differences are fading, the economic imbalance becomes more conspicuous. By becoming almost the only residual difference between the privileged and the under-privileged, the economic disparity becomes the more exposed.

It might, therefore, be said that those who worked out the philosophy of apartheid were basing their experiment, at least in the short run, on sound sociological grounds. If the economic imbalance between the whites and the non-whites was to be stabilized for a while, it made sense to attempt to keep the cultures apart.

And yet such stability can only be a short-term achievement. It is true that Zanzibar remains a tragic case of bio-cultural assimilation gone violent. The population was becoming a relatively homogeneous Swahili speaking people, sharing the same religion as well as the same language. It may also be true that the situation became revolutionary precisely because an economic imbalance based largely on landownership persisted in spite of cultural homogenization.

But the tragedy of Zanzibar may have been the tragedy of a premature racial revolution. Sudan may remain unsure as to whether it is part of the Arab world or of black Africa. But independent Zanzibar could not have sustained its Arab identity for much longer. The mixture of the population internally, the decline of the Arabic language, the emergence of a Swahili culture, and the links which this forged between the island and the black East African mainland, were almost bound to accelerate the dis-Arabization of Zanzibar rather sharply. Indeed, the anti-colonial movement itself had already divided the Arab community between those who continued to take pride in their Arab descent and those who were emphasizing their Zanzibari identity. By the year of independence it was the latter who were winning. Independent Zanzibar would have been the most culturally integrated of all countries south of the Sahara, with the possible exception of Swaziland and Somalia. Just as many Africans in colonial Zanzibar had found it expedient to claim Arab descent, so many Arabs after independence would have found. it expedient to emphasize their African descent.

It should not be forgotten that the "minority" government which was overthrown in January 1964 had obtained 46% of the popular vote only a few months earlier—by no means a "small" minority. In an election seven years before that (in 1957) the school of thought represented by this minority government—"Ours is Zanzibari nationalism"—won less than a quarter of this support. In other words, support for this concept of the *Zanzibar nation* was growing rather than diminishing when the revolution took place. But these trends were never tested under conditions of independence. The Zanzibar revolution took place within less than four weeks of attainment of independence.

But what if Arabism had remained strong in Zanzibar in spite of independence? In such a case the long-term solution would have had to lie in the *ascending* nature of Afro-Arab miscegenation. Let us assume that the Arabs had
remained dominant, had continued to inter-marry, and had still recognized all
children with Arab fathers as Arabs. In such circumstances, and given no
sharp differences in fertility between Arabs and Africans, the proportion of local Arabs to local Africans would have continued to increase. It had certainly
been increasing for the previous three generations, both because of ascending
miscegenation and because the racial composition of Zanzibar was fluid
enough to make it possible for some unmixed Africans to claim Arab descent.
Again, as Michael Lofchie has pointed out, the Arabs were 8.7% of the population in 1924, and had risen to 16.9% of the population of Zanzibar by
1948.[37]

It is precisely this principle of ascending miscegenation which makes a
fundamental difference between prospects for racial mixture in the Sudan today as against such prospects in Southern Africa. Claims that Sudan and
Southern Africa are similar racial situations are, at best, naive, or more likely,
propagandist.

The Portuguese speaking territories in Southern Africa (Angola and
Mozambique) are an imperfect illustration of the *ambivalent miscegenation*
of Brazil, but with greater discouragement of mixed unions than is- now characteristic of Brazil.[38]

Rhodesia/Zimbabwe with its Anglo-Saxon background, started with *descending miscegenation.* A population of Eurafricans had been growing. They
were the offspring of European fathers and African mothers. In the villages
they were accepted in the communal way of life and brought up according to
the custom and language of the mother. But the disintegration of village life,
and the drift towards the cities, have brought to the surface the problem of
these racially mixed people.

While fellow Africans in the villages had readily assimilated the "half-
castes," the Africans in the cities have shown greater distrust of these lighter-
coloured lumpen proletariat.

The Eurafrican has often still had problems with European employers. As
one observer put it some years ago:

> He goes to a prospective employer, but owing to his light skin the white man ex-
> pects him to know English (as all 'Coloureds' do) and generally be more so-
> phisticated than an-African straight from the kraal, which is all he feels himself
> to be. He is again rejected.[39]

But how many Eurafricans are there in Zimbabwe? The exact numbers are
as obscure as they were when the following observation was made

. . . the total Eurafricans in the Native Reserves can scarcely be less than 10,000;
it might be even ten times that number. Nobody knows. But it is growing faster
than ever.[40]

But even at that stage the situation showed signs of future transformation
from descending miscegenation (as in North America) to *divergent miscegenation* (of the South African "Coloured" Model). Eurafricans in Salisbury
had begun to appeal to the Government for recognition as a distinct community, and for compulsory registration as such, and for rights of compulsory education.[41]

When asked if Africans in Rhodesia/Zimbabwe should be denied universal
franchise because one Minister in a black African state elsewhere had tried to
seduce a stenographer, Mr. Ian Smith retorted angrily: "It was not a case of
seduction. It was attempted rape. How would you feel if that had happened to
your wife or daughter?"[42] Ian Smith was trying to stereotype African rulers in
the post-colonial era as both tyrants and rapists.

Such racism contrasts sharply with the problem of Southern Sudan. The
war in the south flared up precisely because the Khartoum Government was
opposed to the idea of maintaining the south as a separate Bantustan.

For as long as the south of the Sudan was kept separate, and assumed that
it would remain separate, tension was minimized. But the very attainment of
independence in the Sudan created in the south fears that southerners would
no longer be left alone, and subsequent policies of deliberate cultural assimilation increased these anxieties. Again, precisely because the Sudan does
not practice apartheid, the danger of tensions between groups emerged
sooner. Converting Southern Sudan into a Bautustan, as the missionaries and
British Colonial authorities had done, had for quite a while delayed the outbreak of hostility, though memories of prior interaction and slave raiding remained potent.

On independence, it was open to the Sudanese government to assure the
south that it would be a Bantustan, left to its own cultural ways under the paternal guidance of Italian missionaries. But it was partly the rejection of religio-cultural apartheid in, the Sudan which opened the way for tensions. And
as the Sudanese now inter-marry, and as Arabic acculturation gathers momentum, the price which will be paid will be in terms of increased social tension, at least for a while.

It is unlikely that asymmetrical miscegenation in the Sudan will ever come
to an end. The Sudanese, as well as the black Africans like the Dinka, are too
patrilineal to evolve a system where both men and women may marry as they
wish across racial boundaries without incurring certain social reservations.
But the system of *ascending miscegenation* guarantees a form of upward mobility which has no equivalent in any other type of racial mixture.

As for symmetry in acculturation, this is more feasible in the Sudan than elsewhere in the Arab world, and has, to some extent, already taken place. The recency of culture contact has produced varieties of Arabic in the Sudan which bear the strong imprint of non-Arabic African languages. The cultural symmetry in the Sudan is not quite of the level attained in Zanzibar or Persia where the local subjugated group profoundly influenced the conqueror culturally, as well as permitted itself to be influenced thereby. Nevertheless, the degree of reciprocity in the Sudan is greater than further down the Nile, or elsewhere in the Arab world now that Zanzibar is no longer part of it. But the most stable of all interactions is a combination of cultural symmetry and economic balance. Where the groups learn from each other as well as teach each other, without creating a society of vast disproportion in economic advantages, the possibilities of a stable society are there.

The emergence of socialistic ideas in the Sudan from time to time may reinforce the leveling tendencies of race mixture. The suspended Sudanese Communist Party is potentially the largest in independent Africa and one of the oldest south of the Mediterranean African countries. The Party's political fortunes have varied from regime to regime, but it has played a part in disseminating more moderate socialistic values to other groups in the Sudan which are less explicitly Marxist.

The triumph of an egalitarian ethic seems likely in the Sudan in the long run. Northern Sudanese intellectuals are disproportionately left of centre, however anti-communist some of them may be.

If the country survives, the Sudan may be the first modern nation in Africa to have creatively used a combination of socialism and sexual "miscegenation" for national integration.

NOTES

1. R. C. Stevenson, "Some Aspects of the Spread of Islam in the Nuba Mountains (Kordofan Province, Republic of the Sudan)," in *Islam in Tropical Africa,* I. M. Lewis (ed.), (London, 1966), p. 209.

2. Consult, for example, H. Bamford-Parkes, *Gods and Men: The Origins of Western Culture* (New York, 1959), Section 3; William H. McNeill, *The Rise of the West* (Chicago and London, 1963), especially Chapter VI.

3. In this paper we use the word "miscegenation" in the full realization that its origins are racist. The whole concept implied by it is based on a disapproval of racial mixture. Our own use of it is, in spite of the origins of the word, intended to be value free. By miscegenation we mean mating between different races, in or out of wedlock, resulting in children of mixed parentage.

4. *Casa Grande E. Senzala* (Rio de Janeiro, 1958), 9th edition, pp. 12–13. Cited by Jose Honorio Rodrigues, *Brazil and Africa,* translated by Richard Mazzara and Sam Heilman (Berkeley and Los Angeles, 1965), p. 55.

5. This sort of answer was given by a Nigerian and by an African American resident in Ghana in discussions in September 1964.

6. For quite a while, the United States' Supreme Court had avoided a direct ruling on the constitutionality of laws which forbade mixed marriage. But those laws began to disappear in the 1960s in spite of the Supreme Court's inhibition. Enough changes were emerging from the political scene to make reforms in this direction inevitable. For a useful background article see Arthur Krock, "Miscegenation Debate," *The New York Times* (Review of the Week) September 8th, 1963. See also the article by Charlotte G. Moulton, published in *The Nationalist* (Dar es Salaam), November 11th, 1964. The Supreme Court finally invalidated anti-miscegenation laws in its decision on Loving vs. State of Virginia, 1967.

7. This distinction between race prejudice based on colour and race prejudice based on purity of blood is also discussed in Mazrui, "Political Sex," *Transition,* Volume IV, No. 17, 1964. The article is reprinted as Chapter 15 in Mazrui, *Violence and Thought: Essays on Social Tensions in Africa* (London, 1969), pp. 306–18.

8. See Jose Honorio Rodrigues, *Brazil and Africa* (Berkeley and Los Angeles, 1965), translated by Richard Mazzara and Sam Heilman, p. 64.

9. Ibid., p. 75.

10. Rodrigues, *Brazil and Africa,* op. cit., p. 75. Consult also Donald Pierson, *Brancos e Pretos ma Bahia* (Sao Paulo, 1945), pp. 186, 188–89.

11. See Pierre van den Berghe, *South Africa: A Study in Conflict* (Berkeley and Los Angeles, 1967), pp. 39–40.

12. Muddathir 'Abd Al-Rahim, *Imperialism and Nationalism in the Sudan: A Study in Constitutional and Political Development, 1899–1956* (Oxford, 1969), pp. 4–5. See also The Republic of the Sudan, Ministry for Social Welfare, *First Population Census of the Sudan: Twenty-one Facts about the Sudanese (1958),* pp. 13, 23.

13. This point is discussed in similar terms in Mazrui, *Towards a Pax Africana: A Study of Ideology and Ambition* (London and Chicago, 1967) p.113. See also Yusuf Fadl Hasan, *The Arabs and the Sudan: From the Seventh to the Early Sixteenth Century* (Edinburgh, 1967), especially Chapter 5, pp. 135–76.

14. Blyden, *Christianity, Islam and the Negro Race* (London: 1887), reprinted in the African Heritage Books, edited by George Shepperson and Christopher Fyfe (Edinburgh, 1967), pp. 24–25.

15. Ibid., p. 19.

16. Dean Stanley, *Eastern Church, p.* 34. Cited by Blyden, ibid., pp. 19–20.

17. McLeod, *The American Indian Frontier* (New York, 1928), pp. 60–61.

18. Ibid.

19. Ibid., pp. 359–60.

20. Herbert Moller, "Sex Composition and Correlated Culture Patterns of Colonial America," *The William and Mary College Quarterly, Vol. II,* April 1945, pp. 131–33; 136–37.

21. Ibid., p. 137.

22. Fadl Hasan, *The Arabs and the Sudan,* op. cit., p. 175.

23. Herbert Aptheker (ed.), *One Continual Cry: David Walker's Appeal to the Coloured Citizens of the World, 1829–1830* (New York, 1965), p. 41.

24. *Black Reconstruction in America, 1860–1880* (1935; reprinted Cleveland and New York, 1962), p. 35.

25. DuBois, *The World and Africa* (1946; enlarged edition New York, 1965), p. 184.

26. See Ordenacoes Filipinas, Book 5, Titles XXIII to XXX. Cited by Rodrigues, op. cit., p. 61.

27. South Africa: A Study in Conflict, op. cit., p. 41.

28. Van den Berghe, *South Africa: A Study in Conflict,* op. cit., 1i. p. 42.

29. Levy, *The Social Structure of Islam* (Cambridge, 1962), p. 137.

30. Levy, ibid., pp. 136, 143 and 138. Consult also Asaf A. A. Fyzee, *Outlines of Muhammadan Law* (London, 1964 edition), especially Chapters 2 and 5.

31. Michael F. Lofchie, *Zanzibar: Background to Revolution* (Princeton and London, 1965), pp. 73–75.

32. Fadl Hasan, *The Arabs and the Sudan,* op. cit., p. 135.

33. Ibid.

34. Fyzee, *Outlines of Muhammadan Law,* op. cit., pp. 95–96. See also Syed Ameer Ali, *Mahommedan Law* (Tagore Law Lectures, 1884), Vol. 1, 4th ed., Calcutta 1912. Also Vol. II, 5th ed., Calcutta 1929. Consult also Dinshah Fardungi Mulla, *Principles of Mahommedan Law,* 15th ed., Calcutta 1961.

35. I am grateful for much of this information to Southern Sudanese informants in Kampala, Uganda.

36. The estimates here are at their most generous, made usually by educated Dinka in exile. The official estimates made twenty years ago are much more modest, placing the Dinka cluster in terms of one and-a-half million or two million rather than four. Consult *Census,* op. cit. Consult also George Peter Murdock, *Africa: Its Peoples and their Culture History* (New York, 1959), especially Chapter 43. The more selective and restricted 1962 estimates made in the Sudan reportedly placed the Dinka at about three million.

37. Lofchie, *Zanzibar: Background to Revolution, op. cit.,* Table 3, p. 74.

38. For a general historical background see C. R. Boxer, *Race Relations in the Portuguese Colonial Empire* (Oxford, 1963). See also Rodrigues, "Influence of Africa on Brazil," *Journal of African History,* Vol. 111, No. 1, 1962; Institute of Race Relations, *Angola: A Symposium* (Oxford).

39. See *Manchester Guardian,* April 28th, 1956. 40. Ibid.

40. Ibid.

41. *Africa Digest,* Vol. III, No. 8, May–June, 1956, pp. 38–39.

42. *East Africa and Rhodesia* (London), October 14th, 1965, p. 95. Disapproval of mixed *marriages* in colonial Rhodesia was even stronger than disapproval of casual mating between the races. A. distinguished United Nations official was once denied a job at the University College in Salisbury because he had a white wife. The man was himself a black Rhodesian (later Zimbabwean).

Chapter Nine

The Multiple Marginality of the Sudan

The bridge concept of the Sudan is fairly common, but it is normally applied to the position of the Sudan in relation to Black Africa on one side and Arab Africa on the other. The Sudan is, therefore, conceived as one of the bridges between two sectors of the African Continent.

But in fact the Sudan serves comparable functions between other segments of the total African pattern. One could see the Sudan as a bridge between Arabic-speaking Africa and English-speaking Africa; between Christian Africa and Muslim Africa; between the Africa of homogenised mass nation-states of the future and the Africa of the deep ethnic cleavage of the present; and finally, between West Africa as a cultural unit and Eastern Africa.

And yet the use of the word 'bridge' is misleading even when applied to Afro-Arab relations. It is not really true that the Sudan plays a role of uniting black Africa with Africa south of the Sahara. Arabs of the north who need to influence the Black Continent do not normally use Khartoum as the route towards that influence, nor do Black Africans who wish to put forward policies that should affect Arab orientations come to the Sudanese Government for advice and the utilisation of its good offices in that cause. The bridge concept of the Sudan claims too much. The Sudan is not bridging a chasm between Black Africa and Arab Africa, nor does it play any special linking or mediating role between these two sectors.

In this chapter, therefore, we have preferred the term 'marginality.' Our sense of the term marginality is not quite the same as that used by Robert E. Park and subsequent sociologists. The sociological meaning of the term normally implies some kind of minority status, or of social deviance. The marginal man is he who hovers on the borderline between those who are in and those who are out, and his behaviour is sometimes motivated by a desire for greater absorption into the dominant community, or at least for greater grudging respect from that community.

Our sense of marginality has things in common with the sociological sense. But it is not our intention to imply any kind of deviance in the status of the Sudan, or lack of acceptance of the Sudan by this or that group. In the ultimate analysis we use the term marginality to denote specific traits in the Sudan which place it significantly in an intermediate category between two distinct sectors of Africa. Sometimes the intermediacy gives the Sudan a double identity as in her capacity as both an African country in a racial sense and an Arab country in a cultural sense. But essentially the notion of marginality we intend is that which places the Sudan on a frontier between two distinct African universe: a frontier which shares some of the characteristics of both of those universes.

THE ARABS AS AFRO-ASIANS

The marginality of the Sudan as between the Arabs and the Africans has links with the marginality of the Arabs themselves, as between Africa and Asia. The Arabs as a race defy continentalistic classification, distributed as they are on both sides of what divides Asia from Africa.

In his more parochialist days (and before the break-up between Egypt and Syria) Chief Awolowo of Nigeria once asserted:

> The United Arab Republic, the pet creature of Nasser, which has one foot in Africa and another in the Middle East, is the very antithesis of a workable African community.[1]

This sort of reasoning is connected with the sentiment which made Nkrumah assert that: 'No accident of history can ever succeed in turning an inch of African soil into an extension of any other continent.'

Nkrumah had in mind the kind of integrationist claims made by France about Algeria, or the claims of Portugal that Angola and Mozambique were part of Portugal. But could North Africa also be regarded as a westward extension of the Arabian Peninsula?[2]

One possible answer is that it depends upon what proportion of the Arab world is now in Africa and how much of it is still outside. At the time of the Arab conquest in the seventh century, it was indeed true that the Arabian Peninsula was extending itself into the Fertile Crescent and into Africa. But had not the balance of preponderance now changed between the different segments? In some ways is this not the equivalent of the change in relationship between England and the United States? The 'mother country' is now overshadowed by her former imperial extension and the danger now is of Britain becoming an extension of the United States, rather than the other way round.[3]

Does the analogy hold in the relationship between Arab Africa and the rest of the Arab world? It certainly holds as between the old Arabian Peninsula proper on one side and Arab Africa and the Fertile Crescent combined on the other. Countries of the peninsula proper, Saudi Arabia especially, from which the Arab invasions of the seventh century originated, are now overshadowed by inter-Arab influence, perhaps by even Iraq and Syria on their own. But in the context of African exclusiveness we would need to put the Arabian Peninsula and the Fertile Crescent together on one side and distinguish them from Arab Africa on the other side of the Red Sea. Yet even here the balance of preponderance is on Africa's side. As Boutros-Ghali put it in a book published in 1963: 'It must not be forgotten that 60% of the Arab community and 72% of the Arab land are in Africa.'[4]

In other words, the situation was such that it had become easier to think of the rest of the Arab world as an extension of Arab Africa than the other way round. But whatever the preponderance, the main issue here is that the Arabs as a race cannot easily be classified either as Asians or as Africans in exclusive terms. In fact Pan-Africanism itself became a major paradox precisely because it involved the Arabs. Pan-Africanism was at once continentally exclusive (in that only African status were eligible) and at the same time a link between sub-Sahara Africa and the world of *Asian* nationalism. The marginality of the Arabs as a people who are neither entirely Asian nor entirely African was decisive in giving the Pan-African movement the paradoxical quality of being both Afro-centric in intention and Afro-Asian in some of its consequences. Tom Mboya of Kenya put his finger on the paradox when he observed:

> From my experience at Pan-African Conferences, and observing their interest in Pan-African matters, I have come to believe that the great majority of Arabs in North Africa look on themselves as African. From our side there has been increasing recognition and acceptance of the Arabs as Africans. . . But if there is hostility between Asia and Africa, there is bound to be a reflection of this conflict between the Arabs of North Africa and the Africans South of the Sahara.[5]

THE SUDANESE AS AFRO-ARABS

But if the Arabs constitute the most important link between Africa and Asia, the Sudanese constitute the most important point of contact between Arab Africa and Negro Africa. There is first the very phenomenon of racial mixture and inter-marriage in the northern parts of the Sudan, coupled with the fact that a large proportion of Arab Sudanese are in fact Arabised Negroes, rather than ethnically Semitic. For many of them the Arabness is a cultural acquisition, rather than a racial heredity.

It is, therefore, the Sudanese more than any other group of Arabs that have given the Arabs a decisive Negro dimension in this racial sense. The distinction between Arabs and Negro-Africa is not dichotomous, but has the complexity of a continuum. That was one reason why the Organization of African Unity is in its composition, 'multi-pigmentational', instead of being a straight division between black Africa and the so-called 'white Africa of the North.' As we have indicated earlier, that Arabs defy continentalistic generalisations, we should remember that the Arabs as a race also defy straight pigmentational classifications. They vary in colour from white Arabs of Syria and Lebanon, brown Arabs of the Hadramaut, to the black Arabs of the Sudan. Within Africa itself, the range of colour among Arabs is also from white to black, though each colour cannot be as smoothly allocated to a specific area. But the stamp of blackness on Arabism comes pre-eminently from the Sudan. The Sudan has made the biggest single contribution to the fact that Arabism includes a Negro dimension. This is the sort of thing which has often impressed American Negroes on their trips through Africa. In the United States the divide between white men and Negroes is more emphatic. While it is possible to meet Negroes who are almost white, it would be impossible to think of an Anglo-Saxon American who was partly black. The dominant group was more purist in its insistence on retaining its own skin personality, but in Africa the continuum between Arab and Negro is smoother, and the Sudan especially has helped to give it this smoothness. And so W.E.B. Dubois, the great American Negro founding father of Pan-Africanism, could make the following observation:

> Anyone who has travelled in the Sudan knows that most of the 'Arabs' he has met are dark skinned, sometimes practically black, often have negroid features, and hair that may be almost Negro in quality. It is then obvious that in Africa the term 'Arab' . . . is often misleading. The Arabs were too nearly akin to Negroes to draw an absolute colour line.[6]

But it is not only the racial mixture and general acculturation in the North which makes the Sudan an important point of contact between Arabism and Negroism. There is also the division between Northern Sudan and the South, giving the country a segment which was not Arabised even culturally.

Indeed, the Sudan as a whole is not quite as Arabised as some northern Sudanese would sometimes prefer. On the basis of the 1955–56 census it has been estimated that of the thirteen million peoples of the Sudan, about forty per cent were Arab, thirty per cent southern, thirteen per cent western, twelve per cent Beja and Nuba, three per cent Nubian, and the rest were foreigners and miscellaneous. When using the language criterion, fifty-two per cent were Arabic-speaking and forty-eight per cent spoke other languages. The twelve years since that census was taken might have made some significant differences in those percentages. In any case, although the Sudan might not be quite as Arab as it is sometimes imagined, what matters sometimes is the phenomenon of self-conception among Sudanese of influence. Distinguished Arabic-speakers of the North, and distinguished southerners, have all been known to exaggerate the ethnic chasm which separates northerners from the peoples of the South. In the words of the then President of the Sudan African National Union (SANU), Aggrey Jaden, at the March 1965 Khartoum Conference on the Southern Sudan:

> The Sudan falls sharply into two distinct areas, both in geograhical area, ethnic group, and cultural systems. The Northern Sudan is occupied by a hybrid Arab race who are united by their common language, common culture, and common religion; and they look to the Arab world for their cultural and political inspiration. The people of the Southern Sudan, on the other hand, belong to the African ethnic group of East Africa. They do not only differ from the hybrid Arab race in origin, arrangement and basic systems, but in all conceivable purposes. . . There is nothing in common between the various sections of the community; nobody of shared beliefs, no identity of interests, no local signs of unity and above all, the Sudan has failed to compose a single community.[7]

This is obviously a hyperbolic formulation of the differences between the Northern Sudan and the South. But when we are discussing the Sudan from the point of view of marginality, this very exaggeration has its uses. For it asserts that one and the same country is, in one area completely Negro, and, in another, completely Arab. The enclosure of these two ethnic personalities within a single territorial entity is itself an approximation to the concept of Afro-Arab marginality for the Sudan. Whether we take the Sudan as a dichotomous duality of the kind claimed by Aggrey Jaden, or we take it as an ethnic continuum, or as an inter-racial mixture, the country still emerges as a paradigm case of an Afro-Arab dual identity.

THE RELIGIOUS FRONTIER

But when we refer to a cultural difference between Northern and Southern Sudan, the difference inevitably includes a religious dimension. No other African country has been as closely identified with a schism between Islam and Christianity as the Sudan has been. The Nigerian Civil War has indeed been sometimes interpreted in neo-religious terms—in terms of vigorous Christian Ibos suffering the wrath of previously humiliated and profoundly conservative Muslim Northerners. But the naiveté of interpreting the Nigerian Civil War in these terms is so easy to expose that only a few popular columnists would now press it. The majority of Federal soldiers are not Muslim, nor of course is the Head of the Federal Government, Colonel Gowon. For the time being the Western Region of Nigeria is on the side of the Federal Government, and that region is decisively Christian in power-structure.

But the naiveté of interpreting the Sudanese problem in religious terms is not quite as easy to expose. Much of the bad press that the Sudanese Government has received in many countries has rested in part on the assumption that southern resistance was aroused as a response to religious persecution. It is true that the figures of the different religious denominations in the South far from established that the South was basically Christian. In 1955 it was estimated that there were 12,000 to 23,000 southern Muslims; 16,500 to 17,500 northern Muslims resident in the three southern provinces; 25,000 to 30,000 Protestants in the South and 180,000 to 200,000 Catholics.[8]

Perhaps only the arrogance of a Christian press could describe a population which is only one-tenth Christian as being 'basically Christian.' What gave the Government's policy the appearance of religious persecution were the expulsions of missionaries and the introduction of measures to put the mission schools under the control of the Ministry of Education. Government control of mission schools is a principle which has been adopted in different forms by other governments in Africa, including the Uganda Government. On the issue of expelling Christian missionaries, again this has not been unknown in Christian countries elsewhere in Africa. A distinction needs to be drawn between religious toleration in the sense of allowing nationals to practise their own religion, and toleration in the sense of allowing missionaries from *outside* to propagate that religion on a particular scale (two-thirds of the missionaries in the Sudan used to be Italians; the rest had been a mixture of predominantly Protestant Europeans).

It is true that there are some dangers in the feelings sometimes expressed by northerners that there is enough division between the two parts of the country without creating a sizable Christian enclave 'within' a Muslim society. But the reasoning is not devoid of sense if it is assessed from the point of view of the demands for national integration. The argument here is that if the southerners have to have their traditional African ways changed, they had better be changed in the direction of greater homogeneity with the North. And this means Arabi-zation and Islamization, rather than Italianization in religious terms. It makes sense, therefore, that governmental policy, committed to the reduction of differences between North and South, should have prescribed the teachings of Islamic students in southern schools.

Western commentators do sometimes assume that while it is fair game to let Christian missionaries loose among simple African villagers, it is sometimes approaching religious persecution to let Muslim missionaries loose within the same population. And so the old idea of making the southern provinces of the Sudan an exclusive preserve of Christian missionaries was seldom challenged. As James S. Coleman put it in referring to a dominant trend in Western attitudes at large:

> Tropical Africa held a special attraction for the [Christian] missionary. The heathen was his target, and of all human groups the Africans were believed to be the most heathen.[9]

In the southern provinces of the Sudan this policy assumed monopolistic dimensions. Islam was deliberately kept out even to the extent of discouraging Muslim names among the southern population, or Muslim dress. In the rest of Africa the great instruments of national or cultural integration have often been the merchants and traders. The spread of certain important African languages or other cultural traits has often been due to the disseminating role of merchants. But in the Sudan the British took a decisive stand. As Sir Douglas Newbold, the Governor of Kordofan in the years 1932–1938, put it once in blunt simplicity: 'We don't want to introduce Arab merchants from the North.'[10]

Given this desire then to bridge the gulf between the North and the South on the withdrawal of British Rule, it was almost inevitable that the North should seek to break the educational and proselytizing monopoly which Christian missions had enjoyed for so long. This determination was accentuated by the memory of the mutinies which broke out on independence as southern dissidents sought to detach the region from the country as a whole if southern autonomy could not be assured otherwise.

It is true that the northerners drifted into excesses in their enthusiasm for greater integration. Several missions were reported to have been told that they were not to treat patients, although no alternative medical facilities were in fact available for the populations concerned. There were also bizarre reports about Christian missionaries being expected to teach Muslim theology.[11]

And then the sheer military repression which has lasted for a decade has some times been ruthless and devoid of adequate moral restraint. The process of integrating the South with the North may not have made much progress in the first decade after independence. It might even have been a case of two steps backwards, one step forward: by no means the most effective way of reaching one's destination if that destination is ahead rather than to the rear.

When on this issue of religion the Sudan and Uganda are classified as one historical entity, a different kind of continuum manifests itself. In Uganda, too, religion has for generations played a part in complicating political issues. Protestants, Catholics and Muslims have competed with each other in Uganda in order to secure greater influence in the nation's affairs. It has been suggested that Islam was once a unifying force in Uganda: it unified Protestants and Catholics into a single political posture. And just as an Arab government and European missionaries have been more recently vying for the control of Southern Sudan, so did Arab settlers and European immigrants struggle for supremacy in Uganda towards the end of the last century. In the words of an official of the British East India Company in 1888 when Arab influence was on the ascendancy in Buganda: 'These events render the question now paramount: Is Arab or European power henceforth to prevail in Central Africa?'[12]

This was, perhaps, the time of maximum amity between Protestants and Catholics in Uganda. When Lugard came he managed to rally the Christian armies of both denominations, and put an end to the Muslim threat and the power of the Muslim Party. But in so doing Lugard 'Thus dissolved the last link binding the Catholic and the Protestants.'[13]

In different forms the division between Protestants and Catholics in Uganda persisted to Independence. Indeed, some of the political parties in Uganda were supposed to be organised on a basis of denominational loyalty. Thus the Democratic Party in Uganda came to be identified with Catholics and to attract wide support from Catholic voters. The party was initially also backed by some of the leaders of the Catholic Church. The Uganda People's Congress, on the other hand, was to some extent identified with Protestants, though this identification was less easily demonstrable than the identification of the Democratic Party with Catholic aspirations. The situation was compounded by the emergence of Kabaka Yekka, a third party whose basis of affiliation was not denominational but regional. Kabaka Yekka—Kabaka Alone—was dedicated to the preservation of the proud autonomy and identity of the Buganda region. Within Buganda itself the Protestants were the elite denomination controlling the establishment. The Catholics were less privileged. But politically the Baganda were more Buganda nationalists than they were either Protestants or Catholics in their ultimate commitment.

The Muslims were much less important in the political sphere, though their influence was sometimes given a boost as a way of gaining support for one Christian sector against another, or for one political party against another.

In an exaggerated kind of way it has been suggested that Uganda was 'the Ireland of Africa', with its division between partisan Catholics and partisan Protestants. In reality the religious dimension is much less prominent, much less deeply rooted than it was in Ireland. Nevertheless, we can speak of Uganda as being, in part, a country of sectarian differences between one Christian denomination and another in the socio-political field.

If we turn our eyes now and look at Northern Sudan, we see sectarian politics at play too: only in this case it is between Muslim denominations, rather than between Christian ones. The political divisions in the first Republic of Sudan following independence had a marked sectarian theme. Even those political leaders who privately deplored the influence of religion on politics started by finding it necessary or expedient to associate themselves with the name of a respected Sayyid in order to win popular support. When the Independence Front, consisting mainly of the Umma party, emerged in 1945 with the support of Sayyid ʿAbd al-Rahmān al-Mahdī, leader of the Ansār (Mahdist) Sect, their opponents, the National Front, claimed the support of Sayyid ʿAlī al-Mirghanī, leader of the Khatmiyya Sect, the other major denominantion in Muslim Sudan. Sayyid ʿAlī himself, while preferring not to make public statements on political subjects, did not deny his association with the pro-Egyptian Front.

What all this means is that Sudanese politics, especially in the first few years after independence, were partly politics between Muslim denominations in competition against each other. By the same token Ugandan politics, especially in the period just before independence, but to some extent also for some time after independence, were politics between Christian denominations in competition with each other. And then between the Northern Sudan and Uganda might be placed the three provinces of Southern Sudan. The provinces constituted to some extent a line of battle between a Muslim government and Christian missions. To the north of these provinces are the politics of Muslim against Muslim. To the south of these provinces in Uganda are the politics of Christian against Christian. And the southern provinces themselves to some extent symbolise Africa's most dramatic confrontation between local Islamic authority and expatriate Christianity.

THE LIMITS OF INTEGRATION

But these inter-denominational differences in the North should not disguise one important aspect of the character of the Sudan. If you took the predominant northern region on its own as a measure, the Sudan is one of the most integrated countries in Africa. The greatest achievement of Islam and Arabic culture in Northern Sudan was, in the words of Yūsuf Fadl Hasan: 'the creation of a feeling of cohesion among the heterogeneous inhabitants of the country.'[14]

In spite of the differences between the Khatmiyya of the Eastern Sudan and the Ansār of the West, and notwithstanding significant tribal feelings among groups like the Nūba and the Beja communities, there has persisted in Northern Sudan a striking degree of national consensus.

For those who regard a capacity for some liberal competitive institutions as an index of a significant measure of national integration, the Sudan affords interesting evidence in that direction. Even the assumption of power by General 'Abbūd in 1958 was by no means an outcome of real parliamentary failure. Sudanese democracy at that time had neither stiffened into the authoritarianism of Nkrumah's regime, nor disintegrated into the corrupt anarchy of the Balewa regime in Nigeria. 'The army [in the Sudan] came to power when one coalition was collapsing and another was about to be formed. The new one between Umma and the National Unionist Party [N.U.P.] was likely to give the stability which the old one had failed to provide. Instead, the Generals took over and the pad of parliament, which softens the blows of sudden change, was lost.'[15]

One need not go quite as far as *The Economist* in the above quotation in favourably assessing the stabilising chances of an Umma-NUP coalition. The point to grasp, however, is that Sudanese democracy had not yet inherently failed when the army took over: except in the somewhat cynical and uncompromising sense that any democracy that is overthrown by soldiers is 'by definition' a failure. The peaceful poll of the February 1958 elections was taken by many observers to augur well for the future.[16]

That nine months later soldiers decided to try their hand at politicizing was not sufficient reason to dismiss the implications of that augury.

In October 1964, General 'Abbūd himself fell from power. 'Abbūd's fall was itself a triumph of public opinion in the North, and an index to some degree of meaningful national consensus. A series of demonstrations in Khartoum, some of which were led by university teachers, shattered the confidence of the military regime. In some ways the fall of 'Abbūd was the most striking manifestation yet of the democratic potential of the Sudan. It is not in every country that the military would bow to popular indignation. It is not in every country in Africa that popular indignation does express itself in spite of possible reprisals from governmental forces. It is true that the military's vulnerability as a regime was partly due to its own internal division. And yet the very divisions within the military forces seemed to have been partly connected with patriotic sentiment and with a reluctance to shed too much Sudanese blood in the streets of Khartoum. One could therefore say that the fall of 'Abbūd in October 1964, was as creditable to 'Abbūd and the military at large as it was to demonstrators in the streets demanding a return to parliamentary politics. In the conditions of Africa today, and indeed of the Middle East, soldiers are to be given national credit when they are too inhibited to slaughter too many of their compatriots.

And yet the inhibitions of the Sudan soldiers do not extend to the South. This is what dramatises the marginality of the Sudan in this area of national integration. On the one hand, the main part of the country has achieved a high degree of cultural cohesion. The North on its own could easily be a nation state in a classical European sense within little more than a generation. On the other hand, relations between the North and the South constitute one of the most acute crises of cleavage in the African Continent as a whole. Sudanese democracy in the North is by no means all that secure and could be overthrown again in the days ahead. But, then, so could French democracy today. But in France, as in the Sudan, there has persisted what *The Economist* once called 'a surprising instinct for democratic forms.'[17] And the instinct might be a measure of the people's capacity to identify with each other, and therefore to refrain from certain excesses of treatment. Yet the Arab-Sudanese democratic instinct has often failed to be effective as a deterrent against Arab brutalisation of the South.

THE SUDAN AND WEST AFRICA

If it was Islam and its culture which partly helped to give Northern Sudan its degree of homogeneity, it was also Islam which has made the Sudan one of the few countries in *Eastern* Africa which has a strong historical connection with the flow of history in *West* Africa. In fact the country today bears the name not simply of a state, but of what has been called a 'civilisation.' In the words of Roland Oliver and J. D. Fage:

> Stretching right across sub-Saharan Africa from the Red Sea to the mouth of the Senegal, and right down the central highland spine of Bantu Africa from the Nile sources to Southern Rhodesia, we find the axis of what we shall call the Sudanic civilization. The central feature of this civilization was the incorporation of the various African peoples concerned into states whose institutions were so similar that they must have derived from a common source.[18]

In some way Oliver and Fage defined the boundaries of the Sudanic civilization in a maximal sense. Saburi Biokabu and Muhammad al-Hājj define a stronger link between the Niger-Chad region on one side and the Sudan on the other. But they also see the Sudanic area as being wider than even that:'The distinction between the two regions is, of course, modern, because to the early Arab geographers, *Bilād al-Sūdān* extended from the Red Sea and the Horn of Africa in the east to the shore of the Atlantic in the west.'[19]

It would be almost true to say that the Republic of the Sudan today is, in an important sense, an extension of West Africa. In its origins the Sudanic civilization might well have spread from the north southwards, and then from the east westwards, making some of the West African kingdoms something

approaching an extension of the Sudanic heart on the Nile. This interpretation
is itself historically uncertain. But even if it were true that the Sudanic
civilization spread, in its second stage, from the east westwards, the fact remains that in West Africa there have been a *number* of nations sharing that
civilization, and there continue to be. This numerical imbalance might force
us to conclude that it is the Republic on the Nile which is an extension of West
Africa, rather than the other way round. But even if that is not admissible,
what matters is that this east-west historical link gives the Sudan one more dimension of marginality. The rising sun on the East Coast and the setting sun
on the West Coast of Africa 'both' momentarily cast rays on a slice of civilization which extends across the whole span of this part of the continent,
from the Red Sea to the Atlantic Ocean.

Controversy about the direction of ideological traffic between Eastern and
Western Sudan is something which has continued to the present day. Which
way did the ideas flow in the Sudanic belt? Biobaku and Al-Hājj first affirm
that there has been 'constant traffic between the Niger-Chad region and the
Sudan from the distant past to the present day.' The purpose of their collab-
orative paper is to attempt to show that the Fulani *Jihāds* had given rise to the
Sudanese Mahdiyya, and that the latter sought support and expansion (outside
the Sudan) mainly in the Niger-Chad region. The two authors go on to argue
that much of the Mahdist literature which was current in the Niger-Chad region in the nineteenth century found its way to the Sudan. They also claim evidence to show that the Sudanese Mahdī, Muhammad Ahmad, was influenced
by ideas from the Niger-Chad region.[20]

But whatever the origins of Mahdism, it was certainly Muhammad Ahmad
of Eastern Sudan who led the most internationally significant Mahdist movement in Africa. In any case, after the original bubble of Mahdist ideas, it became rather difficult to be sure about the direction of the ideological traffic in
this sphere of Muslim activity. Biobaku and Al-Hājj refer to the Sudan's influence on Nigeria. When the Mahdists in the Sudan were again allowed to
function under the leadership of the Mahdī's son, al-Sayyid 'Abd al-Rahmān,
there was 'almost an automatic revival of Mahdism in Nigeria.' The Nigerian
leader communicated with al-Sayyid 'Abd al-Rahmān and acted as his agent
in Nigeria. But the British authorities in Nigeria were more apprehensive than
their counterparts in the Sudan about Mahdism at that period. Malam Sa'īd,
the Nigerian leader of the movement, was therefore arrested in 1923 and deported. The British authorities in Nigeria remained sensitive to the possibilities of Mahdist uprisings, and precautions were taken insofar as this was feasible.[21]

Thomas Hodgkin has argued that Northern Nigeria for a long time remained isolated from the main stream of Islamic reform. Nevertheless, some

ideological interplay between Northern Nigeria and the Eastern Sudan was fairly constant. Even when exploring ways of reforming judicial and legal arrangements in Northern Nigeria, there remained a tendency to take a look at the Eastern Sudan for possible guide-lines on structural changes in this sphere of Islamic life.[22]

Nigeria, of course, is not the only part of West Africa that has had this kind of ideological connection with the Eastern Sudan. The former French Soudan, now Mali, has also displayed manifestations comparable to the events which have taken place in Eastern Sudan and Northern Nigeria. 'In fact, throughout the French-speaking territories of the Savannahland of West Africa, Mahdist manifestations appeared here and there, and from time to time, causing much unrest and agitation.'[23]

It is these considerations which have helped to give Eastern Sudan yet another feature of marginality: at once a piece of the Nile Valley and its heritage, and a piece of the Sudanic civilization which extends to the western coast of Africa.

THE BOUNDARY OF LANGUAGE

Finally a word about the Sudan as a country on a linguistic borderline. We might think of Africa as being divided into three main linguistic segments : English-speaking Africa; French-speaking Africa; and Arabic-speaking Africa. Of course, there is considerable overlapping between these countries, and especially as regards the Maghreb States which are at once Arabic-speaking and French-speaking. But the fascination of the Sudan is that it signifies a borderline case between English-speaking Africa and Arabic-speaking Africa, a rarer phenomenon than the Franco-Arabic duality.

Perhaps this aspect of the marginality of the Sudan has nowhere else been better illustrated than in a simple fact concerning some courses in diplomacy at Makerere University College in Uganda. For a number of years the Department of Political Science at Makerere has organized courses in diplomacy for foreign service officials from a number of African States. In reality virtually all the states that have participated in these courses, or indeed have been invited to participate in these courses, have been English-speaking states. The one exception has been the Sudan. The Makerere Diplomatic Courses have had Sudanese participation all along. This could not be explained simply in terms of the Sudan's nearness to Uganda; for Uganda has other neighbours on its borders who are not English speakers and who are not invited to participate in the Makerere courses. Nor have the Sudanese appeared particularly incongruous in a community of English-speaking Africans. They were near enough as a category to be adequately assimilated into the body of African diplomats attending the Makerere courses.

Perhaps the Anglo-Arabic marginality of the Sudan partly goes back to that historical anomaly of an Anglo-Egyptian condominium over the Sudan. The Sudan was the only country in Africa that was at one and the same time a colony of an English-speaking power and a colony of an Arabic-speaking country. In reality, of course, the imperial control was effectively exerted by Britain rather than by Egypt. But even this factor contributed towards giving meaning to the marginality. After all the English language was up against a pre-existent Arabic presence in the Sudan. It needed a strong English-speaking influence in the Sudan to give English any chance at all as a medium of intellectual discourse. It was, therefore, the preponderance of the British over the Egyptians in the condominium which helped to give the Sudan an Anglo-Arabic duality.

Today Arabic remains definitely the senior partner in this linguistic alliance. Much of the most important Sudanese business continues to be conducted in Arabic. In fact Arabic has been gaining ascendancy since the departure of the British, and has recaptured most of the educational system below university level. From the Sudan, as from India, come reports of a declining mastery of the English language; and debates range as to whether the decline is something worth worrying about. Nevertheless, English does maintain an important place in the Sudan, especially among the graduated intelligentsia.

But the place of English in the Northern Sudan is not the only factor which has given the country as a whole this linguistic marginality. There is also the place of English in the southern provinces to be taken into account. During the colonial period the educational system set up in the South was deliberately committed to the suppression of Arabic as far as possible. This was part of the presumed competition between Islamic culture and British civilisation in this area of Africa. In the words of one British administrator in the course of the preliminary discussions prior to the Juba Conference of 1947:

> We the British, who, whatever our failings, are better qualified than any other race, by tradition and taste and training, to lead primitives up the path of civic progress, are going to stand guard till the South can dispense with a guard, and I am not going to see the South dominated by an Arab civilisation in Khartoum, which is more alien to them than our own.[24]

Caught up in this battle of civilisations was the issue of the medium of education. And so 'the British official and missionary policy was to encourage the use of English rather than Arabic. . .'[25]

Since independence there has been a more concerted attempt by the Sudanese Government to give Arabic a new status in the South. Arab teachers, new Arabic curricula and increased promotion of the teaching of Arabic are all major aspects of the entire Arabisation policy pursued in the South since Independence. The place of English in the next generation of southerners may be less important than the place that English has enjoyed so far among the small group of southern intelligentsia. But whatever the future of English in the Sudan it has so far continued to give this country a quality of linguistic twilight: an intermediate stage between the universe of Arabic in Africa and the universe of the English language.

CONCLUSION

We have tried to demonstrate in this chapter that the Sudan is not simply an intermediate category between Arab Africa and Negro Africa, but is in fact marginal in a number of other ways as well. Even on the issue of Arabism in relation to Negroism there is a double level of marginality. The Arabs, as we have tried to show, are themselves a people who defy classification on the basis of continents. They have nations both in Africa and in Asia. They have a quality of being Afro-Asians.

If the Arabs are Afro-Asians, the Sudanese are Afro-Arabs, both in their internal northern mixture as Arabised Africans, and in the division between Arabic-speaking Northern Sudan and the rest of the country to the south.

As part of this cultural divide there has to be included the position of the Sudan as a focus of what is sometimes interpreted as a confrontation between Islamic Africa and Christian Africa. In reality the confrontation is between a Muslim Government and Christian Missions, or between the new policy of Arabization and the remnants of an old Christian monopoly of education in the South. This whole region of Africa downwards into Uganda has tended to include within it both inter-denominational politics within a single religion and the politics of confrontation between different creeds. The Sudan acquires a borderline quality in this religious sphere as a result.

Underlying it all is the whole issue of national integration in any case. The Sudan represents both an Africa of achieved integration and an Africa of acute structural cleavage. The achieved integration is in the North where the Sudan is well on its way towards becoming a nation-state in a classical sense if it is assessed purely in terms of the cultural homogeneity observable among northerners. But the cleavage with the south puts the Sudan also among those unhappy African countries which have acute ethnic divisions and sometimes raging civil wars.

A fourth area of marginality of the Sudan is in relation to West Africa, whereby this country shares a civilisation which stretches right across the continent, from east to west. In this fourth sense the Sudan is marginal as between the civilisations of the Nile Valley on the one hand and the Sudanic belt of cultural influence on the other. In this sense, the country is also marginal in being almost an extension of West Africa in some important respects.

Finally, we discussed the marginality of the Sudan in relation to Arabic and the English language. The country's history as an Anglo-Egyptian condominium, and its linguistic fluidity when the British took over, enabled the intellectual life of the Sudan to acquire a quality of cultural twilight.

President Nasser once placed Egypt in three concentric circles: the Arab circle, the African circle, and the Muslim one. As an exercise in role theory, President Nasser's formulation was sociologically sound.[26] But the fascination of the Sudan is, in some ways, even more complex. This is not simply a case of a single country playing a role in different circles of allegiance. In the final analysis, the fascination of the Sudan lies in her *profound intermediacy* as she compulsively absorbs into her being a diversity of traits. Parts of Africa which are otherwise vastly different have been known to experience a moment of self-recognition as they cast their eyes on the Sudan.

NOTES

1. See *Awo: The Autobiography of Chief Obafemi Awolowo*, Cambridge: Cambridge University Press, 1960, p. 312.

2. This question is also asked and discussed in similar terms in my book *Towards a Pax-Africana: A Study of Ideology and Ambition* (Weidenfeld & Nicolson & The University of Chicago Press, 1967) pp. 109–17.

3. The best literary expression of this danger is perhaps Bernard Shaw's play *The Applecart.* The United States Ambassador applies to England's King Magnus for permission to join the Commonwealth on the argument that America is a former British possession. But King Magnus saw the danger to his Kingdom, and to the leadership of Britain in the Commonwealth, should the United States become a member of the club.

4. Boutros-Ghali "The Foreign Policy of Egypt" in Joseph Black and Kenneth Thompson (1963*): Foreign Policies in a World of Change,* New York, p. 328.

5. See Mboya (1963): *Freedom and After*, Boston: Little, Brown and Co., pp. 234–35. This point is discussed in a related context in my paper "Africa and the Third World." See Mazrui (1967): *On Heroes and Uhuru Worship*, London: Longmans, pp. 212–13.

6. See Dubois (1965): *The World and Africa*, (first published 1946) New York: International Publishers, (enlarged edition), p. 184.

7. Khartoum Conference on the South, March 1965 Documents: Speech by Aggrey Jaden (mimeo), p. 4, cited by George W. Shepherd, Jr., "National Integration and

the Southern Sudan," The Journal of Modern African Studies, 42 (October 1966) 195, 196. I am indebted to this article for bibliographical guidance and some insights.

8. See *Report of the Commission of Inquiry into the Disturbances in the Southern Sudan during August 1955* Khartoum, (1956) p. See also Shepherd, op. cit., p. 196.

9. See Coleman's chapter on sub-Saharan African in The Politics of the Developing Areas (edited by Gabriel A. Almond and James S. Coleman, 1960): Princeton, N. J. Princeton University Press, p. 278.

10. See K. D. D. Henderson (1953): *The Making of the Modern Sudan*, London: Faber. Shepherd cites Muddathir 'Abdal-Rahīm' The Development of British Policy in the Sudan, 1899–1949, (Central Archives 1965) pp. 10–13, on the same question.

11. See the account in *The Economist* (London) November 19, 1960.

12. Cited by Roland Oliver (1965): *The Missionary Factor in East Africa*, London: Longmans, pp. 133–34.

13. See Oliver, *ibid.*, p. 142.

14. Yūsuf Fadl Hasan (1967): *The Arabs and the Sudan*, Edinburgh: Edinburgh University Press, p. 181.

15. See *The Economist*, November 14, 1959.

16. *The Economist*, March 15, 1958. See also, Harold F. Gosnell, "The 1958 Elections in the Sudan," *The Middle East Journal*, 15 (1958).

17. *The Economist* was referring to the Sudan. See the issue of December 7, 1957.

18. See Oliver and Fage (1962): A Short History of Africa, Penguin Library, p. 44.

19. See Biobaku and Al-Hājj (1966): "The Sudanese Mahdiyya and the Niger-Chad region," in *Islam and Tropical Africa* (ed. I. M. Lewis) published for the International African Institute by Oxford University Press, p. 429.

20. Biobaku and Al-Hājj, "The Sudanese Mahdiyya and the Niger-Chad Region," *op. cit.* pp. 426, 431.

21. See Alan Burns (1948): *History of Nigeria*, London, pp. 182 ff. Also see Biobaku and Al-Hājj, pp. 436–37.

22. For the discussion on Islamic Reform by Hodgkin see, for example, his short piece "Tradition and Reform in Muslim Africa," *West Africa* (Sept. 22, 1956.) See also Hodgkin, "Islam, History and Politics," *The Journal of Modern African Studies*, 1 (March 1963).

23. Biobaku and Al-Hājj, *op. cit.*, p. 437.

24. Letter of 5 January, 1947 from B.G.A. to the Governor of Equatoria Province, Khartoum Conference on the South, March, 1965 documents. Cited by Shepherd, *op. cit.*

25. Shepherd, *ibid.*, pp. 199–200.

26. See also the next chapter.

Chapter Ten

Africa and Egypt's Four Circles: Nasser's Legacy

Egypt will soon celebrate another anniversary of its revolution. The anniversary will take place in the shadow of an Africa vastly different from the one in which the Revolution occurred and a re-examination might perhaps be made of the Egyptian's own conception of his role in the Africa of today and in a world within which Africa is now an active participant.

In his *Philosophy of the Revolution* Gamal Abdul Nasser envisaged Egypt as the centre of three circles—that of the Arab world, that of the Muslim world and that of Africa. His involvement in African affairs, ranging from serving as guardian to Lumumba's offspring to active membership of the radical group of African States, has led to the suspicion in some quarters that it is at best in the President's ' African Circle' that Egypt's hope of leadership might lie. At least, until the Yemen exploded in the Arab world, it was argued that Abdul Nasser had become a pathetic figure of frustration both in the Muslim and in the Arab Circles, and had to turn his attention instead on Africa—of which according to his book, Egypt guarded 'the northern gateway.'

The time is now perhaps suitable to look back and see in what terms Abdul Nasser had envisaged Egypt's commitment in Africa at about the time of the Egyptian Revolution. According to his *Philosophy* the terms were:

> . . . we cannot in any way stand aside, even if we wish to, from the sanguinary and dreadful struggle now raging in the heart of the continent between five million whites and two hundred million Africans. We cannot do so for one principal and clear reason—we ourselves are in Africa.

This was a declaration of intention. The question which now arises is whether the actual performance was, until recently, so poor as to necessitate looking to 'losses in the Arab world' to explain the increased interest in Africa.

Or is the whole drive—as some would have it—a political response to Israeli successes in Africa in recent times?

Both these theories seem to ignore the fact that since everyone's interest in Africa has increased in the last few years, it is very unlikely that Abdul Nasser's attitude would have been the exception—that after declaring for years that 'the era of isolation is gone' and that it was impossible for Egypt to 'stand aside' he would have let Egypt do precisely that—more especially if his prestige in the Arab world had been high enough, or if Israel had never been created.

There is no doubt that Nasser's involvement in Africa had become greater. What major change had taken place between the time Abdul Nasser had declared himself incapable of 'standing aside' and the year 1960 when his campaign in Africa gathered special momentum?

One way of answering this question is to ask another: at the time that he wrote the *Philosophy,* from what in Africa was Abdul Nasser not prepared to 'stand aside'? In the text the answer is, of course, from the struggle against 'five million whites.' The measure of his success is that virtually no white settler in Africa has, for a long time now, considered Abdul Nasser as a neutral in that struggle.

Paradoxically enough, what has changed since Abdul Nasser's pledge is that with so much of Africa already free from imperial rule, the villain of the piece is becoming more and more the white settler himself, rather than the colonial powers and their policies. What this has meant is that the struggle against settler privileges is no longer distinctively nationalistic in the adherents it attracts nor is it peculiarly anti-Western in dynamic. The Colonial Office in London was responsible for breaking up the Rhodesian Federation; Mr. Macmillan publicly expressed his disapproval of *apartheid* in South Africa; and General de Gaulle virtually became an ally of the F.L.N. against the die-hard *colons* of Algeria.

Posing as the champion of the rights of those still under European rule may have been well enough for Egypt for as long as she was one of the few sovereign States on the continent, and at that point Egypt could be confident that many would look to her for leadership, rather than to Liberia or Ethiopia. But then Morocco, Tunisia, the Sudan and Ghana emerged into statehood. Of course, with every new sovereign State on the African scene Egypt found an ally in 'the struggle against colonialism.' But she also found a possible rival for the distinction of being the rallying-point of such a struggle. To put it another way, if Egypt's sovereignty once vested her with the status of a senior partner, the acquisition of sovereignty by others substituted equality for seniority in that partnership.

If the nationalist struggle aimed at precisely such an acquisition of sovereignty by the former colonial territories, why should Egypt's championship of African nationalism be expected to survive the achievement of its goal?

On this point the third All-African Peoples Conference held in Cairo in the spring of 1961 helped to throw some light. It emerged that imperialism was no longer the main threat to African interests. Its place had been taken by 'neo-colonialism'—which the resolutions adopted by the conference generally defined as 'an indirect and subtle form of domination by political, economic, social, military or technical means'—'the survival of the colonial system in spite of formal recognition of political independence.'

The concept was certainly pregnant with possibilities. It introduced both a basis of continuity for anti-colonialist positions and a framework for relating those positions to other roles made necessary by the acquisition of sovereign statehood. For example, one answer to neo-colonialism is to balance one's economic dependence on the West with aid or trade with the East. For this kind of balance only the policy of 'Positive Neutralism' or 'Non-alignment' is considered tenable. And yet positive neutralism is at the same time a way of asserting that a country is not already a victim of neo-colonialism nor being manipulated within alignments. It follows from this that positive neutralism is regarded as both the badge of freedom from neo-colonialism now and a shield against neo-colonialism in the immediate future—pending the attainment of economic maturity at home.

This has opened up a whole new ' Circle' within which Egypt might seek leadership; a Circle not catered for or expounded upon in *The Philosophy of the Revolution.* This is the Neutralist Circle, for which the allegedly more precise term has of late been ' Non-alignment.'

Here again Egypt's geographical position and historical connections place her in a position which could conceivably be portrayed as a ' centre' of that Circle. It is worth recalling that it was to 'Afro-Asians' that China sought to 'justify' her position in her conflict with India. This was, of course, mainly because the Circle of the Non-aligned so far consisted of primarily Afro-Asian countries. Collectively the Egyptians are well qualified as an Afro-Asian voice. They are Africans to the extent that their country stands at the northern gateway of the continent. They are Asians to the extent that the Arabian peninsula from which they claim their spiritual—and at times 'racial' descent—is classified as part of Asia. And they are ' Afro-Asians' both because of the above factors and because of the additional (though related factor) that the Arabs as a race defy simple classification as Asians or Africans, distributed as they are in nation-states across both Asia and Africa. To these qualifications must be added the additional, though very different one—that historically Egypt has had associations with Eastern and Mediterranean Europe from which a European neutralist has emerged in the person of President Tito.

The idea of basing a country's role in the world on historical connections, geographical situation and racial or linguistic affinities is, of course, by no means uniquely Egyptian. The British equivalent of Nasser's Circles, for example, is the view of Britain at once as a European country, as a Commonwealth country and as an 'Anglo-Saxon' or English-speaking country with a special relationship with the United States. In all these three British circles, Britain has at times been no more modest than Abdul Nasser in viewing herself as at least a moral leader—including the idea of the British playing 'Greeks' to American 'Romans.' But whereas Britain seeks to be fully accepted within each Circle by pledging full 'commitment' to each, Egypt seeks to be accepted by affirming ' uncommitedness' or relative freedom of action even within the Circles she wishes to influence. On this hinges the new distinction that Abdul Nasser has drawn between Egypt as a Revolution and Egypt as a State—the former feeling itself free to appeal to the peoples of other countries over the heads of their Governments, the latter feeling itself bound by the shackles of diplomacy.

All this is linked with the search for non-European or non-Western approaches for solving Egypt's own problems at home. And in her concept of 'Arab Socialism' Egypt is now seeking to make herself a model for the policy of ' indigenous answers for indigenous problems.' This domestic 'uncommitedness' is the other side of the coin of ' Neutralism' in foreign relations. It was Algeria's Ben Youseff Ben Khedda who best defined this relationship between internal and external non-alignment when he said:

> Non-alignment implies for each nation the right to establish the type of Government it desires, to freely choose its regime, its economic and social system, and its way of life—in short, to act in accordance with its own guiding spirit unhampered by any pressure from outside.

And musing over Western failures to understand this aspiration, Abdul Nasser was to add: 'People used to say that I was a Communist. Now we read the same thing about Guinea and Sekou Toure.'

Countries like India may themselves restrict their 'non-alignment' to external policy while retaining a basically Western system internally. But 'indigenous' models of Governments are respected even by those who do not seek to devise them for themselves—and Abdul Nasser's model is one more card in the bid for the kind of prestige which throws up leaders within a Circle.

But is the Circle of the externally non-aligned worth leading, after India's experience with China? A leading Indian newspaper, pained by the Indian predicament, was reported to have asked: 'Where are our friends? Where is Tito, Nkrumah, Nasser, Sukarno and all the rest?' The newspaper might well have reasoned that China would have thought twice about violating India's territorial integrity if India had powerful allies to come to her help. The neutralist abroad, on the other hand, might have reasoned that if, after thinking twice, China still decided to invade India and automatically involved the Western Bloc, the crisis for the world would have been greater. And with India as a declared military ally of the West, Russia would hardly have been inclined to retreat into passive embarrassment and relative neutrality in the dispute. India's previous non-alignment, in other words, mitigated the explosive potentialities of her troubles for the world at large, even if it did not eliminate those potentialities altogether. And within the relative calm, Abdul Nasser was among the first to suggest that, short of a prolonged conflict, the two countries might use the non-aligned countries as mediators. He was joined by Tubman of Liberia in this offer of mediation. 'Non-alignment does not mean that we isolate ourselves from problems,' Abdul Nasser had told the Belgrade Conference in 1961, 'It means that we should contribute positively to the consolidation of understanding.' He attempted to apply this aggrieved maxim even when the party was his own friend, Pandit Nehru.

On Cuba the United Arab Republic was also quick to respond—and again in co-operation with another African country. As soon as the American blockade of Cuba was on, the U.A.R. and Ghana were seeking some compromise Security Council resolution which would make it possible for the two big Powers to agree. Along with the Secretary-General, U Thant, the non-aligned in the United Nations (acting on the assumption that the big Powers wanted to avoid war), explored the possibilities of at least helping one of them to save face and so avoid war. For Cuba herself there was some sympathy, but it was a sympathy qualified by the fact that Cuba had violated one of the fundamentals of non-alignment—she had allowed a foreign nuclear base on her soil. In other words, even if the Sino-Indian dispute were accepted as evidence against the wisdom of non-alignment, the humiliation of Cuba was a vindication of at least one tenet of non-alignment. In the autumn of 1962 the United States would presumably have let Cuba alone if Cuba had contented herself with non-alignment—and without foreign bases.

Of course Cuba had to defend herself after the attempted invasion of April of the previous year. But so had Egypt after the Suez adventure of 1956. The United States just before the Anglo-French military action had attempted to 'blackmail' Egypt out of a particular foreign policy position by withdrawing the Aswan High Dam offer. Nevertheless when the British and the French followed this up with military action they did so against the wishes of the United States. This resulted in a tremendous boost to Egypt's prestige among the neutralists all over the world—not least because, unlike Cuba five years later, Egypt vigorously maintained her non-alignment even after economic blackmail by the United States and military bullying by Britain and France. Some time later, when Communism seemed to be threatening Iraq, Abdul Nasser was up in arms against it—and resenting 'Soviet interference in Arab affairs.' He was then to emphasize that distinction to which many neutralists would subscribe—that 'our people do not have to like Communism to feel friendship and sympathy for Russia.'

What all this meant in terms of qualification for leadership in the Neutralist Circle was that in the Suez and Iraqi affairs Abdul Nasser had demonstrated his refusal to be silenced through economic blackmail or forced into an alignment because of aggression by members of one of the World Blocs.

It remains to be seen whether India's non-alignment would survive China's aggression, as Egypt's non-alignment survived Anglo-French invasion—or whether India would succumb, as Cuba succumbed, to formal entanglement with one of the Blocs. So far it is still true to say that if Tito is the neutral of Europe, Abdul Nasser has become the exemplar of Arab and African neutralism combined. With this strength he once sought to make Tito, Nehru and himself the trinity of the new religion in foreign affairs. He still manages to get the neutralist light focused on Cairo, and has at times been in alliance with Belgrade in the vision of 'the Common Market of the Uncommitted.' The reasoning here is that resistance to neo-colonialism and military entanglements should not be undermined by the rising tariff walls of the Common Markets of others.

And what had Israel been doing in the meantime? She was, of course, engaged in active aggression with Britain and France at the time of Suez. Since then the U.A.R.'s argument has been .to emphasize that Suez was no isolated instance of Israel's identity of interests with Europe at large. On the more innocent level there was Israel's representation on the Council of Europe as at least an observer. On the more suspicious level, however, *The Arab Observer* was not slow to note David Ben Gurion's announcement on a visit to Holland in i960 that Israel was a 'European State' and ought to be included in the European Common Market. The major issue of the Arab Circle—Israel—thus makes an energetic intrusion into the Circle of Neutralist fighters against neo-colonialism.

And to bring the Israeli issue into the African Circle as well, Abdul Nasser has argued the case—with some success in terms of converts at the historic Casablanca Conference—that since Israel's own resources were 'not sufficient to balance her own budget,' her aid to the African countries came from other sources. In the words of the official *Arab Observer,*

The money comes from the imperialist Powers, which have been giving Israel financial assistance to the tune of four hundred million dollars annually . . . The imperialists, knowing very well that they are already branded in Africa and that they would be spotted at once if they dealt their cards openly, are hiding behind Israel which is ostensibly a small Power and cannot afford to have imperialist designs.

The argument depends for its persuasiveness on the strong suggestion of indirectness in the concept of 'neo-colonialism'—the Western Powers manipulating African countries through 'the tool,' Israel. To reinforce the argument, attention was drawn to the record of Israel in the United Nations on the issue of Algeria—a record which, in its totality, could conceivably have been interpreted as being partly the outcome of 'excessive dependence' by Israel on France. It is not such a jump as it may appear from portraying Israel as a victim of neo-colonialism (deserving pity) to portraying her as its 'tool' (deserving condemnation)—since it is almost part of the definition of a ' victim' of neo-colonialism that she can be manipulated as a 'tool' against others. Even on the Congo at the time of the Lumumba controversy, Israel was caught on the side of 'the enemies of African Nationalism.' The Cairo line was: ' If the Israeli chiefs really supported the Africans, then why did they not announce their support for the legal power in the Congo, the body on whom depends the victory of the Congo over her imperialist enemies? Instead, the Israeli chiefs supported Moise Tshombe, Prime Minister of Katanga.'

The major enemy of the Arab Circle had thus been made relevant for attack within the African as well as the Neutralist Circles. It may have been a little premature for the United Arab Republic to congratulate herself that 'after the Casablanca Conference Israel has become an African and not only an Arab question.' But what the Conference's denunciation of Israel did illustrate was Egypt's apparent genius for coordinating her external relations in such a way that the advantage of one aspect of those relations could be utilized to reinforce another.

What, however, of that side of Egypt's external relations in regard to which she saw herself as the centre of a Muslim Circle? Jay Waltz of the *New York Times* reported to his paper in January 1961, that 'as part of its drive to win influence in Africa, the U.A.R. plans to exploit Cairo's considerable resources in Muslim teaching and culture.'

This, however, presupposes not only that Egypt has such resources but also that they are great enough to be decisive in shaping the policy of winning influence in other countries. This, in turn, presupposes that there are forces in those other countries which would make it meaningful for Egypt to use these particular resources for gaining influence—that is to say, they must be countries with at least some potential responsiveness to ' Islamic teaching and culture.'

One way, then, of analysing the subject is to take each of the presuppositions in turn and see if together they form a pattern sufficiently meaningful to use as a basis for evaluating this as an instance of Egypt's skill at cross-utilization of the assets of each Circle.

As regards Egypt's Islamic resources there is a sense in which these have lost some prestige in the Arab world generally. With the increasing modernization of so much of the Muslim world, great learning is rapidly ceasing to be automatically equated with religious learning as it was in the past. The occupational structure of many Muslim communities is beginning to change quite perceptibly, and parents are increasingly tending to find a greater incentive for sending their children to secular schools where they can learn some of the new 'skills' than for preparing them for theological discussions in the local mosque between the Maghreb and Ish-a prayers. The young man who returns from a period of study in the United States, Oxford or Paris arrives with a little more prestige than the fresh graduate from Al-Azhar University in Cairo.

A related factor is that this secularization of social prestige and of life generally has taken place in Egypt itself to an even greater degree than almost anywhere else in the Muslim world outside Turkey. Here, then, emerges a paradox in the situation. Al-Azhar has lost some of its hold on the imagination of Muslims abroad because the values of these Muslims have become less religiously-oriented; but it is also losing its hold abroad because Egypt herself is ceasing to be thought of as a model of Islamic society. In other words, just as to the very unorthodox Muslims abroad Al-Azhar is a bastion of obscurantism, so to the very orthodox it is becoming untrustworthy on religious matters since it belongs to a country whose way of life is—if Egyptian magazines and films are anything to go by—being increasingly secularized. The very reforms in religious outlook which have occurred within Al-Azhar itself have alienated the more orthodox Muslims abroad.

All this, however, should not be overemphasized. There may be fewer Muslims today who look to Al-Azhar as the apex of learning, but in absolute numbers, and in terms of geographical distribution, Al-Azhar is producing more graduates for the Islamic world than it has ever done before. Those very reforms that the University has undergone, while alienating the more orthodox, have attracted many. To use the words of Virginia Thompson and Richard Adloff in their *French West Africa*, 'the fact that, as of 1952, 105 French West African students . . . were attending Al-Azhar University indicates the appeal of the radical, nationalistic and reformist doctrines taught there.'

It would probably be wrong to suggest that there is overt and purposeful political indoctrination by the university itself. But the very setting of the university in the heart of Egypt, with all the atmosphere of dynamic nationalism, provides a meeting point between the nationalistic, anti-Western forces of the Arab and African Circles on the one hand, and the aggressively religious forces of the Muslim Circle round Al-Azhar on the other.

Indeed, this interplay of anti-colonialist and Pan-Islamic forces in Cairo itself is, in a sense, a microcosm of what is happening in many parts of Sub-Saharan Africa. And yet, Jay Waltz of the *New York Times* both oversimplified the issue and overstated his case when he suggested some time ago that the United Arab Republic had ' decided to push as hard as possible the argument that Christianity is European and Western and therefore somehow tainted with "imperialism" [while] Islam, on the other hand, is to be presented as a natural faith for free Africa.' What he oversimplified was the extent to which it was open to Egypt to pursue this line of propaganda without risking the alienation of important sections of African opinion.

This is not to deny the temptation inherent in the phenomenon of the spread of Islam in Africa. There is, first of all, the very rapidity of the spread. In 1955 a Lutheran World Congress at Geneva was already expressing alarm at this. Little more than a year later British Methodists were calling for a new and vigorous evangelism to cope with the phenomenon. Early in 1957 the Paris Academy of Political and Moral Sciences received estimates—-based on official statistics—from Mgr. Bressoles to the effect that between 1940 and 1946 the annual increase of professing Muslims in French Africa was 200,0005 that in all Africa the number of Muslims had increased between 1931 and 1951 from 40 million to 80 million in comparison with a Roman Catholic increase in the same period from five million to fifteen; and that of the 130 million inhabitants of Sub-Saharan Africa 28 million were then Muslims, 13 million Catholics, 4 million Protestants and 85 million pagans.

Four years later there were estimates that 'for every African who turns from pagan gods to Christianity, an estimated ten become Muslims.' Even the American evangelist, Billy Graham, returning from Africa in i960, sounded the warning that he had met 'a number of people who think that Africa may eventually be overwhelmed by Islam.'

These reports about the increasing numbers of Muslims in Africa, even if they are at times exaggerated and indifferent to the distinction between the natural increase of a Muslim population and the addition of new converts, would certainly constitute in themselves a temptation to the United Arab Republic.

Another temptation—related, of course, to the rising numbers of Muslims—is the ease with which Christianity can be portrayed as 'the religion of the white man.' Thus ex-Chief Albert Luthuli, the South African Nobel Peace Prize winner, could lament that Christianity was being misunderstood:

> The average African says white man is the cause of all his troubles. He does not
> discriminate between white men and see that some come here for material gain
> and others come with the message of God.

As a citizen of South Africa, Luthuli should have realized that to avoid misunderstanding Christianity, the average African would have to go even further in 'discriminating'—a recurrent word—between white men. Even among those who ' come with the message of God,' the average African would have to discriminate between Calvinists of the Dutch Reformed Church with their open support for separate racial development on the one hand and, on the other, denominations that declare such a policy to be un-Christian. And between these latter in turn the 'average African' would have to discriminate between those who have calmly acquiesced in 'injustices' against Africans (until the Africans themselves started kicking) and those who spoke up for Africans before African nationalism was born.

The 'average African' is further called upon to discriminate between empire-building for the sake of 'the white man's burden' and empire-building for economic exploitation—the missionary being concerned with the former and the settler and trader with the latter. Here again, the distinction is not an easy one to make. One might not go quite as far as Jomo Kenyatta is supposed to have gone once when he reportedly lamented: 'When the white man came to Kenya we had the land and they had the Bible. And now? We have the Bible and they have the land.' Nevertheless, even if the missionary is acquitted of the charge of being an accomplice in the economic exploitation of Africa, it is difficult to acquit him of the degrading implications that flow from the idea of 'the white man's burden.' As James S. Coleman put it in his contribution to *The Politics of the Developing Areas*, 'Tropical Africa had a special attraction for the missionary. The heathen was his target, and of all human groups, the Africans were believed to be the most heathen.

With the rise of nationalism in sub-Saharan Africa there has been a psychological rebellion against the inferiority complex that was built up under this system. Some of the atrocities committed against missionaries in the Congo are, at least in part, explained in terms of this rebellion against the days of what Colin Legum has called 'the Belgian attempt to enforce Christianity on the Congolese.'

One must, of course, be careful not to interpret every African act against Christian churchmen as an act against Christianity. The temporary expulsion in 1962 of the Bishop of Accra, for example, was to be condemned primarily as a violation of freedom of speech rather than as a case of religious persecution—as an old sin of Nkrumah's regime rather than an ominously new one. In other words, the Bishop was temporarily expelled less because of an African distrust of Christianity than because of African sensitivity to criticism from non-Africans.

And yet there is no denying African disillusionment, here and there, with Christian missionaries generally. While Christianity in Ghana was courageously admonishing Nkrumah, Christianity in Southern Rhodesia had seemed at times to have seized on the principle of keeping politics out of the pulpit not because it believed in it but because it found Government policies there acceptable. A Rhodesian African writer in *Zimbabwe News,* the international organ of a banned nationalist party of Southern Rhodesia, may not have been conspicuously out of touch with general African opinion when he wrote: 'We have lost faith [in the missionaries] wholly because of the role they played in suppressing the truth in schools.'

And in French Africa some years ago observers like Thompson and Adloff were already noting that' radical African students view missionaries as the acolytes of imperialism and as bulwarks of colonialism . . .'

To a Muslim there is an element of poetic—if not divine—justice in all this. In British East Africa the major Muslim grievance against Christian missionaries was for years that Christian missionaries used the history of the Arab slave trade in that area to turn Africans against Islam. As recently as September 1960, the author took part in a discussion by Muslims in Mombasa, Kenya, on 'the fallacy of blaming a religion for the sins of those who professed to follow it.'

On the opposite coastline of Africa not much could, of course, be made of the device of identifying Islam with slavery since most of the external slave trade which the West Coast knew was conducted by Christians from Europe. Instead, the following argument was substituted (as it was by J. J. Cooksey and Alexander McLeish in *Religion and Civilization in West Africa):* 'The Berber brought Islam with them from the North, and propagated it among the Northern Negro peoples by the weighty argument of the sword.' From this flowed the line that Islam believed in conversion by the sword; the logic involved being that since the conquerors were Muslims, and proclaimed 'Allah' in their very conquests, Islam was to be equated with the sword.

Where the predicament of the Christian missions in Africa today can be viewed, at least by a Muslim, as a kind of poetic justice is that the same faulty logic is now being invoked against Christianity: 'Since the imperialists were Christians, and proclaimed the white man's Christian burden in the very process of empire-building, Christianity is to be equated with imperialism.'

When to this is added the African search for an 'African Personality,' the rebellion against 'Westernism' extends to the religion that came with it. As in the psychology of the Circle of Neutralism, there is here a groping for the best means of being 'non-Western.'

All this, however, should help Islam only in the negative sense. It may explain why proportionately fewer and fewer Africans turn to Christianity. It might tempt Abdul Nasser to join in discrediting Christian missions. But what could help him put Islam forward as a substitute? Why, for example, is there no large-scale disillusionment with religion as such and a growth instead of extensive atheism? Alternatively, why—if an 'African Personality' is to be emphasized—don't the animists remain animists?

The question is not easy to answer except in very general terms. One relevant factor against any growth of atheism or agnosticism is that essentially these are products of a sophisticated society with a high level of education. In any case, if Christianity is 'Western' so, surely, is atheism—certainly modern agnosticism.

Linked with this foreign origin is the fact that the life of the average African is so closely bound up with what is spiritual that he is unlikely to turn against all forms of religious life just because one form has become identified with colonialism.

More specifically in support of Islam at least when contrasted with Christianity is the case that the editor of an Afrikaans paper *(Dagbreek en Sondagnuus),* put before the Annual Congress of the South African Bureau of Racial Affairs some years ago. Mr. W. van Fleerden's case was:

> Seemingly, the simple principles of the Mohammedan doctrine have a particular attraction for Africa's Negro and Bantu populations. It has the further appeal for them that it recognizes no colour differences. But many observers believe that the most important reason for Islam's success lies in the absence of numerous churches and sects (such as among Christians) which, to the uninitiated, preach confusingly different doctrines.

Here, then, in Islam's favour are the assets of simplicity, of racial integration before God, and of greater consensus between denominations.

As against the tribal religions there is in Islam the attraction of belonging to a world-wide brotherhood which includes countries which have been right in the forefront of the fight against imperialism. It may not have passed unnoticed that the 'most nationalistic' Governments in Africa today—those with the Casablanca spirit—represent predominantly Muslim populations. These are, of course, the United Arab Republic, Mali, Morocco, Guinea and Algeria. (Ghana was the odd-one out in the Casablanca grouping, though the country nevertheless has a sizeable Muslim minority.)

The spread of Islam and the psychological forces at work may indeed tempt a Muslim country like the United Arab Republic to ' push hard the argument' that Christianity is imperialistic and Islam the 'rightful' religion of free Africa. And yet such a line of argument would be faced with the fact that many members of the new elite in Africa are, in fact, Christians—even if all around them they see Muslim numbers rising. The missionaries may have damned themselves, in the way alluded to earlier, to the advantage of Islam. But they also produced an elite that has yet to renounce the Christian religion completely even though it denounces its missionaries. This obviously must dictate caution in any campaign the United Arab Republic might embark upon to discredit Christianity.

That is not to say that Abdul Nasser cannot fulfill his ' obligations' within the Muslim Circle without endangering his plans within the African Circle. No complications need, for example, arise out of the plans of the religions department of the U.A.R., to have a strong Voice of Islam which, in the words of a news-analyst, 'would do in religious spheres what the Voice of the Arabs does in the political propaganda field.' Nor are protests inevitable following the pursuit of the policy of assigning a religious attaché to the U.A.R.'s embassies and legations in Africa and some parts of Asia.

Nevertheless, between his African and Muslim circles Abdul Nasser has to maintain a careful balance. He can hardly afford to forget that in December 1958, the All-Africa Peoples Conference in Accra attacked not only tribalism but also religious separation as evil practices which militated against African liberation and unity.

He certainly may have to exercise the utmost caution in that vision of the Egyptian's role in Africa which his *Philosophy* expressed in the following terms: 'We cannot, under any condition, relinquish our responsibility in helping, in every way possible, in diffusing the light of civilization into the furthest parts of the virgin jungle.'

It is unlikely that Sub-Saharan Africa would warmly embrace the concept of 'the Egyptian's burden' in the very process of renouncing that of the white man! Indeed, it is arguable that the greatest disservice that the Egyptians might do to the spread of Islam in Africa would be to exploit and direct evangelism to such an extent that it became identified with policies in the way that the Christian missions did. Perhaps one of the factors which have helped Islam in Africa is that its recent spread has been mainly through casual individual contact and commercial intercourse with little organized proselytization and only a limited hierarchical bureaucracy. From this particular point of view, Abdul Nasser might perhaps be wise to see that the policy of assigning religious attachés to his embassies does not crystallize into a radical departure from this traditional mode of the spread of Islam.

No less important for the policy's success is that it should not alienate local Muslim opinion in individual territories by offering too persistently the 'model' of Egyptian Islam. J. Spencer Trimingham once observed that ' Islam won its way by making compromises with the forms of religion it encountered.' Just at the time when some Christians are beginning to see the point of such compromises and finding a case for not insisting that Christianity be interpreted only in the way that Europe has interpreted it, it would be ironical if Islam under Egypt's propagation were to engage itself at this late hour in this form of what an American Methodist divine in Japan (the Rev. Dr. John H. McCombe, Jr.) has condemned as 'religious imperialism.'

Along with allowing for such local religious variations, the United Arab Republic must, of course, also allow for the local nationalistic and political sensitivities of the areas concerned—not least because, for better or for worse, there is a sense in which Rupert Emerson is right in contending that 'the universal in religion has been driven to bow to the tribal gods of nations.' All in all it is evidently a delicate undertaking trying to draw Circles of friends round oneself. For these are the different demands they make: to the Eastern Bloc a defier of the West; to the Western Bloc an enemy of Communism at home; to the Arabs ' an Arab first and foremost'; to the Africans ' above all an African'; to the Muslims a 'defender of Islam'; and to Christian colleagues 'a neutral in religion.' Yet Egypt is inescapably poly-cyclic—important as an Arab, as an African, as a Muslim and as a Neutralist nation. So perhaps the villain of the Earl of Avon's (Sir Anthony Eden's) memoirs. *Full Circle,* may yet prove that there is a case, after all, for going round in Circles—provided one manages to keep one's balance.

Chapter Eleven

Afro-Arab Crossfire: Between the Flames of Terrorism and the Force of Pax Americana

International terrorism is one more area of intermingling between the policies of the Middle East and the politics of Africa. Before the end of colonialism and the end of apartheid in Africa, what was described as "terrorism" was as common in Africa as in the Middle East. Since the collapse of political apartheid in the 1990s, the term "terrorism" has more narrowly been focused on the politics of the Middle East. We shall explore the reasons more fully.

TERRORISM AS A TYPE OF WARFARE

Much of the old anti-colonial and anti-apartheid terrorism in Africa in the second half of the twentieth century was targeted against Europeans and the colonial powers. Much of the Middle Eastern terrorism of more recent times has been targeted against the United States and Israel.

In the retrospect of history Africa gained from its own guerrilla movements and terrorist activities against European powers. The Mau Mau war in Kenya did result in Kenya's independence in 1963; the Algerian revolution did result in the liberation of Algeria in 1962; the anti-colonial wars in Angola, Mozambique and Guinea-Bissau did destroy the Portuguese empire in 1974; the anti-UDI struggle in Zimbabwe ended Ian Smith's Unilateral Declaration of Independence, and the anti-apartheid struggle in South Africa finally triumphed against the racial order. Terrorism and guerilla war by Africans against European powers did yield positive results. Terrorism was a form of warfare, and had to be judged in its total political and moral context, and by its ultimate results.

What is more, all forms of warfare kill overwhelmingly more civilians than combatants. The American War in Vietnam killed some four million Vietnamese civilians, against less than sixty thousand American combatants.

However, if anti-European and anti-colonial terrorism in Africa had produced good results in the end for Africa, anti-American and anti-Zionist terrorism in the Middle East has not yet found its moment of triumph. Both the Middle East and Africa have been paying a price for anti-American terrorism. The violent price which the Middle East pays is obvious, especially in Palestine, Iraq and in neighboring Afghanistan. What is the price which Africa is paying for terrorism against the United States?

Firstly, there is the issue of being caught in the crossfire. Africa has been the victim of violent action intended by the terrorists for the United States; Africa has also been a victim of violent action taken by the United States and intended for the terrorists.

In order to kill twelve Americans, Middle Eastern terrorists killed about two hundred Kenyans in the streets of Nairobi a few years ago. This was the attack on the US Embassy in Nairobi in August 1998. There were also Tanzanian casualties when the US Embassy in Dar es Salaam was targeted at the same time.

On the other hand, Sudan was caught in the crossfire soon after when President Bill Clinton ordered the bombing of an apparently harmless pharmacy near Khartoum. President Ronald Reagan, before Clinton, had ordered the bombing of Tripoli and Benghazi in Libya because Reagan thought the Libyans were responsible for a bomb in a German bar which had killed Americans. Violence between Americans and Middle Easterners had been spilling over into Africa for decades—violence from both Middle Easterners and the Americans.

An unknown number of Africans were killed at the World Trade Center, in New York on September 11th—Senegalese hawkers, Nigerian investors, Ethiopian or Eritrean drivers or professionals, Ghanaian students, Egyptian and South African tourists and others. Who knows for certain?

September 11, 2001, has had other consequences for Africa. The Security Forces of Africa have opened their doors to the United States' Federal Bureau of Investigation (the FBI) and the Central Intelligence Agency (the CIA). Africa has fewer secrets from the Americans than ever, if Africa ever had any.

The FBI reportedly arrived in Tanzania after September 11 with 60 Muslim names for interrogation and potential action.

The Kenyan authorities have been so eager to please the Americans that they are tempted to repatriate their own Kenyan citizens to the United States on the slightest encouragement. Fortunately, the American Embassy in Nairobi is sometimes more cautious.

The President of Kenya marched in sympathy with the victims of September 11th. The Muslims of Kenya marched against the American bombing of Afghanistan. President Moi asked "Why didn't the Kenya Muslims march when Nairobi was bombed by terrorists in August of 1998?" The Kenyan Muslims turned the tables on their President "Why didn't President Moi lead a march when Nairobi was bombed in August 1998?"

The President of Tanzania declared a day of mourning for the victims of September 11 in the United States. His critics retorted that they did not remember a day of public mourning in Tanzania when 800,000 Rwandans were killed in the genocide of 1994. Africans grieve when Americans are massacred, but do we grieve as much when Africans are massacred?

There is some anxiety that September 11 and its aftermath may exacerbate tensions not only been pro-Western and anti-Western schools of thought in this continent, but also between Christians and Muslims in Africa. A demonstration by Nigerian Muslims in Kano against the American war in Afghanistan provoked stone throwing by Nigerian Christians in Kano, which flared up into communal riots. Churches and mosques were soon being burnt. President Olusegun Obasanjo had to rush to Kano to contain the tensions before they spilled over into secretarian riots all over Nigeria.

The United States efforts to unite African governments against terrorism may be dividing African people among themselves—a coalition of elites resulting in a contestation at the grassroots.

The pressure on many African governments to enact new legislation against terrorism may pose newer threats to civil liberties in Africa just at the time when democratization was gathering momentum in some African states. Nor must we forget that if America's own democracy decays, it makes it easier for Africa's own dictators to justify their own tyranny. Indeed, the aftermath of September 11th has already been compromising some civil liberties in the United States itself.

1. There are hundreds of people in detention without trial
2. The great majority of those in detention are not publicly announced as being in detention.
3. Out of the hundreds in detention, less than a dozen show any evidence of knowing any particular terrorist suspect or being associated with any movement or charity accused of terrorism.
4. Out of the millions of illegal immigrants in the United States, and those whose visas have expired, the people chosen for detention without trial are almost certainly those with Muslim names or who come from the Middle East.
5. The United States is actually planning to have military tribunals and secret trials for those suspected of terrorism. Even the leaders of Nazi Germany

were given a public trial at Nuremberg after World War II with access to counsel and proper representation. Some of those tried at Nuremberg had been responsible for the death of millions of people.

6. Israel continues to look for old Nazi militants so that they can be tried to-day in a court of law in Israel. Yet Israel feels free to kill Palestinian mil-itants instead of capturing them for trial. Israel tried Adolf Eichmann in 1961 and protected him at the trial with a bulletproof glass cage so that he would not be assassinated. Yet both the USA and Israel in 2001 openly talked about killing terrorist suspects instead of capturing them. And even when Israel has illegally captured Palestinian or Lebanese suspects from across its own borders, the purpose has almost never been to give them fair trial (Adolf Eichmann-style) but to detain those suspects indefinitely with-out trial.

7. U. S. Attorney General John Ashcroft is about to empower the FBI to spy on churches, mosques, and other sacred places to an extent not envisaged in the country for a long time. Places of prayer were once protected from close police scrutiny. However, mosques especially may soon be fair game for police raids in American cities, while Synagogues may enjoy de facto protection even if there is militant Zionism or fundamentalist Judaism be-ing preached inside.

8. Attorney-General Ashcroft wants to breach attorney-client confidentiality if the client is suspected of terrorism. The Attorney General and President Bush repeatedly talk as if those suspected of terrorism were already proven terrorists. What happened to the U.S. principle that a person was innocent until proven guilty?

9. CNN and other major TV networks in the United States were summoned to the White House and warned against giving Usama bin Laden propa-ganda advantage with his videos. Whatever happened to editorial inde-pendence and freedom of the Press?

AFRICA AND THE MID-EAST: DIVERGENT RESPONSES

Why has terrorism continued to escalate in the Middle East while it has de-clined in Africa? Why is Africa talking about "Truth and Reconciliation" with the White man and Reparations from the Western World—while the Arabs and much of the rest of the Muslim world are angrier than ever against the West?

Why do Arab militants regard "Pay Back Time" in terms of retribution against the West—while so many African nationalists regard "Pay Back Time" in terms of reparation from the West?

Let us now look much more closely at the dynamics of politics in Africa and the Middle East from the point of view of reparation versus retribution.

The 2001 conference in Durban against racism and xenophobia took the issues of reparations forward. But the terrorist events in New York on September 11th might have caused a setback to the cause of Reparations. Both Durban and September 11th have demonstrated once again a link between Africa and the Middle East, and the link has been affected by the forces of globalization.

I would like to explore the issue of reparations, on one side, and terrorist retribution, on the other, as alternative methods of "PAY BACK." I would like to place Africa alongside the Middle East in comparative perspective. Africa and the Middle East are in any case overlapping regions. Comparing them in this way is particularly appropriate on a panel on globalization. Imperialism in the Middle East created conditions in which "PAY BACK" time threatened to be revenge. Imperialism in Africa, on the other hand, created conditions in which reparations appeared to be a more appropriate form of "PAY BACK."

Imperialism in the Middle East provoked the worst levels of anti-Western terrorism after formal liberation from European colonial rule. The British had been in power in Egypt, Iraq, Jordan, Sudan and elsewhere. The French had been in power in Syria, Lebanon, Algeria, Morocco, Tunisia and elsewhere. Palestine had been a United Nations trusteeship under British rule.

Imperialism in Africa provoked the worst levels of anti-Western terrorism before formal liberation from European colonial rule: that is to say, before Independence Day.

Let us also relate the comparison to comparative rage. Imperialism in Africa triggered the most explosive anti-Western anger before European colonialism left Africa. Imperialism in the Middle East triggered off the most explosive anti-Western anger after European colonialism had left the Arab world.

What the colonial powers and white minority governments had condemned as "terrorism" in Africa included the Mau Mau war in Kenya and the liberation wars in Algeria, Angola, Zimbabwe, Mozambique, and South Africa. What the Western world has condemned as "terrorism" in the Middle East has included hostage taking in Lebanon, highjacking of planes in the 1970s, as well as suicide bombs in the streets of Israel. The most spectacular was the destruction of the World Trade Center and the attack on the Pentagon on September 11, 2001. In what sense are we to conclude that while the impact of Imperialism in the Middle East created conditions for violent "PAY BACK" against the West, the impact of imperialism on Africa has been to create conditions which are ideal for "PAY BACK" in terms of reparations from the West?

PAY BACK AND SITUATIONAL DIFFERENCES

Some of the differences between Africa and the Middle East are situational, while other differences are primarily cultural. The postcolonial situation in the Middle East included a permanent loss of territory imposed by outsiders.

The postcolonial situation in Africa involved recovery of territory—including recovery of land previously parceled out by apartheid in South Africa. This was won back to Africa.

Africa had also been spared the forceful creation of a Jewish state in Uganda and Kenya earlier in the twentieth century. Joseph Chamberlain, the Colonial Secretary at the time, had offered Theodor Herzl, the leader of the Zionist movement, a piece of Uganda and a piece of Kenya at the beginning of the twentieth century for the creation of a new Jewish state. (The boundaries of Uganda early in the twentieth century included parts of present-day Kenya.)

Had the Zionist movement accepted the offer, and a permanent Jewish state been established in East Africa, it is conceivable that African anger against the West today would be comparable to anti-Western rage in the Middle East.

But the Zionist movement in 1903 could not reach consensus about creating "Israel" in East Africa—and therefore the postcolonial situation in Africa today involves no permanent loss of territory.

A related situational difference is that while the postcolonial conditions in Africa meant a clear end of foreign occupation, the postcolonial situation in the Middle East carried new forms of foreign occupation. It involved NOT just the creation of the state of Israel but also the occupation by Israel of the West Bank of Jordan, the occupation of Gaza, the annexation of the Golan Heights of Syria, the annexation of the whole of Jerusalem and the occupation of a piece of Southern Lebanon for a while. While the postcolonial period in Africa is truly post-occupation, the postcolonial period in the Middle East has entailed new forms of territorial annexations.

Where does the United States fit into this equation? When European powers occupied Africa and parts of Asia, the image of America was that of an anti-colonial force in world affairs. The United States put a lot of pressure on its European allies to speed up the process of giving independence to the colonies.

Even as late as 1956—when Britain, France and Israel invaded Egypt in response to Egypt's nationalization of the Suez Canal—the Eisenhower Administration turned against its allies. The United States forced Israel to withdraw from Sinai, and forced Britain and France to give up Port Said in Egypt. The British Prime Minister had a nervous breakdown—Anthony Eden gave way to Harold McMillan. Egypt's Nasser emerged as a world figure—partly because the United States would not support the Anglo-Franco-Israeli invasion of Egypt. Nasser had been militarily defeated, but emerged politically triumphant. The Eisenhower administration—wittingly or unwittingly—had helped the Egyptian president rise to global stature.

John F. Kennedy as President dismissed the concerns of the white settlers elsewhere in Africa when they objected to the phrase "AFRICA FOR THE AFRICANS." Kennedy insisted "Who else would Africa be for if not for Africans?" The United States was on the side of the aspirations of African nationalists.

But two things were happening which future historians would later have to dis-entangle. The United States was expanding towards greater globalization and expanding role of interventionism in other parts of the world.

In the second half of the 20th century the United States began to be seen more and more as an imperial power, and a supporter of Israeli policies of occupation and repression.

WHY IS THE U.S. being blamed for Israeli policies? Where is Osama bin Laden's anti-Americanism coming from?

1. Massive economic aid from the United States to Israel in billions
2. Provision of sophisticated American weapons to Israel
3. The United States' shielding Israel from U.N. censure
4. The United States making U.N. Security Council impotent in punishing Israel.
5. The United States weakening anti-Israeli Arab forces by buying off the government of Egypt with a billion U.S. dollars every year. Egypt is the largest Arab country and used to be the biggest single threat to Israel militarily. The U.S. largess has bought off Egypt effectively.
6. Preventing Iraq from rising as an alternative to Egypt in challenging Israel.

Taking advantage of Iraq's invasion of Kuwait to weaken Iraq permanently—whereas Pearl Harbor was not used to weaken Japan permanently, nor was Hitler's aggression used to weaken Germany permanently.

The United States is the main source of military support for the enemy of the Arab World, Israel, and the USA is also the main destroyer of Arab capacity to rise militarily. This latter policy includes weakening Egypt and enfeebling Iraq.

The American base in SAUDI ARABIA since 1991 is perceived as turning sacred Islamic soil into an extension of the PENTAGON. The American base in Saudi Arabia is seen not as a shield against such external enemies as Saddam Hussein, but a shield against an internal Iran-style Islamic revolution in Saudi Arabia.

A situation of gross military frustration has been created, especially in Palestine and Iraq, but also on the sacred sands of Saudi Arabia.

PAY BACK AND CULTURAL DIFFERENCES

But the differences between Africa and the Middle East in relation to political rage are not only due to divergent post-colonial situations.

There are also basic differences in culture between the Arabo-Hebrew Semitic peoples (both Arabs and Jews) on one side, and the majority of Black people in sub-Saharan Africa.

One major difference is the martyrdom complex which is much more developed among Middle Eastern peoples than among peoples of sub-Saharan Africa.

The Jews have developed memories of the Holocaust into a major doctrine of Jewish martyrdom in history. As for readiness to commit collective suicide, the Israeli nuclear program is partly based on the premise of the Samson option—a readiness to defend Israel even if means destroying it and much of the rest of the region.

Among Muslims of the Middle East (both Arab and Iranian), there is the martyrdom complex in varying degrees. Historically it has been more developed among Shia Muslims than among Sunni. Suicide bombers against Israel and American troops in Lebanon started among Shiite Lebanese.

But anger against Israel and the United States has now resulted in the extension of the martyrdom complex to the Sunni population of the Middle East.

It is probable (though not yet proven) that the daredevils who destroyed the World Trade Center and the Pentagon were indeed Middle Easterners.

Because culturally the Middle East has a martyrdom complex which is much more highly developed than among any groups in sub-Saharan Africa, it is the Middle East which has been readier than Africa to commit suicidal political violence against the West. In the postcolonial period it is the Middle East, more than Africa, which has been ready to engage in acts of suicidal terrorism against the West.

Another major cultural difference between the Middle East and Africa concerns comparative hate retention. Cultures differ in hate-retention. Some cultures preserve a grudge across centuries. The Irish of Northern Ireland quarrel every year about a Protestant victory of the Orange Order against Catholics four centuries ago. The Irish have a high hate-retentive capacity.

The Armenian massacres of 1915 by the Ottoman Empire are still remembered bitterly by Armenians—and from time to time this memory results in the assassination of a Turkish diplomat somewhere in the world.

The Jews also have high hate-retentiveness, but they have sublimated it through the martyrdom complex. The Holocaust is given a sacred meaning rather than merely remembered as hate.

Because the Arabs have a vastly different history from Jews in the last fourteen centuries, the Arabs' experience as a persecuted people is relatively recent. Their hate-retention and their martyrdom complex is not as well developed or as sophisticated as that of the Jews. But Arabs and Jews do both share a fascination with the martyrdom complex.

Now contrast this culturally with Black Africa. A major reason why Black Africa has not produced postcolonial political violence against the West is Africa's short memory of hate.

Mahatma Gandhi used to prophesy that it would probably be through Black people that the unadulterated message of soul force [satyagraha] and passive resistance might be realized. If Gandhi was indeed right, this could be one more illustration of comparative hate-retention.

The Nobel Committee for Peace in Oslo seems to have shared some of Gandhi's optimism about the soul force of the Black people. Africans and people of African descent who have won the Nobel prize for Peace since the middle of the twentieth century have been Ralph Bunche (1950), Albert Luthuli (1960), Martin Luther King Jr. (1964), Anwar Sadat (1978) Desmond Tutu (1984) and Nelson Mandela (1993). And now Kofi Annan and his UN leadership have joined the galaxy (2001). Neither Mahatma Gandhi himself nor any of his compatriots in India ever won the Nobel Prize for Peace, though Indians have won other categories of the Nobel Prize. Was Mahatma Gandhi vindicated that the so-called "Negro" was going to be the best exemplar of soul force? Was this a case of African culture being empirically more Gandhian than Indian culture?

In reality Black people have been at least as violent as anything ever perpetrated by Indians. The Horn of Africa has had its fair share of violence. So have other parts of black Africa. What is distinctive about Africans is their short memory of hate. Jomo Kenyatta was unjustly imprisoned by the British colonial authorities over charges of founding the Mau Mau movement. A British Governor also denounced him as "a leader unto darkness and unto death." And yet when Jomo Kenyatta was released he not only forgave the white settlers, but turned the whole country towards a basic pro-Western orientation to which it has remained committed ever since. Kenyatta even published a book entitled Suffering Without Bitterness.

Ian Smith, the white settler leader of Rhodesia, unilaterally declared independence in 1965 and unleashed a civil war on Rhodesia. Thousands of people, mainly Black, died in the country as a result of policies pursued by Ian Smith. Yet when the war ended in 1980 Ian Smith and his cohorts were not subjected to a Nuremberg-style trial. On the contrary, Ian Smith was himself a member of parliament in a Black-ruled Zimbabwe, busy criticizing the post-Smith Black leaders of Zimbabwe as incompetent and dishonest. Where else but in Africa could such tolerance occur?

The Nigerian civil war (1967–1970) was the most highly publicized civil conflict in postcolonial African history. When the war was coming to an end, many people feared that there would be a bloodbath in the defeated eastern region. The Vatican was worried that cities like Enugu and Onitcha, strongholds of Catholicism, would be monuments of devastation and blood-letting.

None of these expectations occurred. Nigerians—seldom among the most disciplined of Africans—discovered in 1970 some remarkable resources of self-restraint. There were no triumphant or triumphalist reprisals against the vanquished Biafrans; there were no vengeful trials of "traitors."

We have also witnessed the phenomenon of Nelson Mandela. He lost twenty-seven of the best years of his life in prison under the laws of the apartheid regime. Yet when he was released he not only emphasized the policy of reconciliation—he often went beyond the call of duty. On one occasion before he became President white men were fasting unto death after being convicted of terrorist offences by their own white government. Nelson Mandela went out of his way to beg them to eat and thus spare their own lives.

When Mandela became President in 1994 it was surely enough that his government would leave the architects of apartheid unmolested. Yet Nelson Mandela went out of his way to pay a social call and have tea with the unrepentant widow of Hendrik F. Verwoed, the supreme architect of the worst forms of apartheid, who shaped the whole racist order from 1958 to 1966. Mandela was having tea with the family of Verwoed.

Was Mahatma Gandhi correct, after all, that his torch of soul force (satyagraha) might find its brightest manifestations among Black people? Empirical relativism was at work again.

In the history of civilizations there are occasions when the image in the mirror is more real that the object it reflects. Black Gandhians like Martin Luther King Jr., Desmond Tutu and, in a unique sense, Nelson Mandela have sometimes reflected Gandhaian soul force more brightly than Gandhians in India. Part of the explanation lies in the soul of African culture itself—with all its capacity for rapid forgiveness.

Yet "PAY BACK" as an African demand is a claim for Reparations—contrasting sharply with "PAY BACK" as political retribution against the West by other damaged regions of the world. The West should respond positively to this softer, gentler version of "PAY BACK TIME" between the West and the Rest. Better the music of reparations than the drums of terror.

Finally a word about terrorism and germ warfare. How does bio-terrorism relate to the African condition and Pax-Americana? Let us now explore this dimension.

BETWEEN AIDS AND ANTHRAX

Those who are campaigning against AIDS and HIV are jealous of the attention and publicity anthrax is getting. Bill Clinton tried to make AIDS a national security issue. George W. Bush has more success with mobilization against anthrax.

There is a widespread belief among Black people that HIV and AIDS are part of a racial bacteriological or viral war. Since AIDS has hit Black people so disproportionately, especially on the African continent, there is a strong temptation to conclude that HIV is viral or bacteriological ethnic cleansing. Is somebody trying to shrink the population of Black people?

In the middle of this inconclusive debate as to whether AIDS is part of a racial war there has now surfaced the question as to whether anthrax and other bacteria are part of a war between civilizations. Is the recent scare of anthrax connected with the horrendous atrocities of September 11th in New York, Washington, and Pennsylvania? And are those atrocities part of a clash of civilizations? Or are they homegrown aberrations?

Thabo Mbeki, the President of South Africa, has attributed AIDS not to viral or bacteriological ethnic cleansing but to a class war between the Haves and the Have-nots. Mbeki has argued that the collapse of immune systems in Africa is at least as likely to be due to poverty and deprivation of nutrition as to HIV. To Mbeki AIDS could be one of the latest manifestations of the global class struggle between the Haves and the Have-nots.

Westerners opposed to Saddam Hussein in Iraq have long suspected him of developing bacteriological and chemical weapons designed to be used against Israel and the Western world. And yet when Saddam Hussein was being humiliated with a devastating defeat in 1991, he never resorted to either chemical weapons or germ warfare. Saddam Hussein may be rational enough to threaten germ warfare, yet not so irrational as to carry out the threat when the chips are down.

The return of germ warfare to the Americas at a time when the United States has the most Hispanic-friendly President (George W. Bush) in a century is replete with ironies. The destruction of the original indigenous American civilizations in North America was as much due to new diseases which the white man had brought with him to the New World as to any gunpowder. Indeed, there is evidence to suggest that just when the Aztecs were about to defeat the Spaniards in Central America a single Spanish soldier with smallpox helped to decimate a third of the Aztec population four centuries ago.

Let us hope the new bacteriological threat to North America through modern day terrorism does not materialize as a new version of Montezuma's revenge. Far from the Western world being a cause of AIDS and ethnic cleansing in Africa, Africa needs the West to help control the AIDS pandemic. The threat of anthrax is a diversion from older and more fundamental problems. These older problems include not only Thabo Mbeki's concern about poverty and health, but also international concern about the festering wound of Palestine and its potential for global instability.

The Kenyan medical authorities claimed in October that Kenya was the second country after the United States to be targeted with anthrax. Kenya was a choice which could not have been made by the same mind which chose the World Trade Center as a symbol of America's economic might and the Pentagon as America's military might. The choice of the American targets was made by a brilliant military tactician, however evil.

Sending anthrax to a developing country like Kenya, and to an ordinary citizen instead of a high profile Kenyan, could only have been done by a much more mediocre tactician, or by a copy-cat. It made no sense whatsoever for Al-Qaida to have chosen Kenya for a major anthrax attack instead of Great Britain or Israel. Since then almost every Western country has witnessed copycat alarms and false alarms. But why pick Kenya before Britain? Was the whole scare in Kenya a fake?

Yet whoever is experimenting with "germ warfare," whether by a major organization or as a private vendetta, should be hunted down as a criminal of the first order. What we should avoid is mistaking scapegoating for genuine criminal investigation.

Let us now return to relations of war and peace between Africa and the Middle East. In the year of the Prophet Muhammad's birth [570 C.E.] Mecca was attacked by Abyssinians (Ethiopians) riding elephants. The Qur'an says that Mecca was saved by a flock of birds from Heaven throwing pebbles at the invaders. The "birds and pebbles" are widely interpreted as an outbreak of pestilence among both elephants and the invaders. (See Sura Al-Fil or the Elephant, Qur'an, 30.105). Could the pestilence have been anthrax? The Ethiopian invasion of Mecca was foiled.

Less than fifty years later Ethiopia provided asylum to Muslims on the run from persecution in pre-Islamic Arabia. Thanks to pestilence among their elephants Ethiopians failed to conquer Mecca. Yet two generations later Ethiopians were helping to save nascent Islam. Africa and the Middle East had once again played their convergent roles in the history of civilization.

Chapter Twelve

Eurafrica, Eurabia, and African-Arab Relations: The Tensions of Tripolarity

The tripolar world of Europe, Africa, and Arab countries has a number of asymmetries. Economically Europe and the Arab countries do constitute a regional subsystem. The flow of commodities, capital, technology, and to some extent labor is sufficiently regular to constitute a systemic pattern. The concept of *Eurabia*—linking Europe with the lands of the Arabs—is therefore systemically coherent.

What about the relations between Africa and Europe? Here, too, there is pattern and regularity. The whole colonial experience had forged African economies in Europe's image. Trade, investment, and aid have together created structures of uneven interdependence between Africa and Europe. Those two regions together do constitute an international subsystem. The concept of Eurafrica—signifying a special relationship between those two continents—is therefore also systemically coherent.

What about relations between Africa and the Arab world? Is there sufficient pattern or regularity in economic relations to convert the two regions into an international subsystem? The answer in this case is less clear-cut. The two regions of Africa and the Arab world are overlapping categories. North Africa is of course overwhelmingly Arab in population, although it is also an integral part of African realities. Politically Africa and the Arab world have been strengthening their links. There are also overlapping institutions and organizations, including the OAU. But in the economic sphere, interactions between the two regions are still either modest or irregular. The concept of *Afrabia* is therefore inchoate and premature at the present moment.

The triangle connecting Europe, Africa, and the Arab world has two thick, and sure lines, connecting Europe with Africa on one side and Europe with the Arab world on other. But the third line between Africa and the Arab world is, at least in the economic domain, still thin and uncertain. The question for the future concerns, among other things, how best to complete and even out this particular eternal triangle.

Curiously enough, the process by which this triangular exercise is to be accomplished does itself involve other triangles or triads. These are sometimes cultural in nature, sometimes economic, sometimes political and diplomatic. The tripolar world of the Arabs, the Africans, and the Europeans lies in the shadows of a history that is almost an echo of the Christian doctrine of three in one and one in three.

In this chapter I will address myself especially to-seven triads that have conditioned relations between Africa, Europe, and the Arab world.

THE TRIAD OF LOCATION

In a novel I wrote more than thirty-five years ago, set in the Hereafter, I referred to "the Curse of the Trinity." A Nigerian poet had been put on trial in the Hereafter for deciding he was an Ibo first and an artist second, thus betraying poetry and dying for Biafra. The trial was conducted before nine Elders of After-Africa, where all dead Africans go. On the day of judgment men and women, drawn from all the centuries of Africa's human existence, sat there in the Grand Stadium, attentively awaiting the considered wisdom of the Elders after hearing all the evidence. The Elder on the fifth throne first explained what it was that had influenced the Council of Grand Trials to decide on making a special case of the poet Christopher Okigbo and the Nigerian civil war. "It occurred to us that this whole tragedy was once again the Curse of the Trinity unfolding itself in the drama of Africa's existence. Let us remind ourselves, Oh fellow citizens of After-Africa, of the meaning of the Curse of the Trinity in relation to this old continent of ours."[1] The Elder on the fifth throne continued to explain that the Christian story of three in one and one in three had in part, been a prophecy about Africa, and in part a postmortem on Africa. At the structural level there was the Trinity as the basis of Africa's geography—the Tropic of Capricorn, the Equator, the Tropic of Cancer. Of all the continents of the world only Africa was central enough to be traversed, by all the three basic latitudes. The Equator almost cut the African continent into two halves—such was the centrality of Africa to the global scheme of things.

Since then I have further developed this triad of location. Of the three ancient continents of Asia, Africa, and Europe, Africa has often played the role of a link, and sometimes a mediator, between the Occident and the Orient. In history it has never been quite clear whether Africa was indeed part of the Orient or whether it should be included in the universe of the Occidentals.

So ambivalent has the status of this continent been that its northern portion, North Africa, has changed identity a number of times across the centuries. At one time North Africa was an extension of Europe. This goes back to the days of Carthage, Hellenic colonization and, later, the Roman Empire. The concept of Europe was at best in the making at that time. In the words of historians R. R. Palmer and Joel Colton: "There was really no Europe in ancient times. In the Roman Empire we may see a Mediterranean world, or even a West and an East in the Latin-and-Greek-speaking portions. But the West included parts of Africa as well as of Europe. . . ."[2]

Even as late as the seventeenth century the idea that the landmass south of the Mediterranean was something distinct from the landmass north of it was still a proposition that was difficult to comprehend. The great American Africanist, Melville Herskovits, once reminded us that the Geographer Royal of France, writing in 1656, described Africa as "a peninsula so large that it comprises the third part, and this the most southerly, of our continent."[3]

This old proposition that North Africa was the southern part of Europe had its last desperate fling in the modern world in France's attempt to keep Algeria as part of France. The myth that Algeria was the southern portion of France tore the French nation apart in the 1950s, created the crisis that brought Charles de Gaulle into power in 1958, and maintained tensions between the right and the left in France until Algeria's independence in 1962. This bid to maintain Algeria as the southern portion of a major European nation had taken place at a time when in other respects North Africa had become substantially an extension of Asia. From the seventh century onward the gradual Islamization and Arabization of North Africa helped to prepare the ground for redirecting North Africa's links more firmly toward West Africa, without necessarily ending residual interaction with South Europe. The Arabs themselves had become a bi-continental people, traversing both Africa and Asia. By the twentieth century the majority of the Arab *people* were in fact within the African continent, although the majority of Arab *states* by the last quarter of the twentieth century were in West Asia.

If in some respects and at certain periods in history North Africa has virtually been the southern extension of Europe, and if since the Muslim conquest it has been the western extension of Asia, it has all along also remained the northern portion of Africa. The greatest theater of interaction between Europe, Africa, and the Arab world has been the Mediterranean coastline of the African continent.

For reasons of both geographic contiguities and historical continuities one would have expected the structural relations between the Africanness of

North Africa and its Arabness to be closer than between its Arabness and its European orientation. But so great has been the impact of European imperialism on North Africa that the European orientation is deeper than the African.

THE TRIAD OF ACCULTURATION

The second basic triad concerns three civilizations-Western civilization, Islamic civilization, and the interrelated cultures and civilizations of Africa south of the Sahara.

Religion is one aspect of these civilizations. Here again there are dissimilarities in the three regions that we are examining. Europe is in a sense religiously homogeneous. Where people are still religious in Europe, they are far and away most likely to be Christian, although the denomination may vary. Similarly, the Arab world is basically homogeneous in the religious sense. The overwhelming majority of Arabs are Muslim. Even in Lebanon the demographic balance has now shifted in favor of Muslims .

But unlike both Europe and the Arab world, Africa is religiously heterogeneous. The continent has not only its own indigenous traditional religions; it has also accommodated different versions of both Christianity and Islam. Kwame Nkrumah reminded us about these three parts of the soul of Africa:

> African society has one segment which comprises our traditional way of life; it has a second segment which is filled by the presence of the Islamic tradition in Africa; it has a final segment which represents the infiltration of the Christian tradition and culture of Western Europe into Africa, using colonialism and neo-colonialism as its primary vehicles. These different segments are animated by competing ideologies.[4]

The original intrusion of Islam was mainly through North Africa, although there is some evidence of Muslims arriving in the Horn of Africa almost from the beginning of the Muslim era. Two processes of acculturation got under way fairly early—Islamization and Arabization. I use the term Islamization here to denote conversion to Islam as a religion. I use the term *Arabization* to imply the process of becoming an Arab through *linguistic* socia*lization*. The majority of Egyptians today are not former migrants from the Arabian peninsula; they are descendants of people who were in Egypt from the days of the Pharaohs. The Muslim conquest of Egypt in the seventh century did not result in either the expulsion or the liquidation of the population of ancient Egypt. What the Muslim conquerors did over time was gradually to transmit not only their religion but also their language and identity to the conquered people. In time, Islamized Egyptians came to think of themselves as Arabs.

Curiously enough, where only the language was transmitted, but not the religion, the recipients did not become fully Arab. This is the case of the Copts in Egypt. Over the centuries they became Arabic speakers but not Muslims. They therefore fell short of becoming fully Arab. What this demonstrated is that Arabization as a process could not be fully consummated without Islamization.

The twin processes also occurred in Libya, Northern Sudan, and the Maghreb. The majority of the inhabitants in these parts of Africa gradually witnessed a change in self-identity—and saw themselves as Arabs.

In West Africa, on the other hand, the process was mainly that of Islamization—the conversion to the religion of Islam without necessarily indigenizing the Arabic language. Although North Africa could not become fully Arab without adopting Islam, West Africa could become Muslim without Arabizing its identity.

Somalia, in a cultural sense, falls somewhere between North Africa and West Africa. The Somalis are as Muslim as, say, the emir of Kano in Northern Nigeria and Anwar Sadat in Egypt. But the Somalis are less Arabized than Anwar Sadat was and more Arabized than the emir.

But although the Arabic language has not been indigenized in places like Northern Nigeria and Tanzania, the language has had a profound effect on some indigenous languages in both West and East Africa. Indeed, the most important indigenous languages in the African continent are probably Kiswahili in East Africa and Hausa in West Africa—both languages that have been deeply influenced by both Arabic and Islam. In the case of Kiswahili, even the name of the language is derived from the Arabic word "coast." And up to one-fifth of the basic vocabulary of Kiswahili is also derived from Arabic. Of course the structure of the language is still Bantu—but Arabic is to Kiswahili what Latin is to the English language, a source of great enrichment in vocabulary.

But how was Kiswahili to be written? At first, along the coast of East Africa, written Kiswahili used the Arabic alphabet. Some of the earliest documents available in Kiswahili are indeed in Arabic script. But then European imperialism came to East Africa, and new approaches to literacy were in time adopted. Kiswahili came to be written in the Roman alphabet. In fact, given the nature of the sounds of Kiswahili, this author believes that the Roman alphabet is more efficient for Kiswahili than the Arabic script. But it is illustrative of the triad of cultures, in East Africa that this major Bantu language should have had to choose between the alphabet of the Arabs and the alphabet of Western Europe to express its African self in writing.

The triad of cultures now also increasingly emerges from further changes in the language. More and more words of European languages, especially English, are entering Kiswahili as loan words. These coexist and sometimes compete with words of Arabic derivation on one side and words drawn from indigenous languages on the other.

In some African countries even the political culture sometimes reflects that historic interplay between and among the three civilizations we are examining. The British policy of indirect rule and its aftermath are particularly interesting from this point of view. Britain's colonial policy of indirect rule was born out of a marriage between Islam and the Anglo-Irish philosopher, Edmund Burke. In a sense the legacy of Edmund Burke is what British political culture is all about. As a rule of political prudence Burke advised: "Neither entirely nor at once depart from antiquity. If a society does aspire to change direction, it would be a mistake to do it either totally or in one sudden move." Political prudence, according to Burke, requires political sensitivity to history. As he put it again: "People will not look forward to posterity who never look backward to their ancestors."[5]

British political, culture is a reflection in part of this broad political philosophy. The British are reluctant to turn their back on antiquity either entirely or at once. So they maintain ancient institutions and modernize them as they go along, and they are slower to modify traditional habits than many of their peers.

This same Burkean gradualism in British domestic political culture came to influence British colonial policy. Indirect rule was based on a Burkean principle of gradualism. Many colonial policymakers felt convinced that you could not persuade Africans to look forward to posterity unless you respected their tendency to look backward to their ancestors.

But British indirect rule assumed, the presence of defined institutions in African societies, rooted in the history of those societies. And yet many African societies were relatively decentralized, without the statelike institutions of authority that the British would have preferred to use for purposes of governing. Where was indirect rule to find its paradigmatic formulation? Lord Lugard, the architect of Britain's policy of indirect rule, found those institutions in the emirates of Northern Nigeria. The legacy of Islam in Northern Nigeria, implanted several centuries before the British took over, provided a fertile ground for the implementation of the legacy of Edmund Burke in a colonial setting. Lugard found a "well-organized fiscal system, a definite code of land tenure, a regular scheme of local rule through district Heads, and a trained judiciary administering the tenets of the Muhammedan law."[6]

The British used the institutions they found for their own purposes. The native institutions of Northern Nigeria, if used properly by the new conquerors from Europe, could ensure that the people there were "neither entirely pushed nor at once pressured into turning their backs on their own antiquity."[7] A colonial doctrine was born within the wedlock of Burkean philosophy and Nigerian Islam.

The consequences of British colonial policies in places like Nigeria are of course still unfolding. Some are good and some evil. Some have been disruptive and some moderating and civilizing. What is clear in Nigeria is precisely the dramatic interplay of three civilizations—the culture and technology of Europe, the culture and religion of the Arabs, the culture and personality of Africa.

What should be remembered is the basic asymmetry in the relations among these three civilizations. The Europeans and the Arabs have both lent to each other and borrowed from each other. Europe today uses the Arabic numerals, and uses words like algebra, amalgam, and chemistry borrowed from Arabic and Islamic science. On the other hand, the world of the Arabs in the last two centuries has been considerably conditioned and influenced by the science and technology of the Western world. Intellectually and scientifically it is possible to argue that the cultural interchange between Europe and the Arab world has been basically reciprocal.

What about the cultural relationship between Europe and Africa or between Africa and the Arab world? In these two areas there is considerable unevenness. Although the religion of the Arabs is in the process of converting nearly a third of the population of black Africa, the religions of black Africa have had little influence on the Arabs. Similarly, while the Arabic language has profoundly conditioned such African media as Kiswahili and Hausa, the languages of Africa have made little reciprocal impact on mainstream Arabic.

A similar unevenness is evident in Africa's relationship with Europe. European Christianity has made impressively rapid progress in black Africa in a single century. Indeed, Christianity now is virtually an Afro-Western religion—since all Christian *nations* are either in the Western world or in Africa. Asia has millions of Christians, but almost everywhere Christianity in Asia is a minority religion, with the exception of the Philippines. But in Africa, within a few decades, whole societies have come to regard themselves as Christian. In contrast, African traditional religions are not only despised in the Western world; they are often also despised by the newly Christianized Africans.

Linguistically, Europe's impact on Africa has also been colossal, considering the brevity of European colonial rule. Almost everywhere in Africa south of the Sahara the natives who have acquired competence in European languages exercise disproportionate political influence and enjoy disproportionate prestige. The official language in most black African countries is a European language.

Where parliaments still exist, the language of discourse is a European language. Indeed, the continent itself identifies the different countries partly in terms of whether they are English-speaking, French-speaking, and now Portuguese-speaking. In contrast, Africa has exercised little linguistic influence on Europe. Once again the relationship is decidedly asymmetrical.

The two main policy issues that emerge from the triad of acculturation are, first, the problem of synthesizing the three civilizations within Africa and, second, the problem of reciprocating the penetration of Africa by the other two civilizations.

Nkrumah put the first problem of internal African synthesis at its most ambitious. As he formulated it:

> With true independence regained . . . a new harmony needs to be forged, a harmony that will allow the combined presence of traditional Islamic Africa, and Euro-Christian Africa, so that this presence is in tune with original humanist principles underlying African society. Our society is not the old, but a new society enlarged by Islamic Christian influences. A new emergent ideology is therefore required, an ideology which can solidify in a philosophical statement at the same time an ideology which will not abandon the original humanist principles of Africa.[8]

The idea of synthesizing the Western heritage, the Islamic civilization, and African cultures appears not only ambitious but perhaps unnecessary. What is necessary is a broad *modus vivendi* as a basis of coexistence and interaction among the three cultures—the foundations of a more balanced tripartite heritage. In Nkrumah's words again:

Practice without thought is blind: thought without practice is empty. The three segments of African society . . . co-exist uneasily; the principles animating them are often in conflict with one another. . . What is to be done then? I have stressed that the two other segments, in order to be rightly seen, must be accommodated only as experiences of the traditional African society. If we fail to do this our society will be racked by the most malignant schizophrenia.[9]

As for the task of redressing the balance of influence between Europe and Africa and also between the Arab world and Africa, this to some extent hinges on a process that I have christened *counterpenetration*. Africa has for too long been penetrated by others without attempting counterpenetration in return. Over the centuries the continent has been invaded from outside by foreign travelers, traders, slave-dealers, explorers, missionaries, colonizers, and teachers. Africans have often been passive receivers rather than active interventionists. The question that arises is how the process of acculturation can be reciprocated. As Africa gets increasingly Westernized, is there a chance that one day the West might be to some extent Africanized?

Apart from the influence of such artists as Picasso, the most important transmission belt of African culture into the Western world has been the black population of the United States. The black American impact on the musical culture of the United States especially has had worldwide reverberations. Black America in this sense is a crucial instrument of Africa's cultural counterpenetration into the Western world. Young people from Vancouver to Rio de Janeiro, from New York to Tokyo, from London to Belgrade, have often danced to jazz tunes that bear the unmistakable stamp of the black experience in the Western diaspora.

But what about former black slaves in the Arab world? Why did not people of African ancestry imported into places like Saudi Arabia become in turn transmission belts of African culture deep into the heritage of Islam?

One reason might well be Islam's profound distrust of certain art forms, including the performing arts. Although Western civilization and African cultures gave instrumental music a role to play even in prayer and worship, Islam as a religion tended to keep instrumental music at bay, while putting some value on the human voice for recitation of the Qur'an and hymns.

The first great *muezzin* of Islam was a man of African ancestry—Bilal,. He seems to have had a powerful voice. In my imagination I tend to see Bilal as the Paul Robeson of Mecca and Medina. Here was this black Muslim, equipped with a vibrant voice and a considerable personal presence. The voice was used not to sing 'Ol' Man River" but to summon believers to prayer in the very first years of Islam.

The constraints that Islam imposed on artistic culture not only narrowed the areas of creativity of the Arabs themselves, in areas where Islamic orthodoxy prevailed, but also significantly reduced the potentialities of Africa's counterpenetration into Islamic culture. What Africa had to offer to the Muslim world often lay in precisely those areas where the Muslim world was austere and puritanical. Africa's genius for rhythm and dance, the obsession with the drum, did not entirely miss the Arab world. Some elements of counterpenetration did take place in spite of the haughty puritanism of Islamic orthodoxy. Nevertheless, the contribution was not as striking as Africa's impact on America's musical culture on the opposite side of the globe.

The search has to continue for greater balance, greater mutuality of influence, between African civilization on one side and the civilizations of Europe and the Arab world on the other.

THE TRIAD OF PIGMENTATION

The third salient triad in relations between Europe, Africa, and the Arab world concerns issues of race and color. Technically the Arabs are part of the Semitic races, the Europeans part of the Caucasian, and the black Africans are deemed to be Negroid. Three "racial stocks" seem to be involved in the triangle of Africa, Europe, and the Arab world.

Historically, there was once again an important asymmetry in relations among these three peoples. Both the Europeans and the Arabs once raided black Africa for slaves and exported them to different regions under their control. But there was no instance of black Africans counterraiding either Europe or the Arab world for retaliatory enslavement. Europeans and Arabs were slavers and slave traders. Black Africans were primarily slaves, although parts of the African continent did perpetuate domestic slavery of an indigenous kind.

Between the European slave trade and the Arab slave trade there were some basic differences. The European slave trade in the modern period was much more race-specific, and even Afrocentric, than the Arab slave trade was. In other words, in the modern period, Europe had decided that the people most deserving of enslavement were those who were furthest away from Europeans in pigmentation or color of skin. Theoretically Europe could have invaded India for slaves, or the Middle East, or China, or indeed the Amerindian civilizations of the Americas. But for a variety of reasons, from the sixteenth century onward Europeans decided that the most deserving of enslavement of all people were in fact the black people.

In contrast, the Arab slave trade right into the twentieth century has continued to be racially ambivalent. According to the Arab system, white slaves were not a contradiction in terms. The traffic in slaves looked to the Near East, to Europe, to Asia, to the Arab world itself, as well as to Africa, for slaves. In the last three hundred years the bulk of the male slaves who went into the Arab world were perhaps from Africa, although figures are very difficult to compute. However, it is possible that the majority of female slaves during same period came from outside black Africa.

Aristotle had once suggested that some people were born to be slaves, while others were destined to be masters. Modern Europeans until the nineteenth century interpreted this to mean that some races were born to be slaves and others to be civilizing conquerors. However, the Arabs were seemingly accepting of Aristotle's position that some people might indeed have been destined to be slaves, but the Arabs rejected the proposition that the dividing line between slave and master was in terms of skin color and racial origin. Arab slave trade was pigmentationally diverse, a multicolored phenomenon. European slave trade in the modern period was overwhelmingly targeted at the black peoples.

With regard to the interplay between slavery and sexuality the two "master" races also had divergent inclinations. One interesting contrast from this point of view is between the eunuch *culture* in Middle Eastern slavery on one side, and the stud culture in Western slavery on the other. Middle Eastern cultures were inclined to overprotect their free women. If male slaves were to guard these women, how could temptation be controlled? One brutal answer was to make the male slaves incapable of "abusing" the women sexually. These specific males were therefore sexually mutilated as part of the process of preserving the chastity and dignity of the harem. What should be noted is that the custom of eunuchs is a product of Middle Eastern folk culture and is not sanctioned by Islam as a system of laws.

While Middle Easterners were making their males slaves incapable of sexually abusing their free women, Westerners were converting some of their male slaves into special studs to help produce good specimens. In North America especially, good strong male slaves were specially commanded to mate with diverse female slaves with a view to producing more highly marketable stock. The beginnings of eugenics in the Western world, in the field of human breeding, lie in the special utilization of strong "Negro" specimens as breeding studs. Among the factors that in the twentieth century have led to black excellence in sports and athletics in the United States might conceivably be counted the special breeding system that U.S. slavery sometimes encouraged. Indeed, by the early nineteenth century, some plantations in the South had become primarily "nigger farms" in which the main concern had shifted from producing cotton to producing physically more attractive slaves.

What all this means is that Middle Eastern Slavery included in its culture the brutalities of eunuchry. The masculinity of the male slaves was so distrusted that, when the slave was put in charge of a free harem, that masculinity had first to be destroyed. On the other hand, Western slave trade included in its culture the crudities of eugenics—the masculinity of the male slaves was sometimes so admired that a market value was put on it, and the potency of the man used for purposes of procreating more marketable progeny. Morally, it is difficult to be sure which was a greater insult to the male slave—destroying his capacity to produce children or forcing him to produce children for sale. On balance, the male slave in the Arab world was as badly off as the male slave in the West.

What about the state of the female slaves? On this issue Arab slavery was on the whole morally superior at least to the slavery of the Anglo-Saxons. Under Islamic law a slave woman who is sexually used by her master moves upward halfway toward freedom, and any children she might have with the master become absolutely free. In contrast, children produced as a result of mating between the master and his women slaves in the United States were themselves slaves. Alex Haley's character Chicken George, in *Roots*, was the child of a white master who raped one of his slave girls. Therefore Chicken George became a slave. His own father later sold him to a British slaver who took Chicken George beyond the seas. Under Islamic law, such a situation would have been indefensible. Chicken George, whose father was a free man and owner of his mother, would himself have been legally free.

This is linked to wider systems of lineage in the three civilizations of Africa, the Muslim world, and Europe. They encompass the rules of "miscegenation"—mating and procreating across racial lines. Let us recap here briefly the four systems of "miscegenation" in respect of lineage and descent of the children.

In a system of *descending miscegenation*, the offspring of a racially mixed parenthood is relegated to the status of the less-privileged parent. Thus, in the United States a child who has one parent black and the other white is categorized as black, regardless of whether it was the father or the mother who was black. The child descends to the status of the less privileged parent.

In contrast, Semitic civilizations observe a system of qualified *ascending miscegenation*. A child of racially mixed parenthood can move upward to the status of the more privileged parent, depending upon whether the parent who is more privileged is the mother or the father. Thus, in Israel, if the mother is Jewish the child is Jewish. The child ascends to the status of the mother in a society where Jews have a privileged position. In the Arab world, on the other hand, it is the father who decides the lineage. If the father is Arab the child is Arab—virtually regardless of the race or nationality of the mother. The child thus ascends to the status of the father.

That is one reason why the Arab world has such a multicolored composition. It includes white Arabs from Syria and Lebanon, brown Arabs of the Hadhramout and the Yemens, and the black Arabs of the Sudan. Indeed, the Sudan itself is an interesting laboratory of this principle of ascending miscegenation. In purely racial terms the so-called Arabized North is, on balance, more Negroid than Semitic. The balance of the races in the North is in favor of the blacks, but because of the lineage system, and of cultural and linguistic assimilation, the cultural balance in the North is in favor of Arabism. The remaining one-third of the Sudan is indisputably Negroid. What remains to be seen is whether this portion of the Sudan also will in time become Arabized as a result of both racial intermingling and general acculturation. In the latter process the principle of ascending miscegenation so characteristic of the Arabs would constitute a major aspect of the racial transition.

The third system of racial mixture important in Africa is *divergent miscegenation*. Under this lineage, a product of racially mixed parenthood constitutes a separate group. Thus a child with one parent black and the other white becomes classified as a third category. A particularly important illustration in Africa is the Cape Coloureds of the Republic of South Africa. This is a community consisting of people of mixed racial origin. For the time being they are deemed to be neither white nor African. In the United States they would be classified as black, but officially in South Africa they are not now so classified.

On the contrary, their fate could go in either direction as the situation in the republic polarizes. The great majority of the Coloured population in South Africa are culturally Afrikaners. In other words, the white part of their ancestry is predominantly from the whites known as Afrikaners. The native language of the great majority of the Coloureds is Afrikaans—the language of the Afrikaners. Some reformers in South Africa have suggested that the Coloureds should be reclassified and considered as Afrikaners. If this was accepted, the Coloureds would in fact be beneficiaries of ascending miscegenation, becoming part of the privileged class. In the struggle of the whites against Africans this would increase the number of those who are classified as, in some sense, white. And in the electoral struggle between Afrikaans-speaking and English-speaking whites the ascent of the Cape Coloureds to Afrikanerdom would double the number of Afrikaans-speaking whites in their rivalry with the Anglophones.

On the other hand, many Coloureds in South Africa have recently been in rebellion against white privilege and power. Some of them have even begun to identify themselves with the Africans. Indeed, a few analysts of the South African situation have started a redefinition of the vocabulary of racial analysis in South Africa. For such analysis the term *blacks* in South Africa should now mean not merely Africans but also Coloureds or people of mixed origin. This analysis would transform the lineage system of South Africa into something similar to the situation in the United States. There are even some analysts who would recommend the inclusion of people of Indian origin under the rubric of black.

The term *African* would refer to that section of the black population that is totally indigenous and racially unmixed.

It remains to be seen whether such a new vocabulary of the racial politics of South Africa will gain credence and replace the present one that differentiates between blacks, whites, Coloureds, and Indians. If the racial polarization of South Africa really gets under way, the people of mixed parenthood may indeed be forced to choose among ascending miscegenation, descending miscegenation, and divergent miscegenation.

Elsewhere in the African continent the interplay between ascent and descent has sometimes coincided with the period after independence and the period before. The first military coup in black Africa took place in Togo in 1963. The founder-president, Sylvanus Olympio, was assassinated in January 1963, and a man of racially mixed ancestry took over as head of state of Togo. Before independence, when Africans were the less privileged race, the categorization of this particular individual as an African was a case of descending miscegenation. But in 1963, when he assumed supreme authority as head of an independent African state, the racial ancestry had in this case become an instance of ascending miscegenation. Part of his parenthood was African. Therefore he was African himself. Therefore he had a right to assume supreme command in an African state.

In 1979, a similar situation seemed discernible for a while in Ghana. A soldier of mixed racial parenthood (Scottish to some extent) staged a coup against a military government. He then proceeded to execute three former presidents of Ghana, all of them much more purely African than he was. He succeeded in doing this in a manner that won him acclaim from millions of "pure Africans." Thus a product of mixed parenthood in independent Ghana as late as 1979 could be deemed to be so acceptable as an African that he could even execute former African presidents of the same country with impunity. Before independence this would have been a case of descending miscegenation. In the independent West African state of 1979 it was a striking case of ascending miscegenation.

Although in reality the basic systems of lineage and miscegenation do themselves constitute a triad (descending, ascending, and divergent) there is a residual fourth category, which we might call *ambivalent miscegenation*. Under this category a child of mixed parenthood could move up or down, following either the more privileged or the less, depending upon a number of indicators. Sometimes the indicator could be class-related; if the "half-caste" was economically poor, he just mingled with the blacks and became black. On the other hand, if he became economically prosperous he could mingle with the whites and become white.

A second indicator is the shade of skin color itself. If the "half-caste" was quite fair in appearance he could enter the white circuit, although everybody in that circuit knew that his parenthood was mixed. On the other hand, if that child was pretty dark, he might drift into the universe of the black, population.

A third indicator after economics and skin shade is education and culture. Two brothers with identical parents could be racially designated differently. The highly educated surgeon, even if his color was dark, could to all intents and purposes live as a white man. On the other hand, his brother—working as a trade unionist at the docks, or relegated to the ghettos—might live as a black man although he was a shade fairer than his sibling.

Within Africa itself ambivalent miscegenation is more discernible in Portuguese-speaking Africa than anywhere else, although at least as strong in some societies is the divergent phenomenon of mulattoes in Latin America.

THE TRIAD OF STRATIFICATION

Issues of race and racism in our tripolar world would have included questions of rank and the pecking order. In the modern period, partly because of their technological power, the Europeans have successfully managed to lay claim to the highest positions in international ranking. Africans on the whole have usually been condemned to the bottom position—while the Arabs have sometimes been almost white in the privileges they have enjoyed and sometimes been almost black in the exploitation and humiliation to which they have been subjected.

But stratification is not simply a question of race; it is more often a question of class and status. In postcolonial Africa the three most important classes have been the peasantry, the new bourgeoisie, and the emerging proletariat. Numerically the peasants are the most important—they constitute the majority of the population in most African countries. But in terms of power the new bourgeoisie, almost by definition, has managed to amass a disproportionate share.

But what is this new bourgeoisie in Africa and to what extent is it a product of the impact of Europeans and Arabs upon the continent? It is not often realized that class formation in Africa is not simply a matter of economics; it is also an outgrowth of culture. Class formation is not simply a question of "who owns what?" but also a question of "who knows what?" Among the areas of knowledge that have been particularly important in African stratification is knowledge of European languages. In one African country after another the imported imperial language is the official language of the nation-used by a small elite at the top to conduct the central political and diplomatic business of the society. In most African countries, people cannot become members of parliament unless they have a command of the relevant European language in the country. For the acquisition of ultimate political power in an average black African country, the only alternative to competence in European verbal skills is relative command over imported Western military hardware. The latter basis of power is what all military coups in Africa are all about. To penetrate the citadels of political power in an African country one must have a good command of either the barrel of the gun or the flow of words.

Europe's impact on the Arab world in the cultural sphere is less consistent than Europe's impact on Africa. Although countries like Algeria are still struggling to find the right balance between the role of Arabic, the role of French, and the role of the Berber language, the Arab world as a whole has managed to escape black Africa's fate of conducting the most important national business in a European language. The Arabs have succeeded in retaining Arabic as the primary instrument of national politics and administration. The fact that the Arab world is, by definition, much more linguistically homogeneous than black Africa can claim to be is certainly an important part of the explanation.

What about the impact of Arab culture on the stratification systems of black Africa? In those African countries that are primarily Muslim there is indeed a tendency toward a stratified triad of cultures. More often than not, those who are Westernized still have disproportionate influence and power. Second in importance from this point of view are those who are substantially Islamized. At the bottom of the pyramid of power and influence are the purer indigenes—the local "natives" who have not been assimilated into an alien culture.

What should be borne in mind is that Islamization and Westernization often compete for the top positions of influence in such black African countries as Senegal, Mali, and. even Nigeria. On balance those who were Westernized tend to have the best chances in the system, but by no means invariably. Those who are within the Islamic power structure in Northern Nigeria or Senegal are sometimes as powerful as anybody else within the system.

Throughout Africa there are occasions when the three cultures (indigenous, Islamic, and Western) are associated with specific occupations. A certain level of Westernization is often associated with white collar work. An African child who completes secondary education in a Western-style institution is often reluctant to consider any job that is not white collar. If the parents had made sacrifices to enable a child to complete secondary education, they in turn would feel betrayed if the child did not do his best to get a clerical job, instead of helping with the farm at home. Westernization carries occupational expectations that sometimes make young Africans prefer unemployment and social redundancy rather than an "inappropriate" job outside the culture of offices.

Islamization, on the other has often been associated with trade rather than white collar work. Migrant Hausa traders in West Africa are part of speakers on trading routes in East Africa are part of this association of Islam with commerce on foot.

In religiously heterogeneous African countries, it has also made sense to leave the business of meat selling and butchery to Muslims. Since Muslim customers insist on a particular way of killing the cow or the goat if the meat is to be halal (legitimate as diet), and African Christians and followers of African religions are neutral on how the animal is killed, it is only common sense to let the Muslim part of the population take care of the business of butchery and meat distribution. This has certainly tended to be the pattern in Eastern Africa. In Uganda, under the political leadership of Benedicto Kiwanuka at the beginning of the 1960s, the principle of a Muslim monopoly of the meat trade was temporarily repudiated by the government. But since then the Muslims have reasserted their control of a disproportionate share of the meat trade.

As for those Africans who have not been assimilated into either Western or Islamic culture, it is easier to refer to occupations from which they are excluded than to specific occupations with which they are associated. Africans who are completely non-Westernized are very unlikely to enter the general field of white collar professions. Africans who are neither Westernized nor Islamized are unlikely to become administrators or bureaucrats. The great majority of such Africans are peasant farmers, but many have also become traders and some have been recruited into the newly emerging proletarian class.

But stratification is not merely at the national level or the level of the class designation of individuals. Stratification is also an international phenomenon. Whole societies can be classified and ranked.

Ahmed Sekou Toure, president of Guinea (Conakry), has sometimes referred to Africa as "a continent of the proletarian peoples." Toure's view is different from the view that sometimes sees Africa as "a classless continent." A "proletarian Africa" is virtually a class in itself—a class within a global system of stratification.

Julius K. Nyerere also has been sensitive to the fact that wealth differentials are not simply between individuals but also between societies. As Nyerere put it in the year of Tanganyika's independence:

> Karl Marx felt there was an inevitable clash between the rich of one society and the poor of that society. In that, I believe/ Karl Marx was right. But today it is the international scene which is going to have a greater impact on the lives of individuals [in Tanganyika] than what is happening within Tanganyika. . . . And when you look at the international scene, you must admit that the world is divided between the "haves" and "have nots.". . . And don't forget that the rich countries of the world today may be found on both sides of the division between "Capitalist" and "Socialist" countries.[10]

If black Africa is basically part of the "have nots" of the world, and the Europeans are part of the "haves," where do the Arabs fit in? If Africa is part of a global proletariat, and Europe indisputably part of the global bourgeoisie, to what global class do the Arabs belong?

Until oil wealth affected the destiny of some of the Arab states, it was easy to think of the Arab world as part of the "have nots" in the economic sense. Indeed, until the 1970s the terms *underdeveloped countries* and poor countries were almost interchangeable.

But the emergence of oil power has shattered the easy equation. Virtually all Third World countries are still technically underdeveloped, but only some of them are now poor. South Yemen and Tanzania are still good illustrations of the old equation. They are both poor and underdeveloped. But since the '1970s it has become difficult to think of Saudi Arabia as a "poor country." This is one of the best-endowed countries in the world in oil wealth and dollar reserves, yet at the same time one of the least developed.

We said earlier that class formation within African societies was often a matter of "who knows what" rather than a matter of "who owns what." The question that now arises is whether the '*international* stratification system is based on know-how (especially technology) or on wealth.

The concept of the Third World is normally associated with technical underdevelopment rather than dollar reserves in the bank. There is therefore the First World of technically advanced capitalist countries (the West and Japan); then there is the Second World of technically advanced socialist countries (the Soviet Union and its European allies); and lastly, there is the Third World of technically underdeveloped countries of Africa, Asia, and Latin America. The stratification here is decidedly in terms of modern and developmental know-how rather than in terms of idle petrodollars languishing in Swiss banks. Under this technological definition, the Arab countries and black Africa belong to the same global class.

But if one adopted a system of global stratification based on the per capita income of societies, Saudi Arabia would belong to a decidedly different class from Tanzania. What should be remembered is that Nigeria would belong to a higher class than North Yemen. And Kuwait and Saudi Arabia would both belong to a higher class than Great Britain.

On balance, a global stratification based on income per head of population is less credible than a global stratification based on technical development and know-how. Under the latter structure Egyptians, Nigerians, Tanzanians, and the ordinary people of Saudi Arabia are all part of an exploited and underdeveloped stratum of an international pyramid of privilege and power.

It is of course possible to think in terms of a Fourth World. Under this scheme the Third World would consist of those countries that are technically underdeveloped but at the same time resource-rich. The term *Fourth World* would be reserved for those countries that are both technically underdeveloped and resource-poor. Saudi Arabia and Nigeria would thus become part of the Third World, while Tanzania and South Yemen would be classified as members of the Fourth World.

There are two or three objections to this sub-division, some political and some intellectual Politically it can be asserted that the whole technique of separating resource-poor underdeveloped countries is a device of resource-rich underdeveloped countries is a device of the North to turn underdeveloped countries against each other. It is the old technique of "divide and rule."

Secondly, using resources as way of defining the world's global system makes the system appear more fluid than it really is. Niger lacked uranium a decade ago and has since discovered it. Has Niger really shifted in international affiliations? The copper market was booming a few years ago and has drastically declined. Did Zambia really belong to a higher class a few years ago than it does now? If the Western powers succeeded in developing alternative sources of energy, and the world had a surplus of oil, would OPEC members really undergo downward social mobility in class terms?

The trouble with stratifying the world in terms of mineral resources is that we would need to reclassify countries every time there is an oil strike in a particular society in the South or every time commodity prices on the world market rise or fall dramatically. In reality the global stratification system is much less flexible and more obstinate than this kind of analysis would imply. There is not enough structure at the global level in a class system based on income per head of population, drawn from a fluctuating or perishable commodity.

If Saudi dollars are languishing in Western banks, instead of being used to transform Saudi society, one reason could be Saudi Arabia's incapacity to absorb that wealth. There is a technical gap that requires more than the availability of dollars to fill it. If Saudi Arabia's oil has to be used in the streets of Tokyo and Philadelphia and is inadequately utilized for the internal industrial development of Saudi Arabia, one reason might be the preexistent technological underdevelopment of the society.

Perhaps at the global level, as well as in internal domestic arrangements in formerly colonized countries, class formation is decidedly not merely a question of "who owns what"—but is ultimately a consequence of "who knows what." The North's leadership in technology guarantees it leadership in power for at least the rest of this century. In that sense the Arabs and the black Africans are in the same boat—and their boat is definitely not the flagship.

A TRIAD OF CONFRONTATIONS

So far we have discussed direct relations between Europeans, Africans, and Arabs. In the long run perhaps these are the most important relations. What should be remembered constantly is the influence of other parties on these tripartite contacts.

In the political domain, a major variable has been the role of adversaries of each of these regions. As far as Western Europe is concerned, the most important political adversary is the Soviet Union. As far as the Arab world is concerned, the adversary that commands the greatest hostility is still Israel.' As . far as black Africa is concerned, the remaining symbol of racial humiliation on the continent is the white-dominated Republic of South Africa. In other words, each of our three regions has one particularly visible adversary.

Its own relations with that adversary have had repercussions in its relations with the other two regions.

The Soviet Union has been an imperialist power in Europe, a. liberating force in Africa, and a force with a mixed record in Asia. In Europe the USSR allowed itself to be heir to both the Czarist and the Nazi empires. What the Czars acquired territorially and incorporated into the body politic of Russia, the new Communist regime after 1917 retained. What the Nazis occupied in the course of World War II and the Soviet troops ostensibly liberated, the Soviet Union continued to dominate. Soviet allies in Eastern Europe are mainly countries that had once been under the Nazi yoke—and now remain under Soviet hegemony.

But in Africa the Soviet rule has been—whatever the motives of Moscow— basically liberating. The liberation of countries like Zimbabwe, Angola and Mozambique would have taken at least a generation longer to accomplish if the Soviet Union had not supported the liberation fighters with weapons and other forms of assistance. No Western government would have provided to African liberation fighters the scale of military support they received from the Soviet Union. And elsewhere on the African continent the political and diplomatic rivalries between the West and the Soviet Union have been major contributors to the decolonization process. The West's commitment to decolonization needed the impetus of Soviet rivalry in the quest for friends in Africa.

As for the Soviet Union's record in Asia, this has been mixed. It has included the constructive role of helping Vietnam defeat its Western imperialist enemies. On the other hand, the Soviet role in Asia has also included acquiring new territory. Among the more blatant imperialist roles that the Soviet Union has played recently has been its role in the invasion of Afghanistan. On balance Soviet occupation of Afghanistan is strikingly reminiscent of the Italian occupation of Abyssinia (Ethiopia) in 1935. Both Afghanistan and Abyssinia were relatively backward societies that had nevertheless managed to maintain a degree of ferocious independence across the centuries. Some of their institutions were feudal and outmoded, yet they seemed to retain legitimacy for a while in their own populations. But Abyssinia was then crushed by the Italians, and Afghanistan by the Russians.

However, most African leaders have been relatively mild in their condemnation of Soviet intervention in Afghanistan—even though it is a massive retrograde step in the history of imperialism in the second half of the twentieth century. One reason why African leaders have been relatively insensitive on the issue of Afghanistan is simply the record of the Soviet Union in helping African liberation. While Westerners have been slow to recognize the rights of blacks in Southern Africa, the Soviets have been in the forefront of sympathetic support for many years.

The second critical adversary involved in this drama is Israel as an adversary of the Arabs. If the West has been strengthening the Republic of South Africa economically, Israel may have been strengthening it militarily. Speculation about Israel's military relations with South Africa has focused on two aspects—counterinsurgency and nuclear power. The Israelis have been singularly successful in virtually every battle they have fought with Palestinian insurgents. Israel as a country may one day lose the war for its survival, but for the time being Israel has managed to win the battles. This posture of heroic and lonely battles against "terrorism" has inspired many whites in Southern Africa. Diehard Afrikaners in the Republic of South Africa are sometimes both anti-Semitic and pro-Israel. They dislike their own Jews domestically while strongly admiring Israel's glories of heroic isolation. As a result the Pretoria government has sought to learn from the Israelis the techniques of counterinsurgency and antiterrorism.

The second major military area of collaboration between Israel and South Africa is nuclear collaboration. When in September 1979 the United States announced that a nuclear device had been exploded not far from Southern Africa, the immediate suspicion was that the Republic of South Africa had at last gone nuclear. South Africa vigorously denied this. The United States then hesitated on its own evidence and allegedly seemed unsure. Subsequent speculation seemed to indicate that if there was a nuclear explosion, it might have been primarily Israel's with the support of South Africa, rather than South Africa's with the support of Israel. If the explosion was primarily Israel's, Washington had additional reasons for suddenly pretending it was not sure if any nuclear device had exploded at all. Washington's fear of nuclear proliferation becomes even stronger in the case of proliferation in the Middle East. Has a conspiracy of silence developed to disguise Israel's nuclear capability? Is South Africa an ally in all this?

In the last ten years the broader politics of black Africa have certainly intermingled with the politics of the Middle East. One aspect of this intermingling has been the growing cordiality between Israel and South Africa. It would not be correct to say that Israel has drawn nearer to South Africa only because the majority of black, African states decided to break off relations with Israel in 1973. There was already evidence of very rapid increase in trade and economic cooperation between the two countries well before the outbreak of the October War. Again, before black Africa broke off relations, Israel had decided to raise the level of its representation in Pretoria, and Ambassador Michael Michael was designated. This trend antedated black Africa's severance of relations and therefore was clearly independent of it. Nevertheless, the outbreak of the October War and Africa's decision to declare its solidarity with the Arabs against Israel provided an additional linkage between the politics of the Middle East and the politics of Africa.

Some Western and African commentators have suggested that the Arabs owed the Africans financial and economic reciprocity—that in return for African support over Israel the Arabs should extend greater economic and financial support to African development. There is certainly a compelling case for Arab contributions to African development, but the case should not depend primarily on African support for the Arabs in their confrontation with Israel. In exchange for that African support, the Arabs should maintain and increase their own support for African liberation in Southern Africa. Indeed, the Arabs had been substantially supportive of the African cause in Southern Africa at least a decade before the majority of African states discovered that there was a Palestinian cause worthy of their moral interest. The relevant *modus vivendi* in African-Arab politics is the mutual recognition of each other's primary adversaries—African support against Israel in exchange for Arab support against white minority rule in South Africa.

As for that third adversary, the Soviet Union, it encountered certain setbacks in the Arab world in the 1970s. Not long after the death of Nasser, Egypt drifted out of the Soviet sphere of influence. This was a major reversal in the Soviet Union's diplomatic offensive in the Arab world. And although Egypt would not have had the modest success it had in the October War of 1973 without Soviet support, the trend throughout the 1970s was toward widening the gap between Cairo and Moscow.

Then, on the Western extremity of the Mediterranean world, another event seemed to open a new opportunity for the Soviet Union when a historic military coup took place on the Iberian peninsula. This was the coup in Lisbon in April 1974. The overthrow of the legacy of fascism soon resulted in the collapse of the Portuguese Empire. The Soviet Union had a new opportunity to compensate for losses in the Arab world. Marxist regimes seemed to be on the horizon in Portuguese-speaking Africa. Henry Kissinger woke up one day to discover a "Soviet threat" in a previously undisputed "Western sphere of influence." The West sat up at last and took more the issue of residual liberation in Southern Africa much more seriously than it had ever done before. The Soviet Union as a superpower had to some extent compensated in Southern Africa for the serious setback it had suffered in North Africa when Egypt expelled the Russian advisers and later repudiated the treaty of friendship between the two of countries.

The politics of linkage had once again brought together three different confrontations—the West versus the USSR, the Arabs versus Israel, and the Africans in opposition to white minority rule in the southern portion of their continent.

THE GLOBAL CONTEXT: A TRIAD OF ALLEGIANCE

Many of the triads discussed above have had an ideological component. In both Africa and the Arab world there is a good deal of ideological fluidity—partly because of the impact of European ideas. Governments and the intelligentsia are, on the one hand, sensitive to the need for authenticity and autonomy and, on the other, responsive to the spell of Western-derived systems of thought—especially liberal capitalism, socialism, and nationalism.

Underlying the ideological fluidity in Africa and the Arab world are the dynamics of three forms of loyalty—to the individual, to the group, and to the nation. Loyalty to the individual, creates a predisposition toward liberalism. Loyalty to the nation can sometimes become a form of nationalism. As for group loyalties, these range from ethnicity to class solidarity. The latter sometimes leads to debates about the comparative relevance of liberal capitalism and socialism.

The African and Arab response to European colonialism included elements of all three forms of loyalty—individual loyalty, group solidarity, and national allegiance. Particularly potent as a force against colonialism was African and Arab nationalism.

But is not nationalism inward-looking and tending toward isolating these peoples? That depends upon the type of nationalism. Both Pan-Africanism and Pan-Arabism are major regional movements involving many countries. They also tend to have a built-in global consciousness, if only of a defensive kind. Pan-Africanism and Pan-Arabism are in part a response to an unfavorable distribution of power in the world. Both movements include an anti-imperialist tradition and an ambivalent attitude toward the Western world.

Pan-Africanism and Pan-Arabism have found institutional expression in the OAU and the League of Arab States, respectively. The league has been in disarray since 1977 because of the Sadat peace initiative and the consequent isolation of Egypt in the Arab world. But that debate itself is probably a product of nationalism at two levels. Was the Sadat initiative partly a child °f Egyptian nationalism? Was it a child of Egyptian weariness at having to pay the price of Arab leadership? Is there a continuing basic clash between Egyptian and Arab nationalism?

In addition to these clashes between national and transnational loyalties, there are the subnational conflicts in both Africa and the Arab world. Sometimes these are also forms of nationalism. Nigeria fought a civil war because of Ibo nationalism. And Uganda continues to be centrally affected by the nationalism of the Baganda.

But where does Europe fit into all this? For one thing the nation-state system is itself a child of Western diplomatic history and Western statecraft. The legacy of the Treaty of Westphalia of 1648, when sovereign statehood was inaugurated, has now been globalized. Concepts of nationalism, sovereignty, statehood, and liberty on the world scene have never been the same again. The rhetoric and paradigm of nationalism in both the Arab world and Africa in the twentieth century have shown the marks of the European impact.

Another effect of Europe's influence on our tripartite concerns is that it has helped to reduce the danger of a clash between Pan-Africanism and Pan-Arabism. As I indicated, the Arab slave trade still casts its shadow on African perceptions of the contemporary Arab world. But the legacy of shared European imperialism and the continuing economic hegemony of the Western world have, on the whole, continued to give Pan-Africanism and Pan-Arabism a semblance of comradeship-in-arms against Northern hegemony.

Not that tensions are entirely absent from African-Arab relations. The OAU, OPEC, and the League of Arab States have overlapping memberships. The African states have sometimes attempted to turn the OAU into a lever to extract *economic* benefits from the oil-rich Arabs and their allies. The Arab states have at times attempted to turn the OAU into a lever to extract political benefits from black Africans, especially one the issue of Israel.

As for OPEC, it is both admired and resented in much of the Third World. It is admired as an instance of the Third World's potential power; OPEC is the most powerful instrument that the Third World has produced in the twentieth century. But OPEC is also resented by poorer Third World countries for being inadequately sensitive to the catastrophic impact of oil prices on many of the economies of the Third World.

In black Africa OPEC is sometimes popularly equated with the Arab world. And yet the most important Arab member of OPEC is more opposed to high oil prices than is the most important black African member of OPEC. Saudi Arabia is more of a price "dove" in OPEC than is Nigeria; Nigeria is more of a price "hawk" than Abu Dhabi.

But in the ultimate analysis, what makes African-Arab solidarity survive is a continuing and growing awareness by the two regions that they continue to be dominated by the North.

This brings us to the fourth variety of nationalism. We have so far discussed state-specific nationalism (like Egyptian nationalism), regionwide nationalism (like Pan-Arabism) and substate forms of nationalism (like Ibo, Ganda, and Kurdish brands of nationalism). What has been emerging more recently is what one might call *hemispheric nationalism*. The Third World has been evolving a level of solidarity that is partly a form of nationalism across three continents and partly a form of class consciousness on the global scale. It manifests itself most sharply within the U.N. system—from UNCTAD sessions to the general conferences of the United Nations Educational, Scientific and Cultural Organization

(UNESCO), from special economic sessions of the U.N. General Assembly to the search for a New International Information Order.

We need to place these developments within a global, overlapping systemic triad—the wider state system, the U.N. system, and the system of transnational, nongovernmental movements and trends. In the twentieth century the wider state system has been fostering *global ethnicity*. The idea of the nation-state has on the one hand resulted in such transnational movements as Pan-Africanism, eager one day to produce a United States of Africa. It has also produced Pan-Arabism, with endless experiments in federations and confederations. But the same idea of the nation-state has inspired substate units— such as the Ibo, Kurds, and some Welsh-speaking Welsh nationalists—that have dreamt about forming their own nation-states. Centrifugal and centripetal varieties of nationalism in this context are what *global ethnicity* within the *first system of nation-states* is all about.

The second global system is that of the United Nations. My thesis here is that the second system generates the nearest thing to global class consciousness that we have witnessed so far. The United Nations converts the whole world into an arena of scarce resources. The United Nations also provides the forum of debate and the battlefield of at least political confrontation. In such a situation of global sociology the possibilities of perceiving planetary resources as being subject to distributive justice are enhanced; they are sometimes even maximized.

What all this means is that the U.N. system is in a sense the most important "proletarianizing" factor on the global scene. It helps to enable poor societies to sense their predicament in a planetary context. Hence the emerging Third World solidarity—however fragile—in the U.N. system.

In this context the Arabs and Africans find themselves part of the underprivileged "class" of the world—even when the Arabs are rich in *dollars*. Why should they not be rich in their *own* currencies? Because the monetary system of the world has a stratified system of exchange—the dinar, for example, are not valued independently but only in relation to the dollar. There is a pecking order of currencies. There is also a pecking order of technology. Higher development amid energy deficit is more powerful than energy surplus in the midst of primitive technology.

The third global system of transnational, private, nongovernmental movements and institutions unfortunately is predominantly Northern, made up especially of Northwestern movements like independent trade unions, peace research movements, transnational corporations, and liberal movements on human rights. Many of these movements (although not all) are instances of *globalized individualism and planetary private initiatives*.

What all this means is that the first system of Westphalia—the nation-state—has been promoting forms of global ethnicity. The second system of the United Nations has been promoting global class consciousness, ranging from UNCTAD debates to those of special economic sessions of the General Assembly. The third system of transnational nongovernmental movements includes a tendency toward globalized individualism and planetary private initiatives.

Europe is strong on this last ideological tendency—leaning toward individualism, private enterprise, and human rights. This is the heritage of liberalism. The Arab world and Africa are strong in this period of history on the rights of groups. Arabs and Africans are also strong, as new converts to Westphalia, on the rights of nation-states.

The struggle for the future is to convert Arabs, Africans, and Europeans to *planetary* concerns. How can we create the context for planetary interchange and global cooperation? It may well be that an intermediate stage is a triad of dissent. Let us now turn to this triad.

THE GLOBAL CONTEXT: A TRIAD OF DISSENT

But even beyond the specific national adversaries of each of our regions, there are the broader social forces at work in the world as a whole. The historical context, as intimated earlier, includes the rise of the West into global hegemony. Western technology, culture and power began to conquer much of the world. Western ideas, languages, systems of education, m odes of engineering and production, patterns of consumption, and even rules of behavior began to penetrate societies originally vastly different from those of the West.

What has emerged in recent times are three major challenges to Western hegemony—the challenges of Marxism, Islam, and nationalism in the Third World. This is the global triad of dissent.

Marxism's main attack is on the West's economic hegemony. The Marxist paradigm highlights economic factors and traces power to the fountainhead of basic production. The attack on capitalism and economic imperialism is an inevitable outgrowth of the paradigm. The Islamic challenge, on the other hand, is directed more at the West's *cultural* hegemony than at its economic domination. The revolution in Iran is the epitome of this cultural challenge. The nationalism of the Third World started off as being aimed primarily at the West's *political* hegemony. The anticolonial movements were seeking to enter the arena of Western-style diplomacy—from flags to diplomatic immunity, from national anthems to membership in the United Nations.

The question arises whether Third World nationalism will learn from Marxism and seriously challenge Western economic hegemony. The question also arises whether "Third World nationalism will learn from Islam and begin to challenge the West's cultural hegemony.

Africa and the Arab world are two of the arenas where these battles of dissent are being fought out. Europe, on the other hand, is part of the dominating presence of the Western world as a whole.

In the quest for equity at the global level, the other triads discussed raise policy issues. I mentioned that Europe's relations with the Arab world are structural, and so are Europe's relations with Africa. What are not as yet adequately structured are the relations between the Arabs and the Africans on their own. The triangle needs to be completed. The Arabs have had three major roles in their relations with Africa across the centuries. They have been accomplices in Africa's enslavement and exploitation in the past, allies in Africa's liberation from the Western world more recently, and potential partners in Africa's development. The completion of the triangle may require an expansion of the role of the Arabs as partners in development in the years ahead.

With regard to the triad of acculturation, we noted that the penetration has been from Europe into Africa much more than from Africa into Europe. It has also been from the Arab world into Africa much more than from Africa into the Arab world. The policy issues that arise for the future are whether this asymmetry is inevitable, or whether a process of Africa's counter-penetration into Europe and the Arab world can in fact be inaugurated at a new level. Such counterpenetration by Africa could take cultural, economic, or political forms. A fusion of economic and political counter-penetration can take place when an African country succeeds in converting a particular commodity from a basis of great dependency upon Europe into an instrument of political leverage. Oil was once primarily a basis of dependency; it has now become an instrument of power and influence in the hands of those who possess it. Niger discovered uranium—but its dependency upon France did not lessen, very significantly. It is conceivable that Niger could transform its uranium resources into a basis of countervailing power.

With regard to the Arab world, there has been some counterpenetration of the Gulf by Swahili culture in the last twenty years. Many East Africans, especially from Zanzibar, went looking for jobs or political refuge in the Gulf States after the Zanzibar revolution, in 1964, Some of these Swahili-speaking East Africans hold important jobs in Oman, Abu Dhabi, and even, some towns in Saudi Arabia. One can overhear a conversation in Kiswahili in the Hilton Hotel in Abu Dhabi or in the streets of Muscat. This is a form of counterpenetration, form of counterpenetration, and East Africa should facilitate it.

The triad of pigmentation may be the most finite of them all. A revolution in the Republic of South Africa could occur within the next generation. And racism as an institutionalized phenomenon may in any case be on the way out of human history. In the decades ahead Arabs, Africans, and Europeans will probably quarrel less and less on issues of race and color and more on issues of resources and jobs. The basic policy issue here therefore is to promote those forces that are battling against racism. The Arabs should go beyond diplomatic support for movements against apartheid and commit greater economic resources to the tasks of liberation. Greater pressures on Western oil companies to stop or reduce the illicit flow of oil to the Republic of South Africa would also be a major contribution to the fight against institutionalized racism.

It would also make sense to revive the battle of denouncing Zionism as a form of racism. Zionism started off with religious and nationalist connotations, but it has developed into a racial ideology. Indeed, its insistence on separating the Jews into a distinct Jewish state is very similar ideologically to the commitment by apartheid to create a separate homeland for each cultural group in South Africa. Israel was created as a kind of "Bantustein." The Arabs and Africans should not be "terrorized" by Western governments and media into giving up the struggle against the racial aspects of Zionism.

But more long-lasting than issues of race are issues of stratification and domestic triad of stratification and class formation. The domestic triad of stratification—peasantry, bourgeoisie, and proletariat in Africa especially—is bound to undergo significant changes in the rest of the century. The proletariat will grow, and so will the bourgeoisie. The persistent question is whether the peasantry will succeed in protecting its economic interests and enhancing its political participation as Africa undergoes the twin processes of proletarianization and embourgeoisement.

As for the triad of international stratification, the Muslim world has become part of the vanguard of dissent. Although Islam's main preoccupation is indeed cultural, particular Muslim countries vary in the foci of their efforts. As we indicated, Algeria took the lead in the struggle for a New International Economic Order. It is feasible to argue that militant Iran and militant Libya are both involved in challenging the foundations of traditional international law and aspire to create a new international legal order.

NOTES

1. Ali Mazrui, *The Trial of Christopher Okigbo* (London: Heinemann Educational Books, 1971), p. 135.

2. See R. R. Palmer in collaboration with Joel Colton, A History of the Modern *World,* 2nd ed. (New York: Knopf, 1962), 13. This issue is also discussed in the Introduction to

Ali Mazrui, *The African Condition: A Political Diagnosis* (London: Heinemann Educational Books; New York: Cambridge University Press, 1980) (the B.B.C. Reith Lectures), ix–x.

3. See Herskovits's contribution to *Wellesley College Symposium on* Africa (Wellesley, Mass.: Wellesley College, 1960), p. 16.

4. Kwame Nkrumah, *Consciencism: Philosophy and Ideology for Decolonization and Development with Particular Reference to the African Revolution* (London: Heinemann Educational Books, 1964), p. 69–71.

5. Edmund Burke, Works, Vol. 4, *Reflections on the Revolution in France* (1790) (London: World's Classic Edition, 1907), p. 109.

6. Hugh, Lord Hailey, *An African Survey*, rev. ed. (London: Oxford University Press, 1957), p. 453–54.

7. This doctrinal marriage is also discussed in Mazrui, *The African Condition*, 97–99.

8. Nkrumah, *Consciencism,* p. 70.

9. *Ibid*, 78.

10. Julius Nyerere, "The Second Scramble," a speech delivered at the opening of the World Assembly of Youth Seminar in Dar es Salaam, 1961.

THE SEMITES BETWEEN
SIN AND VIRTUE

Chapter Thirteen

Comparative Slavery: Western, Muslim and African Legacies

In 1992 the Heads of State of Africa, at their summit meeting in Dakar, Senegal, appointed twelve "Eminent Persons" to explore the modalities and logistics of a future campaign for reparations to compensate Black people for centuries of enslavement and exploitation.[1] By that date the world was already familiar with German reparations to the Jews for the Holocaust under Nazi Germany.[2] Koreans were demanding reparations from the Japanese for the brutal Japanese version of imperialism. Korean women exploited in World War II as "comfort women" (sex objects) for Japanese soldiers were demanding restitution.[3] And of course Kuwait was receiving reparations for a brief Iraqi occupation (1990–1991).[4]

But what happened to centuries of Black enslavement and exploitation? African Presidents in 1992 wanted to know if there was a case for Black compensation.

In preparation for the task of determining the case for reparations, we need to understand the types of slavery to which Africans were subjected. The most notorious was the trans-Atlantic slave trade which exported millions of Africans to the Americas.

And yet we know that there was such a thing as the Arab slave trade. How did that compare with the trans-Atlantic slave traffic? We also know that indigenous Africans themselves were not total strangers to mutual enslavement. How did that indigenous slavery compare to the other two systems of servitude?

We need to examine all three systems of slavery before we decide which system should be the first to be held accountable for reparations. Are there different degrees of culpability for slavery?

Modern African history can indeed be viewed as an interplay between three major civilizations—the indigenous, the Islamic and the Western legacies. The traditions and customs of Africa have often responded to or recoiled from the stimuli of the Arabs and the Europeans. There have been occasions when Africa has in turn counterpenetrated the cultural citadels of its conquerors— exerting reverse influence. What has been taking root on African soil itself is the reality of an African triple heritage. The three legacies of Africa, Islam and the West have begun to undergo their own special dialectic of thesis, antithesis and synthesis.[5]

In this paper we apply the concept of the triple heritage to the distinctive experience of slavery. We propose to demonstrate how that experience has indeed encompassed three distinctive traditions of slave culture—indigenous, Islamic and Western. We shall conclude with observations about how the evil of slavery yesterday has nevertheless resulted in forging a potential global role for the Africa of *tomorrow*.

ON SLAVERY AND RACE

Let us first spell out the comparative agenda for our examination of slavery.[6] To begin, indigenous slave-systems in Africa tended to be *uniracial* or *mono-racial*. The masters were of the same race and colour as the slaves. It follows therefore that indigenous slave-systems in Africa were, by definition, the least racist in orientation and attitudes between victors and victims.[7]

In polarised contrast, the Western trans-Atlantic slave-trade was *bi-racial*— targeted at producing a plantation civilization which had white masters and black slaves. Western slave-systems, especially in North America and the Caribbean, became the most racist of all forms of modern slavery. Basically two races confronted each other across the evil institution of slavery. The establishment and growth of slavery owed a great deal to writing—particularly by Christian theologians—that legitimized the racial inferiority of blacks.[8]

Slavery as practised in the Muslim world was *multiracial*. Both the masters and the slaves could be almost of any race. An Arab master could own slaves who came from Africa, Europe or Asia. Indeed, the Arab master could at one time also own Arab slaves. Turks owned Baluchi or Albanian slaves and Syrians owned Indian or Greek slaves.[9] Although slavery as practised by Muslims often included prejudice against this or that ethnic group or caste, skin-colour was not the central divide between masters and slaves. There was no theory which characterized one race as natural slaves and another as natural masters. The slave-system in the Muslim world was not rooted in a basic philosophy of racial stratification, as was the case with the trans-Atlantic slave-trade.

To summarize the argument so far, while indigenous slave-systems were *uniracial* (Black masters, Black slaves), and while trans-Atlantic forms of slavery were *biracial* (white masters, Black slaves), the versions of slavery evident in the Muslim world were *multi-racial* (encompassing diverse races among both masters and slaves).[10] The most race-conscious slave-systems were the trans-Atlantic varieties, with a racial bipolarity as their basic cultural foundation.

The trans-Atlantic slave trade was also the most highly *commercialized* of all forms of slavery in modern history. It went further than any other system to reduce slaves to chattels and commodities. The trans-Atlantic system delved deeper than any other form of slavery into linking slave-labour with related forms of profit-making—from sugar to textiles, from rubber to construction. The slave trade became part of an emerging capitalist world economy.[11] Slaves were both commodities and creators of other commodities. African slaves were at once products and producers.

The *least* commercialized of the slave-systems experienced by Africa were the indigenous versions. Slaves were more likely to be prisoners of war rather than captives for trade.[12] It is true that *some* economic exchange did take place even in indigenous slave patterns. There were some "barter" transactions—slaves in exchange for cattle, or even exchanging slaves for such decorative commodities as cowries. But trade and commerce were modest in indigenous slave systems. In many African societies money had not even been invented yet.

If indigenous slave traditions were the *least* commercialized, and Western capitalist slavery the *most* commercialized, slavery under the Muslims was somewhere *in between*. Trade was a much more developed activity in the history of Islam than it was in most indigenous African societies. Indeed, trans-Saharan trade was much older than Western capitalism. Some Western cultures were first introduced by Islam to long-distance trade and to the use of gold as a medium of exchange.

Indeed, the Prophet Muhammad himself was the first Muslim with experience in commerce and trade. He had served as commercial agent and partner to his own wife, Khadija—travelling long distances on their behalf between Mecca and Damascus in the days before he came a religious leader. In short, Muhammad had been a trader before he "founded" one of the great civilizations in world history. Indeed, Islam is arguably the only great world religion founded by a businessman in partnership with his wife.[13]

With this commercial background, it is not surprising that Islam developed a complex commercial history of its own long after the days of its prophet. Arab slavery itself became commercialized in subsequent centuries after the prophet—often in spite of constraints imposed by Islam rather than because of Islamic permissiveness. But even at its most ambitious, trade in slaves among Muslims was only a fraction of the scale of the trans-Atlantic slave trade under Western capitalism.

The demographic balance towards the end of the twentieth century bears testimony to that difference in scale. By the 1990s there were well over one hundred million people of African ancestry in the Americas. And yet there were only about a couple of million people of African descent in the Arabian peninsula in the concluding decade of the twentieth century.[14] This difference in scale was in spite of the fact that the Arab slave trade was supposed to be more than a thousand years older than the trans-Atlantic slave trade.

Where had the slaves captured by the Arabs gone to? In reality the Arab slave trade bore no comparison with the much more extensive transactions in human merchandise which the Western world perpetrated from the sixteenth century onwards.

This brings us to the third factor of comparison after relative racism and relative commercialization. The third issue concerns comparative territorial distribution in the three traditions of slavery under review. We are up against the *geography of slavery*. Indigenous slave-systems were basically *unicontinental*. The slaves did not have to traverse long distances. There was no equivalent of the middle passage across the Atlantic, with all its horrors.

For every trans-Atlantic slave who was finally put on the market in the Americas, one additional African died somewhere between the slave raid and the final auction in the New World. An alarmingly high proportion of the deaths were actually in transit. Distance was therefore in itself a major killer in slave transportation.[15] The very fact that indigenous slavery was often a case of "neighbourhood bondage" without the cruelties of long-distance exportation, made native versions of slavery geographically more benign.

Slave trade under Muslims was once again somewhere between the terrors of the trans-Atlantic middle-passage and the more benevolent conditions of native neighbourhood bondage. If indigenous slavery was basically *unicontinental*, Muslim slavery was basically *bicontinental*. The Arab slave trade was itself basically a transaction between Asia and Africa—though some of the slaves in the Muslim world were also of European descent. Islam itself is essentially an Afro-Asian religion in distribution. Almost all members of the Organization of the Islamic Conference (a recent global fraternity of Muslims) are either African or Asian.

There are indeed a few million Muslims in other continents—in North America as well as in Europe.[16] But apart from Albania, Bosnia, and, to a partial extent, Turkey, all Muslim *countries* are either in Africa or Asia. Much of the trade done by the Muslim world historically was not necessarily limited to fellow Muslim countries—but it did tend to be limited to the two largest continents of Africa and Asia.

Of course, the distinction between the Arab slave trade and the trans-Atlantic slave trade was not absolute. Some of the slaves captured by the Arabs were in fact for Western markets—in spite of Western hypocritical denunciations of the Arabs. But the bulk of the slaves in the Muslim world across the centuries traversed distances either within Asia or within Africa separately, or *between* those two continents. It was in that sense that the Muslim legacy of slavery was essentially *bicontinental*—though simultaneously *multi-racial*.

Modern Western slavery, on the other hand, was truly *multi-continental*—though basically *biracial*. Almost all the captives of Western slavery were, as we indicated, *black*. Almost all masters in the Western slave systems were *whites*. And yet this racial bipolarity engulfed four continents—Africa, Europe, North America and South America. It also engulfed related islands—from Gore off Senegal's coastline to Jamaica in the Caribbean.

The *history* of slavery has been cruel enough; the *geography* of slavery has sometimes been just as devastating. Proverbially, distance may lend enchantment to the view or distance may make the heart grow fonder—but in the annals of the slave trade, distance added the anguish of transit to the agony of enslavement. By being *multicontinental*, the Western slave trade came the closest to a global enterprise. It also came closest to a globalized trauma in human relations. The geography of bondage has taken its toll.

SERVITUDE AND COMPARATIVE ASSIMILATION

A fourth arena of comparison among the three legacies of slavery concerns relative assimilation and absorption. There has been considerable discussion about the degree to which indigenous slavery was the most ready to permit the assimilation of slaves into the "extended family" of their masters. Lord Lugard, Britain's greatest colonial administrator in Africa, was particularly keen to emphasize one crucial point about domestic slavery in Africa:

> ... whether the slaves in question are *aliens*, acquired and imported and retained as slaves by people with whom they have nothing in common—no community of language, customs and prejudices—or whether they are 'sons of the soil' of the same race as the masters, and merely merit the term 'slaves' because their chief has an absolute right over them, and because they are compelled to work, not for any fixed wage, but for contingent and equally definite advantages and form, in fact, but the lowest grade in the social scale. In the first case, there is an *apriori* probability that the slave will be more harshly treated and more readily sold; in the second case, the probabilities are the reverse.[17]

Lugard was part of a whole school of comparative social analysis which came to conclude that indigenous domestic slavery in Africa was essentially less malignant than trans-Atlantic chattel slavery—partly because indigenous slavery was more assimilationist and integrationist. Lucy Mair lent additional support to this thesis in her study of indigenous slavery among the Baganda in eastern Africa.

> Certain duties, it is true, were specifically allotted to slaves, but, for the greater part, they shared in the ordinary life of the household, were described by the head as 'his children' and a stranger would not be aware that they were his slaves unless this was expressly explained by him. Captured women were taken at once as wives, and except that they had no relatives to go to in case of ill-treatment or their husband's death, their different status ceased to have much importance. Girls might be married to their master's family or might marry other slaves; the latter on marriage set up their own houses, described themselves as members of their master's clan, and observed its practices. They differed from 'free men' in that they could not leave him and that they could not inherit from a real member of the clan.[18]

Next in absorptive and integrationist capacity was Muslim slavery. This was facilitated by the strong patrilineal tendency in Arab traditions of lineage. If the father was Arab, the child was deemed to be Arab regardless of the racial identity of the mother—and regardless of whether the mother was originally a slave. Such a system might be described as *ascending miscegenation*. In a racial mixed marriage, or in the case of mating between a master and his slave-concubine, the offspring ascended to the more privileged parent. The power of patrilineal descent pulled the progeny *upwards* to the status of the father. This was in sharp contrast to Anglo-Saxon slavery in North America—where children of cross-racial mating between a white master and a black slave *descended* to the slave status of the mother, and were deemed marketable.

Of the three slave-systems under review the Islamic tradition displayed the most astonishing capacity of upward social mobility. *Slaves* under Islam were capable of becoming *Sultans*—not just briefly but for long dynastic periods.

It all began with the concept of *slave soldiers* and the origins of *military coups* in Islamic history. Muslim societies did not just assign slaves to roles as plantation labourers or domestic housekeepers. The use of slaves as a distinct component of Muslim *armies* can be traced back to the 9th century of the Christian era. It originated in Baghdad under the Abbasid Caliph al-Mutasim (833–842 A.D.). The idea rapidly spread to many other parts of the Muslim world.

Seldom in human history has the word for "slave" been so indistinguishable from the name of ruling dynasties over centuries. *Mamluk* is an Arabic word meaning "slave" or "he who is owned." And yet *Mamluk* is also the name of a dynasty which ruled Egypt and Syria from 1250 A.D. to 1570 A.D., and whose descendants remained a major force in Egypt under Ottoman rule from 1517 to 1798.[19] Indeed, when Napoleon invaded Egypt in 1798 he found himself up against neo-Mamluk armies under what was basically a neo-Mamluk state. Perhaps never in human history were slaves a more integral part of the power of the state as they were within Islamic civilization.

As historians the *Mamluks* were prolific chroniclers, encyclopaedists and biographers. The greatest social scientist produced by the Mamluk civilization was Ibn Khaldun, one of the founding fathers of modern historiography.[20] In architecture the *Mamluks* have bequeathed to Cairo some of its most striking monuments.

In terms of *horizontal* assimilation into the general populace, indigenous African culture was perhaps particularly hospitable to slaves. But in terms of *vertical* upward social mobility to the pinnacles of control and the commanding heights of the economy, it was Islamic civilization which opened the doors to power to some of its lowliest slaves. Indigenous cultures opened the doors of shared identity; Islam opened the doors of shared empowerment.

The least absorptive and assimilationist of the slave-systems under review was the trans-Atlantic slave system. Precisely because the Western slave traditions were the most *race-conscious*, they exhibited strong resistance to both horizontal absorption and vertical social mobility. There was no Western equivalent of the *Mamluks*. The doors to ultimate commanding heights of either the polity or the economy were closed by the West to precisely those people who were the property of others—"the owned ones." Islam compensated the slaves with the opportunity for ultimate power. Will the Reverend Jesse Jackson or General Colin Powell be the Western world's first *Mamluk* in supreme authority?

Jesse Jackson is the first descendant of a Black slave to make a serious bid for the highest office in the land—the Presidency of the United States of America. The chances of his securing the nomination of the Democratic Party, let alone winning the final electoral vote of the American people, are still very slim indeed. But General Colin Powell may stand a better chance of getting the Republican nomination. America is not yet ready for the rule of a single Mamluk—let alone a Mamluk Dynasty. In the final analysis Anglo-Saxon racial culture still permits far less upward social mobility today than Islamic culture has done for more than a thousands years.

IS SLAVERY A SIN?

Debates about slavery in Africa in the 1990s have focused on reports from Sudan and Mauritaria. In Sudan the question is partly about whether there is slavery at all. In Mauritaria the debate is partly about whether the stratification which exists there is a form of slavery or something else.

This is not a chapter about present day Sudan and Mauritania. It is a chapter about Islam and slavery in the wider historical and sociological perspective. However, the chapter may also help to put Sudan and Mauritania in a broader context across space and time.

Does Islam condone slavery? Is slavery a sin? There is a sense in which all great religions have condoned slavery. The Ten Commandments did not include the commandment "Thou shalt not enslave another." Judaism did not outlaw slavery.

Jesus talked about the meek and the poor—but did not have much to say about the *enslaved*. On the contrary, Christian nations in subsequent centuries engaged in the most extensive trade in slaves in human history—the trans-Atlantic slave trade. In scale, the Christian slave-system was in a class by itself.

Since both Christianity and Judaism are centuries older than Islam, they inevitably tolerated slavery centuries longer than did Islam—by definition. Christian slavery existed for at least four centuries longer than any slavery associated with Islam. Judaism condoned slavery two millennia longer than did Islam.

If all religions condoned slavery in some degree or another, was there a significant difference in degree between religions on that issue? I propose to demonstrate that Islam went further than others to encourage *emancipation* of slaves.

But if that is the case, how is it that it was Christian nations in the nineteenth century which took the lead in the abolitionist movement? One could argue that Christian nations became more abolitionist when they became more industrialized and more secular. It was the industrial revolution rather than a Christian revival which gave birth to the abolitionist movement in the West.

In relation to the morality of abolitionism, the Muslim world had been *doctrinally* ahead—but industrially behind the West. In its message the Muslim religion had been more abolition-friendly than its religious peers—but the West stole a march when the industrial revolution made slave labour less efficient than wage labour.

Wage labour could be hired and fired at will, especially in the nineteenth century before labour unions could fight back. Employees could be laid off (or "down-sized") in times of recession—whereas those who owned slaves found it doubly hard to get rid of them when the economy was depressed. As for inventions such as the cotton gin, this dramatically reduced demand for slave labour on plantations. Technological change was making it easier for the West to have a conscience about the slave-trade.

ISLAM AND ABOLITIONISM

But in what sense was the message of Islam abolition-friendly? The message of Islam was conveyed to the human race by three different ways. These were as follows:

1. *Outright declaration* of what was a sin and what was a virtue, what was discouraged and what was recommended
2. *Cumulative examples* to suggest the ideal in the eyes of God
3. *The planting of moral seed* to be harvested by future generations

through *ijtihad* or judicial review.

These were the three main transmission belts for the ethical message of Islam—preparing the ground for a new moral order for the human race. A moral precept openly declared; a moral precept cumulatively illustrated; and a moral precept planted as a seed for future harvest.

There is no doubt that sins like homicide, adultery, gambling, drinking alcohol were outlawed through *actual declaration* by the Qur'an and/or through the *hadiths* of the Prophet Muhammad.

What about enslaving others or owning another human being? This particular message of Islam has been conveyed through the other two means or transmission belts:

1. By *cumulative examples* to suggest God's ideal
2. By *the planting of a moral seed* for future harvesting.

Islam did not directly declare that slavery was a vice. But it did often declare that setting slaves free was a virtue—the other side of the coin. Islam did not directly declare that enslaving another person was highly unethical— but it did repeatedly demonstrate that setting the person free was highly ethical. Islam was emphasizing this fourteen centuries before William Wilberforce in England or Abraham Lincoln in the United States did so during the West's industrial revolution. Islam was not overtly anti-slavery; yet it was emphatically pro-emancipation.

But in what ways did Islam recommend emancipation? Through the device of repeatedly emphasizing that promoting manumission was meritorious. Setting a slave or captive free is prescribed as part of what we would today describe as "friendly fire"—unintended homicide against a member of one's own side.

Never should a Believer kill a Believer except by mistake. And whoever kills a Believer by mistake, it is ordained that he *should free a believing slave*, and pay blood-money to the deceased's family, unless they remit it freely. If the deceased belonged to a people at war with you, and he was a Believer, the freeing of a believing slave (*is enough*). . . .Allah hath all knowledge, and all wisdom.[21]

Setting a slave free is also one way of atoning for violating one's vow made in the name of God. Breaking a promise to God carries a penalty in the here and now:

Allah will not call you to account for what is void in your oaths, but he will call you to account for deliberate oaths; for expiation, feed ten indigent persons, on a scale of the average for the food of your families, or clothe them; *or give a slave his freedom.* . . . Thus doth Allah make clear to you His signs, that ye may be grateful.[22]

The Qur'an enjoins the freeing of slaves as charity, elevating such manumission to the level of the criteria of righteousness. To the question "what is righteousness?," the Holy Qur'an included the following in its answer:

To believe in Allah, and the Last Day, and the Angels and the Book, and the Messengers; to spend your substance, out of love for Him, for your kin, for orphans, for the needy, for the wayfarer, for those who ask, *and the ransom of slaves*; to be steadfast in prayer, and give Zakat . . . such are the people of truth, the God-fearing.[23]

Is freeing slaves a possible key to paradise? Another verse in the Qur'an distinguishes between the easy path of vice and the difficult path of virtue. The difficult highway of virtue requires discipline and self-sacrifice. Among the sacrifices enumerated for the virtuous is indeed the freeing of slaves. In this particular sura the manumission is elevated even higher in importance as a sacrifice in the difficult path of virtue.

> And what will explain
> To thee in the path that is steep?-
> *(It is) freeing the bondman*; or the
> giving of food in a day of privation,
> To the orphan who claims of relationship,
> or to the indigent (down) in the dust. . .
> Such are the Companions
> of the right hand.[24]

Children of a slave woman and her master are free—they ascend to the legal status of the master. Unlike in the United States before emancipation where Chicken George (Alex Haley's grandfather) descended to the slave status of the mother and could be sold by his white father.

The status of the mother of free children itself changes half way to freedom—but not to complete freedom until the death of her master. The slave woman who bore her master a child was umm walad. She could not be sold or pawned.

The integration of ex-slaves into Muslim society sometimes went to the extent of raising them to very high office. It began with BILAL (bin Rabah) the first great muezzin of Islam, who became an influential companion of the Prophet. Bilal was a freed Ethiopian slave. He remained an influential Muslim after Muhammad's death, subsequently dying in Syria. Bilal is probably buried in Aleppo, though some claim his body is in Damascus.[25]

In the earliest days of Islam slavery was without racism. Many of the slaves were fellow Arabs. The evil of slavery was not linked to the aggravating separate evil of racism.

By a special contract a slave could buy his or her freedom and owners were encouraged to agree. The payments could be in three installments. The master had no right to revoke the contract—but the slave could change his or her mind.

In Islam a pious slave is preferable as a marriage partner to an impious free person. So piety or righteousness confers a separate rank order.

In practice (though not necessarily by the letter of the law) slaves could own some private property—though upon their death the property was inherited by the owner. Islam, through the Qur'an and the Prophet, repeatedly declares that freeing slaves, or ameliorating their condition, were meritorious acts. ('itq)

The question which now arises is whether all these factors added together constituted a *cumulative message* which was abolition-friendly. The question also arises whether they constitute the planting of a *moral seed* to be harvested by future generations through *ijtihad*.

Is this similar to the way the U.S. Constitution has been interpreted to have contained the moral seed of the right to privacy although the Constitution does not explicitly discuss privacy? Indeed the U.S. Constitution has even been interpreted to include a woman's sovereignty over her reproductive rights—although none of these were in the mind of the founding fathers.

Another distinction which needs to be borne in mind is between slavery as a product of the war system and slavery as a product of the economic system. Slavery in the early history of Islam was a child of the war system—prisoners of war being used as enslaved captives.

Much of indigenous slavery in traditional Africa was on the whole also a product of inter-ethnic conflicts—captives of war. That includes the origins of serfdom and caste in *Mauritania*.

Does that war-slavery include stories of slavery in *present-day Sudan*? Is that a revival of Islamic slavery or a revival of indigenous slavery? The evidence can support either proposition.

One remaining ethical issue which arises is whether there are different moral degrees of enslavement. Under United States' law there are certainly different degrees of homicide. There is first degree murder and second degree murder, and even lower degrees of homicide, such as manslaughter. The penalties under U.S. law have varied according to degree of murder.

Are there also moral degrees of slavery? Are some systems of enslavement more evil than others? We have attempted to demonstrate that there are indeed such variations in the evil of slavery. In the case of Africa, three systems of slavery have been experienced. These have been indigenous, Arab-Islamic and Euro-Christian. In what particulars have these three different legacies of slavery differed? Do those differences justify ranking them as first degree, second degree and third degree slave-systems? Let us explore other aspects of this triple heritage of sin.

BETWEEN SEXUALITY AND ECONOMICS

What about the motives for the original enslavement? What was the balance between *sexual* exploitation and *economic* exploitation in the three systems of slavery—African, Islamic and Western?

Economic production and biological reproduction are perhaps the two most fundamental forces in human history. When the quest for economic production is perverted, it becomes *greed*. When the drive for biological reproduction is perverted, it becomes lust.

On the evidence available the most purely *economic* of the three varieties of enslavement was the Western system. This was particularly true of the more mature capitalism of the Anglo-Saxon world. The slaves were needed more for their labour, for the sweat of their brow, rather than for their sexual value. It is true that once they were bought, women were often sexually abused and exploited in any case. But the dominant motive in Anglo-Saxon slave transactions was economic rather than sexual.

The Latin-speaking Europeans, on the other hand, often combined sexual considerations more openly with economic ones. The Portuguese and Spanish slavers marketed *sexual* merchandize as well as extra *labourers* for the plantations. Like other Latin whites, the Portuguese and the Spaniards had fewer complexes about inter-racial mating than did the Anglo-Saxons. Black women in Latin cultures were valued as much for their sexual attractions as for their utility as domestic workers.

Even more sexually motivated was Africa's indigenous slave culture. War captives after "native battles" were often disproportionately *women*—their men having been either killed or successfully chased away. African kings and noblemen often had large numbers of wives and "concubines," many of them former slaves. Suna II of Buganda has been described as having been "excessively interested in women." He had 148 wives, two thousand "reserve wives" and 18,000 *abazaana* (female servants).[26]

What should be borne in mind is that African women were seldom mere sex objects. Christopher Wrigley has correctly estimated that along the northern shores of Lake Victoria, one woman was often able to feed 8 or 10 men, thus releasing them for statecraft and diplomatic pursuits.[27]

Before African slavery got commercialized as a result of contact with other cultures, a disproportionate number of captives from rival "tribes" were indeed *women* (and children). On the other hand, a disproportionate number of slaves captured for the Americas were *men*. The gender balance in the Americas was restored later—partly as a result of inter-racial mating and natural selection. Women were also needed to "breed" more slaves on the plantations. The female disproportion among captives under *indigenous* culture is evidence of its higher sexual motivation. The male disproportion among trans-Atlantic captives was partly due to the higher economic motivation of the plantations of the New World.

Slavery in Muslim societies was perhaps more evenly divided between sexual and economic motives. In the Middle East especially inter-racial mating had considerable legitimacy—at least as much as it had among the Portuguese and the Spaniards of the New World. Women were as often bought for their sexual credentials as for their economic exertions.

But there is one major difference between Islamic culture and indigenous African culture. Unlike Suna II of Buganda, no Muslim dignitary was permitted to have "148 wives and 2000 reserve wives." Islam limited the number of *wives* to *four*—though many a Muslim ruler found a convenient *fatwa* (legal opinion) to permit him to have many *suraya* (concubines) in addition to wives.

Moreover, slave culture in Muslim societies produced one particularly reprehensible sexual aberration—the *castration* of those who guarded the *harem*. The sub-culture of the *eunuch* in Muslim societies started more than a hundred years after the Prophet Muhammad's death. Historians have traced the eunuch tradition in Islam to about the year 750 A.D.[28]

Was it a peculiar product of the culture of the *harem*? In reality castration was more Mediterranean than Islamic. It was certainly practised in the Roman and Byzantine empires. And the Italians practised castration of boys for aesthetic reasons—in order to train them as soprano singers (*castrati*).[29] It was Pope Leo XIII who banned this practice in Italy as recently as 1878.

In Christianity castration was sometimes self-inflicted as a method of conquering temptation. Christian self-castration goes back at least to the theologian Oriegen (A.D. 185–254). In early Christianity there were even sects which deliberately practised self-castration, under the inspiration of Matthew

[19: 12, 5: 28–30]. In the third century of the Christian era the Valesii sect not only castrated themselves but also their guests.

In short, the practice of castration—though widely practised in Muslim slave systems on men entrusted with guarding the harem—was in fact a product of Mediterranean traditions long before Islam. Within Muslim culture the eunuch did not become a factor until more than a century after the death of the founder of Islam. In Christianity self-inflicted castration was practised long before the birth of Islam.

FROM EUNUCHS TO EUGENICS

What persisted among Christians into the twentieth century was another sexual aberration—*eugenics*, or special breeding for human physical "improvement." In a sense, the idea of eugenics in European civilization began with Plato's *Republic*, where an ideal society was portrayed as having an agenda for improving human beings through selective breeding. With the influence of the Age of Discovery, the inexorable march of the British Empire, and the influence of theorists like Darwin and Herbert Spenser, it rapidly gained ground, particularly in Britain and the Continent.[30] But it was not until 1883 that the word *eugenics* itself was coined by the British scientist Francis Galton, whose own book, *Hereditary Genius*, a few years earlier (1869) had recommended arranged marriages between brilliant men and rich women as a strategy of producing a talented race.[31]

In the history of trans-Atlantic slavery eugenics was used not to create a better endowed ruling class *mentally* but to develop a better endowed labouring class *physically*. Selective breeding of slaves was sometimes invoked as a method of producing either stronger specimens or physically more attractive ones.[32] Black domination of some physical sports in the United States in the twentieth century can, in part, be traced back to special breeding under slavery, reinforced by other factors. Black fighters have dominated the boxing ring through much of the twentieth century. And tall and powerful Black players have shown dazzling physical prowess and mental calculation in American football and basketball, at least in the second half of this century. In spite of poverty and undernourishment, the African-American population in the twentieth century has produced a remarkable proportion of resilient and impressive physiques. How much of that physical Black heritage was, in part, a product of selective breeding under slavery?

The obscenities of eugenic experiments under slavery included special inter-racial mating in order to produce lighter-skinned Blacks, who were preferred for certain domestic duties. Lighter-skinned women-slaves were also preferred *sexually* by their white masters.

But who were the white mates who engaged in cross-breeding with slaves in order to produce lighter-skinned human merchandize? Sometimes it was the white members of the slave-owning family themselves who mated with their bonded victims—and then sold their own "half-caste" offspring. This is the *chicken-George* syndrome. Alex Haley's great grandfather was the product of mating between the master himself and one of his slave women. This did not stop the master from selling his own son to an overseas buyer resident in Scotland. George's lighter skin was apparently an asset to his marketability.[33]

Under Islamic law the chicken-George syndrome was inconceivable. A child of a master with one of his slaves was legally free. And the mother herself was at least partially liberated by bearing her master a child. In Islam eugenics between masters and slaves as a method of producing "better" slaves was a legal abomination, totally inadmissible.

Eugenics in the United States persisted in other forms long after slavery was abolished. The American Eugenics Society was established in 1926, committed to the proposition that the privileges of the upper classes were justified by their "superior" genetic endowment.[34] The Society wanted the Immigration Laws of the United States to protect the genetic strength of the existing population—keeping out not only non-whites but also such allegedly "inferior" white stock as Italians, Greeks, Poles and other Slavs.[35]

American eugenic culture had moved from the task of breeding stronger slaves to the mission of breeding more intelligent rulers. Sterilizing even retarded white citizens of the United States, or white epileptics, or the insane, continued in parts of the United States into the 1970s.[36] But the earlier racial agenda of the American Eugenics Society was partly discredited by the eugenic horrors perpetrated in Germany by the Nazis, resulting in the extermination of Jews, Gypsies and such sexual minorities as homosexuals. The Nazis carried eugenics on humans further than any other regime in world history. By so doing the Nazis helped to discredit at least the racial versions of eugenic programmes in the Western world.[37]

If the Western slave-systems were sometimes distorted by *eugenic sexuality*, and slave-systems under Muslim rule were flawed by the *eunuch sub-culture*, indigenous slave systems in Africa were compromised by *sexual promiscuity*. Even when Africans became collaborators with the trans-Atlantic slaver traders, and captured fellow Africans for sale to white slavers, very often the African collaborators retained a high proportion of the female captives for themselves:

> . . . the relatively dense population of the Angola-Kasanjo-Matamba region was a direct consequence of the slave trade; female slaves were incorporated into local society, while males were exported. . . . The Gold Coast, Bight of Benin and Bight of Biafra areas—where a majority of slaves came from—were also some

of the most densely populated parts of Africa. If a disproportionate number of women and children were retained at the same time that males were exported, as was the case in Angola, then the population of the slave-exporting societies would have increased.[38]

It is one of the blots on the history of Africa that so many Africans collaborated in the trans-Atlantic slave trade. But Africa's polygyny, combined with love of children, spared millions of *female* captives the horrors of the middle passage across the Atlantic. Women captives stood a better chance of remaining in Africa—and sometimes contributing to the population growth and density of precisely those societies which exported slaves.

Trade with the Muslim world, on the other hand, did have a preference for women slaves—while the Americas continued to clamour more for male slaves. Because the Islamic slave-trade was much smaller in scale than the export of slaves to the Americans, the net-result was still a bigger export of men than of women:

> In the trade across the Sahara, Red Sea, and Indian Ocean, there was a much higher proportion of females and children, while in the trans-Atlantic trade many more slaves were male than female. . . . Very few slaves in either trade appears to have been more than thirty. . . . In the areas catering to the Islamic trade, where there was also a strong domestic preference for women and children, the structure of the market consistently reflected a price differential based on age and sex. Males, unless they were castrated, were usually cheaper.[39]

We are back to the proposition that women slaves were strongly preferred in indigenous and Islamic forms of slavery in Africa—reflecting in part the greater relevance of sexual motives in these two slave-systems. Male labourers were disproportionately preferred in the trans-Atlantic slave trade—reflecting the more purely economic motives of Western capitalism. Sexual and economic forms of exploitation in all three systems were always intermingled, but the balance between sensuality and greed differed from system to system.

CONCLUSION

We have sought to demonstrate in this chapter that Africa's experience of slavery came through three different legacies of servitude—indigenous, Islamic and Western. Indigenous slavery was *uniracial* (Black masters, Black slaves), Muslim slavery was *multiracial* (multi-coloured slaves and masters) and the trans-Atlantic system of slavery was essentially *biracial* (White masters, Black slaves). Indigenous and Islamic slavery were assimilationist and integrationist, often absorbing slaves into the "extended family" of the master. Trans-Atlantic slavery was more segregationist—keeping slaves and their *race* at a social distance.

Although indigenous slavery also allowed upward social mobility (from *captive* to *captain*), Islamic forms of slavery permitted the highest degree of upward social mobility historically—from *serf* to *sultan*. In the case of the *Mamluks*, former slaves ruled parts of the Muslim world not just for a decade or two, but for centuries.

Indigenous forms of slavery in Africa were highly *culture-conscious*—permitting cultural assimilation as one route for the slave's emancipation. Islamic slavery was *religiously conscious*—often outlawing the enslavement of a Muslim by a fellow Muslim:

> Whoever is captured in a condition of non-belief, it is legal to own him, whosoever he may be, but not he who was converted to Islam voluntarily, from the start, to any nation he belongs, whether it is Bornu, Kano, Songhai, Katsina, Gobir, Mali and some of Zakzak [Zazzau]. These are free Muslims, whose enslavement is not allowed in any way.[40]

In other words, prior conversion to Islam in Africa was often a protection against enslavement by fellow Muslims. On the other hand, subsequent assimilation into the culture of the master was often an important key to emancipation under the rules of indigenous slavery.

If the Islamic system was *creed-conscious*, and the indigenous system was *culture-conscious*, the Western system was *race-conscious* in the extreme. "For Europeans, slaves were perceived as racially distinct; despite acculturation, slaves were even more clearly defined as outsiders, thereby guaranteeing that the acquisition of rights in European society would be severely limited."[41]

In other words, the Western slave-system was the least absorptive and permitted the least social mobility. Even Brazil—though more absorptive than the United States—has been far less integrationist than has slavery been in Kuwait or Buganda. It remains to be seen whether someone like the Reverend Jesse Jackson or General Colin Powell will be permitted to become the first Western equivalent to a *Mamluk* ruler. Descended from a slave, Jackson or Powell could become Head of State—traversing the social distance from "owned property" to "honoured president." But he is up against the accumulated heritage of a biracial slave system—with all its polarized prejudices.

Meanwhile, history sits in judgment on slavery. What are the different scales of restitution? If murder can be first degree and second degree, what about slavery? In degree of sinfulness, perhaps the indigenous slavery of the Africans themselves was third degree. The slave-system maintained by Muslims was second degree. Muslims had defied the Quranic encouragement of emancipation, especially ever since Islam went dynastic and monarchical with the Umayyad (A.D. 661–750) and Abbasid (A.D. 750–1258) Dynasties.

As for the trans-Atlantic Western slave-system—the most extensive traffic in human merchandise in the history of the world and the most racist in character—the probable verdict of history is likely to be "slavery most foul." History as jury is likely to proclaim emphatically: "guilty in the first degree." Should the campaign for reparations begin with this first degree of Black exploitation?

The Blacks of the world are indeed a people of the day before yesterday and a people of the day after tomorrow. Before slavery was commercialized, Blacks lived in one huge village called 'Africa.' And then strangers arrived— and took some of the people away, marketing them in diverse parts of the world. Before the dispersal Africans regarded their village as the whole world; many of them knew no other. But the triple heritage of slavery has scattered Africans so widely that the sun never sets on the descendants of Africa. Instead of the African village being regarded as the whole world, planet Earth has now become itself the equivalent of an African village. Descendants of Black slaves have become Ministers on the Arabian Gulf and have begun to become Governors in the United States. Is not this reparations enough? Is a new and more humane dynasty of the *Mamluks* at hand in a global context? Are the serfs of yesterday destined to become the sultans of tomorrow? Or is this mere tokenism, signifying the success of isolated Black individuals while the massive moral debt of Black enslavement remains unpaid?

Millions perished in the slave trade. Millions more suffered on plantations. Millions even more have yet to find redemption. Should the historic reckoning of restitution begin?

NOTES

1. The OAU's Group of Eminent Persons is charged with devising strategies and modalities for a campaign to obtain reparations for colonialism and its aftermath, as well as for enslavement.

2. On the discussions on reparations to Israel by Germany, consult Ronald H. Zweig, *German Reparations and the Jewish World: A History of The Claims Conference* (Boulder, CO: Westview Press, 1987).

3. For brief reports on these payments, see, for instance, issues of the *Far Eastern Economic Review,* February 18, 1993: pp. 32–4; February 25, 1993: p. 26; and *The Economist,* January 18, 1992: p. 32.

4. See the *UN Chronicle* 29 (December 1992), 26–30; and for an exhaustive discussion, Rodney J. Morrison, "Gulf War Reparations: Iraq, OPEC and the Transfer Problem," *The American Journal of Economics and Sociology* 51 (October 1992), pp. 385–99.

5. Consult Ali A. Mazrui, *The Africans: A Triple Heritage* (London: BBC Publications and Boston: Little, Brown Publishers, 1986) a companion volume to a BBC/PBS Television Series of the same title (1986).

6. An earlier such examination may be found in Robin Winks, *Slavery: A Comparative Perspective* (New York: New York University Press, 1972).

7. On slavery in Africa, see, for example, John Ralph Willis, ed., *Slaves and Slavery in Muslim Africa* (London and Totowa, NJ: F. Cass, 1985) and Janet Ewald, "Slavery in Africa and The Slave Trades from Africa," *The American Historical Review* 97 (April 1992), pp. 465–85.

8. See, for instance, Samuel Seabury, *American Slavery Distinguished From the Slavery of English Theorists, and Justified by the Law of Nature* (New York: Mason, 1861); John H. Van Evrie, *White Supremacy and Negro Subordination* (New York: Negro Universities Press); and George D. Armstrong's *The Christian Doctrine of Slavery* (New York: C. Scribner, 1857); Armstrong was pastor of a Presbyterian Church in Norfolk, VA.

9. Works that emphasize the Arab role in slave trade and slavery include Bernard Lewis, *Race and Slavery in the Middle East: An Historical Enquiry* (New York: Oxford University Press, 1990) and Gordon Murray, *Slavery in the Arab World* (New York: New Amsterdam, 1989).

10. For another comparative analysis of the slave trades, see Patrick Manning, *Slavery and African Life: Occidental, Oriental, and African Slave Trades* (New York: Cambridge University Press, 1990).

11. Consult, relatedly, Barbara L. Solow, "Capitalism and Slavery in the Exceedingly Long Run, *Journal of Interdisciplinary History* 17 (Spring 1987), pp. 711–37; Joseph E. Inikori and Stanley L. Engerman, eds., *The Atlantic Slave Trade: Effects on Economies and Peoples in Africa, The Americas and Europe* (Durham, NC: Duke University Press, 1992); and the classic by Eric Williams, *Capitalism and Slavery* (London: Andre Deutsch, 1944, 1987).

12. See, for instance, Suzanne Miers and Igor Kopytoff, eds., *Slavery in Africa: Historical and Anthropological Perspectives* (Madison, WI: University of Wisconsin Press, 1977), pp. 13–14.

13. For a biographical treatment of Muhammad, see W. Montgomery Watt, *Muhammad, Prophet and Statesman* (Oxford: Oxford University Press, 1961).

14. A distribution of the African diaspora may be found in Gerard Chaliand and Jean-Pierre Rageau, *The Penguin Atlas of Diasporas* (London: Penguin, 1995).

15. On the Middle Passage, see Herbert S. Klein, *The Middle Passage: Comparative Studies in the Atlantic Slave Trade* (Princeton, NJ: Princeton University Press, 1978).

16. For a somewhat dated but still useful indicator of Muslims in the Western world, see John Weeks, "The Demography of Muslim Nations," *Population Bulletin* (1988), 43, p. 4 (Special Supplement).

17. Lugard, *The Rise of Our East African Empire* (1893), pp. 169–70.

18. Lucy Mair, *An African People in the Twentieth Century* (1934), pp. 31–33.

19. A historical treatment of the Mamluks of Egypt may be found in David Ayalon, *Studies on the Mamluks of Egypt* (London: Variorum Reprints, 1977).

20. For a biography of Khaldun, see Muhammad Abd Allah Inan, *Ibn Khaldun, His Life and Work* (Lahore: Sh. Muhammad Ashraf, 1962).

21. See Verse 92, *Surat Al-Nisa, Al-Qur'an*. The translation is based on the English version prepared by the King Fahd Holy Qur-an Printing Complex, Al-Madinah Al-Munawarah, Saudi Arabia, 1411 H., pp. 242–243. The above emphasis within the quotation is ours.

22. *Surat Al-Ma'idah*, verse 89. For English translation, *ibid*, pp. 314–15. The emphasis within the quotation above is ours.

23. *Surat-el-Baqara*, verse 177, *ibid*., pp. 71–72. The emphasis within the quotation is ours.

24. *Surat al-Balad*, chapter 90, verse 13. The emphasis in the quotation is ours.

25. For a fascinating account of this close associate of the Prophet Muhammad, see H. A. L. Craig, *Bilal* (London and New York: Quartet Books, 1977).

26. Sir Apolo Kagwa, *The Customs of the Baganda*, trans, by Ernest Kalibala (New York, 1934), 51. I was stimulated by Michael Twaddle, "Slaves and Peasants in Buganda," paper presented at the annual meeting of the Canadian Association of African Studies, 1983.

27. Christopher C. Wrigley, chapter in *The King's Men*, edited by Lloyd A. Fallers (London, 1964) p. 18. I am indebted to Michael Twaddle for bibliographical guidance.

28. On the important places occupied by eunuchs in Muslim societies, especially in Saudi Arabia and Egypt, consult Shaun Elizabeth Marmon, *Eunuchs and Sacred Boundaries in Islamic Society* (New York: Oxford University Press, 1995).

29. See Angus Heriot, *The Castrati in Opera* (London: Secker & Warburg, 1956).

30. A useful survey is Pauline M. H. Mazumdar, *Eugenics, Human Genetics, and Human Failings: The Eugenics Society, Its Sources and its Critics in Britain* (London and New York: Routledge, 1992).

31. Francis Galton, *Hereditary Genius: An Inquiry Into Its Laws and Consequences* (London and New York: J. Friedmann and St. Martin's Press, 1978).

32. See William H. Tucker, *The Science and Politics of Racial Research* (Urbana: University of Illinois Press, 1994), p. 51.

33. Alex Haley, *Roots* (New York: Doubleday, 1976).

34. Consult Ellsworth Huntington, *Tomorrow's Children: The Goal of Eugenics* (New York and London: J. Wiley & Sons, Inc., and Chapman & Hall, Ltd., 1935) for their point of view.

35. Tucker, *The Science and Politics of Racial Research*, pp. 77–83.

36. See Ruth Macklin and Willard Gaylin, eds., *Mental Retardation and Sterilization: A Problem of Competency and Paternalism* (New York: Plenum Press, 1981).

37. On the Nazis and their eugenics programs, see Gotz Aly, *Cleansing the Fatherland: Nazi Medicine and Racial Hygiene* (Baltimore: Johns Hopkins University Press, 1994); and on the connection between the Nazis and American racism in this

regard, see Stefan Kuhl, *The Nazi Connection: Eugenics, American Racism, and German National Socialism* (New York: Oxford University Press, 1994).

38. Paul E. Lovejoy, *Transformations in Slavery: A History of Slavery in Africa* (Cambridge and New York: Cambridge University Press, 1983), pp. 64–65.

39. Lovejoy, *Transformations in Slavery*, *ibid*, p.62. Consult also Martin Klein and Claire Robertson (eds.), *Women and Slavery in Africa* (Madison, 1984).

40. Ahmad Baba, *Mi'raj.* Cited by Lovejoy, *ibid*, p. 30.

41. Lovejoy, *ibid*, 3. Consult also Martin Klein and Paul E. Lovejoy (eds.), *The Uncommon Market: Essays in the Economic History of the Atlantic Slave Trade* (New York, 1979).

Chapter Fourteen

Comparative Racism: Zionism and Apartheid

After the Middle East October War of 1973, Israel and Apartheid South Africa were drawing close together. The interaction has ranged from cultural and sporting exchanges to the restoration of full ambassadorial relations, from consultations on techniques of counter-insurgency to cooperation in the production of steel and now, even preliminary nuclear consultation. The visit of the South African Premier to Israel in 1976 was symbolic of this new *entente cordiale* between Israel as a child of Zionism and South Africa as the father of apartheid.

By a curious historical destiny 1948 was a critical year for both Zionism and apartheid. In that year Israel was born, having previously won a majority in the United Nations in its favor. In that year also the National Party in South Africa was engaged in an electoral campaign on the policy of "apartheid," defined as a more rigorous separation of the races and cultures of South Africa. The National Party under Dr. Malan captured power, and Afrikaaner nationalism as an ideology began to be more systematically operationalized.

But is there much more between Israel and apartheid than the coincidence of a "shared birthday" in 1948? Is there much more between Israel and South Africa than the coincidence of a shared predicament in the 1970s and 1980s?

This chapter will focus especially on four factors—situational similarity between Israel and South Africa, normative congruence between Zionism and the ideology of apartheid, the trend toward greater economic cooperation between Israel and South Africa, and the issue of greater military consultations between the two.

This chapter accepts that the reasons behind the new entente cordiale between South Africa and Israel are indeed partly situational. But we hope to demonstrate that the situational similarity has its roots in a prior ideological congruence between Zionism and apartheid. The sense of isolation which Israel now shares with South Africa is a consequence of parallel efforts to implement culturally separatist ideologies at the wrong time in history.

Let us therefore first examine these deeper normative similarities between Zionism and the ideology of apartheid before we turn to their political and structural consequences.

THE GERMANIC ROOTS OF ZIONISM AND APARTHEID

It is important to remember that apartheid as an ideology is not just another word for "racism." It is a philosophy which defines nationality in terms of cultural homogeneity and racial distinctiveness. As a policy apartheid is committed to the separate development of different cultural groups. It conceives of citizenship not as a legal contract between the individual and his state but ultimately as a cultural bond between the individual and his community.

There is little doubt that apartheid as an ideology is partly a child of nineteenth century European conceptions of nationality. Mazzini was not the only nationalist prophet who linked nationality to divine purpose. According to Mazzinii, God "Divided Humanity into distinct groups upon the face of our globe, and thus planted the seeds of nations."[1] In its alliance with the Dutch Reformed Church of South Africa, Afrikaaner nationalism embraced this linkage between national differentiation, ethnic separatism, and divine purpose.

The apartheid program as a policy includes the ambition of *macro-segregation*—the creation of separate monoracial and unicultural "homelands" for each group. The Transkei, given "independence" in October 1976, was supposed to be the first of such Bantustans. But the apartheid program also includes "micro-segregation" operationally. Micro-segregation has entailed such legislation as the Group Areas Act committed to residential separation, the Bantu Education Act designed to arrest cultural convergence between Blacks and Whites, the Population Registration Act to control trans-ethnic movement, the Prohibition of Mixed Marriages Act and many other additional pieces of legislation.

On the whole Zionism has more in common with apartheid on the issue of macro-segregation (separate homelands for culturally distinct groups) than on the issue of micro-segregation (racial separation in towns and localities). What is clear is that both Zionism and Afrikaaner nationalism have borrowed from the anti-pluralistic and exclusivist tendencies of German nationalistic thought as a special case of European nationalism.

Theodor Hertzl, the towering European founder of the Zionist movement, was an assimilated Jew. Born in Hungary, he later imbibed Germanic culture and many of its political postulates. From his professional base in Vienna he looked at European society through both liberal and nationalistic eyes. His liberalism inclined him toward pluralism and heterogeneity. His Jewish nationalism pulled him toward Zionism with all its potential exclusivity. Herzl never resolved the dilemma in his own sensitive mind, but the movement which he helped to create was to lean increasingly toward Germanic doctrines of "the unified soul of the fatherland" and away from liberal diversity.

Herzl, in his original idea of a Jewish home, did indeed see a state populated almost only by Jews at first. But his original solution was in terms of finding vacant territory which the Jews could then populate—"to give to the people without land a land without people." These were the days when Herzl could allow for the possibility of an Israel in South America. But by the time Britain's colonial secretary, Joseph Chamberlain, offered him Uganda, the lure of Palestine as the proper home for the Jews was too strong. And yet to Herzl himself the vision was that of a state where non-Jews might still live in an open society, and where the Jews and their religion would not constitute a privileged group.

> It would be immoral if we would exclude anyone, whatever his origin, his descent, or his religion, from participating in our achievements. For we stand on the shoulders of other civilized peoples. . .What we own we owe to the preparatory work of other peoples. Therefore, we have to repay our debt. There is only one way to do it, the highest tolerance. Our motto must therefore be, now and ever: 'Man, you are my brother.'[2]

Herzl was more liberal but certainly less logical than the Zionists who later triumphed. The idea of having a Jewish home where everybody else was equal, and where others could be admitted even to the extent of tilting the balance of population, was to some extent a contradiction in terms. Morris R. Cohen captured this dilemma when he asked:

> Indeed, how could a Jewish Palestine allow complete religious freedom, intermarriage, and free non-Jewish immigration, without soon losing its very reason for existence? A national Jewish Palestine must necessarily mean a state founded on a peculiar race, a tribal religion, and a mystic belief in a peculiar soil. . .[3]

As Zionism gathered strength a strong preference for a racially and religiously purist state for the Jews began to gain ascendancy, though this concept was up against considerable diplomatic difficulties in the international arena.

The Jewish Agency of Palestine, the shadow Jewish government before the creation of Israel, played down the notion of a racially and religiously purist state. The Agency was even embarrassed during World War II when significant members of the Labor Party in Britain went to the extent of demanding that the Arabs should be forced to leave Palestine to make way for Jewish immigration.[4] Early discussions on the best solution for the Palestine problem sometimes envisaged a federation of Jewish and Arab states. This was deemed to be one realistic solution which would reconcile the interests of both groups, and fulfill the British Balfour Declaration of 1917.

His Majesty's Government views with favor the establishment in Palestine of a national home for the Jewish people, and will use their best endeavors to facilitate the achievement of this object, it being clearly understood that nothing shall be done which may prejudice the civil rights of existing non-Jewish communities in Palestine, or the rights and political status enjoyed by Jews in any other country.

At the diplomatic and international level a compromise seemed to be emerging. In 1947 a United Nations' Special Committee on Palestine (UNSCOP) left to make a new study of the problems involved in Jewish-Arab relations and the conflicting ambitions involved. But when UNSCOP completed its work, it was only the minority report which favored a federation of Jewish and Arab states. On September 3, 1947, the majority report of UNSCOP recommended that the League of Nations' mandate, initiated in 1919 after the Ottoman Empire lost control of its Arab territorial possessions, should now be terminated, and that Palestine should be partitioned into sovereign Arab and Jewish states. That school of Zionism which was militantly purist in its conception of a Jewish home had triumphed. On November 29, 1947, the General Assembly of the United Nations—by a vote of 33 to 13, with 10 abstentions—confirmed their vision. The state of Israel was given a global birth certificate in imminent anticipation. A new political community, explicitly defined in terms of race and biological descent from the ancient Hebrews, was about to enter world history.

What did this concept of an ethnically defined Jewish state have in common with Afrikaaner nationalism in South Africa? Conceptions of citizenship under both ideologies were in an important sense anachronistic. C.G. Montefiore was surely right when he argued as long ago as 1899, in relation at least to Zionism:

There is no *a priori* reason why in any one state men of different races and creeds should not be ardent citizens living in peace and harmony with each other. The trend of modern thought, in spite of backwaters and counter currents, is surely in that direction. A Russia which must be purely Slav and of the orthodox Greek church strikes us as an anachronistic effort which in the long run will inevitably break down.[5]

Such a concepption of citizenship is borrowed from tribal ideas of the past, as well as from German nationalism. Tribal polities were inseparable from kinship. A person could not belong to a social or even ceremonial collectivity if he did not have kinship status. In many an indigenous society both in Africa and elsewhere "there are no non-relatives." All roles are allocated and activities organized in relation to kinship status broadly defined.

This pre-modern conception of citizenship is sometimes better illustrated in some South Pacific island societies and among aboriginal tribes in Australia that in African political communities, but the element of similarity is strongly there all the same. Certainly many societies in Southern Africa before European settlement organized themselves traditionally by kinship, either real or conferred. A new citizen became one either through complete cultural assimilation or through mixing his blood with members of the community concerned. What Meyer Fortes said of Kariera society is true of many traditional political communities in Africa as well.

> . . .outsiders can be incorporated into a society or a community, or more generally, brought into the ambit of sanctioned social relations, by having kinship status ascribed to them. Different communities, even those of different tribal or linguistic provinance, can exchange personnel by marriage, and can fuse for particular ceremonial occasions by, so to speak, intermeshing their kinship field. . .Herein lies the essence of the kinship polity. . .[6]

Here an important difference does present itself between tribal society on the one hand, and Jewish and Afrikaaner conceptions of citizenship on the other. For most African cultures readiness to intermarry is one approach to the forging of a shared community. Those who are unwilling to mix blood, and intermesh their kinship field, are unwilling to share a political community. The Zionist approach to citizenship is in some ways quite the reverse. Among westerners, Jews and Germans are probably the most concerned with sexual exclusivity. The capacity of the Jews to see themselves as a group descended from the ancient Hebrews, and therefore as a group entitled to return to Palestine, was facilitated by their tradition of sexual exclusivity. When religion and race are so intertwined, both racial intermarriage and religious intermarriage become additionally constrained and inhibited. Again Montefiore saw this as a problem for the modern Jew already in the nineteenth century.

> I admit that in the case of the Jews religion and
> race are practically co-extensive. A Roman Catholic
> Czech of Bohemia may perhaps be united, so far as the
> Czech part of him goes, with his fellow Bohemian
> Protestant, and *qua* Catholic he will marry a German

of the same religious denomination! Among the Jews,
religion and race play into each other's hands, and the
common refusal of intermarriage, however justified
as the only means of maintaining the life of a tiny
minority, preserves and strengthens the alleged isolation and
difference.[7]

To some extent the Jewish tradition of sexual exclusivity has been undermined in the twentieth century. Out-marriage amongst British Jews is currently 35 percent; amongst American Jews the figure is similar; amongst German Jews before Hitler's persecution it was higher. But the tradition survives
strongly in Zionist Israel.

Today in Israel problems of defining the rights of Jews as against the rights
of others have been bedeviled both by militarized nationalism and by Judaism's hostility to interreligious marriage. Cases have come before the
courts in the last few years in Israel involving children of mixed descent. The
political forces that are still capable of being mobilized against the liberalization of Israel's laws of descent are still significant. Both the government of Israel and the courts in Israel have felt the pressure of racial purity as a political force in the Jewish state. These pressures emanate in part from religion
and in part from the psychology of the garrison state.

The orthodox Jewish concept of citizenship is no less purist than the
Afrikaaner approach. For both Jews and Afrikaaners, kinship is ultimately de-
signed to maintain internal cohesion. After all, had not the K'ai-feng Jews of
China disappeared from the map of world Jewry mainly because they had
permitted themselves to intermarry freely with the Chinese? And had not the
Jews of Northern Ethiopia become so *black* that for centuries Rabbis had
found it difficult to accept them as Jews? It was not until 1972—the year of
Idi Amin's expulsion of the Israelis and the Asians from Uganda—that the
Sephardic Grand Rabbi Ovadia Yosseff, decided to save the black Jews from
the fate of the Chinese Jews—total disappearance. Recognition was at last re-
luctantly conceded to the 25,000 members of the Falasha tribe of Northern
Ethiopia as a group biologically descended from "genuine" Jews who went to
Ethiopia centuries ago.[8]

But did not German ideas of nationality and exclusivity also influence Arab
nationalism? European nationalism generally has had a pervasive intellectual
influence on much of the Third World, including the Arab world. And the
German factor in global nationalist philosophy has been pronounced. But it
was not the Arabs who rejected the idea of Arabs and Jews living together in
a united Palestine. It was the Jews. It was not the Arabs who insisted on partition. It was the Zionists and their supporters. The principle of national exclusivity in the Middle East was much more a feature of Jewish nationalism

than of Arab nationalism. Arab actions against their own Jewish citizens were a response to Zionist exclusivity rather than an independent doctrine within Arab ideologies.

We next turn to the role of religion in statecraft, from the Middle East to Southern Africa.

RELIGION, THE STATE AND THE MARTYRDOM COMPLEX

A special primordial feature of the normative convergence between Israel and Apartheid South Africa lay in the impact of religion upon the ruling ideologies in the two societies. Zionism is the offspring of a marriage between Judaism and the legacy of the 1648 Treaty of Westphalia; apartheid is the offspring of a marriage between the Dutch Reformed Church and the legacy of race consciousness. Judaism in search of statehood resulted in the creation of Israel. The Dutch Reformed Church in search of descendants of Ham and Sham as racial categories, stumbled on the doctrine of apartheid.

The champions of both Zionism and apartheid have invoked the Old Testament as solemn witness to their doctrines. In the case of Israel the biblical influence is sometimes relatively mild, especially among the more secular citizens of the Jewish state. But the very notion of "returning" to Israel, the fanatical commitment to the retention of Jerusalem as the "capital," and the choice of the name of "Israel" for a twentieth century nation-state are all symptoms of an underlying merger between biblical nostalgia and Jewish nationalism within the ethos of Zionism. Not unexpectedly, given this framework, Prime Minister Begin invoked the Old Testament to justify Israel's territorial claims on the West Bank of the Jordan River and Gaza Strip.

Similarly, in the case of Afrikaaner nationalism, the Old Testament has been used to validate racial segregation and white supremacy. In August, 1982, at a meeting in Ottawa, Canada, the two Dutch Reformed Churches of South Africa (NGK and NHK churches) were at last suspended from the World Alliance of Reformed Churches on the grounds that apartheid as a religious doctrine was a heresy.[9] The stage was thus set for a more complete break between the Afrikaaner church and the international alliance of churches.

In addition to the doctrinal aspects of Afrikaaner and Zionist fundamentalism, there is the common phenomenon of the *martyrdom complex* in both Boer and Jewish nationalism. The martyrdom complex in Jewish experience has had varied manifestations across the centuries, going back to the myth of the exodus from Egypt. But the martyrdom complex found a more compelling expression after the ghastly genocidal horrors and obscenities of Hitler's concentration camps. Hitler was at once the greatest enemy of the Jews in history and the greatest (but unconscious) friend of the concept of "Israel." The horrors he perpetrated resulted in a great boost for the Zionist movement. Western Jews who had previously had reservations about the movement, were now more firmly converted. And Western governments were now readier to ignore Arab wishes in favor of Zionist aims.

In the West Hitler's holocaust created a pervasive sense of guilt which for a long time was used as a resource which the new Jewish state could draw upon. For two or three decades Western liberals were often afraid of voicing reservations about Israel's behavior lest this be interpreted as a form of anti-Semitism. American Jews committed themselves more firmly than ever to Israel, partly because of a sense of guilt arising out of not having done enough for Jews under Hitler's terror a few years earlier. Opposition to Zionism by a Jew was now interpreted as "Jewish self-hate" and anti-Zionism in a gentile was interpreted as anti-Semitism, plain and simple.

In leaders like Menachem Begin the martyrdom complex of Jewish nationalism has reached fanatical proportions. Heads of government of even friendly countries in Europe have been denounced in "holocaust" terms if they showed any sign of deviating from policies preferred by Israel. And when the Pope agreed to give an audience to Yassir Arafat, the Vatican was denounced by Begin's government and accused of having failed to utter a word against the massacre of Jews in Europe under Hitler. The wording of the Vatican's rebuttal rejecting the Israeli charges showed signs of the Polish Pope's own hand:

> These comments are surprising, almost incredible. They overlook — possibly under the impact of an emotion which itself is hardly justified — all that the Pope and the Vatican have done to save thousands upon thousands of Jewish lives before and after the Second World War. . .[10]

The Vatican's strong reply not only emphasized the Church's role in saving Jews, but went on to quietly remind Israelis that it was not just Jews who were massacred by the Nazis.

Afrikaner nationalism has a martyrdom complex of its own with the British in the role of German Nazi. The Dutch had colonized South Africa before the British. British imperialism later on compelled Afrikaaners to vacate some of their original settlements and trek north in 1835. This trek was the equivalent of their exodus — a major symbolic event in Afrikaner mythology, as the migrants traveled north to create the Dutch republics of the Orange Free State and the Transvaal.

By the turn of the century British-Boer relations had reached another point of supreme crisis. The Boar War broke out — a dirty war even by colonial standards. Thousands of Afrikaner women and children were herded into concentration camps, where it is estimated that 26,000 perished. There were no gas chambers, but there is evidence of widespread use of starvation as a political weapon. The Boer War left a deep martyrdom complex in the Afrikaner psyche.[11]

The British won the Boer War and maintained control until 1910, but it was not until 1948 that Afrikaner nationalists at last captured political state power over South Africa as a whole. However, unlike Zionism, Afrikaner nationalism did not have a fund of guilt-feelings even in Britain to draw upon for very long. The Afrikaner's new ideology of apartheid was less respectable than the ideology of the Zionists. Israelis could count on fellow Jews world-wide for moral and often material support; Afrikaners could not even count on fellow Dutch in the Netherlands for sympathy in their predicament. Jews outsider-Israel were among the vanguard defenders of Zionism; the Dutch outside South Africa were often among the vanguard *critics* of apartheid. As a result, the martyrdom complex of Afrikaners found a new intensity arising from South Africa's increasing international isolation and its status as an ideological heretic.

The most frightening thing about the martyrdom complex is what it does to those who control the machinery of the state. The *state* is a principle of power and authority; the *nation* is a principle of identity. There is only one thing worse than the state and that is a state which insists on becoming a "pure" *nation*-state, which insists on attaining cultural or ethnic homogeneity within a single generation.

The martyrdom complex leads to a fortress mentality, which in turn reinforces ethnic exclusivity. Israel insists on its being a *Jewish* state; Afrikaners insist on creating tribal "homelands" separate from "White" South Africa. In pursuit of those aims both Israel and South Africa have been quite ruthless. Indeed, by the 1980s, Israel was on its way to becoming the most arrogant nation-state since Nazi Germany. The earlier invasions of Lebanon, the 1981 bombing of Beirut, the destruction of the Iraqi nuclear plant, the 1982 invasion of Lebanon, and the cynical use of Christian rightists to do the dirty work of "clearing" the Palestinian refugee camps of "terrorists," were all symptoms of the moral corrosion of the *state* of Israel under the control of rulers who were particularly haunted by the Jewish martyrdom complex. By 1982 Israel seemed ready to preside over a Palestinian holocaust. The wheel of genocide seemed to have come full circle—the victim was about to become the perpetrator.

On this issue of the value of human life, apartheid may even have a more humane record than Zionism. Since 1948 far fewer civilians have *died* as a result of the implementation of apartheid than as a result of the defense—of Zionism. The Sharpeville massacre of 1960 in South Africa is supposed to fee one of the most costly acts of barbarism in that country against unarmed civilians. The number of dead was put at 69, the number of wounded at over 150.

By the standards of what the Israeli army kills, Sharpeville was a Sunday afternoon picnic.

The Soweto riots were in fact more costly than Sharpeville, but still mild by Israeli standards of reprisal. In short, since 1948, far more *Palestinians* have been killed by the State of Israel than *Black South Africans* have been killed by the Government of South Africa. Yet the population of Palestinians is only a fraction of the population of Black South Africans.

In at least this respect then, the state has been even more cynically amoral in the hands of the Zionists than it has been in the hands of champions of apartheid.

EXPORTING REFUGEES AND IMPORTING LABOR

The logic of ethnic exclusivity has had still other profound consequences both for Zionism and apartheid. South Africa's solution to the problems of the plural society was an elaborate system of pass laws to discourage "excessive penetration" of white areas by Blacks. Israel's solution to the "threat" of cultural mixtures was even more drastic.

The ethnic "purification" of Israel after its creation in 1948 was helped considerably by the military ineptness of the Arab states. The original Israeli boundaries as defined by the United Nations gave Israel 5,400 square miles with a population of 963,000, of whom 500,000 were Jewish. The Arab state partitioned out of Palestine had 4,500 square miles with a population of 814,000 of whom 10,000 were Jewish. Jerusalem, with a population of 2CT6,000 had 100,000 Jews—and was turned into a separate body.

On May 14, 1948, the day on which the state of Israel was formally proclaimed, the Arabs launched a military attack. They were defeated before they could even get near the controversial borders of partitioned Palestine. The Israelis had their first moment of triumphant expansionism. They occupied more than half the territory allotted to the Arabs, and increased the size of their state from 5,400 to 7,722 square miles.

Technically their territorial expansionism should have resulted in a further racial dilution of the population of the new Israel. After all, the original Israel had little more than half its population Jewish, while the new lands which were conquered had a preponderance of Arabs.

But the Arabs of both the newly conquered territories and the original Israel were encouraged to flee. Who encouraged them to become refugees? The Israelis claim that Arab broadcasting stations instigated the flight of the Arab inhabitants within areas controlled by Israel. But there is evidence that the Arabs had begun to run before the fighting broke out, partly as a result of the conditions of terror deliberately created in some areas by Israeli militants. One of the most notorious of such operations of intimidation was the "Deir Yassin Massacre," committed on April 9, 1948, which cost 245 lives.

One of the most thorough investigations made into whether Arab broadcasting stations had instigated the Arabs of Palestine to flee was made by the Irish journalist, Erskine Childers. From the records of the British Museum Childers examined and listened to all the tapes of Arab radio stations monitored during the first Arab Israeli war in 1948 Childers found nothing to substantiate the Israeli claim that the Palestinian refugee problem was created by Arab radio stations.

The Israeli government had promised Childers concrete proof about these broadcasting instigations. Childers visited Israel again in 1958, but were shown no proof of the point in dispute. On the contrary, he had found upon listening to the broadcast tapes evidence of appeals from Arab countries asking the Palestinians to stay put as a way of ensuring their claims.[12]

The refugees have swollen in numbers since 1948 to over two million. Technically some of these refugees should indeed be regarded as Israeli citizens, to the extent that they were part of the population of Israel on the day Israel was created and were deemed by the United Nations to be citizens of the country. The United Nations was the body which had brought the state of Israel into being. The Geneva Convention which Israel signed in 1949 recognized the right of refugees to return to their homeland, whatever the reasons for which they originally fled.

But the doctrine of an Israel consisting of Jews was not easily compatible with the readmission of thousands of non-Jewish citizens. The Israeli immigration laws—especially from 1950 with the Law of Return—are prepared to admit large numbers of Jews from Russia, Eastern Europe and elsewhere, and even complain that the Russian government makes it difficult for those Jews to get to Israel. And yet the same government so keen on Jewish immigration is at the same time militantly opposed to the resettlement of some of its own Arab citizens who fled in a moment of terror some three decades ago. The Jews of Russia have never known Israel, and would technically be alien to that part of the world. But the Arabs in tents next door to Israel were part of Palestine until Zionism triumphed, and a radically exclusive state came into being. The Israeli government says they have no responsibility for the Arabs that had fled from Palestine, since Israel has replaced them with Sephardic Jews from Arab countries. The doctrine of racial purification continues to color the ideological legitimation of the Jewish state.

Israel has continued to have its Enoch Powells, its defenders of a racially exclusive state, to the present day. There are strong voices not only defending permanent exclusion of those non-Jews that were terrorized into leaving the country in previous years, but also urging the further de-Arabization of Israel as it now exists. Life as a garrison state has taken its toll of Jewish tolerance. More than two decades of continuous military preparedness have sharpened Israeli chauvinism and Jewish consciousness.

Of the present population of three million in Israel, ten per cent is Arab. But an additional one million Arabs have fallen under Israeli control as a result of the new lands conquered by Israel during the 1967 June war. The Jews still outnumber the Arabs almost two to one even including the conquered territories. But many Israelis are already worried about the survival of Israel's Jewishness. A survey commissioned by the Israeli government in 1972 pointed out that the Arab population was growing faster than the Jewish, and that by 1985, if present trends continued, the Arabs would constitute forty per cent of the combined population of Israel and the occupied lands. This is what has come to be called "the demographic nightmare."

Pinas Sapir, Finance Minister under Golda Meir, represented an important school of thought among Israelis when he said that he would rather give up most of the territory now conquered since 1967 than see the Arab population of Israel come up to forty per cent before the end of this century. In a television interview in 1972 he said:

> If I have to choose between a binational state which will include the town of Hebron, in the West Bank, and a Jewish state without Hebron, I shall prefer the latter.[13]

Sapir has repeated that a binational state would be a "tragedy." The late Defense and Foreign Minister Moshe Dayan was in some ways less purist in his conception of Israel than are some of his compatriots. He would rather keep the conquered lands even if he had to put up with non-Jews. There was a time when Dayan believed that after ten years of economic union with Israel, the occupied Arab lands might voluntarily want to remain part of the Israeli state. But even Dayan had to think in terms of a solution which would ensure a permanent Jewish majority in the Israeli state.

In reality Dayan's vision included a preference for the availability, of cheap labor within Israel or cheap labor for Israeli industry within the occupied territories in a manner fundamentally similar to the migration of cheap labor from Turkey into the Federal Republic of Germany. Currently, 75,000 laborers, or approximately one-third of the total Arab work force of the West Bank and Gaza Strip territories commute to Israel In some forms of unskilled labor, such as that found in the building trades and the service sector, Palestinians make up as much as 30 percent of the work force. Within Israel itself, it is quite clear that these workers would be the first to be laid aside should there be a major economic recession, for Palestinian wages are not covered by Israeli trade-union agreements Nor are Palestinians eligible for the basic social welfare benefits given Israeli workers similarly, the Israeli National Insurance system does not include West Bank-Gaza residents. It is quite true, however, that the Arab workers are better off with the wages that they earn than they would be in their original areas, as employment in Israel accounts for 30 percent of the total income of West Bank and Gaza Strip Palestinians. But the large number of workers who go into Israel also affects the local Palestinian economy; since most of these workers come from the agricultural sector, the area under cultivation in the occupied territories has been reduced by 35 percent.[14]

Profound moral as well as economic problems are raised by a situation where cheap labor is imported on a temporary basis, and on the clear understanding that never would it be allowed to affect demographically the Jewish racial nature of the state. In this instance the Israelis want to have their cake and eat it too. They want the availability of non-Jewish labor, on the one hand, and the guarantee of perpetual Jewishness of their state on the other. The dilemma has posed much moral unease for many Israelis and humanitarians elsewhere.

The similarity with South Africa here lies South Africa's readiness to import personnel from other parts of Africa, on a temporary basis, provided the long term white power in South Africa is not compromised.

But Israel and South Africa want to combine the economic blessing of alien personnel without compromising the ultimate racial principle of their own conceptions of statehood.

The Pretoria regime has at times sent recruiting agents to a number of different African countries, expressing a preference for imported labor but still unwilling to give up the basic assumptions of white supremacy. Black labor pours into South Africa from Malaw and Botswana, from Zambia and Namibia. Even Marxist Mozambique maintains a contract of cheap labor with South Africa in exchange for gold. There is no doubt at all that South Africa excels in the arts of exporting refugees and importing cheaper labor than is locally available. More so even than South Africa, the foreigners Israel recruits constitute a pool of cheap labor.[15] They come in the early morning, before most Israelis are awake, from the West Bank of the Jordan River and the Gaza Strip. Wearing Arab headdresses and work boots, they commute each day in overcrowded buses and taxis to construction sites and factories all over Israel. They are Israel's migrant workers—about 50,000 to 60,000 Arab laborers from the occupied territories who have come in steadily increasing numbers since the 1967 war to find jobs in Israel's overheated economy. In the last few years they have become an indispensable ingredient in Israel's economic boom—the cheap labor on which the economy has vaulted forward since the six-day war.[16]

The principle of the ethnic polity is up against the dictates of economic convenience in both Israel and South Africa. Economy and culture exert a mixed influence on these racial approaches to statecraft.

An additional irony in South Africa itself has been the prosperity of the local Jews against the background of the exploitation of both local and imported Blacks. The Jews in South Africa have shown themselves to be among the most liberal of Whites. From among South Africa's Jewry comes many a voice of sanity and humane realism.

But when all is said and done, the Jews in South Africa are at the heart of the country's economy. Their developmental contribution is central to the controversial prosperity of South Africa. There is no doubt that the Jews have played an important role in the development of the region as a whole, though they have managed to couple it with relatively liberal racial attitudes.

It is also quite clear that the Jews have had a much bigger share of the economic wealth of Southern Africa than the Afrikaaners. Jewish South Africans have on the whole been part of the English-speaking South African community, and have been among the most influential members of that community. But, as Colin and Margaret Legum once argued, if the Marxists were right in their assertion that power lies among those who control the means of production, Afrikaanerdom would not today be ruling the Republic of South Africa. The Legums pointed out that the key "means of production, distribution and exchange" and the most important section of the Press, were in the hands of the English-speaking South Africans.

> The disparity between capitalist power and political power in South Africa is clear. English-speaking South Africans control 99 percent of mining capital, 94 percent of industrial capital, 88 percent of finance capital, and 75 percent of commercial capital. But the political interests they support have no chance of achieving power as things stand today. Nor can this disparity be explained in terms of the diffusion of capitalist power. The bulk of it is controlled by seven financial houses. Between them they control over a thousand of the largest companies, with combined financial resources exceeding 1,000 million.[17]

Not all this wealth was of course Jewish, but the Jewish component seemed to have been particularly conspicuous. The Legums pointed out that in its early struggles to achieve power, Afrikaanerdom caricatured this powerful financial complex as "Hoggenheimer"—the "foreign, imperialist and capitalist octopus." The Legums continue:

> (Akrikaanerdom) looked upon this fat, cigar-smoking, diamond-studded, *hook-nosed*, oligarch as the heir of Cecil John Rhodes, still regarded as Afrikaanerdom's greatest enemy."[18]

The biggest Jewish name in the industrial complex of Southern Africa is Oppenheimer. When Sir Ernest Oppenheimer died in 1957, Harry Oppenheimer inherited three major business empires—De Beers, Rhodesian Anglo-American, and the Anglo-American Corporation of South Africa. What should be noted is that Harry Oppenheimer is Jewish by ethnic descent but converted to Christianity. Through the empires he has exercised some control over the world diamond market, the world's largest gold-producing group, and much of the copper output of Southern Africa. His interests include uranium, coal mines, lead, zinc, real estate, railways, ranching, fertilizers, chemicals, explosives and munitions among others. "His ninety-odd companies have a market value of more than 500 million; they produce between 15 and 20 million in profit a year."[19] Oppenheimer is a product of the contradictions of the south African situation—English prosperity and Jewish ethnicity.

The late Kwame Nkrumah, first president of Ghana, was also staggered by Oppenheimer's economic omnipresence in such a large part of the African continent. In the last book he wrote while still in office Nkrumah attempted to carry Lenin's thesis on imperialism a stage further. Lenin had described imperialism as the highest and most elaborate stage of capitalism. But Lenin had not addressed himself to neo-colonialism, a form of economic control which falls short of territorial annexation. It is to this phenomenon that Nkrumah addressed himself in his book Neo-Colonialism, *The Last Stage of Imperialism*. In this book Nkrumah had a good deal to say about what he called "The Oppenheimer Empire." Nkrumah said:

> The king of mining in South Africa, indeed in Africa, is Harry Frederick Oppenheimer. One might almost call him the king of South Africa, even the emperor, with an ever extending empire. There is probably hardly a corner of Southern Africa's industrial and financial structure in which he has not got a very extended finger of his own or the hook of some affiliate or associate. These fingers and hooks attach the Oppenheimer Empire firmly to other empires as great or greater.[20]

Nkrumah went on to say that Mr. Oppenheimer was director, chairman or president of some seventy companies. "These directorships as well as those held by important colleagues and nominees, whose names recur monotonously on the boards of an ever-extending complex of company boards, give the lie to the fiction of respectable separateness, even where there is no obvious financial link."

In the following chapters of his book Nkrumah provided facts and figures about what he also called the Oppenheimer "octopus," asserting that through affiliate companies, the economic tentacles of this octopus has extended and touched a far-flung parts of Africa, including "Tanganyika, Uganda, the Congo,

Angola, Mozambique, West Africa, and even into the Sahara and North Africa."[21] Harry Oppenheimer is in fact a good example of the ethnic Jewish liberal who is caught in between. But his vast empire is precisely what comes into conflict with that liberalism in race relations. He does believe in some degree of racial equality, but is also concerned to protect his economic interests in Southern Africa and beyond. His behavior as an investor sometimes clashes with the broader vision of justice. In 1963 he decided to spend 10 million to build a munitions factory in order to enable South Africa's armies to become independent of external imports. The company, Afrocan Explosives, seemed to many African nationalists a military consolidation of white power.

Three years before that, the Sharpeville shootings of defenseless Africans had led to world indignation and domestic fear of an uprising in South Africa. Morale fell and capital started leaving South Africa. The economy was in danger of a serious slump. It took Oppenheimer's personal intervention in the financial world to help restore confidence and reattract investment into South Africa. Oppenheimer went to the United States to arrange a $10 million loan for one of his companies. The successful negotiations for a massive loan to support business interests in South Africa helped to clear the economic cloud and restore some confidence in the security of investment in South Africa. "Oppenheimer needs to maintain international confidence for the interests and policies which he is committed to supporting—even if the result assists Verwoerd. This is Oppenheimer's real dilemma: the more successful he is as a financier, the less successful he is as a radical politician."[22]

As we know the famous Balfour Declaration was addressed to Lord Rothschild. The Rothschilds have also been important in the business world of Southern Africa, with special reference perhaps to the Rhodesian Selection Trust. These are all part of the impressive Jewish participation in the industrial development and financial growth of Southern Africa.

It is partly because of this impressive economic performance that South Africa's Jews provide the second largest private financial contribution to Israel—second only to that provided by American Jews. Jewish prosperity in South Africa helps the survival of Israel. Israel has demonstrated Jewish power at the expense of the Palestinians. South Africa has witnessed Jewish prosperity against the background of black cheap labor—both local and imported.

MILITARIZED ZIONISM AND IMPERIAL APARTHEID

The strategy of maintaining relative ethnic exclusivity with the assurance of relatively cheap labor has required policies which are both imperialistic and militaristic. Apartheid South Africa and Israel devised divergent policies but in pursuit of comparable goals. It is arguable that on the issue of territorial expansionism since the Nationalists took over power in 1948, South Africa has been a more civilized country than Israel. Israel's territorial expansionism started in the very year of its creation. With almost every new war with the Arabs, Israel has grown in size. In 1956 it was only because of the angry insistence of the United States under Eisenhower that Israel relinquished the large areas of the Sinai that she occupied as part of her conspiracy with Britain and France in the Suez war. In 1967 Israel got another chance to reconquer the Sinai. It took another war, in 1973, before Israel returned a little territory to Egypt. And after the Camp David Accords the whole of the Sinai reverted to Egypt. On the other hand, since Camp David, the Golan Heights of Syria have been annexed by Israel, East Jerusalem incorporated, and Jewish settlements in the West Bank vastly expanded.

While Zionism has continued its hunger for more land, apartheid in its philosophy envisaged surrendering land for the different "Bantustans," and even land for neighboring Swaziland.[23]

Apartheid South Africa had indicated some readiness to give up direct occupation of territory, but without giving up indirect control over what goes on in that territory. South Africa's readiness to give "independence" to Bantu "homelands" is an assertion of this readiness to relinquish direct occupation. The Transkei's "independence" in 1976 was the first of these moves. South Africa's Machiavellian plans for Namibia also include the prospect of a partial end to direct occupation.

And yet the kind of ethnic Balkanization envisaged for Namibia is bound to make a mockery of the country's prospective "sovereignty." South Africa intends to reduce occupation of Namibia, but without losing control.

As for Transkei, its dependence on South Africa is well and truly assured by physical fragmentation of territory, combined with ethnic dispersal. As a British commentator put it:

> The Transkei, made up of three unconnected areas totaling the size of Denmark, can never be economically independent of South Africa. Physically the least fragmented of South Africa's black homelands, it is the only one capable of achieving sufficient economic self-reliance to improve its economic relationship with the republic from one of complete subservience to self-respecting interdependence. However, the odds are stacked against it. . . Vorster plans to give Transkei and other homelands a kind of freedom while tying them to the necessity to export their black workers to the white republic for jobs where they will have minimal rights. A quarter of a million Traskeians will have to go to white areas to work.[24]

In its more conciliatory moments, especially under American pressure, the Labour Israeli government also indicated periodically a readiness to give up part of the West Bank of Jordan "in the context of a general peace settlement." But even the Israeli Labour Government would still want to maintain control over the West Bank either through institutionalized arrangements or through the militarily weak government of Jordan. Israel under Labour would at times even consider a kind of "Bantu homeland" for Palestinians—provided it was decidedly *not* a sovereign state, or an autonomous political actor. Hence Israel's insistence that even in peace negotiations, the Palestinians should somehow be represented as part of Jordan's delegation.

But the paramount imperative of ethno-cultural exclusivity continues to bring the ideology of apartheid closer to the ideology of Zionism in spite of divergent techniques of implementation. South Africa's "homelands" policy seeks to strip South African citizenship from those that are deemed to be of a Bantustan. Thus all Xhosa are declared to have ceased, or are in the process of ceasing, to be South African now that Transkei has attained "independence." This applies even to those Xhosa who are still living in the heartland of South Africa and have been outside the Transkei all their lives.

Thus the dream of apartheid is to have, the heartland of South Africa "white." The richest and largest part of the country is to be reserved for the privileged immigrant Caucasian minorities.

Similarly, the logic of creating a Jewish state in Palestine has all along required that the great majority of citizens should be Jewish by one means or another.

There are two main approaches to such contrived ethnic preponderance. One is to increase the population of the privileged ethnic population. The other approach, as we indicated earlier, is somehow to reduce the population of the unwanted ethnic groups.

Both Israel and Apartheid South Africa devised ways of experimenting with the two approaches. On the strategy of increasing the population of the privileged group, both Israel and South Africa have had elaborate immigration laws which are ethnically discriminatory. As we argued before, that is what Israel's Law of Return is all about. Whether one defines Jewishness in religious or in ethnic terms, there is no doubt that Israeli immigration laws are comparable in their exclusivist implications to the old "White Australia policy." As we indicated, a Jew from, say, Eastern Europe who has had no connection with Palestine except for a tenuous myth two thousand years old has had almost automatic access to Israel—whereas an Arab who was born in Palestine, and fled in 1948, can enjoy no right of literal return. The logic of the Jewish state has sanctioned the kind of discriminatory laws which the Jews themselves would condemn were they applied against them by some other state. If the United States' Congress were to adopt immigration statutes for America which gave priority entry to white Anglo-Saxon Protestants, Jews all over the world would be among the first to protest. Yet Israel has laws which, by the very logic of creating a Jewish state, discriminate against both Christians and Muslims in favor of Jews.

The logic of white supremacy in South Africa had similarly resulted in immigration practices which encourage white settlers and discourage all other potential immigrants. Both Israel and South Africa have thus strongly promoted policies which aim to increase the population of the "master race" within the total citizenry at the expense of other groups.

What about the parallel strategy of trying to reduce the population of the unwanted ethnic groups? Let us return to this theme in greater detail. On this issue, Israel has once again turned out to be as brutal as South Africa. Neither country has succeeded in "purifying" itself ethnically. Apartheid has not managed to do without large numbers of black people in "white" areas. And we know that Israel is still landed with a population which is still one tenth Arab.

Yet white South Africa cannot be accused of the kind of tactics which Zionists used in 1948 to get as many Arab Palestinians as possible to flee for their lives. Those tactics, ranged from threatening ghetto-dwellers in cities with "the outbreak of cholera and typhus" to brutal intimidation by Jewish troops in the Lydda-Ramle. In such areas Arab Palestinians, all destitute, were given an hour to leave.

We have already referred to the worst single event in those early days—the notorious massacre of Arab villagers at Deir Yassin. Those who were killed by Jewish fanatics were *old* men, women and children. They were brutally and deliberately butchered. Many were stripped and sadistically mutilated. Some were thrown into a well in sheer random cruelty. Arthur Koestler described the Deir Yassin massacre as "the psychologically decisive factor in this spectacular exodus." It certainly contributed to the de-Arabization of Palestine as frightened inhabitants scrambled for refuge in neighboring countries.

The Jewish state which was envisaged by the United Nations upon voting in favor of its creation in 1947, would have contained a 45 per cent Arab population. With a birth rate higher than that of the Jews, the Arabs in Israel might well have begun to equal if not outnumber the Jews by the 1970's—just as Muslims had begun to outnumber the Christians in Lebanon by the same period. But Zionist tactics in the early years of Israel's existence were so successful that a larger Israel in the 1980's has nevertheless a much smaller proportion of Arabs. Nothing that South Africa under the Nationalist Party has ever done is remotely comparable as a brutal strategy of demographic manipulation. The regime in Pretoria since 1948 has often dreamt of the day when the heartland of South Africa would be completely white, but the regime has yet to engineer a nightmare to send Blacks fleeing to their "home-lands." On this issue of demographic manipulation there is little doubt that Zionism since 1948 has been more ruthless and cynical than apartheid.

Once the Israelis succeeded in reducing the Arab population of their country to less than a quarter of what it would otherwise have been, they could then simply take a stand against letting them come back to Israel. The Israelis have argued that it was up to other Arab countries to absorb these refugees. After all, they were fellow Arabs. Why should they go back to what was once Palestine? In the words of Abba Eban to the United Nations in 1957 on the issue of Palestinian refugees:

> The responsibility of the Arab governments is threefold. Theirs is the initiative for its creation. Theirs is the onus for its endurance. Above all—theirs is the capacity for its solution.[25]

Abba Eban's assumption here is that because the Palestinians were Arabs, it was up to countries like Jordan, Syria and Lebanon to absorb them into their own societies. It was like the Government of Pretoria arguing that because a Xhosa or Zulu was an African, it was up to Angola, Mozambique and Zambia to integrate them as fellow Africans. But Xhosa and Zulu of South Africa were not merely black; they were also South Africans. Why should they be satisfied with being absorbed into Zambian or Angolan societies? Similarly, Palestinians were not merely Arab—they were also Palestinians. Why should they be satisfied with absorption into present-day Syrian, Lebanese or Jordanian societies?

> These Arabs, in short, are displaced persons in the fullest, most tragic meaning of the term. . . Unlike other refugees, *these refuse to move, they insist on going home*."[26]

It is because of these factors that strictly on the issue of displacement, the plight of Palestinians has been more tragic than that of the Zulu, Xhosa and other South African Blacks.

Yet the fate of these South African Blacks is tragic enough. They may not have been induced to scream for safety to their "homelands," but they have been made to feel humiliated, brutalized and wantonly exploited. In the ultimate analysis the ideology of Zionism does converge with the philosophy of apartheid—they are both discriminatory ideologies whose implementation inevitably and logically necessitated strategies of repression and ethnic exclusivity.

Yet internally in their own societies the privileged groups have been relatively humane. White South Africa within itself is one of the more liberal polities on the African continent. The white newspapers within South Africa are among the freest in the region; the judges are among the most independent, the white workers are among the most privileged.

Similarly, Israel within itself is the most liberal polity in the Middle East. But although both white South Africa and Israel score high in their treatment of their own "Kith and Kin," the logic of their ethnic exclusivity prevents them from being humane to their own neighbors.

The result for each of them has been regional isolation. Sometimes they see this isolation in heroic terms. There is, for example, the image of Israel as a courageous immigrant community which has managed to defy a hostile environment and survive with honor. This hero-image of Israel has been important both for white South Africans and for white Rhodesians. *Die Bruger*, for instance, draws inspiration from Israel's example of victorious loneliness in these words:

> We in South Africa would be foolish if we did not at least take account of the possibility that we are destined to become a sort of Israel in a preponderantly hostile Africa, and that fact might become part of our national way of life. . .[27]

It is partly this sense of shared isolation that has led in the 1970's to a new *entente cordiale* between the land of apartheid and the land of Zionism. This has included reports that South Africa was prepared to finance "an expansion of Israel's arms producing capacity"—partly in exchange for South Africa's purchase of Israeli-built jet fighters.[28]

More immediately controversial in terms of Israeli-American relations has been the news that Israel was building two missile boats for delivery to South Africa. American officials in the State Department were becoming concerned about aspects of Israeli-South African relations, according to "usually reliable sources."

> The sources expect more U.S criticism of the links between Israel's state-owned Military Industry and South Africa.[29]

Israel is said to have been advised that deals like the missile boat arrangement with South Africa could hamper the efforts which Americans were making to help reduce Israel's international isolation. In some circles there has also been a fear that Israel's increasing friendship with South Africa could strain relations between American Jews and American Blacks.

> Direct (U.S.) aid to Israel would certainly be viewed by many black observers here as indirect aid to the hated South African regime . . . (According to some blacks) pro-Israeli policies (could) become by extension pro-South African policies.[30]

Behind it all was the rapid evaporation of Israel's early idealism and moral fervor. Israel was becoming another *paragon of commercialized warfare and arms trade*. The little country was, per capita, trying to outstrip France as a cynical dealer in the arts of destruction. But the main difference was that Israel's clients—unlike those of France—were disproportionately reactionary.

> A list of (Israel's) clients that includes South Africa and Bolivia, and a sales catalogue with counter-insurgency weapons, does not sit too well with liberals anywhere.[31]

But the most ominous of all the cynicism is the apparent nuclear collaboration between Apartheid South Africa and Israel. Is Israel's technological expertise entering into an alliance with South Africa's financial power to create parallel nuclear capabilities in the two countries? Circumstantial evidence in support of this thesis has increased, especially since 1979.

In reality nuclear power may be more relevant for the survival of Zionism than for the survival of apartheid. Zionism's most dangerous adversary lies outside Israel—in the determination of the Palestinians and their prospective military and economic allies. But apartheid's most dangerous adversary is within South Africa—in the form of internal black militancy. Israel could conceivably use military nuclear weapons against her external adversaries, but the architects of apartheid could hardly threaten nuclear annihilation against the restless masses of Soweto. In the ultimate analysis, apartheid is vulnerable from *within*—where nuclear weapons are largely irrelevant. But Zionism is, in the first instance, vulnerable from without. In those circumstances a nuclear capability could at least delay the final day of reckoning for Jewish exclusivity.

But despite this asymmetry in nuclear relevance between the techniques of Zionism and the strategies of apartheid, a momentous alliance has nevertheless emerged since the 1970's between Israel and Southern Africa.

A joint military-industrial complex between Israel and South Africa is in the making. The South African Iron and Steel Corporation is already cooperating with Israel' s Koor enterprise. And trade between the two countries has quadrupled since 1973. Alongside this industrial and commercial cooperation is the growing interaction in militarily relevant areas, from counter-insurgency to preliminary nuclear consultations.[32] Israel's sales to South Africa rose from $8 million to $11.8 million in the same period.[33]

CONCLUSION

When the Nazis asserted their control in Germany in the 1930fXf and proceeded to put their racist doctrines against the Jews into practice, the Nationalist Party in South Africa responded in sympathy. Dr. Malan's "apartheid" movement helped to work up an anti-Semitic hysteria in South Africa, and provided an umbrella of semi-legitimacy to such fascist groups in the Union as the Greyshirts, the Blackshirts and the Brownshirts. The centenary celebration of the Great Trek in 1938 aroused renewed racist fervor among Afrikaaners, and Dr. Malan appealed to "the spirit of Blood River in a new Trek" in terms which were basically neo-Nazi.[34]

Malan and his comrades were the architects of apartheid. These were the people who were trying to rally white South Africa behind the ideals of Nazism—urging South Africans at least to remain neutral in World War II. But for a while Malan and his party lost—and Smuts carried white South Africa with him on the side of Britain. The vote in the South African parliament was relatively close. But the outcome delayed the worst excesses of apartheid for another decade.

However, while Dr. Malan and his fellow racial purists in South Africa awaited their chance to capture power, the Jews in Germany were suffering precisely from doctrines of racial purity and exclusiveness. In the words of Rupert Emerson of Harvard University:

> It is to Hitler and the Nazis that we are indebted for the full development of the appalling potentialities of the national concept in both its personal and its territorial aspects. . .Under the spell of the Nazi racial doctrines, Germany moved to a ruthless implementation of the dogma that only the proper German was a member of the nation, entitled to an equal share in the state. . . . The Nazis likewise developed the fullest application of the idea that all persons whose origins were in the German community continued to be members of the *Volk* whatever their present residence and citizenship.[35]

What about all persons of Jewish origin regardless of their present residence and citizenship? On this issue Zionism had even more in common with pan-Germanism than does Afrikaaner nationalism. The Jewish victims of Nazi exclusivity were driven to seek a new refuge in Palestine—based in turn on their own ethno-cultural exclusiveness. Those who ran away from the brutality of a "pure Germany" sought to establish for themselves a "pure Jewish State." But on what principles could the Jews do this? Rupert Emerson answered in the following terms:

> The conception of creating a Jewish national home in Palestine could not possibly be squared with the principle of self-determination, or for that matter, of democracy, on the basis of any of the generally accepted criteria. The Arabs. . . received neutral support from the King-Crane Commission sent by President Wilson to ascertain the state of affairs in Syria and Palestine. Asserting that the Zionists looked to practically complete dispossession of the non-Jewish inhabi-

tants of Palestine, this Commission found nearly nine-tenths of the population to be non-Jewish and emphatically opposed to the entire Zionist program. . . To the Arabs it (turned out to be) a prolonged and tragically successful invasion of an Arab country by an alien people under Western imperialist auspices, ending in the expulsion of most of the people whose country it was. No suggestion of a plebiscite accompanied the General Assembly's proposal that Palestine be partitioned.[36]

By the 1980's the logic of Zionism had come full circle. The successors of Dr. Malan in South Africa, once fervent in supporting Hitler's anti-Semitism, áre now in alliance with the successors of Chaim Weizmann and Ben Gurion. The strategy of displacing Palestinians has found a point in common with strategy of stripping Xhosa of their South African citizenship. The policy of opposing the creation in Palestine of a "secular, democratic State in which Jews, Muslims, and Christians might live together" is now allied to a philosophy which opposed the creation of a diverse, democratic state in which Boer, Bantu and Briton might live together. The anti-pluralist element in Zionism is now aligned with the anti-pluralist element in apartheid. Somehow the ghosts of Auschwitz in Germany, of Deir Yassin in Palestine, and of Sharpeville and Soweto in South Africa, are suddenly in bewildered communion with each other. In the nightmare of historical change, those who might once have made strange bedfellows are now rudely transformed into natural if pathetic allies.

NOTES

1. For further citations from Mazzini and other thinkers who relate nationality to divine purpose see Boyd C. Shafer, *Nationalism: Myth and Reality* (New York: Harcourt, Brace and Company, 1955), chapter 11, "Some Metaphysical Myths."

2. Cited by Hans Kohn, "Zion and the Jewish National Idea," the *Menorah Journal*, 1 and 2, Autumn-Winter, 1958, p. 46.

3. Morris R. Cohen, The Faith of a Liberal (New York: Holt, 1946).

4. Dan Kurzman, *Genesis 1948, the First Arab-Israeli War* (New York: The New American Library, 1970, p. 23.

5. See C.G. Montefiore, "Nation or Religious Community?" reprinted in *Zionism Reconsidered*, edited by Michael Selzer (London: Macmillan, 1970), 61. Montefiore's discussion of these issues originally appeared in *Transaction of the Jewish Historical Society of England*," 4, 1899–1901 (London, 1903).

6. Meyer Fortes, *Kinship and the Social Order* (Chicago: Aldine Publishing Company, 1969), p. 104.

7. C.G. Montefiore (Note 5), p. 51.

8. See "Israel Acknowledges Jewishness of Tribe of Northern Ethiopfe," *The Washington Post*, January 5, 1973. For an alternative interpretation of why the K'ai-feng Jews

were assimilated in China, consult Song Nai Rhee, "Jewish Assimilation: The Case of Chinese Jews," *Comparative Studies in Society and History*, 15, 1, January 1973, pp. 115–26. A major reason why Jews look more like other people in the specific countries they have adopted than like each other lies precisely in the history of "illicit" race mixture On the question of: the limits of the cultural assimilation of the Jews in foreign lands consult also Maurice Samuel, *I, The Jew* (1927), (Harcourt Brace, 1954 edition).

9. For a discussion of Childers findings and their relevance for the present militancy of the Palestinian refugees consult the illuminating series of articles carried by *The Guardian* (London) in October 1972. See especially Paul Balta, "Palestinian Refugees: A Growing National Consciousness," The Guardian, October 21, 1972.

10. See article by Yuval Elizur (Washington Post special) *Chicago Sun Times*, August 16, 1972.

11. Consult Terrance Smith, "Israelis Debate Morality and Economics of Using Arab Laborers," *The New York Times*, April 12, 1972.

12. For a discussion of Amin's efforts as an attempt to transcend dependency consult Mazrui, "Racial Self-Reliance and Cultural Dependency: Nyerere and Amin in Comparative Perspective," *Journal of International Affairs* (Columbia), 27, 1, 1973.

13. Terrance Smith, *The New York Times*, April 12, 1973.

14. Colin and Margaret Legum, *South Africa: Crisis for the West* (London: Pall Mall Press, 1964), pp. 107–108.

15. Ibid., 108. The emphasis is mine. Pierre van den Berghe curiously plays down these aspects of the race situation in South Africa in his otherwise stimulating book, *South Africa: A Study in Conflict* (Berkeley and L.A.: University of California Press, 1967).

16. *Ibid.,* pp. 117–18.

17. Kwame Nkrumah, *Neo-Colonialism, The Last Stage of Imperialism* (London: Thomas Nelson and Sons, 1965), pp. 110–19, 127.

18. *Ibid.*

19. *Ibid*, pp. 121–122 For examples of Oppenheimer's liberalism consult his T. B. Davie Memorial Lecture at the University of Cape Town, *The Conditions for Progress in Africa* (University of Cape Town Press, 1962) and his *Towards Racial Harmony* (Johannesburg: Frier and Munro, 1956) Nkrumah's estimate of number of Oppenheimer's companies is twenty fewer than that of Legum's—without lowering the impact.

20. For some discussion of the principle of Macro-segregation and its logic of repression see Pierre Lvan den Berghe, *Race and Racism: A Comparative Perspective* (New York: John Wiley & Sons, 1967), pp. 108–10.

21. *The Sunday Times* (London), August 15, 1976. For a broader introduction see Ezekiel Mphahlele, "South Africa: Two Communities and the Struggle for a Birthright," *Journal of African Studies*, 4, 1, Spring 1977, pp. 21–50.

22. Erskine Childers, "The Other Exodus," *The Spectator* (London), May 12, 1961. For some of the wider moral issues touching on the issue of the Jewish conscience in relation to Israel consult Irving Louis Horowitz, *Israeli Ecstasies/Jewish Agonies* (New York: Oxford University Press, 1974).

23. *Ibid*. The emphasis is original.

24. See *Die Transvaler*, December 17, 1960, and *Die Burger*, March 13, 1962.

25. *New York Times*, April 18, 1976.

26. Jason Morris, "Israel-South African Deal Stirs Debate," Christian Science Monitor (Washington), August 12, 1976.

27. *The Washington Post*, April 21, 1976.

28. *The Sun* (U.S.A.), August 18, 1976.

29. After 1973 trade between Israel and South Africa began to expand dramatically. South Africa's exports to Israel tripled (from $11.6 million in 1972 to $32.4 million in 1973).

30. See, for example, Ronald Segal, *The Race War* (New York: Bentham Book under the Viking Press, 1967), pp. 77–78.

31. Emerson, *From Empire to Nation* (Cambridge: Harvard University Press, 1960).

32. *Ibid*.

33. *Ibid.*

34. *Ibid.*

35. *Ibid.*

36. *Ibid.*

Chapter Fifteen

Comparative Terrorism: Arab, Jewish and African (Usama, Sharon and Shaka)

The word "terror" in the modern political context was born out of the French revolution in the eighteenth century.[1] Terror and revolution became intertwined and synthesized. A modern social revolution was born.

A TYPOLOGY OF TERROR

In this chapter we distinguish between firstly, revolutionary terrorism, going back to the French revolution; secondly, racial terrorism which in the twentieth century included the Ku Klux Klan in the United States and apartheid in South Africa. And thirdly, there is religiously inspired terrorism, which includes Al-Qaeda but has also manifested itself among followers of almost every major religion: Christianity, Judaism, Sikhism, and Hinduism.

Yes, religious zealots from the Islamic background killed Anwar Sadat. But we should remember also the religious zealots from the Sikh background who assassinated Indira Gandhi, as well as the Jewish assassin of Yitzhak Rabin.[2]

There is the question of whether state terrorism is a different category, or whether it is a difference in method. For example, did the apartheid state commit state terrorism—or was it a vision of racially-inspired terrorism? Has Israel been guilty of state terrorism? Ariel Sharon, when he was Defense Minister in 1982, could even engage in surrogate terrorism in Sabra and Chatila. He facilitated the massacre of Palestinians by Phalangist right-wing Christian militia in Beirut.[3] Was this a combination of racial and religious terrorism?

After he became Prime Minister of Israel in 2001 Sharon became similarly reckless with the lives of Palestinian civilians in response to attacks on Israelis by Palestinian suicide bombers. When in July 2002 an F-16 fighter plane fired a rocket into a civilian residential building in Gaza in order to kill one adversary, and killed nearly ten innocent children as well, Ariel Sharon described the Israeli mission as one of Israel's greatest military successes.[4] [His Foreign Minister was more apologetic and circumspect in his utterances.]

There is no doubt that Ariel Sharon's attitude to civilian life on the Palestinian side has a terrorist-style of recklessness.[5] He has been kept in check by the wider democratic culture of Israel, and by the constraints of the opinion of the United States and by the reactions of European allies. Under Sharon Israel has drifted towards periodic state-terrorism and war-crimes.

Having differentiated revolutionary, racial, state and religiously inspired terrorism, we should also note that each of those in turn includes two sub-varieties—heroic terrorism and horrific terrorism.

Heroic terrorism is of the kind whose aims are noble and may even be humane, but whose means are morally ignoble and often physically cruel. Horrific terrorism, on the other hand, lacks legitimacy at the level of both the goals being pursued and the means being employed. Both ends and means are ignoble.

In our own day there is a debate about whether suicide bombing by oppressed Palestinians are a case of heroic terrorism. Many people in the countries which have been bombed by the United States in the last forty years may also wonder whether the attack on the Pentagon on September 11, 2001, was not a case of heroic terrorism—since the Pentagon is widely viewed as a war machine and therefore a legitimate military target.

However, there may be a general international consensus that the attack on the World Trade Center in New York on the same day was a clear case of horrific terrorism. What makes the means being used illegitimate is sometimes the test of proportionality. The means used against the World Trade Center was out of all proportion to the end envisaged—even by the Machiavellian standards of the end justifying the means.

I became politically conscious in colonial Kenya against the background of the Mau Mau war of the 1950s. The British colonial authorities condemned Mau Mau as a terrorist movement. If it was a terrorist movement, it was of a revolutionary variety rather than a racial variety.

If Mau Mau was a terrorist movement it has to be regarded as a case of heroic terrorism.[6] Liberation struggles which resort to terror may have disgraced their methods, but surely not their goals.

The trouble with apartheid in the history of South Africa was that both the goals and the means were illegitimate. The goals were racial segregation within each city internally, and the pursuit of territorial ethnic cleansing as a long-term strategy of separate development.[7]

The means was an elaborate structure of racial control, and the disenfranchisement and intimidation of all the races but that of European stock.

Apartheid started off as tyranny without terror—white dictatorship without daily violent intimidation. But it did not take long before apartheid became tyranny plus terror.

The more the internal opposition to apartheid grew, the more the system became a regime of horrific terrorism.

Did the opposition to apartheid also resort to terrorism? The answer is YES. But there were two differences. Firstly, terrorism perpetrated by African National Congress (ANC) followers was not systemic to the movement. There were incidents of terror rather than a mapped out strategy of terror. ANC terror was episodic.

Necklace burning of presumed Black traitors, for example, was a form of terrorism.[8] But such incidents were often happening in spite of the policies of the ANC and in spite of the preferred goals of the leadership.

The second difference between apartheid terror and opposition terror is that movements like the ANC were seeking to democratize South Africa. The goals remained noble and even humane. The means were occasionally a case of heroic terrorism.[9]

Israeli terror against Palestinians is, on the whole, episodic rather than systemic. Occupation of another people is a form of tyranny but not necessarily a form of terror. But Israeli occupation is drifting towards terror, even systemically.

FROM SHAKA TO OSAMA BIN LADEN

Perhaps even more fascinating from this point of view is the significance of Shaka Zulu in the history of terror. Was Shaka the first heroic terrorist of modern African history? Was he also the first revolutionary terrorist of modern Africa?

Shaka was a military genius but also a control freak. Militarily he did have brilliant ideas of formation and organization. He was an innovator in weaponry. But can he be compared with Osama bin Laden? It partly depends upon the difference between trying to build an empire, and trying to dismantle an empire. Shaka Zulu was a heroic terrorist who had sought to construct a new and glorious Zulu Empire.[10] Was Osama bin Laden a heroic terrorist who has sought to bring down the American empire?

Some have admired Shaka Zulu because he began life as a fatherless child and rose to become one of the great warrior-kings of all time. Others have admired Osama bin Laden as a millionaire who decided to live in caves in Afghanistan for a cause much bigger than his millions. Shaka moved from the cave to the palace; Osama moved from the palace to the cave.

Shaka Zulu was not, of course, himself a writer. But he has fascinated writers and induced creativity in others. He was a figure of contradiction—an innovator and a destroyer, a man of passionate love and infinite cruelty.

Some writers have described Shaka as Africa's answer to Machiavelli—a Prince who truly believed that power stood on the pillars of fear rather than the foundations of love. Shaka practiced what Machiavelli had once preached—that great ends justified any means.

Léopold Sédar Senghor, founder-President of Senegal, composed a dramatic poem for several voices in honor of Shaka, but dedicated to "The Bantu Martyrs of South Africa." In the poem Senghor has a white voice taunting Shaka for the murder of Noliwe. The white voice accuses Shaka of having killed his fiancé in order to escape from his wider public conscience.

Shaka answers: *And you talk about conscience to me? Yes, I killed her, while she was telling of the blue lands; I killed her yes! My hand did not tremble; a flash of steel in the odorous thicket of the armpit.*

White voice: *So you admit it Shaka? Will you admit to the millions of men you killed*
Whole regiments of pregnant women and children still at breast?
You, provider-in-chief for vultures and hyenas, poet of the Valley of Death.
We looked to find a warrior. All we found was a butcher . . . .

Shaka:
The weakness of the heart is holy . . . .
Ah! You think that I never loved her
My Negress fair with Palm oil, slender as a plume
Thigh of startled otter, of Kilimanjaro snow . . . .
Ah! You think I never loved her!
But these long years, this breaking of the wheel of years,
This carcan strangling every act
This long night without sleep. . . .
[You think I never loved her?]
I wondered like a mare from the Zambezi running and rushing at the stars,
Gnawed by nameless suffering like leopards in the trap
[You think I never loved her?]
—I would not have killed her if I loved her less.[11]

We have here a fusion between the sadism of murder and the masochism of suicide. He killed Noliwe to escape his own love for her. He killed many

Black people because he was wanted to make their nation truly great. Shaka
betrayed the Black in order to raise them high. In the words of Senghor's
Shaka:

I had to escape from doubt . . .
From love of Noliwe
From the love of my black-skinned people.[12]

Shaka Zulu has become almost a Muse unto himself—stimulating poets
like Mitshali, scholars like M. Kunene, playwrights like Wole Soyinka, comparative analysts like Michael Chapman, statesmen like Léopold Senghor, literary pioneers like Thomas Mofolo, and more recently television work like
the popular South African television series (SATV) on Shaka.

Physical destruction is often manure for artistic creation. Jean Giradoux
caught this paradox with a brilliant hyperbole when he said in 1944:
As soon as war is declared it will be impossible to hold the poets back.
Rhyme is still the most effective war drum.[13]

On the eve of the year 2000 the British Broadcasting Corporation [World
Service] asked me to choose my African of the millennium. I insisted on
choosing two Africans—one great African of thought and one great African
of action.

For my African of thought of the last thousand years I chose Ibn Khaldun,
the North African widely regarded as the founding father of modern social
science. His book Al-Muqaddimah (written in the fourteenth century) is still
widely read in universities worldwide.[14]

Arnold Toynbee, himself a major macro-historian of great distinction, had
the following to say about this book by the Tunisian, Ibn Khaldun.

"Undoubtedly the greatest work of its kind that has ever been created by any
mind in anytime or place . . . the most comprehensive and illuminating analysis
of how human affairs work that has been made anywhere."

[Toynbee, The Observer (London)]

If my choice of African of thought of the last thousand years was Ibn Khaldun, my African book of the period would be Al-Muqaddimah—alongside St.
Augustine's City of God of the preceding thousand years.

But what was my choice of the African man of action of the last one thousand years? In the BBC interview I chose Shaka Zulu as my African of action
of the millennium. As a Western commentator has put it:

Shaka stands out as the greatest of them all—both Romulus and Napoleon to the
Zulu people—and his legend has captured the imagination of both European

and African writers, inspiring novels, biographies, and historical studies in sev-eral tongues. As a violent autocrat he is both admired and condemned: admired by those who love conquerors, condemned by those who hate despots.[15]

Let us now cross the Atlantic and look more closely at the American experience of terror, much of it going back to Shaka's own lifetime and beyond. Long before Osama bin Laden, America had suffered from terrorists.

KU KLUX KLAN AS A TERRORIST MOVEMENT

The history of terror in the American experience is a transition from individualized terrorism from within the United States to collective terrorism from outside the United States. Individualized terrorism is the tormenting or killing of individual civilians by other civilians for racial, ideological, or other political reasons. Under this definition Ku Klux Klan (KKK) was a terrorist organization—designed to create terror and consternation among particular vulnerable groups in the society.

The Ku Klux Klan was the most durable and longest surviving terrorist organization in the history of the United States. More than a century before Al-Qaeda, there was Al-Klan. More than a century before Osama bin Laden there was the Grand Wizard Nathan Forrest. In 1867 the Klan was declared "the Invisible Empire of the South" at a convention in Nashville. Nathan Bedford Forrest was the first Grand Wizard. In the nineteenth century, the KKK started as a social club by Confederate veterans in Pulaski, Tennessee in 1866. The name was apparently derived from the Greek Kykos, meaning approximately "circle." Indeed, the English word "circle" is derived from it. Indeed, the English word "circle" is derived from it. The "suffix" Klan was added for alliterative reasons.[16]

KKK became a vehicle for Southern White underground resistance to Radical Reconstruction. The KKK struggled to restore White supremacy in the South by whipping and killing freed Blacks and their White supporters. They wore white robes and sheets to maximize the terror to their Black victims.

In night raids they did not cry out "Allah Akbar" (God is great), but they often used the burning cross for further intimidation. White supremacy in Tennessee, North Carolina and Georgia was indeed restored partly as a result of Klan action.

In response to continuing violence among local KKK branches, the US Congress started legislating in ways which threatened the civil liberties of White folk. Congress passed the Force Act of 1870 and Ku Klux Klan Act of 1871 authorizing the President to suspend the writ of habeas corpus, suppress KKK disturbances by force, and impose heavy fines on such terrorist organizations.[17]

President Ulysses S. Grant sent federal troops to some areas, suspended habeas corpus for some counties in South Carolina, and detained hundreds of Southerners for conspiracy.[18] Such strong measures against White people was something new.

However, in 1882 the U.S. Supreme Court declared the KKK Act unconstitutional—and the KKK subsided to rise another day. The Supreme Court's decision legitimizing the KKK was made in the case the United States versus Harris of 1882.

In the nineteenth century civil liberties were curtailed by an act of Congress. Since September 11, 2001, civil liberties are curtailed at the initiative of Attorney General, John Ashcroft.[19]

1. There have been hundreds of people in detention without trial virtually on Ashcroft's orders, or his Department of Justice's commands.[20]
2. The great majority of those in detention are not publicly announced as being in detention, nor given access to a lawyer.[21]
3. Out of the hundreds in detention, less than a dozen show any evidence of knowing any particular terrorist suspect or being associated with any movement or charity accused of terrorism.[22]
4. Out of the millions of illegal immigrants in the United States, and those whose visas have expired, the people chosen for detention without trial are almost certainly those with Muslim names or who come from the Middle East. A new version of racial profiling is being implemented.[23]
5. The United States is actually planning to have military tribunals; the Bush administration once considered secret trials for those suspected of terrorism.[24] Even the leaders of Nazi Germany were given a public trial at Nuremberg after World War II with access to counsel and proper representation. Some of those tried at Nuremberg had been responsible for the death of millions of people.[25]
6. The culture of assassination at home subsequently killed King, John F. Kennedy and Malcolm X. Have Israel under Sharon and the United States under Bush adopted assassination as an instrument of foreign policy?[26] Israel continues to look for old Nazi militants so that they can be tried today in a court of law in Israel. Yet Israel even before Sharon's premiership has felt free to kill Palestinian militants instead of capturing them for trial. Israel tried Adolf Eichmann in 1961 and protected him at the trial with a bulletproof glass cage so that he would not be assassinated.[27] Yet both the USA and Israel in 2001 openly talked about killing terrorist suspects instead of capturing them. And even when Israel has illegally captured Palestinian or Lebanese suspects from across its own borders, purpose has almost never been to give them fair trial (Adolf Eichmann- style) but to detain those suspects indefinitely without trial.

7. U. S. Attorney General John Ashcroft has empowered the FBI to spy on churches, mosques, synagogues and other sacred places to an extent not envisaged in the country for a long time. Places of prayer were once protected from close police scrutiny. However, mosques especially may soon be fair game for police raids in American cities.[28] Will synagogues enjoy de facto protection even if there is militant Zionism or fundamentalist Judaism being preached inside? Will Ashcroft's own church be exempted?

8. Attorney-General Ashcroft wants to breach attorney-client confidentiality if the client is suspected of terrorism.[29] The Attorney General and President Bush repeatedly talk as if those suspected of terrorism were already proven terrorists. What happened to the U.S. principle that aperson was innocent until proven guilty?[30]

9. CNN and the other major TV networks in the United States were summoned to the White House and warned against giving Osama bin Laden propaganda advantage with his videos. Whatever happened to editorial independence and freedom of the Press?

10. President Bush described the attacks of September 11 as "an act of war" and responded with war in Afghanistan. Yet Al-Qaeda and Taliban fighters who are prisoners are denied the rights of prisoners of war according to the Geneva convention.[31] Even U.S. allies in Europe are disturbed that the U.S. is slipping away from civilized standards and from obeying international law. What kind of legal advice is Attorney General Ashcroft giving President Bush?

Yet in most of the twentieth century the terrorism of the KKK encountered few of such tough preventive measures from the Federal Government. In the 20th century the new KKK rose near Atlanta, Georgia, in 1915. This was before Martin Luther King was born. But at its peak this terrorist organization in the United States had four million members nation-wide. Its agenda of prejudice had widened. In addition to being anti-Black it became anti-Catholic, especially in 1928 when Alfred E. Smith, a Catholic, won the nomination of the Democratic Party for President. The new KKK was also anti-Jewish, anti-immigrant, and against organized labour.[32]

For actual lynching by KKK, the victims were overwhelmingly black.[33]

Lynchings continued into the second half of the twentieth century, though their numbers had drastically declined. Writing about the lynching of blacks in the United States, John Hope Franklin and Alfred A. Moss, Jr., pointed out that, "The new century [1900] opened tragically with 214 lynchings in the first two years."[34] Some of the lynchings were perpetrated by supporters of KKK who were not necessarily members. NAACP organizers were killed in Mississippi while trying to register Black voters in the 1950s. These included

Reverend George W. Lee and Lamar Smith.[35] Martin Luther King was killed the following decade.

The most shocking lynching of the 1950s was the 1955 murder of a fourteen-year old Black boy Emmett Till, who was visiting Mississippi from Chicago, and was dared by other Black boys to say something courageous to a White woman in a shop. Emmett Till gathered enough courage to say to the White woman "Bye, Baby"! As a Northern boy from Chicago he was showing off he could do something daring to a White woman.

Those two words not only cost the boy's life. He was picked up, tortured, had an eye pulled out, shot in the head, chained to a seventy-five pound cotton gin and thrown into a river to sink. The body surfaced a few days later and was identified. An all-White jury returned a verdict of "Not guilty" on people who had kidnapped Emmett Till and must have been the ones who killed him. They were even acquitted of kidnapping.

But for the first time in the history of Mississippi, a Black man testified against an accused White man. Mose Wright, Emmett's uncle, found the courage to identify the White folks who had picked up his nephew. Courage is different from fearlessness. Courage is to be afraid and still be able to do what needs to be done. Mose Wright was courageous in that court as he pointed out the kidnappers of his nephew.[36]

It took the murder of a White woman ten years later in Alabama before the President of the United States would go on television to publicly denounce the Ku Klux Klan. President Lyndon Johnson at last condemned the organization in March 1965 in a nationwide television broadcast. He also announced the arrest of four Klansmen for the murder of the civil rights worker—a White woman in Alabama.[37]

Yet even the 1990s it was still possible for a Black man to be tied at the back of White man's truck and dragged on the ground until his head rolled off his body. Individualized racial terrorism was still alive and well in the United States when in 1998 James Byrd Jr. was chained behind a pick-up truck in Jasper, Texas, and mutilated in this manner by a couple of White racists.[38] As for racially inspired police brutality in the 1990s, this included the forty-one shots fired by the police, which killed an unarmed West African immigrant standing outside his home in New York—a Muslim casualty of New York police brutality. The policemen were acquitted. There was also the brutal sodomization of the Haitian Louima also by New York police officers.[39]

Nevertheless, September 11, 2001, took terrorism to entirely new levels of destructiveness. It was not the terrorism of the powerful against the vulnerable, as in the case of the KKK violence against underprivileged Blacks. September 11, 2001 was terrorism against the most powerful in the world. The Pentagon was a symbol of America's military might. The World Trade Center was a symbol of America's economic might. If Al-Qaeda were the terrorists of September 11, 2001, this was action by cave dwellers against the super-rich and the super-powerful. It was criminal and cruel, but it was David fighting Goliath, and in this case David came to pay a heavy price.

While the KKK picked on vulnerable minorities to terrorise, Al-Qaeda has picked on the mightiest power to challenge. If the KKK was racially inspired, Al-Qaeda was religiously motivated. The result has been catastrophic for both sides.

COUNTERTERRORISM: MARTIAL AND MORAL

Let us now turn to two forms of counter-terrorism. Martial counter-terrorism involves use of weapons and confrontational politics. Moral counter-terrorism involves passive resistance and ethical struggle. In the United States George W. Bush symbolizes martial counter-terrorism especially against religiously inspired terror. Martin Luther King Jr. represented moral counter-terrorism, especially against racial terror.

Let us also remember the link between terrorism and assassination (as with the deaths of Anwar Sadat and Indira Gandhi).

I was privileged to meet Dr. Martin Luther King Jr. when I was a graduate student at Columbia University in New York. King was already sensitive to issues beyond the American shores. The period was 1960–1. African Davids were fighting European imperial Goliaths.

Let me repeat that Dr. King and I talked about the Kenyan leader called Tom Mboya, at that time the second best known East African politician after Jomo Kenyatta. Mboya and King were about the same age. Of course, we had no idea that the lives of both King and Mboya would be cut short by an assassin's bullet before the decade of the 1960s was out. They were victims of individualized terrorism

But although Martin Luther King was so sensitised quite early to issues beyond these shores, was his dream too parochial? Was his dream too U.S.-based? Perhaps King never became as Pan African as Malcolm X did. Nevertheless, King did respond quite early to intellectual influences from beyond the American shores. He particularly emphasized his moral debt to Mahatma Mohandas Gandhi, the Indian leader of resistance against British rule in India. King once observed: "It is ironic that the greatest Christian of the modern age was a man who never embraced Christianity"[40]—that is, Mahatma Gandhi.

As the author Keith D. Miller has reminded us, Gandhi's protest against British repression was done in such a way that it was "a collective expression of Christ-like love."[41] Martin Luther King's life was transformed by that one single and particular Indian. King learnt moral counter-terrorism from Mohandas Ghandi.

Did King first get interested in Gandhi when he heard Mordecai Johnson of Howard University preach about Gandhi's achievements? The presentation was to King "so profound and electrifying" that King "bought a half-dozen books on Gandhi's life works."[42]

But was King inadequately attentive to the larger questions of the world? DID KING have the wrong dream? Should he have gone global—and dreamt about the end of the Cold War—East and West, Socialist and Capitalist, reconciled at last? Was he inadequately attentive to the North-South divide?

"Free at last! Free at last! Thank God, Almighty, we are free at last!" Was King less internationalist than Malcolm? The great reconciliation of the last decade of the 20th century was not racial, but ideological. Martin King did start agitating against the war in Vietnam before he died—was he getting internationalized? The ideological Cold War seems to have given way to what Samuel Huntington has called "a Clash of Civilizations."

Was that dream too parochial, too U.S.-based? And even within the U.S.A., what is the balance sheet today? How much of that dream has been realized? There have in fact been gains and losses since the 1960s.

The Black predicament in the U.S.A. is full of contradictions. Martin Luther King preached non-violence but saw Blacks disproportionately represented in the U.S. Army. Was Muhammad Ali a better Gandhian when he refused to fight in Viet Nam? Is violence in uniform less violent than violence in the streets? With the end of the ideological war, is there an intensification of the racial war world-wide?

There is the possible birth of GLOBAL APARTHEID. In the aftermath of September 11, the white world is closing ranks. There is now greater Pan-Europeanism than anything since the Holy Roman Empire. The European Union is admitting new members.[43] The Cold War has ended a deep ideological split which once existed within the white world. Is the shadow of global apartheid looming over us—a new racial hierarchy on a global scale? Is there a new clash of civilizations between the darker races and the fairer ones? Is this clash of civilizations more imminent after September 11 and George Bush's martial counter-terrorism?

TOWARDS GLOBALIZING KING'S DREAM

Yes, Martin Luther King Jr. was politically molded by two personal forces external to the Black experience. In the case of King the two external personalities were Jesus Christ and Mahatma Gandhi.

Many people believe that Lenin operationalized Marx from the world of ideas to the world of policy. King believed that Gandhi operationalized the love-ethic of Jesus from the world of ethics to the world of action.

Both of Martin Luther King's ultimate mentors were, in a sense, assassinated. The Jesus of Christianity was assassinated through the crucifixion. Mahatma Gandhi was assassinated by a bullet from a fellow Hindu. *Was the crucifixion of Jesus an act of state terrorism? The assassination of Gandhi was privatized terrorism.*

King used the legacy of soul-force from Jesus and Gandhi as a means to an end. The end was the liberation and dignification of Black people. For Martin Luther King Jr., the union between Jesus Christ and Mohandas Gandhi was indissoluble. If Christianity had been—like Hinduism—a religion based on reincarnation, Reverend King would have wondered whether Mohandas Gandhi was a reincarnation of Jesus Christ. At least so far the union between Jesus and Gandhi has turned out to be more truly indissoluble than the union between Marx and Lenin.

Martin Luther King's dream remains relevant, but it needs to be globalized. It needs to reconcile not just different races, but different civilizations. This is particularly urgent since September 11, 2001.

So let freedom ring from the shores of Somalia and the high plateaus of Ethiopia, let freedom ring from the deep valley of the Brahmaputra and Euphrates, let freedom ring from the isles of the Caribbean and the deep recesses of the Amazon, let freedom ring from Hungary to Harlem, from Palestine to Chechnya, from the snows of Kilimanjaro to the winds of Chicago. As we continue to paraphrase Reverend King, let freedom ring from Kashmir to Capetown. We need a global coalition for moral counter terrorism, and not merely a global alliance of martial terrorism.[44]

And when this happens, and when we have allowed freedom to ring in every village and every city, in every country and every continent, we will speed up the day when all God's children—Indo-Guyanese and Afro-Guyanese, indigenous and immigrant, men and women, White and Black, Jew and Gentile, Afghan and American, Hutu and Tutsi, Palestinian and Israeli, Sharonites and Arafites, Muslim and Christian, Ashcroft and the legacy of Malcolm X, Hindu and Buddhist, Saint and Sinner, will be able to join hands and globalize both Martin Luther King and Malcolm X—"Free at last, Free at last, Thank God Almighty! We are free at last!"

Yet even that powerful line needs cultural globalization—a world beyond either heroic or horric terror; a universe beyond revolutionary, racial, state and religious violence.

> Thank God Ruhanga, Almighty, we are free at last;
> Thank Jehovah, Almighty, we are free at last;

Thank Bhagwan, Almighty, we are free at last;
Thank Omuchwezi, Almighty, we are free at last;
Thank Ogun, Almighty, we are free at last;
Thank Mwenye ezi Mungu, we are free at last;
Thank Allahu Akbar, we are free at last;
Thank the heavens, thank the stars, we are free at last.
AMEN to One, Amen to all.

A CONCEPTUAL CONCLUSION

We have sought to demonstrate in this chapter that terrorism has a variety of doctrinal stimuli—the most common of which are racial, religious, statist and revolutionary stimuli. Racially inspired terrorism has ranged from the Ku Klux Klan in America to apartheid in South Africa. Religiously-stimulated terrorism has included Sikh terrorism in India, Al-Qaeda from the Muslim world, the Irish Republican Army's role in the "Troubles" of Northern Ireland, and Zionist terrorism before and after the creation of the state of Israel.

Revolutionary terror in its modern guise probably started in the French revolution in the late eighteenth century. In Africa Shaka Zulu unleashed revolutionary terror in a bid to create a new Zulu political order.

Terror by the State has included the right-wing variety of the Nazis and the left-wing variety by Stalinists and Maoists. Less drastic have been terrorizing techniques by the Israeli state especially under Ariel Sharon—targeted killings, use of missiles on civilian neighborhoods, collective punishment through demolition of homes, and cruel general repression by an occupying power.

All these four categories (race, religion, revolution and the state) are sources of doctrinal stimulation to terrorism. But terrorism can also be distinguished by pervasiveness. Supporters of the African National Congress in South Africa resorted to "necklace lynching" as a method of executing those accused of treason to the cause of liberation. Such incidents constituted episodic terrorism. On the other hand, the racial order of apartheid and its police-machinery were eventually founded on systemic terrorism. Apartheid had evolved from racial tyranny to racial terror.

The third area of differentiation in terrorism is ethical in judgment rather than doctrinal in-inspiration. Heroic terrorism has noble goals but ignoble means. Horrific terrorism, on the other hand, is illegitimate at the level of both ends and means. Palestinian suicide bombers may be engaged in heroic terrorism. Palestinians are an oppressed people whose dreams of liberation are legitimate, though their means are sometimes ignoble.

On the other hand, there is almost universal consensus that the destruction of the World Trade Center in New York on September 11, 2001, was a case of horrific terrorism.

A fourth distinction to be borne in mind is between individualized terrorism, perpetrated by one person or two, and terrorism by a movement. The uni-bomber in recent American history was the supreme case of individualized terrorism. The anthrax scare in 2001–2002 might also turn out to be a case of individualized terrorism. The destruction of the Federal Building in Oklahoma City in 1995 was probably half-way between individualized terror and a movement.

On the other hand, Al-Qaeda in the new millennium and the Mau Mau in Kenya in the 1950s have been cases of movement-terrorism.

Finally, this chapter has also drawn a distinction between martial counter-terrorism and moral counter-terrorism. The martial variety invokes military power and emphasizes the use of physical force. George W. Bush and his team have led an alliance of martial counter-terrorism against Al-Qaeda, the Taliban and others.

Moral counter-terrorism, on the other hand, is what Mahatma Gandhi called satyagraha (soul force) in the face of violence verging on terror. Among Gandhi's most distinguished non-Indian disciples was, of course, Martin Luther King Jr., who mobilized "soul force" against the legacy of the Ku Klux Klan and against officially sanctioned segregation in the southern states of the United States. Moral counter-terrorism has often relied on passive resistance and appeal to a higher moral order.

In this chapter, we also described the crucifixion of Jesus Christ as a case of state terrorism. Why was the crucifixion "terrorism" instead of just an act of state violence? Because the Roman policy of crucifying offenders and letting them hang until they died was indeed intended to create terror as a form of judicial deterrent. Although Jesus Christ was the most famous victim of crucifixion of all history, crucifixion itself was a relatively common form of judicial terror in parts of the Roman Empire. [For purposes of analysis we are accepting the Christian tradition about the crucifixion.]

Although the phenomena of terror and terrorism go back to ancient times, their study is a relatively recent area of investigation. State terrorism especially goes back to the earliest days of the state and of empires. On the other hand, revolutionary terrorism is more modern in orientation, probably emerging out of the French revolution.

What is much more recent is what might be called TERRORSMOLOGY — not the study of terror but the study of terrorism as a strategy of combat in an ideological context.

This chapter has been part of the quest for a paradigm of terrorsmology, a quest for exploring the doctrines, methods, ethics, and causes of an emerging system of warfare. The science of terrorsmology is still in its infancy.

NOTES

1. See, for instance, Albert Parry, *Terrorism: From Robespierre To Arafat* (New York: The Vanguard Press, 1976).

2. Rabin was assassinated by a Jewish law student called Yigal Amir who was part of a group of Jewish fundamentalists, although he claimed he acted alone; see Laura Blumenfeld, "Slain Leader's Legacy Lives On, Assassin Admits," *Washington Post,* May 14, 1999, p. 1 and Abraham Rabinovich, "Yitzhak Rabin, The Sabra, the Mensch," at http://info.jpost.com/1998/Supplements/Rabin/7.html in a special supplement of *The Jerusalem Post.* The context of Amir's actions is provided by Ehud Sprinzak, "Israel's Radical Right and the Countdown to the Rabin Assassination," in Yosam Peri, ed., *The Asssassination of Yitzhak Rabin* (Stanford, CA: Stanford University Press, 2000), pp. 96–128.

3. As Gerald Butt, in a profile of Sharon for the *British Broadcasting Corporation* (BBC) reminded listeners:

> As defence minister, and without explicitly telling Prime Minister Menachem Begin, he sent the Israeli army all the way to Beirut, a strike which ended in the expulsion of Yasser Arafat's Palestine Liberation Organisation (PLO) from Lebanon. The move stopped the PLO using Lebanon to launch attacks against Israel, but also resulted in the massacre of hundreds of Palestinians by Lebanese Christian militiamen in two Beirut refugee camps under Israeli control.

BBC News, "Ariel Sharon: Controversial hardliner." Tuesday December 4, 2001. For more, visit http://news.bbc.co.uk/2/hi/in_depth/middle_east/2001/israel_and_the_pales tinians/profiles/1154622.stm
A commission appointed by the Israel government, the Kahan Commission, found Sharon "indirectly responsible" for the massacre; see Anita Miller, Jordan Miller, Sigalit Zetouni, *Sharon: Israel's Warrior-Politician* (Chicago: Academy Chicago Publishers and Olive Publishing, 2002), p. 170.

4. *CNN.com* reports that "Israeli Prime Minister Ariel Sharon has described an attack on a residential area of Gaza City which killed at least 15 people, including seven children, as "a great success" because it killed its target—a Hamas military leader." "Sharon Praises airstrike 'success.'" *CNN.com* July 23, 2002. See http://www.cnn .com/2002/WORLD/meast/07/23/mideast.reaction/ for more details on this incident.

5. Sharon's history of conflict with the Palestinians is recounted in Baruch Kemmerling, *Politicide: Ariel Sharon's War Against the Palestinians*, (London, New York: Verso, 2003).

6. Relatedly, consult Wunyabari Maloba, *Mau Mau and Kenya: An Analysis of a Peasant Revolt* (Bloomington, IN: Indiana University Press, 1993), and Marshall S.

Clough, *Mau Mau Memoirs: History, Memory, And Politics* (Boulder, CO: L. Rienner, 1998).

7. See Barbara Rogers, *Divide & Rule: South Africa's Bantustans* (London: International Defence and Aid Fund, 1976); and for some general overviews of apartheid, consult Nigel Worden, *The Making of Modern South Africa: Conquest, Segregation, and Apartheid*, 3rd ed., (Oxford, UK and Malden, MA: Blackwell Publishers, 2000) and Philip Bonner, Peter Delius, Deborah Posel, eds., *Apartheid's Genesis, 1935–1962* (Braamfontein and Johannesburg, South Africa: Ravan Press and Wits University Press, 1993).

8. Even today, people impatient with the failure of the South African police system to punish criminals continue to periodically engage in this type of "informal justice," as reported by the BBC Monday, 14 January, 2002 http://news.bbc.co.uk/1/hi/world/africa/1759954.stm.

9. Frustrations leading to violence may also have been due to the failure of passive resistance in the early history of the ANC; see Edward Feit, *African Opposition in South Africa: The Failure of Passive Resistance* (Stanford, CA: Hoover Institution, Stanford University, 1967) and also Peter Walshe, *The Rise of African Nationalism in South Africa: The African National Congress, 1912–1952* (Berkeley, CA: University of California Press, 1971).

10. A portrait of Shaka may be found in E.A. Ritter, *Shaka Zulu; The Rise of the Zulu Empire,* (New York: New American Library, 1973, 1955), and for an interesting brief analysis, also see James W. Fernandez, "The Shaka Complex," *Transition*, No. 29. (Feb.–Mar., 1967), pp. 10–14.

11. Leopold Senghor, "Shaka" in John Reed and Clive Wake, eds. and translators, *Senghor: Prose and Poetry,* (London: Oxford University Press, 1965) pp. 143–145.

12. Leopold Senghor, Ibid.

13. From a French-language work which was translated by Christopher Fry as *Tiger at the Gates* (New York: Oxford University Press, 1963).

14. For an English translation, see N. J. Dawood, ed., *The Muqaddimah, An Introduction To History,* transl. Franz Rosenthal, (Princeton, N.J.: Princeton University Press, 1969).

15. Eugene Victor Walter, *Terror and Resistance: A Study of Political Violence with Case Studies of Some Primitive African Communities* (London and New York: Oxford University Press, 1959 and 1972) pp. 109–10.

16. Details on the origins of the Klan may be found in Chester L. Quarles, *The Ku Klux Klan and Related American Racialist and Antisemitic Organizations: A History and Analysis* (Jefferson, NC and London: McFarland and Co., Inc., Publishers, 1999), pp. 27–34.

17. Consult Everette Swinney, *Suppressing the Ku Klux Klan: The Enforcement of the Reconstruction Amendments, 1870–1874* (New York and London: Garland Publishing, 1987), pp. 57–102.

18. *Ibid,* pp. 203–237.

19. Even the Inspector General of the Department of Justice has commented harshly on the circumstances of the arrests, flimsy evidence, and post-arrest treatment of the September 11 detainees: consult the report of the Inspector General of the

Department of Justice: United States. Department of Justice, *The September 11 Detainees: A Review of the Treatment of Aliens Held on Immigration Charges in Connection With the Investigation of the September 11 Attacks* available at http://www.usdoj.gov/oig/special/0603/full.pdf (2003).

20. *New York Times* (November 29, 2001), p. 1.

21. In legal battles under way, even the courts appear to be sympathetic to the arguments proffered by the US government against releasing the names of prisoners; for one such court in NJ, see *The Washington Post* (June 13, 2002), p. 18.

22. Indeed, of the 762 detainees investigated in the Department of Justice report cited above, none were found to have links with terrorism. See the op-ed piece by Richard Cohen, "Ashcroft's Attitude Problem" *The Washington Post,* (June 10, 2003), p. 21.

23. Chisun Lee writes that, Sin Yen Ling, a lawyer for the New York-based Asian American Legal Defense and Education Fund pointed that "Since December [2001], Ling says, she has personally represented as many as 40 immigrants, all but one of Middle Eastern or Muslim extraction. And the flow has not lessened." "The Name Game." *The Village Voice* (August 14–20, 2002). Further, the demographics of the 762 detainees in the report of the Department of Justice, *The September 11 Detainees,* illustrated in Figure 2, p. 21, are completely different from those of the 9/11 hijackers. For instance, the largest number of the detainees (254) were Pakistanis, and while the largest number of the hijackers were Saudi Arabians, more Indians and Turks were arrested than Saudi Arabians!

24. See the concerns raised by critics in a report in the *New York Times* (December 29, 2001), p. B7.

25. For one discussion of the issues at Nuremberg, consult Alan S. Rosenbaum, *Prosecuting Nazi War Criminals* (Boulder: Westview Press, 1993).

26. Although the word "assassination" is rarely used, the Bush administration is not coy about using targeted strikes to kill those who may be perceived as "terrorists." Indeed, Bush himself said in his 2003 State of the Union Address: "All told, more than 3,000 suspected terrorists have been arrested in many countries. Many others have met a different fate. Put it this way: They're no longer a problem to the United States and our friends and allies." See http://abcnews.go.com/sections/nightline/World/iraq_assassination030315.html for more.

27. For details, see Moshe Pearlman, *The Capture and Trial of Adolf Eichmann* (New York: Simon and Schuster, 1963).

28. New guidelines were issued permitting these activities, although FBI Director Robert S. Mueller III denied that the guidelines would be used to do widespread surveillance of mosques; see the *Washington Post* (June 6, 2002), p. 1.

29. See the press release from the American Civil Liberties Union, and other members of a coalition regarding this issue at http://archive.aclu.org/news/2001/n122001a.html

30. See relatedly, the op-ed piece by Jean AbiNader and Kate Martin, "Just the Facts, Mr. Ashcroft," *The Washington Post* (July 25, 2002) p. 21

31. There is some concern about the legal rights that are afforded to even U. S. citizens who are presumed to be part of Al Qaeda or Taliban by the Ashcroft Justice De-

partment; see a report in *The Washington Post* (June 20, 2002), p. 1; an editorial in the same publication (June 20, 2002), p. 22; and an op-ed piece by a former Marine, *The Washington Post* (June 25, 2002), p. 19.

32. See Quarles, *The Ku Klux Klan and Related American Racialist and Antisemitic Organizations,* pp. 53–75.

33. For an overview of lynching, consult Philip Dray, *At the Hands of Persons Unknown: The Lynching of Black America* (New York: Random House, 2002).

34. John Hope Franklin and Alfred A. Moss, Jr., *From Slavery to Freedom: A History of African Americans.* Seventh Edition. (New York: McGraw-Hill, Inc. 1994), p. 263.

35. Dray, *At the Hands of Persons Unknown,* p. 422.

36. For one account of the Till tragedy, see Stephen J. Whitfield, *A Death in the Delta* (New York and London: Free Press and Collier MacMillan, 1988).

37. See Merle Miller, *Lyndon: An Oral Biography* (New York: G. P. Putnam's Sons, 1980, p. 443.

38. The Byrd case is described in Dray, *At the Hands of Persons Unknown,* pp.458–60.

39. Elizabeth Kohler, in "The Perils of Safety," *The New Yorker* (March 22, 1999), pp. 50–58, argues that it is hard to see the Diallo case purely in terms of racism, unlike the case of Louima.

40. Keith Miller, *Voice of Deliverance: The Language of Martin Luther King, Jr., and Its Sources* (New York; Toronto: Free Press; Maxwell Macmillan Canada; Maxwell Macmillan International, 1992) p. 92.

41. *Ibid.*

42. *The Papers of Martin Luther King, Volume IV: Symbol of the Movement* (Berkeley and Los Angeles, CA; London: University of California Press, 1992), pp. 477–478.

43. The following nations: Slovenia, Hungary, Poland, Slovakia, Cyprus, Czech Republic, Estonia, Latvia, Lithuania and Malta have been invited to join the European Union in 2004. See T. Fuller, "The next Europe: At What Price A Bigger EU?" *International Herald Tribune.* (June 13, 2002).

44. In a slightly different vein, Tony Blair, British Prime Minister and one of the few European leaders who supported the Iraq War has recognized that arms and weapons alone cannot defeat terrorism. In an address to a joint session of Congress, July 17, 2003, Blair said:

> This is a battle [against terrorism] that can't be fought or won only by armies. We are so much more powerful in all conventional ways than the terrorists. Yet even in all our might, we are taught humility. In the end, it is not our power alone that will defeat this evil. Our ultimate weapon is not our guns, but our beliefs.

CBSNews.com, "Full Text of Blair Speech, July 17, 2003." Readers interested in the full speech may consult the http://www.cbsnews.com/stories/2003/07/17/iraq/main 563816.shtml website.

Chapter Sixteen

Black Intifadah: The Mau Mau War and the Palestinian Uprising

The Palestinian tragedy had two illegitimate parents—one parent consisted of the pro-Jewish policies of the British Mandate and the second parent were the anti-Jewish policies of the Nazis. The aftermath of two political texts have led to the heavy burden of the Palestinian people—the pro-Jewish text of the Balfour Declaration of 1917 and the anti-Jewish text of Hitler's Mein Kempf of 1938.

The Jewish friendly legacy of the Balfour Declaration led to the disempowerment of Palestinians. Hitler's atrocities against the Jewish people enhanced the case for a separate home for the Jews. The Nazi Holocaust made the world more receptive to the aspirations of the Zionists.

Lord Balfour and Adolf Hitler were the historic architects of the 1948 creation of Israel. Balfour was the Dr. Jekyll and Hitler the Mr. Hyde of the Palestinian calamity.

But our story in this chapter goes back further than either Hitler or Lord Balfour. It goes back to the time when the British were ready to offer parts of Africa to the Zionist movement for Jewish settlement and occupation. However, the British later attempted to turn Kenya into a white man's country instead of a Jewish homeland.

But this chapter is also about the contradictions in the attitudes of postcolonial countries towards the Palestinian tragedy. Some of these post-colonial states see their history in the present predicament of the Palestinians. But other post-colonial states including some Arab countries, collaborate with Western powers, with Pax Americana and with the Zionist global lobby.

Kenya has included both aspects of post-coloniality—solidarity with Palestinians as fellow victims of occupation and dependent solidarity with Israel as an extension of Western hegemony. The dialectic is still unfolding.

One of the questions hanging over the post-KANU Kenya is whether the new regime under President Mwai Kibaki in Nairobi will be less Pro-Israel in its Middle Eastern policies than the governments of Daniel arap Moi and Jomo Kenyatta had been when the Kenya African National Union [KANU] was the ruling party. It is one of the ironies of Kenya that the land which had virtually invented African versions of the anti-colonial guerrilla war had for so long been out of step with the Palestinian struggle against Israeli occupation. Why was Kenya's Jomo Kenyatta so different from South Africa's Nelson Mandela on the issue of sympathizing with the Palestinians?

Palestine and East Africa have been historically linked in at least FOUR distinct additional ways. Firstly, both Palestine and East Africa experienced European colonial rule and racial betrayal. Tanganyika, like Palestine, was even declared a Mandate of the League of Nations and later a trusteeship of the United Nations.

Secondly, both Palestine and parts of East Africa had historically been considered for Jewish settlements. The British Colonial Secretary at beginning of the twentieth century had offered parts of Uganda and Kenya to the Zionist movement as a basis of a new Jewish state. Joseph Chamberlain's life spanned from 1836 to 1914. He nearly created an Israel in Africa.

Thirdly, both Palestine and parts of East Africa had subsequently engaged in armed resistance and liberation struggle. The Mau Mau movement in Kenya in the 1950s turned to armed struggle and even terrorism in order to end White settlements on African lands and terminate British occupation of Kenya as a whole.

The Palestinians intifadah in the last quarter of the twentieth century and the first decade of the twenty first century had also sought to end with armed struggle foreign settlements (Jewish) in Arab lands and terminate Israeli occupation of what remained of Palestine. The Mau Mau movement in Kenya had exploded in 1951–1952 only three or four years after Israel was created. Mau Mau was a Black Intifadah against white settler rule in Kenya—a struggle which lasted nearly a decade.

The fourth link between Palestine and East Africa concerned the extension of the Palestinian struggle to include East Africa as a battlefield. Has the Palestinian struggle exploded beyond its own borders end encompassed some of the former battlefields of Kenya's own Mau Mau movement—from the streets of Nairobi to the beaches of Mombasa?

In terms of a macro-comparison across history, the Mau Mau struggle in Kenya was a national uprising in the context of North-South relations. The Palestinian intifadah has been an international struggle in the context of global relations.

Let us look more closely at these four or five links between the tragedy of Palestine and the experience of East Africa.

THE ZIONISTS AND THE ZINJI?

The offer of fertile parts of Uganda and Kenya was made to the Zionist movement by Joseph Chamberlain as British Colonial Secretary in the first decade of the twentieth century. Theodor Herzel presented the offer to the Zionist movement. At that time the Jewish dream was to find for a people without land (the Jews) some land without people. The British authorities regarded Eastern Africa at the time as "land without people"—partly because they did not recognize the "natives" as real "people."

And since Palestine was still under Ottoman Muslim rule, it seemed easier to settle Jews in fertile East Africa, distant form Ottoman complications.

And so, on December 21, 1902, Joseph Chamberlain made the following entry into his diary: "If Dr. Herzel were at all inclined to transfer his efforts to East Africa, there would be no difficulty in finding suitable land for Jewish settlers."

Theodor Herzel, the founding father of Zionism, subsequently recorded in his own diary that Chamberlain had indeed offered him "Uganda." After consideration and debate among Zionists, it was concluded that "Uganda" was a possible extension of a future Jewish homeland rather than the core. Herzel wrote: "Our starting point must be in or near Palestine. Later on we could also colonize Uganda; for we have vast numbers of human beings who are prepared to emigrate."

Julian Amery, a distinguished British public intellectual, later wrote a biography of Joseph Chamberlain. In the biography Avery insists that what Chamberlain offered to the Zionists was not really what today we regard as "Uganda." It was the cool and fertile highlands of Kenya. According to Avery, "there is no better white man's country anywhere in the tropics."[1]

God had offered the followers of Moses a promised land across the Red Sea from West to East. Great Britain in 1902 offered the followers of Moses a new promised land across the Red Sea in the reverse direction of East to West.

The ancient Jews had sought escape from enslavement in North Africa and followed Moses into the unknown. At the beginning of the twentieth century the modern Jews were invited to seek security and asylum in Eastern Africa under the umbrella of Pax Britannica.

Some Zionists were tempted by Joseph Chamberlain's offer. The Zionist figuratists believed that the new Israel could figuratively be anywhere on God's earth which afforded safety to God's Chosen People. But the Zionist literalists insisted that the new Israel had to be literally close to where ancient Israel once flourished. The Zionist literalists were often less secular and more nationalistic than the figuratists.

In the end the Zionist movement turned down the British offer of what was then regarded as "Uganda." The boundaries of Uganda at that time included what is today's Kenya. The British colonial authorities later reserved the best of that land in Kenya for European settlement rather than Jewish settlement. The land became the so-called "White Highlands of Kenya" instead of "Jewish Homeland." It was precisely this reservation of the best land in Kenya for whites only which helped to precipitate the Mau Mau intifadah. Like the Palestinian uprising, the Mau Mau war was unequal in military weaponry. While the Israelis have used tanks and rockets, the British in Kenya in the 1950s used airplanes and aerial bombardment of the Abedaire Mountains.

While Mau Mau did not produce suicide-bombers, the fighters did resort from time to time to other forms of terrorism—such as targeting a white farming family in the White Highlands for total elimination. Almost all armed liberation movements of the twentieth century all over the world included terrorist actions from time to time.

The absence of suicide bombers among the Mau Mau fighters was partly because Mau Mau was not in possession of the kind of explosives which would have made suicide a viable method of targeting the enemy. In any case, indigenous Kikuyu culture does not lend itself as readily to suicidal martyrdom as Semitic cultures (both Arab and Jewish) have done in history.

But Mau Mau did demonstrate that those who made the most sacrifices in a liberation movement were not necessarily those who benefit the most from the fruit of liberation.

The Mau Mau fighters were militarily defeated, but their goals of ending white settlements and terminating British occupation of Kenya were triumphant. Other Kenyans benefited from Mau Mau sacrifices—although Mau Mau warriors remained unsung heroes for fifty years.

The fertile soil in East Africa which Joseph Chamberlain had once offered to the Zionist movement, and which subsequent British Colonial Secretaries had reserved for European farmers, was finally returned in the 1960s to indigenous ownership and control.

Had Theodor Herzel and the Zionist movement accepted the British offer of East Africa for Jewish settlements, apartheid as a system would have started earlier in African history than it did. The creation of a Jewish state in East Africa would have been the equivalent of dividing a country into separate homelands according to ethnicity. East Africa would have had a religio-cultural apartheid, separating Jews from Black gentiles (so called Zinj) long before South Africa had a racial apartheid, separating white skin from black skin.

But the racial apartheid of South Africa had proven easier to dissolve than the creation of a Jewish state in East Africa would have been. "Zionist versus the Zinj": This would have been a more deadly racist confrontation.

Yet the creation of Israel from Mandated Palestine has not completely protected East Africa from the consequences of Zionist triumphalism. In the 1970s a Jewish-owned hotel in Nairobi, the Norfolk, was partially damaged by a bomb planted by an Arab nationalist who had stayed there.

Was Kenya being punished for being pro-Israel? Could the reason have been that the people who inherited power in Kenya from the British Raj were not the same people who militarily fought the British rulers and white settlements in central Kenya?

In South Africa power passed from the architects of apartheid to those who had picked up arms against apartheid. In post-colonial Kenya power bypassed the Mau Mau fighters and was given instead to those who had denounced or disowned the Mau Mau liberation fighters when the war was being fought.

In August 1998 the American Embassies in Nairobi and Dar es Salaam were destroyed seemingly by Middle Eastern terrorists—killing hundreds of East Africans and fewer than two dozen Americans. Had Kenya been targeted because it was perceived as an ally of Pax Americana?

FROM THE TORAH TO THE TERROR

The problem was compounded by the pro-Zionist tendencies of postcolonial Kenyan governments. Had independence in Kenya been handed over to those Kenyans who had directly fought against British rule and while settlements, post-colonial Kenyan governments would probably have been as sympathetic to the Palestinian struggle as most Black fighters against apartheid in South Africa had been. But the beneficiaries of the Mau Mau war were not the fighters themselves but were sometimes even the collaborators with the British rulers.

Kenya collaborated with the Israelis in the Entebbe raid by Israeli troops against Idi Amin's Uganda and against pro-Palestinian hijackers in July 1976. Nairobi was used as a re-fuelling stop for Israeli planes after the raid and as a stop for medical treatment for any Israelis wounded from Entebbe.

Because the rulers of postcolonial Kenya were not the Mau Mau fighters themselves, the Kenyan government was not even minimally neutral when the Kurds of Turkey were engaged in their own liberation movement. The Kenyan authorities helped to capture and hand over to Turkey the leading PKK Kurdish leader Abdullah Ocalan who was at the time hiding in Nairobi. The capture dealt a death blow to the Kurdish resistance in Turkey.

Postcolonial Kenya's continuing collaboration with Pax Americana, Pax Britannica and Zionism continued to make Kenya a target for Middle Eastern resistance movements. In November 2002 Kenya was once again a battleground for Middle Eastern conflicts. A suicide bomber targeted the Israeli owned and Israeli occupied Paradise Hotel in Mombasa, killing nearly twenty people. Twice as many Kenyans as Israelis were killed in the attack.

Once again a country which had been spared the fate of becoming an African Israel was not spared the consequences of the equally unjust creation of Israel in Palestine. Jews as children of the ancient Torah became parents of the modern terror in the Middle East. Postcolonial Kenya was caught in the crossfire.

Also in November 2002 there was a failed attempt in Mombasa to shoot down an Israeli plane with tourists on board. In the 1950s the Mau Mau never attempted to shoot down a British plane. Although Mau Mau were themselves bombed by British planes, they did not have the technology to shoot them down.

On the other hand, a liberation movement in Rhodesia (later Zimbabwe) twenty years later did have the technology to shoot down an airplane with whites on board. Joshua Nkomo's ZAPU party did have surface to air missiles. In 1978 they did shoot down a civilian airline with white folks on board. Nkomos's liberation fighters even attempted to kill the survivors after the crash.

Outside Africa the Israelis did shoot down in 1973 a civilian Libyan airline with 108 passengers, ostensibly because the Israelis thought the plane was a military threat. In 1988 the Americans shot down an Iranian civilian aircraft in the Gulf area, again pleading an honest and regrettable mistake. There were 292 civilians on board. The Russians were less hypocritical when in 1982 they shot down a South Korean airplane over Soviet territory because they were convinced that the plane (though civilian) was nevertheless engaged in espionage on behalf of the United States. Some 290 people were killed including a member of the U.S. Congress.

There is also the debate about Pan-American flight 103 over Lockerbie in Scotland in 1988. In spite of the verdict by a Scottish Court on a Libyan suspect, confusion has persisted whether the real culprits were Iranians (avenging the shooting down of their own civilian craft) or pro-Palestinian Arab saboteurs.

The 2002 attempt to shoot down a civilian passenger plane in Mombasa was unprecedented in Kenya, the land of Mau Mau, but it was not unprecedented in either Africa as a whole or within the global aviation history.

But the events in Mombasa in the last week of November 2002 did once again illustrate that the land of Mau Mau and the politics of the Palestinian intifadah continued to be interlocked. The ghosts of Joseph Chamberlain and Theodor Herzel continue to haunt the land which nearly became a tropical Israel in the shadow of Mount Kenya; an Israel along the shores of Lake Victoria.

Chapter Sixteen

THE GLOBAL CONTEXT

By a strange twist of destiny, Kenya in 2001 was coming to terms with its Mau Mau history at about the same time as the United States was engaged in its war on terrorism. The Mau Mau movement against white settler rule in Kenya in the 1950s had been widely denounced by its critics as a terrorist movement. African loyalists to the British colonial regime were sometimes assassinated by Mau Mau, and from time to time a European farming family would be wiped out in a midnight raid by Mau Mau. By October 1952 the British Governor of Kenya, Sir Evelyn Baring, was forced to declare a state of emergency in the colony.

As the fiftieth anniversary of the outbreak of Mau Mau war was approaching, the Kenyan authorities started contemplating in the year 2001 major gestures to honour Mau Mau as a movement of patriotic heroism and nationalist sacrifice. The British had arrested and executed Dedan Kimathi, a Mau Mau "commander" in the forest. In the year 2001 Kenya was considering turning into national monuments the place where Kimathi was arrested and perhaps the place where many Mau Mau fighters were once detained.

There is also a movement to seek out Dedan Kimathi's remains, give him a hero's funeral and build a special Mausoleum. Certain Kimathi enthusiasts are even demanding a Kimathi Day annually as a day to honour those who gave their lives in the liberation war for Kenya's independence in the 1950s.

Almost exactly fifty years later the atrocities of September 11, 2001, occurred at the World Trade Center in New York (a symbol of American economic might) and at the Pentagon (Department of Defense, a symbol of American military might) in Washington, D.C. A third plane, probably intended by the terrorists for either the White House or the Congressional building (the Capitol), was aborted and crashed in a field in Pennsylvania.

International terrorism is one more area of intermingling between the policies of the Middle East and the politics of Africa. Before the end of colonialism and the end of apartheid in Africa, what was described as "terrorism" was as common in Africa as in the Middle East. Since the collapse of political apartheid in the 1990s, the term "terrorism" has more narrowly been focused on the politics of the Middle East. This is unfair to Middle Eastern liberation fighters.

Much of the old anti-colonial and anti-apartheid terrorism in Africa in the second half of the twentieth century was targeted against Europeans and the colonial powers. Much of the Middle Eastern terrorism of more recent times has been targeted against the United States and Israel.

In the retrospect of history Africa gained from its own guerrilla movements and terrorist activities against European powers. The Mau Mau war in Kenya did result in Kenya's independence in 1963; the Algerian revolution did result in the liberation of Algeria in 1962; the anti-colonial wars in Angola, Mozambique and Guinea-Bissau did destroy the Portuguese empire in 1974; the anti-UDI struggle in Zimbabwe ended Ian Smith's Unilateral Declaration of Independence; and the anti-apartheid struggle in South Africa finally triumphed against the racial order. Terrorism and guerilla war by Africans against European powers did yield positive results. Terrorism was a form of warfare, and had to be judged in its total political and moral context, and by its ultimate results.

What is more, all forms of modern warfare kill overwhelmingly more civilians than combatants. The American War in Vietnam killed some four million Vietnamese civilians, against less than sixty thousand American combatants.

However, if anti-European and anti-colonial terrorism in Africa had produced good results in the end for Africa, anti-American and anti-Zionist terrorism in the Middle East has not yet found its moment of triumph. Both the Middle East and Africa have been paying a price for Israeli repression and the anti-American terrorism. The violent price which the Middle East is paying is obvious, especially in Palestine, Iraq and in neighboring Afghanistan. What is the price which Africa is paying for terrorism against the United States?

Firstly, there is the issue of being caught in the crossfire. Africa has been the victim of violent action intended by the terrorists for the United States; Africa has also been a victim of violent action taken by the United States and intended for the terrorists.

In order to kill twelve Americans, Middle Eastern terrorists killed, as we indicated, about two hundred Kenyans in the streets of Nairobi a few years ago. This was the attack on the US Embassy in Nairobi in August 1998. There were also Tanzanian casualties when the US Embassy in Dar es Salaam was targeted at the same time.

On the other hand, Sudan was caught in the crossfire soon after when U.S. President Bill Clinton ordered the bombing of an apparently harmless pharmacy near Khartoum. President Ronald Reagan before Clinton had ordered the bombing of Tripoli and Benghazi in Libya because Reagan thought the Libyans were responsible for a bomb in a German bar which had killed Americans. Violence between Americans and Middle Easterners had been spilling over into Africa for decades—violence from both Middle Easterners and the Americans.

Since the destruction of the Israeli Paradise Hotel in Mombasa in November 2002, matters have continued to move from bad to worse in Palestine. However, there is a chance that matters are moving from bad to better in Kenya following the ouster of the Kenyan African National Union and the end of the legacy of Daniel arap Moi.

Jomo Kenyatta had had a better influence on the history of Kenya than Moi had but Kenyatta's legacy was also of collaboration with the West and with the Zionist lobby in Nairobi.

Both Kenyatta and Mandela had been imprisoned by their respective white adversaries—but Mandela had never disowned the armed struggle against apartheid, while Jomo Kenyatta had persistently denied any connection with Mau Mau even after he became President of Kenya.

Had the real Mau Mau fighters inherited postcolonial power in Kenya, the history of Kenya's relations with the Palestinian movement would probably have been dramatically different. The land which nearly became Africa's Israel might well have become a land more truly sympathetic to the Palestinian cause.

Yet it is not too late. Kenya after KANU may learn to be more independent of both the West and the Zionists. Kenya may become another African ally to the Palestinians.

Countries like Kenya were spared the fate of an African Israel on their soil, but have not been spared the global repercussions of the unholy alliance between the legacy of Lord Balfour and the aftermath of Adolf Hitler.

The pro-Zionist policies of the British Mandate, and the anti-Jewish policies of the Nazis were the two forces which together created a world more receptive to the creation of a Jewish state. The aftermath has been disastrous for Palestinians, for Israelis and for the world. Humanity needs to find a way out of this monumental tragedy.

NOTES

1. See Julian Amery, *The Life of Joseph Chamberlain,* Vol. IV (London: Macmillian 1951) especially pp. 262–5. Kenya as a separate country had not yet been created in 1902. Much of what is today Kenya was included by the British within the boundaries of what they called "Uganda" at the time.

Chapter Seventeen

Between Intifadah and Al-Qaeda: East African Perspective

This chapter is a work in progress. It was offered as a basis of discussion at a seminar on "Islam in Africa" held in Nairobi, Kenya, December 4–5, 2006, sponsored by the British Foreign and Commonwealth Group on Engagement with the Muslim World. The seminar is also co-sponsored by the British High Commission in Kenya. The author's views are not necessarily those of the sponsors of the symposium.

In the years since the end of the Cold War there have been two radicalizing forces in the Muslim world—the humiliation of fellow Muslims abroad and the oppression of local Muslims in their own country. For example, young Pakistanis are radicalized both by the injustices in their own society (a local force) and by what they regard as the humiliation and oppression of fellow Muslims in Palestine, Kashmir, Afghanistan, Iraq, and as far away as Chechnya. The injustices committed against Muslims worldwide constitute the external radicalizing force. The Muslim ummah is felt to be under siege.

This chapter focuses on the potentially radicalizing experiences in a post-colonial African country in which Muslims are a minority. Muslims in Kenya are internationally conscious and do share the global Muslim anger over such issues as Palestine and Iraq. We may take that as a given.

But we also need to examine the internally radicalizing elements of the condition of Muslims as a minority in Kenya. Can Muslim grievances be addressed in advance in order to avert radicalization? Is pre-eventive action possible to ensure that both the Muslims of the Kenya Coast and the Somalis of North-East Kenya remain firmly within the bounds of the law?

Kenya shares borders with both Somalia and the Sudan—two countries which have experienced major political convulsions involving Muslims. What can be done to prevent a spill-over effect into Kenya in such a violent neighborhood?

The worst acts of international terrorism in Black Africa within the last ten years have occurred in Kenya. In August 1998 the U.S. Embassy in Nairobi was bombed, and over 200 people were killed. Less than fifteen of the casualties were Americans. The great majority of the victims were Kenyans, caught in the crossfire.

In November 2002 the Israeli-owned Paradise Hotel in Mombasa was targeted by a suicide bomber. Three times as many Kenyans as Israelis were killed. Again the locals were caught in the crossfire.

If there were Muslim terrorists in Kenya, were they locally born and bred—or were they Al-Qaeda immigrants on an anti-American and anti-Zionist mission in Kenya? The evidence seems to suggest an external penetration into Kenya. The local Muslims are increasingly politicized—but they are not yet radicalized. They certainly fall far short of bearing arms.

But while Kenya Muslims are indeed law-abiding and much prefer peaceful methods, they should not be taken too much for granted. Recent raids of Muslim and Arab farms by "squatters" at the Kenya Coast may feed into an already deep sense of political alienation among under-employed Muslim youth and their parents.

While a full-blown Black Al-Qaeda is unlikely at either the Kenya Coast or among the Kenyan Somali, a potential Black Intifadah is a distinct possibility. A Black Al-Qaeda carries the risk of violent conspiracy and terrorism; a Black Intifadah is an open uprising of stone-throwing youth, rather than of weapon-wielding revolutionaries.

Al-Qaeda operations are not only violent, they are also basically conspiratorial and leaning towards methods of terror. Intifadah operations are more like the revolt of the Chinese youth at Tiananmen Square in Beijing in 1989. The classic Intifadah was the first uprising of the Palestinians towards the end of the twentieth century.

The second Palestinian Intifadah was more violent than the first. In desperation, and in the face of escalating Israeli brutalities, Palestinians may be in the process of being radicalized from the level of Intifadah to the level of Al-Qaeda. Efforts should be made to reduce their desperation before the worst comes to the worst.

Radicalized East Africans are still below Intifadah level of revolt, let alone Al-Qaeda. But the causes of Muslim disaffection need to be addressed.

Although the Mombasa riots of the 1990s and 2002 are over, Kenya does face the risk of a Black Intifadah, or an uprising at the Coast (similar to the Palestinians) unless some serious problems of the people of the Coast are addressed. There is a lot of anger at the Coast.

It is estimated that the unemployment rate among young Muslim males at the Coast is about twice the national average. Bearing a Muslim name in Kenya is often an economic, social and political liability.

Of course, there are a lot of Coastal people who are not Muslims. But because the people in power in Nairobi are not Coastal, many of the best jobs at the Coast go to the ethnic communities who are powerful in the capital city hundreds of miles away. Non-Muslim Coastal people suffer almost as much as Muslim wana-nchi.

In the academic professions, the doors are closing for Muslim Kenyans. The Muslim Kenyans who are currently at the top of the liberal professions were almost all educated during the British colonial period when there was less discrimination against Muslims as such. Those successful Kenyan Muslims include a former Dean of Arts at the University of Nairobi, a former Head of College of Science also at Nairobi, a number of Ambassadors, a former Deputy Governor of the Central Bank of Kenya, a number of professors in Kenyan institutions etc., etc. Jomo Kenyatta University of Agriculture and Technology, Thika, has a Kenya Muslim as Chancellor from the same generation.

But who will replace these Muslim Kenyans at the top? Let us now take a closer look at my own history, but as described by anonymous biographer.

As for Ali A. Mazrui, there is absolutely little doubt that he would never have had a university education as a Muslim student under most postcolonial African governments. Mazrui would have remained a bank clerk or teller in Mombasa all his life. A Muslim student with Third Grade School Certificate results (which is what Mazrui had) would have been confined to the dustheap of academic history, under a government led by either Jomo Kenyatta or Daniel arap Moi, and probably even under Mwai Kibaki.

To that extent, Mazrui was lucky that his academic fate was decided in the last few years of colonial rule. A colonial government could have faith in a Muslim student with third grade results in the Cambridge School Certificate—and could give him a scholarship to study in England, in spite of poor secondary school results. But Mazrui is convinced that a postcolonial government would have relegated him to oblivion.

ISLAM AND PARTY-FORMATION

By some estimates, the Muslim population of Kenya is about the same as the Jewish population of the United States—some six to seven million. And yet the total national population of Kenya is only a tenth of the national population of the United States, 30 million Kenyans as against three hundred million Americans. Obviously, the percentage of Muslims in Kenya is ten times the percentage of Jews in the United States. And yet, while American Jews are true activists in American politics, Kenyan Muslims are often nonentities in their own country.

And then President Moi tried in his 1992 Madaraka Day speech to divide Muslims who were once slaves from Muslims who were once slave-owners. This was similar to the attempt by KANU to divide Kikuyu who were once "Mau Mau" from Kikuyu who were once "loyalists" to the British. Was Moi dividing collaborators from resisters? Divide and Rule?

Is there a case for an Islamic party in a postcolonial African country? The U.S. Jews have certainly not formed a Judaic Party in the American process. Instead, the Jews have sought to influence the system by infiltrating the two dominant parties in the United States—Republicans and Democrats. American Jews have perfected the art of lobbying and pressure-group tactics.

To avoid the risk of a Black Intifadah in Kenya, there is a case for creating a League of Muslim Voters committed to influencing all parties from an Islamic perspective, and committed also to arousing the political and electoral consciousness of Muslim voters. This could turn Muslim voters into a swing-vote from time to time. If Kenya Muslims develop a vested interest in the political process, they would be less likely to be radicalized. But should political pluralism permit political parties based on religious values?

I personally believe that such parties should be permitted provided they are also committed to the democratic process. After all, Italy and West Germany had been ruled by the CHRISTIAN DEMOCRATS for many years each.

Will Africa produce Christian Democratic Parties and Islamic Democratic Parties? Uganda has produced a Christian Democratic Party in all but name. The Democratic Party in Uganda, especially in the First Republic of Uganda under Milton Obote's first Administration, was basically a Catholic Democratic Party. Political pluralism can accommodate parties which salute sacred ideologies— but on condition that those parties are also committed to the democratic process.

Christian Democrats and Islamic Democrats in Africa may be some of the parties which African pluralism has to accommodate in the days ahead.

Tribe is a form of identity; religion is a kind of ideology. Political parties based on "tribe" and ethnicity can create identities in collision. Political parties based on religion are a special kind of ideological organization. Provided such religious parties respect the rights of others and comply with the democratic process, they should surely enjoy every right to compete in the electoral arena and contend for influence in the marketplace of policies. The democratization of Kenya Muslims may help avert their radicalization.

ETHNICITY AND RELIGION: IS KENYA A FUTURE LEBANON?

But is there not a danger that religious parties will eventually turn Kenya into another Lebanon—torn deeply in civil strife?

What could turn Kenya into another Lebanon is not rival political parties, but rival armies. And, so far, the danger of rival armies does not lie in churches and mosques, but in ethnicity and tribalism.

Nowhere in Black Africa has there been a civil war which has been primarily religious. All civil wars in Black Africa have been primarily ethnic, tribal, racial or regional—but not religious. This applies to the Nigerian Civil War (1967–1970), the Angolan Civil War from 1975–76 onwards, the Mozambican Civil War from the 1970s onwards, the recurrent civil strife in Rwanda and Burundi, Nkata versus the African National Congress in apartheid South Africa, the wars in Chad, the long war in Eritrea (1962–1992), and even the different wars in the Sudan. The fundamental divide between North and South in the Sudan is infinitely more than religious—it is cultural, linguistic, civilizational and sometimes quasi-racial. On the other hand, the Darfur war has been Muslim against fellow Muslim.

In the 1990s, the main mediator for peace between North and South in Sudan was a Muslim—i.e., President Ibrahim Babangida of Nigeria in his capacity as Chairman of the Organization of African Unity at that time. General Babangida's administration had been trying its best to make the North-South reconciliation in the Sudan a crowning achievement. This was long before the explosion of the Darfur conflict.

Nigeria's own problems are first ethnic, secondly regional and only thirdly religious. Time and again in Black Africa the religious factor has been far less divisive than many other factors—and certainly less so than ethnicity (tribalism) and clan.

In Somalia religious homogeneity has failed to keep the nation together. Although the country is overwhelmingly Muslim, the citizens have butchered each other almost as mercilessly as have the Sudanese next door.

George Bernard Shaw used to say that the British and the Americans were a people divided by the same language. It is more tragically true that the Somali are a people divided by the same culture. Islam has failed to bind them together. So has the Somali language.

But if Somalia is a case where religious sameness has failed to unite, Senegal is a country where religious difference has failed to divide. With over 90 percent of the population consisting of Muslims, Senegal had a Roman Catholic President not for five years, not for ten, not for 15 years, but a whole 20 years—without cries in the streets screaming out, "Jihad fi sabil el Llah" [Jihad in the path of God]. The Senegalese Muslims respected the democratic process. In religious toleration, they were in fact far ahead of most Western nations.

On the other hand, it was not until 1960 that the U.S.A. "elected" its first non-Protestant (i.e., a Catholic) President. But was Kennedy really "elected"—or did he only become President by an electoral numerical error?

A Jewish President of the United States is unlikely in the near future. Indeed, until this past decade, the Jews had avoided bidding for the Presidency out of fear of unleashing the Demon of Anti-Semitism.

What about a Muslim President of the United States? There are now as many Muslims as Jews in the U.S.A.—although the Muslims are, of course, much less visible or influential. A Muslim in the Oval Office is unlikely to take over in the lifetime of my grandchildren, although an Arab-American (Ralph Nader) did run for U.S. President in the years 2000 and 2004. But Nader was a Christian.

And yet here was Muslim Senegal accepting a Roman Catholic President for two decades.

From 1980 Senegal had a Muslim President at last. But guess what? The First Lady from 1980 to 2000 was a Roman Catholic. I wonder when a Head of State in the Western world is likely to have a Shiite woman for his First Lady?

THE PRICE TAG OF THE KENYA COAST

What is distinctive about the Coast of Kenya? What does the Coast bring to the national heritage which is uniquely Coastal?

First, the Coast brings to the national table the national language of Kiswahili—the most successful indigenous language on the African continent. This linguistic legacy was not forged just by the Waswahili. It was shaped and influenced by all Coastal peoples—the Giriama and the Digo, the Taita, as well as all the Mijikenda. In the Kenya context the Coast is the fountainhead of the national language.

Secondly, the Coast offers its national features for sport—the splendor of its beaches. Thirdly, the exceptional utility of its harbors has made Mombasa the gateway to the outside world for centuries. Without Kilindini Harbor in Mombasa, the economies of Kenya, Uganda and elsewhere would be in serious trouble. Without the beaches of Malindi and other coastal playgrounds, Kenya's tourist industry would diminish. Without Kilindini, Kenya's economy would shrink. No other part of Kenya can make the same contributions to Kenya's economy. If the Coast generates wealth, but its Muslim population is underprivileged, is an Intifadah on the horizon?

The fourth area of uniqueness of the Kenya Coast is its historicity. Of course, all parts of Kenya have a history, but there is something about the history of the Coast which is captured not only in the oral tradition, but also in stone, in written documents hundreds of years old, in the ruins of ancient cities like Gedi, and in the living continuities of ancient city-states like Lamu.

No other part of Kenya brings this kind of legacy to the national heritage. Indeed, the Coast was the first part of Kenya to be literate, but will the Coast be the last to be given a university of its own? Mombasa has been ignored as a university city.

Fifthly, the Coast is unique in Kenya in being the fountainhead of East African Islam as a faith, as a culture and as a civilization. In the Kenya Coast the muezzin was calling Muslim believers to prayers hundreds of years before the Protestant Reformation in Europe. It is arguable that Islam is older on the Kenya Coast than it is in some areas of the Middle East. No other part of Kenya brings the Islamic legacy so decisively to Kenya's national heritage as the Coast does.

To summarize, why is the Coast unique?

It is the fountainhead of the national language, Kiswahili.

It is the gateway from East Africa to the outside world, through its harbors, especially Kilindini.

It is the playground of beaches and water sports—so vital to the tourist industry.

It is unique in its historicity—from the ruins of Gedi to Fort Jesus, from ancient written documents to remnants of a city-state like Lamu.

It is Kenya's fountainhead of Islam. The mosque on the Kenya Coast goes back to the earliest centuries of the Islamic calendar. The Coast was the first region of Kenya to learn to read and write hundreds of years ago, but is in danger of being the last to have a university of its own.

What do non-Coastal Kenyans feel about this five-sided distinctiveness of the Coast? Perhaps the nation has come to value the national language, Kiswahili. Perhaps the nation appreciates its great dependence on Kilindini Harbor. But is there a tendency to take the Coast for granted?

Moreover, the least appreciated of the Coast's five contributions to the national heritage is Islam. And yet Islam is also part of the ancestry of Kenya's national language. Kiswahili was born out of a meeting of two civilizations, African and Islamic.

Islam is also part of the historicity of the Coast—from the Swahili city-states to the fluctuating fortunes of Fort Jesus across the centuries.

In short, of the five aspects of uniqueness which the Coast brings to the national banquet, three aspects are profoundly influenced by Islam (language, history and religion).

Can Kenya afford to despise Islam and still save the other four legacies of the Coast—language, national gateway, tourist playground, and monumental historicity?

The Waswahili are still by far the most gifted users of the national language, Kiswahili. And the Waswahili are, in their great majority, Muslims. A repressed Swahili community is unlikely to be a major agent for enriching the national language.

Although the proportion of Muslims in the population of Tanzania is larger than the proportion of Muslims in Kenya's population, the proportion of non-Muslim experts of Kiswahili in Tanzania is paradoxically also larger than the proportion of non-Muslim Swahilists in Kenya. Julius Nyerere, for example, was not a Muslim. But he also happened to be one of the most brilliant users of the Swahili language in Tanzania. He had even translated William Shakespeare into powerful Kiswahili.

As compared with Tanzania, Kenya has a smaller percentage of Muslims. But for the enrichment of its national language, Kenya is in reality more dependent on Muslim Swahilists than Tanzania is. In Kenya to repress the Waswahili is to impoverish the Swahili language.

In Kenya to repress the Muslims is also not only to risk Islamic radicalization. It is also to detract from the special historicity of the Coast. For much of what is distinctive about the history of the Coast is the profound interaction between the African peoples there and the Islamic culture. For more than a thousand years the Kenya Coast has been not only part of the history of Africa. It has simultaneously been part of the history of Islam worldwide.

What about the Coast as a gateway into and out of East Africa? What about the Coast as a tourist playground? How would the repression of Islam affect those?

The last thing any patriotic citizen would want is a situation where there is so much discontent among the local people of the Coast that it begins to show first in escalating social deviancy, then in escalating crime, and finally in escalating rebellion and rioting. We must avert an Intifadah, let alone conversion to Al-Qaeda. Joblessness corrupts; absolutely joblessness corrupts absolutely. If the Coast were to become ungovernable, Kilindini Harbor would be endangered, the railway artery would be at risk, the peaceful beaches would be in turmoil, and the historic sites could be a nightmare. The Coast is too valuable to Kenya to be taken for granted. An Intifadah must be averted. So, of course, must Al-Qaeda.

CONCLUSION

Radicalization among Muslims in recent times has been precipitated by two major forces. The internal force consists of domestic injustices at the expense of Muslims and a deep sense of deprivation among the youth. The external cause of Islamic radicalization can be traced to the sense of helplessness among Muslims in the face of the perceived humiliation of Muslims in societies which have ranged from Palestine to Bosnia, from Iraq to Afghanistan, from Kashmir to Chechnya. Iran is the latest Muslim country to be under threat.

The global ummah appears under siege. Among politically conscious Muslims including those in Kenya and the rest of Africa—there is palpable anger.

But this paper has not addressed the wider global causes of Muslim rage. We have limited ourselves to potentially radicalizing grievances within the Muslim minority in postcolonial Kenya. Muslim areas in Kenya which are wealth-generating are disproportionately at the Coast. Yet the most valuable tourist facilities and Coastal residences and hotels are overwhelmingly in the hands of non-Coastal people. A deep sense of relative deprivation is created among Coastal indigenes. Land-grabbing by others is notoriously recurrent. And discrimination against Muslims in the distribution of jobs, scholarships, and large-scale trading licenses is widely manifest.

The most disadvantaged of Kenya Muslims are the Somalis of the North-East—although individual Somalis have sometimes risen high in the institutions of the Central Government. Calamities which have befallen the Somali people in recent years (be they natural disasters or social conflicts) have seldom aroused a sense of urgency in Nairobi. A great sense of being neglected is pervasive among Kenya Somalis.

The possibility of an Intifadah either among Coastal Muslims or among the Kenya Somalis is by no means remote if the grievances are not addressed. But the possibility of Kenya recruits into Al-Qaeda is a nightmare still mercifully distant. The Lord be praised.

Section V

ISLAM IN WORLD AFFAIRS

Chapter Eighteen

Muslims in a Century of Four Ethical Revolutions

The United Nations was born out of the ravages of war. The British Commonwealth was born out of the ravages of imperialism. At one time Britain either ruled or controlled nearly two-thirds of the Muslim world. Both the UN and the Commonwealth have now become forces for globalization. The Commonwealth dropped the word "British" from its name, as its membership got more global.

Globalization consists of those trends in the world which are fostering, wittingly or unwittingly, such tendencies as economic interdependence on a global scale, cross-cultural awareness, and global institution-building to regulate both inter-human relations and the exploitation of the world's resources. Globalization does include international currency upheavals like the recent ones in Asia, but those will not be the focus of this paper.

The twentieth century was the century when war went global. The human race fought two world wars. World War I gave birth to the League of Nations, which was primarily a European Club. Almost the whole of Africa, much of Asia and the Muslim world, and the United States were outside the League, though the reasons for their absence from the League differed.

It was World War II which gave birth to a more credible world body—the United Nations—though it took two decades after its formation before its membership became truly universalized.

One particular force was vital for the universalization of the United Nations and the global expansion of the Commonwealth—the force was decolonization. This particular push of history liberated more and more countries—and made the new states available for membership of the United Nations and for accession to the Commonwealth. Today more than a billion Muslims are represented in the United Nations and about half of those are also represented in the Commonwealth, including the Muslims of Pakistan, India, Bangladesh, Nigeria and Malaysia.

But behind these political trends have been equally fundamental ethical trends in the twentieth century. These ethical transformations have changed the nature of the Commonwealth and of the world. Let us look at them more closely.

TOWARDS MORALLY ACCOUNTABLE ECONOMIES

Four ethical revolutions have characterized the twentieth century. In the first third of the twentieth century we witnessed in the Northern hemisphere revolutions against laissez-faire economics and increasingly in favor of morally accountable economies. These trends ranged from socialism to the New Deal, from V.I. Lenin to John Maynard Keynes. The Trades Union Congress in Britain united with the small Independent Labour Party at the beginning of the century. By the end of World War I the Labour Party was large enough to become the official opposition. Muhammad Ali Jinnah, future founder of Pakistan, felt some of the Fabian influences of this period during his years in Britain.

In approximately the second third of the twentieth century the dominant revolution was racial. It challenged white supremacy world wide, and undermined the legitimacy of European empires. The revolution galvanized anti-colonial struggles and energized human rights movements. The European Empires experienced wide-ranging struggles for greater racial justice. From Indonesia to Algeria colonised Muslims sometimes resorted to armed struggle.

In approximately the last third of the twentieth century two revolutions have captured the imaginations of reformers—the green revolution in defence of the environment and the gender revolution in pursuit of the empowerment of women. Has the Muslim world kept pace with these latest revolutions as well?

The twentieth century has sought morally responsible economies (spearheaded in the first third), racially responsible societies (spearheaded in the second third) and a world attentive to the empowerment of women and the defence of the environment (spearheaded in the third of the century).

How has the Commonwealth been affected by these four revolutions in the twentieth century? How has the Muslim world responded to them?

Let us look at these momentous trends at both their global and Commonwealth levels more closely.

It is not often recognized that laissez fair economics was probably born out of religious pantheism in the same sense in which Marxian material dialectics were born out of Hegelian Idealist dialectics. Pantheism found in Alexander Pope a powerful poetic voice. In Pope's An Essay on Man we hear:

> All are but parts of one stupendous whole,
> Whose body Nature is and God the soul.
> All nature is but art unknown to thee,
> All chance direction which thou canst not see,
> All discord harmony not understood,
> All partial evil universal good.
> Whatever is, is right.[1]

This philosophical complacency was repugnant to Islamic ethics, but became quite influential in parts of the West. Adam Smith took this optimism from the religious-philosophical
universe and focussed it on economics.

If you let economic and market forces operate unimpeded, all discord would in reality be "harmony not understood," all "partial evil" would be "universal good." An invisible hand would see to that. While Muslim economies were subject to rules against riba and reckless profiteering, Western economies entered the era of laissez-faire.

To quote and paraphrase another thinker, "All is for the best in this best of all possible economic worlds"—provided the market had free reign.

This optimism about the benevolent consequences of unimpeded market forces dominated economic thought in the West until approximately the first third of the 20th century. It may now be struggling to come back, to some extent.

The principle of laissez-faire at one time opposed the establishment of a minimum wage, or the regulation of the employment of children. The campaign to save English children from the grime and soot of chimneys did not come into law until much later.

Even the formation of trade unions was once regarded as a conspiracy to sabotage the economy, punishable by terms of imprisonment.

The most sustained theoretical challenge to laissez-faire philosophy did come in the nineteenth century with the rise of socialist thinkers, including Karl Marx. Many Muslim thinkers flirted with socialist ideas also.

But it was in the first third of the 20th century that anti-laissez-faire economic and political thought began to have a direct influence on the fate of governments and their policies.

At one level it led to the most momentous revolution of the 20th century— the Russian communist revolution of 1917. This was a total rejection of laissez-faire market forces.

Less drastic was the challenge posed to laissez-faire by Keynesian economics. The state could intervene in the economy and regulate it—but in order to save capitalism rather than to destroy it. John Maynard Keynes helped to give capitalist respectability to state participation in the economy. State intervention to create jobs and assist the unemployed was also calculated to alleviate the suffering of their children.

In the United States the divergence from laissez-faire came with Franklin D. Roosevelt's New Deal policies which were designed to help the poor and the unemployed during the Great Depression. Roosevelt faced considerable opposition from a more conservative Supreme Court. But the New Deal of the 1930s muted the philosophy of laissez-faire in the United States at least until the mid-1990s. Is the principle of a morally accountable economy about to be overthrown by Republicans in the United States? Or will their bark turn out to be harsher than their bite?

TOWARDS MORALLY ACCOUNTABLE IMPERIALISM

How did these trends in the wider world affect the future Commonwealth and the Muslim world? The nature and mission of European colonialism began to change. The evolution of the welfare state in the West gave birth to a kind of welfare imperialism for the colonies. Great Britain was later to establish the Colonial Development and Welfare Fund. The poorest Muslim countries under British rule were among the beneficiaries.

The old mission of Pax Britannica which emphasized law and order in the colonies gave way to a greater commitment to the material welfare and development of the native peoples. Welfare imperialism abroad accompanied the British welfare state at home.

But all this was itself setting the stage for the great ethical revolution of the second third of the 20th century—the racial revolution. While Islam itself is doctrinally non-racial, most Muslims had been under European racist rule. This second major ethical revolution of the century intensified anti-colonial struggles in Asia and Africa, increased and deepened Afro-Asian nationalism world-wide, sparked off the civil rights movement in the United States, and created both white apartheid and its militant Black adversaries. Muslims in South-East Asia had to fight not only European imperialism but also Japanese.

Curiously enough, World War II played a direct and sometimes positive part in this second revolution of the 20th century—the racial revolution.

If we blame the horrors of World War II on the Germans it is still amazing how beneficial some of the long-term consequences of that war were for the future Commonwealth. This is the silver lining of the cloud of the Third Reich.

There is no doubt that the World War played a decisive role in undermining the foundations of the old European empires in Asia, Africa and the Americas. The war accelerated the independence of the Asian part of the British empire—resulting in the independence of India and Pakistan in 1947 within two years of the end of the war. The liberation of South Asia was an important precedent for the liberation of Africa a decade later. And South Asia had a huge concentration of Muslims.

The German military challenge undermined Britain's imperial will and impoverished the British exchequer. The Germans also humiliated France and undermined the myth of French grandeur and invincibility. After all, the Germans had defeated France with unexpected ease. The mythology surrounding France in Africa was never the same again. In less than a decade after the end of World War II mujahiddeen in Algeria were fighting for their independence.

World War II had also knocked Western Europe (including Germany) out of the League of first-rank world powers—and revealed more clearly the temporary bipolar succession of the United States and the Soviet Union as the new superpowers on the world stage. Countries like Pakistan and Egypt learnt to exploit this superpower rivalry while it lasted.

World War II had been fought as a crusade against tyranny and dictatorship. This crusade carried anti-colonial implications. If German occupation of Poland or Belgium was wrong, what about British occupation of Nigeria, Malaya, Algeria, and India? The moral rhetoric against the Germans boomeranged against British and French imperialists.

The Atlantic Charter signed in 1941 by President Franklin D. Roosevelt and Prime Minister Winston Churchill was widely interpreted as the Magna Carta of self-determination for all societies (including the colonies)—in spite of Winston Churchills' attempt to exclude the British Empire from the liberating implications of the Atlantic Charter.

The war against Germany and its allies expanded the political horizons of the African and Muslim soldiers who had fought in it. These soldiers had seen more of the world, and had witnessed the human weakness of the white man's fear in war, sometimes cowardice in a white officer. The white man was cut-down to size from demi-God to fellow human being. So what gave him the right to dominate and exploit Arabs or Black folks? African and Arab veterans of World War II were some of the catalysts of nationalism in this phase of struggle.

Then there was the impact of World War II on the birth of the United Nations' Organization which in turn played a role in the decolonization of Africa, Asia and the Caribbean. Some countries which were once colonies of Germany before the end of World War I became trusteeships of the UN after World War II. These countries included Tanganyika, Cameroon, Togo, Ruanda-Urundi and South-West Africa (now Namibia).

The UN was for a while a benign collective imperial power. But on the whole the over-all impact of the UN on Africa, Asia and the Caribbean was in the direction of greater decolonization. Most former British colonies joined the Commonwealth. Muslim members (with years of entry) include Malaysia (1957), Nigeria (1960), Pakistan (re-entered 1989) and, in a sense, India (1947).

With the disintegration of political apartheid in South Africa in the 1990s, a very important battle has been won. Canada played a big role against the apartheid regime. But the war against racial injustice in South Africa is surely not over. Political apartheid may be over, but economic apartheid is alive and well. As President, Nelson Mandela refused to turn his back on those Muslim leaders who had once supported him, such as Muammar Qaddafy of Libya and Yassir Arafat of the Palestine Liberation Organization (PLO).

The great wealth of that great country is still mal-distributed along racial lines. Whites in South Africa own the best land; whites own the mines and most of the mineral wealth; whites have disproportionately the best jobs in industry, commerce and the civil service. And whites still have the least unemployment and the best salaries and wages for the same kind of work.

Economic apartheid is still intact. With the peaceful formation of a multiracial government of national unity, political apartheid died in 1994. A major battle has been won; but the war is inconclusive. The Commonwealth as a whole fought to end political apartheid. Is there a role for the Commonwealth in the struggle against economic apartheid? Many Muslim governments helped in the crusade against white minority rule. Can Muslims still help in the new economic struggle?

Indeed, in South Africa, the anti-laissez-faire revolution may lie in the future rather than in the past. It may lie in the first third of the 21st century rather than the first third of the 20th century as it did in the West.

The sequence of the four revolutions in South Africa were simply distorted by the aberration of racism, whose institutionalized form lasted longer in South Africa than anywhere else.

Outside South Africa the second ethical revolution of the twentieth century was indeed a racial revolution and was primarily in the second third of the century from the mid-1930s to the mid-1960s. For Africa and the Muslim world this revolution was, as we indicated, particularly wide-ranging. Armed struggle in Africa and the Arab world came to benefit considerably from the support of the Soviet Union and its allies at the time. What had happened in the anti-laissez-faire revolution of the first third of the 20th century fed into the racial struggles of the later part of the century.

In the United States the racial revolution included such momentous Supreme Court decisions as Brown versus the Board of Education in 1954 which ended the era of "Separate but Equal." The racial revolution in the African Diaspora also included the civil rights movement in the United States and the role of Dr. Martin Luther King Jr. in it. Was the civil rights movement in the USA helped by the anti-colonial movement in Africa in the second third of the 20th century? The symbiotic relationship between anti-racism and the anti-colonialism is still to be conclusively studied.

Another anomaly worth noting is that none of the Arab countries previously ruled or controlled by Great Britain applied to become members of the Commonwealth. While the Muslim world is well represented in the Commonwealth (nearly 500 million people) the Arab world is grossly under-represented. Countries like Egypt, Sudan and Iraq regarded Commonwealth membership as incompatible with Pan-Arabism. It would be ironic if in the 21st century the first Arab member of the Commonwealth became the new Palestine state.

THE GENDER REVOLUTION

As for last third of the twentieth century, this has witnessed two other ethical revolutions—a concern for the rights of women and a concern for the ecology, including other living creatures. How has the Commonwealth been influenced by these latest twin revolutions—gender and ecology? Is the Muslim world a mere bystander?

The gender revolution in the West has helped African and Muslim children more than African and Muslim women. Liberated Western women have been an important additional lobby in support of the rights of children in Asia and Africa. Western influence in defence of African and Asian children is culturally less offensive than Western efforts in defence of African and Asian women. When the Nigerian Military Government of the late General Sani Abacha sent out feelers about outlawing female circumcision in November 1994, the regime did so in the context of the rights of children rather than the rights of women. Female circumcision was seen as a violation of the rights of children (since it was done in childhood) more than a transgression against the rights of women. Although General Abacha himself was a Muslim, female circumcision in Nigeria was practised by both Muslims and non-Muslims. It was more a "tribal" rite than a religious one.

General Abacha's government was also considering outlawing scarification (tribal marks on the face). Again, if outlawed by his successors, the decree would be in the name of the rights of children who are scarred as minors.

In the phenomenon of women in top positions in politics, it is arguable that the Commonwealth has led the world. It did not begin with Margaret

Thatcher as prime minister of Great Britain. It began in 1960 with Sirimavo Bandaranaike as Prime Minister of Ceylon (later Sri Lanka). Indeed, Mrs. Bandaranaike started the overwhelmingly Commonwealth phenomenon of female succession to male martyrdom. This is a situation where a woman attains ultimate political office but in succession to a heroic male relative, usually martyred. Mr. S.W.R.D. Bandaranaike was assassinated in 1959—and the widow, Mrs. Bandaranaike, was swept into ultimate political prominence soon after.

Jawaharlal Nehru died in 1964 and in 1966 Indira Gandhi, his daughter, became prime minister of India. Zulfikar Ali Bhutto was executed in Pakistan in 1979—and eventually Benazir Bhutto became prime minister for the first time in 1988. She has continued to be in and out of power. Pakistan is the first Muslim country in modern history to have a head of government who is a woman.[2] In Bangladesh Sheikh Mujibur Rahman of the nascent nation was assassinated with his wife and five of his children in August 1975, and eventually one of his surviving daughters became leader of the Awami League and finally Prime Minister in 1997.

Also in Bangladesh President Ziaur Rahman was assassinated in May 1981. Ten years later his widow was sworn as prime minister. Bangladesh is the first Commonwealth country to have had two women prime ministers in succession, belonging to opposing parties. Bangladesh is also the first Muslim country to have achieved such female empowerment at the top.

Across the world is the only South American member of the Commonwealth—the Cooperative Republic of Guyana. Cheddi B. Jagan was sworn in on October 30, 1992, in succession to Hugh Desmond Hoyte. Cheddi Jagan died in March 1997. In December 1997 his widow Janet Jagan was elected president—amidst charges that since she was foreign-born, she was not qualified to be Head of State in Guyana. (Mrs. Jagan was born as a white American in Chicago.) Most Muslims in Guyana seem to have voted for Mrs. Jagan.

The one remarkable Commonwealth female leader who was in no sense a successor to a heroic male relative was Britain's Margaret Thatcher, who became Prime Minister in May 1979, and maintained her top leadership for eleven years.

But Margaret Thatcher was a case where the two revolutions of the twentieth century sometimes dramatically clashed—the struggle for gender equality and the struggle for racial equality. Although she herself symbolized the ultimate empowerment of a woman, and she may well be regarded by historians as the most powerful single woman in any part of the twentieth century, she was less than lukewarm in the struggle for racial equality.

Within the Commonwealth she was sometimes isolated in her refusal to impose economic sanctions on the apartheid regime in South Africa. She would dig her high heels in—at once a symbol of female power and a symbol of refusal to fight apartheid.

A Commonwealth female leader who had reservations about the first ethical revolution of the twentieth century was Dame Mary Eugenia Charles of Dominica in the West Indies. As a politically successful woman she signified the march of the gender revolution in the century. But as leader of the Dominica Freedom Party (DFP), she represented a right-wing alliance which was associated with the propertied class at Rosenau. Mary Eugenia Charles was Prime Minister from July 1980 until 1994.

Eugenia Charles' right wing tendencies was a factor behind Dominica's enthusiastic participation in the multinational force which, under U.S. leadership, invaded Grenada in October 1983. Once again, within the story of Eugenia Charles we find the gender revolution of female empowerment running counter to the earlier revolutions in defence of the economically and racially underprivileged. Grenada was at the time a country trying to create a morally accountable economy through socialism. It paid the price of a U.S.-led invasion.

Canada experimented briefly with a woman prime minister when Brian Mulroney resigned in favour of Kim Campbell in 1993. It was not a good time to have the first woman prime minister. Kim Campbell was confronted with an anti-Conservative tide which she could neither contain nor reverse. Her Party (the Progressive Conservative Party) suffered the worst defeat to any ruling party in Canadian history—shrinking from 153 to 2 members in the House of Commons. She was Prime Minister for a mere 134 days. She resigned as party leader on December 13, 1993.

In spite of all this unevenness, the Commonwealth (including its Muslim members) has indeed been in the vanguard of the struggle for the political empowerment of women. Scandinavian countries have provided striking models of their own, and have set a good example to the rest of the world. But their international visibility is modest in comparison to the leading members of the Commonwealth. Within the Commonwealth at least one-fifth of the human race has been ruled by a woman at sometime or another in the last forty years. In South Asia over three hundred million Muslims have known rule by a woman. And if Sonia Gandhi—the widow of the assassinated Rajiv Gandhi—does eventually become India's second woman Prime Minister, the achievement will be both trans-gender and trans-racial. Sonia Gandhi is ethnically Italian, as well as being a remarkable woman. Her party (Congress) is widely regarded as Muslim-friendly.

Finally, we should remember that the Commonwealth may be the only male-dominated multinational club which has had a woman for its Head for more than four decades. The Head is, of course, Queen Elizabeth II. The only reservation Muslims might have is that the Head of the Commonwealth is simultaneously the Head of the Church of England. The British monarch has to serve both roles. For once, it is the Muslims who might prefer a separation of church and state.

THE GREEN REVOLUTION

If the initial three ethical revolutions of the twentieth century were socio-economic, racial and gender, what is the nature of the fourth revolution and how has it affected the Commonwealth?

The green revolution of the last third of the twentieth century has sought to protect rivers and hills, air and water, Indian and Malaysian tigers and African elephants. Sometimes the struggle against environmental degradation and the struggle for morally accountable economies are inseparable. Particularly poignant in 1995 was the plight of the Oguni people of Nigeria and the brutal fate of Ken Saro-Wiwa in the full glare of a Commonwealth conference in New Zealand. The environment of the Oguni villagers was devastated by the oil industry in their area—and Ken Saro-Wiwa and eleven others were executed partly for protesting in ways which were unacceptable to the military in Nigeria. Because President Sani Abacha was a Muslim and the executed Ogoni activists were mainly Christian, the brutal incident had sectarian reverberations in Nigeria.

The green revolution has also sought to protect the dwindling legacy of wild animals against the greed of hunters, poachers and corrupt politicians. But is there also a danger that as far as Westerners are concerned, "one hippo is worth two Hutus!"? In other words, are the agricultural and pastoral needs of Africa's expanding populations being sacrificed to the whims of nature lovers? The rate of population growth among Sub-Saharan Muslims has been particularly high.

There is indeed a genuine dilemma. In many African countries, independence for African people (Muslim and non-Muslim) has meant less freedom for African animals. Widening political horizons for African people have coincided with narrowing physical horizons for African animals. Post colonial African authorities have been far less effective in protecting African animals than the colonial authorities had been. What nature lovers sometimes forget is that post-colonial African authorities have been less effective in protecting African people too. The cost of learning how to govern ourselves has sometimes been high. But we do need to learn self-government in any case. It is a stage we have to go through.

On the other hand, the African animals have been lucky that the post-colonial era has coincided with the new ecological revolution. Post-coloniality has coincided with the rise of the green movements.

While some human beings are indeed fast depleting the heritage of Planet Earth, other human beings are on greater ecological alert in the last third of the twentieth century than ever before in history. However un-Islamic when taken literally, Alexander Pope's couplet has been given a new ecological meaning:

> "All are but parts of one stupendous whole
> Whose body Nature is and God the Soul"

The environmental depletion is worse today than ever in history. But the environmental defenders are more active than ever before, in history. On balance the Asian and African environment has suffered because of independence but the Asian and African environment would have suffered even more if the era of independence had not coincided with the newly energized environmental consciousness world-wide. Indonesia under President Suharto was too permissive towards environmental degradation of the tropical rain forest. Fires have taken a high toll.

The ethical revolution of environmentalism is partly helping to discipline the earlier ethical revolution of race. The struggle for the rights of people of colour is by no means over yet. But now there is concern for the rights of the leopard and the rhino, the rights of fish in the rivers and oceans, the green rights of valleys and hills.

Other environmentalists go further. There are even Muslim environmentalists who share William Wordsworth's belief that Nature's grand design is predicated on joy and wonderment.[3]

Genes are a memory of ancestry. The duty of a Muslim father is to bring up good children (father as disciplinarian). The duty of a Muslim mother is to bring up happy children (mother as a fountain of sympathy). If children are an insurance for old age, mothers are greater beneficiaries. Women in the Muslim world and Africa live longer and are more likely to benefit from the children's care in old age. If children are a passport to immortality, fathers in Africa and the Muslim world have access to more passports. Polygamous fathers can have up to 50 children; whereas no woman is ever likely to be a biological mother to more than about 12 children at the most. The role of children as insurance here on earth serves mothers better than fathers. The role of children as a heavenly insurance for immortality in African traditional religion gives fathers an edge—since per person African fathers have more children than African mothers.

For every human being there is an economically pre-productive age, which is followed by a productive age and which in turn is followed by a post-productive age.

Clearly a newly-born baby is not economically productive. If it is being breast-fed, it is not even a direct economic consumer except in number of nappies or diapers it goes through.

In Western societies children below the age of about 7 are hardly ever economic producers. They are in the pre-productive age. In Nigeria and South Asia the pre-productive age may be children below the age of about 4 years old. After that they may be involved in serious economic activities on the farm or the household.

Although the productive age in Africa and South Asia begins early—perhaps at the age of 4—the productive age also ends relatively early. Going into serious retirement at the age of about 55 is quite common in Asia and Africa. People are regarded as "old" in Nigeria and Pakistan earlier that they are in the United States and Western Europe. The post-productive age in Africa and Asia is allowed to start sooner than necessary.

But in addition the population of the elderly is in any case expanding much faster in the West than in South Asia and Africa—Western men and women live longer. And so the population of the post-productive sector is becoming a bigger percentage of the total Western community.

In Africa, on the other hand, fertility rates are much higher than they are in the West. As a region Africa has the fastest growing population rate in the world. Therefore the pre-productive sector of Africa's population is bigger than it is in the West—just as the post-productive sector in the West is bigger than it is in Africa. The West has a disproportionate number of elderly people, while Africa has a disproportionate number of children and minors.

In the 21st century the West has to solve a compelling dilemma—is it enough to delay death without delaying aging? People in the West live longer but the aging process continues relentlessly—until the elderly become decrepid and overwhelmingly dependent. The West has found the secret of living longer but not the secret of stopping the aging process. The Western world is not yet James Hilton's Shangri-La, where both death and aging are delayed.[4]

A BRIDGE BETWEEN GENDERS

But the quest for balance in the 21st century is not only between races, classes and generations. It is also between men and women. Politically how should Africa and the Muslim world respond to the gender revolution? Africa and Asia should work out institutions in the political process which permit the following phases of parliamentary participation:

PHASE I: We should have gender reservation of seats under which both the candidates and the voters would be women. Some Muslim countries have made a start.

PHASE II: The seats would still be reserved for women candidates, but this time they would need to cultivate the support of both male and female voters. The electoral roll would now be universal. Iran is feeling its way towards such a system.

PHASE III: This would be a stage when there is confidence that female parliamentary candidates can compete without protection or reservation of seats. All parliamentary seats would therefore revert to a common electoral universal roll, free for all. Turkey believes it has reached such a stage. But although Turkey is another Muslim country which has produced a woman Prime Minister [Tansu Cïller], women members of parliament are still few in Ankara.

India worked out a formula of reserving seats for women in the Lower House, but so far no government has followed through with required legislation. On the executive branch, the aim everywhere in the Commonwealth and the Muslim world should be to plan for at least a third of the cabinet and the bureaucracy to consist of women by the year 2025 or soon after. Gender revolution or not, Muslim and most Commonwealth women may never want to be as much as fifty per cent of either the political or the military professions— 30% women in both professions could be optimum.

On the other hand, by way of compensation, women should own and control more than 50% of the economy before the middle of the 21st century. In some African countries women already do the bulk of the agricultural work. What is needed is to give them greater rights of ownership of land and greater access to independent credit.

As for enhancing female participation in the judicial branch of government, this can best be achieved by encouraging and subsidizing more and more women to study the law—and help them establish themselves in the face of stiff masculine competition. From the wider legal profession women could then increase their numbers in the judicial system of judges and district attorneys and make a greater impact on the country's system of justice. New fatwas in the Shari'a may be needed to permit Muslim female judges. Can the legal testimony of a woman continue to have half the weight of a man's testimony in economic cases?

In September 1994 The United Nations Cairo Conference on Population was agonizing about how many new children would have been born thirty years from then. In Addis Ababa at about the same time another conference was agonizing about how many of those children would be born as refugees either as children or as adults. Should the Ummah have a High Commissioner for Refugees of its own?

The Cairo conference was about new babies being born in normal circumstances. In Addis Ababa the UNHCR/OAU conference was in part about new babies born in refugee camps. What did reproductive health mean in refugee camps in Pakistan, Afghanistan or Tanzania? Is there a definition of refugee which would take into account whether the child is wanted or not? Perhaps every unwanted child, anywhere in the world, is a political refugee.

This applies to unwanted children of parents who are not themselves refugees. Unwanted new babies of Tutsi or Hutu in Tanzania are therefore refugees twice-over. Unwanted rape babies in Bosnia are refugees. International law and practice have tended to define a refugee in relation to whether a state tolerates him or her as a citizen. Should we include in the 21st century in the definition of a refugee the issue of whether the parents want the child as a member of a family? If the world is a global village, is it also to become a global cradle? When will every unwanted baby have global foster parents? Is the 21st century the relevant era? Should the Muslim world consider having a High Commissioner for Children and Orphans?

In response to both the gender and ecological revolutions, we need a global population policy, rather than just a policy for the growth rates of the Third World. Every child born in the United States is multiple times a greater threat to the Planet Earth than a child born in Nigeria, Bangladesh or Egypt.

The child born in the USA will consume a bigger share of the world's resources, generate more carbon dioxide into the atmosphere with his cars and gadgets, contribute more to the greenhouse effect, be a bigger threat to the ozone layer, generate more toxic and nuclear waste without adequate means of disposal, and perpetrate a continuing use of sophisticated military arsenals several times every decade.

The 1994 Cairo Conference on Population had many speakers who regretted population growth in countries of low gross national product like Pakistan and Nigeria. There were very few voices who regretted population growth in countries of high national consumption like the United States. According to Paul R. Ehrlich and Anne H. Ehrlich in their book The Population Explosion:

> . . . a baby born in the United States represents twice the destructive impact on the Earth's ecosystems and the services they provide as one born in Sweden . . . . 35 times one born in India, 140 times one in Bangladesh or Kenya, and 280 times, one in Chad, Rwanda, Haiti or Nepal.[5]

While the global reformers should indeed champion reduced population growth in Asia andin the 21st century, they should also champion measures for minus-zero population growth in the industrialized world, and greater control of rates of consumption. But within that larger global policy on population, refugees and orphans the Ummah and Commonwealth should work out roles for themselves—sensitive to the four ethical revolutions of the twentieth century.

CONCLUSION

Early in 1998 I was attending the World Economic Forum in Davos, Switzerland, the largest and in some ways most important economic conference of its kind. The theme for this 1998 World Economic Forum was based on a consciousness of the new century, and the new millennium. The forces of globalization were in the Davos air.

From Commonwealth Africa the Davos Forum invited some of the men who represented a new generation of leadership, fit to prepare Africa for the new millennium.

The Forum was addressed by President Yoweri Museveni of Uganda, who defended his vision of an economy without the state, and a state without political parties—Uganda as a no-state economy and a no-party state. The Forum was addressed by President Jerry Rawlings of Ghana, a former military ruler who had been creatively recycled into a democratic ruler. Is this a new wave into the twenty-first century? Is Jerry Rawlings the second Kwame Nkrumah of Ghana's history?

The World Economic Forum was also addressed by Thabo Mbeki, President of the African National Congress in South Africa and almost certainly the next President of South Africa after Nelson Mandela. This Deputy President of South Africa discussed the pitfalls as well as the promise of globalization for the twenty-first century.

Representation from the Arab world included the distinguished Palestinian woman activist, Hanan Ashrawi, as well senior ambassadors from diverse countries.

Nawaz Shariff was the most senior statesman from the Muslim world at the World Economic Forum. The Prime Minister of Pakistan called upon international investors to distinguish between short-term political problems in South Asia and long-term economic opportunities. They should rise to the challenge of long-term optimism. Iran was represented by the woman Vice-President, Masoumeh Ebtekar, Vice-President of the Islamic Republic of Iran and Head of the Organization for the Protection of the Environment and Kamal Kharrazi, Minister of Foreign Affairs of the Islamic Republic of Iran.

In this chapter our longer term perspective concerns four ethical revolutions which have unfolded in the 20th century—the revolution of moral accountability; the revolution of racial equality; the revolution of gender equality; the revolution of ecological balance.

In the first revolution of morally accountable economies, thinkers within the Commonwealth provided some of the best answers to the challenge of MORALLY ACCOUNTABLE CAPITALISM.

The most influential of the thinkers in the Commonwealth was perhaps John Maynard Keynes whose theories helped capitalism find its own enlightened self-interest, a formula for its survival. It was in the interest of capitalism to avert abject poverty and prevent class-polarization. But capitalism can only do so with the help of the state. Selective state intervention became a lifeboat for the survival of capitalism during the Depression. Most of the Muslim world was already under capitalist direction.

Keynsian theories later resulted in major developments in the construction of welfare states in the Commonwealth—helped by the landslide victory of the British Labour Party after World War II. Muslim thinkers were influenced by such Western schools of socialism.

Canada later blazed the trail in morally accountable economies in the Americas, capping it with the most responsible National Health Scheme in North America. In the British Empire morally accountable power resulted in such innovations as the Colonial Development and Welfare Fund and other experiments which sought to tame colonial exploitation with colonial development and imperial responsibility. It also helped to speed up the process of turning the British Empire into the Commonwealth.

As we enter the new millennium we know that the process of creating morally accountable power is reversible. There has been a partial dismantling of the welfare state in some Commonwealth and Muslim countries. We are unlikely to relapse ever again into laissez-faire—but nevertheless, capitalism has sought to free itself recently from some of the moral fetters of social democracy in a number of countries in the Commonwealth.

The question for the Third millennium is which tendency is more enduring—the pull towards a social democratic order and a morally accountable economy or the pull towards the sovereignty of the market and reduced moral accountability.

In the second ethical revolution of the 20th century (the struggle against racism), the Commonwealth has also been in the vanguard. Some of the greatest fighters against racism have emerged out of the womb of the Commonwealth. They have ranged from Mohandas Gandhi in South Africa to Muhammad Ali Jinnah in British India; from Barbara Castle in Britain to Winnie Mandela in apartheid South Africa; from General Abdel Nasser in

Egypt to Shridath Ramphal of Guyana; from Mahathir Mohammad of Malaysia to Robert Mugabe of Zimbabwe. Mahatma Gandhi and Nelson Mandela are widely regarded as the moral giants of them all—whose ethical message has resonated and resounded around the world. Most Muslims will accept the choice of Mandela; but some Muslims may have reservations about Mohandas Gandhi.

Will the 20th century hand over to the 21st century a world with little or no racism? Or will the second millennium hand over to the third a different kind of racism instead? We are beginning to suspect that a classless society in the 21st century is most unlikely. But is a raceless society in the twenty-first century at least conceivable?

The four revolutions themselves will continue to be needed. Economies need to be socially accountable. Societies need to be racially equitable. The world needs to be gender egalitarian. And the human race needs to be ecologically responsible. The Commonwealth and the religion of Islam itself are bound to play a part.

The Commonwealth is caught in the vortex of those four revolutions of the 20th century as we approach the new millennium. Islam is bound to be one of the most influential sets of values unfolding upon the new configuration.

Is there a fifth revolution waiting to be born in the 21st century? The world needs to be culturally more balanced—restoring validity to traditions which have been marginalized, cultures which have been eclipsed, and languages which have been diminished by the aggressive expansionism of Western civilization. W.E.B. Du Bois once argued that the ultimate problem of the 20th century was the problem of the colour line. Perhaps the ultimate problem of the 21st century will be the problem of the culture line. The Commonwealth and the Muslim world are bound to be in the middle of it all. But that is a subject for another study.

NOTES

1. Alexander Pope, *An Essay on Man* (1733–34).
2. Pakistan pulled out of the Commonwealth in 1971 in protest against international recognition of the independence of Bangladesh (formerly East Pakistan). The new Pakistan was readmitted to the Commonwealth in 1989.
3. William Wordsworth, *Lines Written in Early Spring* (1798).
4. See James Hilton's novel *Lost Horizon* (London, 1944 edition).
5. Paul R. Ehrlich and Anne H. Ehrlich, *The Population Explosion,* (New York, NY: Simon & Schuster, 1990) p. 134.

Chapter Nineteen

Africa and Islam in Search of Seven Pillars of Wisdom

The year 2004 marks the ninetieth anniversary of the outbreak of World War I. That First World War resulted in the collapse of Islam's last great imperial order. The story of Islam's relationship with the Western World in the last one hundred years can be viewed as a transition from the final collapse of the Ottomans to the spectacular rise of the American empire.

The decision of the Young Turk Triumvirate to enter World War I on the side of Germany and Austria unleashed forces which were going to affect the Muslim world for the rest of the twentieth century and beyond. As the Ottomans were being defeated Lord Balfour, then British Foreign Secretary, issued his historic Balfour Declaration expressing British support "for the establishment in Palestine of a national home for the Jewish people." The declaration was affirmed in a letter from Arthur James Balfour to Lionel Walter Rothschild, the 2nd Baron Rothschild, a leader of British Jewry.

Lord Balfour little realized that he was setting the stage for the most enduring conflict between Muslims and Westerners since the eighth crusade led by King Louis XIV in the thirteenth century. Some have even argued that the Arab and Muslim struggle against political Zionism is the belated nineteenth crusade for the control of the Holy Land.

In some of the medieval crusades Muslims and Jews were on the same side against the Christian invaders. From the Balfour Declaration onwards the new crusade has been a case of support for Jewish occupation and displacement of Muslims. After all the Balfour Declaration was a friendly exchange between a Christian aristocrat (Balfour) and a Jewish aristocrat (Rothschild) at the expense of an Arab people.

T. E. LAWRENCE AND THE DECLINE OF ISLAM

Enter T. E. Lawrence, otherwise known as Lawrence of Arabia! He had been commissioned into the British security forces in 1914, and was officially attached to the Hejaz Expeditionary Force under the command of General Wingate. His mission was to unite the Arabs, but not against the emerging force of Zionism but against the older adversary of Ottoman occupation. Lawrence promised the Arabs that if they united and revolted against the Turks, Arab freedom and a united Arab nation would be supported by Great Britain.

T. E. Lawrence was probably sincere in wanting to help the Arabs become a free and united people. But Lawrence's country, the United Kingdom, was far less sincere. Great Britain encouraged the Arab revolt against the Ottomans as one of the strategies of winning World War I. Once the Ottoman Empire collapsed, Arab countries became the loot of the victorious European powers. Much of the Arab World felt under European rule either as outright colonies, or as protectorates, or as Mandates of the League of Nations. That included Palestine, which fell under British administration, ostensibly answerable to the League of Nations. The ghost of Lord Balfour hovered over the British mandate in Palestine. British trusteeship failed to protect the freedom and integrity of the Palestinian people—with long-term disastrous consequences for the history of the world.

Had Lawrence's dream of a united Arab nation materialized, perhaps Palestine would never have been partitioned. Alternatively, if Lawrence and Great Britain had failed to destroy the last great Muslim empire in history, subsequent relations between Islam and the West might have been less acrimonious.

What the Arabs had needed was liberation from the Turks without recolonization by the British, the French and subsequently the Americans. The Arabs did succeed in jumping out of the Ottoman frying pan—but only to fall into the fires of Euro-American domination. T. E. Lawrence helped the Arabs jump out of the Ottoman frying pan—only to see Arab dreams perish in the new fires of Western imperialism.

According to Lawrence, Freedom itself is "the seven-pillared worthy house," a structure of glory resting on seven pillars. But Lawrence knew that in the Bible the seven pillars upheld the house not of Freedom but of Wisdom. In the words of the Book of Proverbs (ix, I): *"Wisdom hath builded a house: she has hewn out her seven pillars."*

Lawrence wrote his book, Seven Pillars of Freedom partly at All Souls College, Oxford. He had lost much of his draft at Reading Station, while changing trains in the Christmas season in 1919. Three years later All Saints hosted Lawrence to help him complete his book. This remarkable stranger among the Arabs was only one of the actors who helped to change the relationship between the Arabs and the West. But perhaps Lawrence was the most romantic of all the relevant actors. To use his own words:

> All men dream but not equally. Those who dream by night in the dusty recesses of their minds wake in the day to find that it was vanity: but the dreamers of the day are dangerous men, for they may act their dream with open eyes, and make it possible. This I did. I meant to make a new nation, to restore a lost influence, to give twenty millions of Semites the foundations on which to build their national thoughts.

Lawrence saw the Arab liberation fighters as responding to what Lawrence called "the inherent nobility of their minds." Lawrence felt that the Arabs were betrayed for the sake of what he called "the British petrol royalties in Mesopotamia," an old name for Iraq. Lawrence lamented, " *We pay for these things too much in honour and in innocent lives . . . Arab help was necessary to our cheap and speedy victory in the East, and that better to win and break our word than lose.*"[1]

Lawrence tried to reject honours and rewards for his role in the Arab revolt. He was so ashamed of the British Adulation of "Lawrence of Arabia" that he even changed his name for a while to T. E. Shaw. While the British and the French were fragmenting the Arab world, a British imperial presence was astride Iraq, Kuwait, Jordan, and the Gulf as a whole, in addition to the older British occupation of Egypt. A French imperial presence was astride Syria and Lebanon, as well as the older French colonization of the Maghreb in North Africa.

As for the legacy of the Balfour Declaration, it was increasingly interpreted as a green light for Zionist ambitions in spite of Lord Balfour's proviso that "nothing shall be done which may prejudice the civil and religious rights of existing non-Jewish communities."

The old allegory of the camel and the Arab's tent assumed the dimensions of a political allegory. It was cold in the desert at night. The camel begged the Arab to permit its head into the tent for shelter and warmth. The Arab thought compassionately about a stranger in distress. Then the camel asked for shelter in the tent for its neck. Then the camel's shoulders begged for shelter. By the time the camel was asking for shelter for its second hump, there was little room left in the tent for the original Arab occupant in the tent. The camel was the Zionist movement. The tent was Palestine. Lord Balfour was being invoked to strengthen the Zionist movement. Hundred's of thousands of Palestinians were subsequently displaced! A new heritage of hate was created.

The collapse of the Ottoman Empire had also resulted in the collapse of the Islamic Caliphate for the first time in thirteen centuries. Turkey, which had been the strongest link of Muslim solidarity under the Ottomans, became instead the strongest expression of neo-Muslim secularism under the new Turkish Republic.

The ending of the Caliphate deprived Muslims of a global institution of shared allegiance. The political secularization of Ataturk's Turkey also deprived the Muslim ummah of the strongest Muslim military power in the Middle East. The negative long-term consequences of World War I for the Muslim world continued to pile up.

But it was not just the Ottoman Empire which collapsed after World War I. It was also the German Empire in Africa under the Kaiser. And just as Ottoman rule in the Arab world was rapidly replaced by British and French imperialism, so was the German empire in Tanganyika, Ruanda-Urundi, South West Africa, Cameroon and Togoland rapidly replaced by mandates administrated by Britain, France, Belgium and White South Africans. Like Arab subjects of the Ottoman Empire, African subjects of German colonies fell out of the frying pan of one empire into the fires of an alternative imperial order.

By the end of the twentieth century all of Africa and most of the Arab world were at least nominally independent of old-style colonialism. But a whole new phenomenon had emerged—a different kind of empire under the United States of America. The end of the Cold War had ended older concepts like "balance of power." The world had lost its global checks and balances. The United States had become the mightiest power in human history. It certainly had more military might than the next ten countries added together. Economically it is in a class by itself. It is taking more than a dozen European countries to constitute a union which could adequately challenge the economic influence and power of the United States.

This mighty country was still a democracy at home in spite of the recent erosion of civil liberties since September 11. Domestically the United States does have a system of checks and balances. But externally the United States has become an empire, only marginally subject to checks and balances. Domestically the American system is still predicated on rights. Internationally American behavior is predicated increasingly on might.

The greatest military casualties of the new Pax Americana are Muslims. The greatest economic casualties of an American-led globalization are Africans. The rules and priorities of a globalizing international economy are leaving Africans more and more marginalized. The erosion of rules in the use of military power are leaving Muslim countries more and more vulnerable to Pax Americana.

In the face of this new international disequilibrium, humanity needs a new Global Ethic. There is a compelling need for new criteria of right and wrong across civilizations. One approach is to rediscover the seven pillars of wisdom and redefine them in the context of the new imbalances in the world system.

In this chapter we use the term "strangers in our midst" to refer to people whom we do not regard as part of the "we" in the we/they equation. Their identity is perceived as different—either by race, religion, ethnicity, and nationality, gender or by some other criteria of differentiation. The search for a Global Ethic is partly a search for how to deal with "strangers in our midst" ethically and in solidarity.

This chapter is primarily about this search for standards of interhuman relations, combined with how we treat the ecology which our species has to share with other creatures.

The human species is the only one which can consciously choose standards of ethical behaviour. The burden of moral choice is upon us. Quo vadis? Where do we go from here?

The human race needs to identify seven principles. Every civilization in the world has elements which can be used to consolidate those principles of a Global Ethic. In this lecture we shall use two civilizations as case studies— Islam and African values. How can these two civilizations contribute to the pillars of the new Global Ethic?

The first pillar of wisdom is tolerance. Which of the values of Africa and Islam are supportive of tolerance? Both Africa and the Muslim world seem to be conflict-prone. Does not conflict signify a breakdown in tolerance? Are Africans often prone to interethnic violence? Muslims are accused of the Jihad mentality.

PILLARS OF A GLOBAL ETHIC

The behaviour of every people is only partially determined by the ethical standards of its culture. Some cultures are born intolerant, some become intolerant and some have intolerance thrust upon them. How much of the violence in the Muslim world is native born and how much has been thrust upon Muslims?

Right now there are three Muslim countries under military occupation— Iraq, Afghanistan and Palestine. Lebanon is periodically devastated, if not destroyed, by Israel. There are other Muslim populations forcefully and sometimes brutally integrated into wider state-systems. This includes the Chechens under Russian occupation, the Kashmiris under Indian rule, the ethnic Albanians in Kosovo under international trusteeship with no hope of self-determination. In the last three years at least two hundred thousand Muslims have been killed in Afghanistan, Iraq, Gujarat, Kashmir, Palestine, Chechnya. In the period since the 1991 Gulf War we may have to add a million more killed by United Nations sanctions in Iraq and by Serbian brutalities in Bosnia, Kosovo and elsewhere, and by the merciless Israeli occupation of the West Bank and Gaza. Counting the number of dead in the world as a whole since 1990, Muslims are a people more sinned against than sinning.

But there is a lot in the ethical code of Islam which recommends forgiveness and compensation rather than revenge. In Chapter 2 Surat el Baqara the Qur'an does not recommend turning the other cheek. It does allow for the legitimacy of retaliation [Al-Qisas] if the injustice is clear, but the surah recommends compensation and forgiveness as a better alternative. [See Sura 2 and such verses as 178]. Indeed, the same Surah goes on to emphasize.

> *"Kind words and the forgiving of faults are better than charity followed by injury." [Surah 2, verse 149]*

And when the Prophet Muhammad conquered Mecca from the ruling Quraysh, he did not issue playing cards of the fifty most wanted Quraysh, as the Americans issued 50 cards of wanted Baathists in Iraq. Muhammad did not imprison thousands as some conquerors have done. The Prophet Muhammad conquered Mecca, granted amnesty to all Quraysh who entered the sacred mosque for asylum, or stayed peacefully in their homes, or found their way to the home of the paramount Quraysh leader, Abu Sufyan—Muhammad's former enemy.

As for the importance of asylum in Islam, it is captured in when the Islamic calendar begins. The Islamic calendar does not begin from when the Prophet Muhammad was born (the year 610 c.e.), or from when the Prophet Muhammad secretly left Mecca in search of asylum in a safer place. The Hijjrah from Mecca to Medina in the Miladiyya year 610 was a quest for religious refuse. The whole Islamic calendar is therefore a celebration of asylum.

In Africa's ethical code, tolerance is partly captured in Africa's short memory of hate. While Islam recommends compensation and forgiveness as a better response than retaliation, Africanity recommends a return to normality without hate after each conflict. The Nigerian civil war of 1967–1970 ended without reprisals and without an African equivalent of the Nuremberg trials. Ian Smith unleashed a racial war on Zimbabwe and lived to sit in Zimbabwe's parliament and criticize the successor Black regime. Nelson Mandela lost twenty-seven of the best years of his life under a white racist regime, and emerged ready to have afternoon tea with the widow of the architect of apartheid, Mrs. Verwoerd.

Jomo Kenyatta was imprisoned by the British and denounced by a British Governor as a "leader unto darkness and death." He emerged from detention and turned Kenya towards a pro-Western orientation in which it has tragically persisted. Kenyatta even published a book entitled Suffering Without Bitterness.

Africans fight deeply and passionately, sometimes ruthlessly, in defense of either their identities or their values. But when the fighting is over, African cultures have a low level of hate-retention. Potentially this could be part of Africa's contribution to the principle of tolerance in the Global Ethic.

The second pillar of wisdom is the optimization of the economic well being of the people. The Muslim world has been privileged to have a disproportionable share of the oil wealth of the human race. Saudi Arabia is a country which accommodates the holiest sites of Islam (Mecca and Medina), but it is also a country which is blessed with the world's greatest oil reserves. Iraq, which accommodates some of the holiest sites of Shia Islam, also accommodates the second largest oil reserves in the world. And the Organization of Oil Exporting Countries is at least two thirds Muslim in composition.

Traditional Islam is basically pro-profit but anti-interest. The oil wealth of the Muslim world challenges Muslim believers to find out where legitimate economic returns end, and illegitimate usury and exploitation begin. Ancient laws of zakat (religious tax) and sadaqah (charity) may need to be transformed for the age of petroleum. But the blessing of oil-wealth can also be the curse of vulnerability to the global strategy of the American Empire.

African economic ethics go back to the concept of ujamaa in Julius K. Nyerere's prescription for postcolonial Tanzania. While the West in the twentieth century had evolved the concept of the welfare state, Africans had evolved even earlier the concept of the welfare tribe. Long before welfare socialism in Britain, Africa had developed a defecto system of collective responsibility for orphans, for the infirm, for the aged, and for the needy. African communities had historically looked after their most vulnerable members.

From former German East Africa (Tanganyika), Julius K. Nyerere expanded this African sense of family (ujamaa) into the basis of modern socialist ethic of sharing. In our own lecture today we go a step further and globalize ujamaa into an ethic for the human family as a whole.

RACE BETWEEN AFRICANITY AND ISLAM

The third pillar of wisdom is social justice. It is a struggle to reduce ethnic and racial inequalities and a quest for a more humane equilibrium. If in terms of political violence in the world Muslims are a people more sinned against than sinning, Africans are similarly more sinned against than sinning in terms of racial prejudice and discrimination. Black people across the centuries have been humiliated, enslaved, colonized, castrated, marginalized and spat upon. The tormentors of Black folks have sometimes been Muslims, sometimes Christians, sometimes others. Blacks have been racial victims per excellence.

The Qur'an tells Muslims that when confronting injustice, reparation is often better than revenge. But Black people are only just beginning to mention the word "reparations" for outright enslavement or for the obscenities of apartheid. In 1992 a summit meeting of the Organization of African Unity appointed a Group of Eminent Persons to explore the modalities and strategies for claiming reparations for Black enslavement. I was among those appointed. One of the biggest problems faced by our Reparations Committee was the relative lack of support from Africans themselves for the reparations crusade.

In terms of the Global Ethic perhaps there should be reparations for Black people, just as there has been reparations for the Jewish people. But reparations can take different forms. For the Jews it consisted of capital transfer from Germany to Jewish survivors and to the State of Israel. For Black people another form of reparations could be skill-transfer—a major global effort in genuine capacity building among devastated Black people. A third kind of reparations could be power sharing—increasing African power in those institutions which have extra power over Africans. There should increased African representation in the governing bodies of the World Bank and the International Monetary Fund, and a permanent seat for Africa on the Security Council. These measures would constitute an attempt to empower Africans after centuries of enfeeblement.

A new kind of Black empowerment is symbolized by Secretary of State Colin Powell, followed by Secretary of State Condoleeza Rice of the United States. These are descendants of slaves who have come to wield power among white people who had once enslaved their ancestors. In other words, one form of reparations is the empowerment of Black people in countries which had previously traded in slaves or practiced slavery.

One day in the future Africans and Arabs would need to negotiate what kind of reparations is feasible for the Arab slave trade. Among the factors which make the Arab slave trade a different system is the Arab lineage system; which regards a child as Arab if the father is Arab, regardless of who the mother is. Thus Sheikh Saad Abdallah Salim al-Sabah became Prime Minister of Kuwait though descended from a Black mother. Anwar Saadat was President of Egypt and was not faulted for having a Black mother. Prince Bandar bin Sultan could be a long-lasting distinguished Saudi Ambassador in Washington DC and be genealogically half African. There are millions of people of mixed blood in the Arab world who are classified as Arabs. This is vastly a different system from the United States where a child is Black if either parent is Black, even if the father is a White Anglo-Saxon Protestant (a WASP).

In the Royal Houses of Kuwait and Saudi Arabia, where some of the princes have African mothers, which prince would pay reparations to which? A wholly different formula would have to be devised if any reparations were to be negotiated in the future concerning the Arab slave trade.

As for the position of the Islamic religion on the race question, it is arguable that Islam is the most racially egalitarian of all three Abrahamic religions—Judaism, Christianity and Islam. Judaism has a doctrine of "the Chosen People" which has often been genealogically interpreted. European Christianity has a long history of racial segregation, including the racial segregation of churches. Such church segregation has persisted to the present day in the United States. To the best of our knowledge the twelve disciples of Jesus were all genealogically Hebrew. But the Prophet Muhammad's disciples—the Sahaba—were multicultural in composition, including the famous Black Sahaba, Bilal son of Rabah, who was the first to call believers to prayer at the great Kaaba in Mecca when Muslims reconquered it from the Quraysh. Bilal was a companion of the Prophet Muhammad, and is widely revered today as the first Black man to embrace Islam.

The Qur'an tells Muslims that they have been created into nations and tribes mainly so that they could know each other.[2] And the Prophet Muhammad said to his followers, more explicitly:

> An Arab is not superior to a
> non-Arab, nor a red man
> to a black man except
> through piety and virtue

Islam thus brings to the Global Ethic a doctrine of racial egalitarianism which goes back fourteen centuries. Where the historical record of Islam is less impressive is with regard to the fourth pillar of wisdom—equality between men and women. Let us turn to this issue of gender in the experience of both Muslims and Africans.

GENDER BETWEEN AFRICANITY AND ISLAM

In addition to the disciplines of the clock, the calendar, the numerals and the letters, has Islam also introduced into Black Africa a new discipline of gender? Indigenous cultures in Africa gave more roles to women than Islam did, while Islam gave more rights to women than indigenous culture had.

On the whole, the gender discipline of Islam in Black Africa had, on the whole, been negative. Under Islamic influence the roles of women in Black Africa have become more restricted as compared with indigenous culture. But the rights of women in inheritance have improved under Islam than under indigenous traditions. Women are owning more under Islam than under native customary law. But what about the role of women in the wider Islamic experience? Africans and Arabs should pay attention to trends in the wider Muslim world.

Although the Prophet Muhammad's widow Ayesha set the precedent of Muslim women in combat roles on the battlefield, there is general consensus among Muslim jurists that killing women or children is beyond the pale.

This has to be seen in the context of three varieties of sexism evident in human behavior, not uniquely Islamic. Benevolent sexism is a form of gender discrimination which selectively favors the otherwise disadvantaged gender. For example, when in 1912 the captain of the Titanic decided that the limited space on the lifeboats was to be reserved for women and children, that was a form of benevolent sexism with which most cultures would agree. The safety of women and children came first.

Most cultures would also agree that while women may have a duty to die for their faith or for their country, women do not have a duty to kill for their faith or their country. Even in the West drafting women for direct combat has been culturally repugnant. Forcing women to go and kill has tended to be avoided in most cultures, including Western and Islamic, least until recently.

In spite of Ayesha's role in the Battle of the Camel, benevolent sexism in Islam has spared women obligatory combat roles. African Muslim women have similarly been demilitarized, except perhaps in Somalia from time to time.

In addition to benevolent sexism, there is benign sexism. This benign sexism is of differentiation rather than of discrimination. A policy of different dress codes for men and women has been part of the sexism of differentiation in Islam. There are different rules of modesty for male and female. In most cultures women are expected to cover more of their bodies than men. The Swahili buibui is part of the local female dress code.

In addition to benevolent sexism and benign sexism, there is the third version of malignant sexism. This is the kind of gender discrimination which results in sexual exploitation, economic marginalization, cultural subordination or political disempowerment. Although many Muslim countries are guilty of such versions of malignant sexism, there are paradoxes in the Muslim world. In no Muslim country are women more liberated than women are in the United States, but in some Muslim countries women have been more empowered than women have been in the United States.

Right now two Muslim countries outside Africa have women as heads of state or heads of government. Indonesia, the largest Muslim country in population, has a woman as President—Megawati Sukarnoputri. In Bangladesh both the Head of Government and the leader of the Opposition have been women—Sheikh Hasina Wajed and Begum Khaleda Zia have alternated in political power for more than a decade.

Two other Muslim countries outside Africa have had a woman chief executive at the top of the political process. Benazir Bhutto has been Prime Minister of Pakistan twice. And Ms. Tansu Ciller has been Prime Minister of Turkey, a far cry from the political culture of the Ottoman Empire.

All these cases of Muslim women at the top have occurred long before the United States has had a woman president, or Germany a woman Chancellor, or Italy a woman Prime Minister, or Russia a woman President. But Asian Muslims have been ahead of Africans in this empowerment.

While serving as heads of government such Muslim women in those countries have been de facto Commanders-in-Chief. Were they continuing in the tradition of the Prophet's widow Ayesha in the middle of the Battle of the Camel way back in the fist century of the Hijrah calendar, the seventh century of the Christian era?

Have any of these Muslim women in power had to contend with terrorism by fellow Muslims? Bangladesh has had conflicts, coups and assassinations over the years, but neither Sheikh Hasina Wajed in power nor Begum Khaleda Zia has had to fight terrorism.

On the other hand, Megawati Sukarnoputri in Indonesia had been under enormous pressure to act against Islamic militants, especially since the devastating terrorist bombs in the resort town of Bali.

Muslims are not unique in resorting to terrorism in a bid to redress wrongs perpetrated against them. But terrorism by Muslims gets far more publicity as a rule than terrorism by others. What all cultures and all religions are being forced to scrutinize more closely than ever are the detailed ethics of terrorism. Black Africa is caught up in the crossfire between Middle Eastern militancy and the American war on terror. In Eastern Africa Uganda has led the way in the political empowerment of women. It was a Muslim President of Uganda, Field Marshall Idi Amin, who appointed the first woman Foreign Minister in Eastern Africa. This was two decades before Bill Clinton appointed the first woman Secretary of State in American history. And Liberia has at last elected Ellen Johnson-Sirleaf as the first woman president in Africa.

Although appointed by a Muslim Head of State, Foreign Minister Elizabeth Bagaya of Uganda was not herself a Muslim. President Yoweri Museveni has since carried female empowerment in Uganda even further. Uganda under Museveni has known a woman Vice-President long before the United

States has had one. Yet once again the highest ranking Ugandan women have not yet been Muslims. In Africa as a whole the political empowerment of Muslim women still has a long way to go, though military regimes have sometimes opened more doors to women than have civilian governments. Somaliland, the Anglophone part of Somalia currently separated from Mogadisho, has a very distinguished woman Foreign Minister.

In the experience of both Muslims and Africans the gender question is still problematical. But there are plusses as well as minuses in what these two civilizations can demonstrate to a human race still struggling to achieve gender equity.

THE ECOLOGICAL PILLAR OF WISDOM

Let us now turn to the environmental pillar of wisdom– the quest for ecological balance and the protection of Planet Earth against excessive exploitation and devastation. Muslims have often chosen green as the colour of Islam, partly because green was associated with peace. But from the middle of the twentieth century the colour green has also been adopted by environmental movements, by those who are committed to keep the hills and valleys of Planet Earth forever green. In this ecological sense we may indeed ask: how "green" is Islam doctrinally and in practice? And how ecology-friendly is African culture?

Environmentally there is a remarkable contrast between the ancestral homeland of Islam and the ancestral core of sub-Saharan Africa. Islam was born in a region which was ecologically sparse and dry. Equatorial Africa, on the other hand, is a region of lush natural abundance, including equatorial forests. The Arabian peninsular as the birthplace of Islam is a region of limited natural rainfall and limited water supply. Equatorial Africa, on the other hand, is a region of tropical downpours and some of the greatest rivers and lakes on the face of the world.

It is in that sense that the dry geography of Islamic origins and the abundant geography of equatorial Africa have represented striking contrasts in the ecological heritage of Planet Earth.

There is a related paradox with regard to the geographical origins of Islam. The Arabian lands which were so short of water during the Prophet Muhammad's time were destined to become lands of abundant oil fourteen centuries later. Lands which once celebrated oases of water became lands which celebrated oases of oil. The greatest oil reserves were discovered beneath the ground where the Prophet and his companions once walked. A religion which taught its followers how to clean themselves with sand (tayamam) when they ran out of water later discovered God's petro-bounty beneath the sand.

A more negative paradox about petroleum is the extent to which it has often been a threat to the "greenness" of Planet Earth. While Arabia itself has
been less environmentally damaged by petroleum than, say, Ogoniland in
Nigeria, petrowealth in Saudi Arabia has been culturally corrosive. Much of
the pristine Islamicity of the Arabian Holyland has been compromised by
grotesque buildings and the glittering names of Western tourist hotels. The
days of water shortage in Arabia were more spiritually authentic than the new
era of the abundance of oil.

Unlike Islam, Africa's traditional religion draws no sharp distinction about
where the Creator ends and the created begins. More clearly in African religion than in Islam particular rivers and hills may be sacred, particular trees
like the baobab may be worthy of awe.

Islam has profane animals (especially the pig) but no sacred animals (such
as the cow in Hinduism). African traditional religions, on the other hand, have
both sacred and profane animals. Indeed, some African ethnic and clan cultures have totems which identify with particular animals (e.g. the owl totem
for a clan, or a totem of the hippo or monkey).

Sometimes the struggle against environmental degradation and the struggle
for morally accountable economies are inseparable. Particularly poignant in
1995 was the plight of the Ogoni people of Nigeria and the brutal fate of Ken
Saro-Wiwa in the full glare of a Commonwealth conference in New Zealand.
The environment of the Ogoni villagers was devastated by the oil industry in
their areas—and Ken Saro-Wiwa and eleven others were executed partly for
protesting in ways which were unacceptable to the military in Nigeria.

The green revolution has also sought to protect the dwindling legacy of wild
animals against the greed of hunters, poachers and corrupt politicians. But is
there also a danger that as far as Westerners are concerned, "one hippo is worth
two Hutus!"? In other words, are the agricultural and pastoral needs of Africa's
expanding populations being sacrificed to the whims of nature lovers?

There is indeed a genuine dilemma. In many African countries independence for African people has meant less freedom for African animals. Widening political horizons for African people have coincided with narrowing physical horizons for African animals. Postcolonial African authorities have been
far less effective in protecting African animals than the colonial authorities
had been. What nature lovers sometimes forget is that post-colonial African
authorities have been less effective in protecting African people too. The cost
of learning how to govern ourselves has sometimes been high. But we do
need to learn self-government in any case. It is a stage we have to go through.

On the other hand, the African animals have been lucky that the post-colonial era has coincided with the new ecological revolution. Post-coloniality
has coincided with the rise of the green movements.

While some human beings are indeed fast depleting the heritage of Planet Earth, other human beings are on greater ecological alert than ever before in history. Alexander Pope's couplet has been given a new ecological meaning:

> "All are but parts of one stupendous whole
> Whose body Nature is and God the Soul"

The environmental depletion is worse today than ever in history. But the environmental defenders are more active than ever before, in history. On balance the Asian and African environment has suffered because of independence but the Asian and African environment would have suffered even more if the era of independence had not coincided with the newly energized environmental consciousness worldwide.

The ethical revolution of environmentalism is partly helping to discipline the earlier ethical revolution of race. The struggle for the rights of people of colour is by no means over yet. But now there is concern for the rights of the leopard and the rhino, the rights of fish in the rivers and oceans, the green rights of valleys and hills. These two are "strangers in our midst," deserving asylum.

The environmental revolution and the gender revolution are interlinked at various points. But they are interconnected most poignantly through the issue of population and the whole culture of having and rearing children. It is to this area of convergence between gender, population and environment that we must now turn.

Many African countries have been witnessing their population double every 20 years. Children under 15 years of age probably account for 45% of the populations of Africa—as compared with 37% in Asia and 40% in Latin America.

Infant mortality is still very high. In some years Black Africa accounts for 5 million out of 7 million annual infant deaths—although Black Africa has less than one-sixth of the population of the developing world and only about a tenth of the population of the world.

Africans have many children for a variety of reasons, including, on the one hand, the assumption that children are an insurance for old age when parents will need to be looked after and, on the other hand, the belief that children are (in African tradition) a passport to immortality beyond the grave: We are not dead as long as our blood flows in the veins of the living. This is the phase of Sasa: The living dead still being remembered by their descendants.

Genes are a memory of ancestry. The struggle continues.

THE AESTHETICS OF THE ENVIRONMENT

The environmental movement of the twentieth century was only partly inspired by a concern for population growth, planetary survival, and an economic cost-benefit analysis. It was also inspired by the aesthetics for conservation. The concept of "endangered species" has been a deference of biodiversity, rooted in the belief that a world with fewer species of animals and a smaller range of plants was a less beautiful world.

On this issue of natural beauty one question which has arisen is whether the love of flowers was culturally relative. Jack Goody, the distinguished Cambridge anthropologist, has strongly argued that although Africa is rich in plants, African culture is not fascinated by flowers.

> . . . the peoples of Africa did not grow
> domestic flowers, nor yet did they make
> use of wild ones to any significant
> extent in worship, in gift giving or in
> the decoration of the body. . . . But what is perhaps
> more surprising is that flowers,
> neither domesticated nor wild, play
> so little part in the domain of
> design or the creative arts.[3]

Jack Goody goes on to observe that African sculpture provides no striking floral designs. And even in African poetry, songs and proverbs, flowers are relatively absent unless there is a prior stimulus of Islam or some other external aesthetic.

George Bernard Shaw was once visited by a flower-loving aristocratic fan. The lady visitor observed that there were no flowers inside Shaw's home. "Mr. Shaw, I am surprised to see no flowers in your beautiful home. Don't you love flowers, Mr. Shaw?"

Bernard Shaw responded: "Indeed I do love flowers, dear lady. I also love children. But I do not go around chopping off their heads for display in my living room!" Shaw was asserting that a genuine love of flowers required our leaving them to prosper as plants in the soil. There is a sense in which African attitudes to flowers is organic in the same sense.

Yet this does not explain the more limited use of the imagery of flowers in either African plastic art or African verbal arts.

Shakespeare urges us not to attempt to beautify what is already naturally beautiful:

> *To gild refined gold, to paint the lily,*
> *To throw a perfume on the violet*

> *To smooth the ice, or add another hue*
> *Unto the rainbow . . .*
> *Is wasteful and ridiculous excess.*[4]

In African poetry and song is there an equivalent use of flowers as metaphors "to point a moral or adorn a tale"?

If it is true that African culture underutilizes flowers for either art or ritual, what are the underlying social and aesthetic reasons? One possible explanation would take us back to Bertrand Russell's assertion that "civilization was born out of the pursuit of luxury." It is possible to see civilization as a relentless quest for beauty. It is a sense of "civilization" which produced the Taj Mahal, the sunken churches of Lalibela, the Palace of Versailles, and the spectacular temples of Abu Simbel at Aswam built by Ramses II. Such splendor illustrates what Bertrand Russell regarded as "the pursuit of luxury."

Before European colonization were the cultures of equatorial Africa inadequately motivated to pursue luxury? Was that why there were so few indigenous palaces and monuments outside the Nile Valley? Was the psychology of not constructing beautiful structures related to the psychology of inadequate attention to flowers?

Another possible explanation for the deflowering of African cultures is that so many flowers on the equator were potential fruit in the process of formation. A planted seed begins to germinate into a plant; the plant produces a bud; the bud blossoms into a flower, and the flower culminates into a fruit. Africa celebrates the end product [the fruit] rather than the intermediate stage (the flower). Africa may be poor in names for flowers. In most indigenous cultures there is no tropical equivalent of such range of names as, the lily, the violet, the tulip, the orchid, the daffodil. But African languages are fully competitive in names of fruit:

> —*chungwa, chenzi, embe, bungo, kitoria, nazi, kanju, ndizi, kunazi, fenesi, buyu and many others.*

More recent African loan words for fruit (usually borrowed from Arabic) include *nanasi* (pineapple) and *tufaha* (apple).

In the history of Islam the garden and ecological beauty were initially assigned to paradise in the Hereafter where rivers, lakes, flowers and beautiful women awaited the faithful. However, in the history of Islam and Planet Earth the heritage of flowers initially came more from Persia than from the Arabian Peninsula. The heritage then spread to North Africa. What came to be regarded as distinctively Islamic gardens developed in Tunisia in the ninth century of the Christian era. Jack Goody refers to the evidence of a Flemish traveler in about the year 1470, who seemed to have counted four thousand individually owned, irrigated gardens around the city of Tunis—"full of fruit and with flowers perfuming the air."[5]

The enclosed garden behind walls became a feature of aristocratic residences in the Middle East. Both women and flowers were protected behind enclosures. Among the most spectacular of the gardens of Islamic civilization were the Moorish ones of Alhamra in Southern Spain, whose scale can be gleaned to the present day.

The representation of flowers in pictures and drawings was doctrinally discouraged by some denominations of Islam. Live gardens were fully permitted, but their artistic representation of flowers flourished in the arts of carpet making in Persia, Turkey and elsewhere. Indeed, aristocratic homes in much of the Muslim world were full of representational art, including sinful lewd pictures and pornographic paintings.

A cost-benefit analysis needs to be done as to whether Islam's encouragement of gardens and discouragement of organic representation is compatible with the fifth pillar of the Global Ethic. Similarly is Africa's coolness towards flowers and Africa's warmth towards fruit ecologically friendly? Such aspects of Islamic and African cultures need to be studied and evaluated from the perspective of the Fifth Pillar of Wisdom (Ecological).

INTER-FAITH RELATIONS: GAINS AND LOSSES

No Global Ethic is sustainable without involving the great religions of the world. How has the preceding century affected the chances and quality of inter-faith dialogue? In order to answer that question we need to return to the long-term consequences of World War I and the mission of T. E. Lawrence in the Middle East—the subject with which we opened this chapter.

We mentioned earlier that the collapse of the Ottoman Dynasty marked the last of the great Muslim empires in world history. It led to the end of the Caliphate, which had been a symbol of Muslim solidarity for thirteen centuries. It led on to the secularization of Turkey, thus depriving the Muslim Middle East of a great military power. And in the course of World War I, and with the prospect of Ottoman defeat, Lord Balfour issued his momentous Declaration about national home for the Jews.

How World War I ended was one of the major causes of World War II. The humiliating conditions imposed on Germany created the sense of outrage in Germany which facilitated the rise of Hitler. In World War I Germany had lost her African empire. In World War II under Hitler, Germany sought to create an empire in Europe.

How have these events affected inter-faith dialogue? Hitler's slaughter and brutalization of the Jews severely damaged relations between Christian churches and the Jews in the short run. But in the longer run the scale of the Holocaust and the martyrdom of the Jews under the Nazis brought Jews and Christians in the Western world closer together than they had ever been since the days of the Roman Empire. It is unlikely that Mel Gibson's film, The Passion of the Christ, would affect the rapronhent. One healthy reason for the Christian-Jewish rapprochement was a heightened Western awareness of the evil dangers of ethno-religious bigotry. But there was an unhealthy reason also for the Christian-Jewish rapprochement. This was the enormity of guilt felt by Western Gentiles—a depth of guilt so great that Western support rapidly grew for the creation of a national home for the Jews, provided such a home was not created on European soil.

The Zionist movement had previously received offers of territory for Jewish settlement in Uganda, Kenya, South America. These offers of other people's land for a national home for the Jews were made mainly by European leaders. Britain's Colonial Secretary Joseph Chamberlain offered parts of Uganda and Kenya to the Zionist movement early in the twentieth century. What European leaders never offered European Jews was a piece of Europe for the creation of a national home for the Jews. Creating Israel on a piece of German territory after World War II would have been poetic justice indeed.

Instead Palestinians paid the ultimate price for the atrocities and brutalities of the Nazis against the Jews. This diversion of "the Jewish Question" from Europe to the Middle East helped Christian-Jewish rapprochement in Europe. Western gentiles were so afraid of being accused of anti-Semitism that the State of Israel could do no wrong. Never since Hitler's Germany had a state behaved with such impunity towards its neighbors as Israel has been in recent decades. Ordinary citizens and the media in European countries have begun to raise their voices against Israel's brutal occupation of Palestine, but one keeps waiting for a public reprimand of Israel from a major Western leader.

Unfortunately, the creation of Israel and its aftermath have put unprecedented stress between Muslims and Jews. Relations between the global ummah and world Jewry have probably never been under greater strain in fourteen centuries than they are today. Two major reasons have poisoned Muslim-Jewish understanding. One is the behavior of the State of Israel. The second is the almost spontaneous tendency of world Jewry to rally behind Israel and attack those who criticize it.

Western sense of guilt over the Nazi Holocaust has on the whole helped relations between Christians and Jews, but Western appeasement of the Zionist movement have damaged relations between Muslims and Jews. About ten years separated two documents of momentous consequences for the Middle East—one was indeed the Balfour Declaration of 1917 and the other was Hitler's Mein Kampf of 1927. The Balfour Declaration was controversial but was in the tradition of "the British fudge." Mein Kampf by Adolf Hitler was a work of evil. But in their vastly different ways the two documents unleashed forces which favored the long-term aims of the Zionist movement. Israel was indeed created, and the world has never been the same since.

In the days of T. E. Lawrence Jerusalem was "sacred but squalid." In the words of Lawrence of Arabia:

> . . . Jerusalem was a squalid town which every Semitic religion has made holy. Christians and Mohammedans came here on pilgrimage to the shrines of their past, and some Jews looked to it for the political future of their race. These united forces of the past and the future were so strong that the city almost failed to have a present.[6]

Jerusalem is still excessively preoccupied with the past and the future. But it also has a present, however tumultuous and painful.

We have argued that since the days of Lord Balfour and Hitler relations between Christians and Jews have improved enormously, while relations between Muslims and Jews have deteriorated. But what about relations between Muslims and Christians?

There has been some stress on relations between the Muslim world and the West, but the tensions are not between churches and mosques, but between Muslims and Western secular power. In this case the central cause of tension and hate is not Israel alone, but also the United States as a hegemonic power. America's pro-Israeli policies are part of the problem but not the only one.

Increasingly, in the course of the twentieth century the United States became a new kind of empire. The new American Empire is an empire not of occupation, but of control; not a land-hungry hegemone but a resource-hungry colossus.

Militarily American might adds up to the military power of the next ten countries added together. In global reach, the United States has some degree of military presence in nearly one hundred countries already.

In production, the American economy is the indispensable engine of the world economy. Technologically, the U.S. is not only independently triumphant; it is also a major magnet of the technological expertise of the rest of the world. There was a time when the brain drain consisted of talented people migrating physically to the West. But now the technological skills of South Asians can be used by American industry without having to import the South Asians to the United States. The West is buying the brains of India without buying the bodies.

Lord Lugard, Britain's greatest colonial administrator, devised a strategy for British colonial rule in Africa. Lugard called the policy "Indirect Rule," which became the guiding principle of governance in British Africa.

Lugard's idea was that the British should seek to rule Africans through their own "Native Authorities" as much as possible. Subject peoples were best ruled through institutions and customs which they understood. But in the final analysis, British rule required the military might of Pax Britannica to keep control.

The question arises whether the new American Empire is a latter-day case of "Indirect Rule." Are "Native Authorities" allowed to remain in power, but only as long as they do not stray far from the designs of Pax Americana? The new strategy of regime-change is the latter-day equivalent of destooling a recalcitrant African Chief. The foreign policy of the United States seems to be driven by a latter-day Lord Lugard.

Iraq and Afghanistan have been invaded partly to effect regime-change. The United States has sought to marginalize Yassir Arafat as a partial regime change in Palestine. Libya has given up its right to pursue weapons of mass destruction, perhaps partly out of fear of regime change. The Bush Administration has recommended regime change in Iran. Israel has recommended regime change in Syria. This is becoming a pattern of destooling uncompliant chiefs.

At least as distressing are the Muslim chiefs and emirs who are protected by the United States against change. Many undemocratic Muslim regimes derive part of their stability from the United States. A significant number of Muslim countries are de facto American protectorates, although their people are against American control.

FROM BALFOUR TO BUSH

Anti-Western sentiment in the Muslim world is just a version of anti-American sentiment. Even the new Anglophobia in the Muslim world is a derivation of Blair-phobia—an angry disgust with Tony Blair. Blair seems to be less afraid of regime change in Britain by the British electorate than an imaginary regime change in Britain by American power. The ominous shadow of George W. Bush is upon Tony Blair.

Mainstream Christian churches in the West are much more Muslim-friendly today than they were in the days of the Ottoman Empire. But there are fringe evangelical movements in the United States which have become more Islamophobic than ever. The Prophet Mohammad has been given worse names since September 11 than at any time since the days of anti-Turkish sentiment at the beginning of the twentieth century. Ironically, the Ottoman Empire had a more humane system of autonomy for religious minorities (the millet system) than that practiced by any Western power either at that time or since then.

The contradictions have persisted from the old days of the Ottoman Empire to the new era of the American Empire. It is arguable that while the Ottoman Empire was bad for the Arabs, it was good for Islam in world affairs. T. E. Lawrence helped the Arabs against the Ottomans, but he may at the same time have harmed Islam in the long run. The Ottomans had kept Turkey Muslim and independent of the West. The Turkish Republic is making Turkey secular and part of the West. Turkish women have won the freedom to be members of Parliament, but they have lost the freedom to cover their heads with a scarf.

Underlying it all is a monumental transition from the era of Lord Balfour as a representative of the old British Empire to George W. Bush as a symbol of the new American Empire.

As for relations between Christianity and Islam in Africa, both religions are expanding in numbers and growing in influence. But can they co-exist peacefully? Christianity and Islam are divisive in Africa only if they reinforce prior ethnic and linguistic divisions.

In Nigeria almost all Hausa are Muslims, almost all Igbo are Christians, and the Yoruba are split in the middle. Thus Islam reinforces Hausa identity; Christianity reinforces Igbo identity and Yoruba nationalism unites the Yoruba regardless of religion.

Islam and Christianity divide Northern and Southern Sudan mainly because the two regions were already divided by even deeper cultural differences. The two regions belonged to two different indigenous civilizations even before they were either Islamized or Christianized.

On the other hand, Muslims in Senegal repeatedly voted for a Christian president. For twenty years Leopold Sedar Senghor, a Roman Catholic, was President of a country which was over ninety percent Muslim Abdou Diouf. Leopold Senghor was succeeded for another twenty years by a Muslim president of Senegal. The Muslim president had a Roman Catholic First Lady. This degree of ecumenical democracy has not been achieved in the Western world. No Western democracy has ever elected either a Jew or Muslim for President. Joseph Lieberman, a distinguished Jewish Senator in the United States, trailed far behind in his bid for the Democratic presidential nomination in the 2003–2004 primaries.

As for the distinguished British Tory Benjamin Disraeli, there is general consensus that he would never have become Prime Minister of Great Britain in the nineteenth century had his Dad, Isaac D'Israeli, not quarreled with his Synagogue of Bevis Marks, and then decided to have his children baptized as Christians. After all until 1858 Jews by religion were not allowed even to run for parliamentary elections in Britain, let alone become ministers.

On the other hand, Tanzania has had a religiously rotating presidency. Julius K. Nyerere, a Catholic, was succeeded by Ali Hassan Mwinyi, a Muslim, who in turn was followed by Benjamin Mkapa, a Christian. Will the next Tanzanian president be Salim Ahmed Salim, a Muslim? The religious rotation may indeed continue.

Nigeria has not yet developed a religiously rotating presidency. But there are advocates of a regionally rotating Nigerian presidency, alternating between the north and the south. Such regional alternation could, de facto, be a religious alternation in the Nigerian presidency.

Africa had no religious wars before the arrival of Islam and Christianity. But now that Africa has embraced its own Islam and Christianity, the Africans are developing ecumenical attitudes to religion which are far ahead of the rest of the world. The ecumenical spirit of Africa may be part of its contribution to the Global Ethic and to the sixth pillar of wisdom.

TOWARDS GREATER WISDOM: THE SEVENTH PILLAR

The seventh pillar of wisdom is a relentless quest for greater wisdom. An important part of this area of wisdom is the pursuit of creative synthesis. The synthesis may be between ethics and knowledge, between religion and science, and between one culture and another. It is arguable that Islam was historically at its most creative when it was ready to learn mathematics from India, philosophy from ancient Greece, architecture from Persia, science from the Jews, and jurisprudence from the legacy of Rome.

Muslims believe that God's first words to the Prophet Muhammad were indeed about knowledge; and God's first command to the prophet was the imperative Iqra ("Read"). These earliest Qur'anic verses linked biological sciences with the sciences of the mind.

Moreover, by proclaiming that all knowledge is ultimately from God, these verses warned against the arrogance of pseudo-omniscience among humans. Science was morally accountable:

1. *Read in the name of thy Lord who created—*
2. *Created the human person out of a mere clot of congealed blood;*
3. *Read and thy Lord is most bountiful;*
4. *He who taught by the pen;*
5. *Taught man that which he knew not.*
6. *Yet man does transgress all bounds.*
7. *In that he looketh upon himself.*
8. *Verily to the Lord is the final return.*

[Sura Iqra or Alaq, verses 1–8]

God "taught by the pen." In contemporary terms, "the pen" could be extended to include teaching by the computer and the Internet. God taught human beings "that which they knew not." Within the last one hundred years alone this has included splitting the atom, landing a man on the moon, sending a spacecraft to Mars, cloning a sheep and exploring cyberspace.[7]

The distinctive aspect of early Islam as a civilization was precisely this readiness to synthesize what was best from other cultures. Those early Qur'anic verses stressed that all real knowledge came fro God regardless of which human being (ominsaan) discovered it. Every successful scientific discovery helped to reveal more of God.

This early Muslim readiness to learn from other civilizations declined. By the second half of the Ottoman era in the eighteenth century the Muslim world was getting to be scientifically marginal. By the nineteenth century the Ottoman Dynasty was widely regarded as "the sick man of Europe." The corruption of Muslim rulers, the walls of theological legalism against innovation, the increasing Ottoman tendency to imitate the West rather than learn from the West, had weakened the Dynasty long before it collapsed during World War I. Hypothetically, Ottoman creativity could have been rehabilitated with new and better leadership. But World War I, the Arab revolt and T. E. Lawrence deprived the Ottomans of any further opportunities to re-invent themselves.

Unfortunately the Arab nations which emerged out of Ottoman and European colonization did not fare much better scientifically or technologically. The heavy hand of cultural obscurantism continued to impede Arab advancement.

In this new millennium The Arab Human Development Report 2003 criticized "the alliance between some oppressive regimes and certain types of conservative scholars"—an alliance which seemed to lead to "interpretations of Islam which . . . are inimical to human development particularly with regard to freedom of thought, the accountability of the regimes to the people and women's participation in public life."[8]

The report on Arab Human Development discusses "the knowledge gap" in the Arab world in spite of petrowealth. According to the report, only 53 copies of newspapers are sold per 1,000 people in Arab countries, compared to 285 in the West. Less than two percent of the Arab population had Internet access. There are only 18 computers per 1,000 people as compared with a global average of 78.3.

As for scientists and engineers in the Arab world, there are only 371 in research and development per million resident citizens as compared with a global average of 979 per million. How much of this knowledge gap and intellectual deficit is due to a version of Islam which is no longer responsive to creative cultural synthesis?

In South Asia Pakistan has broken through the nuclear barrier and succeeded in giving the Muslim world its first nuclear power. In other respects
Malaysia had been the most successful Muslim—led country in the world.
Yet Prime Minister Mahathir Mohamad used his Swan song of retirement in
2003 to call upon fellow Muslims to close the knowledge gap between themselves and such adversaries as the Zionists. Mahathir Mohamad knew only
too well that even in Malaysia itself he had had a tough time trying to close
the knowledge gap between Muslim Malays and non-Muslim ethnic Chinese.
Economically and technologically Malays had still lagged behind their ethnic
Chinese compatriots. All evidence suggests that the Chinese had been better
at "creative synthesis of cultures" than the Malays had been.

Paradoxically the Prophet Muhammad had called upon his followers to
pursue knowledge "even as far as China." That was fourteen centuries earlier.
Was the message of Muhammad prophetic for Malay's relations with ethnic
Chinese in both Malaysia and Indonesia? Or did the Prophet anticipate
Samuel Huntington's worry at the end of the twentieth century about an
emerging alliance between Islam and countries of the Confrican heritage?

First the angel Gabriel calls upon the Prophet Muhammad to read in the
name of God who had taught by the pen. Then Gabriel assures Muhammad
that all knowledge comes from God anyhow. Then the Prophet calls upon his
followers to pursue knowledge as far as China. And on the eve of the twenty-
first century Samuel Huntington worries about an alliance between China and
the Muslim world, while others identify active collaboration between North
Korea and Pakistan. Is the Prophet Muhammad's prophecy in the process of
fulfillment?[9]

The question arises whether the Global Ethic would be better served by a
new multipolar world than by a world with only one superpower. Does the
Global Ethic require global checks and balances which would include the influence of China, the leverage of the Muslim world, as well as the power of
the West?

As for African, its credentials for a global role in the twenty first century
are still in terms of natural resources and intrinsic cultural values, rather than
in technological skills.

But Africa thinkers are in disagreement about the relationship between wisdom, on one side, and technical skills, on the other. Philosophers of romantic
gloriana emphasize the monumental achievements of Africa's past, ranging
from the pyramids of Egypt to the brooding majesty of Great Zimbabwe.
Without necessarily realizing it, such gloriana thinkers seem to share part of
Betrand Russell's conviction that civilization is the pursuit of luxury.

The greatest of Africa's postcolonial gloriana thinkers was Cheikh Anta
Diop of Senegal, who emphasized ancient Egypt's pivotal role in the origins

of world civilization as a whole. Diop saw the River Nile as the mother of the earliest human achievements.

The other major African school of civilizational theory has emphasized not the grand monuments of Africa's structural achievements but the wisdom of being non-technical. In the words of the Black poet of Martinique, Aime Cesaire:

> *Hooray for those who never invented anything!*
> *Hooray for those who never discovered anything;*
> *Hooray for joy, hooray for love;*
> *Hooray for the pain of incarnate tears . . .*
>
> *Honor to those have invented neither powder nor the compass;*
> *Those who have tamed neither gas nor electricity;*
> *Those who have explored neither the seas nor the skies . . .*
>
> *My negritude [my Blackness] is neither a tower nor a cathedral;*
> *It plunges into the deep red flesh of the soil.*[10]

Western thought has a sub field called the "philosophy of science." What this simplifying school of African thought represents is a philosophy of unscience. As Jean-Paul Sartre pointed out, this African reveling in not having invented either powder or the compass is a proud celebration of non-technicalness. It is a salute to the wisdom of closeness to nature.[11]

The greatest African thinker of this simplifying school was also Senegalese. The late Leopold Sedar Senghor, who was President of Senegal from 1960 to 1980, was a philosopher and a poet, as well as a statesman. Senghor argued that while Cartesian epistemology starts from the premise "I think, therefore I am," African epistemology starts from the vastly different source of self-awareness—"I feel, therefore I am." Senghor belonged to the philosophy of unscience, in contrast to his gloriana compatriot, Cheikh Anta Diop.[12]

As we seek to construct a Global Ethic based on seven pillars of wisdom, we need to listen to those two competing philosophies about the relationship between expertise, on one side, and genuine wisdom, on the other. We need also to listen to Africa's song of self-affirmation as captured in the following poetic prose:

"We are a people of the day before yesterday and a people of the day after tomorrow. Long before slavery we lived in one huge village called Africa. And then strangers came into our midst and took many of us away, scattering us to all the corners of the earth. Before those strangers came, our village was the world; we knew no other. But we are now spread out so widely that the Sun never sets on the descendants of Africa. The world is now our village, and we plan to make it more human between now and the day after tomorrow."[13]

Wisdom begins when we understand ourselves. Wisdom matures when we aspire to higher human standards. How we treat strangers in our midst is the ultimate humane standard.

CONCLUDING SUMMARY

We have interpreted the history of the relations between the Muslim world and the West as a tumultuous transition from the collapse of the Ottoman Empire after the end of World War I to the rise of the American Empire after the end of the Cold War. The collapse of the Ottoman Empire was in part of fragmentation of the Arab world, its recolonization by Britain and France, and the demise of the Caliphate. The rise of the American empire subsequently exploited the Arab fragmentation. Muslims also confronted the alienating consequences of the end of the Muslim Caliphate. Lord Balfour's Declaration of 1917 unleashed forces which culminated in the creation of Israel.

T. E. Lawrence [Lawrence of Arabia] contributed to the collapse of the Ottoman Empire. Lawrence was a "Stranger in the Arab World." He symbolized how strangers in our midst could change the course of our history. Lawrence first published his momentous work, The Seven Pillars of Wisdom, in 1926. This chapter presumes to propose Seven Pillars of Wisdom for the new century.

In the face of the new American hegemony, the new pillars of wisdom need to add up to a Global Ethic. The first of our new pillars of wisdom has to be a quest for tolerance and minimization of violence. Are Africa and Islam conflict prone? Who forged the link between terrorism and political Islam? We have addressed some of those questions.

The second new pillar of wisdom is surely the optimization of the economic well being of the people. T. E. Lawrence lived through the Russian revolution and its aftermath of ideological egalitarianism. How egalitarian are the cultures of Islam and Africa? We have touched upon the political economy of Islam and the African experience.

The third new pillar of wisdom is the quest for social justice. It is a struggle to reduce ethnic and racial inequalities and a quest for a humane equilibrium. We have found Islam to be the most egalitarian of the Abrahamic religions. We have found Africa worthy of reparations for centuries of racial injustice.

The fourth new pillar of wisdom is a basic gender equality. This is a major change from the world of T.E Lawrence. How have Islam and Africa treated women? We have examined gains and losses for women in Africa and the Muslim world.

The fifth pillar of wisdom is a quest for ecological balance. T. E. Lawrence was enchanted by the culture of the desert. What is strongly needed is a wider responsiveness to ecological conservation and environmental balance, ranging from population policy to the culture of flowers. Even the wild animals are "strangers in our midst," seeking asylum. Is Africa ecology-friendly? Is Islam "green"?

There is also the sixth pillar of inter-faith dialogue and cooperation. Islam reaffirms that "there is no compulsion in religion. What about tensions with Christians and Jews? There were no religious wars in Africa before Christianity and Islam arrived.

The seventh pillar of wisdom is the quest for further wisdom. This is a struggle for new knowledge, restrained by humane wisdom. The Prophet of Islam urged his followers to seek wisdom as far as China. Was the Prophet predicting a future alliance between Islam and modern China?

Perspectives on these new seven pillars of wisdom have to respond to the Middle East as a normative center of global culture and to Africa as a challenge to the global conscience. Lawrence of Arabia initiated a process. Whither the AMERICAN EMPIRE? How is it affecting the future of Islam and the African condition? The search for greater wisdom continues.

NOTES

I am indebted to Thomas Uthup and Muhammad Yusuf Tamim for research and bibliographical assistance.

1. T. E. Lawrence, Seven Pillars of Wisdom (Privately Printed 1926, published by Jonathan Cape in 1935 and by Penguin Books in 1962) See Introductory Chapter.

2. Details to follow.

3. Jack Goody, *The Culture of Flowers* [Cambridge Press, 1993] pp. 12–13.

4. King John, Act IV Scene 1.

5. Jack Goody, *The Culture of Flowers* Ibid, p. 105.

6. T. E. Lawrence, *Seven Pillars of Wisdom* (first published in 1926) [New York: Penguin Books, Modern Classics, 1976 edition] p. 341.

7. These issues are discussed more fully in Ali A. Mazrui and Alamin M. Mazrui, "Islam and Civilization" chapter in *Dialogue of Civilizations: A New Peace Agenda* eds. Majid Tehranian and David W. Chapell (New York: L.B. Tauris 2002) pp. 139 to 160.

8. See the Report on the website of the United Nations Development Programme (UNDP).

9. See Samuel Huntington, *The Clash of Civilizations and the Remaking of World Order* [New York: Simon & Schuster, 1996].

10. Aime Césaire, "Return to Native Land" ???

11. J. P. Sartre, (1963) pp. 41–3.

12. Leopold Sedar Senghor, See also Ali A. Mazrui and JF Ade Ajayi et al "Trends in Philosophy and Science in Africa," *Africa Since 1935* eds. Ali A. Mazrui and C.Wondjii, *UNESCO General History of Africa*, Vol. Viii. (London: Heinemann Educational Books, 1993).

13. This African song of reaffirmation is paraphrased from programme 9 of Mazrui's television series, *The Africans: A Triple Heritage* (BBC/PBS and Nigeria's Television Authority, 1986).

Chapter Twenty

Islam and the United States: Streams of Convergence, Strands of Divergence

From "The Clash of Civilizations"[1] thesis to September 11, 2001, and from Iraq to the Palestinian-Israeli conflict, the relationship between Islamic values and Western—particularly American—norms in the 20th century appears to casual observers as a story of conflicts. Yet a more careful analysis of the twentieth-century Islamic ummah and Americans suggests a more complex tale of convergences and divergences. Can the 21st century be an era where strands of convergence could overpower the strands of divergence?

We are now able to identify four different phases of relations between America and the Muslim ummah both normatively and politically.

PHASE I

A. Relationships between Euro-American *values* and traditional Islamic *values* were *close* in the first half of the twentieth century. In the areas of sexual behavior, gender roles, alcohol consumption, and the death penalty, Islamic values and Euro-American values converged.

B. Relationships between Euro-American *people* and Muslim *people* as an ummah were *distant* in the first half of that century. Divergences between the two peoples were marked by prejudice and racism.

PHASE II

A. In the second half of the twentieth century, relationships between Euro-American values and traditional Islamic values *diverged*—as America became more ethically and sexually libertarian. Sex, alcohol and drugs were ascending in America. The importance of religion deteriorated markedly in Europe, and to a lesser extent, in the United States. The status of women improved in the Western world.

B. Also in the second half of the twentieth century, relations between the Euro-American people and Muslim people converged—as America became more liberal and the world became more internationalist. The United States (especially after the passage of the Immigration Reform and Control Act of 1965)[2] and Europe began to see large numbers of immigrants from the Muslim world, while more and more Westerners began to visit the Muslim world (particularly the Arab areas) for economic, political, and academic reasons. This was in process from the end of World War II until the end of the 20th century.

PHASE III

A. In this new twenty-first century, the relationship between American values and traditional Islamic values has continued to diverge as America has become even more socially libertarian. America is now flirting with the idea of same-sex marriages—or at least same sex civil unions, truly un-Islamic.

B. Since September 11 the trend of tolerant convergence between American *people* and Muslim *people* has either been interrupted or is being reversed. Most Americans and Muslims [both in the United States and worldwide] are regrettably in the process of being pulled apart. Muslims in the West are routine targets of harassment in various ways, while Westerners in the Muslim world have to be concerned about hatred and consequent physical harm.

PHASE IV

The fourth phase is a deeper democratization of America and the rolling back of the excesses of American social libertarianism. In the Islamic world, there is a recognition of the impotence of current political arrangements to improve economies, and the necessity to reinterpret Islam to bring about the improvement of the human rights of the Islamic ummah. Values on sex, marriage, and gender converge, while differences on democratization and liberalism converge to realize people's differing beliefs and aspirations. People converge through migration, study, and knowledge.

This fourth phase of relations between Euro-America and Islam is really an optimistic scenario about the future rather than a report of what is already happening. In that sense this fourth phase is for the time being perhaps more akin to Martin Luther King Jr.'s "I Have a Dream" speech.

Let us look at these phases now in some detail.

THE FIRST PHASE

In the period between the two World Wars, the social and sexual mores of the United States were much closer to those of a Muslim society than they are today.[3] At the same time, the United States at that time was less tolerant of other races and religions. In social and sexual practices, the US was closer to Islamic values, but in racial and religious prejudice, the two worlds diverged. Let us take a closer look at some of these convergences and divergences.

Sexuality: In the period before World War II, US public mores and opinions opposed premarital sex.[4] The 1920s did see an increase — to almost 50 percent — of women who had premarital sex — but there were limits.[5] There were even laws against sex outside marriage in some states.[6] In the Muslim world, sex before and outside marriage was strongly condemned, with some societies even having "honor killings" for daughters who stray sexually.[7]

Homosexual acts, especially between males, were criminal acts in the United States in the first half of the twentieth century. There are numerous examples of laws that made such activities illegal — some of them until very recently.[8] These acts have been, and remain, illegal throughout most of the Muslim world. For both gay men and lesbians, remaining "in the closet" was the prudent way to live in both Muslim and US societies.

Gender and Family: In the inter-war years the family in America was still as sacrosanct as it is in much of the Muslim world. Unmarried couples living together were rare. Babies born out of wedlock still suffered from social stigma. And the very idea of same-sex marriages or even "civil unions" had not even been conceived.

Families in America in the interwar years still believed in having a head of the family with authority — usually the father or the husband. Unfortunately, both in America and the Muslim world, women were still subordinate.

In the United States, women did not get the vote until after a Constitutional Amendment in 1920. The coming of the franchise for women was sometimes as slow in coming to the Western world as it was in the Muslim world.[9] For many Americans in the interwar period, the idea of a female president was unthinkable. In 1936, the percent of Americans who would vote for a woman if she were qualified to be president was at about 31 percent.[10] The first stirrings of anti-colonial sentiment brought forth a slew of male leaders in much of the Muslim world who would go on to lead their future countries in the immediate aftermath of the post colonial era.

In the economic sectors of society, both in the United States and in the Muslim world, female participation was also very low. In 1936, only 18 percent of Americans approved of a married woman working even if she didn't have to do so for economic reasons.[11] World War II and the rise of "Rosie the Riveter" as a icon of female participation in the labor force was an immediate catalyst for significant female participation in the US labor force.[12] But the return of the men after World War II reversed many of these gains.[13]

What is at stake here is that on the issue of women's liberation, the United States and the Muslim world were on the same stage of relative sexism early in the twentieth century.

Against Alcohol: A less enduring normative convergence was *the ban on alcoholic drinks in the history of the United States.* This value was truly neo-Islamic. Initially, prohibition of alcohol was by individual states. The first state law against alcohol was passed in Maine in 1850,[14] and was soon followed by a wave of comparable legislation in other states—rising up to 33 states affecting 63 percent of the population by the end of World War I. Orthodox Muslims around the world probably cheered when they heard about this trend against alcohol in America.

Meanwhile, a campaign for alcoholic prohibition at the *Federal* level had been gathering momentum. A constitutional amendment against alcohol needed a two-thirds majority in Congress and approval by three quarters of the states. Such a constitutional change was ratified on January 29, 1919, and went into effect on January 29, 1920, as the Eighteenth Amendment of the United States' constitution.[15] On the issue of alcohol, the United States became almost Islamic.

Death Penalty: Another area of convergence between Islamic values and American values has been in the acceptance of capital punishment as one of the answers to human depravity.

The most controversial elements of the Sharia are the *hudud* (Islamic physical punishments for criminal offenders). One of the principles the American judicial system continues to share with majority opinion in the Muslim world is the acceptance of the death penalty.

The most controversial of Islamic applications of the death penalty relates to the sexual offense of adultery. The most controversial of American applications of the death penalty relates to killing the mentally retarded and to the execution of juvenile offenders.

At least in Muslim countries, there appears to be little favoritism in the application of the death penalty. Saudi Arabia has been known to put to death even a Princess on charges of adultery.[16] On the other hand, one of the more pernicious practices in the United States is the disproportionate number of African Americas who have been subjected to the death penalty or are on "Death Row."[17]

Attitudes to Differences of Race and Religion: On the single pervasive issue of racism and race-relations, the United States has been much worse than the Muslim world both in the years between the two World Wars and in today's world after the Cold War. But the U.S. itself was much more racist in the 1920s than it is today. This was the era of sweeping segregationist measures, the rise of racist leaders to high political office, and "Jim Crow" laws designed to subjugate African Americans. Lynchings and the "Tuskegee Experiments" typified the parlous condition of African Americans. There were also laws forbidding sex and marriage across the racial divide, and it took a Supreme Court decision (*Loving v. the State of Virginia*)[18] to make them unconstitutional. The decline of racism also led to greater tolerance of interracial marriage.[19]

Religious minorities also suffered from prejudice. In the latter part of the eighteenth century and even during the beginning of the 20th century, Jews and Roman Catholics were victims of violence by the KKK, discriminated against in university admissions, and anti-Semitic statements by prominent authors such as H. L. Mencken were hardly questioned. In this environment, the American lack of tolerance towards Muslims was not surprising. Muslims were profiled as a different race,[20] and various depictions of "Mohammeddans" were often viciously pejorative.

Of course, race in the Muslim world was not much of an issue. It must be remembered that Bilal, one of the closest associates of the Prophet Mohammad, was probably black. The coming together of various races who comprised the Islamic ummah, manifested in the diverse array of colors gathered at the Hajj in Mecca, was not affected even by the centuries of colonial rule and white supremacy. Indeed, for many in the world, this was one of the more attractive features of Islam.[21]

When it came to religious minorities under Islam, the Muslim world practiced the tolerance emphasized by the Quran. Religious minorities such as Jews and Christians lived and flourished in much of the Islamic world.[22] The millet system of the Ottoman Empire exemplified the openness of Muslim societies towards Jews and Christians. Although there were some discriminatory measures (such as the jizya tax), religious minorities such as the Jews did not face organized mass murder, mass pogroms, and state-directed genocides in any Muslim state but did face them in Eastern Europe and Germany. Even in the United States, there was resistance to Jewish immigration.[23]

Overall, in this first phase, the major convergences between the Islamic world and the United States occurred in the areas of sexual behavior, sex roles, alcohol consumption, and the death penalty. The major divergence was on the treatment of racial and religious minorities. Social conservatism of the United States permitted these strands of convergence and divergence with the Islamic world. However, the fabric of some of these conservative values began to fray in the second half of the twentieth century.

THE SECOND PHASE

In the second half of the twentieth century, Euro-American values and Islamic values began to diverge. Of course, many of the seeds for these divergences were laid earlier, but they really began to bear fruit in this period. Again, we may look at the issues of sexual behavior, sex roles, alcohol and drugs, the death penalty, race and religion.

Sexuality: Personal mores and family values have changed rapidly in America since the two world wars. The norms and mores have become less and less akin to Islamic values. Sex before marriage, with parental consent, became common.[24] The erosion of social disapproval of premarital and extramarital sex, and advances in contraception, played a large role in contributing to sexual freedom. The "sexual liberation" of the sixties was largely confined to the Western world. The invention of the birth control pill contributed to the sexual empowerment of women, who were free from the fears of pregnancy. Sexuality has been cheapened in America and female bodies are exploited in a wider range ways than ever—from easily available pornographic movies on television to techniques in advertising that promote an idealized version of female beauty, from high class prostitution to the objectification of women.[25] This is more distant from Islamic values.

While American culture does give greater freedom to women than does Muslim culture, American culture extends less dignity to women than does Muslim culture.

Sons in America respect their mothers less than sons in the Muslim world; husbands in America respect their wives more than husbands in the Muslim world.

Sex roles: American culture on gender has become more and more different from Muslim culture on gender. On the positive side, American women are more active in the economy and in the political process and have made enormous progress in the quest for equality. For instance, between 1936 and 1996 the percent of Americans who approve of a married woman working even if she doesn't have to do so for economics has gone from 18 percent to 81 percent.[26] And in the same time period, the percent of Americans who would vote for a woman if she were qualified to be president has increased from 31 percent to 96 percent.[27]

By the measurement of women's liberation America now has outstripped the Muslim world; but by the yardstick of the empowerment of women, has the Muslim world outstripped America?

The United States has never had a female president. Yet two of the most populous Muslim countries—Pakistan and Bangladesh—have had women prime ministers. *Benazir Bhutto* headed two governments in Pakistan, and *Khaleda Zia* and *Hassina Wajed* have served consecutively in Bangladesh.

Turkey too had a woman Prime Minister, *Tansu Ciller*. And Indonesia, the most populous Muslim country of them all, now has a woman Head of State, President *Megawati Sukarnoputri*. Muslim countries seem to be ahead in female empowerment, though still behind in female liberation. Four Muslim countries have experienced highest female political leadership long before the United States, France, Italy and Russia have had a female President, and long before Germany has had a female Chancellor.

Alcohol and drugs: The Prohibition movement in the United States did not last for very long, and early in the twentieth century, the movement began to repeal the 18th Amendment. In February 1933 Congress adopted a resolution proposing a new constitutional amendment to that effect. On December 5, 1933, Utah cast the 36th ratifying vote in favour of the Twenty-first Amendment. At the federal level alcohol was legal again[28]—breaking the link with Islamic culture.

A few states in the Union continued to be "dry states," and chose to maintain a statewide ban. But the disenchantment that the Federal-level prohibition had created adversely affected attitudes to temperance even in those states, which had once led the way in favour of prohibition. It is arguable that prohibition at the state-level might have lasted much longer if the original asymmetry (some states for and some states against) had been respected and allowed to continue. The Eighteenth Constitutional Amendment was a pursuit of national symmetry in American attitudes to alcohol. The Eighteenth Amendment sought a premature national moral consensus on alcohol—and thereby hurt the cause of temperance in the country as a whole. By 1966 virtually all the fifty states of the Union had legalized alcoholic drinks—though some preferred that drinking be restricted to homes and private clubs rather than be served in public bars and saloons.

Drugs have become a major issue in both urban areas and rural areas in the United States, despite several "drug wars," incarceration of drug users and dealers, and attempts to interdict supplies from Latin America, Southeast Asia, and Southwest Europe. While drugs are not absent in Islamic societies (qat, for example, in Yemen and Somalia), parents in many Islamic societies do not have to worry about their offspring using drugs—to the extent that parents in the West do—unless they send their children abroad for education.

Death Penalty: As mentioned previously, America had been executing the mentally retarded and juveniles who committed crimes as minors. Indeed, as one liberal critic has pointed out, in the execution of mentally retarded and juveniles, the United States shares the practices of only five Islamic countries—Iran, Nigeria, Pakistan, Saudi Arabia, and Yemen.[29] Various Supreme Court decisions provide hope to those who hope to change these practices.[30]

Although Muslim countries do share in the imposition of the death penalty, there are encouraging signs where the penalty is not pursued. Nigeria, for example, has decided not to execute *Amina Lawal* on the charge of adultery.[31]

America is still divided on the death penalty with some states upholding it and others rejecting it as "cruel and unusual punishment." It seems almost certain that the United States will abolish the death penalty long before the Muslim world as a whole is similarly converted to the proposition that the death penalty in the 21st century is not the best solution to human depravity.

Secularism and Political Action: The First Amendment permits religious minorities to practice their religions in relative peace. Of course, like all doctrines, secularism has its fanatics who sometimes want to degrade the sacred rather than permitting it.[32] But at its best a secular state is a refuge of safety for minority religions. It is in that sense that American secularism is a friend of Muslims living in the United States.

But while secularism is a divorce from formal religion, *Muslims see socio-sexual libertarianism as a dilution of spirituality*. Socio-sexual libertarianism makes America less and less Islamic. One can be without a formal religion and still be deeply spiritual in a humanistic sense. John Stuart Mill and Bertrand Russell were without formal religion, yet each had deeply spiritual values. Albert Schweitzer, the Nobel Laureate for Peace, was at times an agnostic, but he was deeply committed to the principle of reverence for life—even protecting the lives of insects in Africa.[33]

In discussing the role of American Muslims *qua* Muslims (heirs of the Hijrah), we have to look more closely at their moral concerns in relation to American culture. Curiously enough, and in spite of Muslim opinion, American secularism is indeed good news for Muslims in America. The bad news is the expanding arena of American socio-sexual *libertarianism*, which has resulted in greater divergence in values. Secularism in the political process does indeed help to protect minority religions from the potential intrusive power of the Christian Right. On the other hand, expanding American socio-cultural libertarianism in such fields as sexual mores alarms both the Christian Right and Muslim traditionalists in the United States. Social libertarianism is what has eroded what American values have in common with Islamic values.[34]

These moral concerns in turn have consequences on how American Muslims relate to the wider political divide between Republicans and Democrats in both foreign and domestic policies.

From the 1990s onwards more and more American Muslims have apparently been registering to vote and seeking to influence candidates in elections.[35] On such social issues as family values and sexual mores, Muslims often find themselves more in tune with Republican rhetoric and concerns. On the need for a more strict separation of church and state, which helps to protect religious minorities, it is the more liberal Democrats who offer a better protection to Muslims. Let us look at these contradictions more closely.

The Democratic Party in the United States is more insistent on separating church from state, including its opposition to prayer in schools. This draws African American Muslim parents even more towards the Democrats, since the Muslim parents do not want their kids to be under peer pressure to attend Christian prayers. More recent immigrant Muslims from the Middle East or of Asian descent regard prayer in school as potentially more Islamic.[36] These latter Muslims may be drawn to the Republicans.

On the other hand, the Republicans are stronger on traditional family values and are more opposed to sexual libertarianism. This draws many Muslims (especially immigrant Asians) to the Republican Party. Most Muslims share Republican concerns about abortion and gay rights.[37]

In the United States Western secularism has protected minority religious groups by insisting on separation of church and state. That is a major reason why the Jews in the United States have been among the greatest defenders of the separation of church and state.[38] Any breach of that principle could lead to the imposition of some practices of the religious majority—like forcing Jewish children to participate in Christian prayers at school.[39]

Religion has been declining in influence in the West since the days of the Renaissance and the Enlightenment.[40] But it is mainly in the 20th century that *spirituality* in the West has taken a nose-dive. From an Islamic perspective, America has become not only less religious, but also dangerously less spiritual. America has become not only more secular but dangerously more socially libertarian.[41] Again we use the term libertarianism more in the sense of minimum ethical restraint and not in the sense of minimum political control.

Muslim parents particularly fear that American socio-cultural libertarianism is likely to influence the socialization and upbringing of the next generation of Muslim children—excessive levels of acquisitiveness, consumerism and diverse forms of sexuality.[42]

It is because of all these considerations that Islam within the United States feels threatened less by American secularism than by American socio-sexual libertarianism. And American socio-sexual libertarianism is what has made United States mores more and more un-Islamic.

However, in a few other respects, relations between the Euro-American people and the Islamic ummah converged. Let us look more closely at some of these convergences.

Convergence of Political and Economic Interests: In the post-War period, and especially during the Cold War, much of the devout regions of the Muslim world had deep antipathy toward the atheistic Communist ideology propagated by the Soviet Union, and to a lesser extent, China. The United States and other Western countries were happy to build military and strategic alliances with anticommunist regimes in Muslim countries to prevent communism from spreading. Of course, especially in the case of the Middle East and North Africa, there was also a convergence of economic interests between Western countries and regimes in Muslim countries. Western consumers' demand for oil and gas could not be met cheaply enough from domestic resources, while Middle Eastern ample oil and gas supplies could only be extracted with the help of Western corporations.

There were a few exceptions to this convergence. Much of the Muslim world and the US found themselves on opposite sides of the Arab-Israeli dispute, and the 1973 oil embargo threatened the cordial economic ties that had developed between the two sides.

Population Movements: Nevertheless, population movements between the two worlds helped to promote greater understanding and tolerance. Many universities in the United States began Middle East Studies and Islamic Studies programs leading to scholarly visits and exchange. Trade between some Islamic countries and the West began to boom. Unlike in the past where Westerners ventured into the Muslim world with the gun and/or the Bible, in the second half of the 20th century, Western visitors appeared with aid, trade, books, and technology. Guns and tanks and airplanes were only brought at the request of the regime in control.

From the other side, the need for cheap labor in the West and the pull of economic benefits began to attract Muslim immigrants to the Western world. Germany, France, and the UK were the destinations for Muslims from Turkey, North Africa, and South Asia. Europe and the United States also attracted Muslim students, scholars, and elite tourists from the oil-rich countries.

In the United States, the formerly European–dominated immigration flows decreased as people from the Third World were permitted easier entry into the US after passage of the Immigration Reform and Control Act (IRCA) of 1965. IRCA allowed immigration from every country and gave each country the same amount of immigration. Significant Asian and African immigration resulted.[43] The civil rights movement, the decline of racism, and the recognition of the important contributions of immigrant Muslims in America have all contributed to greater tolerance of Islam.

The years under President Bill Clinton were a measure of the growing American acceptance of Islam in fits and starts. President Clinton sent greetings to Muslims during the fast of Ramadhan from 1996. We should also note how Hillary Clinton hosted a celebration of Idd el Fitr (the Festival of the End of Ramadhan) in the White House in April 1996 and 1998. Vice President Al Gore visited a mosque in fall 1995. And the first two Muslim chaplains (one in the Army and the other in the Navy) to serve the 10,000 Muslims in the US armed forces were sworn in under Clinton's watch.[44]

President Clinton received in the White House a delegation of Arab Americans to discuss wide-ranging issues, domestic and international. The National Security Advisor, Anthony Lake, received a delegation of Muslims (including this author) in 1996 to discuss the ramifications of the Bosnian crisis.

The Clinton gestures towards Muslims were sufficiently high profile that a hostile article in the *Wall Street Journal* in March 1996 raised the specter of "Friends of Hamas in the White House"—alleging that some of the President Clinton's Muslim guests were friends of "Arab terrorists," and supporters of the Palestinian movement. The critic in the *Wall Street Journal* (Steve Emerson) had a long record of hostility towards U.S. Muslims. His television programme on PBS entitled *Jihad in America* (1994) alleged that almost all terrorist activities by Muslims worldwide were partially funded by U.S. Muslims. President Clinton's friendly gestures to Muslims probably infuriated this self-appointed crusader of Islamophobia.[45] Yet Clinton's Muslim-friendly strategy continued. This friendliness was also apparent in the larger population. Generally speaking, there was acceptance of American Muslim women wearing head-scarves or *hijab* in their day-to-day lives, unlike in France.

Normative divergence between Islam and Euro-American values once coincided with a convergence of tolerance between Muslims and Americans. Should American Muslims help to reverse this divergence in values without triggering off the return of those darker forces of racism and intolerance of those yesteryears? Can American Muslims help to remind America of what was best in its own quality of life once upon a time—without completely negating the pre-September 11 trend in tolerance, which America had once achieved?

If such is the destiny, which awaits American Muslims, theirs will be a marriage of the heritage of the Hijrah with the legacy of the Mayflower.

THE THIRD PHASE: DIVERGENCES

In the 21st century, there has been an increasing gap between Islamic values and Euro-American values, especially in the area of norms relating to homosexuality and gender roles, and the death penalty. Some of these areas have been dealt with earlier, but let us survey some potential areas of discord between Islam and Euro-American values.

Attitudes towards homosexuality have also changed in the West. Indeed, a majority of Americans and Europeans would say today that laws against homosexual sexuality are a violation of the rights of gays and lesbians.[46] There has been speculation that the *Lawrence* decision may mean that North America may be edging towards same-sex marriages within a decade or two.[47] Religious bodies such as the Episcopalians have struggled with the ordination of openly gay bishops.[48]

There have been no comparable pressures on Islamic societies, marriages, and the ulema, apart from gay Muslims who live in the West.[49] Although the Qur'an is explicit in its condemnation of homosexuality, in practice, temporally and spatially, there appears to be tolerance of homosexuality. The prevailing attitude appears to be a variation of the Catholic Church's treatment of homosexuality and homosexuals, urging the homosexual to confess and be celibate. In Islam, there appears to be more of an emphasis on repentance than confession.[50]

> There are, in fact, some interpretations that argue that the Prophet Muhammad did not view sexual relations between men as severe as other offenses against sexual propriety such as adultery and fornication.[51]

On gender roles, the divide between Islam and the West continues to bedevil relations among Muslim women themselves, as well as between Muslim women and their Western counterparts. An outstanding example of this is the controversy over the proposal to ban headscarves in French public schools. Muslim women were on both sides of this issue, as were various Western women.[52] While Muslim women continue to rule and run for political office, there has been a backsliding in the position of women in some countries such as Iraq and Algeria.[53] American women themselves are beginning to question the two-earner household, and some professional women are beginning to abandon their careers to get on the "Mommy Track."

While the divide between Islamic values and Euro-American values in these areas of social values may not be immediately harmful to the tolerant convergence of Muslims and Americans, the aftermath of September 11 and accompanying political changes have interrupted or reversed the trend towards convergence. Muslims and Westerners—particularly Americans—in many areas are regrettably heading toward mutual distrust, if not hostility. We can briefly survey these under three areas: the violence of terrorism, the violence of occupation, and an environment of harassment.

The Violence of Terrorism: By the year 2000, it appeared as if violence against Americans and terrorism against American interests was low in comparison to previous years.[54] But September 11, 2001 changed this perception violently. Not since the Civil War had American lives been lost in such magnitude on a single day.[55] The images were horrific, and imprinted on the nation's psyche.

Americans had to get used to the kind of surveillance and lifestyle of people in many other countries—such as the United Kingdom and Israel—that have had to deal with terrorism on a much more intimate level. Subsequent bombings, kidnappings, and other acts of violence have made many Muslim countries such as Indonesia and Saudi Arabia dangerous for Americans to visit, and the routine subject of travel advisories from the State Department.[56]

Muslims have also been the victims of violence due to terrorism. Indeed, the bombings in Saudi Arabia claimed more Muslim lives than American lives. In a sermon in early 2004, the Imam of the Grand Mosque in Mecca asked Muslims to foreswear violence.

> Islam seeks moderation. Those who deviate from moderation and try to incite Muslims against their rulers are seeking discord and anarchy through destruction, terrorism, bombings and shedding the blood of Muslims and those under the protection of the state.[57]

American and Israeli responses to terrorism have often led to the death of innocent civilians in the West Bank, Gaza, Iraq, and Afghanistan. In addition, the practice of "rendition," where people who are suspected of terrorism are turned over to governments who have less qualms about torturing them, has also led to Muslims being victimized by the security services of these governments. A prime example of this was the September 2002 incident of a Syrian-born Canadian citizen, Maher Arar, who was sent to Syria where he was reportedly tortured and imprisoned for ten months.[58]

Violence of Occupation: Recent revelations about the lack of Weapons of Mass Destruction (WMDs) in Iraq have left the Bush and Blair administration struggling to come up with alternative rationalizations for the rush to war in Iraq. The Bush administration cited intelligence to assert that Iraq had not destroyed WMDs and had enough of a stockpile to present an imminent danger. However, former chief weapons inspector David Kay's investigation revealed not only that Iraq did not have stockpiles of WMDs at the time of war, but also that the Hussein regime had destroyed these weapons well before the war.[59]

The violence of occupation has resulted in both American and Iraqi casualties during the Iraq war and subsequent occupation. The number of Americans and Iraqis wounded is likely to be much higher.[60] Although Afghanistan has been overshadowed in the news, Americans and Afghans are also getting killed and wounded there regularly. The relatives and friends of those Americans killed or wounded in Iraq and Afghanistan are not likely to become the best friends of Muslims.

Americans however also have reason to worry about the lack of friendship from Muslims in many other countries—not just Iraq and Afghanistan—who feel that US aid and support for their enemies is perpetuating violence and hardship for them. Muslims under direct military occupation include Iraq, Palestine and Afghanistan. Muslims militarily struggling for self-determination include Chechnya and Kashmir. Muslims on the radar screen for possible military intervention by Western powers include Iran, Syria, and Somalia. Muslims being harassed under new anti-terrorist legislation already include Tanzania, Kenya, potentially South Africa and a host of other countries under pressure from the Bush administration.

Environment of Harassment: It has now almost become a cliché to say "September 11 changed everything"—particularly in regards to the attitudes of Americans toward Muslims. But perhaps what is more worrisome is the official attitudes and policies that may even be encroachments on the Bill of Rights and leave dark smudges on the beacon of American democracy.

Muslims harassed at American and international airports are beginning to multiply.[61] On August 3, 2003, on arrival from overseas, I was detained at Miami airport for seven hours and subjected to repeated interrogation.[62]

The aftermath of September 11 has already been compromising some civil liberties in the United States to ominous proportions:[63] Muslims have been particularly targeted.

1. The US Senate Finance Committee has asked the Internal Revenue Service to turn over financial records, including donor lists, of Muslim charities and foundations. The list of organizations includes several that are under separate investigations by the Treasury Department, the FBI, and other agencies. Muslim leaders feel that this will chill charitable giving by donors to legitimate causes.[64]
2. Visitors to the United States from countries in Africa, the Middle East, Asia, and South America are being digitally photographed and fingerprinted on arrival, but visitors from European countries are being exempted. Privacy advocates are disturbed by this plan and another plan to collect personal information on passengers on domestic flights to assess their security risks.[65]
3. On and off there are hundreds of people in detention without trial under American jurisdiction. They are overwhelmingly Muslim.[66] The great majority of those in detention are not publicly announced as being in detention.[67] Out of the hundreds in detention, only a handful show any evidence of knowing any particular terrorist suspect or being associated with any movement or charity accused of terrorism. Muslims are targeted.[68]
4. Out of the millions of illegal immigrants in the United States, and those whose visas have expired, the people chosen for detention without trial or

instant deportation are almost certainly those with Muslim names or who come from the Middle East.[69] The INS has been singling out particular nationalities (mainly Muslim) in the United States for discriminatory treatment, illegal harassment and unconstitutional imprisonment.[70]

5. The United States has considered having military tribunals and secret trials for those suspected of terrorism. Many of these suspects are lodged in Guantanamo Bay, Cuba, and the level of justice envisaged for them has led to searing critiques. As a leading British judge, Johan Steyn, has said

   The question is whether the quality of justice envisaged for the prisoners at Guantanamo Bay complies with the minimum international standards for the conduct of fair trials," Lord Steyn said. "The answer can be given quite shortly. It is a resounding, 'No.'"[71]

   Even the leaders of Nazi Germany were given a public trial at Nuremberg after World War II with access to counsel and proper representation. Some of those tried at Nuremberg had been responsible for the death of millions of people.[72]

6. The United States has supported Israel's search for old Nazi militants so that they can be tried today in a court of law in Israel. Yet just as Israel kills Palestinian militants instead of capturing them for trial, the United States has started killing al-Qaeda suspects in Afghanistan, Iraq and Yemen.[73] Israel tried Adolf Eichmann in 1961 and protected him at the trial with a bulletproof glass cage so that he would not be assassinated.[74] Yet both the USA and Israel from 2001 onwards have killed terrorist suspects instead of capturing them. And even when Israel has illegally captured Palestinian or Lebanese suspects from across its own borders, the purpose has almost never been to give them a fair trial (Adolf Eichmann-style) but to detain those suspects indefinitely *without trial*.

7. U. S. Attorney General John Ashcroft has given the green light to the FBI to spy on churches, mosques, and other sacred places to an extent not envisaged in the country for a long time.[75] Places of prayer were once protected from close police scrutiny. However, mosques especially may soon be fair game for police raids in American cities, while *Synagogues* may enjoy de facto protection even if there is militant Zionism or fundamentalist Judaism being preached inside.

8. Attorney-General Ashcroft wants to breach attorney-client confidentiality if the client is suspected of terrorism.[76] In the case of the detainees at Guantanomo Bay, some regulations relating to the eavesdropping between lawyers and clients have been relaxed, although their day in court is still a long way away.[77] The Attorney General and President Bush repeatedly talk as if those *suspected* of terrorism were already *proven* terrorists. What happened to the U.S. principle that a person was innocent until proven guilty?[78]

9. CNN and other major TV networks in the United States were summoned to the White House and warned against giving Osama bin Laden propaganda advantage with his videos. Whatever happened to editorial independence and freedom of the Press? Self-censorship by the American media is still disconcertingly rampant.

10. The PATRIOT Act provides the US government with a lot of power against even citizens, including the permission for federal agents to "sneak and peek" at citizens' private records; enter citizens' homes in secret; and hold citizens indefinitely without access to legal counsel or a hearing before a judge.[79]

The administration of George W. Bush humiliated Muslims in the White House at the beginning of his administration. At a meeting of US Muslims with the Office of Faith-Based and Community Initiatives, Secret Service agents removed an American citizen who was Muslim.[80] In the aftermath of 9/11, while President Bush did take pains to assure Muslims that the war against terrorism was not a war against Islam, other administration officials were not so charitable. Lt. Gen. William G. Boykin, the Pentagon's deputy undersecretary for intelligence, discussing a 1993 battle with a Muslim militia leader in Somalia, said, "I knew that my God was bigger than his. I knew that my God was a real God, and his was an idol."[81]

Many Americans may have to brace themselves for a less free America than the one, which closed the twentieth century, but an America more *religion-conscious* than the one, which opened the third millennium. If the erosion of civil liberties is justified on the grounds of the war against terrorism, this is a war with no recognizable finality of either a peace treaty with the enemy, or a demand of unconditional surrender.

What would constitute the end of this war? Would we be able to have a victory parade, open bottles of halal champagne or hug each other with joy in the streets? After World War II there was VE Day (Victory in Europe) and V-J Day (Victory in Japan). What would constitute such finality in the war on terrorism?

We must not forget that if America's own democracy decays, it makes it easier for the Third World's own dictators (Muslim and non-Muslim) to justify their own tyranny.[82] When the American government itself erodes American freedoms, its credibility in promoting freedom and democracy abroad is substantially eroded.[83] People have begun to question if the Bush administration is really committed to promoting democracy: as Fred Hiatt has pointed out, ". . . the struggle against intolerant and violent strains of Islamism is going to be a long one, and it is set back when the United States falters in supporting democratic values."[84]

THE FOURTH PHASE:
DEMOCRATIZING THE US, EMPOWERING ISLAM

This fourth phase is a scenario for the future rather than a report of historical trends. The United States needs greater political democratization and reduced social libertarianism. United States policy, even when cloaked in the benevolent clothes of promoting democracy abroad and preventing terrorism at home, must be restrained. Minorities may play a crucial role in view of their own experience with the American democratic experiment. Corporate and media power to promote rampant consumerism and sexuality will need to be countered.

The Muslim world needs greater doctrinal liberalization and deeper intellectual modernization. On the path of empowering Islam, the varieties of Islam must be enlisted to reinterpret Islam for the modern era. Crucial in this regard will be promoting an Islam that is not obscurantist and promotes knowledge and intellectual freedom; an Islam progressive in relation to gender roles and basic human freedoms; and perhaps even an Islam tolerant about difference on such matters as sexual orientation.

Rolling back American socio-sexual libertarianism would require new discipline in the areas of:

1. Greed, corporate and personal. This would require stricter controls over corporate corruption, accounting fraud, and exorbitant compensation paid to CEOs. The scandals at Enron, WorldCom, Tyco, and other companies have been examples of such greed.[85] Personal greed has been manifested in the culture of cheating that results in people cutting corners to get ahead.[86]
2. Consumerism and depletion of the world's resources. Any comparative survey of the consumption of Americans vis-à-vis other cultures points to the huge appetite of Americans for consumption of the world's resources. For instance, per capita US energy consumption in 1996 was 43 times that of Yemen.[87]
3. The rules of sexuality. Perhaps the extreme level of this has been Massachusetts, which has moved towards declaring that gay marriages have to be allowed to avoid the "separate but equal" classification of "civil unions" that some states such as Vermont have permitted for gay unions.[88] On the other hand, there appears to be a backlash in other states, such as Ohio, which recently became the 38th state to ban same-sex unions.[89] The Alliance for Marriage, a bipartisan coalition of more than 50 religious leaders, including Roman Catholics, Protestants, Jews and Muslims is seeking a constitutional amendment that would ban gay marriage but not

stop states from enacting civil unions for same-sex couples.[90] Also, according to the Centers for Disease Control, there has been a 30 percent decrease in the teenage birthrate over the last decade, and this is not just due to better protection. Recent studies have shown that teenagers are having less sex than their parents think, and are more conservative on sex than their parents.[91]

4. Hedonistic inebriation and medical lifestyle enhancements (alcoholism and drugs). Colleges and universities are confronting issues of binge drinking by young people. Some regions of the US have considered decriminalizing the use of marijuana, especially for medical reasons. Commercials on television advocate the use of drugs, although with prescriptions, to combat impotence.

As for the greater democratization of America, it is tied up with America as Empire.[92] Although Americans are reluctant to think of their actions as that of an imperial regime, as Dimitri K. Simes has put it, "Whether or not the United States now views itself as an empire, for many foreigners it increasingly looks, walks, and talks like one. . ."[93]

The United States as an Empire can only be checked by the United States as a democracy. African Americans, Latinos and Muslim Americans have a lot to learn from Jews about how to be empowered Americans. So indeed do women of America of all races. American women are substantially liberated, but they have yet to penetrate the citadels of power. Jews have been staggeringly successful not only politically in America, but also economically, educationally and culturally.[94] Jews are the supreme example and ideal model of an American minority that has successfully used the American system to its full advantage. Jews have also exploited the American system for the benefit of Israel.[95]

If African Americans, Muslim Americans, Arab Americans, Latinos and women of all races became half as successful as the Jews in influencing directions of American policy, their effect would probably be towards liberalizing the foreign policy of the United States. Many African Americans and Native Americans are quite aware of the excesses of America as empire themselves. As the renowned African American novelist Walter Mosley said recently:

> Blacks do not see America as the great liberator of the world. Blacks understand how the rest of the world sees us, because we have also been the victims of American imperialism.[96]

At the moment America is torn between a domestic philosophy based on *rights* and a foreign policy based on *might*. America is an empire abroad and struggling to be a democracy at home. Demographic changes in the United States may tilt the balance towards a better and more humane equilibrium.[97]

A new global clash of civilizations has indeed begun, with the United States at the center of it. But the seeds of redemption may also lie in America. Those seeds are carried by emerging populations potentially more responsive to other cultures and civilizations than the contemporary U.S. power-elites seem to be. The imperial tunnel is still dark — but the light of a more inclusive American democracy can be seen at the end of this tunnel.

A particularly important issue is whether Muslims can use their present pain and anguish as a basis of a new sense of unity. The unity needs to be constructive rather than destructive, benevolent rather than malevolent, determined to protect Muslims rather than harm others.

Who knows? Perhaps out of such unity of anguish there will subsequently emerge the unity of achievement, a triumphant American Muslim identity at long last, combining faith in Islam with what is best about America.

As for a future Islamic Renaissance and liberalization, this may one day have to be led by Muslims receptive to other cultures, like those in the West. For our purposes in this dialogue, we may distinguish among three schools of Islam — Orthodox, modernist and liberal.[98]

Orthodox Islam is literalist in its interpretation of the Qur'an and the Sunna, ritualistic in its observances, traditionalist in gender relations, with an emphasis on a *God of Justice*. On the whole, such Orthodox Muslims are far less receptive to other cultures.[99]

Modernist Islam seeks to bring Islamic beliefs closer to modern science, technology and the expansion of human knowledge. Modernist Muslims put less emphasis on Islamic rituals and more emphasis on Islamic rationalism. The modernist Allah is a *God of Enlightenment*. Beliefs about Satan, jinn, devils and spirits are interpreted metaphorically rather than literally. Even angels are seen as figurative manifestations of God. Perhaps Abdolkarim Soroush of Iran is a modernist Muslim.[100] Modernist Muslims also include most theorists of the Islamization of knowledge.

Liberal Islam is less concerned with updating Islam scientifically and more concerned with updating Islam *ethically*.[101] The Liberal Muslim is less worried about whether Iblis exists physically or only figuratively. Islamic liberalism is anxious that Muslim women be treated as equals; that slavery be declared *haram* under *any* circumstances; that the amputation of hands of thieves be relegated totally to history; and that the death penalty be either abolished completely or be limited to such egregious offenses as first-degree murder (and never be imposed on adulterers). To liberal Muslims, Allah is a *God of Compassion*. Perhaps Fatima Mernissi of Morocco is a liberal Muslim.[102]

The modernization of Catholicism has been relatively easy because the Roman Catholic Church has a spiritual head who enjoys some "divine infallibility" in some of his interpretations of the faith. The modernization of other branches of Christianity had to ride on the immense cultural revolution of the Protestant Reformation. The modernization of Judaism occurred mainly in the Jewish Diaspora as the Jews engaged in brilliant cultural synthesis. Modernization in Islam could occur in the Muslim Diaspora in those countries where Muslims have freedom to speak and debate intellectual and theological matters without fear of physical harassment.

IN SEARCH OF ISLAMIC CONSTITUTIONALISM

How can Muslims either modernize or liberalize Islam without having a Muslim Pope, or a Muslim Protestant Revolution or a new Muslim cultural synthesis? First and foremost, Muslim liberal thinkers and modernist theologians need to be assured greater intellectual freedom, without the fear of harassment or the risk of violent bigotry. Secondly, the liberal thinkers and modernist theologians need to invoke *idjitihad* more systematically in order to address the contradictions between ancient doctrine and modern realities. Thirdly, these new ideas should be made more accessible to the wider Muslim ummah, taking advantage of the new "information superhighway" and the computer revolution.

The three schools of Islam (Orthodox, Modernist and Liberal) are not to be conceived as *madhahib*. They can be reformulations of some of the existing *madhahib*. It is possible to modernize Sunni Islam and liberalize Shiism.[103]

Let us agree that a good Muslim cannot deny, disobey, contradict or neglect Allah's commands. But the whole point of this debate is whether a good Muslim can *re-interpret* God's command in the light of new evidence or changed circumstances.

Of course the word of God is infallible, but those who interpret it are *not*. Unlike Christians, Muslims do not believe that God walked among men and conversed with human beings directly (Jesus as "the word of God made flesh"). But even for Christians, God is not personally available on earth *today* to give lessons on how to interpret their scripture.

The Qur'an is infallible, but those who have interpreted it are fallible human beings. The United States' constitution was drafted by Founding Fathers who were not themselves necessarily lawyers. However, those who interpret the Constitution *today* are judges who live in the twenty-first century. Since the adoption of the U.S. Constitution in the eighteenth century, slavery has been declared unconstitutional, segregated schools declared illegal, women and Blacks have been given the vote, and the right to privacy has been read into the Constitution through judicial review. The fundamental law of the country has been repeatedly re-interpreted by its judges without abandoning the sanctity and dignity of the Constitution.

There is a debate about the U.S. Constitution comparable to our own debate about how to interpret the Qur'an. There are conservative jurists even on the Supreme Court itself who insist that the text of the Constitution should be interpreted as closely as possible to the original intent of the founders. There are others who believe that the U.S. Constitution is a *living guide* to the nation and is therefore subject to reinterpretation according to changing social and political realities.[104]

Minorities like Black people and Muslims in the United States have benefited far more from the second juridical school (historically relative) than by the first (constructionist and orthodox). The gains of the Civil Rights Movement were mainly under the Warren Supreme Court, which was historically relative and reformist. Since then the U.S. Supreme Court has been moving back to rightwing orthodoxy.[105]

We need to distinguish between rules of evidence and fairness of punishment. Even if one of our loved ones had adversely satisfied the rules of evidence on adultery, would we still be comfortable with their being executed for adultery? We must remember that such sins as adultery or homosexuality in Dar el Islam might have been committed by one's cousin or one's brother, or even by one's father. We must remember the words of the Prophet. The relevant Qur'anic verse that is cited in the case of homosexuality is:

> If two men among you
> Are guilty of lewdness
> Punish them both.
> If they repent and amend
> Leave them alone; for Allah
> is oft-Returning, Most Merciful (Qur'an 4: 16)

Quranic verses 4: 15 and 24:4 suggest that for the severe punishments envisaged for adultery, four witnesses are required. Even if the rules of evidence were satisfied, would one still regard such punishments as fair in the twentieth or twenty-first century? Individual Muslims must reflect carefully and be honest with themselves before they answer. Would they be prepared to kill one of their brothers for adultery if four witnesses had witnessed his sin physically? Islamic modernism and Islamic liberalism would not seek to end a human life for a sexual offense, however revolting.

The Qur'an and the Sunnah are the sources of the Islamic Constitutional Order. The Qur'an is older than the U.S. Constitution by more than a thousand years. If things in the world have changed a lot since the days of Thomas Jefferson, how much more have they changed since the days of the Prophet Muhammad (pbuh)? If American jurisprudence is allowing itself to learn from the lessons of the two hundred years of history, why cannot Islamic jurisprudence learn from fourteen centuries of historical change? Muslims must always remember once again that while the word of God is infallible and immutable, the human interpreters of the word of God are not. New Muslim intellects should review the doctrines once again.

IS RELIGION IN CONFLICT WITH SCIENCE?

Narrow orthodoxy is precisely what has left Muslims behind and made Muslims vulnerable to being humiliated and brutalized by others. Nor must we forget that Black people have also been under-achievers and that women have been left below the commanding heights of science and philosophy.

However, there has never been a time when women were at the pinnacle of global power, or when Black people were at the center of the global equation. But there was a time in history when *Muslims* were globally triumphant. Why did Muslims decline so disastrously? And why have they continued to be marginalized? Is it possible that Muslim refusal to let the message of Islam be re-interpreted is at the core of the retardation of the Muslim world? Is orthodoxy a disservice to Islam?[106]

During the one hundred years of the existence of the Nobel Prize, Muslim winners of the Nobel Prize in the Sciences (chemistry, physics and medicine) can be counted with the fingers of one hand. Jewish winners are in their dozens. Christian winners are probably in their hundreds. The few Muslim winners of the scientific Nobel Prizes are not products or alumni of Islamic universities. They are almost always products of Western education.

A publication of the Third World Academy of Sciences has estimated that less than one percent of world scientific publications are published in the Arab world, in spite of oil wealth. Even rich Arab states spend one seventh of the global average spent by other nations on research and development.[107]

There are indeed two ways for Muslims to judge themselves. One is to look at those who have outperformed us—such as Jews and Euro-Christians. The other is to look at those who have performed worse than ourselves in the sciences, such as Black people, women and perhaps the Chinese. Are Muslims sure that they would like Islam to be judged on the basis of below-average performance? Women and Black people have a more solid excuse for underperformance than Muslims have. The Chinese may be facing the same dilemmas as the Muslim ummah. Why has China been outperformed by the much smaller Japan? The Muslim world has also been outperformed by a Japan, which is less than a tenth of the Muslim population of the world. Muslims need to address the issue of why we are so far behind. Liberal Muslims believe that the ummah has refused to change in the light of expanding knowledge and changing circumstances. What do Orthodox Muslims believe are the causes of our retardation?

My late father of blessed memory used to argue that Muslims were left behind when they stopped observing the tenets of their religion. But Jews and Christians observe the tenets of Islam even *less*. Why have Jews and Christians forged ahead in science and technology in spite of their not being Muslims at all? Modernist Muslims are urging a review of our dogmas.

Muslim doctrines, which have hurt our progress, have included the concept of *bid'a*. Originally intended to protect the young religion from premature reform and distortion, *bid'a* became a symbol of Muslim distrust of all kinds of innovations and inventions. While the word *innovation* has positive connotations in the English language, the word *bid'a* in Islamic discourse carries negative and sinful implications. The concept of *bid'a* came to symbolize a fundamental Muslim resistance to change. Orthodoxy defended itself against innovation.

On the other hand, the highly progressive Muslim principle of *Idjitihad* has been grossly under-utilized. Indeed, among Sunni Muslims, the doors of *idjitihad* have been closed in reality, though not necessarily in theory. Had the doors been open, there would have been more than four Sunni denominations in Islam by now.

Sudan's Mahmoud Muhammad Taha should be counted among Muslim *ulamaa* who invoked *idjitihad* in a bid to reinterpret Islam. Taha paid with his life in 1985 under Jaafar Nimeiry's version of the *hudud*.[108]

The future of the human race may depend upon the gradual restraint of the United States, on one side, and the gradual empowerment of the Muslim world on the other. But the Muslim world will never be empowered until it understands the dynamics of human knowledge.

The origins of Islam rest on *the miracle of wisdom without formal qualifications*. Islam is the religion of a man who could not read or write and yet helped to produce the most influential book in its original language in human history. [The Bible is the most influential book *in* translation.] Islam is a religion of a man who, when commanded by an angel to read [*"Iqra"*], confessed meekly that he could not read. That exchange between Gabriel and Muhammad broke the link between inspiration and instruction forever. Illiteracy can be the mother of supreme wisdom. I affirm that in spite of my being a professor with multiple degrees and author of more than twenty books.

But the future of Islam needs to narrow the gap between religious ritual and intellectual rationalism, and bridge the gap between faith and reason. Only then will Muslims be able to defend Islam not just with word of mouth but also with the power of knowledge. Only then will Muslims be able to fight for Islam not by terrorizing the enemy but by educating the adversary.

CONCLUSION

We have tried to identify in this chapter four phases in the history of relationships between Islam and the Western world, with particular reference to the Americo-Islamic interaction. The paradox of the first half of the twentieth century was a convergence in values between Islam and Euro-America, but a divergence of empathy between Muslims and Westerners.

The sanctity of the family, the distrust of extra-marital sex, the rejection of homosexuality, the emphasis on modesty and chastity, were all values shared by Islam and the Euro-American experience. The United States even went to the extent of prohibiting alcohol through a constitutional amendment in the years between the two world wars—a major convergence with Islam as a profoundly anti-alcohol culture.

Yet those years of Americo-Islamic convergence in values were also the years when Americans regarded Islam as the equivalent of the anti-Christ. American racist culture dismissed Muslims among the darker and ominous races of humankind. Similarity of values coincided with hostility in relationships between the two peoples.

In the second half of the twentieth century, the paradox was reversed. Euro-American political values became more and more liberal, improving the relationship between Westerners and Muslims as human beings. On the other hand, the social, sexual and family values of Westerners (including Americans) became more permissive and open. In the West pre-marital sex, extra-marital fornication, homosexuality and lesbianism, alcoholism and marijuana moved closer to cultural acceptance. Dress culture for women became less modest as miniskirts, tight pants, and low necklines became the order of the day. A cultural divergence was occurring between the new Euro-American norms and the more conservative values of Islamic traditions.

On the other hand, the relationship between the American *people* and the Muslim *people* in the second half of the twentieth century became increasingly more positive. America seemed to be in the process of accepting Islam not as an alien intrusion but increasingly as part and parcel of the American mosaic. Islam was becoming "indigenous" to American pluralism.[109]

The third phase in Americo-Islamic relations is now unfolding since September 11, 2001. The new Bush administration would like to trade in the currency of *fear* in order to mobilize political support. This is a far cry from the anguish of Franklin D. Roosevelt after the Japanese attack on Pearl Harbor. Roosevelt proclaimed: "The only thing we have to fear is fear itself."

With George W. Bush's administration, it has become a different silent imperative—"The only thing we have to *sell* to the American people is fear itself." Former Vice President Al Gore put it bluntly: "The last three years have seen the politics of fear raise its ugly head again."[110] As Thomas L. Friedman has noted in his column in *The New York Times:*

"We have stopped exporting hope, the most important commodity America has. We now export only fear, so we end up importing everyone else's fears right back."[111]

In spite of assurances that the war on terrorism is not a war on Islam, Muslims are paying a disproportionate price for this latest American campaign—from the war on Afghanistan and Iraq to the harassment of Muslim citizens of the United States.

The fourth phase of Americo-Islamic relations requires the taming of the imperial power of the new United States following the collapse of the Soviet Union and the end of the Cold War. America's own internal democracy needs to develop the skills of restraining America as an empire. In the final analysis, only America as a democracy can effectively control America as an empire.

Yet one additional force is needed for restraining the United States. That other future force is the potential power of the Islamic civilization when its petrowealth is combined with a truly emergent Islamic renaissance. Such an Islamic rejuvenation may be needed to help the global system realize the virtues of checks and balances once again.

Insha Allahu Taala.

NOTES

1. See Samuel P. Huntington, *The Clash of Civilizations and the Remaking of World Order* (New York: Simon and Schuster, 1996).

2. Unlike in previous immigration legislation, the Immigration Reform and Control Act of 1965 did not have race as a category for immigration and naturalization decisions; a detailed analysis of this Act may be found in Cheryl Shanks, *Immigration and the Politics of American Sovereignty, 1890–1990* (Ann Arbor, MI: University of Michigan Press, 2001), 144–86.

3. Compelling histories of sexual customs in the United States are drawn in Jon D'Emilio and Estelle Freedman, *Intimate Matters: A History of Sexuality in America*

(New York: Harper & Row, 1988); David Allyn, *Make Love, Not War: The Sexual Revolution, An Unfettered History* (Boston: Little, Brown, 2000), and Kevin White, *Sexual Liberation or Sexual License? The American Revolt Against Victorianism* (Chicago: Ivan R. Dee, 2000).

4. For example, Bertrand Russell's appointment to the City College of New York was rescinded because of his defense of sex prior to marriage; see Allyn, *Make Love Not War*, 16.

5. These limits are explored in D'Emilio and Freedman, *Intimate Matters*, 256–65, and White, *Sexual Liberation or Sexual License?* 77–78.

6. Many of the laws against adultery were enacted under the pressure from female moral reformers; see D'Emilio and Freedman, *Intimate Matters*, 144–45.

7. See Geraldine Brooks, *Nine Parts Of Desire: The Hidden World Of Islamic Women* (New York: Doubleday/Anchor, 1995), 54. For a more general survey of "honor killings," consult L. A Odeh, "Crimes of Honour and the Construction of Gender in Arab Societies," In: Mai Yamani and Andrew Allen, eds., Feminism *and Islam: Legal and Literary Perspectives* (Berkshire, UK: Ithaca Press, 1996), 141–94.

8. The Supreme Court decision in *Lawrence v. Texas* (2003) striking down anti-sodomy laws alarmed conservatives; see a report in *The Washington Post* (June 27, 2003), 1.

9. For a chronology of female suffrage, consult Jane Hannan, Mitzi Auchterloine and Katharine Holden, *International Encyclopedia of Women's Suffrage* (Santa Barbara, CA: ABC-Clio, 2000), 339–40.

10. Niemi, Muller, Smith, *Trends in Public Opinion*, 22 and Mitchell, *American Attitudes*, 334.

11. Niemi, Muller, Smith, *Trends in Public Opinion*, 225 and Mitchell, *American Attitudes*, 340.

12. For some fascinating stories about female workers in the World War II period, see Nancy Wise and Cheryl Wise, *A Mouthful of Rivets: Women At Work in World War II* (San Francisco: Jossey Bass, 1994), and for a scholarly analysis, consult Maureen Honey, *Creating Rosie the Riveter: Class, Gender and Propaganda During World War II* (Amherst, MA: University of Massachusetts Press, 1994).

13. Wise and Wise, *A Mouthful of Rivets,* 188–06. Over the longer period, the reversal after World War II in female participation was temporary, as evinced by statistics covering the 1870–1986 period in Barbara Bergman, *The Economic Emergence of Women* (New York: Basic Books, 1984), 20.

14. See K. Austin Kerr, *Organizing for Prohibition: A New History of the Anti-Saloon League* (New Haven and London: Yale University Press, 1985), 35.

15. Consult Thomas M. Coffey, *The Long Thirst: Prohibition in America 1920–1933* (New York: W. W. Norton & Co., 1975) and Kerr, *Organizing for Prohibition*, 185.

16. Based on this incident, a docudrama entitled *Death of A Princess* (1980), directed by Antony Thomas, caused a major controversy when it was shown in the West.

17. Statistics on race and the death penalty can be found at http://www.death penaltyinfo.org; according to recent estimates, about 45 percent of death row inmates are African American.

18. For an overview of this case, see Allyn, *Make Love, Not War: The Sexual Revolution, An Unfettered History* (Boston: Little, Brown, 2000), 85–92. Excerpts from the decision may be found in Abraham L. Davis and Barbara Luck Graham, *The Supreme Court, Race, and Civil Rights* (Thousand Oaks, CA: Sage Publications, 1995), 214–16.

19. Public opinion has changed dramatically in this regard. The number of whites who thought that there should be laws against interracial marriage has declined from 59 percent in December 1963 to 11 percent in 1996; see Richard G. Niemi, John Mueller, Jon W. Smith, *Trends in Public Opinion: A Compendium of Survey Data* (New York, Westport, CT and London: Greenwood Press, 1989), 170, and Susan Mitchell, *American Attitudes: Who Thinks What About the Issues That Shape Our Lives* (Ithaca, NY: New Strategist Publications, Inc., 2000), 194–95.

20. Racism toward immigrant Muslims was exacerbated by immigrant legislation, which was racist; see Richard Wormser, *American Islam: Growing Up Muslim in America* (New York: Walker & Co., 1994, 2002), 13. For a quick overview of the history of Islam in the US, consult Bret E. Carroll, *The Routledge Historical Atlas of Religion in America* (New York and London: Routledge, 2000), 102–03.

21. Malcolm X was one such example. On the religious transformation of Malcolm, see Louis A. DeCaro, Jr., *On the Side of My People: A Religious Life of Malcolm X* (New York: New York University, 1996).

22. Relatedly, consult Youssef Courbage and Philippe Fargues, *Christians and Jews Under Islam* (London and New York: Tauris, 1997).

23. This resistance was in the context of European refugees fleeing the war and persecution of the Nazi advances, and many of these refugees were Jewish; see the note in Shanks, *Immigration and the Politics of American Sovereignty, 1890–1990,* 333.

24. Indeed, as late as the seventies, only 26 percent of surveyed Americans thought sex before marriage was not morally wrong, but this had increased to 42 percent in 1996; see Niemi, Muller, Smith, *Trends in Public Opinion*, 193 and Mitchell, *American Attitudes*, 416.

25. Relatedly, consult Martha A. Fineman and Martha T. McCluskey, eds., *Feminism, Media, and the Law* (Oxford and New York: Oxford University Press, 1997) and Lisa M. Cuklanz, *Rape on Prime Time: Television, Masculinity and Sexual Violence* (Philadelphia: University of Pennsylvania Press, 2000); and for one alternative example, see Lori M. Irving and Susan K. Berel, "Comparison of Media-Literacy Programs to Strengthen College Women's Resistance to Media Images," *Pyschology of Women Quarterly* 25, 2 (June 2001), 103–11.

26. Niemi, Muller, Smith, *Trends in Public Opinion*, 225 and Mitchell, *American Attitudes*, 340.

33. Consult David Kingsley, *Ecology and Religion: Ecological Spirituality in Cross-Cultural Perspective* (Englewood-Cliffs, NJ: Prentice-Hall, 1995), 123.

27. Niemi, Muller, Smith, *Trends in Public Opinion*, 22 and Mitchell, *American Attitudes*, 334.

28. Coffey, *The Long Thirst,* 315.

29. Michael Moore, *Stupid White Me: And Other Sorry Excuses for the State of the Nation* (New York: Regan Books, 2001), 206.

30. The Supreme Court has decided to take up the issue of the death penalty for juvenile offenders at the current time; see *The New York Times* (January 27, 2004), 1.

31. Amina may not have been in any danger of being executed at all, and even under the Shariah, the case against her was flawed. See the opinion piece by Helon Habila, "The Politics of Islamic Law: Shariah in Nigeria," *The International Herald Tribune*, 7.

32. At this time, the French National Assembly has decided to ban the head scarves worn by Muslim females in public schools; for a French explanation of the feelings behind the ban, see the op-ed piece by Guy Coq, "Scarves and Symbols," *The New York Times* (January 30, 2004), 21.

33. Consult David Kingsley, *Ecology and Religion: Ecological Spirituality in Cross-Cultural Perspective* (Englewood-Cliffs, NJ: Prentice-Hall, 1995), 123.

34. Jane I. Smith, *Islam in America* (New York: Columbia University Press, 1999), 127.

35. See the *Christian Science Monitor* (November 2, 2000), 18; and more recently, Arab Americans have been approached for their political support, since their numbers may be pivotal in some battleground states in the 2004 Presidential race; see the reports in *The Washington Post* (October 18, 2003), 7; (October 19, 2003), 5; (December 7, 2003), 1; and David Broder's op-ed piece, "Mobilizing Arab Americans," *The Washington Post* (October 22, 2003), 29.

36. According to one survey of US Muslims, 30 percent are black, 33 percent South Asian, and 25 percent Arab (the survey did not include followers of the Nation of Islam); see *The Baltimore Sun* (April 27, 2001) 4.

37. A poll by the American Muslim Council in 1999 showed that 53 percent of Muslims identified with the Democratic Party, while 47 percent identified with the Republican Party; see the *Denver Post* (December 18, 1999), 26.

38. A key tenet of American liberalism is the separation of Church and State, and Jewish political activity has tended to be more liberal; see Lena Stein, "American Jews and Their Liberal Political Behavior," in Wilbur Church, ed., *The Politics of Minority Coalitions* (Westport, CT, and London: Praeger, 1996), 196.

39. For some instances in the 1990s, see Frank S. Ravitch, *School Prayer and Discrimination: The Civil Rights of Religious Minorities and Dissenters* (Boston: Northeastern University Press, 1999), 9–12. Relatedly, on the Jewish position on religion in public schools, see Jonathan D. Sarna and David G. Dalin, *Religion and State in the American Jewish Experience* (Notre Dame, IN: University of Notre Dame Press, 1997), 239–240.

40. There has been a decline of religion—particularly Christianity—in Europe; see *The New York Times* (October 13, 2003), 1.

41. See Kambiz GhaneaBassiri, *Competing Visions of Islam in the United States: A Study of Los Angeles* (Westport, CT: Greenwood Press, 1997), 44–45.

42. For some discussions of these fears, see Smith, *Islam in America*, 120, GhaneaBassiri, *Competing Visions of Islam in the United States,* 78–84, and the *San Francisco Chronicle* (January 17, 1999), 1.

43. Shanks, *Immigration and the Politics of American Sovereignty, 1890–1990,* 144.

44. Groups and organizations established by Muslims in the United States to correct stereotypes and influence policy include the Council for American Islamic Relations,

based in Washington, D.C. and the Muslim Public Affairs Council; see "Muslims Learn to Pull Political Ropes in US," *Christian Science Monitor* (February 5, 1996), 10. Also, on the chaplains, see Jane I. Smith, *Islam in America* (New York: Columbia University Press, 1999), 159.

45. Emerson's article appeared in the *Wall Street Journal* (13 Mar. 1996), 14.

46. Leading human rights publications now routinely survey the state of laws against gays and lesbians. See, for example, Human Rights Watch, *World Report 2002* (New York, Washington, DC, Brussels: Human Rights Watch, 2002), 602–08. Ronald Inglehart and Pippa Norris have argued in "The True Clash of Civilizations," *Foreign Policy* (March/April 2003) Issue 135, 62–70, that a country's treatment of homosexuals is indicative of its level of tolerance, and that the differences between the Islamic world and the West on this issue and gender rights mark the dividing line between Islam and the West.

47. There is a strong effort in Canada to legalize same-sex marriages although there has been opposition, notably from the Catholic Church; see *The International Herald Tribune* (August 11, 2003), 7.

48. On the decision by the Episcopalians, see Michael Massing, "Bishop Lee's Choice," *The New York Times Magazine* (January 4, 2004), 32–40.

49. One such person, a lesbian Canadian Muslim, Irshad Manji, has recently been in the news with her *The Trouble With Islam: A Muslim's Call For Reform In Her Faith* (New York: St. Martin's Press, 2004).

50. See Khalid Durani, "Homosexuality and Islam," in Arlene Swidler, ed., *Homosexuality and World Religions* (Valley Forge, PA: Trinity Press International, 1993), 184; and for a longer study of Islamic homosexuality, see Stephen O. Murray and Will Roscoe, *et al*, *Islamic Homosexualities: Culture, History, and Literature* (New York and London: NYU Press, 1997).

51. Jim Wafer, "Muhammad and Male Sexuality," in Murray and Roscoe, et al, *Islamic Homosexualities*, 87–90.

52. *New York Times* (February 4, 2004), 8.

53. For an example in Iraq, see *The Washington Post* (February 3, 2004), 2.

54. See the op-ed piece by Larry Johnson, "The Declining Terrorist Threat," (July 10, 2001).

55. The September 11 attack caused the largest loss of American lives on a single day on American soil since the Civil War, when there were battles that claimed thousands of lives on a single day, and the war itself claimed 623,000 lives; see Philip S. Paludan, *A People's Contest: the Union and Civil War, 1861–1865*, Second Edition, (Lawrence, KS: University of Kansas Press, 1996), 316 for a comparative casualty count of major US wars.

56. A majority of the countries under US travel advisories currently have Muslim majority populations or substantial Muslim populations; a list of the advisories may be found at http://travel.state.gov/warnings_list.html 16 of 27; Americans are advised to avoid traveling to these countries.

57. *New York Times* (February 2, 2004), 3.

58. See *The Washington Post* (November 19, 2003), 28 for a report on the incident.

59. The Kay revelations may be found in *The Washington Post* (January 28, 2004), 1.

60. In an NBC interview with President George W. Bush February 7, 2004, the number of US deaths and casualties by interviewer Tim Russert was put at about 530 deaths and 3000 "injuries and woundings;" a full transcript of the interview is at http://msnbc.msn.com/id/4179618/; and an estimate of Iraqi civilian deaths ranges between 8,000 to 10,000, according to http://www.iraqbodycount.net/.

61. Many Muslims from other countries who have been subjected to a special registration procedure, including the taking of fingerprints and photographs, have decided to boycott visiting the United States. For instance, a Pakistan-born Canadian citizen professor who was asked to go through this procedure on his way to the United States decided to stay away from the United States till the procedure was removed. See *the Washington Post* (November 11, 2003), 17.

62. For a report on the difficulties faced by Muslim travelers at airports—including this author—see *The Washington Post* (September 14, 2003), 8.

63. For general accounts of the encroachment on civil rights, see Nat Hentoff, *The War on the Bill of Rights, and the Coming Resistance* (New York: Seven Stories Press, 2003); David Cole, *Enemy Aliens: Immigrants' Rights and American Freedoms in the War on Terrorism* (New York: New Press 2003); David Cole and James X. Dempsey, *Terrorism & the Constitution: Sacrificing Civil Liberties in the Name of National Security* (New York: New Press, 2002) 2nd rev. ed. 2002; and Wendy Kaminer, *Free For All: Defending Liberty in America Today* (Boston: Beacon Press, 2002). For a specific report on the circumstances of the arrests, flimsy evidence, and post-arrest treatment of the September 11 detainees, see the highly critical report of the Justice Department's own Inspector General: consult Inspector General of the Department of Justice: United States. Department of Justice, *The September 11 Detainees: A Review of the Treatment of Aliens Held on Immigration Charges in Connection With the Investigation of the September 11Attacks* available at http://www.usdoj.gov/oig/special/0603/full.pdf (2003).

64. *The Washington Post* (January 14, 2004), 1.

65. *The Washington Post* (January 12, 2004), 1.

66. See the op-ed piece by Jean AbiNader and Kate Martin, "Just the Facts, Mr. Ashcroft," *The Washington Post* (July 25, 2002) 21.

67. The Supreme Court has refused to hear challenges to the arguments proffered by the US government against releasing the names of prisoners; see *The Washington Post* (January 13, 2004), 18.

68. Also, of the 762 detainees investigated in the Department of Justice report cited above, *none* were found to have links with terrorism. See the op-ed piece by Richard Cohen, "Ashcroft's Attitude Problem" *The Washington Post,* (June 10, 2003), 21.

69. See the concerns raised by critics in a report in the *New York Times* (December 29, 2002), B7.

70. Chisun Lee writes that, Sin Yen Ling, a lawyer for the New York-based Asian American Legal Defense and Education Fund pointed that "Since December [2001], Ling says, she has personally represented as many as 40 immigrants, all but one of Middle Eastern or Muslim extraction. And the flow has not lessened." "The Name Game." *The Village Voice* (August 14–20, 2002). Further, demographics of the 762 detainees in the report of the Department of Justice, *The September*

11 Detainees, illustrated in Figure 2, 21, are completely different from those of the 9/11 hijackers. For instance, the largest number of detainees (254) were Pakistanis, and while the largest number of the hijackers were Saudi Arabians, more Indians and Turks were arrested than Saudi Arabians!

71. Quoted in *The New York Times* (December 1, 2003), 5.

72. For one discussion of the issues at Nuremberg, consult Alan S. Rosenbaum, *Prosecuting Nazi War Criminals* (Boulder: Westview Press, 1993).

73. Although the word "assassination" is rarely used, the Bush administration is not coy about using targeted strikes to kill those who may be perceived as "terrorists." Indeed, Bush himself said in his 2003 State of the Union Address: "All told, more than 3,000 suspected terrorists have been arrested in many countries. Many others have met a different fate. Put it this way: They're no longer a problem to the United States and our friends and allies." See http://abcnews.go.com/sections/nightline/World/iraq_assassination030315.html for more.

74. For details, see Moshe Pearlman, *The Capture and Trial of Adolf Eichmann* (New York: Simon and Schuster, 1963).

75. New guidelines were issued permitting these activities, although FBI Director Robert S. Mueller III denied that the guidelines would be used to do widespread surveillance of mosques; see the *Washington Post* (June 6, 2002), 1.

76. See the press release from the American Civil Liberties Union, and other members of a coalition regarding this issue at http://archive.aclu.org/news/2001/n122001 a.html

77. A report on the relaxation of the rules may found in *The Washington Post* (February 6, 2004), 11.

78. See relatedly, the op-ed piece by Jean AbiNader and Kate Martin, "Just the Facts, Mr. Ashcroft," *The Washington Post* (July 25, 2002), 21.

79. *The Washington Post* (November 12, 2003), 2. Even New York City, the site of the 9/11 attacks, has formally condemned the Patriot Act; see *The Washington Post* (February 5, 2004), 11.

80. See the report in the *New York Times* (June 29, 2001), 14.

81. An investigation was launched into the general's remarks; see *The Washington Post* (October 22, 2003), 2. Boykin is supposed to work with Muslim countries on anti-terrorism efforts, and quite apart from being inflammatory, his words displayed appalling ignorance about the essentially same God that Muslims, Jews, and Christians worship; see the op-ed article by John Kearney, "My God Is Your God," *The New York Times* (January 28, 2004), 25.

82. A Human Rights Watch report pointed out that country leaders were taking advantage of the anti-terror campaign to suppress dissent and abuse human rights; see *The Washington Post* (January 18, 2001), 12.

83. See Tom Malinowski, "Absent Moral Authority," *The Washington Post* (February 2, 2004), 17.

84. See Fred Hiatt, "Democracy on Hold," *The Washington Post* (October 6, 2003), 23.

85. A readable account of some of these misdeeds may be found in Roger Lowenstein, *Origins of the Crash: The Great Bubble And Its Undoing* (New York: Penguin Press, 2004); and for a briefer example, see his "The Fall of the House of Rigas," *The*

New York Times Magazine (February 1, 2004), 26–32, 42–3, and 62.

86. See David Callahan, *The Cheating Culture: Why More Americans Are Doing Wrong To Get Ahead* (New York: Harcourt Press, 2004).

87. This example is cited in Rafael Reuveny, "Economic Growth, Environmental Scarcity, and Conflict," *Global Environmental Politics* (February 2002), Volume 2, Number 1, 93.

88. A report on the Massachusetts Supreme Court's decision may be found in *The Washington Post* (February 5, 2004), 1.

89. The Ohio bill was sweeping—it would also prohibit state agencies from giving benefits to both gay and heterosexual domestic partners; see *The New York Times* (February 3, 2004), 12.

90. The Alliance was in the news recently when one more mainstream Islamic organization, the Islamic Society of North America, withdrew after being accused of links to extremism; see *The Washington Post* (February 8, 2004), 15.

91. See the comment by Charles McGrath, "Arrested Developments," *The New York Times Magazine* (January 4, 2004), 8.

92. Critical discussions on the American empire may be found in Chalmers Johnson, *Blowback: The Costs and Consequences of American Empire* (New York: Henry Holt, 2001, 1st Owl Books ed.) and Michael Parenti, *Against Empire* (San Francisco, CA: City Lights Books, 1995).

93. Dimitri K. Simes, "America's Imperial Dilemma," *Foreign Affairs* (November–December 2003), Volume 82, Number 6, 93.

94. For a discussion about the successes and reasons for Jewish success in American society, see Steven J. Gold and Bruce Phillips, "Mobility and Continuity Among Eastern European Jews," in Silvia Pedraza and Rubén G. Rumbaut, eds., Origins and Destinies: Immigration, Race, and Ethnicity in America (Belmont, CA: Wadsworth, 1996), 186–88.

95. An overview of the American Jews' role in American foreign policy toward Israel may be found in Steven L. Spiegel, "Israel and Beyond: American Jews in U. S. Foreign Policy," in L. Sandy Maisel and Ira N. Forman, eds., Jews in American Politics (Lanham, MD: Rowman & Littlefield Publishers, 2001), 251–69 and for an alternative argument positing that the extent of their influence on US policy to Israel may be declining, consult Steven T. Rosenthal, *Irreconcilable Differences?: The Waning of the American Jewish Love Affair With Israel* (Hanover, NH: Brandeis University Press: Published by University Press of New England, 2001).

96. This quote is from an interview with Walter Mosley in *The New York Times Magazine* (February 8, 2004), 17.

97. The demographic changes in the United States of the 21st century pose several challenges; see, for example, Nancy A. Denton and Stewart E. Tolnay, eds., *American Diversity: A Demographic Challenge for the Twenty-First Century* (Albany, NY: State University of New York Press, 2002) and Neil Smelser, William Julius Wilson, and Faith Mitchell, eds., *America Becoming: Racial Trends and Their Consequences*, 2 volumes (Washington, DC: National Academy Press, 2001).

98. For a slightly different discussion of the "Islamic spectrum," see Seyyed Hossein Nasr, *The Heart of Islam: Enduring Values for Humanity* (San Francisco, CA: Harper San Francisco, 2002), 57–112.

Chapter Twenty

99. Wahhabi Islam in Saudi Arabia, and The Taliban in Afghanistan may be examples of such Orthodox Islam. Brief descriptions of the rise of the Wahhabis in Saudi Arabia may be found in William L. Cleveland *A History of the Modern Middle East* (Boulder, CO: Westview Press, 1994), 116, and Nasr, *The Heart of Islam*, 69–70.

100. Readers interested in Soroush may consult Reason, *Freedom, & Democracy in Islam: Essential Writings of 'Abdolkarim Soroush*, translated, edited, and with a critical introduction by Mahmoud Sadri and Ahmad Sadri, (Oxford and New York: Oxford University Press, 2000).

101. Guides to some of the views in liberal Islam may be found in Charles Kurzman, ed., *Liberal Islam: A Sourcebook* (New York: Oxford University Press, 1998).

102. Ms. Mernissi has been a prolific author on issues involving Islam, women, and Morocco. Some of her major works include *Scheherazade Goes West: Different Cultures, Different Harems* (New York: Washington Square Press, 2001); *Islam and Democracy: Fear of the Modern World*, transl. Mary Jo Lakeland (Reading, MA: Addison-Wesley Pub. Co., 1992); *The Veil and the Male Elite: A Feminist Interpretation of Women's Rights in Islam*, transl. Mary Jo Lakeland (Reading, MA: Addison-Wesley Pub. Co., 1991); *Women and Islam: An Historical and Theological Enquiry*, transl. Mary Jo Lakeland (Oxford: Basil Blackwell, 1991); *Doing Daily Battle: Interviews With Moroccan Women*, transl. Mary Jo Lakeland (London: Women's Press, 1988); *Beyond The Veil: Male-Female Dynamics in Modern Muslim Society* (Bloomington: Indiana University Press, 1987 edition, Rev. ed., 1st Midland Book ed).

103. Iranian President Mohammad Khatami may be an example of a Shiite cleric and politician who is attempting to bring about change in Islam; see his *Hope and Challenge: The Iranian President Speaks* (Binghamton, NY: Institute of Global Cultural Studies, 1997).

104. Relatedly, consult the following: Keith E. Whittington *Constitutional Interpretation: Textual Meaning, Original Intent, And Judicial Review* (Lawrence, KS: University Press of Kansas, 1999); Terry Eastland, ed.,; foreword by Griffin B. Bell, *Benchmarks: Great Constitutional Controversies In The Supreme Court* (Washington, DC and Grand Rapids, MI: Ethics and Public Policy Center and W.B. Eerdmans Pub. Co., 1995); and William F. Harris, II, *The Interpretable Constitution* (Baltimore: Johns Hopkins University Press, c1993).

105. In comparison to the Warren Supreme Court, the Rehnquist Court has become more conservative, for the most part. See, for instance, David Kairys, *With Liberty and Justice for Some: A Critique of the Conservative Supreme Court* (New York: The New Press and Nortons, 1993); William Mishler and Reginald S. Sheehan, "*The Supreme Court as a Countermajoritarian Institution? The Impact of Public Opinion on Supreme Court Decisions*," *The American Political Science Review* (Mar., 1993), Volume 87, Number 1, 87–101;Tracey E. George and Lee Epstein, "On the Nature of Supreme Court Decision Making," *The American Political Science Review*, Volume. 86, Number 2. (Jun., 1992), 323–37; and Richard C. Kearney and Reginald S. Sheehan, "Supreme Court Decision Making: The Impact of Court Composition on State and Local Government Litigation," *The Journal of Politics*, Volume 54, Number 4. (Nov 1992), 1008–025.

106. Perhaps the most well-known—but also controversial—explanation for the stagnation of the Muslim world is Bernard Lewis *What Went Wrong?: Western Impact and Middle Eastern Response* (Oxford and New York: Oxford University Press, 2002); but also consult Hilal Khashan, *Arabs at the Crossroads: Political Identity and Nationalism* (Gainesville: University Press of Florida, 2000); Michael Field, *Inside the Arab World* (Cambridge, MA: Harvard University Press, 1995); and Olivier Roy, *The Failure of Political Islam*, translated by Carol Volk Cambridge, MA: Harvard University Press, 1994).

107. Ehsan Masood, "Faith, Reason, and Science," *TWAS Newsletter* (April–June 2003), Volume 15, Number 2, 5.; also see Thomas L. Friedman, "Courageous Arab Thinkers," *The New York Times* Week in Review Section (October 20, 2003), 11.

108. On Taha's views and execution, consult Abdel Salam Sidahmed, *Politics and Islam in Contemporary Sudan* (New York: St. Martin's Press, 1996), 122–23 and 136.

109. The harassment of Muslims seems to have mobilized several groups to involve themselves politically. See the reports in *The Washington Post* (December 7, 2003), 1; (October 18, 2003), 7; (October 19, 2003), 5; and David Broder's op-ed piece, "Mobilizing Arab Americans," *The Washington Post* (October 22, 2003), 29.

110. Gore made these comments in a Tennessee Democratic gathering in a fiery speech; see the report in *The New York Times* (February 8, 2004), 18.

111. Thomas L. Friedman, "On Listening," *The New York Times* (October 16, 2003), 31.

Section VI

CONCLUSIONS

Chapter Twenty-One

The Semitic Impact on Africa: Arab and Jewish Influences

In this chapter we are looking at the issue of identity in Africa from a particular perspective. We are focusing especially on the impact of the Semitic peoples (especially Arabs and Jews) upon the cultural personality of the continent.

Contemporary Africa's triple heritage of indigenous, Islamic and Western legacies is just, the modern culmination of a much older triple heritage — the heritage of indigenous, Semitic and Greco-Roman influences on Africa.

The ancient Semitic strand has now narrowed and focused more firmly on Arab and Islamic influences; the ancient Greco-Roman strand has now expanded to encompass wider European and American intrusions.

The expansion of the Greco-Roman strand is probably irreversible. But is the reduction of the Semitic strand to the Arabo-Islamic trend now under challenge? Is the Semitic factor in Africa's political experience destined to re-incorporate a Jewish element in the years ahead?

The best, embodiment of the ancient triple heritage (indigenous, Semitic and Greco-Roman) are North Africa and Ethiopia. The best embodiment of the modern triple heritage (indigenous, Islamic and Western) is Nigeria.

The whole cultural history of Africa is captured in the transition from the triple ancient personality of North Africa and Ethiopia to the triple modern personality of Nigeria.

In population Ethiopia is probably the second largest African country south of the Sahara. Nigeria is indeed the largest. Culturally, the two countries together probably tell the whole story in their own way.

The Jewish impact on African identity has taken a variety of forms, of which the most, important are:

1. The actual presence of Jews in Africa.
2. The direct, religious impact of Judaism.
3. The indirect religious impact, of Judaism through Christianity and Islam.
4. Jewish experience as a comparative metaphor for Africa.
5. Jewish economic and political penetration of Africa, especially in the 20th Century.

Of all parts of Black Africa, Ethiopia has probably experienced the most direct impact of Judaism. We shall return to this shortly.

Almost, the whole of the rest of Africa has experienced the indirect religious impact of Judaism through Christianity and to some extent through Islam. But first let us examine the actual presence of Jews in Africa—beginning with the observation that Africa accommodates, on the one hand, some of the richest Jews in the world and, on the other, some of the poorest.

The two main divisions of World Jewry have also been well represented in Africa. North Africa has accommodated clusters of Ashkenazic Jews, mainly immigrants from Europe who entered Africa in the nineteenth and twentieth centuries. Outside the Republic of South Africa, the numbers of these European Jews in sub-Saharan Africa are modest. But in countries like Kenya, Jews are often influential and some are exceptionally wealthy.

The biggest numbers of Jews in the Arab world today are in Morocco. Before the creation of Israel, Morocco had more than a quarter of million Moroccan Jews and a few European Jews. By 1956 well over 60,000 Jews had emigrated to Israel. Some also left for France. Every Arab-Israeli war created new fears among Moroccan Jews. The number of Jews now remaining there are probably in the region of, at the most, fifty thousand.

Egypt had approximately a hundred thousand Jews before World War II. There are now very few Jews left in Egypt. As for Algeria, there were more than 130,000 in 1960:

> Mass exodus of the Jewish population began in May 1962 after the signing of the Evian Agreements which secured independence for Algeria. Within a few weeks, from May to July, almost all of Algeria's Jews left, the country; they were joined by most, of the Europeans. Being French citizens more than 125,000 went to France and about 10,000 to Israel.[1]

The history of the Jews in Algeria—almost all of them Sephardim—goes back 2000 years. Most of them acquired French citizenship through the Crernieux Decree of 1870. In time Sephardic Jews in metropolitan France may become indistinguishable from Ashkenazim.

But let us now take a different look at the Jewish presence in Africa from the unusual vantage point of a comparative study—a vantage point which includes issues of race, class and power.

COMPARATIVE JEWRY

The Jewish presence in Africa, though much more modest than that of the Arabs, has had a fascination of its own. The most black of all Jews are of course the Falasha of Ethiopia—self-conceived as the lost tribe of Israel (Beta Israel). A majority of them were at last transferred to Israel in 1985 in the wake of the Ethiopian famine. Economically the Falasha in Ethiopia were among the poorest of the poor. They were neither Sephardic nor Ashkenazic. Politically they were often persecuted under a Christian theocracy. Religiously they continue to be despised even by fellow Jews. It was only in the 1970s that Israel's Law of Return was at last allowed to be selectively applicable to the Falasha Jews. They could "return" to Israel, but under careful conditions. It took a large seal ecological "holocaust" in Ethiopia in 1985 to tilt the balance of Israeli sympathy.

Ethiopia is the only African country which for centuries has had not only Black Christians and Black Muslims, but also Black Jews. All the three Semitic religions have, through sheer length of time, found indigenous roots in Ethiopia.

But a more interesting juxtaposition is between the Falasha Jews of Ethiopia and the white Jews of the Republic of South Africa. That juxtaposition captures more clearly many of the issues of race, class, religion and continental identity mentioned earlier.

The Falasha of Ethiopia even after transferred to Israel are among the poorest of all Jews. I visited a Falasha village in Ethiopia in 1984. Even by African standards, the poverty was stark, the sanitation abysmal, the living conditions primordial and rudimentary. The only abundance were the clouds of flies, everywhere!

On the other hand, among the richest, of all Jews of the world are those of the Republic of South Africa. What they contribute to the treasury of Israel is next only to the contribution of the Jews of the United States. And among white South Africans, the Jews have a higher per capita income than the ruling and politically more influential Dutch-speaking Afrikaners. In class terms, what this means is that the Falasha Jews have been either serfs or peasants across the Centuries—while the Jews of South Africa have been in the main either in the liberal professions or members of the commercial bourgeoisie.

Until 1985, the Falasha were disadvantaged Jews in a land ruled by privileged Black gentiles—from Black Emperors of the past to Black Marxists of latter years. South African Jewry have been privileged white Jews in a land ruled by privileged white gentiles—bound together by the bonds of racial advantage.

The Falasha were racially part of a Black majority—but religiously a minority. On the other hand, South African Jews are racially part of a white minority—though religiously also a minority.

The Falasha were for a long time Jews under a Christian theocracy, a state based on sectional religious supremacy. South African Jews have been part of white supremacy—a state based on sectional racial supremacy. The Blacks in South Africa are religiously closer to the ruling class than the Jews are—but the Jews are of course racially closer to the ruling class than the Blacks are. In other words, South African Blacks are Christians like the Dutch-speaking Afrikaners. If South Africa had been a theocracy, the Black gentiles would have been above white Jews.

On the other hand, if Ethiopia had been a state of racial supremacy, the Falasha would have had access to the Black ruling class. But because Ethiopia was for centuries a theocracy, Black Jews failed to benefit. And because South Africa has been a state based on white supremacy, Black gentiles have failed to benefit. The Falasha were politically submissive in Ethiopia, though remaining religiously distinctive across millenia. South African Jews have remained ideologically liberal and sometimes progressive and radical—while still remaining religiously distinctive.

In relation to Israel, all that the Falasha can contribute to Israel is their own population. "Open your doors, O Land of Israel." And yet the Falasha were marginalized by the Law of Return until the ecological holocaust of the 1980s.

What the South African Jewry can contribute to Israel is, as we indicated, the second largest donation after the U.S.A. Indeed, per head of the population, the donation of South Africa's Jewry has in some years been larger than that of American Jews. Rich Jews are, de facto, privileged under Israel's Law of Return. Abba Eban, formerly of South Africa, is only a modest illustration of this tendency.

The Falasha Jews briefly gained from a leftwing revolution in Ethiopia—but lost through a rightwing swing in Israel under Menachem Begin. The Marxist regime in Ethiopia was beginning to treat the Falasha with a greater sense of equal citizenship than almost any of the previous Ethiopian governments across the centuries. On the other hand, the Orthodox rightwing in Israel have tended to be more anti-Falasha than the secular Jews. The Jewish purists often regard the Falasha as unacceptable Black pretenders if not heretics.

But while the left, wing radicalization of Black Ethiopia did briefly aid the fortunes of the Falasha, the future leftwing radicalization of a Black revolution in South Africa is bound to hurt white Jewry as well as white Gentiles. A large part of South Africa's Jewry seems to be inevitably destined for settlement in Israel within the next generation. And yet the two Jewish communities of Africa (Falasha and South African) have posed problems about the definition of an African. The Falasha were indigenous by every appearance, but they insisted that they were immigrant. They were "the Lost Tribe of Israel." Indeed, the name "Falasha" itself means strangers or exiles in Amharic. The group is sometimes hostile to the name "Falasha"—and yet they thought of themselves doctrinally as exiles from Biblical Israel.

On the other hand, South African Jews are immigrant by every appearance, but they increasingly claim that they are no less indigenous to South African soil than Blacks claim to be. The whites claim that many of the Blacks came from the north of the continent at just about the same time that whites arrived from across the seas.

And yet it seems very obvious that the Falasha (even when transferred to modern Israel) are culturally African in almost, every respect—while the South African Jews are almost, completely European culturally. The Falasha claim to be alien—while their culture betrays their indigenous reality. South African Jews claim to be African—while their culture betrays their Eurocentric actuality.

We are back to the triple definition of Africa. Is Africa a continent, a race, or a power structure? The question of whether a Falasha Jew is less African than a South African Jew is caught up in the dynamics of that, interplay between Semitic identity as race, Semitic-identity as religion, and the triple heritage of Africa itself.

It is clear that the issue of how "African" white Jews are to be related to the question of how "black" Africa generally is. If we have accepted that Arabs are Africans, how can we reject North African Jews? After all, Jewry in the African continent is older than Islam. We have already referred to the history of the Jews of the Maghreb—a history which goes back two thousand years. That is five hundred years older than the history of Islam. How can we accept Muslim Arabs as Africans—if we reject the Jews, who were in Africa before the Muslim conquest of North Africa?

On the other hand, how can we accept the Jews of South Africa and reject the Dutch-speaking Afrikaners? What would ever make a white man an "African"? Is the definition subjective—demanding that the person must feel African? Or is the definition temporal—depending upon whether whites have become African by sheer durability and time in Africa?

One solution is to insist on both subjective and temporal criteria of Africanity. The remaining Jews of Arab Africa, especially those who are definitely Sephardim, qualify as "Africans" under the combined subjective and temporal criteria. But the European Jews of sub-Saharan Africa, the Ashkenazim Jews, are in the same situation as the rest of the white presence in Africa. They have to demonstrate a sense of belonging to an African society—as well as demonstrate a long period of geographical location in Africa. Having a South African passport, or having South African citizenship is not, the equivalent of belonging to an "African society"—especially since all genuine Africans in South Africa are gradually being forced into either the homelands or statelessness. Alas, the Ashkenazim Jews of South Africa may not have enough time to be Africanized—before the Black-White holocaust.

As for Jewish experience as a comparative metaphor, this ranges from its impact on beleaguered Afrikaners in South Africa to the theme of Black Zionism in Liberia.

Jewish economic and political penetration into Africa is specially relevant in the twentieth century—from Jewish investment in Southern Africa to the Arab-Israeli factor in Africa. We shall return to this modern phase later on. But historically and culturally, the main embodiment of Judaism in African life-styles is still to be found in Ethiopia. The Falasha are only part of Ethiopia's rendezvous with Judaism. Let us now turn to the other aspects of Ethiopia's links with Semitic traditions.

THE STAR, THE CROSS AND THE CRESCENT

Every society tends to have two paramount myths—the myth of ancestry (how the society started and developed) and the myth of mission or purpose (what is special about that society in terms of human values).[2]

Ethiopia's myth of origin is heavily Hebraic. Even under a Marxist regime most Ethiopians probably believe that their overthrown Royal House could trace its origins to King Solomon and the Queen of Sheba, and that the Emperor's title of "Lion of Judah" was historically valid with regard to the link to "Judah."

Historians of Africa have speculated about King Solomon's Empire. Did it expand to Southern Arabia? Did some Jewish migration take place from Southern Arabia to Aksum, the heartland of ancient Ethiopia? Did these early Jewish immigrants into Africa help to shape future Ethiopian history?

Ethiopian Christianity is Black Africa's oldest. Christian legacy—is Judeo-Christian in more than the usual sense. In some ways it is reminiscent of the religion of the Christian Jews of Jerusalem in the first century after Jesus, Christians who incorporated a lot of Jewish practices into their Christianity (in contrast to the less Judaic Christians of Antioch).

Ethiopian Christianity (like the Christian Jews of the first century) did practise circumcision—and Ethiopian Christianity did also adopt some of the dietary practices of Judaism. However, we should also note there is a persuasive school of thought that says Ethiopian circumcision is pre-Christian.

In spite of the Hebraic elements in Ethiopian Christianity, the Ethiopian orthodox church was not particularly tolerant across the centuries towards Ethiopia's Black Jews, the Falasha. The Falasha had defiantly rejected Christianity—and the Christian theocracy, while it lasted, was not amused.

The Jewish influence on Africa is also indirect—through both Christianity and Islam. Virtually all Jewish prophets are honoured by both Christians and Muslims in Africa. And the Jewish myth of origin—Genesis and Adam and Eve—has been replacing Africa's own tribal myths of origins from one corner of the continent to the other. Monotheism has been conquering Africa under the banner of either the cross or the crescent—but behind both banners is the shadow of Moses and the Commandments he conveyed.

The third Jewish impact, on Africa is through the Jewish experience as a metaphor for the African predicament. The Jewish release from Egypt under Moses' leadership has captured the imagination of many an African nationalist. South Africa's Albert Luthuli, Black Nobel prize winner for peace, entitled his book Let My People Go, after Moses' demand to the Pharaoh.

On the other hand, Luthuli's own Dutch oppressors in South Africa, saw their own trek north from British control as the equivalent of Moses' exit from Pharaonic Egypt. The Afrikaners' more recent situation of isolation among hostile neighbours is often equated with Israel's "heroic isolation" in the Middle East.

This brings us to the fourth impact of the Jews on Africa—the economic and political penetration, especially in the twentieth century. Joseph Chamberlain, as Colonial Secretary, offered the Jewish movement, of Zionism parts of Uganda and Kenya for the establishment of the state of Israel. Theodor Herzl, the Leader of the Zionist movement, preferred to keep East Africa as a potential colony of Jewish surplus population—but the initial Jewish home had to be Palestine. East Africa was thus spared a long-term Israel in its midst.

In 1948 Israel was created in Palestine rather than in Eastern Africa. Much of Africa was still under European colonial rule in any case. Israeli penetration of Africa had to wait, until Africa's independence. In 1957 Ghana became independent under Kwame Nkrumah, and the Israelis wasted no time in cultivating the new African leadership. The decade 1957 to 1967 was the honeymoon of African-Israeli relations—as Israel committed itself to a variety of African development projects, providing mainly expertise rather than capital, while the setting was one of rivalry with the Arabs. The historic competition between the two Semitic peoples—the Jews and the Arabs—had entered a new phase, with Africa as the theatre of rivalry.

THE ARABS IN AFRICAN HISTORY

More weighty than the Jewish factor in Africa's historic experience has been precisely the Arab factor, of which the most pervasive element has been the wide-ranging impact of Islam on Africa.

But what forms did the Arab impact take on Africa's history? The most fundamental aspects of the Arab impact on Africa included the following:

1. The biological impact: Arab intermarriage with Black Africans, creating new Africans in North Africa, the Nile Valley, Swahili City states and elsewhere.
2. The linguistic impact: This includes the role of Arabic in strengthening fellow Semitic or neo-Semitic African languages such as Hausa and Amharic. In Nigeria a curious factor emerges. The Fulani are closer to the Semites biologically (physical features etc.) but the Hausa are closer to the Semites linguistically (linguistic structure etc). A new breed called the Hausa-Fulani captured this dual bio-linguistic heritage of the two amalgamated "tribes."

In addition to the Arab impact on fellow Semitic or neo-Semitic languages within Africa, there is the direct impact of Arabic on the emergence of new languages altogether. The most important of these new languages is Kiswahili. There is little doubt that Kiswahili is the product of interaction between Arab culture and African linguistic structures. Though "new" in this sense, Kiswahili can be traced back at least five centuries.

Thirdly, there is the direct impact of Arabic on pre-existent African languages which are not Semitic. The impact of Arabic on Somali is a particularly striking illustration. Somali is not a Semitic language (unlike Ethiopia's Amharic, which is a Semitic language). And yet the impact of Arabic on Somali imagery and vocabulary is comprehensive. Fourthly, there is the indirect impact of Arabic through other languages already influenced by Arabic. Kiswahili in East Africa has influenced many other African languages, bequeathing to them loan words and Swahili imagery in a variety of forms. Hausa in West Africa has influenced many neighbouring languages. There is also the danger that Arabic-influenced languages like Kiswahili and Hausa may—in their own success—cause the death of dozens if not hundreds of other smaller indigenous languages in their shadow. The death of a language in Africa is often the death of an ethnic identity—with mixed consequences for the cause of national integration.

Fifthly, there is the role of the Arabic language itself as a medium of communication. Are more and more Africans learning it as a language in its own right? Is it being introduced into more universities in Africa as a special area *of* study? Is the proportion of African Muslims who have a command of Arabic increasing?

What is clear is that Arabic is already, in terms of speakers, the most important single language in Africa. At least one out of every five inhabitants of the African continent speaks Arabic.

Sixthly, there is the receding impact of the Arabic alphabet south of the Sahara. Kiswahili is abandoning the Arabic orthography in favour of the Roman. The Somali, after decades of hesitation, have at last chosen the Roman alphabet instead of the Arabic.

And yet the actual creation of new Arabs is still continuing. Let us now turn to this remarkable process of "Arab-formation" across the centuries.

THE BIOLOGY OF ARABIZATION

The Arab conquest of North Africa in the seventh and eighth centuries initiated two processes—Arabization (through language) and Islamization (through religion). The spread of Arabic as a native language created new Semites (the Arabs of North Africa). The diffusion of Islam created new monotheists, but not necessarily new Semites. The Copts of Egypt are linguistically Arabized but they are not of course Muslims. On the other hand, the Wolof and Hausa are preponderantly Islamized—but they are not Arabs.

The process by which the majority of North Africans became Arabized was partly biological and partly cultural. The biological process involved intermarriage and was considerably facilitated by the upward lineage system of the Arabs. Basically, if the father of a child is an Arab the child is an Arab—regardless of the ethnic or racial origins of the mother. This lineage system could be described as ascending miscegenation—since the offspring ascends to the more privileged parent. This is in sharp contrast to the lineage system of, say, the United States where the child of a white father and a Black mother descends to the less privileged race of that society. Indeed, in a system of descending miscegenation like that of the United States, it does not matter whether it is the father or the mother who is Black. An offspring of such racial mixture descends to Black underprivilege. The American system does not therefore co-opt "impurities" upwards across the racial barrier to higher status. It pushes "impurities" downwards into the pool of disadvantage.

It is precisely because the Arabs have the opposite lineage system (ascending miscegenation) that North Africa was so rapidly transformed into part of the Arab world (and not merely Muslim world). The Arab lineage system permitted considerable racial cooptation. "Impurities" were admitted to higher echelons as new full members—provided the father was Arab. And so the range of colours in the Arab world is from the whites of Syria and Iraq to the browns of the Yemen, from blond-haired Lebanese to the Black Arabs of the Sudan.

Within Africa the valley of the White Nile is a particularly fascinating story of evolving Arabization. The Egyptians were of course not Arabs when the Muslim conquest occurred in the seventh century A.D. The process of Islamization in the sense of actual change of religion took place fairly rapidly after the Arab conquerors had consolidated their hold on the country.

On the other hand, the Arabization of Egypt turned out to be significantly slower than its Islamization. The Egyptians changed their religious garment from Christianity to Islam more quickly than they changed their linguistic garment, from ancient Egyptian and ancient Greek to Arabic. And even when Arabic became the mother tongue of the majority of Egyptians, it took centuries before Egyptians began to call themselves Arabs.

But this is all relative. When one considers the pace of Arabization in the first millenium of Islam, it was still significantly faster than average in the history of human acculturation. The number of people in the Middle East, who called themselves "Arabs" expanded dramatically in a relatively short period. This was partly because of the exuberance of the new religion, partly because of the rising prestige of the Arabic language and partly due to the rewards of belonging to a conquering civilization. Religious, political and psychological factors transformed Arabism into an expansionist culture which absorbed the conquered into the body politic of the conquerors. In the beginning there was an "island" or a peninsula called "Arabia." But in time there were far more Arabs outside Arabia than within. At the end of it all there was an "Arab world."

Along the valley of the White Nile Northern Sudan was also gradually Islamized—and more recently has been increasingly Arabized. Again a people who were not originally Arabs have come to see themselves more and more as Arabs.

The question which arises is whether there is a manifest, destiny of the White Nile—pushing it towards total Arabization. It began with the Egyptians and their gradual acquisition of an Arab identity. The Northern Sudanese have been in the process of similar Arabization. Are the southern Sudanese the next, target of the conquering wave of Arabization within the next hundred to two hundred years? Will the twin forces of biological mixture (intermarriage between Northerners and Southerners) and cultural assimilation transform the Dinkas and Nuers of today into the Black Arabs of tomorrow? It is not inconceivable, provided the country as a whole holds together. As intermarriage increases, Northern Sudanese will become more Black in colour. As acculturation increases in the South, Southerners will become more Arab. Biological Africanization of the North and cultural Arabization of the South will reinforce each other and help to forge a more integrated Sudan. Southern Sudanese are *the* only sub-Saharan Africans who are being Arabized faster than they are being Islamized. They are *acquiring* the Arabic language faster than they are *acquiring* Islam. This is in sharp contrast to the experience of such sub-Saharan peoples as the Wolof, the Yoruba, the Hausa or even the Somali—among all of whom the religion of Islam has been more triumphant than the language of the Arabs. This rapid Arabization of the Southern Sudanese linguistically has two possible outcomes in the future. The Southern Sudanese could become Sudan's equivalent of the Copts of Egypt—a Christian minority whose mother tongue would then be Arabic. Or, the Arabization of the Southern Sudanese could be followed by their religious Islamization—in time making Southern and Northern Sudanese truly intermingled and eventually indistinguishable.

Meanwhile, the Swahili language has been creeping northwards towards Juba from East Africa as surely as Arabic has been creeping southwards from the Mediterranean. The Swahilization of Tanzania, Kenya, Uganda and eastern Zaire has been gathering momentum. With Arabic coming up the Nile towards Juba and Kiswahili down the same valley, Southern Sudanese will find themselves caught between the forces of Arabization and the forces of Swahilization. Historically, these two cultures (Arab and Swahili) can so easily reinforce each other. It is because of this pattern of trends that the manifest destiny of the Valley of the White Nile appears to be a slow but definite assimilation into the Arab fold over the next century or two.

But racial ambivalence will maintain a linkage with Africanity. Indeed, the Southern Sudanese are *bound* to be the most negritudist of all Sudanese—even if they do become Arabized. There is a precedent of Black nationalism even among Northern Sudanese. It is not often realized how much Negritude kind of sentiment there is among important sectors of Northern Sudanese opinion. Muhammad al-Mahdi al-Majdhub has been described as "probably the first Sudanese poet to tap the possibility of writing poetry in the Arabic language with a consciousness of a profound belonging to a 'negro' tradition."[3]

The poet al-Mahdi has indeed affirmed:

In the negroes I am firmly rooted though the Arabs may boastfully claim my origin. . . . My tradition is: beads, feathers, and a palm-tree which I embrace, and the forest is singing around us.[4]

Muhammad Miftah al-Fayturi is another Arab negritudist. Information about his ancestry is somewhat contradictory. His father was probably Libyan and his mother was Egyptian but of Southern Sudanese ancestry. In his words:

Do not be a coward
Do not be a coward

say it in the face
of the human race:
My father is of a negro father,
My mother is a negro woman,
and I am black.[5]

In some notes about al-Fayturi's early poetic experiences there is the anguished cry: "I have unriddled the mystery, the mystery of my tragedy: I am short, black and ugly."[6]

Then there are *the* Arab negritudists who sometimes revel in the fact that they are racially mixed. They can also be defiant and angrily defensive about their mixture. Salah A. Ibrahim, in his piece on "The Anger of the Al-Hababy Sandstorm," declared:

Liar is he who proclaims:
'I am the unmixed. . .' Yes, a liar![7]

In the Sudan of the future there may be even less room for such "lies" than there is at present. After all, Arabization is, almost, by definition, a process of creating mixture—and its relentless force along the White Nile is heading southwards towards Juba and beyond.

THE RELIGIOUS IMPACT OF THE ARABS

There is a school of thought which regards the religious penetration of the Arabs as the most important Arab influence in Africa. Certainly the population of Africa converted to Islam is far greater than the population linguistically or biologically linked to the Arabs. And Islam is a form of identity as well as a religion.

The distribution of Islam in North, Western and Eastern Africa leaves Southern Africa almost, untouched, but not quite. In May 1983 President Banana of Zimbabwe addressed an Islamic Conference in Harare. The delegates represented the Muslims of Southern Africa. Zimbabwe alone had 800,000 Muslims. It is in West Africa, however, that Africa's new Triple Heritage can be studied at its most vigorous. If Ethiopia is the laboratory of the ancient Triple Heritage (indigenous, Semitic and Greco-Roman) south of the Sahara, Nigeria is the grand laboratory of the new Triple Heritage (indigenous, Islamic and Western). Sometimes the different identities are in conflict with each other—the split personality of a nation.

Estimates of Nigeria's population of Muslims vary considerably -from a third of the population to an absolute majority. The Organization of the Islamic Conference (OIC) has reportedly re-classified Nigeria from the category of "country with Muslim minority" to "Muslim country." Although not a member itself, Nigeria has been granted observer status by the OIC.[8]

Certainly the Islamic presence in Nigeria is considerable -especially in the North and West of the country. Listening to any national news bulletin in Nigeria any evening reveals a significant number of national figures who are Muslims or bear Muslim names. Every time Nigeria has had a general election since independence, the federal government has passed into the hands of a Muslim-led political party. In 1981 Nigerians topped even Pakistanis as the largest contigent of pilgrims to Mecca from any part of the world. This pattern would probably have continued but for new foreign exchange regulations in Nigeria in 1982 which resulted in a federally-imposed rationing of number of pilgrims per state.

Other ways of controlling the number of Nigerian pilgrims to Mecca have been devised by the Muslim-led Federal Government. The conditions announced for the registration of pilgrims in 1983 included the automatic disqualification of any one who had been to Mecca on pilgrimage in the preceeding three years. There was also the sectarian disqualification of Muslims who were of Ahmadiyya persuasion (an evangelical proselytizing Muslim movement which was founded by Mirza Gulam Ahmed in British India and has been doing missionary work in different parts of Africa).

The daily paper, The New Nigerian, carried the report of the new Hajj conditions as the main headline story of the day. The paper dates each issue according to both the Gregorian and Islamic calendars. This report was in the issue of Wednesday, Shaaban 20, 1403 A.H. (June 1, 1983, A.D.).

All these are illustrations of an Islamic presence in Nigeria which is dynamic and vigorous—at times a little too vigorous. In distribution at least half the Yoruba are probably Muslim and so are *an* overwhelming majority of the Hausa and Fulani. In other words, if Nigeria had consisted only of its three largest, "tribes" (Hausa, Yoruba and Ibo) over two thirds of the country would have been Muslim. It is basically the presence of smaller "tribes" in Nigeria (the so-called "minorities") which has reduced the percentage and proportion of the Islamic presence in the country. Yet even among the minorities in the North and West both Christianity and Islam continue to make in-roads. On the whole the European colonial impact failed to arrest the spread of Islam in West Africa, though it may have slowed it down in some parts of the sub-region. It is estimated that Senegal is over 80% Muslim, Guinea (Conakry) over 90%, Mali over 80%, Sierra Leone over 50%, the Ivory Coast some 30%, Cameroon over 40%, Niger over 90%, Chad over 60% and so on. The heartland of Black.

In East Africa (as distinct from the Horn and Nile Valley) European colonial rule was more successful in arresting the spread of Islam. In Uganda,

Kenya, Rwanda, Burundi and Zaire Islam remains at best a minority religion, though often politically significant. Indeed, under Idi Amin, the Muslims of Uganda were a politically privileged and powerful minority for eight years.

In Tanzania there are probably more Muslims than Christians numerically, but there are still large numbers of Tanzanians who do not belong to either category and continue to uphold their own traditional creeds and beliefs. Christians in Tanzania are a powerful and privileged minority, but a large one at that.

In the Horn of Africa and the Nile Valley Islam is numerically preponderant, though patchy in Southern Sudan and uneven in Ethiopia. The population figures of Ethiopia have so far been particularly hazy, but the Muslims are estimated to be in the region of 50%, in spite of the long history of Ethiopia as a Christian theocracy. The ruling or central ethnic group, the Amhara, are of course preponderantly (Coptic) Orthodox, but Islam is strong among many other ethnic groups, including the separatist regions of Eritrea and the Ogaden.

In the Sudan and Egypt Islam is more clearly triumphant, though both countries have large non-Muslim minorities. Egypt's Christian minority has strong cultural ties with Europe; the Sudan's Southern minorities have strong cultural ties with the rest of Black Africa. The expansion of Islam within Egypt has probably reached its limits—it is unlikely to make further inroads into the Coptic population. However, the expansion of Islam in the Sudan will probably continue. The process of Islamizing and Arabizing the South may no longer be the official policy of the central government in Khartoum especially now that Nimieri is no longer in power, but the sociological context of the South in a country under ultimate Arab rule is almost automatically receptive to further spontaneous acculturation.

The impact of Islam on Zaire is more modest and is unlikely to expand to any significant extent except in the east. An off-shoot of Islamic culture in eastern Africa, the Swahili language is one of the major languages of Zaire, but the religious presence of Islam in Zaire is more limited.

The white presence in Southern Africa arrested the spread of Islam further south. But indeed there are Muslims in Malawi, Zimbabwe and Mozambique especially in the northern parts. The question which arises is whether it is a shrinking or expanding population.

Islam in the Republic of South Africa is a significant phenomenon mainly among the Coloureds, the Indians and the Malays. It is weak in the Black African population, but there have been inroads even there. A rise in conversions as a result of disenchantment with white-dominated Christianity may already be under way, but the scale is likely to be modest. This then is the approximate spread of Islam as a religion. The religion captured Saharan Africa and parts of the Nile Valley before it captured West Africa. It penetrated parts of Eastern Africa and trickled further inland and further South.

But Islam is not just a religion. It is a whole civilization. Among the aspects of that civilization which have had an impact on Africa is architecture. It is to that aspect, that we must, now turn.

THE ARCHITECTURAL IMPACT OF THE ARABS

Mansa Musa (1312–1337 A.D.), ruler of ancient Mali, left his country in 1324 on a pilgrimage to Mecca. He had one hundred camels, each laden with three hundred pounds of gold. Five hundred slaves accompanied him, each bearing a golden staff. He passed through Cairo on his way to Mecca. His impact has fascinated historians ever since. He "went to town" in the bazaars of Cairo — one of the most lavish spending sprees of all time. His generosity in Egypt became legendary — a display of hospitality and generosity which was of pharaonic proportions. The lavishness was great enough to cause an alarming depreciation of gold on the Cairo exchange.

But what did this Muslim ruler of ancient Mali bring back from his trip to Arab lands? From Mecca he brought back piety and a greater dedication to Islam. He also brought back Muslim scholars from the Middle East to enhance the sophistication of Mali Islam.

But perhaps the most enduring legacy he brought, back from his Arabian travels was his sponsorship of a man called Abu Ishaq as-Sahili, a poet and architect from Andulasia. The identity of a civilization is partly expressed through its skyline. As-Sahili laid the foundations of the Islamic and Arabian styles of architecture in parts of Western Africa. The Gao mosque was a particularly impressive legacy of as-Sahili's. Today the range of Islamic architecture in Western Africa is from the domestic architecture of the Hausa-Fulani in Nigeria to great. mosques in Dakar, Senegal, and from the ruins of Timbuktu in Mali to the Emir's Palace in present-day Zaria.

In East Africa architecture often included a particular concern for the point of entry into a building structure. Out of this concern emerged the special art of what are called "Lamu doors" — heavy and wide doors decoratively carved out in wood.

Is Islamic architecture purely the architecture of mosques? The answer is of course "No." Because Islam is a whole civilization, the architectural impact is quite diverse in Muslim Africa. Interesting architectural experimentation took place in pre-revolutionary Zanzibar -of which the most famous is Bait-el-Aiaib (House of Wonders) which is now the Zanzibar headquarters of the ruling Chama cha Mapinduzi of Tanzania, party of the revolution.

Zanzibar also has the ruins of Sultan Barghash's special palace for his
Harem—as well as an Arab fortress or two.

But, on the whole, European colonial rule tended to demesticate (dis-do-
mesticate) Islamic architecture. It became less and less the architecture of ordinary family residential houses, and more and more reserved exclusively for
public buildings and structures. Islamic architecture in Africa became more
and more the architecture of mosques, palaces, fortresses, educational buildings and other public structures.

In terms of the triple heritage, the architecture of the Mombasa Institute of
Muslim Education in Kenya was particularly remarkable. The architect was
an Englishman; the location was Africa; the architecture was Islamic. Captain
Beaumont—British to his toenails, artistocratic to his monocle, imperial to
his helmet—designed the most elaborately Islamic of any colonial complex
of buildings in Mombasa.

There was a purpose to this apparent, madness in confluence of cultures. A
British Governor of Kenya, Sir Philip Mitchell, wanted to establish a technical institution of learning for muslims of Eastern Africa to help them catch up
realistically with Christianized Africa. Sir Philip wanted Muslims to catch up
especially in the fields of technology—electrical, mechanical, civil and other
branches of engineering.

This Muslim Institute hired Europeans mainly as instructors in these technical fields. The students were Muslims of Eastern Africa (Kenya, Tanganyika, Zanzibar, Uganda and Somalia especially). The triple heritage was
captured in that very composition of students and staff.

But in addition there was in the background a confluence of a British architect, and an Islamic style of architecture while Africa provided the construction labour and of course the location.

In the post-colonial era *the* Mombasa Institute of Muslim Education has
now become the Mombasa Technical Institute. But the architecture is the least
changeable aspect of the Institute—defiantly Islamic to the end. In solemn
recognition of this fact the institution's motto is retained in its Arabic form
above the gate of entry: "ENDEAVOR AND ACHIEVE" in Arabic words and
letters.

Further north in Kenya the tourist imperative of the modern age has capi-
talized on Arabian romance. A number of hotels in Malindi have used a partially Islamic motif. One hotel is called after Sindbad, the sailor. And the leading tourist hotel in Lamu is named after the Swahili word for the Islamic
paradise, Peponi. The architecture of this Lamu luxurious hotel is neo-Islamic.

In short, Islamic architecture even in Kenya alone ranges from the ruins of
the Swahili City State of Gedi to the design of some of the most modern

tourist hotels in Malindi and Lamu. The architecture also ranges from the structural complexity of the Mombasa Institute of Muslim Education (now Mombasa Technical Institute) to the elaborate designs of Lamu doors into private houses all along the Kenya Coast.

ISLAM'S IMPACT ON AFRICAN POLITICAL CULTURE

Yet another impact of Islam on Africa is in the realm of political culture. This includes Islam's impact on political values, institutions, and vocabulary. Again identity, political identity especially, is at stake.

The origins of the state in West Africa were partly Islamic. Before European colonization, there were West African states or empire-states. The nation-state had yet to develop fully. Empire states like ancient Mali and ancient Songhai were products of interaction between Islam and indigenous culture. Sometimes the rulers were strong Muslims and became patrons of Islamic scholarship in court and beyond. In turn the scholars could sometimes be strong influences in court and in policy formulation. Examples which spring to mind include the Court of Muhammad Toure in his rule in Songhai from 1492 to 1528 A.D. and the Court of Idris Alooma (1571 – 1603 A.D.) of the Kanem-Bornu empire.

By the time the European colonizers arrived in the nineteenth century, experience in statecraft had accumulated in West Africa—though not uniformly. As history would have it, it was the Islamic Emirates of Northern Nigeria which had the most enduring consequences for the colonial order. The British empire builders were impressed by the political structures which the Hausa-Fulani had already evolved. The British conqueror of Northern Nigeria, Lord Lugard, was inspired enough by these institutions to develop a whole new doctrine of colonial rule -the doctrine of indirect rule. As Lugard's compatriot, Lord Hailey, came to put it in his class, An African Survey:

> It was in northern Nigeria that this procedure of using Native Authorities was given a systematic form by Lord Lugard during the years which followed the declaration of the protectorate in 1900. The area which was brought under British protection was the scene of the most effectively organized system of indigenous rule to be found south of the Sahara. Most of the old-established Hausa Kingdoms had embraced the Islamic faith, and under its influence there had by the early 16th century developed a well–organized fiscal system, a definite code of land tenure, a regular scheme of local rule through appointed District Heads, and a trained judiciary administering the tenets of Mohammedan Law.[9]

Indirect rule as a doctrine had repercussions elsewhere in Africa. This doctrine of using Native Authorities did not work effectively everywhere—but the fact that it was attempted at all was born out of the British response to the Islamic state structures discovered in Northern Nigeria.

Aspects of Islamic law, the Shari'a, were respected by the Colonial Order wherever there were Muslims in any significant numbers. My own father was Chief Kathi(or Grand Kadhi) of Kenya in the 1940s. His was the appeal court for cases decided under the Shari'a in different, parts of colonial Kenya. His court was mobile. He travelled to different parts of Kenya to hear the appeals. At times I travelled with him.

The Shari'a is still operative in post-colonial Kenya in aspects of personal and civil law, though the trend in independent Kenya is towards a gradual integration of Islamic, indigenous and Western-derived law. This is an ambition to synthesize the triple heritage in law. The latest effort has been a quest to establish an integrated law of succession and inheritance. The Government of Kenya has of course tried to consult Islamic opinion and the opinions of African customary law specialists. Although consensus has been elusive, the present Kenyan regime remains obstinate in its pursuit of integrated national law as a long-term objective. The triple heritage in law is in search of a synthesis in a number of African countries. Kenya is part of the search.

But the impact of Islamic culture has not only been in the areas of political institutions and law. It has also been in the field of political ideas and political vocabulary.

In the field of vocabulary, languages like Hausa and Kiswahili still look to the Arabic language and Islamic history as a source of new words for political discourse. In Kiswahili concepts like constitution (katiba), independence (uhuru), and republic (iamuhuri), are *all* Arabic- derived.

Sometimes the contrasts of *borrowings* from indigenous and Arabic sources are *themselves* fascinating. The Swahili word for king (mfalme) is Bantu or indigenous while the word for president (raisi) is Arabic-derived. Indeed, while the word for king is indeed Bantu, the word for Queen (malkia) is Arabic-derived.

The word for monarchy (ufalme) is Bantu while the word for republic (jamuhuri) is Arabic-derived. The word for slavery (utumwa) is Bantu, while the word for freedom or independence is Arabic-derived (uhuru).

Since independence there has developed the language of "East/West relations" and "North/South Dialogue." The former refers to the ideological divide between Western countries and Communist countries; the latter refers to the economic divide between the industrialized countries of the Northern hemisphere and the developing countries of the South.

In Kiswahili the original words for East and West (mashariki and magharibi) are *Arabic*-derived; while the words for North and South (kaskazini and kusini) are *probably* Bantu-derived.

The words for writing and reading (andika and soma) are *Bantu* while the words for book and letter (kitabu and baruwa) are *Arabic*-derived.

The verb to enquire (uliza) is Bantu but the verb to answer (jibu) is Arabic-derived. But it should be noted that the nouns "question and answer" could be both Arabic-derived (swali and jibu).

The word for the executive branch of government (serikali) is Muslim-derived (Turkish and Arabic)—whereas the word for the legislative branch is bunge, a Bantu word.

Members of the executive are *also* Arabic-derived, such as ministers (mawaziri), army (jeshi), policeman (askari).

In Tanzanian Kiswahili the word for socialism (ujamaa) is Arabic-derived whereas the word for capitalism (ubepari) is Bantu. One of the reasons why, Nyerere's translation of Shakespeare's Merchant of Venice appears ideologically inspired is because Nyerere entitled the translation Mabepari wa Vanisi (sic) (capitalists of Venice).

Indeed, the term ujamaa in Tanzanian Kiswahili is itself a fusion of the triple heritage. The word itself is Arabic-derived. It. refers to the indigenous phenomenon of ethnic solidarity or the solidarity of the extended family. And yet Nyerere's intention was to find an African equivalent of the European concept of "socialism." The word ujamaa is Islamic, the ancestral phenomenon of solidarity is indigenous, and the conceptual metaphor equates African family hood with European socialist fellowship.

The word for friendship in Kiswahili (urafiki) is Arabic derived whereas the word for brotherhood (udugu) is Bantu. Tanzanians have started to use the word "ndugu" as the equivalent of "comrade." In this context the word for socialism is still Arabic-derived, but the equivalent of the word "comrade" in Dar es Salaam is thus Bantu.

In Luganda the ethnic identification is so close that the word for brother is "Muganda" (which also means member of the Ganda tribe). When a Muganda introduces a male friend who is so close that he is the equivalent of a brother, the friend has to be introduced as a Muganda.

Curiously enough, Lusoga (related language of the Basoga) heavily influenced by Luganda, also uses the word "Muganda."

With regard to sisters in Luganda, the vocabulary emphasizes descent from the same mother rather than shared membership of the same "tribe."

Luganda also has elaborate vocabulary to distinguish siblings of a shared mother from siblings of a shared father. Luganda is also strict in forbidding certain forms of internal intermarriage (endogamy). Cousin marriages among the Baganda are *much* more restricted than among the Waswahili. The richer vocabulary of relationships in Luganda is in part a function of endogamy and the need to be precise about those relationships.[10]

Finally, it should also be noted that while the word for politics in Kiswahili (siasa) is Arabic-derived, the word for economics (uchumi) is Bantu.

CONCLUSION

Africa is a cultural bazaar. A wide variety of ideas and values, drawn from different civilizations, compete for the attention of potential African buyers. This marketing of cultures in Africa has been going on for centuries—but a particularly important impact has come from the "Semites" (especially Arabs and Jews) and the "Caucasians" (especially Western Europeans).

In sub-Saharan Africa it goes back to the ancient triple heritage of indigenous traditions. Semitic influences and links with the Greco-Roman world. The Semitic strand was partly Jewish, hence, some Hebraic practices very early entered Ethiopian Christian civilization. This is quite apart from the presence of the Black Jews (the so-called "Falasha") in the country across the centuries.

Jewish influence is also discernible in a number of otherwise indigenous myths of origin, from Yorubaland to Abysinnia (upper Ethiopia).

Jewish ideas have also entered Africa indirectly through Christianity and Islam, both of which have strong links with Judaism. As for the experience of the Jewish people themselves across the centuries, from early religious persecution in Pharaonic Egypt to the Nazi holocaust, this has sometimes influenced Africa as a comparative metaphor. Jewish martyrdom and Africa's history of humiliation have sometimes been seen as parallel agonies. And even the Afrikaners of South Africa have sometimes seen themselves as beleaguered "Israelis" of Africa. The most recent Jewish impact on Africa has been due to Arab-Israeli rivalries. The Afro-Israeli honeymoon was, in a sense, from 1957 (with Ghana's independence) to 1967 (with the June Arab-Israeli war). From 1967 to 1973 a deterioration in Afro-Israeli relations was discernible. But it took the October War of 1973 to shake most of Africa into breaking off diplomatic relations with the Jewish state.

In May 1982 President Mobutu Sese Seko of Zaire resumed relations with Israel. Did he do it to impress Americans and win more friends in the U.S. Congress? Did he do it to improve security in Zaire? Was he exasperated with the Arabs? Or was he simply following "brother Sadat's" lead? In August 1983 President Doe of Liberia followed suit and recognized Israel. Did he do it as protection against "Libyan subversion"? Was he also looking for additional funds from Capitol Hill? Was it a way of telling Americo-Liberians (descended from Black Zionist returnees) that all was forgiven?

At any rate, Israel seems to have had some success in reducing its isolation in Africa, however modestly. Was this a revival of the Jewish component in Africa's Semitic equation? It is too early to be sure.

But while Israel can compete with the Arabs for political influence, and for a role in Africa's development programmes, it has no chance of catching up with Arab cultural influence and the impact, of the Arabs on African identity. The modern triple heritage of Africa has produced approximately a hundred million Muslims south of the Sahara. This is a cultural reservoir for the Arabs for which the Jews have no real equivalent. In any case, Judaism is a more exclusive religion than Islam—and Judaism is therefore offering no competition to either Islam or Christianity in the scramble for Africa's soul.

Nor can Hebrew ever rival Arabic as a major force in Africa's cultural experience, and as a source of words for indigenous African languages. And is there such a thing as Jewish architecture which can influence African design, or even Jewish art, to compete with Islamic architectural and cultural influences? Is there such a thing as Jewish dress to compete with neo-Islamic dress culture in Africa?

With regard to intermarriage, Jews are *more* exclusive than Arabs. The "Semitic" blood which mingles with African blood will remain overwhelmingly Arab, not only because Jews are *much* fewer than Arabs in absolute numbers, but also because Jewish endogamy and lineage are less receptive to intermarriage than are Arab kinship patterns.

On the other hand, those Jews that are part of Western civilization are major carriers of Western ideas and major innovators in the Western idiom. Nobel prize winners almost, every year include laureates with Jewish names. Ethnic Jews in history who have shaped the modern intellect include Karl Marx, Sigmund Freud and Albert Einstein. The greatest impact of Jews in the modern period has been in their capacity as innovative Westerners, rather than as Jews. In the equation of the triple heritage, Western Jews are more Western than Jewish; they are carriers of Western culture rather than transmitters of Semitic traditions. Marxism—from the barracks of Ethiopia and Mozambique to the cafes of Dakar—is probably the most important legacy from a Western Jew to have influenced twentieth century African history.

In ancient and medieval Ethiopia, the Jewish contribution was part of the Semitic aspect of the ancient triple heritage (indigenous, 36 Semitic, and Greco-Roman). In Ethiopia since the revolution of 1974, the Jewish component (including Marxism) is part of the Western leg of the new triple heritage (indigenous, Islamic and Western).

The Semites—both Arab and Jew—continue to be a major aspect, of Africa's problems of identity and Africa's political and cultural history. The range is from the muezzin calling Africans to prayer to the radical trumpet calling Africans to revolution, from Africa's shared nationalism with the Arabs to Africa's shared martyrdom with the Jews.

NOTES

1. Consult *The Jewish Communities of the World*, (London: Andre Deutsch, 1971) prepared by Institute of Jewish Affairs in association with the World Jewish Congress, Third Revised edition.

2. For America's twin myths consult Max Lerner, *America as a Civilization: Life and Thought in the United States Today* (New York: Simon and Schuster, 1957) p. 162.

3. See Muhammad Abdul-Hai, *Conflict and Identity: The Cultural Poetics of Contemporary Sudanese Poetry* (Khartoum: Institute of African and Asian Studies, University of Khartoum, African Seminar Series No. 26 1976) pp. 26–27.

4. *Nar al Majadhib*, (Khartoum, 1969). p. 195, 287. See also page 24.

5. Cited by Abdul-Hai, *op.cit.*, pp. 40–41.

6. *Ibid.*, p. 42.

7. *Ghadhbat al Hababy* (Beirut, 1968) Abdul-Hai, *ibid.* p. 52.

8. *Europa Yearbook*, 1984 (London: Europa, 1984).

9. Lord Hailey, *An African Survey* (London: Oxford University Press, revised edition, 1957) pp. 453–4.

10. I am indebted to Sam Max Sebina and Brenda Kiberu for explaining to me the nuances of Kiganda terms of endearment.

Chapter Twenty-Two

Euro-Jews and Afro-Arabs in World History: A Conclusion

We have sought to demonstrate in this volume how Arabs and Jews started off as one Semitic family–and then radically diverged. We have also noted how Arabs and Africans started off as different people–and have since converged across the centuries into an Afrabian commonwealth.

The Jews diverged increasingly towards Europe and the wider Western world. In spite of periodic pogroms and centuries of discrimination, European Jews became deeply assimilated and, after a while, became almost indistinguishable from their white Christian neighbors.

The religious legacy which Jews brought with them into Europe became a major cause of their social isolation and communal marginalization. They became vulnerable partly because they were associated with a religious tradition which had historically rejected Jesus and betrayed him to the Romans.

On the other hand, the religious legacy which the Arabs imported into Africa became a stimulus of their upward mobility and helped to propel them into conquerors. Judaism, as practiced by Jews in Christian Europe, helped to condemn the Jews to marginality for centuries. Islam, as practiced by Arabs, both in Christian Africa (such as Egypt before the Arab conquest) and in polytheistic sub-Saharan Africa, turned the Arabs into an African aristocracy.

Over time, the Arabs became accomplices in Africa's exploitation, partners in Africa's development and, more recently, allies in Africa's liberation. As accomplices in Africa's exploitation, the Arabs engaged in the trans-Saharan slave traffic and the Indian Ocean slave trade and exploited Africans in other ways as well.

Arabs as partners in Africa's development helped to stimulate the growth of cities and city-states like Kano, Bornu and Lamu; enriched African languages like Kiswahili, Somali and Wolof; transformed African legal and judicial systems; and promoted literacy in societies which previously possessed no written word. Islam and Arab culture influenced African architecture, dress code, business practices, manners and statecraft.

Arabs as allies in African liberation became especially important in the wake of the European colonization of Africa and of much of the Muslim world. Nationalists in Africa and in Arab countries found common cause in their joint struggle against European colonialism. President Gamal Abdel Nasser of Egypt (reign 1952–1970) used Egyptian resources for anti-colonial broadcasts beamed into European African colonies south of the Sahara. Nasser helped educate in Egypt a generation of African youth and provided asylum to African revolutionaries on the run.

Libya under Muammar Qaddafy was in the forefront against the forces of apartheid in South Africa. African liberation fighters against white minority rule and against Portuguese imperialism in Southern Africa often found their greatest supporters in such Arab countries as Algeria, Libya and Iraq. Such Arab support included Arab financial contributions to such movements as the African National Congress in South Africa and the South West African People's Organization (SWAPO) of Namibia.

Indeed, there developed a strong diplomatic alliance between Arab champions of the Palestinian cause and African supporters of liberation movements in Southern Africa. Most of the time, Arab and African states voted on the same side on issues concerning Palestine, on the one hand, and concerning the fight against apartheid and white minority rule in Southern Africa, on the other. This Afrabian joint alliance remained strong until Anwar Sadat of Egypt broke ranks and made unilateral peace (however uneasy) with Israel.

But by the second half of the twentieth century such an Afro-Arab alliance against Israel was no match for the Judeo-Western alliance in defense of the Jewish state. Jews in the Western world, and especially in the United States, had become part and parcel of Western global might. Arabs and Africans, on the other hand, were still part of the Third World of underdeveloped societies.

In the struggle against apartheid, the Jews of South Africa had become so Europeanized that they counted as white people in South Africa's stratification system.[1] Indeed, white South Africa and Israel empathized with each other as pockets of "Western civilization" under siege against non-Western "barbarians." White South Africa and Israel even collaborated with each other in a mutual development of nuclear capability.[2] White South Africa and Israel both managed to build nuclear weapons.

In the days of apartheid in South Africa, the Japanese were accepted as white people, while the Chinese were not. Similarly, the apartheid regime accepted its local Jews and Israelis as white people, whereas the members of the other branch of the Semitic people (the Arabs) remained people of color.

However, it is important to remember that while all Arabs were regarded as "people of color" by the apartheid regime, not all Jews were acceptable as white folks. The least acceptable were the Ethiopian Jews (the so-called Falasha). For a long time they neither qualified as Jews to the state of Israel nor qualified as white people to the logic of apartheid. The Ethiopian Jews were Black and culturally Amhara except for their religion. It took large-scale famine in Ethiopia and strong lobbying by American Jewish leaders to convince the state of Israel to arrange an exodus of the Falasha from Ethiopia to Israel, beginning with Operation Moses in 1985 and operations Joshua and Solomon later.[3]

North African countries like Egypt, Algeria and Morocco had had Arabized Jews for centuries.[4] The Jews of Algeria regarded themselves as French in the twentieth century and migrated to France as white French people when Algeria became independent of France in1962. Most of the Jews of Egypt migrated to Israel after the creation of the Jewish state in 1948 and in response to the Arab-Israeli conflict which ensued. In the second half of the twentieth century Arabized Jews from Morocco or Egypt rapidly became European Jews if they went to the Western world. But a majority of Jews from the Arab world became Israelis instead. On balance, access to a European identity was relatively open to all Jews in the second half of the twentieth century with the obvious exception of the Ethiopian Jews.

While in the twentieth century Jews could rise high in Europe and the Western world while still remaining adherents of Judaism, Arabs in the Western world could only reach the political pinnacles of Western power if the Arabs were Christian. During the Presidency of George W. Bush in the United States, the House of Representatives had a number of Arab-Americans. These included Darrell Issa of California, Charles Boustany of Louisiana, Nick Rahall of West Virginia, and Ray LaHood of Illinois. John H. Sununu had been a high profile Arab-American in the Executive Branch (chief of staff under President George H. W. Bush) and his son, John E. Sununu, is currently a Republican Senator from New Hampshire.[5]

George W. Bush's election in both 2000 and 2004 had included an Arab-American challenger to the Presidency—Ralph Nader, who lost to Bush. On the other hand, President Bush did appoint Arab-Americans to high positions—such as Spencer Abraham as Energy Secretary. None of these Arabs would have made it if they were Muslim.[6]

On the other hand, the membership of the U.S. Senate is on some occasions one tenth Jewish (ten Senators out of a hundred).[7] None of these particular

Semites have needed to renounce Judaism in order to be elected to the American legislature.

As for the comparative impact of Arabs and Jews on Western civilization, the Jews have impacted the West from within, while the Arabs have stimulated the West from without. Arabs and Muslims historically helped to teach Europeans mathematics (hence the Western use of "Arabic numerals" and such Arabic words as algebra). The Arabs and Muslims helped Europeans to rediscover the intellectual riches of ancient Greek civilization. Western academic traditions including bibliographies, gowns for graduation, spire and quadrangles in architecture, were essentially inspired by ancient Muslim academies. More recently Arab petroleum is indispensable to Western prosperity.

The impact of the Jews on Western thought has been even more staggering and has been overwhelmingly from within. There is, of course, the pervasive impact of the Old Testament on Western thought. There is also the legacy of Jesus (as a Jew) and the Old Testament attributed to him. And the more recent Jewish geniuses who have shaped the modern mind—have ranged from Karl Marx to Freud, from the rationalist Spinoza to the physicist Albert Einstein. The West has been plagiarizing from the Semites for centuries. Westerners have plagiarized from the Arabs through the Arab external impact on Europe. They have plagiarized from the Jews through internal penetration of Jewish ideas into the Western world view.

This book of ours is about how Jews became substantially European and how Arabs became partly African. But it is also obvious that Europe became partly Jewish just as Jews became Europeanized. The Arabs penetrated and Islamized much of Africa. Today if there is any city which is the capital of the Arab world, it is Cairo—influencing the rest of the Arab world from the reverberations of the African continent.

On the issue of culture and power, no cultural group in the world (per head of population) has exerted more influence than the Jews. The total number of Jews worldwide is less than fourteen million[8]—yet Jewish contributions to higher education, high culture, journalism, diplomacy, statecraft, politics and science has been staggering.

There are more than twice the number of African Americans than there are Jews in the world added together—and yet the influence of African Americans on U.S. politics and policies is only a fraction of the influence of their Jewish compatriots.

Jews outperform not just Americans of color, but also White American gentiles, per head of population. This is the phenomenon of Jewish exceptionalism (Jewish intellectual edge) which has produced a staggering number of Jewish winners of the Nobel Prize for (a) Literature, (b) Chemistry, (c) Physics, (d) Medicine and (f) Peace.[9]

Is the explanation genes or culture? It is culture, but with a strange combination. It is overwhelmingly Western Jews who have performed so superbly. Western Jews perform better than Westerners who are not Jews and better than Jews who are not Westerners. It is the synthesis of Jewish tradition and Western civilization—a kind of creative impurity.

Over 80% of the Jews of the world are Westerners or white folks. The largest Jewish country in population is not Israel, but the United States. The U.S. has about six million Jews.[10] According to 2002 estimates, Israel has just over five million. The third Jewish presence is in France (over 500,000). The fourth is in Canada (over 350,000). The fifth is in the United Kingdom (275,000). The sixth is in Russia (265,000). Other predominantly European (racially) Jews may be found in Australia, Ukraine and Germany—all of whom are estimated to have about have about 100,000 Jews—and Hungary (with over 50,000 Jews) and Belgium (with over 30,000 Jews).

One Latin American country is estimated to be the seventh in number of Jews (with less than 200,000)—Argentina. Brazil has about half of those.

In Africa the largest concentration of Jewish presence is in South Africa. In the year 2002, South Africa was the twelfth/ninth country in the world in number of Jews (over 70,000).[11]

In some respects, Jews can be compared with the Japanese in history. There is such a thing as Japanese exceptionalism. Japan became leader of the industrial revolution in Asia and is now the second industrial power in the world. Japanese culture synthesizes the following elements:

Hierarchy and order
Thrift and savings
Work ethic
Social cohesion

In technology, the genius of Japanese exceptionalism is the genius of efficient improvement, rather than the genius of original invention. The exceptionalism of the Jews, on the other hand, is quite often the genius of original invention. Three of the following five makers of the modern mind were Jews:

Isaac Newton (1642–1727)
Karl Marx (1818–1883)
Charles Darwin (1809–1882)
Sigmund Freud (1856–1939)
Albert Einstein (1879–1955)

And yet the Chosen People of History were not the Jews alone. They were the Jews and Arabs combined. Between them these Semites produced two and a half billion followers of monotheistic religions. Judaism, Christianity and Islam have helped give birth to diverse civilizations, to shape the moral standards of the human race, to stimulate new languages, and to construct physical wonders which have ranged from Al-Hamra in Spain to the Taj Mahal in India, and from the Jewish Wall and Al-Quds in Jerusalem, to the grand mosques in Senegal.

As Arabs intermingled with Africans, a fertile new Commonwealth of Afrabia emerged. And as Jews intermingled with Europeans, new pinnacles of human achievement were reached.

> *The blood of experience meanders on,*
> *In the vast expanse of the valley of time,*
> *The new is come and the old is gone,*
> *And life abides a changing chime.*

NOTES

1. On Jews in South Africa, see, for instance, Gideon Shimoni, *Community and Conscience: The Jews in Apartheid South Africa* (Hanover, NH and Glosberry: Brandeis University Press published by University Press of New England and David Philip, 2003) and Sergio DellaPergola and Allie A. Dubb, *South African Jewry: A Sociodemographic Profile* (Jerusalem : Institute of Contemporary Jewry, Hebrew University of Jerusalem, 1988).

2. For accounts of this nuclear collaboration between the two states consult David Fischer, "South Africa," in Mitchell Reiss and Robert S. Litwak, Eds., *Nuclear Proliferation After the Cold War* (Washington, DC: Woodrow Wilson Center Press and The Johns Hopkins University Press, 1994), pp. 209–213; Joel Peters, *Israel and Africa: The Problematic Friendship* (London: British Academic Press, 1992), pp. 159–161; and Benjamin M. Joseph, *Besieged Bedfellows: Israel and the Land of Apartheid* (New York: Greenwood Press, 1988), pp. 57–71.

3. A description of Operation Solomon may be found in Stephen Spector, *Operation Solomon: The Daring Rescue of the Ethiopian Jews* (Oxford and New York: Oxford University Press, 2005).*Operation Solomon: The Daring Rescue of the Ethiopian Jews* (Oxford and New York: Oxford University Press, 2005).

4. The mother of former Senator George Allen (R-VA), Etty Allen, was raised as a Jew in Tunisia but reportedly chose to conceal it after her arrival in the United States, leading to a controversy about Senator Allen's Jewish roots in his Fall 2006 campaign for reelection to the US Senate. For more on the controversy, see Michael D. Shear, "Allen's Mother Revealed Jewish Heritage to Him Last Month," *The Washington Post* (September 21, 2006).

5. The first Senator of Arab-American descent was James George Abourezk (Democrat, South Dakota), and other former Senators of Arab-American descent include

James Abdnor (Republican, South Dakota) George Mitchell (Democrat, Maine) and Spencer Abraham (Republican, Maine).

6. President Clinton did appoint Donna Shalala, who has Lebanese Jewish ancestry.

7. A complete roster of Jews in all major political positions is available in Sandy Maisel and Ira N. Forman, Eds., *Jews in American Politics* (Lanham, MD: Rowman & Littlefield Publishers, 2001), pp. 449–470. Indeed, the Senate beginning in 2007 will have thirteen Jewish Senators, according to the on-line encyclopedia Wikipedia at http://en.wikipedia.org/wiki/List_of_Jewish-American_politicians, accessed December 3, 2006.

8. Jewish population estimates vary. One source lists the number of Jews world-wide at 14.4 million; see John W. Storey and Glenn H. Utter, *Religion and Politics: A Reference Handbook*, (Santa Barbara, CA: ABC-CLIO, 2002), p. 119. Noted Jewish demographer Sergio DellaPergola has put the population at 13.2 million world-wide, as a rough estimate; see his "World Jewish Population at the Dawn of the 21th [sic] Century," in Eliezer Ben-Rafael, Yosef Gorny, and Yaacov Ro'I, Eds., *Contemporary Jewries: Convergence and Divergence* (Leiden and Boston, MA: Brill, 2003), p. 49.

9. Columnist Charles Krauthammer has pointed out that 20 percent of Nobel winners have been Jewish; see his "Everyone's Jewish," *Washington Post* (September 25, 2006).

10. One estimate puts the number of Jews in the US population at 6.06 million, amounting to about 2.2 percent of the US population, according to a table in *The Statistical Abstract of the United States* (Washington, DC: Bureau of the Census, January 2002), p. 56. It was estimated to be at 5.7 million in 2002 by DellaPergola, "World Jewish Population at the Dawn of the 21th [sic] Century, "in Ben-Rafael, Gorny, and Ro'I, Eds., *Contemporary Jewries*, p. 51.

11. These figures are for 2002 and are drawn from DellaPergola, "World Jewish Population at the Dawn of the 21th [sic] Century, "in Ben-Rafael, Gorny, and Ro'I, Eds., *Contemporary Jewries*, p. 51.

Appendix One

Prosperous Minorities as Targets of Prejudices

When is racism provoked by the material or intellectual success of a minority? When is a minority under certain social conditions too successful for its own good?

Jealousy, envy and relative deprivation can be trigger mechanisms of prejudice on the part of majorities against overly successful minorities. But the minority may also be at fault by being too socially separate from the majority. Jews in the West have been a remarkable minority.

Prestigious eastern private institutions in the U.S.A. began to impose quotas on admissions of Jews after World War II—the discrimination hidden under the term, "character." Sometimes a university would set up a committee of alumni to screen out allegedly unattractive applications.

Columbia University had a 40% Jewish student body when it imposed its quota in 1920. Within a couple of years enrollment dropped to 22 percent. In nearby City College of New York and Hunter College, Jewish enrollment continued at about 80%.[1]

In the 1970s Everett Carll Ladd, Jr. and Seymour Martin Lipset said that 80% of college-age Jews were in college, whereas only 40% of all college-age Americans were in college. In the 1950s 62% of college-age Jews were in college, when only 26% of all college-age Americans were in college. The gap is narrowing—not because fewer Jews are in college, but because more gentiles are now enrolled.

There is some disagreement as to whether a bigger percentage of Jews than gentiles make straight As in grade. But there is less disagreement about the fact that a much higher proportion of Jewish students (40%) are attending "high ranking" institutions (as contrasted with 13% of the gentile population).[2]

The down-side of this impressive performance is that dialogue between civilizations and cultures is inhibited by uneven distribution of incomes and uneven distribution of skills.

Prejudice against Jews because of their success has declined in the United States. But prejudice against Korean Americans because of their success is still alive and well. This also affects other East Asians.

The prejudice manifests itself at the elite level in certain professional schools. And it manifests itself at the inner city level with prejudice against Korean shopkeepers in minority neighborhoods.

Dialogue between cultures is again hampered by uneven distribution of skills and uneven levels of income. Israelis and Arabs continue to be uneven in skills. The ethnic Chinese in Indonesia have repeatedly paid a high price, partly because of their economic success.

In 1965 a million Chinese were killed in Indonesia for two totally contradictory allegations—that the ethnic Chinese Communist Party were about to stage a Communist revolution and that the ethnic Chinese were the vanguard of successful capitalism.

Dialogue between two major cultures—Chinese and Malay—was sabotaged by the disruptive forces of uneven incomes, uneven skills and ideological insecurities.

This contradictory role also affected colonial Malaya. The British authorities fought a Communist movement which was overwhelmingly Chinese in composition. And yet ethnic Chinese were simultaneously developing into very successful entrepreneurs.

Since independence, Malaysia experienced its worst anti-ethnic Chinese riots in 1970. Since then affirmative action policies by the Malay-dominated government in favor of Malays has diffused the ethnic tension against Chinese. The Chinese are still far and away the most prosperous.

In West Africa the Igbo became too economically successful for their own good, especially in Northern Nigeria, which is mainly Hausa territory. The explosive economic situation was aggravated by a military coup in Nigeria in 1966 which killed Hausa leaders but spared Igbo ones.

Anti-Igbo riots broke out in Northern Nigeria later in 1966 and killed thousands. Minorities condemned for their prosperity may find themselves condemned to uglier fates as well.

The great paradigm of all these different cases has been the experience of the Jews. The Igbo in Nigeria were often referred to as "the Jews from the East" (meaning from Eastern Nigeria). The ethnic Chinese of Indonesia and Malaysia have also often been regarded as the equivalent of the entrepreneurial Jews of the Western world.

The Jews of Europe especially have become the supreme example of a talented minority who have, from time to time, been too successful for their own good. Yet the Jews have risen again and again from the ashes, and demonstrated how invincible the human spirit can still be. The struggle continues.

NOTES

1. [Truman] President's Commission on Higher Education, *Higher Education for American Democracy*, Vol. I (Washington, D.C., 1947), 27, Vol. II, 1. Also, Levine, *American College and the Culture of Aspiration*, 137–37. Cited by Richard Nelson Current, *Phi Beta Kappa in American Life: The First Two Hundred Years* (New York: Oxford University Press, 1990), pp. 220.

2. Stephen Steinberg, *Academic Melting Pot in the 1970s*, p. 109. Ladd and Lipset, *The Divided Academy* (New York, 1975), p. 150.

Appendix Two

Is "Jewish Uniqueness"
a Dangerous Doctrine?

I have been stimulated by both students and faculty in the debate on comparative suffering and the concept of holocaust. Of course the Jewish experience was unique at some level. There is no such thing as identical suffering between any two sets of people. The scale of destruction of the native peoples of this hemisphere was also unparalleled. Also unique were the brutality and racism of the trans—Atlantic slave trade, including the horrors of "the middle passage" across the Atlantic on crowded ships. Should we have coined a special word exclusively for Black slavery under white domination? No other kind of enslavement included those horrors. There are degrees of uniqueness. I have come to the conclusion that to regard the Jewish holocaust (with or without a capital H) as QQ unique is not only inaccurate: it is downright dangerous. If the concept of "the Jewish Holocaust" becomes a doctrine, it would be a claim not only that such suffering has never happened to any other people in the past, but that it can never happen to any other people in the future. Would we be encouraging a future Hitlerian lunatic to try and invalidate Jewish uniqueness by annihilating another people in a comparable way? If the concept of "the Jewish Holocaust" is already a doctrine, are we inviting complacency about future genocidal dangers to other people? Are we modernising the doctrine of "the Chosen People" at the risk of other societies?

If uniqueness is a matter of degree, I personally have long been convinced that the Jews are especially unique. Per head of population no other people in history has had a greater impact on human affairs across time. The Jews do not need to monopolise the concept of "holocaust" in order to be unique. Uniqueness is not absolute. The Jews do not have to feel insulted when their suffering is compared with the suffering of fellow human beings. And yet many Jews feel precisely that.

In 1985 I visited a slave cell in Elmina Castle in Ghana. I knew that African slaves awaiting trans—Atlantic shipment were once packed in such cells very close together—sweating upon each other. The captives were often sitting on their own urine and filth. If cholera broke out a whole cell could be wiped out. I reflected on all this horror in my television series, The Africans: A Triple Heritage. I then went on to say the following in program 4 of my TV series, my voice choking with rage:

> As a African visiting a place like this [in Ghana] seeing all this, I begin to have some kind of idea of what a Jew might feel like if he visits Auschwitz or some other Nazi German concentration camp and sense those powerful emotions of bewilderment, of anger, of infinite sadness.

I thought that such reflections on trans—cultural martyrdom would bring Jews and Blacks together. And yet the Public Broadcasting Service in the United States (PBS) received complaints from some Jewish viewers. Those particular Jews regarded any comparison between Jewish suffering and Black suffering as a demeaning of the Jewish experience. That millions of Blacks were not only enslaved but actually died in the "middle passage" across the Atlantic was regarded by some Jews as a trivialization of their own Semitic suffering. "Trivialization"? For every African who was finally marketed in chains, another died somewhere between the slave-raid in Africa and the plantations in the Americas. Millions perished—as millions were enslaved. Does a comparison with this scale of Black suffering "trivialize" the Jewish experience? Is this the latest game of "trivial pursuits"?

I have argued elsewhere that for native Americans and African—Americans there has been no newly created "State of Israel" to compensate for the indignities and cruelties of the previous holocaust. The holocausts of the Americas have continued to the present day to inflict pain and humiliation on its victims and their descendants. Approximately 40% of prisoners on death–row in the United States are African—Americans. The jails, mortuaries and police cells still bear anguished testimony to the disproportionate suffering of victims of American holocausts. Jewish suffering under the Nazis came to an end. The suffering of native Americans and descendants of slaves in this hemisphere still continues. In the United States today there are more male descendants of African slaves in prison than in college. How about new measurements of comparative suffering? How about new measurements of uniqueness?

I have no quarrel with reserving the Hebrew word Sho'ah or Hurban exclusively to the martyrdom of the Jews under the Nazis even when we are speaking English. After all, the English language has adopted the quasi-Arabic word Hah to refer exclusively to the Muslim pilgrimage to Mecca. The generic word "pilgrimage" is available for other uses. Similarly the Greek-derived word holocaust should remain a generic metaphor and be applicable to other large — scale atrocities, as well as to the martyrdom of the Jews under the Nazis.

I personally feel closest to the Jews on two types of occasions. Firstly, when I reflect on how many of my most cherished values were in fact historically influenced by Jewish thinkers. Secondly, when I reflect that Jews have at times suffered as much as Africans. Why should I be denied this second reason for feeling close to the Jews?

Appendix Three

The Nuclear Club: Is there a Judeo-Christian Monopoly?

In international relations the ultimate confrontation between issues of power and issues of conscience lie in the nuclear arena. In 1998 the land of Satya-graha (soul force) and the land of the rising crescent of South Asia lost their nuclear innocence.

The country of Mahatma Gandhi, India, declared itself a nuclear power in May 1998. Who was in opposition? One answer was the Islamic Republic of Pakistan which detonated its own nuclear devises also in May 1998 in direct response to the Indian nuclear initiative.

A different answer to the question of "who is in opposition" to the nu-clearization of Hindu India and Muslim Pakistan is the present nuclear Club of Five. While it is true that bombs have no religion, four Christian-majority nuclear powers (the United States, the United Kingdom, France and Russia) and one Confucian-Buddhist-Communist country, (The People's Republic of China) have claimed a monopoly. Four Christian countries are far and away the most important nuclear powers in the world—the U.S., the U.K., France and Russia—in spite of the fact that the use of nuclear weapons is funda-mentally un-Christian.

It was nearly twenty years ago that I first raised in the Western media the spectre of a nuclearized Africa. I even presented to Westerners the scary sce-nario of an Idi Amin "doing a war-dance with a nuclear device." Idi Amin was the erratic dictator of Uganda in the 1970s.

I gave my warning when I gave the 1979 BBC Reith Lectures under the ti-tle of "The African Condition: A Political Diagnosis." But in reality I was not thinking of Idi Amin's Uganda as a future nuclear power. I speculated about a Third World challenge, including a future Nigeria, a future South Africa and conceivably even a future Zaire if that large and wealthy country succeeded in re-inventing itself at long last.[1] In fact the Congo was the first African country to have a nuclear research reactor nearly forty years ago.

In the nearly twenty years which have elapsed since my BBC Reith lectures, Nigeria and Zaire (now Congo) have moved further away from being potential nuclear powers. Their infrastructures have been allowed to decay dismally, and so much of their scientific talent has gone into exile.

As for the Republic of South Africa, as soon as the bomb was in danger of falling into Black hands, F.W. DeKlerk and later Nelson Mandela and his colleagues were persuaded to sign the Nuclear Weapons Nonproliferation Treaty.

Although the ideas I proposed in the BBC Reith Lectures in 1979 about a nuclearized Africa are now further away from fulfillment rather than nearer, we should on the eve of the new millenium re-open the question — especially against the background of India's and Pakistan's accession to the status of declared nuclear-weapons states. But where does the United States fit in all this? And how relevant is Christianity?

THE DEMOCRATIZATION OF THE NUCLEAR WORLD?

In terms of majority of population, the United States is the largest Christian country in the world. But it is also the only country to have used nuclear weapons on people (mainly civilians) — killing and maiming thousands in Hiroshima and Nagasaki in 1945. American political culture is sympathetic to the principle equality in many different areas. After all, it was the American Declaration of Independence which declared that "all men are created equal and are endowed with certain inalienable rights. . . ." Many have linked American egalitarianism to American versions of Christianity. Yet the America of conscience is constantly in a tense relationship with the America of power.

But the most obstinate areas of resistance to equality in American experience have been resistance to racial equality in domestic policy and resistance to military equality in foreign policy. The latest version of U.S. resistance to military equality includes U.S. commitment against nuclear proliferation without much U.S. effort to achieve universal nuclear disarmament. The largest Christian country in the world is also the largest nuclear power — and the most jealous of nuclear monopoly.

The U.S. seeks to guarantee a system of nuclear apartheid — according special nuclear monopoly to the U.S., the U.K., France, Russia and China to the exclusion of all others. To use a Hindu idiom, this is the world of nuclear Brahmins with full entitlement to weapons of mass destruction.

If Africa cannot be taken seriously through the technologies of production and information, should it try to be taken seriously through the technology of destruction?

What India and Pakistan have done with their nuclear tests in May 1998 may have lessons for Africa. Although India is approximately the same size as China demographically, and will outstrip China in population in another twenty to thirty years, successive U.S. governments have treated China with far greater seriousness than they have treated India.

They have saluted India for being the largest democracy in the world, and then proceeded to ignore it. The West have tended to compare India only with Pakistan—which is less than one seventh the population of India. There is a reluctance to regard India as a rival to China.

On the eve of attainment of Black rule, South Africa allowed itself to be pressured into signing the Nuclear Nonproliferation Treaty instead of supporting India in its opposition to nuclear apartheid. Racial apartheid was ending in one country; nuclear apartheid persisted at the global level.

Nuclear apartheid is a world which consists, on the one hand, of Nuclear Haves who are under no special pressure to give up their own weapons of mass destruction, and, on the other, of nuclear Have-Nots who are punished when they presume to go nuclear or build arsenals of mass destruction.

Iraq has been threatened and bombed a number of times for presuming to have weapons which every permanent member of the Security Council (the U.S., the U.K., France, China, and Russia) have had with impunity. Four Christian countries and one Confucian-Marxist power have asserted nuclear monopoly.

While in the world as a whole the nuclear monopoly is controlled overwhelmingly by countries with Christian majorities, in the Middle East the nuclear monopoly is reserved for the single Jewish nation. In the 1980s I once served as Chairman of a United Nations Committee on Nuclear Proliferation. Even as long ago as the early 1980s there was no doubt among us that Israel was, to all intents and purposes, a nuclear power militarily. But our Committee softened our conclusion in order not to give the other countries of the Middle East justification to pursue the nuclear option in competition with Israel. As Chairman of the UN Committee, my hands were tied—but I knew I was helping to legitimize a Jewish monopoly of nuclear weapons in the Middle East.

Western powers have started reducing some of their arsenals—but for the wrong reasons. They are reducing them not because the Western powers now regard nuclear weapons as evil but because the threat to their own security has eased since the collapse of the Soviet Union. In other words, if there is a new threat to the West, the West will re-nuclearize vertically.

Well, other countries have security problems too right now. What is nuclear sauce for the Christian goose, should it not also be nuclear sauce for the Hindu and Muslim ganders?

The North Atlantic Treaty Organization does not need three nuclear powers— the United States, Britain and France. It would reassure the world that the five permanent members of the Security Council would like to keep the number of nuclear powers to a minimum if Britain and France gave up their own. One way of stopping nuclear proliferation is to engage in nuclear dis-proliferation— reducing the number of Nuclear-Haves already in being. Will Britain and France de-nuclearize? If they do not, the following scenario is likely:

> The regime of nuclear apartheid in the twenty-first century will be shaken in three stages. First, by the twin-rivalries between India and Pakistan, on one side, and between India and China, on the other. This could include a nuclear arms race in the region as a whole. Second, by the potential nuclearization of Iran and Iraq. Third, by the re-nuclearization of South Africa in the twenty-first century.

The regime of nuclear apartheid needs the culture shock of nuclear proliferation to cause enough consternation for the pursuit of universal nuclear disarmament. Nuclear weapons are evil. But in order to get the present nuclear-haves to give them up, we may have to scare them with additional nuclear countries.

But Africa would stand no chance of playing any historic role of breaking the global regime of nuclear apartheid unless it creates conditions which would help not only stem the domestic brain drain but drastically reverse it. We need to move from brain-drain to brain retain—the retention of our best trained minds. We also need to add to brain retain the further accomplishment of brain-return—the repatriation of brain power back to Nigeria, Southern Africa, Kenya and the rest of Africa.

It has been estimated that up to a quarter of the best trained Nigerian brain power may be in exile by now—working in laboratories, factories, schools, and commercial enterprizes in North America, Europe, Southern Africa and elsewhere. More talent is moving out of Nigeria and Africa.

How can we achieve brain-repatriation? How can we tempt back home the African emigres? Many may not want to return permanently, but may be prepared to come and serve their country on specific assignments from time to time for periods of two, or three or more years. Brain-return is needed for general development, and not merely for nuclear research.

Many are eager to help rebuild their country and society—but the atmosphere has to be welcoming, the political conditions relatively transparent, and the economic policies less arbitrary and less prohibitive. The nuclear breakthrough for both India and Pakistan was achieved when some of their best scientists decided to go back home to their own countries.

Nuclear weapons are still disproportionately in the hands of countries with Christian majorities—the United States, the United Kingdom, France and Russia. But the weapons are themselves un-Christian, un-Islamic, un-Judaic and evil. Yet the Judeo-Christian monopoly may need to be broken by proliferation to more and more non-Judeo Christian countries—before we can achieve the Christian and Abrahamic ideal in which nuclear weapons are banished from all countries for all time.

But when can the world of power and the world of conscience be persuaded to reach such a rational goal?

NOTE

1. The lectures were published as a book the following year. See Mazrui, The African Condition: A Political Diagnosis (New York: Cambridge University Press, 1980).

Index

Abrahamic peoples, 129; belong to inter-related languages, 129; and Semetic people, 129

Abrahamic religions, 3–4, 129

Afrabia, vi, 4, 11–17, 37, 132; and the Red Sea divide, 136–38, 140; Resolving Africa-Arabia divide, 137

Afrabians-types of, 16–17, 37–38, 133–34; alliance against Israel, 440; and creation of new ethnic communities, 135; and linguistic ties, 136; and population movement between Africa and Arabia, 135; between geography and culture, 134–36; fusion of African-Arab identity, 133; genesis of, 133; Islam in Africa, 135

Africa: and the Middle East, 31; Arab influence, 417, 437; Arab impact, 417–32; caught in Middle-East conflict, 320–22; collapse of German Empire, 355; cultural Arabization of, 131; intellectual liberation, 61–62; Islamic impact on, 131, 135; Jewish economic and political, 422–24; Jewish influence, 417–22, 436–37; Jewish presence in, 418–19, 421–22, 441; linguistic Arabization of, 131, 135; nuclearization of, 455, 456;

Mazrui, A. A. 1979 Reith Lectures, 455; penetration by Arab ideas, 131; semitic influence, 417; Triple Heritage in, 417, 428, 435

Africa-Europe-Arab relations, 219; influenced by seven triads, 219; of location, 219–21; of acculturation, 221–26; of pigmentation, 226–31; of stratification, 231–36; of confrontation, 236–39; of allegiance, 240–43; of dissent, 243–45

African-Arab relations (strengthening of): and terrorism, 132; and economic relations, 132–33, 141; and Islam, 132; economically fragile, 218; political links, 218

African-Americans: and Black Jews, 97; and Rastafaria Movement, 97; and USA political parties, 105; and Islam, 97–98; diversity in, 96–97; intellectuals, 110; religious impact, 97

African-American Muslims: as bridge with other Muslims, 75, 97; as bridge with African-Americans, 75; as disadvantaged religious group, 101

African diaspora: Re-Africanization of, 71; via Pan-Islam, 71–72, 74, 98; via Pan-Africanism, 71–72, 74, 98

African epistemology, 45–46, 54
Africans-as casualties of
	marginalization, 38
Afro-Arab crossfire, 206
Afro-Arab reconciliation, 134
Afro-Jewish tensions in USA, 56–58
Al-Azhar University, 199
Al-Qaeda, 304–9, 330–31
Arabia: Cultural integration with Africa,
	138–39; By Arabization, 138–39; By
	Islam, 138–39; Reluctance to
	embrace Afrabia, 140
Arab-Africa racial mixture, 143, 150;
	compared to other communities, 143,
	144; ascending miscegenation, 156,
	229; ambivalent miscegenation, 147,
	159–60, 230, 231; descending
	miscegenation, 147, 229; divergent
	miscegenation, 148–49, 158, 229,
	230; inter-marriage: attitude of
	traders, 152; attitude of
	agriculturalist to, 152–56; attitude of
	white women to, 154–55
Arab-penetration of USA power, 131
Arab-Americans, 80, 131
Arabs-Africanization of, 4, 38, 129,
	131; demographically, 131;
	territorially, 131
Arabs and Africa-linguistic ties, 11,
	424–25, 434–35
Arabs and Africa-pre-Islamic ties, 11–12
Arabs-architectural impact on Africa,
	431–32
Arabs-as Afro-Asians, 176–77
Arabs-as casualties of marginalization,
	38
Arabs-as exploiters of Africa, 439
Arabs-as liberators of Africa, 440
Arabs-developmental role in Africa,
	439–40
Arabs-Euro-American domination of,
	353–54
Arabs-growth in Africa, 12–14, 24
Arabs-impact on Africa, 417, 424–32

Arabs-impact on Western thought and
	civilization, 442
Arabs-influence on Africa, 417, 437
Arabs-intellectual influence on Africa,
	14–15
Arabs-USA political influence in, 441
Arabs-religious impact on Africa,
	428–30, 439
Ashcroft, J., 302–3, 394

Bagby, I., 106
Balfour Declaration and Lord
	Rothschild, 285, 314, 352, 354
Bin Laden, O., 117, 298–300
Black influence on USA politics, 65,
	67–68, 75, 76–82, 104–6
Black Intifadah, 314, 324, 330, 331
Black Liberation Front, 57
Black Muslim Movement-and
	sacralization of Black
	Consciousness, 63
Black power and brain power, 56
Black studies: and intellectualisation
	Blackness, 63; and Negritude, 51–55;
	and race relations in USA, 55–56;
	and sacralization of Black identity,
	46, 51, 63; and Talmudic tradition,
	56–57, 62–63
Blacks: comprehensive discrimination,
	61; intellectual pursuit, 48–50;
	scientific marginality, 50–51, 59–62
Blyden, Edward, 151

Cantor, E., 105
Cesaire, A., 52, 376
Chamberlain, N., 316
Childers, E., 280
Clinton, B.-attitude to Muslims, 79, 83
Counter terrorism-African impact, 31, 38

Darlington, C. D., 50
Deir Yassin Massacre, 280, 288
Democratic Party-attitude to Muslims,
	83, 85–87

Dialogue between cultures: inhibited by uneven income distribution, 448–49; inhibited by uneven distribution of skills, 448–49

Digital revolution and Islam, 25–26

Digital revolution-in Nigeria, 26

Dinka-marry Arab women, 166

Diop, Cheikh Anta, 375–76

Du Bois, W. E. B., 53

East Africa-caught in Middle-East conflict, 315–21

East Africa and Palestine, 315

Egypt and Pan Africanism, 145

Egypt as centre of three circles, 192–94; Africa, 192; and Israeli involvement in Africa, 197–98; and Islamic involvement in Africa, 197–98; Arab-world, 192; as a neutralist, 194, 196–97, 205; as champion of African nationalism, 193–94; as Afro-Asian voice, 194; as Pan-Islamic force, 199–200; caught between Africa and Muslim circle, 204; Muslim world, 192, 198–204; Non-aligned position, 196–97; status in Muslim world, 199–200

Ethical revolutions-types of, 336–37, 350; and Commonweath, 335–38, 341, 343, 350–51; and gender revolution, 341–44; female political leadership, 342–44; Muslim response, 346–47; population control, 348–49; and green revolution, 344–46; and morally accountable economies, 336–38; and morally accountable imperialism, 338–41; and Muslim world, 336–41; and South Africa, 340

Ethiopia-Christian presence in, 422

Ethiopia-Jewish presence in, 419–22

Ethiopia-re-Africanization of, 139

Eurabia, 218

Eurafrica, 218

Euro-Jews convergence (*see also* Jews-Europeanization of): due to cultural Westernization, 131–32; due to political penetration by the West, 131–32

Falasha Jews, 419–21, 441

Freud, S., 10

German paronia, 118–19

Ghandi, M., 35–37, 305–7

Global Apartheid, 306

Global ethic, 356–78; seven pillars of: tolerance, 356–58; economic equality, 358, 377; social justice, 358–60, 377; gender equality, 360–63, 377; ecological pillar, 363–68; inter-faith relations, 368–73; quest for wisdom, 373–78

Globalization-economic, 23

Globalization-and cultural re-tribalization, 23

Globalization-and Islam, 24–25

Globalisation and Shariah, 29

Globalization-impact on Africa, 23, 25–26

Globalization-semitic causes of, 24, 38

Globalization-types of, 23–24

Goody, J., 60, 366–67

Group of Eminent Persons, 249

Haley, A., 74–75

Hasan, Fadl, 163, 183

Herzl, T., 272–73, 316

Ibn Battutah, 15

Ibn Khaldun, 15, 300

Indirect rule, 433–34

Islam: and the Black experience in USA, 68, 71, 106–7, 109–12; and the Jewish experience in USA, 106–12; decline of, 353; early spread in Africa, 12; impact on African political culture, 433–34; in Nigeria,

429; in South Africa, 430; in the Caribbean, 72–73, 98–99; compared to Islam in USA, 72–73, 98, 99
Islam in Africa Seminar, Nairobi, December 2006, 323
Islamic Caliphate-collapse of, 355
Israel-and ethnic cleansing, 122
Israel-and South Africa interaction, 270–92, 440–41
Israel-creation of, 273–74
Israel-as cause of anti-Semitism, 122–25; in Britain, 122–23
Israel-as Jewish state, 280–81
Israel-as threat to USA democracy, 115–16, 124
Israel-as threat to Israeli democracy, 116
Israel-Kenya relations, 318, 322

Jackson, J., 255
Jaden, A., 179
Jensen, A., 48
Jewish-admission USA universities, 447
Jewish Agency of Palestine, 272–73
Jewish diaspora, 4–5, 17
Jewish economic and political influence in Africa, 423
Jewish emigration USA to Israel, 58
Jewish exceptionalism, 442–43, 449
Jewish-hate retention, 213
Jewish history-Hegelianization of, 7–9
Jewish holocaust: and diaspora Jews, 130; as dangerous idea, 451; compared to African suffering, 453; compared to Trans-Atlantic slave trade, 452; supporting Zionism, 130
Jewish influence on Africa, 417–22, 436–37
Jewish influence on USA foreign policy, 68–69, 105–7
Jewish influence on USA politics, 64–65, 67, 75, 104–5, 107–8, 441
Jewish intellectual pursuit, 47–50, 63–64, 109–10
Jewish penetration of USA power, 131

Jewish prejudice decline in USA, 448
Jewish presence in Africa, 418–19, 421–22, 441, 443
Jewish-self-hate, 277
Jews-and dissident otherness, 9–10
Jews (USA)-attitude to Israel, 105–6
Jews-compared to Japanese, 63, 443
Jews-comprehensive discrimination, 60–61
Jews-control of USA educational institutions, 56–57
Jews-conversion of, 6
Jews-economic role in South Africa, 283–85
Jews-Europeanization of, 4– 6, 17, 38, 129, 130–32, 439; began in Alexandria, 130
Jews-impact on Western thought and civilization, 10, 442
Jews-influence on public opinion in USA, 56
Jews-intellectual influence Muslim world, 14
Jews-religious marginalization in Europe, 439
Jews-selective discrimination, 60–61
Jews-westernization of, 131
Judeo-Marxism and Europeanization of Jewishness, 9

Kaba, A. J., 112
Kashmir, 80–81
Kenya-and Black Intifadah, 324–26
Kenya-as Jewish homeland, 315–17
Kenya-between ethnicity and religion, 326–27
Kenya-caught in Middle-East conflict, 315–21, 324
Kenya Coast: and Al-Qaeda, 330–31; and Black Intifadah, 324, 330–31; Arabs and ethnic fluidity, 160–62; economic alienation, 331; influence of Islam in, 329; racial categorization in, 161–62

Kenya-Israel relations, 318, 322
Kenya-pro-Zionist tendencies, 318, 322
Kimathi, D., 320
King, M. L., 305–7
King-Crane Commission, 292
Ku Klux Klan, 301–4
Krochmal, N., 7

Lawrence, T. E., 353–54
Legum, C., 283
Leibovitz, Y., 118
Levi-Strauss, C., 62
Lugard, J. F., 433
Luthuli, Chief Albert, 200–201

Mahdist Movement, 186–87
Majette, D., 111
Malan, D. F., 292
Malcolm X, 46
Mamluks, 254–55
Mandela, N., 37, 215
Mansa Musa, 431
Marable, M., 110
Marx, Karl, 6–8, 58–59, 64; as last of
   the Jewish prophets, 10; influence of
   European tradition on, 59; influence
   of Talmudic tradition on, 59
Marxism-Judaic impact, 7
Marxism-rabbinic impact, 7
Mau Mau Movement, 297, 320, 322;
   and Palestine Intifadah, 315, 317,
   319, 322
Mazrui, A. A.-Jewish influence on, 453
Mbeki, T., 216
McLeod, W. C., 152–53
Mckinney, C. A., 110–11
Mendelssohn, 6
Miscegnation-and integrated model of
   racial mixture, 163
Mitchell, Sir Philip, 432
Moller, H., 154–55
Mombasa Institute of Muslim
   Education, 432
Muhammed, Elijah, 46–47, 81

Muhammad, Farrad, 81
Muslim culture-spread of in Africa: by
   migration, 152; by proselytization,
   152; by trade, 152
Muslim missionaries in Africa, 151–52
Muslim women in political power,
   362
Muslims: and bida, 402; and innovation,
   402; and science, 401–2; attitudes to
   Christianity, 200–203; empowerment
   of, 396, 402–3; restraining the USA,
   404; view Christians as imperialist,
   203
Muslims in Kenya: and party formation,
   325–26; compared to Tanzania
   Muslims, 330; democratisation of,
   326; economic alienation, 331;
   radicalisation of, 323–24, 331;
   political alienation, 324–25, 331
Muslims in USA: and African-American
   links, 110; threatened by Middle-East
   conflict, 110–11; viewed as threat by
   Jewish groups, 110–11; and Black
   experience 67–68, 104; and identity
   crisis, 67, 69–70, 81, 104, 111; and
   Jewish self-definition, 67–68, 104;
   and links with (USA) Jews, 110; and
   participation crisis, 67, 71, 75–76,
   104; and political parties, 78–80,
   82–83, 85–86, 106; and public
   affairs, 108–9; and racial identity, 81,
   108; and right-wing political shift,
   85–87; and USA foreign policy,
   68–69, 71, 77–78, 80, 89, 105, 107;
   and USA policy formation, 78; and
   value crisis, 67, 82–85, 104, 111;
   caught between Black diaspora, 104;
   caught between Jewish diaspora,
   104; compared to Black experience,
   90, 71–76, 104–12; compared to
   Jewish experience, 67–71, 90,
   104–12; compared to Jews, 69–70;
   immigrant, 83–84, 87–89;
   indigenous, 83–84, 87–89; influence

on USA politics, 65, 67–68, 76–82, 108; organizations, 70

Nasser, G., 33
Nation of Islam: and racial identity, 81; and sacralization of Blackness, 47; and Judaism, 46; characteristics of, 46–47
Negritude, 52–53
Nigeria-indirect rule, 433–34
Nigeria-1966 civil war, 27–28
Nigeria-North-South divide, 26–27
Nigeria-privatization of, 30
Nigeria-rise of, 30
Negrology, 54–55
Nkrumah, K., 284–85
Nuclear Brahmins, 456
Nuclear Club-Judeo-Christian monopoly of, 455–59
Nuclear Club-monopoly threatened, 458–59
Nuclear power: India as, 455–58; Israel as, 457; Pakistan as, 455–58; USA as, 456
Nuclearization-and brain return, 458
Nuclear world-democratization of, 456
Nuclear world-de-nuclearization of, 457–58

Obama, B., 110
Oppenheimer, H., 284–85
Ottoman Empire, 352–53, 355, 368, 372, 377

Palestine and East Africa, 315
Palestine Intifadah, 315, 317
Pay-back time: Africa response to, 210; as reparation, 210–11, 215; and cultural differences, 34–35, 212–13; and hate retention, 35, 213–14; Jewish, 213; and Middle-East matyrdom complex, 213; and situational difference, 32–33, 212–13; and Ian Smith, 36, 214; and Jomo Kenyatta, 36, 214; and

Nigerian 1966 civil war, 36, 214–15; comparative between Semites and Africans, 35; Middle-East response, 210; as retribution, 210–11; M. Ghandi's view on, 35, 214
Pittsburgh Platform, 18
Potter, B., 48–49
Powell, General C., 265

Qaddafy, M.-as Pan-Africanist, 132,

Rastafari movement, 74, 97, 100
Red Sea, 136–38, 140
Reparations, 31–32, 57–58
Reparations and retribution, 209, 210
Republican Party-attitude to Muslims, 83, 85–87
Richardson, L., 110
Romantic gloriana, 73–74, 99, 100
Romantic primitivism, 73–74, 99, 100

Sacks, J., 122
Semitic divergence, 23–24, 38, 129; and Europeanization of Jews,129; and Africanization of Arabs, 129
Semitic people-defined as, 3
Semitic re-convergence, 38
Senghor, L., 52–55, 299–300, 376; On African intuition, 45, 54
September 11, 2001, 304–5
Shaka Zulu, 298, 300; compared to O. Bin Laden, 298–300
Shariacracy, 29–30; and militancy, 29–30; in Northern Nigeria, 29
Slavery: and Arab masters, 157–59; and descending miscegenation, 158; and Islam: abolished by Islam, 257–59; and ascending miscegenation and Islam, 159; condoned by Islam?, 256; damaging Islam, 75; emancipation by Islam, 256–59; harem, 261–62; Mamluks, 254–55; and Triple Heritage, 250; and white masters, 156–58; as a sin, 255, 266; assimilation and absorbtion, 253;

indigenous and assimilation, 253, 255; Muslim and absorption, 254; due to ascending miscegenation, 254; due to patrilineal tendency, 254; social mobility in, 254; war and slavery, 259; Western (Trans-Atlantic), 255; least absorptive and assimilationist, 255; inimical to horizontal absorption, 255; inimical to vertical social mobility, 255; damaging African culture, 75; difference in scale, 252; gender preference, 264; geography of, 252–53; moral degrees of, 259–60; motives for, 260–63; reparations for, 265–66; Trans-Atlantic, 250–51, 255, 262–63; types of, 250; indigenous, 250–51; uniracial or monoracial, 250, 264; culture conscious, 265; Muslim, 250–53, 265; bi-continental, 253; multiracial-not race based, 264; creed conscious, 265; Western (Trans-Atlantic), 250–51, 255, 262–63; bi-racial, 264–65; race conscious, 265

Snow, C. P., 47–48

Spinoza, Benedict de-impact on Western thought, 10

Sudan: Afro-Arabs in, 177–79; and asymmetrical miscegenation, 171; and cultural symmetry, 172; and cultural symmetry and economic balance, 172; and West Africa, 185; as extension of West Africa, 185–86; Arabization of, 426–27; Arabs types of, 176–77, 189–90; as Afro-Arab dual identity, 179; as intermediacy between Black and Arab Africa, 176, 184–85, 187; as linguistic borderline, 187–88; between English and Arabic speaking Africa, 187–88; biological Africanization of, 426–27; integration of, 181, 183–85, 189; linguistic marginality, 187–89; military and politics, 184; Muslims and political

issues, 183–89; Nigeria link, 187; North-South cultural divide, 179, 181; not a bridge between Black and Arab Africa, 175; racial divide,179; religion and political issues, 182–83; religious divide, 179–82; spread of Madhism in, 186–87

Sudan-Northern: Arabization of, 163; Cultural and religious cohesion, 185; ethnic fluidity, 162–63; inter-marriage in, 163; miscegenation in, 163; patrilineal descent in, 163

Sudan-Southern: bio-cultural solution, 163–64; ascending miscegenation solution, 163–66; patrilineal descent as solution, 163–66

Suez crisis, 196

Symmetrical acculturation, 142; descending asymmetry, 143

Symmetrical miscegenation, 142; asymmetrical, 143, 147, 171

Talmudic tradition, 45–47, 62

Terrorism: affect Christian-Muslim relations, 208; Africa-caught in crossfire, 207; African response to, 208; and African civil liberties, 208; and Al-Qaeda, 309; and germ warfare, 215–17; and Mau Mau Movement, 297; and Middle-East conflict, 118, 212; and September 11, 2001, 207; and Shaka Zulu, 298; and USA civil liberties, 208–9; and (1998) USA embassy attack, 207; and USA support for Israel, 118, 212; and USA support for Saudi Arabia, 212; anti-American, 207; anti-Zionist, 207; as anti-colonial struggle, 206; as type of warfare, 206; counter-types of, 305–6, 309; declining in Africa, 209; escalating in Middle-East, 209; racial (Ku Klux Klan), 301–4; religious (Al-Qaeda), 304–5, 308–9; September 11, 2001, 304–5; types of, 296–309

Terrorsmology, 309–10
Triple Heritage, 417, 428, 435

Uganda-as Jewish homeland, 315–17
Uganda-religion and politics, 182–83
USA: and Arab dictators, 116; and
    Muslim dictators, 117; support for
    Israel, 117
Uthup, T., 112
UAR-response to Cuban crisis, 196
USA: and Middle-East conflict, 320;
    and relations with Islam, 380–404;
    four periodic convergence-
    divergence phases of, 380–404; and
    Saudi Arabia, 34; anti-Americanism,
    34; as imperial power, 33–34; as
    cause of anti-Semitism, 124;
    economic action against Africa, 355;
    globalization of, 33–34; military
    action against Muslims, 355; rise of,
    355; support for Israel, 34

White Nile-Arabization of, 426

Zanzibari-racial categorization, 160–61;
    Arabs and assymetrical
    miscegenation, 167; Arabs and ethnic
    fluidity, 160–62; Arabs and
    symmetrical acculturation, 167
Zanzibari revolution, 168–69, 172
Zimbabwe-descending miscegenation,
    170–71; EuraAfricans in, 170–71
Zionism, 17–18; and apartheid, 270–92;
    and Judeo-Nazism, 118–21, 125;
    racialization of, 118–21, 125; stifling
    Israeli democracy, 119–21